The Asian Pacific

Political and Economic Development in a Global Context

Vera Simone
California State University, Fullerton

Anne Thompson Feraru
California State University, Fullerton

Longman Publishers USA

The Asian Pacific: Political and Economic Development in a Global Context

Longman, 10 Bank Street, White Plains, N. Y. 10606

Associated companies:
Longman Group Ltd., London
Longman Cheshire Pty., Melbourne
Longman Paul Pty., Auckland
Copp Clark Longman Ltd., Toronto

Executive editor: Pamela Gordon
Development editor: Susan G. Alkana
Production editor: Linda Witzling
Cover design: Keithley and Associates
Text art: FineLine
Production supervisor: Richard Bretan

Library of Congress Cataloging-in-Publication Data

Simone, Vera.
    The Asian Pacific : political and economic development in a global
context / Vera Simone and Anne Thompson Feraru.
        p. cm.
    ISBN 0-8013-0895-X
    1. Asia—Economic conditions—1945- 2. Economic forecasting—
Asia. 3. Pacific Area—Economic conditions. 4. Economic
forecasting—Pacific Area. I. Feraru, Anne Thompson.
HC412.S583 1994
330.95—dc20   94-15201
                                                  CIP

1 2 3 4 5 6 7 8 9 10-CRS-9897969594

to Lisa, Hans, and Jameen
to Arthur, Robert, and Philip

Contents

Illustrations and Tables

Preface

The Asian Pacific has entered world history as a new frontier. The dynamic center of this new frontier is Japan, a small resource-poor island nation culturally indebted in earlier times to China, for centuries the dominant power in the region. Following its defeat in World War II Japan emerged in the technological forefront of modern know-how and has replaced the United States as the world's leading creditor nation. Not far behind are the newly industrializing countries, or NICs, as they are known. These four "little tigers"—South Korea, Taiwan, Singapore, and Hong Kong—together with Japan have been responsible for much of the current U.S. trade deficit. Equally dramatic is the new wave of Japanese protégés in Southeast Asia—Indonesia, Malaysia, and Thailand. These countries are on the verge of parlaying international capital into worldwide exports on an unprecedented scale. In China, the ancient ideas of the world's oldest continuous civilization are being recast into modern form. Even in China's present transitional state, the sheer size of its material and human resources guarantees it a place among the great powers of the world. And just over its border awaits the Siberian and Far Eastern hinterland of Russia, whose development remains an untapped extension of this new frontier.

The region has become the fastest growing economic area in the world, turning the skyways of the Pacific Ocean into one of the most traveled paths of modern moguls. After being overshadowed in the last few centuries by the dominance of Europe and North America, the countries of the Asian Pacific have come into their own as important members of the global network of economic and political relationships.

This book is designed to respond to, and to stimulate further, the growing interest in this area of the world among students, business people, media practitioners, and the general public. It assumes little prior knowledge of the history, geography, politics, or foreign relations of the region. The geographic area chosen for study here, the "Asian Pacific," is more limited in scope than either the "Pacific Rim" or the "Pacific

Basin." The "Rim" in its broadest definition includes all countries along both western and eastern shores of the Pacific, and the "Basin" adds to these the island countries in mid-ocean. Our choice is to focus on the countries of East and Southeast Asia—China, North and South Korea, Japan, Taiwan, Vietnam, Laos, Cambodia, Thailand, Malaysia, Singapore, Myanmar (formerly Burma), Indonesia, the Philippines, and to a lesser degree Brunei and the colony of Hong Kong. Other countries in the region are brought into the discussion where their actions significantly affect these countries. And of course the impact of American and Russian foreign policy interests and actions is inescapably part of the story.

Justification for adding this book to the already crowded shelves in bookstores and libraries is that it meets the need of nonspecialists for an up-to-date introduction to the politics of the whole region, that it incorporates economics, history, and cultural elements, and that it includes both national and international politics.

Our approach is analytic rather than simply descriptive. Instead of proceeding country by country, we identify and analyze patterns of similarities and differences among them, using descriptive material about particular countries to illustrate the patterns. Our hope is that this strategy will give the reader a grasp of the whole region and sufficient knowledge about each country to serve as the foundation for more intensive study.

The perspective of the book is interdisciplinary, because we are convinced that to understand contemporary politics in Asian countries one needs to know something about their history, especially their experiences with Western colonialism, and about the cultural traditions and modern beliefs that underlie their political institutions. A grasp of the close connection between economics and politics in the socialist countries as well as in those with predominantly market economies is also essential.

Finally, politics as analyzed here crosses over the conventional separation in political science between comparative (that is, internal) politics and international relations. We show how a country's domestic political and economic policies influence its foreign relations and how both are influenced by the actions of other states, all operating within the context of a changing international environment in which they act and are acted upon.

The book is organized into nine chapters. Chapter 1 sketches the demographic and economic features of countries in the region and introduces the major theories of development that are applied and evaluated in subsequent chapters. Chapters 2 and 3 are historical, analyzing the effects of colonialism and the transition from colonial rule to independence. The next three chapters focus on politics, economics, and culture in these countries since independence. Contemporary political institutions and processes are compared in Chapter 4, with discussion of why authoritarianism in various forms characterizes them. Chapter 5 looks at their political economies, considering the reasons for their differing degrees of economic success and whether the Japanese pattern of development is transferable. Chapter 6 concludes the analysis of the process of modernization by showing how traditional Eastern cultures have interacted with Western-derived ideologies to affect political and economic change. The last three chapters shift to foreign policies and international relations. Chapter 7 focuses on the impact of the cold war and the effects of its end on political and military relations among Asian Pacific states and between them and the superpowers. Chapter 8 deals with the international political economy of the region, analyzing patterns of trade, aid, and investment and regional economic integration. In the concluding chapter, after reviewing the progress Asian Pacific countries have made thus far in political and economic development, we look to the future, at problems of succession in leadership, at prospects for human rights, and finally at the changing relationship between the region and the global system.

ACKNOWLEDGMENTS

We are grateful to colleagues and students at California State University, Fullerton, for their support and for the Faculty Enhancement and Instructional Development Grant to develop instructional materials that led to this book. Valuable comments and suggestions were made by Arthur Feraru, Jane Schneider, Martha Winnacker, and the following reviewers selected by the editor:

Jules S. Chan, University of Wisconsin—Eau Claire
Elizabeth Davis, Illinois State University
James Fetzer, SUNY Maritime College
Gary Hawes, Ohio University
Louis Hayes, University of Montana
Ilpyong J. Kim, University of Connecticut
Carmen Baker Lemay, Ball State University
Yogendra K. Malik, University of Akron
Peter R. Moody, University of Notre Dame
Betty Rosser, Nicholls State University
Mark Tilton, Purdue University
Theodore Vestal, Oklahoma State University
Donald E. Weatherbee, University of South Carolina
Allen S. Whiting, University of Arizona

Joyce Rosenblum and Thomas Prendergast of the United Nations Photo Library generously made available many of the photos used here. Special recognition goes to David Estrin, who encouraged us to undertake this project, and to David Shapiro, Owen Lancer, and Linda Witzling, for their patience and expertise in bringing it all together, finally.

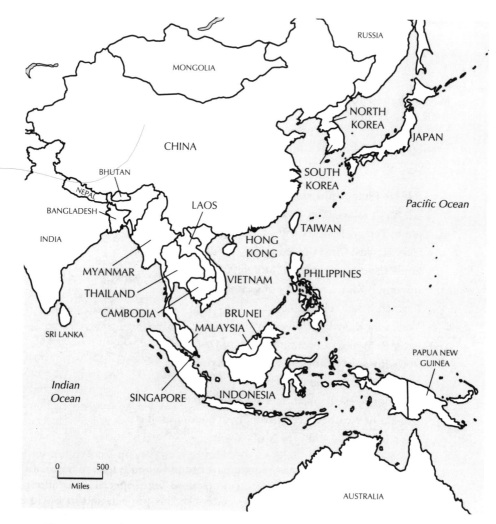

The Asian Pacific

Source: Adapted from John Andrews. *The Asian Challenge.* Hong Kong: Longman Group (Far East) Ltd., 1991.

chapter **1**

Comparing Asian Pacific Countries

Some Facts and Some Theories

One way of learning new things is to make comparisons between what we are familiar with and what we are trying to get to know. Making comparisons involves identifying differences and recognizing similarities between the familiar and the unfamiliar, whether they are kinds of food or colleges or works of art or people or—in this book—groups of people organized into countries. Each country has its own history, worldview, social customs and relationships, ways of producing to meet material needs, ways of distributing and exercising political power, ways of managing relations with other countries. Yet every country is unique, both similar to and different from other countries. That is what comparative political analysis is about: *comparing* political processes, structures, policies, and other features of nation-states. In what ways are they similar? In what ways different? What theories can be used to explain those similarities and differences? We try to make our comparisons *systematically*, not haphazardly, in order to detect *patterns,* to make *generalizations,* to see possible *connections* between politics and economic, cultural, historical, and other characteristics of the countries under study.

Studying the politics of the Asian Pacific region is probably more difficult for Americans and Canadians than studying Europe. There are at least two reasons for that difficulty. One is that Europe is more familiar to most North Americans than Asia; the ancestors of most people in the United States and Canada, their dominant languages, and their political heritage have been from Western Europe; and their educational systems are still decidedly "Eurocentric." Asia, in contrast, influenced by Confucianism, Hinduism, Buddhism, Islam, and the tradition of ancestor worship and ritualized reverence for symbols of authority, is much less familiar to North Americans and more likely to be stereotyped by them as "backward," "inscrutable," "not like us," hence more difficult to understand.

In addition to being culturally different from either Europe or North America, Asian countries are quite a bit more different from each other than are the countries of Europe, especially Western Europe. While Europe has a common religious tradition, Judeo-Christianity, the Asian Pacific has three major religions and one very powerful secular ethical tradition, Confucianism. European countries also have the shared experience of "modernization" and (especially in Western Europe) of "democratization," whether of the liberal or socialist variety; but Asian countries range from "modernized" Japan and Singapore, for example, at one end of the continuum to the traditionalism of Burma (renamed Myanmar in 1989) on the other, from the absolute monarchy of Brunei to the elective politics of the Philippines and Japan.

To help you overcome those initial obstacles to learning about the Asian Pacific and to introduce you to the adventure of comparative political analysis, in this chapter we will do two things. First is a quick introduction to the region with a preliminary sketch in very broad brush strokes of the variety (and some similarities) that characterizes these countries. That preliminary sketch will be filled out in more detail in the chapters that follow, but in this chapter you will be given enough information to begin comparing Asian countries with your own country, and with each other. In the second part of this chapter you will be introduced to two very different theories that have been devised by social scientists to explain the process of "modernization," meaning how "traditional" societies (such as England and France were in the fourteenth century) became "modern" socially and politically and "developed" economically (as Europe, the United States, Canada, and Japan are today). The two alternative theories of modernization presented in this chapter, supplemented by two additional theories explained in later chapters, will be applied to our study of Asian countries and may help to explain how and why some countries have succeeded in modernizing and developing, while others have not.

THE ASIAN PACIFIC REGION: DIVERSITY AND COMMONALITIES

Cultural Heritage

Unlike Europe, the Asian Pacific countries do not share a single common cultural heritage. Several different civilizations have shaped the cultural mosaic that gives Asia its exotic allure for Westerners. East Asia is comprised of countries with a predominantly Confucian culture; Confucianism originated in China and spread to Korea and Japan and into the part of the Indochinese peninsula that today is Vietnam. Hinduism and Buddhism moved eastward from India before the ninth century, shaping the dominant belief systems of Burma, Siam (renamed Thailand in 1939), Cambodia, and the island of Bali in Indonesia, and also gathered adherents to various sects of Buddhism in China, Japan, and Korea. In a subsequent wave of traders from the Middle East and India, Islam found its way into the Asian Pacific, becoming the prevailing religion in Malaysia, Indonesia, Brunei, and the southern part of the Philippines. Christianity followed later, brought in by European and American traders, missionaries, and colonial officials, although it did not supplant the earlier traditions and, except in the Philippines and South Korea, now has only a small number of adherents. Thus the underlying belief systems of the Asian Pacific countries come from more varied traditions than Europe's.

If they can be said to have a common cultural characteristic stemming from that richly diverse past, it is the high value placed on consensus in social relations that distinguishes Asian Pacific peoples from Europeans, Americans, and Canadians. Unlike Westerners, who are accustomed to the rule of the majority in group decision making, in Asian Pacific cultures people prefer to deliberate until decisions acceptable to all can be reached. Consensus serves to maintain harmony among members of the group, who are expected to put the community's welfare above their individual interests. This emphasis on community is reinforced by the ethical beliefs of Confucianism, Buddhism, and Islam, and by the agricultural imperatives of wet rice cultivation practiced in much of the region, which requires community cooperation in maintaining the dikes and controlling the flow of water.

Colonial Experience

Different parts of the region were colonized in modern times by Europeans, Americans, and later Japanese. The Dutch colonized the East Indies (now Indonesia); the Portuguese took modest holdings on the island of Timor, the port of Macao in south China, and Malacca, which later passed to the Dutch and then to the British; the Spanish and later the United States took the Philippines; Britain acquired Hong Kong, Burma, peninsular Malaya including Singapore, Brunei, Sarawak, and North Borneo (now Sabah); France conquered Indochina (now Vietnam, Laos, and Cambodia). Britain, France, tsarist Russia, Germany, and later Japan carved out semicolonial "spheres of influence" in China, and the United States through the Open Door policy exacted access to the spheres held by the other powers.

Thailand and Japan escaped Western colonization. Thailand accomplished this through the wily diplomacy of King Rama IV and the willingness of France and England to have his country serve as a buffer between their holdings in Southeast Asia. Japan, deducing that successful resistance to the West's superior military and economic power required it to emulate the West and become "modern" as rapidly as possible, undertook a crash program that by the early twentieth century had made it powerful enough not only to have escaped colonial rule but also to have acquired Taiwan and Korea as colonies of its own. Further conquests by Japan in the 1930s and 1940s gave large areas of China and Southeast Asia the experience of Japanese occupation.

Although the imperial powers' colonial policies varied in the impact they had on the traditional societies over which they ruled, the Asian colonies shared the common experience of alien domination and contact with modern institutions and Western ideas, especially the institutions of capitalism and the idea of nationalism. That experience stimulated the desire to become technologically advanced and to exercise the right of national self-determination. Nationalist independence movements challenged the legitimacy of colonialism and, after independence was achieved by most of the colonies in the two decades following World War II, those movements provided the first generation of postcolonial political leaders.

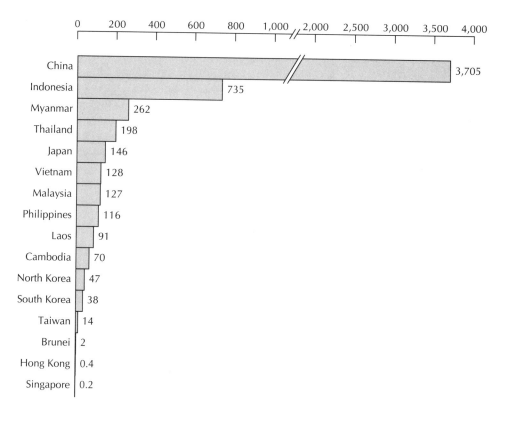

FIGURE 1.1   Land Area (1,000 sq. miles)

Sources: The World Almanac and Book of Facts 1991 and World Fact File.

Geographic and Demographic Features

The countries vary greatly in land area, in population, and in natural resources. As shown in Figures 1.1 and 1.2, China, with a land area similar to that of the United States and with over a billion people, is more than five times larger than the next largest Asian Pacific country, Indonesia, with 735,000 square miles and 181 million people. Other countries with land area over 100,000 square miles are (in descending order) Myanmar, Thailand, Japan, Vietnam, Malaysia, and the Philippines. Between 50,000 and 10,000 square miles in area are Laos and Cambodia, and under 50,000 square miles are North and South Korea, Taiwan, Brunei, the colony of Hong Kong, and the city-state of Singapore.

Population size roughly parallels land area, with some exceptions. The smallest in population is Brunei with over 300,000; others with under 10 million are Singapore, Laos, Hong Kong, and Cambodia. Next are those with 18 to 44 million: Malaysia, Taiwan, North Korea, Burma, and South Korea. From 57 to 68 million are Thailand, the Philippines, and Vietnam. Over 100 million are Japan and Indonesia, and the "giant," China, has over a billion.

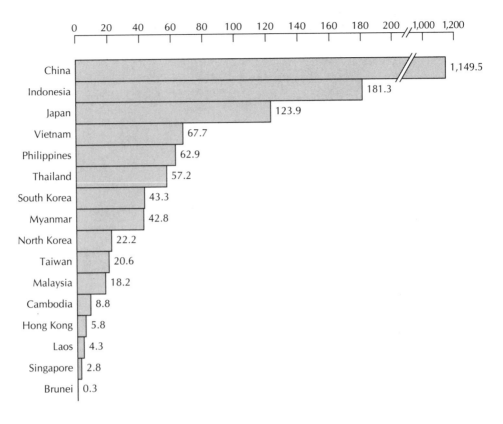

FIGURE 1.2   Population, 1991 (in millions)

Sources: World Development Report 1993 and, for Taiwan, Asia 1993 Yearbook.

The countries also vary in natural resource endowment, another indicator—like land area and population size—of potential for economic development. Rich mineral resources are found in China, Malaysia, Indonesia, and Brunei, for example; natural resources such as good harbors, navigable rivers, and hydroelectric power capability are other potentially significant assets. However, the examples of economic success achieved by relatively resource-poor countries such as Japan, Singapore, and South Korea suggest that having resources in one's own country may be less crucial than having the means to buy them from others.

Apart from sheer numbers, another difference among the populations of Asian countries is in the variety and size of ethnic and religious groups, shown in Table 1.1. In countries like China, Korea, Japan, and Vietnam, which had long precolonial histories as distinct (though not always unified) states, the great majority belongs to a single ethnic group. In contrast, Indonesia and Malaysia, which did not exist as political entities before colonial times, have greater diversity among their people. Divisions along ethnic, religious, and linguistic lines are thought to pose problems in creating national unity and loyalty to the central government and in developing a nationally oriented bureaucracy and nationally based political parties and interest

TABLE 1.1 Ethnic and religious groups in Asian Pacific countries

Country	Ethnic Groups	Percent	Religions	Percent
Brunei	Malay	64	Islam	63
	Chinese	20	Buddhism	14
	Other	16	Christianity	10
Cambodia	Khmer	90	Buddhism	88
	Vietnamese	5	Islam	2
	Chinese	5		
China	Han Chinese	93.3	Atheism, Confucianism, Buddhism, and Taoism	*
	Zhuang, Hui, Miao Yi, Ugyur Manchu, Tibetan Mongol, and Korean	6.7	Islam	1.4
			Christianity	.06
Hong Kong	Chinese	98	Buddhism, with Taoist and Confucian elements	majority
			Christianity	10
Indonesia	Javanese	45	Islam	87
	Sundanese	14	Christianity	9
	Madurese	7.5	Hinduism	2
	coastal Malays	7.5	Buddhism	under 1
	many others	26		
Japan	Japanese	99.4	Shintoism and Buddhism	majority
	Korean	0.6	Christianity	under 1
Korea, N.	Korean	99.8	none	majority
	Chinese	.2	Chondogyo	14
			Buddhism	2
Korea, S.	Korean	99.9	Confucianism, Buddhism, Chondogyo, and Shamanism	67
	Chinese	0.1	Christianity	28
Laos	Lao	50	Buddhism	85
	Tai	20	animism	15
	Phouteung	15		
	Hmong, Yao, other	15		
Malaysia	Malay and other indigenous	60	*peninsular Malaysia:* Islam	majority
	Chinese	31	Buddhism	*
	Indian	9	Hinduism	*
			Sabah:	
			Islam	38
			Christianity	17
			others	45
			Sarawak:	
			animism	35
			Buddhism or Confucianism	24
			Islam	20
			Christianity	16

6

Myanmar	Burman	68	Buddhism	85
	Shan	9	animism	15
	Karen	7		
	Rakhine	4		
	Chinese	3		
	Indian	2		
Philippines	Malay	95.5	Catholicism	83
	Chinese	1.5	Protestantism	9
	other	3.0	Islam	5
			Buddhism	3
Singapore	Chinese	76	Buddhism, Taoism	56
	Malay	15	Islam	15
	Indian	7	Sikh	*
	other	2	Confucianism	*
Taiwan	Taiwanese	84	Buddhism, Taoism, and	
	Mainland Chinese	14	Confucianism	93.0
	aborigines	2	Christianity	4.5
			other	2.5
Thailand	Thai	84	Buddhism	95.5
	Chinese	12	Islam, Hinduism,	
	Khmer, Mon, other	4	Sikh, Christianity, and	
			Confucianism	4.5
Vietnam	Vietnamese	90	Buddhism	majority
	Chinese, Muong,		Taoism,	
	Thai, Khmer, and Cham		Confucianism,	
	mountain groups	10	Hoa Hao, Cao Dai,	
			Islam, and Christianity	*

*percent unknown
Sources: Countries of the World and Their Leaders Yearbook 1992 for data on ethnic groups; *The World Factbook 1992* for Taiwan ethnic and religious groups and for ethnic groups in Brunei, China, Indonesia, and the Philippines; *World Fact File 1990* for data on religions.

groups. Ethnic differences often accompany religious differences within countries, and in a number of cases the religion of the ex-imperial power continues to have practitioners.

Political and Economic Systems

Postcolonial political and economic systems combine, in varying mixes, elements of precolonial traditional institutions with "modern" elements adopted—and adapted—from Western models. China, North Korea, Vietnam, and Laos have "communist" institutions of Soviet origin, with one ideologically based party (though minor "parties" may be allowed to exist, they do not constitute a challenge to the Communist Parties); their economies are centrally planned and publicly owned, though recent economic liberalization in China, Laos, and Vietnam has opened opportunities for private entrepreneurs.

Japan and the Philippines have more recognizably Western democratic features with several major parties, though until 1993 the Liberal Democratic Party held power

Page 8: Some of the ethnic diversity in the Asian Pacific is shown by these portraits of people from Indonesia, China, Japan, Cambodia, and Vietnam.

Sources: Clockwise from top right: United Nations photo 149070/Andrea Brizzi; United Nations photo; United Nations photo by J. Corash; United Nations photo 159497/J. Bliebtreu; photo by Vera Simone. *Center:* United Nations photo/G. Cohen.

in Japan for all but a few months in the postwar period, and in the Philippines electoral competition was suspended during the period of martial law by former President Ferdinand Marcos. Both countries have economies based on private ownership, though in Japan the government has a major role in guiding the economy. That is also true of South Korea and Taiwan, whose governments are bureaucratic, authoritarian regimes in which the military has important influence, although elections in Korea in 1992 brought in the first civilian president in thirty years. The military is also politically involved in Indonesia, Thailand, Myanmar, and the Philippines. Private enterprise characterizes their economies, although in Indonesia the government controls oil and other extractive industries.

Singapore has a one-party-dominant civilian government, actively pursuing policies to promote economic expansion. Thailand and Cambodia are constitutional monarchies; Malaysia has a ceremonial sultan elected by the rulers of the former Malay states now incorporated into the Federation of Malaysia; and Brunei's sultan exercises supreme executive authority. Malaysia's multiethnic society is reflected in a ruling coalition of Malay, Chinese, and Indian parties in which the Malay Party is dominant. Hong Kong, still a British colony, is only now beginning to experience modest steps in the direction of self-government; its economy is capitalist, although the colonial government is heavily involved in providing social services such as public housing.

This quick overview of the variety of political institutions in the Asian Pacific is followed up with a more thorough discussion in Chapter 4.

Economic Indicators

As shown in Figures 1.3 and 1.4, Asian Pacific countries range from "developed" Japan to "underdeveloped" Laos. Japan has by far the largest gross domestic product (GDP) and the highest gross national product per capita or, more simply, per capita income (PCI). Next in GDP is China, with less than one-fifth of Japan's GDP and a low PCI, ranking twelfth of sixteen in the region. Brunei has the second highest PCI, although its total economic output is one of the smallest. South Korea's GDP of $283 billion ranks third highest, and Taiwan's and Indonesia's are also over $100 billion. In PCI Singapore, Hong Kong, Taiwan, and South Korea each top $6,000. With GDPs in the $60–100 billion range are Hong Kong and Thailand; from $20–50 billion are Malaysia, the Philippines, Singapore, and North Korea, and their PCIs vary from a low of $730 in the Philippines to a high of $14,210 in Singapore. At the low end in both GDP and PCI are Vietnam, Cambodia, Myanmar, and Laos.

Labels are usually given to distinguish the levels of economic development thus far reached by the countries. Leading the pack is Japan, a "developed" modern economy, followed by the four "little tigers," the newly industrializing countries (NICs) of South Korea, Taiwan, Singapore, and Hong Kong. In the next rank are those most ad-

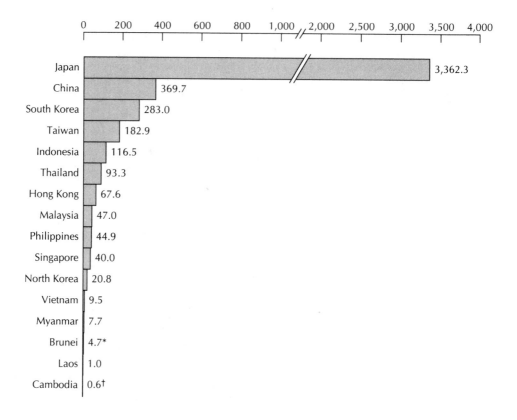

FIGURE 1.3   Gross Domestic Product, 1991 (in $ U.S. billion)

Sources: Asia Yearbook 1993 for Brunei, North Korea, Myanmar, Taiwan, Vietnam; *World Development Report 1993,* Tables 1, 1a, and 3, for other countries.
*1990 figure
†1994 estimate

vanced toward industrialization of the "developing" countries—Malaysia, Thailand, Indonesia, China, and perhaps also North Korea. Then come the more slowly progressing Philippines and at the bottom are the "backward" economies of Vietnam, Cambodia, Myanmar, and Laos. Oil wealth and small size put Brunei in a separate category of "rich but underdeveloped," very similar to Middle East oil sheikdoms.

Summing Up Similarities and Differences

To sum up this brief survey of the characteristics of Asian Pacific countries, we have found that all of them reached the modern era as traditional, agricultural societies with cultures that, although shaped by different belief systems, shared the social value of consensus. Some of them had had long histories as organized and distinct political entities, while others had not established a separate unified identity.

All of them felt the impact of colonialism to some degree. Although a few managed to escape colonial rule, the others did not, and all experienced the traumatic en-

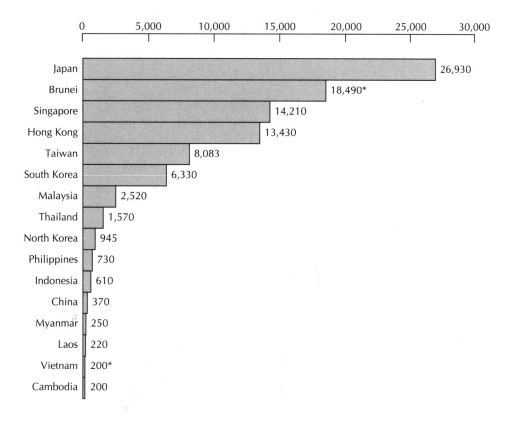

FIGURE 1.4   Gross National Product per Capita, 1991 (in $ U.S.)

Sources: Asia Yearbook 1993 for Brunei, North Korea, Myanmar, Taiwan, Vietnam; *Countries of the World and Their Leaders Yearbook 1992* for Cambodia; *World Development Report 1993,* Tables 1, 1a, and 3, for other countries.
*1990 figure

counter between the indigenous traditional order and the new "modern" ways brought in by the Westerners and later the Japanese. While the colonies each had different imperial masters pursuing somewhat different policies toward their "wards" with varying impact on the traditional political, economic, and social systems in the colonies, the common outcome in all was the awakening, or revival, of a sense of national identity and the demand for independence from alien rule.

When we look at the Asian Pacific countries now, three or more decades after independence was achieved, we are struck by the great differences among them, and generalizing about them is difficult. In the region are very large countries and tiny ones, some resource-rich and others resource-poor, one with a billion people and one with fewer than a third of a million, some with quite homogeneous populations and others a veritable patchwork of ethnically diverse people. The political and economic systems, though also quite varied, are typified by some form of authoritarianism and by a substantial degree of government direction of the economy in both the socialist and capitalist systems. Economic development in these countries is far from uniform; a cluster of affluent countries has reached a level rivaling the older developed states in Europe, a larger group of countries is moving up the economic ladder, and another smaller group is still struggling to raise its standard of living.

Having looked briefly at the variety of characteristics found among countries in the Asian Pacific region, we now move to the second part of this chapter. In it you are given an explanation of two different theories or frameworks to apply in comparing these countries with each other and with your own, the objective being to see which theory better explains why and how some countries have made progress in modernization and development and others have lagged behind.

THEORIES OF DEVELOPMENT

Development is the central organizing principle of this book and is also at the center of theories that have dominated the study of comparative politics in the last four decades. An explanation of how development is defined and why it is the organizing principle of our comparison of Asian Pacific countries is, therefore, in order.

What Is Development and Why Is It Important?

Development, like *modernization,* is a term that describes the structural and behavioral changes that a society undergoes in the process of acquiring an industrial system of production and distribution. Technologically, development requires the knowledge and use of increasingly complex and sophisticated machinery and techniques with which to control the environment and produce a variety of goods and services. Organizationally, development results in the increasingly specialized nature of political, social, and economic institutions and the multiple roles they impose on human beings in the course of carrying out diverse responsibilities as workers, parents, and citizens. Behaviorally, development involves a broad range of new beliefs and attitudes that individuals must acquire to adjust to the demands placed on them by social and geographic mobility, broader political allegiances, economic growth, and a technology that requires literacy, openness to new experiences, punctuality, and working with people in close proximity and under conditions fixed by large organizations rather than landlords and the dictates of nature.

What makes newly independent nation-states like those that are the subject of this book pursue development? Part of the answer is that modern knowledge and technology were almost invariably seen by the conquered as the source of the Westerners' power to subjugate them. This dictated their mastery as a means of sheer survival, their development as a means of self-defense. A second reason that non-Western people aspire to the "modernity" of the Western way of life is the affluence and comfort afforded by modern know-how and organization. The conveniences that those of us who have them consider necessities—plumbing, electricity, refrigerators, telephones, and so on—are compelling wants in and of themselves for most human beings who carry their water from wells, live and work by the light of day, and otherwise labor with primitive tools. It was enough, even without the aid of mass media, to have heard about the exceptional exploits of white men and women. And though not all or even a majority of traditional people living throughout Asia (or Africa or Latin America) necessarily admired or coveted a modern way of life when introduced to it, they were inescapably propelled toward it by the glitter of its promise and its subversion of their traditional way of life.

Out of a complex set of motives and incentives, therefore, Asian Pacific countries, like other countries of the Third World, began their excursion as independent nation-states with "development" as the central item on their agenda. Because there were neither blueprints for erecting such a modern edifice nor even much advice on what materials were necessary or where to begin the process of construction, the nations of the Asian Pacific pursued development in a wide variety of ways.

How to modernize? became the common concern of newly independent nation-states when colonialism came to an end after World War II. But this apparently simple question masked a number of complex theoretical as well as practical issues. How feasible is it to modernize by borrowing the institutions and procedures of highly industrialized countries? What kind of political order most effectively promotes economic growth and social cohesion? Is a market-oriented economic strategy or a state-driven command economy more promising? To what extent does a development strategy closely aligned with international capital inhibit a young state from following independent domestic and foreign policies? How does a state's national security policy affect its developmental strategy? How is a state's need for political order balanced with its need for democratic expression and input?

While policymakers in the new states faced the task of finding practical answers on how best to proceed toward modernization, scholars faced the thorny theoretical problem of how to analyze the politics of "developing" countries with the analytic tools used for comparing modern Western countries. In a world sharply split between the rich modernized nations and the poor backward nations struggling to develop with either hand-me-down colonial institutions or experimental revolutionary ones, comparative politics had to be redefined to focus on modernization. This redefinition led to three major questions: What was the process by which capitalist modernization in the West had originally taken place? How was that process different for latecomers? Why did development occur more readily in some countries than others?

The effort to answer these questions produced two very different kinds of theoretical approach. On the one hand, there was modernization theory, on the other there was dependency theory and world system theory. Though dependency theory has elements that distinguish it from world system approach, in this book the two will be considered as members of the same theoretical family. At the center of both modernization theory and dependency/world system theory are ideas about the function of the state and of the marketplace. Basic to understanding these contemporary theories is a grasp of the European intellectual tradition on which they draw—that is, the theoretical principles, premises, and concepts that laid the groundwork for understanding development in modernizing Europe. The three leading contributors to that tradition are Thomas Hobbes, Adam Smith, and Karl Marx, and it is to their ideas on the modern state and the modern marketplace that we now turn.

Thomas Hobbes's Theory of the State

The concerns that prompted Hobbes to construct his theory of the state in the seventeenth century (he lived from 1588 to 1679) are the same ones that faced the newly independent countries of the Asian Pacific at the end of World War II: civil war, ensuring the stability of a unified state, and securing the legitimacy of its regime. Dismayed at the horror of civil war in England, Hobbes undertook a scientific analysis of the causes of political disorder. Applying logic to the hypothetical situation of a "state of nature," Hobbes described human life without a government to maintain order as "solitary, poore, nasty, brutish, and short."[1] To avoid this perpetual state of civil strife, Hobbes argued, rational individuals agree to relinquish their natural rights to decide for themselves what is in their best interests to a state strong enough to secure political order. Thus Hobbes explained and justified citizens' obedience to a strong, authoritarian, and stable state as a rational alternative to the chaos of all individuals seeking their rights on the basis of might. Each individual with his or her own natural, self-interested agenda of desires and fears enters a social contract with all the others to obey the rules of the state.

Hobbes's objective—to prevent disorder—remains ours, and his solution—a national state strong enough to command political order and stability—has been extraordinarily enduring. Three centuries later Westerners still believe the state gets its legitimate mandate to decide right and wrong for everyone under its jurisdiction from the consent of the individuals over whom it rules. This seventeenth-century social contract conception of the authority of the state based on the self-interest of individuals is one of the two pillars of modern development theory. In its authoritarian form, the Hobbesian idea of the state has particular relevance for studying the varieties of authoritarian nation-states that dominate the Asian Pacific landscape.

Adam Smith's Theory of the Market

The second pillar of modern development theory is the marketplace. If the state provides political order on the basis of individuals' consent, the marketplace provides economic growth on the basis of individuals' choices to produce, sell, and buy. Living from 1723 to 1790, more than a century after Hobbes, Adam Smith laid the groundwork for today's modernization theory. He argued that the "natural" development of the market unencumbered by undue restrictions of the state best provides for economic growth and human welfare; what is in the economic self-interest of each individual operating in the marketplace coincides with the welfare of society as a whole. Indeed, by producing a better mousetrap or a better automobile to outsell your competitor you enrich not only yourself but contribute to the economic growth and prosperity of the entire society

Here too this eighteenth-century Western European theory of the free marketplace assumes extraordinary relevance to the Asian Pacific on the threshold of the twenty-first century. Some scholars have suggested that the phenomenal economic growth of the "four tigers" is attributable to their reliance on Adam Smith's "free marketplace," while others dispute this observation, arguing that in fact East Asian governments have been active players in the market. Thus, the experience of these Asian Pacific nations has assumed particular importance as a test of the validity of Smith's theory, and debate continues on the question of how applicable the free market is as a mechanism for latecomers to modernization. If anything, the debate has been refueled by the recent conversions to marketplace reforms on the part of the communist nations in the Asian Pacific—China, Vietnam, Laos, and even North Korea.

The marketplace and the state are thus at the center of the two dominant and contrasting theories of world "development" today. Contemporary modernization theory, which first made its appearance after World War II at the time the newly independent Asian Pacific nations were searching for solutions to their problems, heralds the marketplace as the universal engine of progress for all states. With the emergence of dependency theory in the 1960s and subsequently world system theory, a counterargument is made to explain why, contrary to the expectations of modernization theory, underdeveloped countries in Latin America (and presumably elsewhere) had actually failed to develop as expected. The dependency argument, which suggests that developing countries become more rather than less impoverished by the gross inequality of their international exchange relationships with the advanced countries, can be considered a forerunner and variant of world system theory. Like the dependency approach, world system theory views the expanding global marketplace as benefiting the rich industrialized "core" at the expense of the poor "peripheral" countries. In contrast to modernization theory, world system theory contends that the world market, even as it expands, causes an invidious division of nations that is akin to the class hierarchy within nation-states, with a "core" of powerful nations at the center, a multitude of weak nations on the "periphery," and the "semi-periphery" of nations moving either up or down the international ladder of wealth and power.

Before further discussion of these two dominant contemporary theories of development, however, one more piece of the Western European Enlightenment tradition must be put into place as the foundation of today's theoretical discussions: the Marxian frame of analysis. World system theory is a descendant of Marx's theory of historical evolution. Without understanding Marx, therefore, the issues separating the two competing theories of development are difficult to comprehend.

Marx's Theory of Historical Evolution

Marx, who lived from 1818 to 1883, was almost as avid an admirer of the marketplace as Adam Smith. He was certainly as devout a believer in progress. But in two important ways his vision of the marketplace was markedly different from Smith's. First, he took a historical view of the marketplace as a relative newcomer itself and therefore as vulnerable to decrepitude as earlier social systems that had disappeared from European history. Just as the bourgeoisie had ushered in the marketplace, according to Marx, the working class would usher in its nemesis: a humanitarian communism. The second characteristic of Marx's vision of the marketplace distinguishing it from Smith's was its ceaselessly dynamic motion. In an endless search for profits, the marketplace was an irrepressible, globally expansive phenomenon that would spread into every nook and cranny of the earth's surface, breaking down national barriers indisiminately and replacing them with an international class struggle of capitalists ainst the working class.

In his view of the state, Marx differed not only from Smith but also from the clas-: contract theory of Hobbes. In contrast to Smith's minimalist notion of the state's role in assuring the needs of an expansive marketplace, Marx saw the state as a pow-erful agent of the capitalist class. If the bourgeois class was the engine of economic progress, of necessity it had to have the cooperation of the state in its activities, es-pecially when it struck out for new lands to conquer and new shores from which to embark on its journeys throughout the world. In contrast to Hobbes's notion of the state as an autonomous neutral force subjecting all individuals equally to its authority, freeing them to participate in the economic activities of the marketplace under secure rules of political order, the state for Marx was an instrument of the business class for whom the market was a private benefit as well as a public arena of economic growth.

This is the root of the opposition between modernization and world system the-ories: In the former, the state when it functions properly represents and serves all people equally, while in the latter, the state when it operates to support the market-place becomes an ally of the capitalist class, which is its major beneficiary. Although access to the state is never formally denied to anybody, the state's interests coincide with the class that makes (and keeps) the state healthy, wealthy, and wise.

Modern Theories of Development

Modernization theory and world system theory are the two most frequently encoun-tered contenders to explain the phenomenon of "development." They may not both embrace progress with the same unalloyed optimism, but they do begin with the same two human constructions—the state and the marketplace—as their Enlightenment heritage. Both understand development as the outcome of the capitalist marketplace's transformation of small-scale subsistence agricultural societies under traditional local forms of rule—kingship, aristocracy, or chiefdoms—into ever expanding large-scale industrial societies with nation-states governed by competitive elections. But two characteristics stand out as sharply dividing these contending theories of develop-ment: their understanding of "time" and their outlook toward national versus global "space." Dependency theory, often considered a third approach, is here treated as an antecedent of world system theory.

Modernization Theory. Modernization theory, like Newtonian physics, does not see the passage of time as changing the fundamental equation of how the capi-talist marketplace works. Nor does it entertain the idea that beyond the individual there is an additional motor of change: corporate bodies. From this perspective of modernization, therefore, it matters little *when* nations embark on the process of de-velopment; the rules, the relationships, and the consequences must of necessity re-main pretty much the same. Countries like Indonesia or Malaysia that pursue modernization in the latter half of the twentieth century confront an agenda similar to that of England, France, or Japan in the eighteenth and nineteenth centuries: capital accumulation, investment, and externally open trade relations relying on unfettered market mechanisms for exchange.

The engine and focus of development, for modernization theory, is always on the internal domestic aspects of national development: streamlining the centralized state so it can protect the nation's economic marketplace and domestic security against external and internal threats, encouraging the education, skills, and opportunities of individuals so they can function in the marketplace. The external or international context of course plays a role in providing opportunities for raising capital, trading, or acquiring resources and markets, but national development, in the final analysis, according to this theory, is internally generated by an enterprising business class and a neutral state apparatus capable of protecting property and securing domestic tranquillity.

The autonomy of the state in modernization theory signifies its distance from all social classes and its effective control of the military. Modernization in this theoretical conception is a *national* responsibility, requiring a state strong enough to promote the marketplace but aloof enough to remain outside the arena of economic policy-making. In the early stage of the modernization process, it is argued, the state is likely to need greater strength to protect its infant development from undue competitive pressures. It may even be bureaucratically authoritarian in its direction of the nation's economic development in its fledgling state. This was certainly the case among the European nation-states in the early stages of capitalist formation when major wars among them served to strengthen the state even further. It is also the theory's explanation of why newly independent nation-states exhibit bureaucratic authoritarian characteristics to a far greater extent than is compatible with the standard of advanced developed nation-states.

In these theoretical discussions of the state's role in the development process, "the state" seems to take on a life of its own, as if it were a single actor. We talk about it as being strong or weak, intervening to a greater or lesser extent in the economy, and so on. For a number of reasons, including the fact that the state plays such an important role in our lives as modern citizens, like a parent writ large who authors the rules that govern society, it may be important to remind ourselves that the state is an abstraction; it does not actually exist as a substantial "thing." As such, it refers to an extraordinarily complex organization made up of many people, often appointed, sometimes elected, usually representing others and functioning in diverse institutional settings that frequently pull in different directions. As a "voice of authority," therefore, it neither speaks in a single voice nor does it actually represent the nation as a whole, except in the metaphorical sense.

World System Theory.   For world system theory, "late developers" face an entirely different dilemma from early developers when they confront the task of modernizing. Their lack of an internal bourgeois-driven developmental dynamic in the first place makes these nations subservient and vulnerable to the depredations of the advanced nations. This results in unequal relationships between strong states protecting the interests of their international investors and weak states unable to protect either their human or material resources from the ravages of an exchange system that favors

[handwritten marginal note: weak players are unable to compete w/ the existing or strong players]

the strong and the wealthy. Because this new dilemma is an internationally determined one in which starkly unequal players compete freely in an open match without handicaps, the weak players never get a chance to strengthen their game, while
the already skillful players win not only all the games but eventually also the other
players and the ballpark.

According to the early dependency version of this theoretical approach, expressed in the 1960s by scholars specializing in the Latin American region, exporting
capitalism becomes part of the problem rather than being part of the solution to
poverty and backwardness. Unlike Lenin's more optimistic scenario of imperialism as
a process in which capitalists turn backward countries into the international equivalents of revolutionary workers who would eventually break the chain of exploitation,
dependency theorists held a pessimistic outlook for the Third World. For Western investors in developing countries, the activity they were engaged in might be conventionally understood as modernizing, bringing new ideas, superior sources of wealth,
and the skills and attitudes required to produce them to backward peoples, but the
dependency interpretation of their consequences was a bleak vision of permanent impoverishment for Third World peoples while further enriching the already prosperous developed nations. The dependency perspective thus dramatically countered the
optimistic liberal prospects of effective charitable assistance to help the weak become
stronger. In its place was a grim depiction of a perverse umbilical cord by which the
strong advanced country saps the nutrients of the underdeveloped dependent nation,
permanently impairing its ability to develop at all.

[handwritten marginal note: dependency they → weak become more weak to help rich. liberalist they → rich help the weak to develop.]

In Immanuel Wallerstein's more fully elaborated theoretical consideration of a
world economic system, the same idea is a premise: that highly developed nations at
the core of the international marketplace operate as an external constraint on the internal economic and political structures of weak, peripheral nations in the international system.[2] But Wallerstein's elaboration of a three-tiered conception of the world
system leaves the theoretical door open to both upward and downward mobility of
individual nations from the lowest and highest tiers to the middle tier, the semi-
peripheral or middle-class level of nations. As scholars began to document incidents
of autonomously acting states in some parts of the periphery that move upward into
semi-peripheral status, world system theory was modified to take them into account.
By generating policies to support local initiatives, even relatively weaker states are
able to increase their bargaining chips in the international marketplace, thus coun-
teracting the pressures from externally powerful players to their own advantage. Such
a modified model of "dependent development" suggests that even weak states can
play a mediating role to forge effective alliances between local bourgeoisie in dependent countries and the powerful multinational bourgeoisie combing the world for investment opportunities.

This less deterministic vision of a global market system, in which less-developed
countries have alternatives to being stifled by the constraints of core countries' profiteering, holds particular promise for understanding the dramatic postwar development of Taiwan, Singapore, Hong Kong, and South Korea into "tigers." According to
Wallerstein's theory, the NICs have been able to catapult themselves up into the middle rank of world nations by means of a strong state capable of mediating between na-

tional capabilities and international opportunities. The state actively fosters its own development by promoting a coalition of indigenous bourgeois elements and transnational corporations in search of new locations for investment and production. This theory "brings the state back in" as an autonomous actor in the global economy.[3] Rather than emphasizing the domination of multinational corporations and the world system needs in controlling the shape of economic progress in less-developed countries, this approach suggests that there may be considerable latitude for a developing nation to adopt a strategy of development that will maximize its strength in aligning itself with particular agents of international capital.

Convergence of the Two Theories. Despite the considerable difference between modernization theory and world system theory, both have modified their original positions, resulting in something of a convergence between the two. The crux of that convergence is the increased role of the state in directing and promoting economic as well as political development. For modernization theory this has meant moving away from Adam Smith's conception of the state as laissez-faire; for world system theory this has meant moving away from Karl Marx's conception of the state as a mere tool of the business class. For both theories the practical successes of Asian Pacific nations in fostering economic growth and development have provided evidence in their favor as well as incentives to modify their arguments.

SUMMARY

The preliminary sketch of the countries in the Asian Pacific covered in the first half of this chapter demonstrates how richly varied the region is in almost all dimensions—area, population, geography, natural resources, cultural legacy, colonial experience, and system of government since independence.

This diversity is in marked contrast to the aspiration all these countries share, that of development into prosperous, modern nation-states. With a resource base ranging from rich (Brunei with its oil) to poor (Japan), with belief systems including among others animism, Confucianism, Buddhism, Islam, and Catholicism, and with colonial structures inherited from Western European countries stretching from Portugal to Great Britain and the United States, it is difficult to imagine a single path of development for them all. And indeed the disparities among them with respect to how prosperous and modern they have become are enormous. If the astounding economic growth of the "four tigers" has made the Pacific Rim a household term in the West, the stagnation of a country like Myanmar or the slow pace of change in a country like Laos raise the question, What factors explain why some countries develop rapidly and others seem to resist the process entirely?

A number of possible answers to this question can be derived from the two competing theoretical frameworks discussed in the second half of this chapter. One theory bases its analysis on the original Western experience with capitalist development, while the other's analysis begins with the difficulties developing countries have had in adopting this model. Despite the great differences between these two theories, however, there is one internal factor that both can agree might well explain why particular countries in the Asian Pacific have developed more rapidly than others: a strong, autonomous, and activist state. In the next chapter the diverse colonial legacy of Asian Pacific countries will be explored as a possible factor that influences how strong or weak modern states in the region are today.

QUESTIONS FOR DISCUSSION

1. In what ways are Asian Pacific countries different from each other? similar to each other? different from your own country? similar to it?
2. What are the differences between living in a "developed" and an "underdeveloped" society? Why is development so appealing to people everywhere?
3. In the rise of modern capitalism in Europe, what contribution did government make? the market?
4. Can developing countries follow that same formula for success?

NOTES

1. *Hobbes' Leviathan* (Oxford: Clarendon Press, 1909), p. 97.
2. Immanuel Wallerstein, *The Modern World-System: Capitalist Agriculture and the Origins of the European World-Economy in the Sixteenth Century* (New York: Academic Press, Text Edition, 1976).
3. Peter B. Evans, Dietrich Rueschemeyer, and Theda Skocpol, eds., *Bringing the State Back In* (Cambridge: Cambridge University Press, 1985).

FOR FURTHER READING

Modernization Theory

Black, Cyril E., ed. *Comparative Modernization: A Reader.* New York: The Free Press, 1976, pp. 25-61 (Samuel P. Huntington, "The Change to Change: Modernization, Development, and Politics") and pp. 62-68 (Dean C. Tipps, "Modernization Theory and the Comparative Study of Societies: A Critical Perspective").

Etzioni, Amitai, and Eva Etzioni, eds. *Social Change.* New York: Basic Books, 1964, pp. 285-300 (W. W. Rostow, "The Takeoff Into Self-Sustained Growth") and pp. 342-61 (Alex Inkeles, "Making Men Modern: On the Causes and Consequences of Individual Change in Six Developing Countries").

Dependency and World System Theory

Evans, Peter. *Dependent Development: The Alliance of Multinational State and Local Capital in Brazil.* Princeton, NJ: Princeton University Press, 1979, pp. 14-54 ("Imperialism, Dependency, and Dependent Development").

Seligson, Mitchell A., and John T. Passe-Smith, eds. *Development and Underdevelopment: The Political Economy of Inequality.* Boulder: Lynne Rienner Publishers, 1993, pp. 217–30 (Immanuel Wallerstein, "The Present State of the Debate on World Inequality").

Shannon, Thomas Richard. *An Introduction to the World System Perspective.* Boulder: Westview Press, 1989.

Wallerstein, Immanuel. *The Capitalist World Economy.* Cambridge: Cambridge University Press, 1979.

Three Theories

So, Alvin Y. *Social Change and Development: Modernization, Dependency, and World-System Theories.* Newbury Park: Sage Publications, 1990.

chapter 2

The Imposition of Colonialism

Modernization in the Asian Pacific begins with colonialism. Although foreign ideas had contributed layers of cultural influence throughout East and Southeast Asia for thousands of years, Western colonialism was unlike anything that preceded it. The Arabs, Indians, Malays, and Chinese who had set themselves up as rulers and had conducted trade and settled throughout the Asian region had never been accountable to monarchs elsewhere; the Europeans who arrived after the sixteenth century came to build empires for their monarchs in Portugal, Spain, England, and France, creating colonies out of other people's territory and incorporating them into the world market system.

The story of how the modern world insinuated itself into Asia, transforming the lives of those it subjugated, is complex. It has been told by different people in different ways and continues to be the subject of intense controversy, although for the most part the outward forms of colonialism have disappeared. The nations that exist in Pacific Asia today are in one way or another products of the intercourse between East and West over the past four centuries. During this time, the system we call colonialism swept the world, altering everything in its course. But in the process of incorporating the world's people into a global economy, the originators of capitalism—Britain, France, the Unites States—were themselves undergoing continual changes that turned modernization at the center into a moving target and resulted in variations of the colonial enterprise on the periphery. Under Portuguese and Spanish rule, colonies fared quite differently than under Britain and France in the nineteenth century and under Japanese and American colonial administration in the twentieth century. Not surprisingly, responses to the challenge of modernization have varied with both time and circumstance.

But for Asians, as for all non-Western people, modernization was brought by outsiders who considered themselves superior both materially and spiritually. The merchant-adventurers from Portugal, Spain, Holland, England, and France were accompanied by Christian missionaries armed with faith that conversion to belief in their God would rescue the heathen Asians from the errors of Hinduism, Buddhism, Confucianism, Islam, or the nature-worship, magical beliefs of animism. By its very nature, the Christian religious enterprise was an economic, political, and social form of Western intrusion quite distinct from the Indianizing influences that had followed in the wake of Arab and Indian trade throughout the region.

Trade and religion brought Western values, ideas, technology, and goods, the instruments for breaking down the natural contours of the old Asian world to prepare the way for a revolutionary process of change that continues to this very day. From Asians' perspective this Western intrusion was at once appealing and threatening to their established way of life. To Westerners, prying open Asian societies was somewhere between a duty and a blessing, bound to yield economic enrichment and spiritual salvation.

Merchants and missionaries were followed, especially in the nineteenth century, by administrators, governors, and resident advisers as well as the armed forces of the Western powers. The idea that political and socioeconomic development would also flow from the contact between Western imperialism and the "backward" peoples of Asia justified taking control of Asia as colonies. Colonialism in this phase entailed the remaking of Asia in the image of the West. By establishing political and administrative rule, Englishmen and Frenchmen would be modeling the benefits of modern society to stir in primitive peoples the desire to become modern. The result would be a world enriched by representative institutions and individual freedoms. We will not elaborate here on the destructive and rapacious aspects of Western colonial rule. The underlying problem for Asians with this benign view of colonialism's purpose was the assumption that modernization meant Westernization. How were Japanese, Chinese, Koreans, Thai, Vietnamese, or Javanese to become modern without also becoming Western? Was it possible to become Western without losing one's own identity? What exactly was the Western experience of modernization that formed the basis of expectations for Asians?

The story of colonialism as the stimulus to modernization in Asia really begins in Europe, where great economic and political changes from the fifteenth century on impelled the people of that continent outward to assert control over the rest of the world. So in the first sections of this chapter, the European roots of colonialism are uncovered and examined in the light of the two theories of development that were introduced in Chapter 1. Then we describe the traditional societies of Asia as they were, before recounting the history of how the Europeans came and carved out their empires in Southeast Asia and exerted their influence in East Asia. The rest of the chapter looks first at the puzzling issue of why China and Japan responded so differently to the challenges of colonialism's demands for modernization and finally at the character of colonial rule in Southeast Asia as experienced by four of the colonies in that region.

EUROPEAN ROOTS OF COLONIALISM

Five hundred years ago living conditions worldwide were very similar; most people did hard physical labor, relying on their own and animal power to raise food and produce necessities for themselves. A few, the elites, did brain work: making political decisions, directing wars, collecting taxes, supervising religious and educational institutions. But the gap between have and have-not peoples was not as great as it is today. One estimate[1] is that before the industrial revolution, differences in income levels between the poorest and the richest countries were in the range of 1.0 to 1.6 and that the standard of living in Europe as a whole was lower than in China and about the same as in the rest of the world. Capitalism changed all that.

Colonialism grew out of the extraordinary changes that ushered in capitalism in Western Europe in the fifteenth century: the scientific, Protestant, and commercial revolutions. The Renaissance had released human energies for improving life on earth rather than preparing for life in heaven. The scientific revolution made the physical world more comprehensible to and controllable by human intelligence. And the Protestant revolution shattered the secular power of the Catholic Church, strengthening the individual nation-states of Europe. When the Portuguese and Spaniards started crisscrossing the seas in search of precious metals, valuable spices, and quality fabrics, they reduced the globe to a single market, centered in Europe. By the middle of the seventeenth century, the king of England had chartered companies to establish colonies in North America and India. Colonialism as the process of incorporating peoples in Asia, Africa, and the New World into the commercialized web of political life in Europe had begun.

The transformation of Europe from feudalism to capitalism occurred in stages. In the mercantilist stage, the precious metals brought to Portugal and Spain from their colonies in the Western Hemisphere went to buy commodities from England and the Netherlands, becoming available as productive capital in those more advanced economies. There feudal manors were giving way to commercialized agriculture, mills, and mines. Merchants and lords were becoming capitalists who no longer saw land as an inheritance to support a way of life but as a means to make a profit. As land was enclosed, peasants were forced into cities where they became wageworkers. Artisans and craftsmen were also driven into the working class when the commodities they produced could not compete with goods produced more cheaply in greater volume in the new factories built by the capitalists.

With the industrial revolution in the late eighteenth century, capitalism moved into higher gear. In this second stage, manufacturing greatly increased productive capacity, and the voracious appetites of machinery for raw materials to continually expand production changed the nature of colonial undertakings. Under mercantilist colonialism, exotic luxury items like tea, porcelain, spices, and silks had been imported from the colonies into Europe. Now with the industrial stage of capitalism, there was a two-way trade. Minerals, fibers for manufacturing, oil, rubber, tin, as well as increased quantities of tea, coffee, and tobacco flowed into Europe and the United States to satisfy the vastly expanded population of consumers and producers. In the other direction cotton goods, iron and steel products, alcoholic beverages, and cigarettes were exported to the colonies. In addition to this European commodity trade, the colonies provided opportunities for lucrative capital investments. Between 1880 and the First World War there was a virtual frenzy of competition among imperialist nations to acquire exclusive control of territory in Asia and Africa.

The colonial knots tied in the late nineteenth and early twentieth centuries are central to the discussion of modernization in non-Western areas. What impact did colonial status have on the traditional economies of non-Western peoples either to impair or enhance the chances of their subsequent ability to modernize? Some scholars deflate the significance of economic exploitation in the colonies, noting that European countries needed neither raw materials nor market outlets for their manufactured goods to any substantial degree.[2] Others argue that mere size (in absolute terms) of foreign trade or investment is not as critical in assessing their importance as their interrelatedness, that is, the degree to which a country has been incorporated as a dependent satellite into the world economic market. These different outlooks are at the core of the two alternative theoretical perspectives introduced in Chapter 1. Each perspective approaches the question of colonialism differently and interprets the facts of the colonial period of Asian history differently, as will be seen in the next section.

TWO THEORETICAL VIEWS OF COLONIALISM

Modernization Theory

Modernization theory approaches colonialism as an export commodity of the Western industrializing nations. Through colonial rule, advanced industrial nations export the productive, scientific, and social potential of modern liberal society to "backward," outlying areas. In their colonial outreach, capitalist nations extend their accomplishments beyond their national boundaries, thus opening up "backward" or traditional societies to the progressive potential of modern development. The initial motivation for foreign capitalist ventures may have been to expand markets and profits for their own domestic benefit, but the long-range consequences were to sow the seeds of modernization among insular and custom-bound peoples in backward parts of the world. The very term *opening* to refer to Western encroachments suggests a liberating force, a loosening of the restrictions of tradition-bound peoples from their ancient moorings.

This does not necessarily mean excusing the more unsavory aspects of colonial exploitation or political subjugation; what it does mean is that colonialism is envisioned as an extension of modern civilization, which confronts traditional societies with the challenge of fundamental changes to their ancient way of life. These fundamental changes are understood as national—not regional or global—developments. As each colony obtains its independence, having spent a tutelary period under the wings of a more advanced industrial nation, it is expected to replicate, albeit in modified form, the original European pattern of national development, following a sequence of steps considered necessary to transform a traditional way of life into a modern one.

In this delineation of the process, colonization makes modernization as a potentiality available to people in "backward" areas of the globe. If countries are unable to benefit from the opportunity, an explanation must be sought in the internal factors that impede progress, the resistance to change of enduring traditions, for example. By focusing almost exclusively on the domestic socioeconomic and political aspects of change, the approach ignores the constraints on developmental resourcefulness that derive from the complex international web of dependency relations.

World System Theory

From the world system perspective, colonialism is the incorporation of new territories and people into the global network of market relationships. When precapitalist societies are brought into the existing order of the world market they come in at the "periphery." In their relationship with the powerful "core" of advanced capitalist nations, these colonies, even when they gain their political independence, remain economically and politically weak. In between core and peripheral nations lies an intermediate or "semi-periperhal" zone of nations either moving up from their backward status as low-production, low-paid economic areas to high-production, well-paid economic areas or moving down from more advanced to less advanced economies.

At its inception in the sixteenth century, the world system was coterminous with Europe. Since then, core nations (or those attempting to move into that position) have used a combination of force and guile to enlarge the global market in order to remain competitive in a dynamically charged international market. This competition among core nations to supersede one another drives the system. For newly incorporated or peripheral countries (whether they are formal colonies or not), however, it means dependence on the core and exploitation as the price of admission. As do lower-class people within capitalist society, this theory suggests, peripheral nations face overwhelming odds against becoming truly independent and prosperous members of the world community. From this perspective, development or improvement is not merely a question of becoming politically independent and modernized; it is a question of how many cards one has to play in the mobility game within a worldwide system, which for the most part is stacked in favor of those who are already on top.

Controversy between advocates of these two theories as applicable to late-twentieth-century economic progress in some Asian Pacific countries has led to a third theoretical perspective centering on *the role of the state* to explain how Taiwan and other newly industrializing countries (NICs) have been able to move from peripheral status as colonies to semi-peripheral prosperity. This "statist" theory of development will be discussed further in Chapter 5.

TRADITIONAL SOCIETIES ON THE EVE OF COLONIALISM

What were societies like in East and Southeast Asia before Western colonialism hit them? Why did some traditional societies succumb more easily to colonial rule than others? To understand the impact of Western colonialism it helps to have an understanding of the sum of earlier influences, sometimes referred to as *traditional society,* that the Europeans discovered when they arrived.

Economically and socially, societies throughout the Asian Pacific were quite similar prior to the seventeenth century. They were agrarian societies, many of them de-

Rice farming requires cooperation to build and maintain the paddies, as in the terraced fields in Indonesia.
Source: United Nations photo 154948/Ray Witlin.

pendent on rice cultivation with its requirements for substantial irrigation, intensive labor, and community cooperation. The family was the basic unit of production; land was divided equally among sons in China but inherited by the eldest son in Japan. Within the family, as in the larger society, rigid social hierarchies favored male over female, old over young.

Belief Systems

The oldest and most enduring beliefs were in spirits attached to the variety of elements upon which people depended but over which they had no control; especially in rural areas these "superstitions" continued to coexist with the more organized and sophisticated religious doctrines that fanned out from the great civilizations in China and India.

Three great religious traditions—Hinduism, Buddhism, and Islam—had spread eastward from India and Arabia throughout Southeast and East Asia, while Confucianism had made its way from China to Korea, Japan, and Vietnam, where its principles were adapted to the distinctive conditions in each society. By the time Europeans began arriving in the sixteenth century, Hindu influence—once pervasive in most of Southeast Asia—was still visible only in Bali. Buddhism, which had followed Hinduism from India, was still dominant in Burma, Thailand, Laos, and Cambodia and had left traces of its presence in parts of Indonesia. Islam, having arrived in the fourteenth century, was established in Malaya, Indonesia, and the southern Philippines. The only place where animism prevailed untouched by any of the major belief systems from either India or China was the Philippines; when Christianity was brought there by the Spaniards it swept through the society like a brushfire.

An ethical system emphasizing propriety in earthly affairs, Confucianism was able to coexist with religious belief systems: in China with Taoism and Buddhism, and in Korea, Vietnam, and Japan with Buddhism. Chinese Confucianism was reshaped into a distinctively Japanese form by the additional influence of Shinto, the belief in the divinity of the emperor, and Bushido, a strong warrior code of honor. Although Confucianism and the religious beliefs of Hinduism, Buddhism, and Islam differ substantially from each other, they share a powerful common denominator: a fatalistic acceptance of the human condition.

Political Organization

In politics, authoritarian rule was the norm among traditional peoples in the Asian Pacific. There were enormous differences in the scale of political organization from the atomistic village communities of the Philippines to the highly centralized state bureaucracy of the Chinese empire. But even in China, where the central government ruled over a large land area, it did not penetrate down into the villages where most of the people lived. And the actual power wielded by the central government waxed and waned over the centuries; when the emperor's power waned, regional leadership exercised by a middle tier of provincial administrators filled the vacuum. In the nineteenth century the Qing or Manchu dynasty's power was on the decline, increasing China's susceptibility to penetration from outside as well as to challenges from within.

Kingdoms similar to the Chinese existed, though on a smaller scale, in the other Confucian states and in Buddhist Burma, Thailand, Cambodia, and Laos, and had existed earlier in Sumatra. The political institutions of Hindu and Islamic societies were typically small in scale as, for example, the Malay sultanates. In all these societies, the village was the lowest level of social organization. In the north and central Philippines, atomistic village communities were the only political structures, and this lack of cohesiveness may have made the Philippines more susceptible to foreign cultural penetration than other more cohesive societies.

The basis of the rulers' legitimacy and the ranking of different classes in the social hierarchy also were influenced by the dominant belief systems. In Hindu, Buddhist, and Islamic politics, divine will legitimized unlimited personalist monarchs, but detachment from worldly affairs kept the Hindu and Buddhist priesthood largely out of the political realm, and they did not challenge kingly authority. Islam, on the other hand, views this world as important and religion as governing all aspects of life, so the notion of separation of church and state is quite alien to the Moslem worldview.

Social Hierarchy

The ranking of classes below the emperor, king, or sultan put the military and merchants higher in the Hindu and Islamic social hierarchies than in the Buddhist; in the simple village structures of the Philippines the village leader, the *datu,* occupied the top of the pyramid. Peasants in all societies were low in rank, the very bottom being occupied by slaves, outcastes, untouchables, and in Islamic societies the non-Moslems, the "infidels." In Confucian China, the emperor's legitimacy rested in practice on performance; if the emperor and his civil service of scholar-bureaucrats met their moral obligations to the classes beneath them, the inferiors owed their superiors obedience and respect. Below scholar-officials in the Chinese social hierarchy, land-owning peasants ranked higher than artisans and merchants, the latter not at all well regarded. Landless workers and servants occupied the bottom position.

In Japan, the Confucian social hierarchy was modified to incorporate the pre-Confucian Shinto belief in the divine descent of the emperor from a sun goddess. Also unlike China, the Japanese emperor had for centuries symbolized the unique identity of Japan, though until 1868 actual power was exercised by the *shogun,* a military leader who reached his preeminent position in wars with several hundred other feudal clan leaders, the *daimyo.* The emperor was the ceremonial head of the social order and the shogun the head of the political order. Next came the daimyo and their armed supporters, the *samurai,* followed by the peasants. Below them—as in China—came artisans and merchants, and at the bottom the *eta* or outcasts, whose low status as the handlers of animal carcasses and leather remains in effect still. In Japan, the military tradition carried on by the shogun, daimyo, and samurai was much more powerful and respected than in China where, although military force played a major role in settling the issue of dynastic succession, the military profession itself was not highly valued.

These characteristics, it is speculated, made traditional societies more or less resistant to Western influence and the conditions imposed by colonialism. Darling[3] ranks China as the most resistant to foreign influence; the Chinese-penetrated states of Korea, Vietnam, and Japan somewhat less so; and the least resistant the Southeast Asian countries that had experienced the cultural impact of Hinduism, Buddhism, and in the cases of Malaya and Indonesia, Islam as well. Cohesiveness of societal structures was highest in Korea, Vietnam, and China and least in the pre-Spanish Philippines and in Japan.[4] Resistance to change may also have been greater in those societies in which people had the collective memory of a long, shared history than in societies of shorter duration. Countries that had existed for a thousand or more years prior to the arrival of Western colonialism include China, Vietnam, Korea, Cambodia, and Japan,[5] although their boundaries were much more fluid and permeable than those of modern European states.

Geography also impeded or enhanced the Western impact. Size may account in part for China's escaping colonization by a single foreign power, and the 3,000-mile extent of the Indonesian archipelago meant that Dutch rule spread only gradually from Sumatra and Java to the other islands. Topography also plays a role: For example, landlocked Laos was relatively inaccessible to the seagoing imperial powers as compared to countries with coasts. The presence of natural resources, such as tin and rubber in Malaya, and soil suited for crops in southern Burma, Java, and Sumatra added to their appeal.

THE CONQUEST OF SOUTHEAST AND EAST ASIA

In colonizing Southeast Asia, Europeans brought people together under one foreign government without regard for either natural boundaries or ethnic affinities. Indeed ethnic, linguistic, and religious divisions among colonized peoples facilitated their subjugation and were reinforced by divide-and-rule colonial policies and the importation of Chinese and Indians to work on the coffee and rubber plantations and in the mines. When these artificially created colonial states later became independent, their governments and leaders inherited all the attendant problems of trying to forge nations out of states arbitrarily imposed to serve European interests.

In China, Korea, and Japan, on the other hand, strong sovereign states with enduring boundaries predated European domination. Each had a long history of unified rule, a homogeneous population, and a highly developed and sophisticated civilization rivaling that of Europe. They were capable of effectively resisting the encroachments of Western colonizers forcing them to pay higher costs for economic and political control. Unlike Southeast Asia, none of the East Asian countries became outright European colonies. Japan escaped colonization altogether and joined the Europeans in their own game, making Taiwan and Korea its imperial possessions. China came close to being colonized; the term *semicolony* seems a fitting description of its status in the nineteenth century, when the European countries (later joined by Japan) carved out for themselves special "spheres of influence" in parts of that vast country.

Western colonialism occurred in two phases, the mercantilist and the capitalist, as different motives reflective of economic changes in Europe impelled Western countries to conquests in Asia. Major events in the history of colonialism in the Asian Pacific are identified in Table 2.1.

The Mercantilist Phase

The Portuguese and Spanish arriving in the sixteenth century plied their trade quite differently from earlier Westerners who, since Marco Polo's time, had traveled overland between the Mediterranean and Asia in pursuit of silks and spices. In this early mercantilist phase of capitalism, the Dutch and the British, following closely on the heels of the Portuguese, vied with one another for control of key ports and sea lanes. Merchants typically negotiated or coerced local rulers into granting them an array of trading rights: the freedom to move in and out of Asian ports, favorable tariff treatment, a small foothold on shore for residence, storage, and ship provisioning. With their modest goal of acquiring desired Asian products, the European traders in this period did not need to penetrate extensively into the hinterland, nor did they usually assume responsibility for carrying on governmental functions. Exceptions were the Spanish in the Philippines and the Dutch East India Company in some of the islands now making up Indonesia, where control was extended in varying degrees.

TABLE 2.1   Important Dates in the Era of Colonialism

1511	Portuguese capture Malacca
1557	Portuguese take Macau
1564	Spanish take the Philippines
1637	Shimabara Rebellion by Japanese Christians against Tokugawa shogunate
1640	Japan bans contact with foreigners
1641	Dutch East India Company takes Jakarta, Malacca, Moluccas
1682	Dutch government takes over from Company
1786	British take Penang
1819	British take Singapore
1824	Dutch and British settle conflict over colonies by agreeing to Dutch control of the East Indies and British control of Malay peninsula
1842	First Anglo-Chinese ("Opium") War; Treaty of Nanjing
1850–1864	Taiping Rebellion against Qing Dynasty
1853	Admiral Perry's fleet arrives in Japan
1857	Second Anglo-Chinese War; Yangtze Valley opened, China cedes territory to Russia
1862	French take Cochin China
1863	French protectorate over Cambodia
1867	British protectorate over Kingdom of Burma
1868	Tokugawa shogunate overthrown; Meiji Restoration
1874	French protectorate over Kingdom of Annam-Tonkin
1885	British abolish Kingdom of Burma and administer as part of India
1887	French consolidate rule over Vietnam
1888	British protectorates over Brunei, North Borneo, Sarawak
1893	French protectorate over Laos
1894–1895	Sino-Japanese War; China cedes Taiwan to Japan; Japan gets rights in Korea, France gets sphere of influence in south, Russians in Manchuria
1896	British establish Federation of Malay States
1898	Spanish-American War, United States takes the Philippines; in China, Germany gets sphere of influence in Shandong Peninsula, Russia in Liaodong Peninsula, French in Guangzhou
1900	Boxer Rebellion (China)
1904–1905	Russo-Japanese War; Japan gets southern Sakhalin, sphere of influence in Manchuria, and more rights in Korea
1910	Japan annexes Korea
1911	Qing Dynasty ends; Republic of China proclaimed
1913	Russia establishes protectorate over Mongolia
1914–1918	World War I; Japan gets German interests in Shandong and influence in eastern Inner Mongolia and in Fujian Province
1917	Russian Revolution; Japan expands influence in Manchuria
1931	Japanese begin military conquest of China
1934	Japanese create puppet state, Manchukuo
1941–1942	Japanese occupy the Philippines, Malaya, Singapore, Indonesia, Burma, French Indochina; by agreement with government, Japanese forces enter Thailand

The Portuguese and the Spanish.   The Portuguese captured Malacca (in what is now Malaysia) from the Malays of neighboring islands (now Indonesia) in 1511. Control over this important collection point for spices enabled them to increase their earnings by making others' ships pay for protection as they passed through the narrow straits into the South China Sea and beyond. The Portuguese extended their interests into the Indonesian archipelago eastward to Timor and north to China, in 1557 acquiring Macao (which they still hold). The Spanish, moving westward from Mexico across the Pacific, took over the Philippines in 1564, holding them until 1898.

The Dutch and the British.   European nations fell over one another in the colonial hunt. The Dutch replaced the Portuguese in the Malay-Indonesian area, taking Jakarta on Java, the port of Malacca, and the Moluccas in 1641. The British successfully challenged the Dutch in the eighteenth century, moving from India on to Burma and down the Malay Peninsula, where local sultans granted them the islands of Penang and Singapore. Competition between England and Holland heightened when they took opposing sides in the Napoleonic Wars and the British occupied Malacca, Java, and Sumatra. The rivals finally settled their differences by an 1824 treaty acknowledging Dutch possession of the East Indies and British dominance in the Malay Peninsula. As the result of wars in 1824 and 1852, the British obtained control of parts of Burma. Meanwhile, beginning in the eighteenth century, French missionaries and traders were displaying interest in the eastern part of Southeast Asia.

China.   China responded with disdain to European traders' demands for entry, granting limited rights first to the Portuguese at Macao and later to the Dutch and British at Canton (now Guangzhou). By the early 1800s, however, the British urgently needed to expand their access to the China market. In an effort to correct a trade deficit caused by their purchases of Chinese tea, for which Britons had acquired an ever growing thirst, the British East India Company brought opium from India to China. When the Chinese, alarmed by the growing addiction of their people, decided to curb that trade, Britain launched the first Opium War and defeated the Chinese handily. By the Treaty of Nanjing of 1842 China agreed to open five "treaty ports" to trade and ceded the island of Hong Kong to Britain outright.

The "Opening" of Japan.   Initially receptive to both trade and Christian missionaries, the Japanese decided on a policy of isolation and by 1640 banished all foreigners except for a small number of Dutch who were allowed to reside on an island in Nagasaki Bay. Japan remained "closed" until 1853, when the American navy came to "open" it. "Manifest destiny" had propelled the United States westward across the continent and around Cape Horn to California and out into the Pacific. With an eye on Japan as a fueling station for ships on their way to Shanghai from San Francisco, the United States sent Admiral Matthew Perry with four warships to ask for better treatment of shipwrecked sailors, for permission for vessels to take on coal and provisions at Japanese ports, and for trade between the two countries. Perry gave the Japanese authorities a year to consider the requests, all of which, except the trade, were

Commodore Perry as portrayed by a Japanese artist.

Source: Detail from the Black Ship Scroll, 1853, with permission from the Honolulu Academy of Arts.

accepted upon his return in 1854. A few years later, however, commercial treaties were signed with the United States, Great Britain, France, Russia, and the Netherlands, opening up certain ports to trade and foreign residents. But Japan managed to avoid the indignity of becoming either a colony or a quasi-colony by purposefully undertaking its own modernization (discussed later in this chapter).

The concessions won by the Europeans in East and Southeast Asia were sufficient to satisfy them until the industrial revolution enlarged their appetite for trade and led to the demand for expanded control over territory. In the latter part of the nineteenth century, colonialism turned into a virtual frenzy of competition for the remaining chunks of Asian real estate.

The Capitalist Phase

Appetites in this phase of colonial expansion were for grain to feed Europe's growing population, raw materials and minerals to feed Europe's mills and factories, markets for their manufactured goods, and places to invest their capital. Simply trading in available goods to satisfy existing needs was no longer sufficient. Supply had to be increased, demand created, and investments secured against civil disorder, war, and default on debt. This required control of areas where rice, tea, coffee, sugar, fibers, and rubber could be intensively cultivated by Asian laborers under European direction; where tin and other mineral resources could be discovered and extracted; where investments could be made in plantations, mines, and the infrastructure of roads, railways, and harbor facilities to bring the local products out and European goods in; and where these varied economic activities could be pursued with a minimum of competition from other foreigners and interference from the Asian authorities. The answer was to make colonies of these areas, either outright or under the fig-leaf guise of "protectorates," drawing borders around them to mark the exclusive jurisdiction of each imperial power, or in the case of China, carving out quasi-colonial spheres of influence for the predator states.

Southeast Asia.   The Dutch, having concentrated their interests on the Indonesian archipelago, extended their effective control from Java and Sumatra to the outer islands, except for parts of Borneo, where between 1846 and 1888 the British established protectorates over North Borneo, Sarawak, and Brunei. They followed up on their earlier acquisitions in Burma by pressuring the king to make his country a British protectorate in 1867. When his successor tried to counter British influence by encouraging French trade and investment, the British invaded and in 1886 annexed Burma to India. Further down the Malay Peninsula, the British meddled in local conflicts among the sultans, giving advice, deposing and replacing rulers, until four of the sultanates came together as the Federated Malay States under a British resident-general. Five remaining Malay states, which had been under loose Thai suzerainty, accepted the status of protectorates. Added to the three Straits Settlements (Singapore, Penang, and Malacca) already under British rule, this completed England's domination of the Malay Peninsula.

France, having lost out to Britain in the competition for India, was busy in Indochina, starting with Vietnam, which it saw as a potential route to trade with interior southwestern China. French advisers and mercenaries aided the emperor of Annam, the central segment of Vietnam, in uniting Cochin China and Tonkin, the southern and northern parts of the country, under his rule. During his reign French traders and missionaries were allowed to enter, but successor Vietnamese emperors imposed restrictions on them and persecuted their subjects who had converted to Christianity. The murder of Christian missionaries provided the French with justification for military intervention, leading to the acquisition of part of Cochin China by cession in 1862 and the rest by conquest later. In 1874 a protectorate was established over the Kingdom of Annam including Tonkin, with French advisers to assist in reorganizing its armed forces, maintain order, and help with government finances. Antagonized by French influence in states it regarded as vassals, China was drawn into a losing war with France in 1883. In Cambodia King Norodom was induced to put his realm under French "protection," permitting the usual rights to residence, missionary activity, and the importation of goods duty free. Conquest of the kingdom of Laos completed France's colonial acquisitions, known collectively as French Indochina.

Thailand, alone in Southeast Asia, managed to escape formal colonization by taking advantage of the rivalry of France and England. Through skillful diplomacy Siam, as it was then known, remained as an independent buffer between British and French colonies. It was, however, pressured to relinquish territory to British Burma and Malaya and to French Laos and to grant extraterritoriality to foreign residents.

To complete the story of colonial acquisitions in Southeast Asia during the capitalist phase, sovereignty over the Philippines passed from Spain to the United States at the end of the Spanish-American War in 1898. Filipino revolutionaries who had fought along with American forces to liberate their country from Spain resisted the imposition of American rule until the armed struggle for Philippine independence was finally suppressed in 1902.

By drawing the strings tightly around Southeast Asia, Western nations were closing in on China. As Burma, Annam, Tonkin, and Laos were incorporated into the colonial empires of England and France, China's influence was further enfeebled. In the last half of the nineteenth century and the first four decades of the twentieth, China's territory and sovereignty were encroached on by competing Western powers, joined at the turn of the century by a newcomer to the imperialist game, Japan. Table 2.2 lists the colonies held by the Western powers and Japan around 1910.

Spheres of Influence in China.   The Anglo-Chinese War of 1857, often referred to as the Second Opium War, illuminated the pattern of collaboration by which Western powers extorted additional territorial rights in China. Initiated by Britain and joined by France, the war ended with China's agreeing to pay a huge indemnity, to open more treaty ports, and to grant rights to trade and travel the length of the Yangtze River deep into the interior of China. For her efforts in mediating the conclusion of the war, Russia received an additional large piece of Chinese territory in the northeast, which became the Maritime Province and included the valuable port of Vladivostok.

The next military encounter, in 1894, pitted China against Japan, challenger to Chinese influence over the Korean Peninsula. Again the Chinese lost to superior firepower, the Japanese getting control not only of Korea, which it annexed in 1910, but the Chinese island of Taiwan and the Liaodong Peninsula at the tip of Manchuria. This dramatic entry of Japan into the imperialist camp was too much for France, Russia,

TABLE 2.2   Colonial Possessions around 1910

Colonial Power	Colonial Possession
France	Cambodia, Laos, Vietnam (Cochin China, Annam, Tonkin)
Japan	Korea, Taiwan
Netherlands	Dutch East Indies (Sumatra, Java, Bali, most of Borneo, Moluccas, western Timor, Celebes, western New Guinea)
Portugal	Macau, East Timor
United Kingdom	Burma, Malay states, North Borneo, Brunei, Sarawak, Malacca, Penang, Singapore, Hong Kong
United States	Philippines (Spanish colony from 1564–1898)

and another newcomer on the scene, Germany, and they used diplomatic pressure on Japan to return Liaodong to China. As a reward the French received various railroad, mining, and tariff concessions in south China adjacent to French Indochina, and the Russians got similar railroad and mining rights to Manchuria. The Germans, after applying additional military pressure in 1898, got exclusive leases on territory in Shandong along with railroad and mining rights, setting off another round in which similar privileges were granted to the Russians in the Liaodong Peninsula and the French on Guangzhou (Canton) Bay in the south. The British were given mainland territory adjacent to Hong Kong Island as well as the port of Weihaiwei in Shandong, from which to keep an eye on the Russians in Liaodong.

Acquisition of exclusive leases in ports and coastal areas signaled the beginning of the struggle for such rights in the interior, which reached a peak in the period 1895–1900. At stake were investment opportunities in the lucrative enterprises of building and operating railroads, which also opened up the hinterland to trade, missionary activity, and the exploitation of mining rights granted along with the railroad concessions. Protection for these substantial interests and the foreigners who came to work in China was provided for by European naval, land, and police forces in China.

Seeing the encroachment of other governments in China, the United States, which had not staked out a claim for itself to a sphere of influence at this point, asked the other powers to pledge themselves to an Open Door policy, that is, not to discriminate against other countries' products in tariffs, harbor duties, and railroad rates in their respective spheres. Competition among the foreign powers was thus moderated by acceptance of each other's concessions and by collaboration in multinational joint financing as well. Their common interest in protecting their positions in China found visible expression during the Boxer Rebellion in 1900, when antiforeign elements attacked the foreign settlement area of the capital, Beijing, and sacked the embassies. With the Chinese authorities either unable or unwilling to stop the rebels, five powers whose diplomats and citizens were under attack—England, Russia, Germany, the United States, and Japan—formed a military force to suppress the Boxers. They then extracted from the Manchu government sizable indemnities for damages, putting China further into debt. Within a few years Japan, with British approval, took on Russia in 1904–1905 and won the war in a costly but spectacular display of naval power. Though drained by the effort, Japan gained control over the southern part of Sakhalin Island and a commanding position in Manchuria.

China continued to suffer losses even after the abdication of the emperor in 1911 and the formation of the Republic of China government. Russia took Mongolia as a protectorate in 1913, and Britain drew Tibet into its sphere. Japan, having joined the winning side in World War I, was rewarded with the German interests in Shandong, gaining as well influence in eastern Inner Mongolia and in Fujian Province on the mainland across from Taiwan. In the aftermath of the 1917 Russian Revolution, Japan expanded its holdings in northern Manchuria and took part in the Allied intervention in Siberia against the Bolsheviks. All these acquisitions were prelude to the military conquest of China by Japan, which began in Manchuria in 1931. The invading forces defeated the Chinese defenders and set up a puppet state, Manchukuo, in 1934. During the rest of the decade the Japanese conquered much of eastern China, evicting the

Westerners from their privileged positions and forcing the republican government to move its capital from Nanjing far inland to Qongqing. The widest extent of Japanese imperialism came in 1940–1942, when its armed forces moved into Southeast Asia and many of the western and central Pacific islands. The effects on Southeast Asia of this relatively brief but significant experience of Japanese occupation will be discussed in Chapter 3.

MANCHU AND MEIJI: ALTERNATIVE RESPONSES TO COLONIALISM

The dramatically different outcome of the confrontation between East and West in China and Japan has intrigued and puzzled scholars for half a century. Why did China, a large and rich country with a more advanced civilization, disintegrate under the weight of Western imperialism while Japan, a small, resource-poor island nation, consolidated its disparate feudal principalities to emerge in the space of forty years as a modern, imperialist aggressor on the doorsteps of Asia? What accounts for Japan's rapid industrialization after the arrival of Admiral Perry while China, like Humpty Dumpty, had a great fall from which it is still recovering? These questions continue to be relevant to understanding the differences and complex interrelationship between Japan and China today. The two countries have followed very different paths to modernization despite remarkable similarities in historical and cultural experiences.

China's and Japan's Early Responses to Western Demands

When the first wave of European merchants and missionaries appeared on the shores of Japan and China, the idea of trade had some appeal, more to the Japanese than to the Chinese, and Catholic missionaries of the Jesuit, Dominican, and Franciscan orders were allowed entry.

Reception of Christian Missionaries.   Among the missionaries, the Jesuits acted as "goodwill ambassadors" for Western learning in both Japan and China, where they were admired for their self-discipline as well as their education. Their rigorous training suited them for their top-down task of converting the Chinese and Japanese populations. Mastery of the language and customs of their hosts gained the Jesuits entry into elite circles as social equals. Father Francis Xavier, founder of the Jesuit order, won the confidence of Hideyoshi, a powerful Japanese general and contender for the position of shogun, who was known for sporting Portuguese clothes and a rosary. In China, another cleric, Matteo Ricci, was honored with a position in the imperial palace on account of his familiarity with both Chinese classics and Western science. Although the Jesuits never made the number of converts they had envisioned, they brought credit to Western civilization among Chinese and Japanese elites in this early period of contact with Westerners.

Japan and the Traders.   To the Japanese, Western trade at first appeared profitable and compelling. The introduction of novelties like tobacco and eyeglasses caught their fancy, setting off a "veritable craze for European things," including Western dress and Portuguese phrases.[6] European weaponry found buyers among feudal clan leaders who put them to use in their conflicts with one another. But the size of the trade with the West remained relatively small, as did the number of resident foreign traders.

But foreign missionaries and merchants soon wore out their welcome in Japan. Conflicts among Europeans of different nationalities and a variety of Christian sects became disruptive, and the tendency of poor Japanese converts to translate the gospel into campaigns against their rich overlords led the daimyo to a change of heart toward Christianity. And when Spanish missionaries from the Philippines arrived, the Japanese began to suspect territorial designs. The shogunate (controlled by the Tokugawa clan after 1603) moved systematically and forcefully to isolate Japan totally from the outside world. European ships were restricted to only two ports, all Japanese were prohibited from going abroad or returning home, and a ban was placed on building ships any larger than the small vessels suitable for coastal transport. When 20,000 Christianized peasants led by unemployed samurai rose in revolt in 1637 against oppressive taxes, the Tokugawa government's worst fears about the subversive effects of Christianity were confirmed. The Shimabara Rebellion, which in its blend of Christianity and demands for economic justice foreshadowed the Taiping Rebellion in mid-nineteenth-century China, led to the expulsion of all foreigners in 1639. For the next 200 years the only contact Japanese had with the outside world was with the handful of Dutch allowed to remain, confined to an island in Nagasaki Bay. Through this window, the Japanese kept up with news from the West.

China and the Traders.   China's reception of European traders up to the nineteenth century swung from first allowing the Portuguese in and then expelling them, to opening Chinese ports to all Western traders and missionaries and, in the eighteenth century, to forbidding Catholicism and confining the merchants to operating under severe restrictions from warehouses (called "factories") outside the port city of Canton.

By the end of the eighteenth century, Great Britain found Chinese restrictions on their trade intolerable. Canton, the exclusive port for international trade conducted on the Chinese side by a number of chartered firms known as cohongs, no longer offered Great Britain sufficient trade opportunities. Three government missions in 1787, 1793, and 1816 were sent to persuade the Chinese government to change this policy. The emperor, with characteristic nonchalance, saw no need for either British representation in Peking or increased trade since "we possess all things . . . set no value on objects strange or ingenious, and have no use for your country's manufactures."[7]

Beneath the polite diplomatic impasse was a profound conflict of cultures. For their part, the British had neither admiration for nor patience with the Chinese, insisting upon their inalienable right to trade. Like other Europeans, without attempting to learn much about Chinese culture, they derided the Asian customs as barbaric.

For their part, the Chinese had for so long been governed by the assumption that for-eigners were inevitably inferior, to be treated kindly but firmly. They saw all foreign-ers as "devils"; the English were "red-headed devils," the Americans "flowery-flag devils." Western dress and manners were a source of amusement to the Chinese, and even Westerners' physical features evoked laughter. The following reaction of a Chi-nese scholar to Western dress is not without wit:

> Their thick coats fit tightly around their arms and body, narrow trousers re-strict the movements of their knees, tough leather pinches their feet, and hats unyielding in shape grip their heads. Their movements, nevertheless, are quick and abrupt; what they would do without the restraint of their gar-ments, I do not fancy; perhaps, these cramping clothes are a necessary check to their fury, instituted by their sages.[8]

The clash between Chinese resistant to the blunt uncultured barbarians and the European determination to do business moved from diplomacy to war in 1839.

Tea and Opium: The Foreigners Come to Stay

However comical their appearance was to the Chinese, the British merchants had a serious reason for wanting to broaden the terms of trade: tea. Not long after tea was first introduced into Europe by the Dutch in 1644, it became Britons' national drink, and imports of tea from China created an unfavorable balance of trade for London. The Chinese felt no need for British woolens, and the market in China for ornamen-tal clocks and curios from England was limited, so there was a huge outflow of silver to pay for the increasing imports of tea. The solution to Britain's problem was opium, grown in India under British East India Company monopoly, shipped to Canton by pri-vate firms under contract to the company, and imported illegally into China. The profit from the opium trade more than paid for the purchase of tea, saddling China with both a balance of payments deficit and a debilitating drug problem. The outflow of silver from China reached giant proportions when the British East India Company lost its mo-nopoly in 1834, and the triumph of free traders opened the flood gates of opium trade.

Chinese efforts to eradicate the opium-smuggling traffic that was undermining both the economy and the morality of China provoked open conflict with the British, at heart a struggle over who would decide important issues of China's domestic affairs. China's defeat in the first of the Opium Wars, 1839–1842, forced the opening of China and signaled the convergence of external colonial interests and the internal sources of weakness that led to the final collapse of the dynastic system in 1911. The intervening period is punctuated by "unequal treaties," each prompted by the recalcitrance of the imperial Manchu government and the retribution of frustrated Westerners.

Politically, these treaties gave free rein to foreign residents in China who were protected by "extraterritoriality," which meant they lived under the laws of their own country, not China's. Entire areas of the treaty ports (Figure 2.1) were outside the ju-risdiction of Chinese courts, which made them a haven for Chinese criminals as well as for Westerners. To the Chinese, the very existence of these islands of foreign na-

Figure 2.1   Treaty Ports and Other Chinese Cities Opened to Foreigners in the Nineteenth Century

tionals without any allegiance to or respect for their civilization was an offense as well as a source of humiliation. The economic advantages these treaties afforded foreign manufacturers and merchants were considerable. Foreigners had control over the tariffs set on goods imported from European factories. This allowed cotton textiles manufactured in England to be sold cheaply enough to compete with homespun materials, undermining the Chinese handicrafts industry, a major supplement to peasants' income. By the end of the nineteenth century, foreign competition from India and Japan resulted in wiping out two of China's traditional exports, tea and silk, worsening China's unfavorable balance of trade. Indemnities attached to each treaty, punishing the Chinese regime for failure to live up to the previous one, further added to China's balance of payments problem.

Not speaking the Chinese language, resident foreign merchants and businessmen depended on Chinese to negotiate both their businesses and their comforts in China. This gave rise to a class of Chinese whose livelihood was providing a wide range of service to Europeans; they were maids, cooks, nannies, and streetsweepers as well as subcontractors, translators, and Chinese who had connections and understood how to do business in China. This latter group who profited from playing by the foreigners' rules became known as *compradors* (or comprador bourgeoisie); as agents of foreign capital these Chinese constituted a class whose well-being was intricately linked to and dependent on the foreigners.

Along with settlements of foreign merchants came a new breed of missionaries, their right to wage war against the cultural fabric of Confucianism protected by treaty. Protestant and Catholic missionaries ran schools, hospitals, and orphanages, making converts by attacking Confucianism as the source of superstition and cruelty. Although they were only somewhat more successful than the Jesuits had been in winning converts, they were far more visible in the society, proselytizing mostly among the common people. On the one hand, their activities provided opportunities for ordinary Chinese to obtain an education and health care otherwise unavailable. On the other, they planted doubts among some Chinese about their own cultural heritage and evoked resentment among others who were quick to suspect the Christians of kidnapping their children or poisoning their relatives.

Rebellion Within: Taiping and Boxers

By the middle of the nineteenth century, the disruptive effects of Christianity and other Western activities along with the Manchu regime's inability to maintain the territorial integrity of the country and growing dissatisfaction with corruption in the bureaucracy conspired to bring the dynasty to the brink of being overthrown by the Taipings in a rebellion that lasted from 1850 to 1864. Founded by a young scholar whose repeated lack of success in passing the arduous civil service examination had led him to convert to Christianity, the Taiping movement combined elements of Christian ideology with an agenda for modernizing China, a traditional scheme fo redistributing the wealth, and some Western ideas about manufactures and weapons. The Taipings came close to toppling the Manchu dynasty and perhaps replacing it with a regime capable of reforming and modernizing China's government. Western powers, at first favorably impressed by the Taipings' Christianity, soon became suspicious of their radical designs and mistaken religious notions, prompting the foreigners to support the Manchus' suppression of the rebellion.

The dynasty continued to decline in the face of military defeat by the British and French in 1857 and by the Japanese, whose victory over the Chinese in 1894-1895 underscored the failure of the government to undertake effective reforms toward modernization. Manchu rulers obstructed and subverted the changes of progressive

Chinese officials with the same determination they deflected Western demands. For example, funds appropriated to build a modern Chinese navy were used instead by the empress dowager to restore the marble boat and the Summer Palace that had been destroyed by Western forces. The final blow to the imperial dynasty came when the empress dowager, against the advice of her officials, gave succor to the Boxer Rebellion, a popular antiforeign and virulently anti-Christian uprising in the northern provinces, and declared war on the foreign powers in June 1900. When the Boxers (the name of their secret society) besieged the foreign legations in Beijing, the Western powers sent an international expedition to rescue their diplomatic personnel. The dynasty once again put its seal on a peace treaty that included a large indemnity.

When the regime was finally left with no alternative but to implement a reform program similar to those attempted prior to the Boxer Rebellion, it was too late. China had already been partitioned into spheres of influence: The French were in Southwest China, the Japanese in Fujian, the British in the Yangtze River Valley, the Germans in Shandong, the Russians in Manchuria, and the United States treated all of China as open to American trade and economic activity.

Tokugawa Japan and the Outcome of Seclusion

While China was on the verge of dismemberment, Japan was emerging from 200 years of self-imposed isolation. During that time internal peace and the far-reaching changes

With funds intended to build up the Chinese navy, the empress dowager had this marble boat reconstructed at the Summer Palace.

Source: Photo by Vera Simone.

brought about by the Tokugawa regime prepared the way for its successors, the Meiji reformers, to carry out "a revolution from above." To centralize the military and political power of the shogunate, the Tokugawa rulers implemented economic and social policies restricting the autonomy of the daimyo, the feudal lords. A substantial amount of their land was transferred or confiscated, more than tripling the size of Tokugawa holdings. The daimyo were permitted only one castle each and only a fixed number of armed men, the samurai. To prevent the formation of political coalitions against him, the shogun insisted on prior approval of daimyo marriage plans, and daimyo were required to spend alternate years in residence at the shogun's capital, Edo (now Tokyo), where they were under surveillance, their wives and children remaining as hostages when they left. By the end of the Tokugawa period, the expenses of maintaining dual residences and traveling back and forth with their retinues drained daimyo finances.

Economic and Social Changes. The long period of internal peace resulting from centralization of power by the shogun transformed the samurai from warriors into paid government administrators residing in the capital of their lord's domain. By freezing class lines and eliminating social mobility while reducing the number of samurai on the land, Tokugawa policies were simultaneously enhancing samurai status and changing their function. With the samurai removed from the land, villages became autonomous units in which wealthy peasants prospered and became rural entrepreneurs engaged in vegetable oil processing, soya sauce production, and other household industries, as well as moneylending. Poorer peasants, on the other hand, left the land and moved into the cities to provide labor for the commerce and industry that developed there. A market network based on money, contractual relationships, and commercialized agriculture made the merchant class wealthier and more powerful, although it remained low in status and under the political control of the daimyo and samurai.

The changes brought about by Tokugawa rule, similar to changes that had occurred in China earlier but over a much longer time, generated serious problems. Samurai found themselves increasingly impoverished on stipends that were frequently cut by their financially pressed daimyo. Both were at the mercy of a fluctuating market, which further oppressed a growing number of poorer peasants while encouraging an increasingly prosperous class of rural entrepreneurs and city merchants. Watching merchants—whose activity they viewed with disdain—prosper, while they—warriors whose life was dedicated to service—became indigent, kindled the discontent of the samurai, who blamed their misfortunes on the corruption and incompetence of Tokugawa officials.

Attempts by the Tokugawa and the daimyo to address the problems of mounting deficits, inflation, and economic chaos failed, except those of the lords of Satsuma and Choshu. Their domains were in southern Kyushu and the western end of Honshu, which, as the map of Japan on page 95 shows, were most remote from the shogun's headquarters in Edo (Tokyo). The two clans adopted innovative programs to cut costs, put finances on a solid footing, and ensure profits. Though different strategies were used to achieve these results, both Satsuma and Choshu exhibited two characteristics that played an important role in shaping the conservative nature of Japan's modernization. One was the dynamic leadership of independent, progressive daimyo who promoted young low- and middle-ranking samurai of talent and ability to positions of responsibility. The second was a strong feudal tradition that had set these two domains in opposition to Tokugawa rule from its inception, placing them on an "outside" list of mistrusted daimyo. The enduring effect of this estrangement from the central government was to perpetuate an adherence to orthodox samurai traditions that, together with the special family ties Satsuma and Choshu enjoyed with the emperor's court in Kyoto, gave a distinctively conservative stamp to the overthrow of the Tokugawa and the Meiji Restoration, which they later led.

Challenges to Tokugawa Rule.   Stimulus to criticism of Tokugawa rule in early nineteenth-century Japan came from two directions: Western influences and Shinto revivalism, a school of thought that glorified the emperor. Foreign books on all subjects except Christianity could be legally imported after 1720, and scholars of "Dutch learning" translated Western works on science, astronomy, and geography into Japanese. They began to write treatises of their own, even turning (at some risk to themselves) to political, military, and economic subjects by the end of the eighteenth century. Some scholars suggested a formula similar to one the Chinese adopted in the 1860s: "Eastern ethics and Western science." Others argued for a synthesis of Confucianism, Bushido ethics, and Shinto beliefs, emphasizing the emperor's unique right to rule by divine descent, as grounds for ousting the shogun. Many of these ideas found acceptance among a wider audience in the aftermath of Admiral Perry's expedition to open Japan in 1853.

Occurring only eleven years after China's humiliating defeat in the Opium War, the armed U.S. expedition left no doubt in the minds of the Tokugawa that they had no choice but to accede to U.S. demands. Yet the popular outcry for expelling the foreigners made the obvious impossible. For the first time in 600 years the shogun's government consulted with the emperor and the daimyo, only to hear the same futile advice: Reject Perry's demands, but avoid war with the United States. The intrigue and internecine conflicts that followed the signing of the treaties with the United States and other Western countries created an irreparable crack in the Tokugawa armor. As the movement to "Revere the Emperor and Expel the Barbarian" accelerated, the leadership in Satsuma and Choshu, whose slogan was "Enrich the country and strengthen the army," moved closer to ending the Tokugawa regime.

Self-Modernization in Meiji Japan

In 1868, with minimal bloodshed, the Tokugawa were ousted by a coalition led by the Satsuma and Choshu clans. Having learned to appreciate the superior weaponry of the Westerners, the new elite, numbering fewer than a hundred people, most of samurai origin, veered away from any attempt to oust the foreigners. Instead, they set Japan on a revolutionary course of self-strengthening by learning from the West. Following the official installation of the Emperor Meiji as direct ruler of Japan and moving the capital to Tokyo, the samurai oligarchy proceeded to dismantle the feudal system and embark on a crash program of modernization.

A few years after Perry's arrival, Japan signed treaties with foreign governments. This is the first Japanese Treaty Commission sent to the United States in 1860, pictured at the Washington Navy Yard.

Source: National Archives photo.

Wielding power in the name of the emperor, using a combination of the carrot and the stick, they abolished the feudal principalities and divided the country into prefectures controlled by the central government. The daimyo were rewarded with "severance" money and newly created titles of nobility. A system of universal military service was adopted to create a powerful new national army and navy modeled on the Prussian military and the British navy. The samurai, already stripped of their warrior function, were now systematically abolished as a class. Their hereditary stipends were first converted into pensions and reduced, then commuted into small lump payments or government bonds. The final symbolic blow to both samurai and the feudal system was the prohibition against wearing their traditional swords. Reduced to ordinary subjects of the emperor, samurai now had to fend for themselves. Many rose in government offices, others used their lump sum payments to start businesses; some entered the professions, joined the new military, or became policemen, which entitled them to wear swords. Those unable to adjust engaged in revolts, the most serious of which occurred in Satsuma in 1877 and was defeated at considerable cost by the new peasant soldiers of the Meiji army.

Modern Political Institutions.   The Meiji years were spent studying, borrowing, and assimilating those elements of the West that fit the leaders' vision of a militarily strong, politically centralized, and economically powerful Japan. They grafted Western institutions of parliamentary government onto the authoritarian imperial system to which Japan was accustomed and in whose name they ruled. A constitution bestowed on the Japanese people by the emperor established a legislature, the Diet, composed of the House of Peers, appointed by the emperor, and the House of Representatives, elected by the highest taxpaying bracket of male citizens, estimated to have been slightly over 1 percent of the population. The cabinet system as well as commercial and civil laws were copied from Germany, criminal law from France, municipal government from Prussia. Political parties formed and elections were held, but the personalities and views of the oligarchs prevailed. Although "a group larger than the original oligarchy now participated in the work of government, . . . the young founders of the new government, now grown to solid middle age, still controlled Japan."[9]

Government and Business. Government played a prominent and pragmatic role in Japanese economic development by creating a new institutional framework and a technologically advanced physical infrastructure. The police, the currency, and the postal system were modernized. A system of universal education was adopted, which made Japan the first country in Asia to have a literate people. A national banking system was adopted along American lines, and the tax system was standardized. To promote investments, the government took the lead in establishing and operating shipyards, mines, munitions works, textile mills, and other enterprises it considered essential to strengthen Japan for which sufficient private capital was not forthcoming. Foreign loans and government subsidies were used to build railways, roads, and telegraphic communications. Advisers, technicians, and other foreign personnel were imported to help with development but were dispensed with as soon as Japanese could be trained to replace them.

By the 1870s and 1880s, when the government found itself in financial difficulties with an adverse balance of trade, serious inflation, and overextended capital expenditures, it auctioned off most of its enterprises (except for munitions) to private businessmen, friends of government leaders, at bargain prices. Mitsubishi, for example, "acquired the Nagasaki [ship]yard for less than half of what the government had invested in it."[10] Through a combination of buying out businesses that were not immediately but could be made very profitable and doing business with the government, huge industrial and financial combines, the *zaibatsu*, emerged. Thus it was during the Meiji period in the late nineteenth century that the association of business with government—business in the service of the state—became the dominant ethos of Japan's economy.

China's Fate and Japan's Fortune:
Some Different Explanations

The contrast between Japan's rapid and peaceful transformation into a modern society and China's painful and protracted collapse under the combined weight of Western pressure and domestic decay is overwhelming. How can this contrast be explained? The Japanese and the Chinese demonstrated the same antagonism towards the Western threat; each expressed profound satisfaction in the superiority of its own way of life in countering the Western challenge. Yet within twenty years of Admiral Perry's visit, the Japanese had done an about-face of unbelievable proportions. How it was accomplished has been described; what remains difficult to explain is what made it possible in Japan and impossible in China.

Different Historical Experiences?   The most obvious answers are also the most alluring. An example is the argument that draws on a difference between Japan's and China's historical experiences. China evolved independently of any external influences, in splendid isolation. Japan, on the other hand, borrowing heavily from China in the development of its civilization, was able to acknowledge the strength of the West, rendering resistance on its part futile and promoting imitation of the West in its stead. The Chinese remained historically so blinded by their own sense of hubris and complacency that neither the appreciation nor the adoption of Western techniques was possible.

The grounds for rejecting the historical argument are numerous, among the most important being that it is a single-factor explanation of an extraordinarily complex issue. But the appeal of such an argument is powerful enough to warrant illustrating the difficulties with it. While it is true that Chinese civilization developed without benefit of self-consciously borrowing from other civilizations, it was nonetheless capable of absorbing influences from outside, even those that might be imposed by force. Wave after wave of foreign influences have not only passed through China but been peacefully absorbed by the Chinese into their civilization. Buddhism and Islam were mentioned earlier; there was even a community of Jews who flourished in the city of Kaifeng in the eleventh century whose only misfortune was to become so accepted that they totally assimilated, losing what had made them different from their Chinese brethren. Twice in Chinese history outsiders, the Mongols and the Manchus, conquered and ruled the Chinese long enough for them to become assimilated and indistinguishable from their subjects. The precedent the Japanese had for so readily adopting the West as a model for change may well be one among many influential factors, but it is not by itself sufficient explanation for the different impacts the West had on China and Japan.

Different Forms of Feudalism?   Clearly, the historical circumstances of the impact of Western colonialism on Japan and China include both external pressures and internal factors interacting in a particular institutional and political environment. Modernization theory, by viewing colonialism as the *pattern* of ideas and practices brought by an advanced nation to "backward" or traditional societies, emphasizes the internal factors within Japan and China as determining their distinctive responses. According to this line of reasoning, since the pattern of modern ideas and practices in Western countries is alike for both China and Japan, it follows that the different responses of these two societies can only be explained by variations in their domestic situations prior to impact.

Adherents of this theory, therefore, point to the differences between feudalism in Japan and feudalism in China as decisive for their different responses to the Western challenge. Feudalism in Japan, it is asserted, was closer to its European form in the fourteenth or fifteenth centuries than to its Chinese counterpart in the sixteenth century. Unlike China, where intellectuals constituted a nonhereditary scholar-official elite, the feudal elite in Japan was a hereditary class of warriors, the samurai. Similarly in the inheritance of land, primogeniture was characteristic of both Japan and Western Europe, where the eldest son inherited the total family holding, while in China, land was equally divided among all the sons. Such internal factors are evidence in support of the explanation of the difference in Japan's and China's responses to the Western challenge from the theoretical perspective of modernization theory.

Different External Pressures?   From the world system perspective, on the other hand, external factors weigh more heavily in explaining the difference between Japan's and China's reactions to Western provocation. Colonialism, viewed through this theoretical prism, is not merely each Western country imposing its particular pattern of modern life on its acquired territories, but an overall *process* by which the international capitalist market as a whole expands. Laying claim to and reordering economic life in distant parts of the world, whether it is done by Portugal, the Netherlands, Great Britain, France, or the United States, is all part of the evolution of a single world-capitalist market system of exchange. Passing through a variety of stages, this world system incorporates more and more of the earth's surface, reorienting the production activities of people towards the international market. At each successive point in time, the demands that steer principal actors in the international market towards one location or another change in accordance with what has already transpired as well as the appearance of new opportunities. Thus it is not only the spatial imagery of a single world economy expanding amoebalike around the globe by bringing more and more actors into its sphere of economic activity that makes world system explanations different from those proffered by modernization theorists. It is also the notion of time, the passage of time, as a causal factor in explaining both the transformations in the world economy and how demands of the world economy interact with the experiences and resources of people at the periphery.

To explain why China resisted and Japan accepted the challenge of incorporation into the world economic system, therefore, hinges on a chronological or historical analysis not only of the conditions existing in peripheral countries like China and Japan, but the exigencies of the international market at different points in time. China was initially a far more compelling market for conquest by core interests than Japan. Because China with its vast market potentiality was a far more powerful magnet for European traders at least a half century before Japan was of much interest, the high cost China had to pay for resisting Western intrusion acted as a cautionary lesson for the Japanese when their island nation became valuable to the United States as a way station for trade with China. Historically, then, because China was first to feel the full brunt of the capitalist world system, external pressure on China was greater than elsewhere at a time when there was no way of knowing the disastrous consequences of resisting Western demands.

The argument from a world system perspective is that variations in its impact on individual countries like China and Japan result from different pressures exerted by *external forces at different times in the evolution of the international political econ-omy.* From this perspective, the internal differences between feudalism in Japan and China are negligible compared to the different pressures exerted on them at different times by the international network of colonial powers. This sheds a different light on a paradoxical observation about Japan's response made by adherents of moderniza-tion theory, that "a milder foreign challenge provoked a stronger domestic re-sponse."[11] For adherents of world system theory this observation, far from being incongruous, is literally accurate: It describes the disparity between the degree of ex-ternal pressure that enabled Japan to respond more effectively than China to a differ-ent vector of global pressures.

COLONIAL RULE IN SOUTHEAST ASIA

Colonial institutions and policies were designed to serve the economic and political interests of the home country, or at least of vocal and influential elements in it. The primary concern, therefore, was to find the most "efficient" administrative means for securing the political stability necessary to exploit the economic resources and secure the maximum cooperation of the indigenous peoples. Although considerable varia-tions among colonies existed, depending on such circumstances as the stage of capi-talist development of the colonizer and conditions in the Asian societies when they were colonized, the process of colonial state formation exhibited certain common fea-tures that will be identified and then illustrated in case studies of four colonies, each under the rule of a different imperial power.

Features of Colonial Rule

Having been created by the use or threat of force, colonial states were maintained by the exercise of coercive power, including military power, over the subject people. Units of the armed forces of the imperial country, sometimes augmented with colo-nials at lower ranks, as well as police, were typical features of colonial administration through which internal order was maintained.

Second, administrative structures were created to raise the revenues necessary for colonies to be self-supporting. Policies were pursued to further the availability of commodities, access to markets, and opportunities for investments. These institutions and policies, designed primarily for the benefit of the imperial center, had unintended and often detrimental effects on the colonized population.

Third, methods of legitimizing colonial rule and winning over the support of in-digenous people were adopted in order to reduce the cost of ruling over populations actively or potentially resistant to alien domination. Techniques of co-optation in-cluded jobs in the colonial civil service, grants of land, and other material advantages, as well as through the psychological bonds of Western education, fluency in a West-ern language, and conversion to Christianity. In some cases native rulers could be per-suaded to accept incorporation into the colonial structure in return for the benefit of retaining, if not the substance of authority, at least some of the perquisites of their tra-ditional position. For the imperial powers, the hope was that "indirect rule," working through precolonial authority structures, would lend legitimacy to the colonial state they had created, thereby reducing the need for and the costs of using coercive means to maintain order.

A final feature common to colonial rule was the effort by the colonizers to intro-duce political, economic, and cultural changes intended to serve their goals while at the same time keeping the colonized societies stable and thus easier and less expen-sive to control. The difficulty was that seemingly modest and even beneficial changes, such as education, simple public health measures, and road building, could have large unintended effects, disruptive to the social fabric of the colonized societies. Even where explicit colonial policy was to leave the traditional order as untouched as pos-sible, the mere presence of outsiders served as a change maker, leading finally—as hindsight reveals—to organized anticolonial resistance under the banner of national-ism. But that outcome is the subject of Chapter 3. Here it remains to bring to life these generalizations about colonial rule by illustrating them with some specific examples of colonial policies and their effects.

The Philippines under Spanish and American Rule

Of the Asian Pacific countries, Philippine society was perhaps the most transformed by colonialism. Living in separate villages, *barangays,* ruled by headmen, *datu,* Fil-ipinos lacked the political and cultural cohesiveness of other Asian societies that had experienced Hindu, Buddhist, or Confucian influences and some degree of unification into small states or larger kingdoms. These factors made the Philippines more vulner-able to Spanish zeal for converting the "heathen" nature worshipers to Catholicism (thus resisting the spread of Islam and carrying on the battle waged successfully in Spain itself to end centuries of Moorish occupation). For similar reasons, the Spanish were able to harness Filipino agricultural labor by putting an end to traditional slash-and-burn subsistence farming on communal lands and turning peasants into serfs on large estates, the *encomiendas,* to produce commodities for the benefit of landown-ers (the religious orders were among the largest) and traders.[12]

The Spanish ruled through a mixture of civil, military, and ecclesiastical institu-tions. A governor-general with a civil bureaucracy assisted by provincial officials was superimposed over the grassroots village-level *datu,* thus incorporating the traditional headman into the Spanish civil structure. The mission of the military was to carry on operations against the Filipino Moslems of Mindanao and Sulu and to suppress na-tionalist unrest when it began to emerge toward the end of the nineteenth century. Catholic religious orders, in addition to being major landowners, spread not only Christianity but also Spanish culture through the educational institutions they created. Over the four centuries of Spanish colonialism the indigenous elites, who became of-ficials and landowners during the expansion of sugar and rice plantations in the nine-teenth century, had totally assimilated, wiping out consciousness of much of the precolonial Malay culture. Their assimilation, paradoxically, also had the effect of awakening in them a sense of Filipino identity, which led in the last quarter of the nineteenth century to a revolutionary movement for independence.

When the United States entered the picture in the war with Spain in 1898, it accepted the help of the revolutionaries in defeating the Spanish forces, but President McKinley rejected the Filipino declaration of independence as a republic and decided instead to make the islands an American colony. The consolidation of U.S. rule was accomplished after several years of warfare against the independence forces of Emilio Aguinaldo at the cost of more than 4,000 American lives and the lives of almost 200,000 Filipino guerrillas and civilians.[13] Within a short time the United States inaugurated steps leading to a large measure of self-government through institutions modeled on the American pattern; an elected legislature, political parties, recruitment of Filipinos into the civil service, an expansive school system using English as the language of instruction, and Philippine control over domestic policymaking all came into operation during the first decades of American rule.

U.S. involvement in the economy was less activist. Large church-owned estates were bought up and sold to Filipinos, but no steps were taken to prevent concentration of the property in the hands of big landlords who became part of the politico-economic elite. U.S. tariffs allowed free trade between the United States and the islands, with the double effect on the colonial economy of encouraging agricultural production for export and retarding the development of manufacturing enterprises unable to compete with imports from the United States. It was not until the depression of the 1930s that domestic economic interests in the United States—the sugar beet industry affected by cheap Philippine sugar cane, dairy farmers unhappy over importation of coconut oil for margarine, trade unions opposed to cheap Filipino labor—pressured the U.S. government to prepare the colony for independence. As a result, a ten-year transitional period of commonwealth status leading to independence began in 1935. A constitution was drawn up by an elected Filipino convention and a president and vice president elected, the constitution and presidential powers modeled on the American pattern. Despite the interruption of Japanese occupation from 1942 to 1945, the process leading to independence was completed in 1946.

Americans often congratulate themselves on having pursued enlightened colonial policies and prepared their wards for self-government and independence. It is true that the legalization of political parties, the establishment of an elected legislature, the opening of public educational opportunities to a wide segment of the people, the indigenization of the civil service, and the rise of a middle class all were positive innovations not often promoted (or as early) in other Asian colonies. But the underlying political reality was, as one scholar puts it, that

> the party system had merely strengthened the political hold of dominant, landed families, which had used quasi-feudal techniques to gain an electoral following and could hold national power through a system of one-party dominance . . . [and that] the primary beneficiaries of American educational, commercial, and agrarian policies were those who already had superior wealth and education, men whose political power grew rapidly under American tutelage.[14]

So during both the Spanish and American colonial periods, but especially during the latter, the Philippine islands were unified for the first time and incorporated into the world capitalist system. The terms of that incorporation advanced the interests of both the colonial power and the elites of the colony at the expense of the peasants, who expressed their discontent violently in the 1930s and continued to do so after independence.

Laos under French Rule

If the Philippines is the Asian Pacific country that experienced the maximum impact of Westernization under colonialism, the other extreme is Laos where, thanks to topography and the limited nature of French objectives, the impact of Western capitalist colonialism was modest. Landlocked and with a small multiethnic population of Lao, Tai, Khmer, and Meo people living in scattered settlements in the narrow valleys, uplands, and forested mountain areas, the country in precolonial times had been the site of a series of kingdoms in the valleys centered around Luang Prabang, Vientiane, and Champassak. These kingdoms survived and fell through a complicated and shifting network of vassal relationships with neighboring Thailand, Burma, and Vietnam.

French interest in Laos stemmed from their colonial control of the regions of Vietnam and Cambodia. Starting with the negotiation of a protectorate over the Laotian kingdom of Luang Prabang, French ambitions were challenged by Thailand and aroused the attention of the British as heirs to Burma's interests in Laos. After several years of demonstrations of force and ultimatums from France, three-cornered diplomacy among France, England, and Thailand decided Laos's fate, fixing its boundaries "in accordance with the desires and accommodations of the European colonialists"[15] and leaving in Thai territory a Lao population larger than that remaining in French Laos.

Selecting Vientiane as the colonial capital, the French divided the country into provinces administered by French *résidents* directed by a *résident supérieur,* who in turn was under the French governor-general for all of French Indochina. By using existing local government structures and by staffing the colonial civil service with Lao people and with imported Vietnamese who also staffed the police force and militia, France was able to run the colony with only a small cadre of French personnel.

Colonial policy was to develop Laos as a hinterland serving the needs of coastal Vietnam. Some roads linking Laos with Vietnamese cities were built using forced labor, but plans to put in a railroad from the coast inland to the Mekong River and to resettle in Laos large numbers of farmers from crowded Vietnam failed to materialize. Development lagged and income from a head tax, forced labor, and the state monopoly on sales of opium were insufficient to meet the costs of administration and public works. A further expense was incurred for military expeditions to suppress periodic rebellions by mountain tribes resentful of the taxes, French interference with their opium trade, and the subordination of their interests to those of the Lao and Vietnamese in the colonial government.

The impact of French colonial rule in Laos up to World War II was minor; most of the population continued to engage in subsistence farming in scattered settlements. Little was done to develop the economy, to encourage industry, to improve agriculture, to provide schools and health care, or to bridge the long-standing chasms dividing the various ethnic and linguistic segments of the population collected haphazardly as the result of past migrations within boundaries set by the colonial powers. Depending on one's perspective, French treatment of their colony could be condemned as neglectfully retarding Laos's development or applauded as benignly, if unintentionally, sparing the country from forced incorporation on unfavorable terms into the world capitalist system.

In Laos, and Cambodia too, French rule did little to promote economic, political, or social change, but in the Vietnamese segments of Indochina, French colonial policies had much greater impact. Railroads were built, mining companies formed, mills and factories established to supply local markets, and sugar, tea, coffee, rice, and rubber plantations were developed by European landowners. Through private commercial and capital investment and public financing of infrastructure, the colonial economy was integrated into the world economy. Those sections of the economy that produced primary commodities for export expanded, while others, like small-scale farming and traditional industries and crafts that competed with French manufactures, lost ground.

French cultural impact was felt strongly in Cochin China and in the urban centers of Tonkin, imparted by civilian and military officials, clerics, French schools, and the University of Hanoi. Some of the Westernized Vietnamese came to resent their colonial status and eventually joined forces with the traditionalists to oppose its continuation.

Malaya under British Rule

In Malaya, the colonial possession that became Malaysia and Singapore after independence, British rule gave the Malays their first experience of political unity, but it also made Malaya a multinational society. Traditional Malay political organization had consisted of many small Islamic kingdoms on the mainland and also on the islands of the East Indies from Sumatra to Mindanao. Despite sharing cultural affinities of religion, language, race, and political organization, the Malay states had not been united in a pan-Malay empire. One result of Western colonialism was to divide the Malay states among the British on the mainland and in north Borneo, the Spanish on Mindanao, and the Dutch in the other islands.

British colonial structures were a complex patchwork combining direct rule over Penang, Malacca, and Singapore, indirect rule over the Federated Malay States, and looser supervision of the four other Malay states in the north. However different these arrangements were in each of the components of British Malaya, they did for the first time link them through the superstructure of colonial rule into a single political entity.

This unity was at the same time challenged by the introduction into Malaya of Chinese and Indians, who played vital roles in the colony's economic development but who were not, both by choice and especially by the British policy of preferential treatment for Malays over non-Malays, assimilated into Malay society. Migration of Chinese into the area began even before Malaya became a British colony, drawn by opportunities to do work shunned by the Malays, who engaged in fishing and subsistence agriculture. The Chinese became traders, construction workers, tin miners, and farmers and by 1858 constituted four-fifths of the population of Singapore, a major entrepôt for trade among India, Southeast Asia, and China. Expansion of tin mining under the British in the second half of the nineteenth century brought even more Chinese as indentured workers recruited mainly by earlier Chinese arrivals who had become well-to-do. The economic effects of the influx of Chinese were quite important but, in the words of one historian, "The political impact of Chinese immigration in the Malay Peninsula was almost as important as the economic. . . . Chinese entry in large numbers generated an increasing amount of friction between sultan and sultan, Malay and Chinese, and, even more seriously, Chinese and Chinese."[16]

The demographic shift caused by the arrival of large numbers of Chinese who outnumbered the indigenous Malays in certain areas aroused British concern about maintaining the social tranquillity needed for profitable economic exploitation of the colony. To counterbalance the Chinese and also to recruit tractable workers for the expansion of coffee and rubber plantations, importation of Tamil laborers from India was officially encouraged under a government-regulated contract system that in principle provided better terms for the Indian "coolies" than the unregulated indenture system the Chinese had known.

The result of the migration of Indians and Chinese was that at the time of independence the Malays constituted slightly under 50 percent of the population. The three major groups lived in separate communities, engaging in different occupations, speaking different languages, practicing different religions, attending different schools, and forming different social organizations. British policy favored high-ranking Malays with Western education and preference in government jobs while encouraging ordinary Malays to be content with schooling in agriculture and the manual arts. Business was the Chinese sphere and the Indians worked as laborers on large estates owned by Europeans and some Chinese. Tensions among these groups retarded the development of the movement for political independence that swept other colonial possessions in Southeast Asia after World War I, and those tensions eventually led to the split of Malaya into two states, Malaysia and Singapore.

The East Indies under Dutch Rule

Across the Malacca Straits from Malaya lies Sumatra, the westernmost of the island chain that became the Dutch East Indies. As with Malaya, the islands lacked the experience of political unification in the precolonial period, although two sizable states, Sri Vijaya and Majapahit, had existed. The former, a maritime trade-based kingdom centered on Sumatra, was at its zenith in the eleventh century, while the latter was a land-based agrarian kingdom originating on Java and reaching its peak somewhat later. Its successor, the Mataram empire, ruled part of Java when the Europeans came, but none of the three kingdoms encompassed all the islands, which were eventually united as the Netherlands East Indies, defining the boundaries of the independent state of Indonesia.

Political unification under Dutch rule came in stages, moving slowly from Javanese coastal footholds acquired to serve as collecting points for spices from parts of the eastern islands to the inland areas of Java and to other islands as Dutch economic interest shifted in the capitalist phase to plantation farming and mineral extraction. The gradual extension, by conquest and by political manipulation, of effective Dutch control over various parts of the island chain was not completed until the twentieth century. This meant that some areas were subject to more than three centuries of colonial rule and others only decades by the time independence came in 1949.

As a result, although under colonial rule the people of the islands experienced unification for the first time, the traditional differences among them continued and were sharpened by differing lengths of subjection to the Dutch, by differing degrees of intrusion into traditional life to serve the colonizers' economic objectives, and by the Dutch policy of differential treatment for various Indonesian ethnic groups and the resident Chinese community. Java was most impacted by colonial policies, and the contrast between it and the other parts of Indonesia became more marked. It was the site of Jakarta, renamed Batavia when the Dutch East India Company chose it for its headquarters; the city later became the capital of the Netherlands East Indies and, as Jakarta again, the capital of independent Indonesia.

The pattern of expansion of Dutch control, the institutions created, the policies pursued, and the effects of colonialism on the islands all were important manifestations of the Dutch reason for being there, which was profit. Unlike other colonial powers, they had no ambition to make the natives into "proper brown Dutchmen" nor, for the most part, to convert them to Christianity nor to transfer the Dutch form of representative government to the colony nor to replace the customary law of the islands with the Dutch legal system. Their goal was to enrich the motherland by making money, first for the company while it ran the show during the seventeenth and eighteenth centuries and then for the Dutch government, which took over when the company was dissolved in 1798. In relentless pursuit of the goal of making money, the Dutch radically transformed the islands' economy, especially Java's.

With economic gain as the prime objective, the company was not really interested in *governing* for its own sake, but rather in controlling the supply of spices and later in introducing the cultivation of sugar and coffee for the global trading network of company ships carrying goods between Europe and Asia and within Asia as well. To keep this trading empire afloat, the Dutch worked at first through local chiefs to whom villagers customarily paid tribute in the form of labor and shares of their crops; the chiefs collected spices produced by their subjects and passed them on to the company. But when the market developed for items not traditionally cultivated, such as sugar and coffee, the company took a more active role, distributing seedling coffee bushes and using village labor supplied by the chiefs under company compulsion to clear land for plantations and build roads. Cultivation of coffee required a heavy investment of capital by the company and by resident Chinese, and thus the fastest-growing segment of the economy came under alien control.

The tribute system worked well enough from the company's point of view, but when its trade hegemony in Asia was successfully challenged by other Europeans, the company dissolved and the Netherlands government took over control of the colony. On the verge of bankruptcy because of debts from the Napoleonic Wars, the government in 1830 instituted the Cultivation System, a new variant of the tribute system for extracting income from Java with the collaboration of the indigenous elite. One-fifth of village lands were set aside for the production of export crops selected by the government; as part of their duty to their chiefs, the villagers cultivated the crops and worked on other projects such as road building, all without compensation. The arrangement was very profitable for the Dutch and benefited the local elites by maintaining their positions of authority and increasing their wealth. For the Javanese peasant, the blessings were mixed: More and more of them, while continuing to live "inside the shell of a familiar cultural and psychological universe," became participants in "one of the world's largest and most modern agricultural industries."[17] Population on Java increased rapidly, but among the costs to the peasants were episodes of famine, as their labor was diverted from rice production for their own consumption, and economic and political subservience bordering on slavery.

A change in government in the Netherlands led to changes in colonial policy and the Cultivation System was gradually dismantled. Payment of taxes in cash replaced payments in commodities; large private estates increased production of export commodities, and the workers on them were paid wages for their labor. This trend away from government monopoly and essentially feudal production toward a freer market and modern agricultural practice spread to Sumatra and other islands. Its success led paradoxically in the early twentieth century to another change in colonial policy.

Initiated by Dutch civil servants, the Ethical policy aimed at returning some of the benefits of increased productivity to the people of the islands in the form of education and other measures to improve their lot. The results were modest, however, limited by the resistance to change of traditional elites, the reluctance of the European business community, and inadequate funding for schools, a public credit program, and other reforms. In the realm of political institutions, this period saw the establishment of local councils elected by taxpaying, Dutch-speaking voters; the councils selected half of the members of a colonywide Assembly to advise the Dutch governor-general, who appointed the other members. A limited number of Indonesians gained experience as civil servants and council members, but most of the opportunities went to the sons of the aristocracy.

The effects of World War I, another change of government in the Netherlands, and the appearance of nationalist organizations demanding further reforms (their rise is described in Chapter 3) all contributed to the demise of the Ethical programs. One scholar offers this assessment of Dutch stewardship in the East Indies:

> In the crucial test of the beneficence of their rule, the Dutch failed, not apparently from any malicious design or from hypocrisy, but rather because the system which they developed was so completely alien to Indonesian experience and desires. . . . The tragedy of Dutch colonial rule was that it afforded little indigenous experience in handling such a system and also it tended to exploit and perpetuate the problems of Indonesian cultural and regional disunity. These problems survived to embarrass the efforts of Indonesia to function as an independent economic and political entity after World War II.[18]

SUMMARY

In this chapter, colonialism as the source of modernization in the Asian Pacific region was traced back to its Western European origins. The differences in the impact of colonialism on Southeast Asia and on East Asia were contrasted. In Southeast Asia the imperial powers had the opportunity to determine the size and ethnic composition of future states by defining the boundaries of their colonial territories. In East Asia, in contrast, preexisting states of long standing resisted colonization, forcing the colonial powers to use different means to gain entry and achieve the purposes that had brought them to the region. A comparison between Japan's and China's confrontations with the West showed the complex interaction between external pressures and internal dynamics in the meeting between ancient and modern civilizations. The contending perspectives on the effects of colonialism provided by modernization and world system theories remind us of the difference the angle of vision makes in the way we see the world, past and present. This difference becomes even more pronounced in the period of nationalist independence movements, which is the subject of the next chapter.

QUESTIONS FOR DISCUSSION

1. What were the Westerners' reasons for acquiring colonies and spheres of influence in Asia?
2. How did Japan and China respond to the threat of colonialism in the nineteenth century? Why did Japan avoid China's fate?
3. What different effects did colonial rule have on the Philippines, Laos, Malaya, and the Dutch East Indies? Why the differences?

NOTES

1. Paul Bairoch, "Historical Roots of Underdevelopment: Myths and Realities," in *Imperialism and After: Continuities and Discontinuity,* ed. Wolfgang J. Mommsen and Jurgen Osterhammel (London: Allen & Unwin, 1986), pp. 192-94.
2. Ibid., pp. 209-10.
3. Frank C. Darling, *The Westernization of Asia* (Boston: G. K. Hall, 1979), p. 75.
4. Ibid., p. 78.
5. Ibid., p. 83.
6. John Fairbank et al., *East Asia: Tradition and Transformation* (Boston: Houghton Mifflin Company, 1989), p. 394.
7. The Emperor Ch'ien Lung's "Mandates," quoted in Vera Simone, *China in Revolution* (Greenwich, CT: Fawcett Publications, Inc., 1968), p. 72.
8. A Chinese scholar's letter, quoted in Roger Pelissier, *The Awakening of China 1793-1949,* ed. and trans. Martin Kieffer (New York: G. P. Putnam's Sons, 1967), p. 45.
9. Edwin O. Reischauer, *Japan: Past and Present* (New York: Alfred A. Knopf, 1947), p. 126.
10. W. J. MacPherson, *The Economic Development of Japan c. 1868-1941* (London: Macmillan Education Ltd., 1987), p. 38.

11. Conrad Schirokauer, *Modern China and Japan: A Brief History* (New York: Harcourt. Brace Jovanovich, Inc., 1982), p. 106.

12. David Wurfel, *Filipino Politics* (Ithaca: Cornell University Press, 1988), p. 5.

13. Ibid., p. 7.

14. Ibid., pp. 11–12.

15. MacAlister Brown and Joseph Zasloff, *Apprentice Revolutionaries: The Communist Movement in Laos, 1930–1985* (Stanford: Hoover Institution Press, 1986), p. 9.

16. John F. Cady, *Southeast Asia: Its Historical Development* (New York: McGraw-Hill Book Co., 1964), p. 443.

17. David Joel Steinberg, ed., *In Search of Southeast Asia: A Modern History,* rev. ed. (Honolulu: University of Hawaii Press, 1987), p. 158.

18. Cady, *Southeast Asia,* pp. 378–79.

FOR FURTHER READING

Bellah, Robert N. *Tokugawa Religion: The Cultural Roots of Modern Japan.* London: Collier Macmillan, 1985.

Fairbank, John K., et al. *East Asia: Tradition and Transformation.* Rev. ed. Boston: Houghton Mifflin Company, 1989, pp. 435–596.

Steinberg, David Joel, ed. *In Search of Southeast Asia: A Modern History.* Rev. ed. Honolulu: University of Hawaii Press, 1987, Parts 1–3.

Wolf, Eric R. *Europe and the People Without History.* Berkeley: University of California Press, 1982.

chapter 3

Nationalism and the Movement for Independence

Nationalism is a powerful and elusive force with roots in the human heart. The emotional attachment individuals can and do feel to their nation and to one another as members of that exclusive association defies rational explanation. Nationalism originated in Europe as a consequence of the creation of the modern state in countries previously divided into feudal domains. When Europeans colonized the Asian Pacific they brought European nationalism with them. So it was only a matter of time before Western-educated colonial subjects applied the nationalist logic to their own situation and began organizing opposition to imperialist rule. For the colonies in Southeast Asia the outcome of this struggle was statehood and political independence. In Japan and Thailand the governments promoted nationalism in the service of a program of self-modernization in order to resist Western colonialism. For China the nationalist movement bifurcated into traditionalist and radical alternatives, impeding both the process of modernization and the resistance to Western and Japanese imperialism.

In this chapter nationalism will be portrayed as an element in the struggle of Asian Pacific peoples to transform themselves into modern nation-states. In the first section nationalism will be defined and its European origins explained. Next, the transmission to Asia of the Western concept of nationalism and the rise of nationalist movements in reaction to colonialism will be discussed in general terms. Then the specific experiences of four pairs of countries will be compared. The concluding section describes the termination of colonial rule after World War II.

NATIONALISM AND ITS EUROPEAN ORIGINS

Two elements converge to form the modern state: the nation and the state. The modern state is "sovereign," meaning that it is the supreme power. Its government is (or is supposed to be) capable of enforcing the state's authority down to the lowest level, the individual, and its rules are binding on all individuals within its borders. While *state* refers to the supreme power exercised within a given territory, *nation* refers to a group of people who feel they are a community and whose membership in that community transcends in importance all local, more parochial attachments such as those of family, clan, village, tribe, or city. *Nationalism* is the emotional attachment an individual feels toward his or her nation; it is expressed in the belief that members of a nation ought to have the right to national self-determination and to a state of their own.

The concepts of nation and nationalism are amorphous, subject to widely varying interpretations, but as one historian says, "The simplest statement that can be made about a nation is that it is a body of people who feel that they are a nation; and it may be that when all the fine-spun analysis is concluded this will be the ultimate statement as well."[1]

When state and nation converge, that is, when all (or a large majority) of the citizens of a state consider themselves members of one nation, then the state is truly a *nation-state*. But not all states are so fortunate. In some, there are several racial or ethnic groups that do not share the sense of belonging to one nation (for example, Malaysia), and two nations, the Chinese and the Koreans, are divided into two states.

The European Origins of Nationalism

Nationalism has its origins in the formation of modern nation-states in Europe after the twelfth century. Although people have undoubtedly long owed loyalty to a "homeland," in Europe the nation-state evolved into a special kind of homeland. Initially the state belonged to the king in the way manors in the Middle Ages belonged to the feudal lords. The state was identified with the person of the king, who set himself above his fellow feudal lords by enlarging his domain, increasing its wealth, and centralizing its administration. In reducing the power of the nobility, the absolute or "divine right" monarchs of Europe allied themselves with the ascendant power of the bourgeois or "middle" (between the nobility and the serfs) classes, for whom a centralized state was a necessary condition for economic development.

In this early stage of state building undertaken by royalty, people of all classes were subjected to the power of the monarch, and in this way parochial loyalties to lesser lords were transferred to the king. Nationalism as a popular force followed, culturally transforming serfs, noblemen, artisans, and merchants into citizens with a national identity. In the early nation-states—England, France, Sweden, and the Netherlands—a substantial core of the population already shared the elements of a single culture, which the state then reinforced and expanded. Although these states represented as yet only the propertied elite among their citizenry, they were able to arouse the masses' national sentiments and loyalties.

Political nationalism followed cultural nationalism as the bourgeois class became economically powerful enough to demand political control of the national assemblies, doing so in the name of all the people. Modern mass nationalism was born in the conflict between the sovereign power of absolute monarchs and the middle-class champions of representative assemblies, in the course of which two kings, Charles I of England and Louis XVI of France, literally lost their heads. To promote their cause, revolutionary leaders ignited ordinary citizens' enthusiasm for a state that would represent the aspirations of all its citizens, not merely the privileged. Thus seized on by revolutionary movements to legitimize their claims against unjust governments, as in the Declaration of Independence by the American states in 1776 and the Declaration of the Rights of Man in France in 1789, modern mass nationalism penetrated the lower classes to become the basis for political revolutions ushering in republicanism and democracy.

Modern Nationalism's Characteristics

As the ideology of cultural and political nationalism spread throughout Europe and to the rest of the world in the nineteenth and twentieth centuries, it exhibited two characteristics that are important to an understanding of its impact on the Asian Pacific. First, it has adapted successfully to the appeal of other modern ideologies such as fascism, conservatism, liberalism, socialism, and communism by allying itself with each of them in various times and places. Nationalism inspired both Hitler's Fascist supporters and his Social Democrat opponents, for example, and in China, nationalism inspired both the National People's (Nationalist) Party and the Chinese Communists in their conflicting programs to rid their country of foreign domination.

The other aspect of nationalism with significance for the Asian Pacific is its contradictory effects on political life. It is both a unifying and a fragmenting force. Within a country, nationalist sentiment can be the cement that binds people of diverse economic and political interests together, as occurs when a divided population goes to war against a common external enemy. More often in today's world, nationalism splits states apart as national groups pit themselves against one another for control of territory, as in the former Yugoslavia, Soviet Union, and Czechoslovakia. Nationalism can be a disruptive force on a vast scale internationally, setting country against country in competition for resources, markets, and international status, perhaps even threatening the entire international system based on nation-states.

THE ROOTS, TRUNK, AND BRANCHES
OF ASIAN NATIONALISM

Western colonialism had the unintended effect of planting the seeds of nationalism in the minds of its subjects. As colonial administrators, the British, Dutch, and French "saw no contradiction between their powers to rule an alien land and their preachments about creating self-government in that country."[2] It was simply a matter of time, therefore, before people in the colonies began to use ideas of nationalism and of the right to national self-determination to challenge the legitimacy of colonial rule. While in some colonies there had been armed resistance to the imposition of colonial control and sporadic outbursts of rebellion afterward, that resistance was typically localized and spontaneous, in response to specific grievances, and ultimately ineffective in the face of colonial military repression.

Once taking root, however, the concept of nationalism opened the way to more systematic, sustained, and finally successful action, not just to resist but to offer an alternative to foreign rule. The contradiction between the Western principle of self-government and the practice of imperialism was obvious. If the English and French and Dutch and Spanish and Americans had the right as members of nations to be governed by their own people and to have their own sovereign nation-states, why were those rights denied to the people in the colonies? Once the colonials became aware of themselves as members of a nation, they could be mobilized more effectively to throw off the yoke of imperialism and exercise their right to self-determination.

Thus the European idea of nationalism served the leaders of anticolonialist nationalist movements in several ways. It could be used to expand the parochial loyalties of their compatriots to embrace an identification with the whole country, creating a nation where none had existed before. The establishment of such an identity would increase the unity and the strength of the resistance to colonialism; and it could be used to demonstrate to the colonial overlords that their rule was both illegitimate and untenable.

Nationalism and Development: Two Views

The significance of nationalism is approached quite differently by the two theoretical perspectives that have framed our comparative analysis of development. The facts are the same for both theories: Nationalism is the means by which people of a country become aware of themselves as a nation and seek political liberation from foreign rule. Having been initiated into the mysteries of modernity by Western colonial rulers, nationalist leaders appropriate the colonial state for their indigenous population. Beyond this, in the interpretation of what nationalism accomplishes in the aftermath of independence, the two theories differ.

Modernization Theory.   Nationalism in this theoretical context authenticates newly independent states, facilitating the national effort to transform traditional peoples into modern unified communities. In an incremental process paralleling the experience of Western nations, new states abolish the traditional rules and institutions that maintained "backwardness," substituting in their place efficient organizations and rational policies to promote development. Political development in this scenario is the prerequisite for economic transformation, establishing the political space for free enterprise to energize the development process. The enemies to be vanquished are the "backwardness" and poverty of precolonial traditional life. Nationalism, in this perspective, is the resource that galvanizes people to support their own state, one that provides a source of leadership for modernization.

World System Theory.   Nationalism, from the world system perspective, is more complex and contradictory in its consequences. It represents a valiant effort to shake off foreign control, but one that can succeed only in raising people's expectations without being able to deliver on its promises. Implied in nationalism is the assurance that economic development and prosperity will follow in the wake of political independence. But when political independence is successfully negotiated and implemented, a fledgling nation-state finds itself poorer and weaker than it was under colonial protection. Unable to provide the level of material and psychic security that its former imperial patrons had furnished, the ex-colony turns to its old masters or some other developed country for assistance, thus resuming informally a neocolonial economic dependence on the "core" of the world system. The economic linkages tying the new state to powerful international patrons after it has achieved formal political independence enfeeble rather than strengthen their capabilities to pursue autonomous economic development. Thus, nationalism in the service of a state incapable of delivering authentic economic progress can become a destabilizing force.

Characteristics of Asian Pacific Nationalism

In its overall appearance, nationalism in the Asian Pacific exhibited characteristics of nationalism elsewhere. It was a reaction to regimes that did not represent or "belong to" the people they governed. Articulated first by intellectuals and espoused by the educated young, nationalism in the Asian Pacific followed the same evolutionary pattern found in other parts of the world. Beginning modestly, nationalism initially expressed cultural claims to a collective identity distinguished by its language, art, religion, or other common bonds. In a second stage, this cultural identity assumed political form in demands for representation in government. Cultural nationalism and representation became in the third stage an overt struggle to replace the government in power.

Also like European nationalism, Asian nationalism emerged as a full-fledged political force at different times among different people with varying degrees of intensity. In Japan and Thailand nationalism was promoted by ruling elites in the nineteenth century as a way of perpetuating themselves in power and in the twentieth century as a way of expanding Japanese power abroad. Malayan nationalism, by contrast, did not materialize until after World War II, when it erupted in conflict between Malays and Chinese—separating rather than uniting them.

And finally the external links of nationalist movements made them susceptible to changes in the international arena. World-shaking events, such as the First World War of 1914–1918, the Bolshevik Revolution of 1917, the worldwide depression of the 1930s, the Japanese invasion of East and Southeast Asia on the eve of World War II, and the cold war that followed in 1947, all left their imprint on the evolution of nationalism in the Asian Pacific.

In two important ways, however, nationalism in Asia was different from its predecessors in Europe. Unlike European nations whose identities emerged in relation to other Europeans in a regional context, Asian national identities emerged in opposition to Western imperialism and in a *world* context. Nationalist movements in Asia reacted against the existing Eurocentric international system and contributed to the creation of an evolving global community. Further, Asians formed their identity in terms of a dichotomy between Eastern and Western people based on profound religious differences and the invidious racial distinction between white people and people of color.

The Rise of Nationalist Movements

Nationalist movements in Asia did not spring full-blown from the head of Zeus. With some exceptions, nationalist organizations took shape gradually, evolving from obscure peasant revolts against the changes imposed by colonial administrations, moving from specific complaints against foreign rule to a generalized awakening of the national character of their purpose. Western imperialists and their Japanese counterparts each contributed to the process by training a select number of "natives" to assist in their colonial administration. In this way a leadership corps for nationalist movements was recruited and trained by the colonizers, often in the language and in the image of the oppressor himself. When this indigenous elite group found itself excluded from the Westerners' charmed circle of power, it also found itself isolated from its own people. Out of this dilemma was forged both the consciousness of a common opposition toward foreign rule and a strategy for bridging the gap between the educated and the uneducated in colonial society.

This strategy and the vision that instructed it will be covered in a series of illustrative comparisons of four pairs of countries: first, China and Indonesia, where communism became embroiled in the nationalist struggle leading to violent confrontations; next, Cambodia and the Philippines, where the movement for independence from France and the United States was nonviolent and encountered little resistance; then, Burma and Malaya, where the development of a national consciousness was impeded by a deeply divisive ethnic pluralism; and finally Thailand and Japan, where the nationalist revolution was launched from the top down by the government in a successful effort to fend off colonization by the Western powers.

THE EVOLUTION OF THE NATIONALIST MISSION IN CHINA AND INDONESIA

Expressions of nationalism emerged in Indonesia and China just after the First World War, when the rallying cry of self-determination reverberated around the world. It struck a responsive chord among Western-educated professionals—doctors, teachers, and in the case of Indonesia government administrators—for whom the colonial experience was both promising and frustrating. As beneficiaries of a modern education that opened their eyes to the potentialities for improvement of their people, these professionals saw foreigners everywhere in control. The very nations that had gone to war for freedom and self-determination in Europe were running the affairs of Asians. How could the people of China and the Indies effectively assert *their* right to be masters of their own destiny?

Early Stages of Nationalism in China

Answers to this question had been sought by Chinese intellectuals for about fifty years. But until 1911 they had been framed by the teetering existence of an "alien" Manchu dynasty the Chinese blamed for permitting Westerners to overrun their country. With the monarchy toppled and China in disarray, intellectuals focused on the backwardness of Confucian culture as the source of weakness. Sun Yatsen, the Western-trained doctor and spiritual father of the National People's Party, the Guomindang, who became president of the new Republic of China, was enormously influential in spreading nationalist ideals. China's 400 million people, in his view, were just "a heap of loose sand." His answer was to create new bonds among Chinese dedicated to building China into a modern nation. Intellectuals, merchants, workers, and students were drawn to the party by the hope that China would be reunified under a government strong enough to eliminate both the foreigners and the warlords who controlled large areas of the country. But only this vague hope united members of the Guomindang. There was no agreement on what kind of state China should have, nor was there a strategy for retaking the provinces from the hands of warlords. Most important of all, the party had no military force to accomplish the reunification of China.

The agreements reached among the victors at the conclusion of World War I to deliver the German-held province of Shandong to Japan rather than return it to China provoked widespread boycotts and demonstrations. This outburst of nationalist energy, known as the May Fourth Movement, generated new organizations in two directions: towards Western individualism and Russian communism. Although the ideas of Western individualism were extremely popular among intellectuals and young people because to them it meant the freedom to choose one's wife, one's occupation, and one's government, the overwhelming fact remained that China was politically weak and divided. The awareness that no number of individual rights would bring about a strong, nationally united China led some intellectuals in the direction of communism.

The communism toward which nationalist Chinese gravitated in the aftermath of May Fourth came from the Soviet Union, where under the leadership of Lenin in 1917, a revolutionary movement had overthrown a culture and an authoritarianism as backward and entrenched as that in China. The idea that peasants in backward countries could join with workers in the Communist Party to overthrow Western imperialists and embark on a program of state-guided modernization offered a powerful solution to China's problem. Communism in Lenin's version provided a vision of nationalism tied to social justice and a strategy based on anti-imperialism. It was not just a theory; it had worked in practice, a point that was brought home by the Soviet Union's unsolicited renunciation of the special rights the tsarist government had in Manchuria, as well as the remaining Boxer indemnity payments.

The first meeting of the Chinese Communist Party was attended by only twelve members representing fifty-seven people. The Communist Party's survival was bolstered by Sun Yatsen's appeal to the Soviet Union for assistance in reorganizing and militarizing his own party, the Guomindang. From its 1894 objective of supporting the overthrow of the Manchu dynasty, the Guomindang had moved first to a cultural critique of China's weakness, then to a political program for nationalist rejuvenation with

Sun Yatsen

Sun Yatsen

Source: Reprinted with the permission of Macmillan Publishing Company from China Revolutionized *by John Stuart Thomson, copyright 1917 by The Bobbs-Merrill Company, Inc., renewed in 1940 by John Stuart Thomson.*

Sun Yatsen is considered the father of modern China by all Chinese and his mausoleum in Nanjing is visited by Chinese from all over the world, whatever their political persuasion. Sun's persistent efforts to free China from the rapaciousness of warlords and the exploitation of foreigners illuminate the darkness of China's humiliation at the hands of Western imperialist powers. His aspirations for China remain those of Chinese today: nationalism, democracy, and socialism at home and a position of strength, independence, and equality among the nations of the world.

Born to a peasant family in 1866 in Guangdong Province on China's southeastern coast, Sun at the age of thirteen followed many others from that region by emigrating overseas. Joining his eldest brother, a successful businessman in Hawaii, he was educated at a conservative, British-run mission school where he excelled at English and developed an avid interest in Western learning. In 1883, discovering that Sun was about to be baptized, his brother sent him home to China, where his ridicule of local village gods resulted in banishment from his village. Continuing his studies in Hong Kong, Sun became a Christian, went home for a marriage his family had arranged for him, and left his bride to return first to Hong Kong and then back to Hawaii. Rather than work in his brother's business, Sun used the occasion to engage in his first fund-raising, enlisting the help of an American missionary and businessmen to raise $300 to return to Hong Kong, where he decided to pursue a medical profession.

In 1885, while attending medical school in Canton, Sun befriended a member of a secret society dedicated to the overthrow of the Manchu dynasty, rekindling a childhood fascination with the Christian Taiping rebel leader, Hung Hsiuchuan. He completed medical training in Hong Kong but was not permitted to practice there, establishing himself in Macao instead. There he became drawn to the idea of contributing his knowledge of the English language and Western science to the reform of the Chinese empire. In 1894, at age 28, he traveled to Beijing to offer his services to Li Hung chang, the principal adviser to the emperor. Arriving in the capital on the eve of China's war with Japan over Korea, Sun never even obtained an audience with Li, and the rebuff, the first of many in his life, prompted him to embark on an independent quest to revolutionize China.

Between 1894 and 1911, Sun traveled from one overseas community to another, using his charisma, self-assurance, and consummate rhetorical skills to raise funds among overseas businessmen in Europe, the United States, Hawaii, Singapore, Vietnam, and Japan to support the formation and activities of an anti-Manchu political organization. With munitions smuggled into southern coastal China, Sun and his supporters attempted ten uprisings, none of which succeeded. Meanwhile, revolutionary groups had sprung up throughout the coastal regions of China, and when a mutiny among imperial soldiers started a chain reaction that resulted in the overthrow of the Manchus in 1911, Sun read about it in a Denver newspaper.

Though he was by then the most widely known Chinese revolutionary, and the only leader capable of holding the disparate groups of Chinese revolutionaries together, Sun had no base of support within China and little credibility among Western heads of state. On his return home, he stopped in Washington, London, and Paris, hoping to obtain the stamp of approval of foreign governments and loans for his party. With neither in hand, he returned to China to a hero's welcome, was elected provisional president of the Chinese Republic but held office just long enough to hand power over to General Yuan Shihkai.

The years between 1911 and his death in 1925 were a difficult period of international turmoil and intense warlord rivalry within China. Impassioned and imaginative but impractical and politically naive, Sun Yatsen spent most of those years in futile attempts to play off warlords and international powers against one another in order to unify China and throw the foreigners out. After 1919, when urban Chinese erupted in mass nationalistic protest against the Western sellout of Chinese territory to Japan, Sun Yatsen's political connections with Japan and the Western powers became liabilities. Increasingly disillusioned with the prospects of gaining Western support for China's territorial integrity, Sun gravi-

Sun Yatsen (continued)

tated towards the Soviet Union for assistance in forging a military and political organization powerful enough to capture power from the warlords and declare China's independence from Western domination. He died without seeing his dream of a strong and unified China achieved.

Western assistance, and, when that was not forthcoming, to an appeal to the Soviet Union for assistance. The result was a merging of the forces of the Guomindang and Communist Parties. Under the stewardship of Soviet advisers, the Guomindang was reorganized along Leninist lines, a military academy was set up, and members of the Communist Party as individuals joined Sun's party in order to unify China militarily under the banner of a united nationalist front.

Early Stages of Nationalism in the East Indies

For the people of the East Indies the answers to why they were powerless subjects of the Dutch and what needed to be done were somewhat different. In contrast to China, where colonialism contributed to *disunity,* the Dutch in a sense "invented" Indonesia by uniting the islands for the first time as their colony. The problem confronting Western-educated protégés of the colonial regime was how to find a single voice for the complex ethnic mosaic of peoples inhabiting the region: Islamic, Hindu-Buddhist, Confucian-Taoist, Christian, and animist; rice cultivators and traders; kingships and kin groups; Javanese and outer-islanders; literate and illiterate. The Western-educated secular elite that had emerged on Java in the forty-five years preceding World War I, though light years apart from the traditional Islamic communities of the outer islands, recognized the need to bridge that distance. And the impact of the war produced the occasion for the first nationalist coalescence of an emerging Indonesia: the mass political organization of Sarekat Islam (SI).

Sarekat Islam.   Founded in 1912 by Javanese traders fearing Chinese penetration of their enterprise, SI brought together the Islamic outer-islander and the secular Javanese strains of nationalist thinking into a broadly based nationalist objective similar to that of the National People's Party under Sun Yatsen: a commitment to carrying out social and economic development. Its popularity spread under the leadership of an aristocratic Moslem civil servant who affirmed national independence as its ultimate aim in 1917; by 1919 it claimed to have a membership of two and a half million made up of both rural and urban followers, religious and reformist Moslems, Social Democrats and Communists. But SI was affected by the proliferation of other nationalist organizations, the Indies Party led by a Eurasian, Douwes Dekker, and the Indies Social Democratic Association (ISDA) founded by Hendrik Sneevliet, a Dutch Communist who later became the first Soviet-sponsored Comintern agent in China. SI's broad appeal and its policy of permitting members of other parties to join it created serious inner tensions between its radical and more conservative elements. At the core of these tensions was the ISDA, which later became the Communist Party.

Social Democrat and Communist Parties.   Like the Communist Party in China, ISDA was an ideologically coherent and organizationally sophisticated party whose members filled official positions in SI, exerting an influence on policy similar to the Chinese Communists in the National People's Party of China. By 1921, a year after ISDA became the Indies Communist Party (PKI), Sarekat Islam stopped allowing members to belong to other parties, effectively ousting the Communist Party from its midst, the parallel of events in China in 1927. After that, the PKI expanded as an independent rival, attracting members away from SI, which began to decline.

Communism in Indonesia was a pervasive element of the nationalist movement, its anti-imperialist analysis carrying a broad appeal for all nationalists. Its social and economic program was more inclusive than the Moslems' goal of an Islamic state and more focused than the vague solidarity of the secular nationalists' state. As a political party, however, Communists in Indonesia as in China faced the problem of steering a hazardous course between socialist revolution and nationalist accommodation. The PKI, after expanding its membership in the mid-1920s, led a series of disastrous revolts in 1926 and 1927. That independent bid for power ended with the Dutch rounding up "13,000 subversives, exiling 1,000 to the malarial swamps of New Guinea,"[3] and crippling the PKI for a generation. Reemerging after World War II the PKI again rose, hitching its star to Sukarno's charismatic leadership of the nation of Indonesia.

Sukarno's Indonesian Nationalist Party.   More than any other individual, Sukarno gave the nation of Indonesia its distinctive spirit or "soul." With the assistance of students returning from Holland and a younger generation of more militantly nationalist youth, Sukarno founded a new, more assertive Indonesian Nationalist Party (PNI) in 1927. A new flag, a national anthem, and a transcendent purpose—"one nation—Indonesia, one people—Indonesian, one language—Indonesian"[4]—reflected Sukarno's flamboyant style, providing the PNI with powerful symbols to appeal to all shades of nationalist thinking. But functioning in an atmosphere of police surveillance and periodic repression that precluded mass political activity, the PNI was only able to project a solidly united Indonesian identity among the urban, educated elite. Actually mobilizing masses of people to act in concert as Indonesians was accomplished later, as a consequence of the Japanese occupation.

The Impact of the Japanese Occupation on the East Indies

When the Japanese took over the Dutch government in 1942, they added their own coercive techniques for actively enlisting the population in the war effort. By whipping up popular participation in support of "Asia for the Asians," they unwittingly supplied Indonesian nationalists with the mass base they needed to wrest independence from the Dutch after 1945. Sukarno and Mohammed Hatta, by collaborating with the

Sukarno

Sukarno

Source: United Nations photo 49998 AF/pcd.

One of the most colorful of the Asian Pacific nationalist leaders, Sukarno earned an international reputation for impassioned promotion of the cause of a united, independent Indonesia, for swaying crowds with his oratory and winning the adulation of the common people, for his charismatic personality and his love of life's pleasures, including the company of women. He was also criticized for his excesses, for collaborating with the Japanese during World War II, for being too willing to negotiate with rather than fight against the Dutch when they returned to the Indies, for being a poor administrator, for decreeing the end of constitutional government and instituting autocratic Guided Democracy, and for thinking that he could by sheer personal magnetism keep the antagonism between the PKI and the army in some kind of balance with him as the balancer. But whatever the assessment, no one can deny that he was the most beloved of the Indonesian nationalist leaders.

Sukarno was born in Java in 1901 to a Javanese Moslem father and a Balinese Hindu mother at a time when such "mixed" marriages were uncommon. Raised in modest circumstances in a small town where his father was an elementary school teacher, as a boy Sukarno absorbed the moral lessons of the *wayang* or shadow puppet plays of traditional Javanese culture to which he often referred in the public speeches for which he later became famous.

In 1916 he left home for a Dutch-language secondary school in Surabaja where he boarded with the family of the leader of the early mass-based nationalist organization, Sarekat Islam. While there he met many of an eclectic mixture of nationalists in SI and had access to a library of the works of various Western political philosophers, whom he later quoted as inspiration for his own ideas. After graduation in 1921, he moved to Bandung to study engineering at the newly founded technical college there, leaving behind the young girl he had married in name only in 1920 and whom he later divorced to marry an older woman in whose home he boarded. His political involvement and education deepened in Bandung as he came to know more of the nationalist leaders and began to form his own adaptation of Marxism to agrarian Indonesian society, emphasizing anti-imperialism and downplaying the idea of class warfare.

After graduating as an engineer-architect in 1926, he taught briefly and opened an engineering business, but soon became involved in a political study club, meeting with Indonesian students returning from study in Europe and writing articles advocating the unification of Marxist and Islamic elements in a broad-based nationalist ideology. One of the founders in 1927 of the PNI, a political organization devoted to independence and building an Indonesian national consciousness, he became its chairman and tried to form a united front of all nationalist groups. Arrested by the colonial authorities in 1929 for making inflammatory speeches, he was imprisoned for two years, during which he studied Islam but never became a devout practitioner.

After release from prison he tried without success to unite the two political organizations that had been established in the wake of the dissolution of PNI after his arrest. Arrested again in 1933, Sukarno was exiled first to a remote island and later to Sumatra, where he worked as a schoolteacher and met the woman who became the third of his seven wives. During the years between his first arrest and the Japanese takeover of the East Indies, Sukarno spent all but twenty months either in jail or in exile away from Java.

Like nationalists in other Southeast Asian colonies, Sukarno cooperated with the Japanese, seeing them as part of the struggle of Asians against Western imperialism and as supporters of the idea of an independent Indonesia. In 1943 Sukarno went with a delegation to Japan, his first trip abroad and his first view of an industrial country. While working with the Japanese occupiers, he strengthened his ties with the people and established himself as the symbol of national unity, which carried over into the postwar period. Sukarno's record as president after independence was finally won in 1949 is discussed in Chapter 4.

Japanese, availed themselves of the Japanese communication apparatus to convey their nationalist message to a vastly expanded audience of Indonesians across the islands. An Indonesian Army was raised with the assistance of the Japanese, who also enabled Indonesians to acquire higher-level administrative experience for the first time. Consequently, when in 1945 the Japanese suddenly withdrew in anticipation of an Allied offensive, the nationalist leadership of Indonesia was poised to declare independence from the Dutch. Sukarno and Hatta assumed the presidency and vice presidency and a constitution was drawn up for the new Indonesian state.

But the British landed troops in Jakarta to support the Dutch determination to reimpose colonial rule. The outburst of nationalist opposition this instigated swept Indonesians into the maelstrom of social revolution while negotiations between the nationalist politicians and the Dutch dragged on for four years. A mass uprising—called the *pemuda* (meaning "youth") movement in reference to the revolutionary youths who led it—erupted in response to the absence of any effective machinery of government under the new republic. Youth from all social classes, highly critical of the older political leaders' reliance on negotiations to settle the question of independence, believed that only force could bring the Dutch to accept Indonesia's independence. These youthful revolutionaries banded together around charismatic leaders, put together a nationalist army out of the disbanded Japanese-led youth and militia units, and discredited all groups and individuals who had demonstrated any support for the Dutch. The Chinese, Eurasians, and traditional elites were particularly vulnerable to abuse.

The violence unleashed by this movement was a double-edged sword for the new Indonesian government. On the one hand, it threatened negotiations with the Dutch as successive cabinets fell in the wake of criticism for having "sold out." On the other, it provided the mass base and military power the new government needed to establish national as well as international credibility for independence. The fruits of this revolutionary nationalist upheaval came when the United Nations and the United States intervened against the Dutch on the side of the nationalists; the Hague Agreement in November 1949 led to political independence for the Republic of Indonesia with guarantees for Dutch investments.

The Impact of the Japanese Occupation on China

The Japanese played an equally decisive role in determining winners and losers among the Chinese nationalist contenders for power in the postwar world. Foreshadowing the military's decimation of the Communists in Indonesia in 1965, the reorganized Leninist-style Guomindang under the leadership of Sun Yatsen's successor, Chiang Kaishek, had massacred thousands of Communists in 1927, thereby consolidating his government's control over the region along China's east coast, which remained a citadel of foreign influence. The Communist Party, virtually abandoned by the Soviet Union, went underground and dispersed to the countryside, where the handful of Communists we have come to identify as the founders of the People's Republic of China—Mao Zedong, Zhou Enlai, Zhu De, and Deng Xiaoping—reorganized the communist movement as a peasant-based nationalist force.

Settling in remote peasant villages often located on the border between provinces, the Communist leadership joined forces with local "bandits" to strengthen their forces and build armed revolutionary base areas in the countryside. They gained popular support among poorer and landless peasants by pursuing land redistribution policies and addressing peasants' economic grievances against landlords and tax collectors. When the first base area in the Jinggang Mountains came under heavy Guomindang attack at the end of 1928, they moved eastward to a new location between Jiangxi and Fujian Provinces, which they set up as center of a new regime, the Jiangxi

Soviet. Learning from their earlier mistakes, the Communists refined their land reform policies on the basis of a better understanding of the subtle gradations of class structure among China's peasantry. They consolidated and trained a fast-moving guerrilla force, the Red Army, and fostered social change by outlawing arranged marriages, promoting equality for women, and teaching literacy.

Though there were at least a dozen regions in which such base areas were established after 1927, they were unable to withstand the economic blockade and military encirclement of the Guomindang. In 1934, after a series of extermination campaigns waged by Chiang Kaishek's forces, intent on eliminating their Communist competitors once and for all, the Communists were finally routed from their rural strongholds. They embarked on an epic Long March 6,000 miles west and north to Yenan, marching on foot and under fire for more than a year while the Japanese planned their conquest of all of China.

As the Japanese advanced through China inciting fierce nationalist opposition, the two rival political parties were tested in the crucible of the anti-Japanese struggle. The Communists behind enemy lines in the rural north gained a national reputation for guerrilla warfare against the Japanese. The Guomindang, retreating from the urban east coast areas where the Japanese concentrated their troops, conserved their military forces for a final showdown with the Communists after the war. In this critical stage, the Communist Party of China became identified as the symbol of nationalist opposition to the Japanese enemy while the Guomindang forfeited its nationalist credentials in the eyes of countless Chinese. While Chiang Kaishek was correct in his prediction that it would take the United States to defeat Japan, he did not foresee the decisive impact his party's failure to oppose the Japanese and support land reform for the peasants would have on his claim to inherit the nationalist mantle of legitimacy.

This became readily apparent in the civil war between the forces of the Guomindang Republican government and the Communist Party of China, which resumed in 1946. The military and logistical support Chiang Kaishek's forces received from the United States was insufficient to compensate for the popular sentiment favoring the Communists. With military hardware captured from their opponents the Communists marched into the capital and, on October 1, 1949, proclaimed the establishment of the People's Republic of China. The significance of the event, aptly described by Mao Zedong, captures the essence of the nationalist purpose in Asia: "Our nation will never again be an insulted nation. We have stood up."[5]

Although China had stood up under the leadership of the Communist Party, the flag of the Republic of China was not hauled down for the last time as were the British, Dutch, French, American, and Japanese flags over Burma, Malaysia, Indonesia, Vietnam, the Philippines, and Korea. Chiang Kaishek, defeated on the mainland, retreated to the island of Taiwan, a province of China since the eighteenth century and a colony of Japan from 1895 to 1945. There, under the gathering clouds of the cold war, Chiang refused to acknowledge that the communist People's Republic had succeeded the Nationalists as China's government, claiming that the Republic of China was still the only legitimate government of all of China. The island-born population on Taiwan, already unhappy with their treatment by the Nationalists after the province was restored to Chinese rule after 1945, resented the influx of Chiang's officials and army in

Mao Zedong

Mao Zedong
Source: Wide World Photo.

Mao Zedong was a man of epic proportions. He was loved and feared as if he were an emperor or a god but his own wish was to be remembered as a teacher. Self-taught and college educated, versed in Western thought and Chinese classics, an accomplished military strategist and a poet, Mao Zedong combined the flexibility and tenacity of a politician with the inspiration of a visionary.

Born in 1893 in Shaoshan, a village in Hunan province, Mao was the eldest son of a poor peasant who worked his way to prosperity. From his tyrannical father, Mao learned his first lesson in the efficacy of rebellion. Having rebuked his father for insulting him in front of guests, Mao threatened to drown himself rather than kowtow in apology. To his surprise, his father relented. "I learned that when I defended my rights by open rebellion my father relented, but when I remained weak and submissive he only cursed and beat me more."

In the autumn of 1911, after refusing to acquiesce to an arranged marriage, Mao left his village to attend school in the provincial capital. There he found himself in the middle of the upheaval to overthrow the Manchus. Convinced of the necessity for reform in China, Mao threw himself into the fray, writing a revolutionary manifesto that he posted on the school wall and joining the revolutionary army. He returned to civilian life when the volunteers were not called into action and embarked on a period of voracious reading on his own. Then in 1913 he enrolled in a teachers' college, where he was exposed to a progressive faculty and students fired up by patriotism and enthusiasm for the New Culture movement. Schoolwork became framed in the context of an active political life:

Mao participated in street demonstrations against Japanese expansionism, organized guerrilla warfare against warlord soldiers billeted at the school, and published revolutionary articles for *New Youth* magazine; his first was an article that promoted physical exercise as an essential step for the self-strengthening of the nation.

After graduating in 1918, Mao chose to remain in China rather than accompany his classmates abroad on government-sponsored work-study programs. He worked in the Beijing University library, joined a Marxist discussion circle, and fell in love with the daughter of his old philosophy professor. In the tumultuous years that ensued, Mao alternately taught school in Changsha, engaging in radical activity against the local warlord and fleeing back and forth to Beijing, Wuhan, and Shanghai in order to escape arrest. In the summer of 1921, Mao was one of the twelve delegates meeting secretly in Shanghai to found the Communist Party of China. As part of the United Front between the Guomindang and the Communists, he engaged in organizational activities in Shanghai, Canton, and Hunan, finally going underground and retreating to the countryside when Chiang Kaishek turned against the Communists in the Shanghai massacre of April 1927.

Throughout the years of revolutionary struggle Mao endured personal losses—his second wife and brother were executed by the Guomindang, a son was later killed in the Korean War—continual bouts with malaria, and contention among his comrades over his last marriage to Jiang Qing, a Shanghai movie actress who unsuccessfully attempted to assume power after Mao died.

Mao ascended to power in the Communist Party by insisting on an independent course for the Chinese revolution. Repeatedly contradicting party directives from Moscow, Mao waited for the practical success of his ideas to win him the leadership of the party. In 1935, on the Long March, Mao's conception of a protracted guerrilla war based on organizing peasant communities into armed revolutionary bases became the accepted strategy for rebuilding the communist movement after its retreat from encirclement by the Guomindang. Reduced after the Long March from ruling over 19,000 square miles, encompassing a population of 3 million, to a single base in China's barren northwest, the Communists in Yanan adopted Mao Zedong's program for a second united front against the Japanese. On this foundation they swept to power.

During the period of relative seclusion in Yanan, Mao articulated his ideas in writing, yielding a body of work that has come to be known as Mao Zedong Thought. The theme of Mao's pursuit of nationalist revolution was one of "people's war." For revolution to succeed in China required a "mass undertaking" demanding that the party serve the people. To adequately prepare party members for this type of leadership, "rectification campaigns" were instituted for which Mao Zedong Thought provided the material. In the end, for better or worse, Mao's life and the people's China are inextricably bound to each other.

1949. The subsequent history of Taiwan's nationalist evolution will be described in Chapter 4.

NATIONALISM AND THE MOVEMENT FOR INDEPENDENCE IN THE PHILIPPINES AND CAMBODIA

Unlike the experience in China and Indonesia, where the anticolonial movement faced formidable opposition, in the Philippines and Cambodia nationalist leaders achieved political independence with little resistance from the United States and France. The Americans early on had declared that the objective of their presence in the islands was to prepare the people of the Philippines for self-government and eventual independence. In 1934 the U.S. Congress set 1946 as the date for independence, and that date was kept despite the occupation of the islands by the Japanese from 1942 to 1945. In Cambodia's case France had not anticipated nor had Cambodians asked for an end to the 1863 French protectorate over the kingdom until the end of World War II, and by 1953 the French were ready to concede independence.

But apart from the relative ease with which political independence was achieved in Cambodia and the Philippines, the two countries (shown in Figure 3.1, the map of Southeast Asia) are quite different in the extent to which nationalism spread and in the form their nationalist movements took in the years leading up to independence. Cambodia had existed as a political entity before the Western colonialists arrived; the Philippines had not. Spain's rule over those islands provided their first experience of a common political identity and had much more intrusive economic and cultural effects on the indigenous society than did French rule in Cambodia. The symbolic form of the Cambodian monarchy was not disturbed under the protectorate nor did the French have much impact on the culture outside the capital city, Phnom Penh, nor on the traditional Cambodian economy. In the Philippines the sense of national identity developed and was expressed in nationalist organizations in the nineteenth century, earlier than elsewhere in Southeast Asia. In Cambodia nationalist sentiments appeared in the 1930s among Buddhist intellectuals, and anticolonialism was expressed by the small number of Vietnamese residents of Cambodia who were members of Ho Chi Minh's new Indochinese Communist Party. During the Japanese occupation armed groups opposed to the French formed, and after the war came political parties advocating Cambodian independence or at least greater autonomy.

The Philippines

The idea of a Filipino identity was created in reaction to Spanish exclusionist policies, spread by American educational policies, and reinforced by Japan's conquest and occupation; it found expression in the late nineteenth century in the formation of nationalist organizations and in the twentieth century in political parties, divided from the beginning along class and ideological lines.

The Spanish Period.   The unwillingness of the Spanish-born officials to welcome island-born people into the government and ecclesiastical bureaucracies

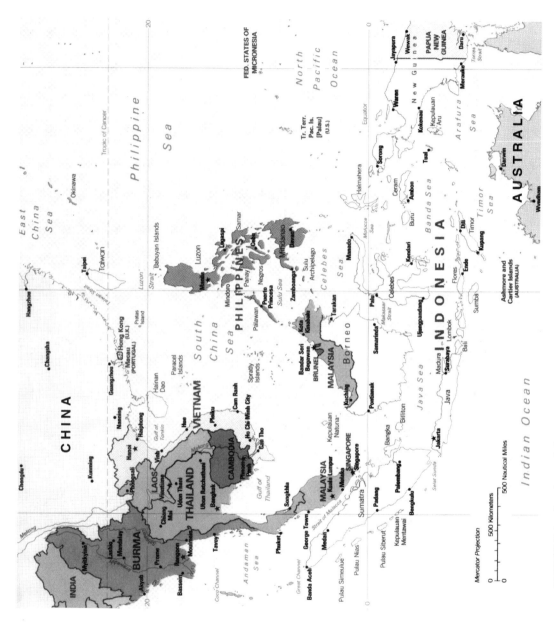

FIGURE 3.1 Southeast Asia

aroused antagonism among the creoles, people of Spanish ancestry born in the Philippines, and the mestizos, people of mixed Spanish, Chinese, and *indio* ancestry. Many of them were members of the emerging local elite of wealthy landowners whose sons came to resent the Iberian Spanish domination not only of the civil service but also of the parish priesthood and the monastic orders, which wielded important economic and political power through their ownership of large estates. In opposition to the Spaniards, the creoles and mestizos found a common identity as Filipinos, and that identity spread to other segments of the population.

Criticism of Spanish rule came from three groups expressing cultural, religious, and political nationalism. The first of these, the *ilustrados,* were the educated sons of the landowning class, many of whom went abroad to escape repression by the Spanish authorities and formed the émigré Propaganda Movement. The objective of that organization was to improve the status of Filipinos in the colony; it advocated equality for them, representation in the Spanish legislature, freedom of speech and assembly, less burdensome taxes, Filipinization of the clergy, and the promotion of a distinctive national cultural identity in literature, the arts, and pre-Hispanic history.[6] One of the leading ilustrados was Jose Rizal, a Chinese mestizo who returned home from exile in 1892 and founded La Liga Filipina to promote a modest program of economic and educational improvements; even that was too much for the Spanish, who promptly arrested him and deported him to the southern island of Mindanao.

The second strain of the nationalist movement involved Filipino clergy who wanted equal opportunity in appointments as parish priests and in the monastic orders. Suppressed by the execution of its leaders in 1872, the movement regained momentum at the end of the Spanish period when Father Gregorio Aglipay established an Independent Filipino Church. The Aglipayans took over churches and lands vacated by the departing Spaniards and at its peak attracted as members a fourth of Filipino Christians.

The third element of the nationalist movement was Katipunan, and its aims were more revolutionary than the other two. Founded by Andres Bonifacio, a Manila clerk, Katipunan advocated political independence from Spain, social revolution to benefit the common people, and seizure of the church-owned estates. Aware of his own limited education and the need to enlarge his base of support, Bonifacio tried unsuccessfully to persuade the ilustrados to join him. A Katipunan-organized rebellion was launched in 1896, and the Spanish authorities rounded up persons suspected of participating, including the ilustrado Jose Rizal. Mistakenly assumed to be the leader of the rebellion, Rizal was executed, providing a martyr for the nationalist cause and radicalizing ilustrados to switch from pressing for more participation in colonial government to pursuing the goal of independence. Leadership of the anti-Spanish revolt was taken over by Emilio Aguinaldo, a local official of Chinese-mestizo stock. But in the face of superior force Aguinaldo negotiated with the Spanish in 1897 for amnesty for his followers and an indemnity and exile for himself, only to be brought back from exile by the U.S. Navy when it arrived in 1898 to pursue the war with Spain. The struggle for independence resumed, this time with ilustrado support. Radical Katipunan economic and social goals were set aside in favor of nationalist political goals, and when the rebels declared the independence of the Philippine Republic on June 12, 1898, the ilustrados exerted the major influence in drafting a constitution for the new government.

The American Period.   The prize of independence was soon snatched from Filipino hands by the Americans, alongside whom they had been fighting. President McKinley decided to keep the islands after the Spanish surrendered, and by early 1899 the forces of the new Philippine Republic were waging guerrilla warfare against the Americans. The unity between Aguinaldo's followers and the ilustrados broke down when the Americans offered to involve educated Filipinos in the shaping of a new government, an offer with great appeal to many ilustrados but unacceptable to others in the resistance. The division was

> not simply a class struggle. It was, among other things, a contest between two world views—the urban, cosmopolitan, and educated versus the rural, unsophisticated, and innocent. . . . The *ilustrados* . . . thought it foolish to continue struggling against the Americans when the opportunities were so great not only for themselves but for what they saw as the best interests of the country. In effect, the Americans made a deal with the *ilustrados.* At the price of collaboration and allegiance, they were offered the chance to fill the vacuum created by the Spanish withdrawal.[7]

The result was that many ilustrados withdrew from the Philippine Republic government they had cooperated in creating and began to participate in the political institutions of the new colonial government. The independence forces were eventually defeated and the short life of the first republic ended.

The Philippine nationalist movement during the American period operated under conditions quite different from those in the Spanish period. Most important was that by 1900 the U.S. government had declared that its policy was to prepare the colony for self-government and independence, so for the Nationalists the question was no longer *whether* but *when* the United States could be persuaded that their wards were ready to stand on their own. Further, the Americans encouraged the formation of political parties, enabling the Nationalists to organize and operate openly. The first parties formed around leading personalities, all committed to political independence and to the forms of United States-style government and representing the landed and nascent industrial elites. Parties on the left, committed to social justice for the lower classes, emerged somewhat later and included the Communist and Labor Parties and Sakdal, created in response to adverse conditions caused by the worldwide depression of the 1930s. But the conservative parties favored by the United States dominated elections and the institutions of self-government; the most influential of these was the Nacionalista Party, led by Sergio Osmena and Manuel Quezon.

American-initiated policies concerning the church and education also affected Filipino nationalism. To counter the appeal of Father Aglipay's Independent Filipino Church, the Vatican acquiesced in the separation of church and state and moved to put more Filipinos into Roman Catholic Church positions and to reduce the church's large landholdings by selling some of them to the colonial government for resale to tenant farmers. Land reform, incomplete though it turned out to be, and the Filipinization of the clergy removed the principal objections of the Nationalists to the Catholic Church and undermined the influence of the breakaway Aglipayans.

In the field of education, American policy was to extend educational opportunities to a broader segment of the population by setting up more schools, staffing them as early as possible with indigenous teachers, and encouraging the teaching of Filipino history. The result was that the sense of belonging to the Filipino nation, which in the nineteenth century had gripped only a small minority, spread widely among the people and gave them a common bond of loyalty, despite the persistence of deep divisions between rich and poor, city and country.

The Japanese occupation during World War II opened up some fissures in the nationalist movement; while Quezon and Osmena left to run the government in exile, others stayed and collaborated with Japan, declaring an "independent" republic in 1943. Armed resistance to the occupation was widespread, led by the leftist People's Anti-Japanese Army, the Hukbalahaps. Both nationalism and pro-Americanism were strengthened by the occupation and the battle to drive the Japanese out.

After the war, Philippine independence was granted on schedule in 1946 and power transferred to the centrists and the leading personalities among them, representing the wealthy and middle classes, while the interests of the masses in countryside and cities remained unarticulated. This class division has continued to haunt postindependence politics, as we shall see in Chapter 4.

Cambodia

The story of the rise of nationalism and the nationalist movement in Cambodia can be told much more briefly because, in contrast to the Philippines, Cambodian nationalism did not really become visible until World War II, just a decade before independence. Such a delayed development might be considered surprising, since the Cambodian kingdom had long existed and at its zenith in the twelfth and thirteenth centuries the Khmer empire extended over much of Southeast Asia. But the glories of the past had been largely forgotten by the eighteenth century, and Cambodia was dominated by its neighbors to the west and east, Siam and Vietnam, until France imposed a protectorate in 1863.

It was not until 1930 that two organizations were founded that became significant in the nationalist movement. One was the Buddhist Institute in Phnom Penh, established by the kings of Cambodia and Laos and the French, with the purpose of fostering Buddhist studies. In fact, it strengthened the ties between the Cambodian king and his people and awakened a sense of national identity among the groups of intellectuals the institute brought together. These included Son Ngoc Thanh, a Vietnamese-Cambodian who started a Cambodian-language newspaper and later became a major figure in the anti-French movement.

A second step in 1930 was the establishment in Cambodia of a cell of the new Indochinese Communist Party. Its founders were Vietnamese residents of Cambodia rather than Cambodians, initiating a pattern of Vietnamese domination of the communist movement in Cambodia that persisted even after the ICP disbanded in 1951 and a separate Cambodian party took shape.

These two embryonic nationalist movements—one communist, the other not—were encouraged by the Japanese to mount demonstrations against the French administration, which Japan left in place to run the daily affairs of the colony. Armed groups under the banner of Khmer Issarak (Khmer Independence) formed in the countryside. In the last months of the war, the Japanese removed the French officials and told the young King Norodom Sihanouk, whom the French had crowned in 1941, that Cambodia was independent. For a seven-month interval from March until October 1945, when the French returned, Cambodians ran their own government. Son Ngoc Thanh, who had fled to Japan in 1942 after an anti-French demonstration, came back to serve first as foreign minister and then prime minister in Sihanouk's government, only to be arrested and exiled again by the French. Khmer Issarak bands continued their resistance in the countryside and managed to take the town of Siem Reap for a brief time in 1946.

Faced with nationalist pressures, the French made some concessions. They gave Cambodia "autonomy" within the French Union, keeping for themselves control of two significant levers of power, the army and the police. They arranged for the election of a constituent assembly to draft a constitution and authorized the formation of political parties. Two were formed: the pro-independence Democratic Party representing the middle bureaucracy, educated youth, and Buddhist monks, many of them supporters of Son Ngoc Thanh; and the more conservative pro-French Liberal Party, toward which the king was inclined. The Democratic Party won elections to the constituent assembly and to the National Assembly that followed, but neither the French nor the king was willing to see the Democratic majority exercise effective control over the government.

Tensions between Cambodian political factions increased in 1951. Thanh returned to a huge welcoming crowd estimated at over 100,000, only to flee to the countryside a few months later. There, refusing to join forces with the Communist-led United Issarak Front formed in 1948, Thanh started his own anti-French, anti-Sihanouk resistance group. That same year the Cambodian Communists established their own party, the Khmer People's Revolutionary Party (KPRP), and Sihanouk began a campaign of his own to mobilize international support for his country's independence. By 1953 the French, preoccupied with holding on in Vietnam against the Viet Minh's struggle to evict them and facing not only pressure from their one-time protégé Sihanouk but also an insurgent movement that controlled large areas of the country, were ready to concede independence to Sihanouk's government. Cambodia's political history since 1953 is traced in Chapter 4.

NATIONALISM AND ETHNIC SEPARATISM IN MALAYA AND BURMA

The British colonies of Malaya and Burma faced formidable obstacles to developing a coherent, inclusive nationalism both before and after independence. Under colonial rule, both these countries became plural societies, a result of large numbers of Indians and Chinese being brought into Malaya and Burma to serve British economic interests. Furnivall's description of multiethnic Burma, equally apt for Malaysia, captures the dilemma of colonized people in a plural society:

> Each group holds by its own religion, its own culture and language, its own ideas and ways. As individuals they meet, but only in the market-place, in buying and selling. There is plural society, with different segments of the community living side by side, but separately, within the same political unit.[8]

Held together by force of the centralized colonial administration of the British, these segregated ethnic communities were often more wary of one another than they were of their European rulers. When nationalist opposition to British rule did emerge, it was the parochial nationalism of the dominant ethnic group in each colony—the Malays in Malaya and the Burmans[9] in Burma—that defined the nationalist cause, lumping together all individuals of foreign descent—Chinese and Indians along with the British—as targets of their opposition. Japanese occupation during the Second World War exacerbated this interethnic animosity, ensuring that once the British left, the ethnic separatism both colonial powers had fostered would remain an enduring problem for postindependence governments to contend with in Burma and Malaysia.

Although ethnic pluralism was common to both societies, there were significant differences between them that affected the course of developing a national identity in Burma and Malaya. The principal religion in Burma was Theravada Buddhism while in Malaya it was Islam. Nationalism emerged early in the twentieth century in Burma and not until after the Second World War in Malaya. In Burma nationalism exhibited a revolutionary ethos, manifested in a broadly based demand for social and economic change along with a complete break with Great Britain. In contrast, nationalism in Malaya was conservative and accommodationist, reflecting the politically privileged position of the Malays encouraged by the British. After independence, Malaya remained a member of the British Commonwealth while Burma refused to join.

For Malays the racial understanding of their own ethnicity played a far greater role than either class or religion in defining their communal interests. Malay nationalism, therefore, was content to restrict the substance of its nationalist demands to the preservation of Malay privileges vis-à-vis non-Malays. In Burma nationalism may have been advocated principally by the Burmans, but the substance of its claims covered an entire spectrum of social and economic changes for a new nation. For them, the goal of nationalism was to create a state at least the equal of its precolonial state under the Buddhist monarchy, while for Malays nationalism had no unified state to look back on, only the feudal rights of the nine sultans who had ruled the region prior to the British colonial administration.

Early Nationalism in Burma

In Burma, as was true throughout Asia, organized nationalism began among an educated elite of Burmans and was initially expressed as a movement to reform or modernize their religion, Buddhism. The events of World War I, as elsewhere, politicized this cultural nationalist movement, the Young Men's Buddhist Association (YMBA), splitting it into pro-British and proactivist organizations. The proactivists who called themselves the General Council of Buddhist (later Burmese) Associations (GCBA) were centered in the university and promoted village-level nationalist organizations ("own-race societies") in rural areas. But as these village-based nationalist organizations came under the leadership of young Buddhist monks, they became more militantly anti-British, creating a breach between the rural and urban segments of nationalist leadership. The rural Buddhist leadership sought to eliminate the colonial government in its entirety while the urban secularist leadership sought just to oust the British while preserving their administrative structure as the foundation of a new nation.

This split *within* the ethnic Burman community, however, must be placed in the larger context of a Burma traditionally divided between the dominant Burmans and the ethnic minorities, which include Chin, Kachin, Shan, Karen, Kayah, and other smaller groups. Relations between them and the Burmans had been troubled since precolonial times, when Burman monarchs on several occasions subdued the peoples on their border, ruling over them for relatively brief periods before their power declined and the conquered areas slipped from their control.

During the colonial period, the division between Burmans and others continued under the British policy of separate administrations for Burma "proper"—the lowland areas where many Burmans lived—and the "frontier areas"—the mountainous regions inhabited by the minorities along the country's western, northern, and eastern borders—as shown in Figure 3.2. The ethnic cleavage between Burmans and the minorities was reinforced by heavily recruiting minorities into the colonial armed forces, by introducing communal representation in the colonial legislature as a form of special protection for minority communities, by the success of Baptist missionaries in converting Karens to Christianity, and by the migration of Indians into the colony.

The picture was further complicated by the fact that politically Burma was administered as a province of India—in effect, a "colony of a colony"—while economically it was exposed to the vagaries of the international market. Using credit provided by Indian immigrants, Burmans expanded their rice cultivation for a booming export economy. But when the rice market collapsed the Indians, who were already in control of commerce, also acquired, along with a few fortunate Burmans, the bulk of the land. Thus by 1938, the largest landowners in the Irawaddy River delta owned two and a half million acres or about 27 percent of all the land in lower Burma.[10] The majority of Burman peasants, on the other hand, fell into debt, foreclosure, and financial ruin, which led to anti-Indian riots and rebellions against colonial taxation and widespread impoverishment. These Burmans supplied a mass base for the radical leadership of the nationalist movement that coalesced just prior to and during the Second World War.

Two major issues divided the urban nationalist leadership in the lively political atmosphere of the 1920s and 1930s: One was whether or not to collaborate with the British-controlled constitutional government introduced in 1923; the other was the question of separation from India. The majority of the GCBA boycotted elections under the new constitution and favored direct action to oust the British, while traditional ethnic minorities who benefited from special representation in the legislative council formed an electoral majority against those Burmans who did enter party politics. Whether or not to separate from India in the struggle against colonial rule was equally divisive, some nationalists favoring freedom from India to obtain home rule on the best possible terms, while others sought alliance with the Indian nationalist movement to hasten the ouster of the British.

When the British decided in favor of separation, granting Burma a more democratic constitution in 1935, the urban nationalist movement split along generational lines.

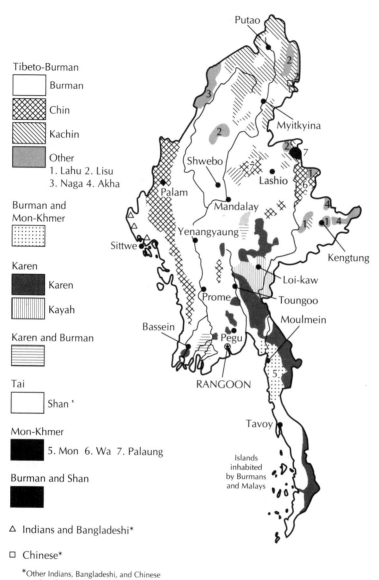

FIGURE 3.2   Ethnic Groups of Burma

Source: From *Burmese Politics* by Josef Silverstein, copyright 1980 by Rutgers, The State University.

The older politicians formed new parties to seek office in the Legislative Council while the militant university students set up their own revolutionary nationalist organizations among workers and peasants. The We Burmese Association, formally organized in 1933, rose to prominence under the leadership of the charismatic Aung San and the All Burma Students' Union after 1938. Calling themselves Thakins ("masters") to suggest they rather than the British were the rulers of Burma, these sons and daughters of the Burmese middle class included the future leaders of independent Burma. They applied Marxist ideas to Burma's colonial situation, organizing labor strikes among the mostly Indian factory workers and encouraging peasant unions with the goal of forcing the British out.

The electoral politics of the older generation of nationalist leaders held little interest for the vast majority of Burmese, whose participation in voting never exceeded 18 percent. The more youthful Thakins with their Marxist orientation, on the other hand, succeeded in arousing popular support from both peasants and workers for a broad range of antigovernment campaigns in the late 1930s. Although these two branches of the nationalist movement differed in principle on the issue of collaboration versus subversion, and in rhetoric between a more British-Labor and a more Marxist class orientation, their broad policy goals were substantially the same: independence, self-determination, and anti-imperialism. These goals were rooted in the question of land for the peasantry, an issue both sides were forced to address.

Thus, nationalism in Burma prior to the Japanese occupation was composed of a number of distinct elements: the professional politicians for whom nationalism became a fight over perks and position in the British-controlled legislature that they hoped to inherit at independence; the youthful, revolutionary Thakins with a strategy for mobilizing the masses of downtrodden for noncooperation with the British; the Burman peasants who violently rebelled against the loss of their land, income, and traditional supports, for which they held both the Indians and the British responsible; and the various groups of ethnic hill people, each protective of their special privileges under the British.

The Impact of the Japanese Occupation on Burma

The Japanese occupation introduced yet another divisive and bewildering dimension to the uncertainties among the diverse Burmese nationalists. A small group of Burmese, including Thakin Aung San, had been trained by the Japanese as an officer corps of a new Burma Independence Army. As it passed through Burma, the BIA grew in size as politically inspired youth joined its ranks. The sight of Burmese participating in the defeat of British colonial rule immeasurably enhanced the power and prestige of the BIA, the more so as its members filled positions of local administration vacated by the mass exodus of British and Indians. Under Japanese control, a government of prewar Burmese politicians was installed and granted nominal independence in 1943.

But it was impossible for the quasi-independent Burmese government to replace the power of the British colonial state and the neutrality of its civil service. When, in addition, the brutality of the Japanese occupation began to cost the Burmese Independence Army its popular support, Thakin Aung San, minister of war in the Japanese-sponsored government, astutely engineered an about-face and joined the Allies to form the Anti-Fascist People's Freedom League (AFPFL).

As in the case of China, the numerous nationalist organizations that cooperated in the struggle against the Japanese in Burma made strange bedfellows: the Communists and Socialists along with the Burmese Independence Army and the AFPFL joined with the Karen National Association, Burma's earliest modern political organization. This brought together Marxist-oriented students, peasants, and Burmese nationalists who sought to *throw out* the British in favor of an indigenously managed independent Burma with the Christian Karen and other ethnic leaders who sought to *bring back* the British to regain and protect their privileged position.

But these coalitions broke apart when the British were dissuaded from reimposing colonial rule by the league's effective organization of popular strikes and demonstrations between 1945 and 1948. When in the interest of achieving independence Aung San, the league's popular leader, demonstrated a willingness to negotiate compromises with the British, the increased likelihood that conservative politicians would be brought back into power alienated the Communists. This in turn caused severe strains in the league, culminating in Aung San's assassination by followers of a former premier, U Saw, some six months before independence in 1948. Thus the one figure capable of uniting the warring political factions in Burma was removed from the political scene. As a result, independence embroiled the new Burmese state in a civil war that echoed the tensions of the international cold war as the two factions of the Communist Party went underground to avoid arrest and pursue through insurrection what had eluded them through the electoral process.

Early Nationalism in Malaya

Colonialism stimulated nationalist sentiment by making Malays aware of themselves as a distinct ethnic group. The new forms of economic activity, urban life, and secular education that non-Malays enjoyed awakened Malays to the realization of their own backwardness. Three strains of nationalist consciousness emerged in the 1920s and 1930s, each appealing to different elements among the elites and with different aims. One was the group of Islamic reformers, inspired by contact with the progressive religious movement in the Middle East. They emphasized the need to purge Malay Moslem practices of their un-Islamic beliefs in magic, superstition, and spirit worship, so that Islam could be a force for modernization among Malays. With that objective, the Islamic reformers ran into opposition from traditional religious leaders and were unable to win over the Malay masses to their cause.

A second group, equally unable to gain a following among the peasant class from which many of them came, was composed of secular intellectuals, mostly teachers and writers. Their radical views included the notion of a pan-Indonesian nationalism uniting Malay people in both British Malaya and the Dutch East Indies. On the eve of World War II they formed the Young Malay Union, a political organization kept under close watch by the colonial authorities.

The third group was conservative in outlook, drawn mainly from British-educated sons of the traditional elite class who had been recruited for administrative positions in the colonial service. Alarmed by the demographic trend that by 1931 showed non-Malays outnumbering Malays, they sought to protect the privileged position accorded Malays by British policy and to increase civil service opportunities, the amount of land reserved for Malays and immigration by their fellow Malays from Java to offset the size of the non-Malay population. Avoiding any undue criticism of their British patrons, they created Malay associations in the separate states, with strong links to the local sultans. These conservatively oriented associations multiplied throughout the Malay Peninsula, extolling the virtues of ethnic Malay consciousness with distinctly hostile overtones towards non-Malays, even those who were Moslem.

While Malays organized in a conservative direction to defend their rights as *bumiputra* ("sons of the soil"), urban Chinese nationalists pursued progressive politics related to their homeland, identifying either with Chiang Kaishek's Guomindang or with the Chinese Communist Party. The Malayan Communist Party, formed in 1930, was active among the mostly Chinese industrial labor force and closely identified with the Chinese community. It had links also to the communist movements in Indonesia and Vietnam. So when the Japanese invaded Malaya in 1941, the Chinese in the colony were obvious targets of suspicion.

The Impact of the Japanese Occupation on Malaya

Under Japanese occupation, the Chinese bore the brunt of Japanese brutality not only because of their support for the anti-Japanese struggle in China but also because they soon became involved in organizing resistance to the occupiers. Because of their early and militant opposition to the Japanese occupation of China, the leaders of the Malayan Communist Party were encouraged by retreating British military officers to organize the Malayan People's Anti-Japanese Army (MPAJA). After receiving training in Singapore, the Communists constituted the core of the MPAJA, which employed the same guerrilla tactics against the Japanese that they were later to use against the British.

In contrast to the Chinese resistance, the Malays were either passive or active collaborators with the Japanese, whose conciliatory policy towards them included promoting them to civil service positions vacated by the British. An interesting question is raised by a former Malay civil servant in his study of communalism in Malaysia:

> It is significant that while collaborating with the MPAJA, the British made little attempt to mobilize the Malays as allies against the Japanese. . . . As one Malay, who was trained as a radio operator before the Japanese Occupation, posed the matter, "Why were not the Malays told to form resistance groups, as the MPAJA were, by the British?"[11]

Thus Japanese occupation of Malaya increased the tensions among the communal groups, hardening the nationalist rivalries into mutual antagonisms. After the Japanese left, a settling of scores between the pro-Japanese and the resistance took place, with Malay collaborators subject to reprisals by the MPAJA.

After the War: The "Emergency"

In 1946 the British announced their postwar plans for a "Malayan Union." In an effort to consolidate the patchwork of political arrangements that the British had made with local rulers a century earlier, the sultans were to relinquish their sovereignty to the

British Crown, and citizenship would be granted to persons born in, or long-term residents of, Malaya. Announcement of the British plan mobilized a storm of Malay nationalist feeling far exceeding any demonstration of national feeling manifested before the war. Within a few weeks a mass Malay movement, the United Malays National Organization (UMNO), had galvanized Malays into action against the British plan, which was hastily abandoned in favor of a return to a federal system recognizing Malay privileges and restricting citizenship.

But independence for the Federation of Malaya was delayed until 1957 by the "Emergency," precipitated by British military action against the Malayan Communist Party (MCP) and the struggle of its Malayan Races Liberation Army (MRLA) to oust the British. The "Emergency" illustrates the conjuncture of international and domestic affairs in the determination of nationalist policy in the postwar world and requires some recapitulation of events.

After the defeat of the Japanese, which they brought about in collaboration with the British, the Communists disarmed and embarked on pursuit of their objective of independence through legal means.

The MCP's efforts to organize the industrial workers, most of whom were Chinese, met with considerable success, and the British began to clamp down on labor unions. By mid-1948 the Malay Communist Party decided to give up constitutional means to achieve power and reverted to armed struggle aimed at interrupting production in the rubber plantations and tin mines.

The "Emergency" was the British military and political war to prevent the Communists from obtaining power. Militarily, the British forced the Communists into the jungle by 1949, while politically they benefited from Malay support, since "most Malays saw the war as preeminently a Chinese attempt to gain control of the state and not only remained loyal to the colonial power but fought actively against the MRLA."[12] Employing pacification techniques that the United States later used during the Vietnam War, the British resettled 500,000 Chinese in more than 400 "new villages" between 1950 and 1952 and deported some 10,000 Chinese to China.

While they were attempting to rout the Communists militarily, the British were preparing for their withdrawal as early as 1949 by encouraging the formation of the noncommunist Malay Chinese Association (MCA) as the Chinese counterpart to the United Malays National Organization. Ironically, closer cooperation between the Malay elite of the UMNO and the wealthy Chinese businessmen of the MCA was brought about (again with British encouragement) in an electoral pact to defeat the Independence of Malaya Party, a noncommunal party formed by Onn b. Jaafar, a founder of UMNO who had left that organization because of its Malay exclusivity. The informal alliance between the two communally oriented organizations, UMNO and MCA, was so successful in gaining the vast majority of seats in Malay's first democratic elections under the new federal constitution in 1952 that the Alliance was formalized in August 1953. When the Malayan Indian Congress agreed to join the Alliance, completing the representation for a stable electoral spectrum established along communal lines, the British felt secure in granting independence to the Federation of Malaya in 1957.

In both Malaya and Burma ethnic pluralism contributed to civil war between the government and its political opponents. In Burma the insurgency came after independence was granted; in Malaya the "Emergency" came before independence and was dealt with by the colonial government. Nationalist movements evolved differently in the two countries. In Burma, the special relationship of the British was with the Karen and Shan minorities rather than with the dominant Burmans, who were hostile to the British. In Malaya, it was the majority Malays whose status and traditions were protected by the British, resulting in an accommodationist form of nationalism. In Burma those who had been thrown onto the mercy of market forces mobilized in support of revolutionary nationalism. In Malaya the Malays, having been shielded from participating in the modern export sector, became proponents of a conservative ethnic nationalism, its principal purpose being to preserve their political privileges from encroachment by non-Malays, in particular the Chinese. Independence was demanded by the majority in Burma and conceded by the British soon after their return at the end of World War II. For the Malay majority, independence from colonial rule was a less pressing goal, and it took more than a decade for a bargain to be struck that enabled the British to turn power over to a conservative coalition dominated by Malays.

NATIONALISM FROM ABOVE IN THAILAND AND JAPAN

As in other Asian countries, Western imperialism stimulated the rise of modern nationalism in Thailand and Japan, even though both of them managed to remain independent. But rather than welling up from below in opposition to government by a colonial power, nationalism in those countries flowed from the top down. The Thai monarchs and the Meiji reformers acting in the name of the emperor undertook a process of self-modernization aimed at strengthening their countries' capacity to resist the threat of forced incorporation into the colonial empires and at reclaiming the sovereignty lost in the unequal treaties. The sacrifices required for modernization were made more palatable to the people by fostering a strong attachment to the nation, by putting loyalty to the monarch above loyalty to the local lord or to one's family, by creating national solidarity in support of the elite's domestic and foreign policy agendas. In both Thailand and Japan, education and religion were enlisted in the service of the nationalist cause. And in both, the ultra-Nationalists gained control of the government in the 1930s, only to lose it when their expansionist mission ended in failure at the end of World War II.

Nation Building by Siamese Monarchs

The integration of Thailand (then called Siam) into the Western-dominated world system began in 1855 with the negotiation of the first of the unequal treaties conceding to Western governments extraterritorial rights for their citizens, unrestricted trade, and low tariffs. The economic and social effects of being swept into the international trading networks were considerable. Siamese peasants began expanding production of rice for export, which gave them income to buy goods imported from the West. Exports of teak, tin, and rubber as well as rice transformed Bangkok into a major trade center. Chinese immigrants came to fill jobs opening up in construction, stevedoring, mills, banks, and offices, creating an ethnic division in Thai society along occupational lines similar to that in other plural societies in Southeast Asia.

Integration into the world system also stimulated the king and court to inaugurate other changes to create a modern nation-state. Governmental reforms were made with an eye to the ever present threat of foreign, particularly British, intervention. The British were on the move in the Malay states to the south and in Burma to the west, and the French were encroaching from the east into areas of traditional Siamese influence in Cambodia and Laos. King Mongkut (1851–1869) and his son and successor Chulalongkorn (1869–1910) assiduously tried to avoid giving the foreigners any justification for taking over their country and at the same time took steps to strengthen the power of the central government over the outlying areas vulnerable to foreign penetration.

Mongkut's initiatives were in the fields of education and religion. Realizing that to deal effectively with the Westerners, the royal family and the nobles needed to learn Western languages and something of Western science and technology, he hired foreign tutors for their children and brought in foreign technical experts to improve the military, the police, and the diplomatic service. Mongkut's influence in the religious sphere stemmed from the quarter of a century he had spent as a Buddhist monk before ascending to the throne; during that period he founded a new Buddhist sect, stripped of the local accretions that had accumulated in Siamese Buddhism over the centuries. Closer to the orthodoxy of early Buddhism, the practices of his Thammayut order were made by his son and grandson the basis for national norms in the selection and training of the Buddhist clergy, becoming one of the unifying elements for Thai nationalism.

During the reign of King Chulalongkorn major reforms were undertaken to strengthen the authority and capacity of the central government. Traditional king-vassal relationships between Bangkok and the outlying areas were replaced by provincial governments under the administrative authority of the national government. The power of the local lords was taken away, and they were either appointed by the central government to positions in the provincial governments or replaced by new officials responsive to Bangkok. The central government itself underwent renovation; functional ministries for interior and defense replaced earlier geographically organized ministries, and the tax system was restructured to bring in more revenue for the expanding bureaucracy and for public works programs such as the extensive railroad network linking parts of the country to each other and to neighboring countries.

Expansion of the power of the central government over the provinces was met with resistance in outlying areas where Siamese rule had previously been indirect and where the people were of different ethnic stock. Rebellions were suppressed by military force, but it was clear that for the newly centralized Siamese state to survive, all the people within its borders would need to be given a sense of membership in the Siamese nation. And this sense of nationhood, as Chulalongkorn, his advisers, and successors saw it, would be fostered by the new form of Buddhism, by extending education to the common people, and by promoting the king as the symbol of national unity. So the Buddhist priesthood was unified under the authority of a supreme patriarch appointed by the king. A state-controlled school system (although not fully in place until the 1930s) began to teach a standard version of the Thai language and a history of Siam stressing the king's rather than local rulers' role, as well as "modern" subjects such as science and math. Chulalongkorn's son Vajiravudh (1910-1925) expanded on his father's efforts to make the monarch more visible to the people. He appeared often in public in the uniform of the Wild Tiger Corps, a paramilitary group he founded, open to commoner and noble alike. The corps and a parallel Village Scout movement for children directed their members' loyalty upward to the monarch as the head of the nation. It was toward the end of Vajiravudh's reign that the Western powers, sufficiently convinced of Siam's modernity, agreed to end most of the restrictions imposed in the unequal treaties.

National Leadership by the Promoters

The Siamese revolution from above produced some remarkable achievements in the nineteenth and early twentieth centuries, but it had left the political core, the absolute monarchy, unreformed. It was not surprising, therefore, that the monarchy itself would be challenged by a new wave of nationalists in the modernized civil and military service the kings themselves had established. Recruited for their ability rather than their connections to the nobility, well educated, often with experience abroad, these people (whom today we would label "technocrats") knew that in the rest of the world absolute monarchies were becoming obsolete. They wanted to further their country's modernization, and expand their own influence, by curbing the power of the king. Under the pressure of a deteriorating national and personal financial situation caused by the world depression of the 1930s, a group of antiroyalist civil servants and military called the Promoters staged a bloodless coup in 1932, forcing Vajiravudh's successor King Prajadhipok (1925-1935) to accept the idea of a limited monarchy. From then on, the responsibility for nation building and national development passed from the hands of royalty to the new elite.

The Promoters and their supporters formed the People's Party and took their place in the government, successfully resisting a royalist countercoup in 1933. They soon split into a liberal civilian faction and a conservative military faction, and the leaders of the two factions, Pridi and Phibun, became rivals for influence in the government for the next two decades. Each man represented a different vision of modern statehood under a limited monarchy. Pridi's goal was to create a liberal constitutional system with the government chosen by and responsible to the electorate. Phibun, in contrast, emphasized the need for a strong state with decisive leadership at the center to direct the process of modernization. Pridi proposed a major role for government in economic planning and the establishment of cooperatives as the preferred form of private ownership. To the conservatives this smacked of communism and they ousted Pridi from the government and forced him into exile. Phibun, an army officer, became prime minister in 1938 and served until 1944. Pridi returned to hold a cabinet position briefly and then became regent for young King Ananda, who was in school in Switzerland until the end of World War II.

Ultranationalism Ascendant in Thailand

The years leading up to and during the war enhanced the influence of the military; ultranationalist ideas, in vogue in Japan and Europe, gained appeal in Siam. Resident Chinese, whose economic power made them visible and vulnerable to nationalist resentment, were restricted from engaging in certain enterprises, and the government created state enterprises to carry on activities formerly conducted by Chinese-owned enterprises. Limits were set on further Chinese immigration and Chinese-language instruction was prohibited. Symbolic of the desire to bring together all Thai-speaking people, including those beyond Siam's borders, Phibun had the country's name changed to Thailand. He followed up on this pan-Thai aspiration with a foreign policy aimed at taking advantage of the European powers' preoccupation with war in Europe to regain territories given up under duress in the late nineteenth century. Incidents along the border with Laos and Cambodia in 1940–1941 led to war with the French colonial government. Japanese mediation resulted in the return of those lands to Thailand, a victory against colonialism that enhanced the prestige of the Thai military.

When the Japanese made their push into Southeast Asia in December 1941, Phibun's government acceded to their demand for passage en route to the conquest of British Malaya and Burma. Riding the wave of Japanese victories, Thailand allied itself with Japan and declared war on the Allies. This move brought short-term territorial and economic gains; Thailand retook areas in Burma and Malaya that it had given up to the British in the nineteenth century, and its economy benefited from increased trade with Japan and provisioning Japanese troops stationed in the country.

But these gains were lost with the Allied victory in 1945. Thailand was forced to return the territories taken from the French and British colonies, and Pridi, who had cooperated with the Allies during the war through the Free Thai underground, was elected prime minister in 1946. The military, temporarily eclipsed as a result of its collaboration with the Japanese, ousted Pridi in a coup in 1947, and he went into exile again. Phibun became prime minister once more in 1948, thwarting a coup attempt the following year by Pridi, who then left the country for good. Phibun remained in office until 1957, when a rival military officer overthrew him and he too went into exile, where he died.

The ouster of Pridi in 1947 marked not only the end of his career in government but the eclipse of the liberal element of modernizing nationalists that he exemplified and the ascendancy of the authoritarian element and military domination of Thai politics. The liberal view did not disappear, but its supporters over the years suffered repression in various degrees of severity at the hands of the military, most recently in 1992, as will be described in Chapter 4.

Nation Building by the Meiji Reformers

In Japan the process of modernization was undertaken from above, by the young samurai who had seized control from the shogunate and ruled in the name of the Em-

FIGURE 3.3 Japan—Principal Islands and Cities

peror Meiji as the symbol of national unity. The nationalism that inspired the creation of a modern state had its foundation in a society more racially and culturally homogeneous than Thailand's, cemented by a confident ethnocentrism and reinforced by national myths about the divine origin of the emperor and his people.

As in Thailand, the stimulus for self-modernization was the need to become strong enough to resist further Western encroachment and eventually to press for termination of the unequal treaties exacted by the imperial powers in the waning years of the Tokugawa. And as in Thailand, the modernizers recognized that national strength required asserting the central government's political, fiscal, and military dominance over the local clans and fostering a sense of national loyalty among all classes of the Japanese people. The Meiji reformers moved quickly to bring the feudal domains under central control. Title to the land was given to the peasants who worked it, and they were required to pay taxes based on the value of the property, in cash directly to the central government, rather than, as before, paying a share of the rice crop to the local ruler. This change assured the central government a predictable revenue source for the increased expenses of modernizing the military and pensioning off the feudal class. The samurai as a fighting force were replaced with a national army recruited by conscription. Although there was some peasant resistance to the draft because it took sons away from work on the farm, military service became a way of forging consciousness of national identity and bonds of loyalty to the emperor and the central government rather than to the local lord.

Religion also was used in building a modern state. From 1868 to 1945, the Japanese government was the patron and advocate of Shinto, whose symbols and practices the state took over and adapted to bolster loyalty to the emperor and the nation. As one scholar puts it, "Shinto, as adopted by the modern Japanese state, was largely an invented tradition . . . to unite disparate elements into a modern nation."[13] Prior to the Meiji period, Shinto was a locally organized religion devoted to worship of many native deities at shrines throughout the country. Its ceremonies were closely intertwined with those of Buddhism, which had higher status during the Tokugawa era. After 1868, the Meiji leaders withdrew state patronage from Buddhism and ordered the separation of the two religions, creating a Department of Divinity to administer national religious affairs and conduct state religious observances. From 1870 to 1884, the government carried on a Great Promulgation Campaign to spread an official creed, teaching respect for the gods, reverence for the emperor, love of country, and obedience to the government. State sponsorship of the campaign "indicates that politicians believed Shinto would be useful in uniting the populace in a common creed that would transcend regional loyalties and differences of class."[14]

While the early Meiji era was a time of extensive borrowing from the West, perhaps excessively emulating Western dress, art, education, and technology to the neglect of Japanese traditions, by the late 1880s the time was ripe for a reassertion of Japanese identity and a renewed interest in Japanese culture. A movement to reverse what the cultural nationalists saw as a decline in morality due to Western influence led in 1890 to the promulgation of the Imperial Rescript on Education, which became the guiding principle for educational institutions. It exhorted the emperor's subjects to maintain harmonious relations with family and friends, to "develop intellectual faculties and perfect moral powers," to be law-abiding, and "should emergency arise, offer yourselves courageously to the State; and thus guard and maintain the prosperity of Our Imperial Throne coeval with heaven and earth." The Rescript concludes, "The Way here set forth is indeed the teaching bequeathed by Our Imperial Ancestors, . . . infallible for all ages and true in all places."[15] These universal values of loyalty and piety were inculcated in generations of Japanese children who participated in ceremonial readings and recited the text from memory, much as American children recite the Pledge of Allegiance. Shinto priests supported the promulgation of the Rescript, benefiting from the popular perception that all Japanese were obligated to observe rites associated with the Rescript and Shinto rites as well.

In the 1890s Japanese nationalism turned outward to the mission of expansion into continental Asia. War with China in 1894, intervention in Korea, and war with Russia in 1904 all elicited wide and fervent support. National pride suffered a series of injuries at the hands of the Western powers. Japan was forced to back down first on its claims to Siberian territory at the end of the Russo-Japanese War and then on some of its twenty-one demands on China during World War I. Its request for the adoption of a clause on racial equality at the Paris Peace Conference was rejected. It was assigned a position in naval power subordinate to England and the United States under the terms of the Washington Naval Disarmament Treaty. Having joined with the United States in sending an expeditionary force to Siberia to rescue anti-Bolshevik Czech military units there, Japan was pressured by the American government into removing its troops, which remained there after the mission was accomplished. Another cause of resentment was American immigration and local laws that discriminated against citizens of Japan.

The almost unanimous support for nationalist goals (dissent was expressed by some Christians, Socialists, and antinationalist Marxist intellectuals) may have obscured the growing differences between the moderate and the radical nationalists over both foreign and domestic policies. Hane[16] characterizes the split as being between the bourgeoisie and liberal intellectuals on one side and the militarists and radical nationalists on the other, between city and country, between Tokyo and the provinces, between the Western-oriented culture and the traditional culture. The radicals gained ascendancy in the 1930s, resorting to political assassination, book banning, textbook revision, compulsory attendance at Shinto services, and other measures to foster national unity and suppress opposition to their actions. Their success can be measured by the enthusiastic support for the decision to go to war in 1941. Japanese nationalism merged with militarism and imperialism to produce Japan's disastrous involvement in the Second World War.

INDEPENDENCE AND THE PROBLEMS OF NATION BUILDING

The surrender of Japan in August 1945 abruptly terminated its colonial rule over Korea and Taiwan, its wartime occupation of coastal and northeast China, the Philippines, the Dutch East Indies, French Indochina, British Malaya, and Burma, and its presence in nominally neutral Thailand. In Southeast Asia Japan's defeat opened the way for the return of the Western powers to the colonies from which they had been evicted in 1940–1942. In China the special privileges accorded foreigners by treaty had been abolished, but the Europeans and Americans returned to resume their commercial and missionary activities in that country.

During the last phase of the occupation and with Japanese encouragement, the Southeast Asian colonies had declared their independence in an abortive move to forestall the return of the former colonial masters. But the latter's military forces soon arrived to reassert control, the question being for how long. The United States' and the United Kingdom's plans for the future of their colonies anticipated independence for the Philippines within a year and for Burma and Malaya somewhat later. The concern was to transfer the reins of government to local people of moderate political persuasion who could be trusted to pursue foreign and domestic policies compatible with the interests of their colonial "tutors" in the art of self-government.

Independence came for the Philippines in 1946 and for Burma in 1948 but, for reasons explained above, was delayed for Malaya until 1957. Singapore was granted self-rule in 1959 and in 1963, along with the British-controlled states of Sabah and Sarawak on the island of Borneo, united with Malaya to form the Federation of Malaysia. Singapore left the Federation under pressure in 1965 and became an independent state. Brunei, the last British colony on Borneo, became self-governing in 1957 and independent in 1984.

In contrast to the Americans and British, the French and Dutch (perhaps to compensate for the ignominy of being occupied by the Germans during World War II) were determined to regain control of Indochina and the East Indies. Resistance was strong in both cases. The Dutch conceded independence to Indonesia in 1949 but kept the western part of New Guinea until 1962, and the Portuguese remained in East Timor until forced out in 1975. Cambodia and Laos became independent of France in 1953 and Vietnam in 1954, with recognition of the existence of two governments, the Democratic Republic of Vietnam in the north and the Republic of Vietnam in the south.

The postwar fates of Japan's two long-term colonies, Formosa and Korea, were determined by three victorious Allied powers. Formosa, the Chinese province of Taiwan given up under duress in 1895, was rejoined to the Republic of China and in 1949 became the site of that government when the Guomindang lost control of the mainland to the Chinese Communists. In Korea, by mutual agreement between the Soviet Union and the United States, American forces entered to accept the Japanese surrender in the southern half of the peninsula, and the Soviet forces did the same north of the thirty-eighth parallel. This division of Korea formed the basis for separate military governments in north and south, which in 1948 were terminated in favor of formal independence for the Democratic People's Republic of Korea in the north and the Republic of Korea in the south.

Japan itself was subjected to American military occupation from 1945 to 1952. During that time, under the direction of the military government with General Douglas MacArthur as supreme commander, constitutional and land reforms were adopted and economic reconstruction from wartime damage begun.

So all the former East and Southeast Asian colonies (except Hong Kong and Macau) had achieved the nationalist goal of political independence; their own flags flew over the capitals, their own compatriots occupied the desks in the government buildings, and the leaders of their independence movements had become the presidents and the prime ministers of the new states. But the tasks of statecraft, of economic development, of political and social modernization, of solidifying a national identity had just begun. And the tasks were complicated not only by internal conditions but also by pressures from beyond their borders. Foreigners might no longer occupy the government positions, but they still had interests they wanted to promote and the political, economic, and military means to promote them. An important aspect of defining those interests was the cold war, which began to chill relations among the major powers almost immediately after the guns of World War II fell silent. That was a major complication, though by no means the only one, facing the governments and the people of the new states.

SUMMARY

The defining attribute of nationalism in the Asian Pacific is that it developed in opposition to Western imperialism. Nationalism, an emotional attachment to the "nation," originated in Europe, and colonialism brought to Asians its message of the right to national self-determination, inspiring demand for independence from foreign rule. In both Europe and Asia, nationalism spread from the top down, combining with a variety of ideologies that offered alternative paths to modernization, forging bonds of unity among members of the nation and becoming a potent source of conflict between nations.

In Japan and Thailand nationalism was promoted by the government as a means to prevent the imposition of colonialism by strengthening the state through a process of self-modernization. Their success in escaping colonization was not matched by China, where the inability of the imperial government to resist foreign encroachment led to its overthrow by republican Nationalists.

Beginning among the Western-educated intellectuals, nationalist sentiments in the colonies moved from cultivating recognition of their national cultural identity to demands for political representation in colonial institutions to insistence on complete independence from foreign rule. Nationalist political movements were affected by both domestic circumstances and international events, most notably the Bolshevik Revolution and World War II. Within each country nationalists were often divided among themselves ideologically and organizationally between Communists and noncommunists, between religious and secular elements, and along ethnic lines, affected by colonial policies and precolonial traditions.

In China, the split between Mao's Communist Party and the Guomindang founded by Sun Yatsen resulted in civil war between the two nationalist movements, ending in communist victory in 1949. Rivalry between secular and religious nationalists, added to Communist-noncommunist differences, delayed independence for Malaya and resulted in postindependence civil war in Burma and Indonesia. Nationalists in Malaya and Burma also divided along ethnic lines, the majority Malays resisting and the majority Burmans leading the move for independence. Cambodian nationalism was slow to develop and also split along ideological lines. In the Philippines, class divisions surfaced in the opposition to Spanish rule; suppression of the populist insurgency in the American period opened the way for co-optation of the Filipino elites and to the peaceful transition from colony to political independence by mutual agreement.

The interval of Japanese dominance during World War II, which demonstrated to Asians the vulnerability of the European imperial powers, had different effects on the nationalist movements. In China, Communists and anticommunists partially and temporarily set aside their differences to fight the common enemy. The Thais, Malays (but not the Chinese in Malaya), and Indonesians collaborated with the Japanese, as did Burmans initially, later organizing resistance. In the Philippines, some leaders collaborated with the Japanese and others fought them.

The end of World War II accelerated the process of decolonization, and in the next decades the nationalists' goal of political independence was achieved. How they managed the tasks of governing is the subject of Chapter 4.

QUESTIONS FOR DISCUSSION

1. What signs of nationalism do you see at work in politics today? Are its effects good or bad?

2. How effectively did leaders in Asian Pacific countries use nationalism in their struggle against colonialism?

3. What was there in the lives of Sun, Mao, and Sukarno that moved them to become leaders of the nationalist movement in their countries?

4. How did World War II accelerate the process of decolonization?

NOTES

1. Rupert Emerson, *From Empire to Nation* (Cambridge, MA: Harvard University Press, 1960), p. 102.
2. Robert H. Taylor, *The State in Burma* (Honolulu: University of Hawaii Press, 1987), p. 67.
3. David Joel Steinberg, ed., *In Search of Southeast Asia: A Modern History* (rev. ed., Honolulu: University of Hawaii Press, 1987), p. 307.
4. Ibid.
5. Quoted in Orville Schell and Joseph Esherick, *Modern China: The Making of a New Society from 1839 to the Present* (New York: Random House, 1972), p. 125.
6. Steinberg, *In Search of Southeast Asia,* p. 269.
7. Ibid, p. 276.
8. Quoted in Taylor, *The State in Burma,* p. 77.
9. *Burmans* is the term generally used to refer to the dominant nationality group in Burma.
10. Steinberg, *In Search of Southeast Asia,* p. 234.
11. James P. Ongkili, *Nation-building in Malaysia 1946-1974* (Singapore: Oxford University Press, 1985), pp. 23-24.
12. Steinberg, *In Search of Southeast Asia,* p. 407.
13. Helen Hardacre, *Shinto and the State, 1868-1988* (Princeton: Princeton University Press, 1989), pp. 3-4.
14. Ibid., p. 59.
15. Ibid., p. 122.
16. Mikiso Hane, *Modern Japan: A Historical Survey* (Boulder, CO: Westview Press, 1986), p. 249.

FOR FURTHER READING

Nationalism

Birch, Anthony H. *Nationalism and National Integration.* London: Unwin Hyman, 1989, part I, pp. 3-74 (definitions and a general discussion of nationalism).

Emerson, Rupert. *From Empire to Nation.* Cambridge: Harvard University Press, 1960, chapters 1-4, 10 (on the development of nationalism in Asia).

Palumbo, Michael, and William O. Shanahan, eds. *Nationalism: Essays in Honor of Louis L. Snyder.* Westport, CT: Greenwood Press, 1981, pp. 3-32 (on the origins of nationalism in Europe).

Nationalist Movements

Drake, Christine. *National Integration in Indonesia*. Honolulu: University of Hawaii Press, 1989, pp. 16-44.

Hane, Mikiso. *Modern Japan: A Historical Survey*. Boulder: Westview Press, 1986, chapters 4-9.

Keyes, Charles F. *Thailand: Buddhist Kingdom as Modern Nation-State*. Boulder, CO: Westview Press, 1987, chapters 3-4.

Ongkili, James. *Nation-building in Malaysia 1946-1974*. Singapore: Oxford University Press, 1985, chapters 1-4.

Osborne, Milton E. *The French Presence in Cochinchina and Cambodia: Rule and Response (1859-1905)*. Ithaca: Cornell University Press, 1969, pp. 175-258.

Sathyanurthy, T. V. *Nationalism in the Contemporary World: Political and Sociological Perspectives*. London: Frances Pinter, 1983, pp. 149-66 ("Anti-Colonialism and the National Movement: the Case of Burma").

Schirokauer, Conrad. *A Brief History of Chinese and Japanese Civilizations*. New York: Harcourt Brace & Jovanovich, 1982, pp. 430-97.

Spence, Jonathan D. *The Search for Modern China*. London: W. W. Norton & Company, 1990, chapters 10-16.

Steinberg, David Joel, ed. *In Search of Southeast Asia: A Modern History*. Rev. ed. Honolulu: University of Hawaii Press, 1987, part 4, chapters 23-33.

Wurfel, David. *Filipino Politics*. Ithaca: Cornell University Press, 1988, chapters 1-2.

Biographies

Legge, J. D. *Sukarno: A Political Biography*. New York: Praeger, 1972.

Schiffrin, Harold Z. *Sun Yat-sen: A Reluctant Revolutionary*. Boston: Little, Brown & Company, 1980.

Schram, Stuart R. *Mao ZeDong: A Preliminary Reassessment*. Hong Kong: The Chinese University Press, 1983.

Terrill, Ross. *Mao: A Biography*. New York: Harper & Row, 1980.

Wilson, Dick, ed. *Mao Tse-Tung in the Scales of History*. Cambridge: Cambridge University Press, 1977.

chapter 4

Authoritarianism in Government and Politics

In the decades since the end of World War II, governments in East and Southeast Asia have wrestled with a formidable array of internal and external challenges. It is not surprising that some degree of authoritarianism is characteristic of each of them, whatever outward form the government takes or official ideology it proclaims. For the leaders of countries freed from colonial control, the central challenges have been to inaugurate ʾself-government, to resist unwelcome interference in their affairs by the former imperial power or other foreign states, to win and hold the loyalty of their people, to meet popular expectations of improved living conditions, and—like incumbents everywhere—to keep themselves in office.

To the countries that had not been colonies—Thailand, Japan, and semicolonial China—the end of World War II also brought challenges. Thailand's government needed to recover internationally from the burden of having sided with the loser in the war; Japan faced the suspension of its sovereignty during six years of American occupation as well as the economic devastation caused both by Allied bombing and the loss of its empire. China underwent political and economic revolution beginning in 1949 and the new communist government had the job of building socialism on the ruins left by the anti-Japanese and civil wars and in a largely hostile international environment. Reunification became a goal for China as for the other divided states, Korea and Vietnam, partitioned as a consequence of the United States-Soviet conflict.

If we fast-forward through the years since independence, two images of government and politics in East and Southeast Asia stand out clearly. One is that modern Western-style institutions appear to have been adopted by most of the countries; the governmental structures of legislature, presidents and prime ministers, cabinets, bureaucracy, and judiciary exist, and elections, political parties, interest groups, and media, which in the West serve as the vehicles for popular participation in the political process, also exist. But—and here is the paradox—the second feature is that all of the postcolonial political systems are to some degree authoritarian, whether under civilian or military rule, communist or noncommunist or anticommunist.

So the central premise of this chapter is that, despite the appearance of modern institutions of democratic government, the reality is that those institutions are the facade behind which the few control the levers of power over the many and the many lack the means or the will to hold the rulers accountable. Authoritarianism, like democracy, lacks a precise, widely agreed-upon definition, and there are gradations in both. Some governments are more "democratic" than others, some governments are more "authoritarian" than others, and the border between the least authoritarian regime and the least democratic one is not an unbridgeable chasm.

In our view, the distinguishing characteristic of authoritarianism is the absence of real competition for political power, the outcome decided by electoral contention between opposing groups, more than one of which has a reasonable chance of getting in power. This is a crucial feature of so-called "pluralist" democracies, such as the governments of the United States, Canada, and countries of Western Europe, where competition at the polls between two or more parties results in switching from time to time from one party or coalition of parties to another. In authoritarian systems, there may be more than one party, there may be interest groups and elections, and the government may have popular support, but the "ins," whether civilians or military officers, capitalists or champions of the working class, don't have *real* competitors.

We see authoritarianism not as the perverse manifestation of megalomania on the part of the few or irresponsibility on the part of the many, but as a way of asserting the authority of the state in societies beset by disintegrative tendencies. Those tendencies, coming from divisions along ethnic, regional, class, or ideological lines, impede national unity and perhaps even jeopardize the survival of the nation-state itself. Authoritarianism seems to its practitioners to offer a solution to disunity by compelling acceptance of the state's primacy over competing claims for obedience. It may be used by the rulers as an instrument to maintain the status quo and to resist pressures for change, or it may be an instrument to bring about change and to overcome resistance to it. But the underlying motivation seems to be the creation or restoration of political unity and stability in situations of disunity and instability.

We begin with a discussion of what modernization theory and world system theory have to say about the kinds of governments likely to have emerged after independence. In the next sections, six different dimensions of authoritarianism are described in the case of individual countries. We conclude by raising the questions of why postcolonial governments in the Asian Pacific are "undemocratic" and whether the trend is away from authoritarianism to democratization.

MODERNIZATION THEORY AND WORLD SYSTEM THEORY PERSPECTIVES ON POSTINDEPENDENCE GOVERNMENTS

As we saw in Chapter 1, both the modernization theorists and world system theorists agree that the government plays a role in economic development. Not just the neutral "keep order, protect private property, and let the free market drive the economy" state of laissez-faire proponents like Adam Smith, nor just the "tool of the capitalists to keep the workers under their thumb" of Marx, the state itself is an active promoter of development, and its policies may in fact benefit the workers as well as the property-owning class, although disproportionately favoring the latter.

Modernization Theory

Initially, modernization theory made the assumption that liberal democratic political institutions are the most appropriate ones to foster development, but this view has been revised in light of a more careful reading of European history and of the phenomenal economic success of the NICs. Early capitalist mercantilism emerged in Europe under authoritarian regimes, and in Asia similarly undemocratic governments such as those in South Korea and Taiwan have presided over the period of rapid development. Accordingly, modernization theorists now take the position that some degree of authoritarianism may be better able in the early stages of development to provide the continuity of direction and the social controls necessary for the massive changes from preindustrial to industrial production.

So while the *form* of liberal politics may exist (legislatures, chief executives, bureaucracy, courts, parties, interest groups, elections), it is likely that full popular participation will initially be curbed by various restrictions on liberties, allowing the modernizing elite to direct the show and to prepare the masses for the responsibilities of eventual self-government.

The expectation is that, as in the historical evolution of the West, the trend will be toward democratization. In Britain and France, the legislature began as a concession forced from a reluctant king by representatives of the aristocracy, who formed political parties; then the middle class, created by and creators of the industrial revolution, demanded representation in parliament; and they were followed by the working class, which expanded the electorate still further. In short, as the economy advances, society modernizes and authoritarianism is expected to give way to democracy.

World System Theory

World system theorists have fewer explicit expectations about politics in peripheral countries, in part because the level of analysis they consider crucial to focus on is the *world* system of international and transnational relationships, rather than on the nation-state and intranational relationships. The world system perspective is skeptical about the notion that government of, by, and for the people has any real meaning in a global capitalist system. Looking at what has happened in the colonial periphery since formal independence, they see governments run by a minority of people linked in one way or another to foreign capitalists; they are the owners of large landed estates raising primary products for export, they own or manage foreign-financed manufacturing enterprises and export-import businesses, or they provide various services to foreign and domestic capitalists. Whether the government in the periphery country is civilian or military, with one or many or no parties, does not matter. Whatever the specifics, the general picture is of a "client" regime, serving the interests of foreign capitalists and their local collaborators. Where development takes place, it benefits the elite and impoverishes the majority of the population. Efforts by the poor to contest this increasing inequality and to demand a larger share of wealth and political power lead to repression by the ruling class in the name of preserving order. External forces and internal interests thus tend to favor authoritarianism.

Now we turn from theory to practice and look at politics as it is carried on in Asian Pacific countries. While all of them exhibit some form and degree of authoritarianism, there is considerable variation from country to country and each has features unique to it. No single pattern typifies the ways by which rulers install and maintain their monopoly of power. Some are civilian regimes and others military, in strong or weak states. Some have revolutionary goals, some reformist goals, and some the goal of preserving the status quo. Some operate through a single-party system, others a one-party-dominant system; others have many parties, and one has no parties at all. There are Leninist-style parties, mass parties, ethnically based parties, and religious parties, to identify some of the varieties. Authoritarianism may be brutal and repressive, relying on force to compel submission, or it may be more gentle and permissive, using subtle pressure and rewards to win compliance. But fear of disunity, insecurity in the face of internal centrifugal tendencies, or vulnerability to outside pressures underlies these regimes.

To organize our comparisons of the diverse forms and degrees of authoritarianism, we have singled out six prominent features shared by two or more of the countries in the region. We begin with the "anachronistic" authoritarianism of an unlimited monarchy in Brunei and a colonial regime in Hong Kong. Next we look at systems in which Leninist-style parties dominate government and politics, with examples from both communist and noncommunist states. Then, in recognition of the prominent role of the military in many countries, we turn to cases in which military regimes have used their power to promote economic development; this we call authoritarianism by military "developers." In some countries deep divisions along ethnic lines have led to authoritarian rule as a means of keeping at bay the disintegrative forces at work in society; we label this "ethnic" authoritarianism. Next we compare the varieties commonly called "hard" and "soft" authoritarianism, and add a "softening" category to characterize systems that seem to be in transition from "hard" to "soft." Our last differentiation is between the forms authoritarianism takes where it operates through a strong state and those where the state is weak. Cambodia is left to the end as a special case where, as of this writing, the government created after UN-supervised elections in 1993 is not yet in effective control of the whole country.

These categories are neither the only way of classifying political systems, nor are they mutually exclusive. A country might fit into more than one of the varieties (Singapore, for example, fits into the category of countries with a Leninist-style party and into the strong rather than weak type of state), and a country might move over time from one variety to another (South Korea, for example, from civilian to military rule and back toward civilian government again and from "hard" authoritarianism toward a "softening" form). But we think you will find the distinctions among different kinds

---

Suggestion to Readers

To update the information about contemporary governments and politics provided in this chapter, you may find it useful to consult sources published after this book was completed in mid-1994. Changes in officeholders and recent developments in domestic and foreign affairs are reported in such sources as the *Statesmen's Yearbook,* the *International Yearbook and Statesmen's Who's Who,* the scholarly journals *Current History* and *Asian Survey,* and news magazines and newspapers, such as the *Far Eastern Economic Review* (which, despite its name, covers political events), the *New York Times,* the *Los Angeles Times,* the *Christian Science Monitor,* and the *Asian Wall Street Journal.*

---

of authoritarian governments a useful device for organizing the descriptions and analysis of countries in the Asian Pacific region.

"ANACHRONISTIC" AUTHORITARIANISM

Brunei's and Hong Kong's governments are survivors from an earlier era when unlimited monarchies and colonies were the common forms of government in most of the world.

Brunei

The most recently independent of the Asian colonial possessions, Brunei is an Islamic monarchy whose hereditary sultan, Sir Muda Hassanal Bolkiah, also holds the post of prime minister. He rules without the restraints of a legislature or political parties.

A colony of Britain from 1888, Brunei became self-governing in internal affairs in 1957, but independence was delayed until 1984 because of the sultan's reluctance to lose the support of the British presence. Under colonial rule, the Malay elite—the royal family and court—with the collaboration of resident Chinese entrepreneurs dominated political life, purposefully insulating the population of Malay peasants and fishermen from the modern oil-producing sector employing foreign personnel.

The traditional elite's dominant position was challenged in the mid-1950s by the formation of the anticolonial socialist Brunei People's Party, representing nontraditional interests and favoring independence and popular participation in government. When the first elections under the 1959 constitution were held in 1962, the People's Party won all the elected seats in a new Legislative Council, and the division between the traditional elite and the challengers deepened. A major policy difference between them concerned the relationship of Brunei with the other British colonies on the island of Borneo, Sarawak and North Borneo, also known as Sabah. While the sultan favored unification of all three territories with Malaya, the other side advocated instead the unification of Brunei with Sarawak and Sabah. An armed rebellion against the sultan broke out in December 1962 and was quickly suppressed with the help of British forces. The Legislative Council was dissolved, party leaders were arrested or fled, and the movement lost its following.

Since then, the monarchy has kept tight control of the reins of government, the sultan holding the post of prime minister and ruling by decree. Public welfare measures, including free education and medical care, were initiated after the 1962 rebellion and help to keep the general population quiescent. Elections were held in 1970 for a new Legislative Council, and again the opposition won and again the monarch dissolved the Council. In 1988 he banned the latest opposition, the small business-backed Brunei National Democratic Party, after it called for him to step down as prime minister.

So, despite fitful efforts to open up the traditional elite's monopoly of political power to participation by other segments of society, Brunei is still under the rule of an absolute monarch.

Hong Kong

A Crown Colony of Britain, Hong Kong is ruled from London through a governor appointed by the British government. Only recently have the residents of the colony been given even very modest opportunities for political expression through election to an advisory council and through the formation of political parties. After a century and a half of colonial autocracy, these small steps in the direction of self-government come rather belatedly. In 1997, under the terms of the 1984 agreement between the United Kingdom and the People's Republic of China, Hong Kong will be returned to Chinese control as a Special Administrative Region with certain protections for property and civil rights.

At present, political power lies in the hands of the governor, currently former Conservative Member of Parliament Chris Patten. He chooses the Executive Council and a third of the members of the Legislative Council, both of which are advisory bodies without the power to make binding decisions. In 1991 for the first time eighteen of the sixty-member Legislative Council (Legco) were elected directly by the residents of the colony; the remaining members are chosen as their representatives by various "functional" occupational groups such as businesspeople, lawyers, and doctors.

The 1991 elections also stimulated the formation of political parties to sponsor candidates. The United Democrats of Hong Kong, headed by Martin Lee, won eleven of the eighteen elective seats; independents won the other six and the pro-business Liberal Democratic Federation failed to win any. Lee's party advocates speedier progress toward democratization before the colony comes under Chinese sovereignty in 1997. He and other victorious candidates are leaders of the Hong Kong Alliance, created to show support for the democratic movement in China after the suppression of demonstrations in Beijing and other Chinese cities in 1989.

Since 1992 there have been heated discussions between the British and Chinese governments and between business and political groups within the colony over proposals by Governor Patten to broaden popular participation in elections to district and

municipal councils and Legco. Beijing's position is that the proposed reforms are con- ·
trary to the 1984 UK-PRC agreement and go beyond the arrangements for Hong
Kong's post-1997 government specified in the Basic Law announced in 1990. Patten's
counterargument is that the changes do not violate prior agreements. Additional subjects of contention between Britain and China involve decisions by the colonial government to undertake major public works projects, such as the construction of a new
airport, that will have fiscal implications for Hong Kong's treasury beyond 1997. China
insists that it be consulted on those decisions, reserving the right after 1997 not to live
up to obligations incurred for projects that it does not approve.

Organized groups in Hong Kong lined up for and against the electoral reform proposals, the Chinese members of the Business and Professionals Federation declaring
opposition, some British members dissenting. The two principal political groups in
Legco, the United Democrats and the Liberals, indicated support for Patten's ideas.
Predictions that the Hong Kong stock market would plunge under the uncertainty
generated by the controversy proved to be unfounded.

Numerous meetings of the UK-PRC Joint Liaison Group in 1993 failed to reach a
compromise on the proposals and each side moved ahead on its own course. Patten
put before Legco a partial election reform bill to lower the voting age from twenty-
one to eighteen, to replace appointed seats on district boards and municipal councils
(which have advisory powers) with elected representatives, and to replace multimember districts with single-member ones. Those proposals were approved by Legco
in February 1994. The Chinese government convened a Preparatory Working Committee with thirty Hong Kong members and twenty-seven PRC members to discuss
what should be done in preparation for elections in 1997.

At the heart of this standoff between Britain and China over Hong Kong elections
seems to be, on the one hand, the British government's desire to demonstrate that it
is leaving the colony honorably, having installed elements of democratic governance.
On the other hand is the Chinese government's resistance to what it sees as unilateral
decisions designed to impose additional restrictions on its authority over Hong Kong
after 1997, beyond those it committed to in the 1984 agreement.

Despite rather last-minute and modest steps undertaken by the British government, the people of Hong Kong (now approaching 6 million) have lacked institutions
through which they can effectively participate in decisions affecting them, including
the timing and terms of the transfer to Chinese rule. For them, 1997 will mean the end
of colonial authoritarianism and adjustment to living under another form, the authoritarianism of the Communist Party of China.

LENINIST-STYLE PARTIES ADAPTED
TO THE ASIAN CONTEXT

The Leninist-style party, which originated in the Soviet Union, has been the prototype
not only for Communist Parties in the People's Republic of China, North Korea, and
Indochina, but also for the Republic of China's Guomindang and the People's Action
Party (PAP) in Singapore.

Designed as an efficient and disciplined instrument for taking power at a time of social disorder and to make the transition from a disintegrating old regime to a new order, this type of party seemed admirably suited to conditions at the chaotic end of colonialism and for political movements intent on making revolutionary changes. For the Chinese, North Korean, and Indochinese Communists, revolutionary change meant following the Leninist pattern of economic, social, and political development; for the Guomindang it meant unifying and modernizing China under Sun Yatsen's and Chiang Kaishek's republican government and then, after the debacle of 1949, developing Taiwan's economy with the eventual goal of returning to power on the mainland. In Singapore, PAP's and Lee Kuan Yew's goal has been to transform that backward and vulnerable Chinese enclave in the Malay Sea into a rich and powerful modern state.

While there are variations from country to country, all share the basic distinctive forms and functions of the Leninist party. The party dominates the state and is organized hierarchically, with decisions coming from the top and followed by the rank and file. These are "cadre" parties, not mass membership organizations; members are screened before admission and expected to accept the discipline necessary to lead the masses in the direction the party has chosen. The Chinese Communist Party and the Guomindang, both heavily influenced by Soviet advisers in their early years, and the Communist Party in Vietnam are the examples chosen to illustrate this variety of authoritarianism.

Party and Government in Communist China: Parallel and Interlocking Hierarchies

China is essentially a one-party state; although minor parties exist and are represented in the national legislature, they are not "opposition" parties, having accepted the leadership role of the Communist Party of China (CPC). Party structures parallel the governmental structures, as shown in Figure 4.1; both are hierarchies of assemblies with the basic-level assemblies electing the next higher level and so on to the highest level, interlocked at the top in the persons of leaders who simultaneously hold party and state positions. Major officials are President and General-Secretary of the CPC Jiang Zemin, Premier Li Peng, and the venerable Deng Xiaoping who, although retired from his official positions, is thought still to be the most influential of the leaders.

Party Membership.   Unlike political parties in the United States, for example, where anyone can "join" simply by declaring a party preference when registering to vote, membership in the Communist Party is selective. (In 1992 there were 52 million members, about 4 percent of the population.) Applicants must be recommended by two party members, investigated and accepted by the local party branch, and approved by the next higher party committee. A member is expected to work for the good of the people rather than for private gain, to follow party discipline, to avoid involvement in factionalism, to study the writings of Mao, Lenin, and Marx, and to set an example for others to emulate.

Because it is both an elite leadership body and the representative of the masses of Chinese citizens, the Communist Party has been the major path by which ordinary

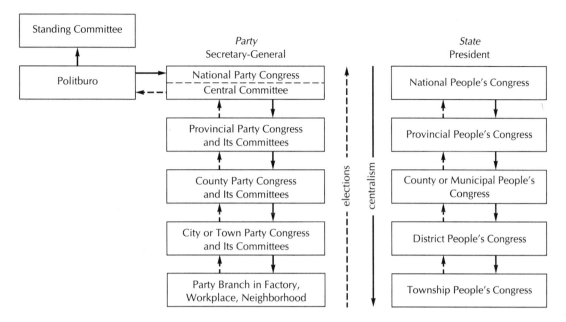

FIGURE 4.1 *CPC and PRC: Principal Party and State Organs*

Chinese could move up in the political world. The level of education and administrative skill of the rank and file has been low, and efforts are being made to upgrade the calibre of party members by providing training at party schools, by recruiting more educated people, and by expelling the unfit as well as the ideologically suspect and those guilty of corruption or other economic crimes. The party's role as central source of authority in society entitles all its members to be considered *cadre,* a term applied to individuals in positions of leadership in other organizations as well.

Cadres (in Chinese *ganbu*) include the local party official in a village, the accountant in a factory, a general in the Army. Those in positions of authority in the military are not necessarily party members. But cadres hold a crucial position in the chain of authority linking policymakers at the center to persons at lower levels who have the responsibility for policy implementation. The quality of the functionaries in the party, central government, provincial and local government, and the military affects the quality of government in China to a degree not equaled in countries where policymaking is more widely dispersed among levels of government and between public and private sectors.

Party Structures and Functions. At the lowest level is the party branch, organized in such places as factories, stores, schools, neighborhoods, farms, and units of the People's Liberation Army (PLA). Led by a branch secretary, the unit's job is to recruit members, maintain party discipline, educate the public about party policies, and provide face-to-face linkage between the CPC and the people.

At each of the higher levels of party organization, as shown in Figure 4.1, there is a *congress,* a large representative body chosen by the level below; the congress meets infrequently for brief sessions, delegating day-to-day supervision of party business to a smaller *committee* and a party *secretary.* At the national level are the National Party Congress, the Central Committee, the Political Bureau (Politburo), its Standing Committee, the Central Secretariat, and in addition the Military Affairs Committee and the Central Commission for Discipline Inspection, national organs for which there are no counterparts at lower levels.

The *National Party Congress* is in principle the highest authority in the party, but since it meets only briefly every five years or so and is quite large (over 1,900 delegates at the 1987 Congress) its supremacy is more formal than real. Its principal functions are to receive reports from the party head and discipline commission, proposals for revision of the party constitution, and economic development plans and to ratify the slate of nominees for the Central Committee prepared by the top leadership (write-ins have been permitted since 1982). Although the National Party Congress does not actively debate policies or overturn what the Politburo has decided, it is an important forum for announcing new policies and directions.

The *Central Committee,* with over 300 full and alternate members chosen at the 14th Party Congress in 1992, usually meets annually to discuss and approve party and state policies and programs. It elects the Politburo, its Standing Committee, and the General Secretary. In the 1980s purposeful efforts were made to retire the older and less-educated Central Committee incumbents and replace them with new talent better qualified to preside over economic modernization. Of the members of the 13th Central Committee chosen in 1987, more than half were new to the position, almost three-quarters had some college education, and about a fifth had specialized postsecondary training; their average age was fifty-five and the single largest group (43 percent) was from local and provincial government, the next (31.4 percent) from the central government and party, and 19 percent from the military.[1] The 14th Central Committee has the same proportion of new and military members as its predecessor.

The *Politburo,* with twenty members in 1992, of whom fourteen are new, and its *Standing Committee,* which does the party's day-to-day business, are at the summit of power over party and government, making personnel and policy decisions for all of China. The Politburo meets often and, after reportedly lively discussion, reaches decisions by consensus. As with the Central Committee, Deng Xiaoping has made efforts to retire other old Politburo members, replacing them with younger men. He has succeeded to some extent; the average age of the 1987 group was sixty-three, compared to seventy-two in 1982; in the changes made at the 14th Party Congress, eight of the elderly Politburo members were removed.

The management of party affairs and the oversight of policy execution are the responsibility of the *Central Secretariat,* organized into departments and run by the general secretary, who is nominated by the Politburo Standing Committee and approved by the Central Committee. Party supervision of the PLA is handled by the *Military Affairs Committee* reporting to the Politburo. Finally, the *Central Commission for Discipline Inspection* investigates charges of breaches of party rules and misconduct by members.

Democratic Centralism.   The party operates according to the Leninist principle of "democratic centralism." The democratic component comes in the form of participation by the rank and file in the selection of delegates to party congresses and in their discussion of policy proposals initiated above and sent down for deliberation before a decision is made. Centralism lies in the top-down screening of candidates to weed out untested or distrusted party members from serving in higher positions and in the fact that central bodies, especially the Politburo, have the final power to make decisions. While consultations down through the ranks precede decisions and are designed to maximize the likelihood that policies will be carried out at the grass roots, once decisions are made at the top all party members are expected to accept the outcome and work unreservedly to implement the decisions. Differences of opinion are not, in principle, to be allowed to solidify into permanent factions; "splittism" is deplored. (But, as we shall see below, the CPC leadership has been and still is divided over important issues of policy and organization.)

The party, especially the top echelon, serves as the executive leadership for the whole country, setting the "general line" that provides the framework for state officials to make their plans and carry them out.

Government Structures and Functions.   The state hierarchy parallels the party's, extending from the local people's congresses elected by the voters to the provincial congress to the National People's Congress, the delegates at each of the higher levels being selected by and from the next lower level.

The *National People's Congress* (NPC), the legislature, meets annually for several weeks to enact laws, adopt constitutional amendments, approve the state budget, and elect a number of executive and judicial officials, including the president, vice president, premier, and other officers of the State Council, or cabinet. The Congress elected in 1988 had just under 3,000 members, about half of them workers, peasants, and intellectuals; the rest were officials from state and party bureaucracy, soldiers, and representatives of minor parties and Chinese living abroad. Such a large body meeting briefly once a year clearly does not function like the smaller full-time legislatures in Britain or the United States, but the NPC does use the occasions afforded by its scrutiny of reports from the government to ask hard questions about policies and performance and to criticize and make recommendations. Between sessions, the NPC Standing Committee acts on its behalf.

Another national deliberative body is the *Chinese People's Political Consultative Conference* (CPPCC), a holdover from the early years after liberation before the first state constitution was adopted and NPC created. The CPPCC is composed of delegates from the minor parties and mass organizations such as trade unions and women's groups and serves both as a link between those groups and the CPC and as a consultative body to the NPC.

The *State Council,* the central executive body, is made up of the premier, vice premiers, and heads of ministries and commissions, many of which have functions relating to the economy, such as planning, finance, agriculture, construction, and various other industries. Reorganization of the ministries and commissions reduced the number of State Council members to 108 in 1988 from its previous 520; even so, the

Council is too large to function as a cabinet, a role performed by an inner group of some fifteen Council members.

So in the division of labor between party and state, party members as the vanguard of the working class provide leadership for the government and the whole society. Although those serving in the state legislative bodies and bureaucracy are by no means all CPC members, the party's influence permeates the state apparatus and the armed forces all the way from the lowest level to the top government positions held by Politburo and Central Committee members.

Intraparty Struggles and Zigzag Policies.   Since liberation, the CPC's goal has been to transform all of China into a modern socialist state, promoting economic and social development within the broad framework of Marxism-Leninism, applying the political experience gained in governing the areas under its control during the 1930s and 1940s. While the commitment to socialism and the leadership of the party was shared by all, differences arose (and continue to exist) over how to achieve the communist objective of economic and social modernization. The sharpest division was between those who favored emphasizing and rewarding technical proficiency (being "expert") and those who endorsed the primacy of loyalty to the values of the revolution (being "red").

The struggles among party members over policy were fierce and resulted in periodic reversals of party line at the top, with sharp swings of the pendulum affecting the entire population. Stirring people up through campaigns to achieve socialist political goals favored the majority of less-educated people, in the process disrupting the orderly economic progress engineered by the experts. But promoting experts to achieve more productive economic organization meant favoring the sons and daughters of the already privileged educated class over ordinary people for whom the revolution had ostensibly been made.

In 1958–1960 and again in 1966–1976 the Maoists gained the upper hand and steered the country through two major social experiments known as the Great Leap Forward and the Cultural Revolution to short-circuit what they saw as the growing entrenchment of the officials in party and state. Mao's argument was that bureaucratization threatened the goals of the revolution, that service to the people was being superseded by the self-serving interests of the officeholders; therefore, a thorough shakeup was required to cleanse the party and government of "counterrevolutionary" elements and through mass campaigns to mobilize popular support for continuing revolutionary struggle.

Great Leap Forward.   For the Maoists, the Great Leap Forward was aimed at arousing mass enthusiasm for new ways of enhancing productivity that did not require capital or resource expenditures. People were encouraged to set ambitiously high production targets and improvise novel collective ways of achieving them. In the countryside, households were joined into large collectives called *communes* and more decision-making responsibility was delegated to grassroots levels. The active participation of everyone was preferred to the overcautious plans of government officials. Those who opposed and were overruled by the Maoists argued that without specialization and incremental production quotas coordinated at the center, chaos would ensue and economic setbacks would occur. When the Great Leap's disastrous consequences became apparent, Mao stepped down and the opposition moved in to put economic development back on an orderly, Soviet-style path once again.

Cultural Revolution. For a second time, in 1966, Mao presided over a campaign to revolutionize popular culture by mobilizing the younger generation to criticize, rebuff, and eliminate Confucian and other "feudal" ideas and artifacts of the older, more educated generation of urban Chinese. Youths were exhorted to form into groups of Red Guards, each competing to outdo the others in revolutionary fervor and loyalty to Mao Zedong's Thought. Mao's writings were condensed and reduced to pithy quotations in a little red book that the Red Guards raised aloft and widely quoted as evidence of political correctness. Young Guards searched people's homes and confiscated and destroyed books, paintings, jewelry, and other symbols of "bourgeois decadence." Factories were reorganized and run by Revolutionary Committees representing workers, technicians, and managers. When turmoil in the streets and factories escalated into civil strife, the Peoples' Liberation Army was called in to reestablish order. Young people were sent from the cities into the countryside to exchange experiences and knowledge with the peasants, thus spreading the damage of the Cultural Revolution. Though officially terminated in 1969, the army's intervention and political uncertainty unleashed by the Cultural Revolution lasted for "ten bad years" until 1976, when Mao, whose illness had precipitated a struggle over succession, died. His widow, Jiang Qing, and three other radical leaders, known as the "Gang of Four," were soon arrested and eventually convicted of plotting against the party's choice of a new chairman.

The Deng Era. Following Mao's death, the anti-Maoists gradually succeeded in wresting control from, though not eliminating, their opponents in the party. Under the leadership of Deng Xiaoping, the Maoist practice of instigating periodic episodes of mass political turmoil was put aside. Economic policies initiated to restore production after the failure of the Great Leap Forward and resumed after the Cultural Revolution became the basis for the Four Modernizations program to modernize agriculture, industry, science and technology, and the armed forces. Self-correcting pragmatism, expressed as "Seek truth from facts," was to guide action, rather than ideological preconceptions. "Redness" alone was not to be valued above "expertness"; the test would be performance. As Deng put it, "Black cat, white cat, what does it matter as long as it catches mice?"

But orthodox elements in the party remained, people commonly identified as "hard-liners" or "conservatives" who feared the effects of loosening controls over the economy and the increased contacts with foreigners that the four modernizations brought. Their fears of "cultural pollution" seemed justified when student demonstrations broke out in 1986–1987 at universities in various cities, calling for reforms in higher education and for political reforms as well. The demonstrations were put down, only to erupt again in May 1989 in Tiananmen Square. Initiated by students at prestigious Beijing University and joined by workers and ordinary citizens in the capital, the movement spread to cities throughout China, coalescing around a multitude of griev-

China's senior leader, Deng Xiaoping, author of the "Four Modernizations" program
Source: AP/Wide World photo Mark Avery, 1989.

ances over inflation, job insecurity, and other economic issues, as well as aspirations for more popular participation in government and a loosening of the party's grip on society. The government's response was slow in coming, reflecting deep divisions over whether to negotiate with the movement's spokespersons or to clamp down forcibly. The latter course prevailed. Martial law was declared and, with the world watching on TV, tanks moved into the city and cleared the square, with considerable loss of life. Many of the activists were arrested, went underground, or fled the country.

Since Tiananmen, the leadership has remained the same, Deng seeming able to hold the hard-liners and the moderates in some semblance of balance. His program of economic reform continues, but political reform, rarely if ever embraced enthusiastically by those in power, is on hold. What will happen when nonagenarian Deng "goes to see Marx" is the subject of speculation. For now, the reins seem to be securely in the hands of the residents of Zhongnanhai, the walled quarter just off Tiananmen Square and next to the imperial palace grounds, where the leaders live and work. The fate of Eastern European communist governments that opened the door a crack to political "liberalization" must surely provide a cautionary lesson for China's leaders to ponder.

Vietnam: War and Unification under the Communist Party

The Socialist Republic of Vietnam, as it has been called since 1976 after the communist Democratic Republic of (North) Vietnam defeated the Republic of (South) Vietnam in 1975 and unified the country, is governed by the Vietnam Communist Party. Prime Minister since 1991 is Vo Van Kiet, former mayor of Saigon (now renamed Ho Chi Minh City), and in 1992 General Le Duc Anh was chosen president. The general-secretary of the party is Do Muoi, who had been prime minister before taking the party post in 1991.

Vietnam's protracted and painful rite of passage from French colony to unified independent state is inextricably bound up with the cold war preoccupation of external actors and therefore it is reserved for fuller treatment later in Chapter 7 on international relations. Here we just give a summary of events in the years from 1945 to 1975 as an introduction to the subject of political developments in the years since unification.

From 1945 to 1975. The Vietnamese celebrate as their National Day September 2, the day in 1945 when Ho Chi Minh declared the independence of the Democratic Republic of Vietnam, but it was thirty years before the DRV actually achieved control over the whole country. First came the period from 1946 to 1954 of war against the French, during which the Viet Minh, a coalition of nationalist organizations, set up a government in liberated areas mainly in the northwest and organized resistance in other areas of the country. That phase of the independence struggle ended with the Geneva Conference of 1954, when France and other states acknowledged Vietnam's independence and gave de facto recognition to two governments, the Democratic Republic of Vietnam in the area north of the seventeenth parallel and the government headed by Emperor Bao Dai in the south. The division was to be temporary, until a nationwide election could be held to determine the country's future government; for reasons described in Chapter 7 that election did not occur.

In the next few years, the DRV established the full panoply of state institutions in the northern part of the country and launched a program of socialist transformation through land redistribution followed by collectivization of agriculture and the development of heavy industry. Peasant objections to land reform and antiparty resistance by Catholics, ethnic minorities in the mountains, and intellectuals all were overcome in this period and party-state control consolidated. In the south, Bao Dai was ousted in 1955 by the United States-backed anticommunist Catholic Ngo Dinh Diem, whose government received economic and military aid and diplomatic support from the United States. When Diem moved to eliminate Viet Minh and other opponents of his government, many went underground to escape arrest.

The war of liberation resumed in 1959 when Viet Minh partisans in the south finally persuaded the leaders in the north, who until then had been counseling them to engage only in political activities, to approve the southerners' use of armed resistance against the government there. War between the Viet Minh and the South Vietnamese army intensified in 1964, when American military and the North Vietnamese army joined in the combat. By 1973, U.S. ground troops were withdrawn. The South Vietnamese government fought on until the spring of 1975, when the country was finally reunited under the Hanoi government. Liberation, as in China, came out of bitter struggle, not just against foreigners, but against compatriots.

After Unification. Political and economic integration of the two parts of the country has not been an easy task. Economic development in the north suffered a severe setback as the result of the material and human costs of the war effort and U.S. bombing. In the south, years of battle raging through the countryside had disrupted the lives of the peasants, bloated the population in the cities, and produced feverish economic activity artificially stimulated by foreign aid and geared to military needs. An ill-conceived effort following unification to collectivize agriculture in the south and the costs of occupying Cambodia and war with China in 1979 also retarded economic progress. Soviet financial aid, given after the termination of Chinese economic assistance in 1978 and the signing of a treaty of friendship between Vietnam and the Soviet Union, became a major source of funds until 1990.

Political unification also posed problems. In addition to the task of "reeducating" officials and supporters of the RVN who had not fled the country, there was the task of reuniting the northern and southern branches of the party into one national body, renamed the Vietnam Communist Party at the Fourth Party Congress in 1976. The government structures of the DRV, Provisional Revolutionary Government (PRG), and the Republic of Vietnam were absorbed into the Socialist Republic of Vietnam. The National Liberation Front (NLF) joined the Fatherland Front, and southern liberation forces merged with the north's People's Army of Vietnam.

Party leadership since unification survived the passing of some of the older generation of wartime leaders and a younger, better-educated generation has gradually taken their place. Factional differences persist within the party between the old and the young, between the veterans of armed struggle and the technocrats, between those who favor self-sufficient national development and proponents of interdependence. There have been debates since the Seventh Party Congress in 1991 and during the 1992 election campaign over whether political changes are required by the economic reform program known as *doi moi*, "renovation," begun in the late 1980s (described in Chapter 5).

So far the dominant opinion in Vietnam as in China seems to be that any goal of a pluralist multiparty system is out of the question and that, up to a point (which Vietnam has not yet reached), it is possible to make economic change without political change. That position was reaffirmed by chairman Do Muoi at the party conference in January 1994.

Some modest political movement has already begun. In the 1992 elections to the National Assembly candidates not screened by the Communist Party were allowed to run as independents, though they were required to get approval from neighbors, coworkers, and the Fatherland Front. The 1992 constitution, while still recognizing the party as the leading force in the state and society, asserts that all party organizations must operate within the framework of the constitution and the law. Political power continues to be monopolized by the Communist Party working through the party, the state, and mass organizations to make, carry out, and mobilize popular support for policies arrived at by the party.

Underlying the issue of political reform in China and the other communist states—North Korea, Vietnam, Laos—are fundamental questions about the role of a revolutionary party after the revolution is won. Once the antirevolutionaries have been eliminated, cowed, converted, or outlived and restoration of the old regime is no longer conceivable, what purpose does the party serve? Is it needed to keep alive the revolutionary vision, to "re-revolutionize" the masses from time to time lest they sink back into privatism and indifference to the collective good? Or, when the goal of society is modernization and development, which require rational and efficient allocation of human, material, and financial resources, is the duplication of party and state hierarchies necessary or a cumbersome waste of talent and energy? Does tight control over decision making in the hands of the people at the top, and unquestioning obedience from below, strangle innovation and creativity in the middle and lower ranks of both party and state? If some decentralization of decision making is desirable, how much can be allowed without risking descent into anarchy? Would the process of economic and social modernization be better served by opening up more positions in government, and even the party, to direct election by the people? Should the leading role of the Communist Party be open to challenge by other organized parties and interest groups? These questions strike at the heart of the system and are not amenable to facile answers, to simple advocacy of "democracy" or other bumper sticker slogan solutions. Nor are they likely to be avoided indefinitely or to go away.

Some of these questions are also relevant to the future of the two anticommunist Leninist-style party states, the Republic of China on Taiwan and Singapore, to which we now turn.

The Guomindang: Leninist Party without Lenin

The Guomindang, the National People's Party, has been the ruling party of the Republic of China since its founding, and the party's Leninist structure dates to the 1920s, when Sun Yatsen invited Soviet help in whipping it into shape for the task of unifying and modernizing China.[2] With the communist victory on the mainland in 1949, the defeated Republic of China (ROC) government, led by General Chiang Kaishek, moved the seat of government to the province of Taiwan, bringing with it the mainland party and governmental structures, the nationalist army and civilian officials. The present president and party chairman is Lee Tenghui and Lien Chan is premier.

The Party.   Like the CPC, the Guomindang is organized hierarchically, with the National Party Congress electing the party chairman and the 180-member Central Committee; it in turn approves the chairman's nominees for the Central Standing Committee. Provincial party structures follow a similar pattern. By the early 1980s party membership had grown to some 2 million, larger in proportion to the total population (20 million) than the CPC, making it—in the words of one observer—"somewhere between a small, tightly organized 'cadre' party and a 'mass' electoral party."[3] The large majority of the members are Taiwan-born, and even in the central standing committee mainlanders were in a minority (fifteen of thirty-two seats) in 1988. Businessmen, technocrats, and local government officials of a younger generation have gradually been brought in as aging mainlanders died or retired.

Factionalism within the ranks of the Guomindang has some similarity to the divisions within the CPC. In Taiwan a central conflict is between old-guard "conservatives," often older and mainland-born, who resist significant political change within the party and government that might loosen the party's traditional power position, and the "moderates," often younger, better-educated people with technical expertise who support gradual adaptation to changes in society that in their view will strengthen support for the party among the voters. Divisions within the Guomindang also surface among the military, the technocrats, and personalist factions organized around leading contenders for top positions. In 1993 a rift opened up over policy toward China, and a group of party members, mostly of mainland origin, who felt the government was not pursuing reunification vigorously enough left the Guomindang and formed the Chinese New Party.

As in the PRC the party on Taiwan maintains its leadership role for the rest of society through its control over nominations for public office, through youth and farmers' organizations, through ownership (though not monopoly) of the media. And, like the mainland, its management of the state is assured by top-level party officials holding prominent positions in government. Chiang Kaishek held both the party chairmanship and the presidency until his death in 1975; his son Chiang Chingkuo succeeded him in the top party post and three years later became president; at his death in 1988 the United States-educated Taiwanese Lee Tenghui took over both positions.

Government Structures.   To maintain the nationalist government's claim to represent all of China (although its effective jurisdiction extends only to Taiwan and a few islands near the mainland), both national and provincial political structures coexist. Under the 1947 constitution still in effect (deliberations on major constitutional revision began in 1992), the national government consists of the National Assembly, which selects the president and is responsible for amending the constitution; a relatively weak Legislative Yuan, which endorses policies initiated in the party and the executive; the premier, appointed by the president, who chooses the Cabinet; the judiciary and an agency that supervises civil service exams, appointed by the president; and the Control Yuan, which monitors the other branches of government through its power to audit their accounts and to censure government officials.

According to the constitution, both the National Assembly and the legislature are elected. The last national elections were held in 1947 and 1948; since then, of course, nationwide elections have not been possible, but "supplementary" elections began in 1969 to fill vacancies occurring as a result of the passage of time. The most recent National Assembly elections were held in December 1991 and Legislative Yuan elections in December 1992. Taiwan's provincial assembly and local councils are elected, as are most local government chief executives; voting for city and county posts took place most recently in November 1993. The provincial governor and mayors of Taipei (the ROC capital) and Kaohsiung (the provincial capital) are appointed by the president, but are to be elected by the voters beginning in 1994.

Political Evolution since 1949.   While still in essence a one-party state, Taiwan's authoritarianism has undergone some modification since 1949. Initially faced with a perceived threat from Communist China and widespread hostility toward the "carpetbagging" mainlanders among the islanders, some of whom actively supported the Taiwanese Independence Movement, Chiang imposed martial law, driving the independence movement underground, suppressing other critics of the regime, curbing the exercise of political rights, and prohibiting the formation of new parties. But the government instituted elections to local assemblies, allowing non-Guomindang "independent" candidates to run, though party members held a large majority of provincial and local positions, except for the lowest-level village assemblies.

Chiang's son and successor, Chiang Chingkuo, against continuing opposition from the old guard mainlanders, brought more young professionals and Taiwanese into the government and party, expanded the significance of local and provincial elections, and tolerated some political activity by "outside the party" (*tangwai*) groups. Political reforms reached a crescendo in 1986–1988 in the Democratic Revolution, which in 1987 ended martial law and allowed demonstrations to occur and the opposition Democratic Progressive Party to organize officially. The trend toward liberalization and "Taiwanization" survived Chiang Chingkuo's death in 1988 when Vice President Lee Tenghui succeeded to the presidency and, despite opposition from the conservative faction of the party, to the chairmanship of the Guomindang. The old guard asserted its influence, however, in the selection of General Hau Peitsun as the premier, a post he lost in 1993. In April 1994 the party's Central Committee endorsed a proposal by Lee for direct popular election of the president, following the trend set for the selection of the provincial governor and mayors.

The Guomindang continues to win at the polls, though its percentage of the popular vote declined from 71 percent in the 1991 elections to 53 percent in the 1992 elections to a low of 47.5 percent in the 1993 elections, and the opposition Democratic Progressive Party's (DPP) share rose from 24 percent in 1991 to 31 percent in 1992 to 41 percent in 1993.

During the 1991 campaign the DPP raised the issue of independence for Taiwan—that is, seeking international and PRC recognition as a separate state—and a sizable pro-independence demonstration was allowed to occur early in 1992. The government, fearful that agitation for such a step would provoke China to a preemptive seizure of the island, warns against too vocal an advocacy of independence by DPP.

The opposition's ability to capitalize on the Guomindang's loosening of controls and its declining share of the popular vote is limited by the fact that the DPP is divided between "moderate" and "radical" factions, the former more willing to work with those in power to get the changes they want, the latter more confrontational and leftist ideologically. So far the Chinese New Party adds little to the challenge to the Guomindang; it won only 3 percent of the vote in its first election contest in 1993 and seems an unlikely candidate for coalition making with the DPP since the two parties' positions on the issue of Taiwan independence are diametrically opposed.

Although mainlander-islander antagonisms persist, it would be an oversimplification to regard the Guomindang as the party of the mainlanders and the DPP as the islanders' party; islanders are a majority in both parties. Nor would it be correct to imply that islanders are all pro-independence and all mainlanders opposed. Although it is unlikely that the Guomindang majority would be willing to abandon their official "one China" stand for explicit support of Taiwanese separatism, they remain wary of unification with a communist mainland and tacitly accept the present de facto "two Chinas" situation. That puts them strategically in the center between the DPP advocates of "one China, one Taiwan" and the Chinese New Party's persistent adherence to the "one China" position.

Despite divisions within and defections from the ruling party and even with the recent softening of curbs on its opponents, the Guomindang's dominance seems secure. Though that dominance has been exercised with a velvet glove in recent years, the Guomindang's capacity and will to use the mailed fist again should not be doubted, if its position is seriously challenged.

Party Systems in Other Asian Pacific Countries

In Singapore the pattern of a Leninist party seems to have been learned by People's Action Party (PAP) founder and long-time leader Lee Kuan Yew in the 1950s, when the British-educated lawyer joined forces with Communists in Singapore to press for independence from Britain. Although once independence was won Lee cut ties with the Communists and became a firm anticommunist, PAP in organization and function closely parallels the CPC. It is described as "a tightly disciplined elitist party, monitored by a small authoritarian leadership and supervised through a cadre system, the identity of whose members is kept a close secret."[4] From the time of independence until 1991, when the opposition won four of the eighty-one seats, PAP was the only party represented in parliament. The power of the state is skillfully used to carry out programs decided on by PAP leadership and to keep the party firmly in control of agenda setting. Its pervasive influence over government, the economy, and the private lives of Singapore's citizens is legendary.

Party systems in other Asian Pacific countries are varied. As noted, above, Brunei bans parties and Hong Kong's fledgling parties as yet have marginal influence in the colonial structure. In Myanmar the proliferation of insignificant parties contributes to their inability to wrest control from the military. Malaysia's communally based parties reinforce the separation of the Malays, the Chinese, and the Indians, although the three ethnic groups' parties are linked in the ruling coalition and in the opposition. Thailand and the Philippines have fluid multiparty systems, organized around leading personalities, mainly civilian in the Philippines and mainly military and ex-military in Thailand. In the one-party-dominant systems of South Korea, Singapore, Indonesia, and Taiwan, opposition parties exist but are eclipsed by the brilliant sun of the government party. That observation was also true of Japan until defections from the dominant Liberal Democratic Party lost it control of the government and a coalition of opponents came into power in mid-1993.

Nowhere in the Asian Pacific do parties, whether organized around ideology, class, ethnicity, personalities, or some mix of those factors, effectively serve to unite the ordinary citizens into political action groups, articulating alternative programs and influencing the making of public policy by electing officials and holding them accountable. Everywhere the liberal and socialist vision of authentic government of, by, and for the people remains unrealized. In a number of countries the military is, or until recently has been, the core element of authoritarian regimes, commonly defining their missions as defense of the state against external enemies and/or internal chaos. Some of them have also successfully pursued the goal of national economic development.

AUTHORITARIANISM BY MILITARY "DEVELOPERS"

Indonesia, Thailand, and South Korea are the leading examples of development-driven military regimes. The first two of them will be examined in this section. South Korea, where the military since the late 1980s has been relinquishing its hitherto visible control to civilian leaders, will be discussed in the later section on "hard," "soft," and "softening" authoritarian systems. The economic development programs and achievements of these military regimes are treated in Chapter 5.

Indonesia's "New Order"

Governing a chain of islands stretching 3,000 miles from Sumatra to New Guinea and with a large ethnically diverse population is no easy task. It requires some strong cement—perhaps a charismatic leader or a compelling ideology or coercion—to hold the pieces together. Indonesia since independence in 1950 has had the first and last, going through three phases in the effort to devise institutions capable of countering the centrifugal forces that threaten the state's existence.

The Sukarno Era.   In the first phase (1950–1957) parliamentary democracy with Sukarno as president was tried, but even his considerable political clout as the charismatic independence leader was not able to get enough cooperation among the multitude of political parties divided along ideological and religious and regional lines to make the parliamentary system work. Immobilism and instability were the result, and the country slid toward disintegration.

In the second phase (1957–1965) Sukarno improvised an authoritarian system he called Guided Democracy; instituting martial law, he suspended parliament, dissolved opposition parties, and tried desperately to balance the growing power of the military by bringing the Indonesian Communist Party (PKI) into his government. Despite its authoritarian nature, Guided Democracy was no more able than the parliamentary system had been to tackle the complex problems of nation building and economic development. Division within the armed forces over Sukarno's militant "Confrontation" policy against the incorporation of British colonies on Borneo into Malaysia and over the perceived "tilt" in foreign policy toward Communist China added to his difficulties. The armed forces' political involvement and the PKI's militancy and strength proved too combustible a rivalry for even Sukarno to keep from exploding. His experiment came to an end in 1965, when leftist army officers attempted a coup. Other military, led by General Suharto, prevented the coup from succeeding and then moved to eliminate PKI as a political force in an orgy of killings carried out by vigilante mobs with army collaboration. In the months following, Sukarno's authority was whittled away, until in 1967 he agreed to turn over presidential functions to Suharto. Banished from taking part in politics, Sukarno died in 1970.

The Suharto Era.   First as acting president and then in 1968 as president, Suharto inaugurated the New Order, which he has directed ever since. The New Order continued the authoritarianism of Guided Democracy and followed Sukarno's strategy of enlisting the support of functional organizations such as labor unions and peasant and other associations. To counter the influence of the old political parties, Suharto formed Golkar, a government-sponsored coalition of several hundred such

Indonesia's President Suharto, who has been in office since 1967.

Source: United Nations photo 177601/J. Isaac.

groups. This umbrella organization became in effect the government's own political party, running candidates and controlling its representatives in parliament. Although most of Golkar's constituent groups are civilian organizations, the military dominates its central secretariat and held the top party post until 1993 when, under pressure for "civilianization" by Suharto, a nonmilitary chairman was chosen to head the party. Since elections were resumed in 1971, Golkar has won substantial majorities.

The old political parties whose disagreements doomed the experiment in parliamentary democracy had already been curbed under Guided Democracy, and Suharto gradually reduced the size and influence of the surviving parties, infiltrating their ranks and restricting their activities. Finally he was in a position to force all the remaining parties to merge in 1973 into two faction-ridden coalitions, the secular nationalist Indonesian Democratic Party (PDI) and the Islamic United Development Party (PPP). Their function as "opposition" parties is severely curtailed by their acceptance of government subsidies and by limitation on campaigning in the villages to a few weeks before elections, in accordance with Suharto's "floating mass" strategy of letting the country masses "float" undisturbed by political waves except for those brief intervals at election time. Like the puppet theater of Javanese tradition, the shadow play of competitive elections is acted out for the benefit of audiences at home and abroad.

In the New Order, the executive holds the reins of power and the legislature is weak. The president is chosen, not by the voters or by parliament, but by a 1,000-member People's Consultative Assembly (MPR), which meets briefly every five years for that purpose. Neither the president nor his cabinet are in effect accountable to parliament, the People's Representative Council (DPR). He appoints 100 of its 500 members, thereby practically assuring a pro-government majority in that body.

The military's participation in politics, enhanced under Sukarno, became domination under Suharto. Justification for such an expanded role is found in the Doctrine of the Dual Function, according to which the armed forces not only have responsibility for internal and external security but also have a legitimate part to play in political and economic life. Foreclosing possible challenges to its rule from nongovernmental groups by incorporating them into Golkar and by selecting party candidates and running their campaigns, the military also controls the civilian bureaucracy. Having purged it of hostile elements soon after coming to power, the military maintains loyalty among civil servants by requiring their support for Golkar, by patronage appointments and by putting officers in administrative posts, all the way from the heads of national ministries to provincial governorships down to positions in local government. Additional levers of power are the central security agency, Kopkamtib (Operations Command to Restore Order and Security), with extensive powers to arrest persons suspected of threatening the New Order, and the territorial military units, based throughout the country and paralleling the civil administrative structure. Although the government retains civilians in positions of authority, the military is clearly dominant in the civilian-military partnership.

Military officers also have significant roles in the economy through their administration of public enterprises and through appointment to the boards of private corporations. These connections generate income for the armed services that is free of legislative scrutiny and for the individual officers as well. Some military and civilian officials get payment for providing protection to Indonesian-Chinese entrepreneurs, always vulnerable to nationalist reprisals and especially so since they have benefited greatly from the economic successes of the New Order.

At the apex of this multilayered structure of economic and political power is President Suharto. He has been able to keep the armed forces under control by advancing the careers of his "political" and "financial" generals, by providing ample funds for the military as well as indirect financial advantages, and by skillful maneuvering to suppress potential challengers to his authority. But there are signs that his power is declining:[5] rival commanders in the armed forces vying for position in the inevitable succession scramble; criticism of corruption and excessive profiteering by Suharto's intimates, especially his children; hostility toward the preeminent position of Chinese businessmen who have flourished under his regime; stirrings among the growing middle class; some Islamic discontent with the secular nature of the state; regional pressures for decentralization of authority; the movement for autonomy among the Acehnese on Sumatra; resistance by the Papuan natives in Irian Jaya to the government's program of relocating large numbers of people from Java there; and the independence movement in predominantly Catholic East Timor, the former Portuguese colony taken by force in 1975.

In Suharto's Indonesia, the visible apparatus of representative institutions—parliament, elections, parties—exists but, in the words of one observer, it "is strictly for show."[6] The reality is rule by a group of military oligarchs claiming to act in the interests of the people while enriching themselves.

Thailand's Military Bureaucracy

Never a colony, Thailand escaped both the exposure to Western institutions by a colonial administration and a struggle for independence that might have stimulated the formation of political parties and a mass nationalist movement. Instead its traditional institutions—the monarchy, the Buddhist clergy, the military and civilian bureaucracies—continued to function without interruption. Comfortable with a centralized hierarchy, none had any particular motivation for challenging the monopoly of power held by the elite. Even the coup of 1932 by progressive modernizing civilians and military officers was aimed at putting the unlimited powers of the king under constitutional limitations. They did not challenge the principle of elite rule; rather, they asked for, and got, an expansion of their share in the elite ranks.

Bureaucratic Dominance.   Since 1932 Thai politics has been "a matter of competition between bureaucratic cliques for the benefits of government. In this competition the army—the best organized, most concentrated, and most powerful of the branches of the bureaucracy—has come out on top."[7] (And a top-heavy "branch" the army is, with more than 600 generals, one for every 300 to 350 troops; in Western armies the average is one general to between 3,000 and 4,000 troops.) Competition among bureaucratic cliques—civilian and military—has played itself out in frequent coups (through 1992, nineteen had been attempted or succeeded) and alternation between military and civilians in the prime ministership; civilians held the position only one-fourth of the time from 1932 to 1991, and some of them were "simply fronts for the military."[8] Justification for autocratic rule by the bureaucracy is that it alone can provide the stability and other requisites for economic development.

The degree of autocracy practiced by the bureaucracy varies over time. When disorder and corruption mount, the reins of control are grasped tightly; elections, parties, and legislatures are suspended. Then when order and cleaner government are restored comes a loosening of control; elected legislatures resume and parties are once again tolerated. But the reins remain in bureaucratic, especially military, hands.

Party Weakness.   Political parties were viewed with suspicion by the first generation of military rulers, and subsequent experience confirmed their view that parties are troublesome and destabilizing. Thai military have not chosen—or been able—to create a single government-sponsored party, as their Indonesian counterparts have done. Individual officers and factions have formed separate parties to further their special interests. Given legal status only in 1955, parties have at times been prohibited and are weak, fragmented, and without mass followings. Bureaucratic hostility and government control of radio and television keep them weak, their fragility weakens the elected legislature, and its weakness further undermines the parties while strengthening the military's contention that democratic party government is incapable of serving the national interest.

The potential of private associations and other interest groups as vehicles for popular participation is limited. The few independent nongovernmental organizations that exist are in the main centered in Bangkok. Out in the countryside, the Ministry of the

Interior controls the village headmen and councils, and the army's civilian affairs · branch has managed to take over existing interest groups, limiting their capacity to act as independent agents on behalf of their members and as challengers of the status quo.

Civilian Interludes. At only two junctures between 1932 and 1991 was military rule temporarily eclipsed. The first such period was in 1944, when the government of Field Marshal Phibun collapsed because it had backed the losing side in World War II. He was succeeded by civilian Prime Minister Pridi until a coup in 1947 brought him back. A second interruption in military rule came in 1973, when a student-sponsored movement for political reform led to clashes on the streets of Bangkok between the police and hundreds of thousands of demonstrators. The military divided over the question of further repression and a civilian government took over until 1976, when the military returned to power after violent confrontations with students at Thammasat University. In each case the civilian interlude was brief. New constitutions were adopted, an array of left, right, and center parties contested elections for parliament and formed transitory coalitions leading to unstable, weak governments and growing ideological polarization. Finally, charging corruption and an impending descent into chaos, the military intervened to bring back order (if not law), and most people seemed at least at first to welcome their return.

Events of 1992. Whether this scenario will be reenacted by the civilian government formed in 1992 is as yet uncertain. It came to power as the result of voter reaction to events following elections in March 1992, when the promilitary parties won a majority in parliament. Their selection of General Suchinda Krapayoon as prime minister triggered large-scale demonstrations in Bangkok, reminiscent of those in 1973 that led to the temporary ousting of the military. Some of the demonstrators in 1992 were ex-activists from that era.[9] This time their grievance centered on the naming of a prime minister who was not an elected member of parliament. The crisis deepened when the military fired on the demonstrators, killing several hundred people, injuring and arresting others. Support for Suchinda evaporated and the king intervened, persuading him to resign. A caretaker government under businessman and former diplomat Anand Panyarachun served until elections in September 1992 gave a coalition of antimilitary parties a small majority in the House of Representatives. Chuan Leekpai, head of the centrist Democracy Party, was named prime minister, and his government, though beset by internal differences among the ruling coalition, managed to survive a no-confidence vote in November 1993, but not to win parliamentary approval of amendments to the constitution aimed at strengthening democratic safeguards. Whether the 1992 election marks the beginning of the end for military domination of Thai politics or is just a temporary setback is as yet unclear.

Military participation in politics takes different forms in different countries; Hernandez[10] distinguishes three kinds of roles: *control, participation,* and *influence. Control* may mean intervention by an openly military junta or with a front of civilian "partners," as in Indonesia since 1965, Thailand since 1932 (perhaps ending in 1992), South Korea since 1964 (perhaps ending in 1988), and Myanmar since 1962. Or the military may play a *participatory* role in a "dual power" relationship where both mil-

*Chuan Leekpai, elected prime minister
of Thailand in 1992.*

Source: United Nations photo 184272/J. Isaac.

itary and civilian leaders are decision makers, the military having an autonomous sphere and a potential veto over the civilians' moves; this seems to be the situation in the Philippines since martial law in 1972 and in the communist governments and Taiwan, whose ruling parties had military origins. In Japan, Singapore, Malaysia, and Brunei, the military has *influence* on the political leadership, but the distinction between the military and the political role is clear and the military accept that distinction, the senior military officers working through channels to provide expert advice to the political authorities and lobbying for their share of the national budget.

While providing leadership and stability for economic development may help explain some cases of military or civilian authoritarianism, in others a more compelling explanation is the need for "glue" to hold together ethnically divided societies. In the next section we look at three examples of "ethnic" authoritarianism.

"ETHNIC" AUTHORITARIANISM

Ethnic minorities are present even in the homogeneous societies of East Asia (Koreans in Japan, Korean and other nationalities in China), and overseas Chinese are scattered in larger or smaller proportions throughout Southeast Asia. In Malaysia, Myanmar, Laos, and to a lesser degree in Singapore, deep divisions between communal groups in these heterogeneous societies contribute heavily to the authoritarian character of their governments. In Malaysia people of Chinese and Indian ancestry constitute over 40 percent of the population; the rest are Malay or non-Malay indigenes in the Borneo states. In Myanmar a third of the people are minorities (Shan, Karen, Chinese, Mon, Indian, and others) and the rest Burman; the Karen have been waging guerrilla warfare against the government for decades. Laos, as the result of boundaries drawn to suit the purposes of the colonial powers, has some forty ethnic groups, with the lowland Lao accounting for a little less than half the population; contacts among groups are limited by language, poverty, and the mountainous terrain. Singapore's Chinese are about three-fourths of the total, the rest mainly Malay and Indian; government policy is to create a "nonracial" Singaporean identity and to assure minority representation in the legislature.

In this section we will look more closely at Malaysia, Myanmar, and Laos as examples of "ethnic" authoritarianism.

Malaysia

A federation of thirteen states incorporating former British territories on the Malay Peninsula (except Singapore) and Sabah and Sarawak on the island of Borneo, Malaysia is a constitutional monarchy. The position of head of state rotates among the sultans of the nine traditional states. The monarch and the state legislatures select members of the upper house of the federal legislature; the lower house is directly elected by the voters and it chooses the prime minister. Dr. Mahathir bin Mohamad has held that position since 1981. The ruling political group is the Barisan Nasional (National Front), a coalition of the United Malays' National Organization (UMNO), the Malaysian Chinese Association, the Malaysian Indian Congress, and other minor parties. This multiethnic coalition, in which UMNO is dominant, has been in power since independence in 1957. Other parties exist but are weak, except in the states of Sabah and Kelantan.

The Ethnic "Bargain." The most salient feature of Malaysian politics since independence is the maintenance of a precarious balance between the conflicting interests of the Malay majority and the Chinese and Indian minorities, particularly the Chinese. Ethnic tensions are in part a legacy of the British colonial policy of keeping the ethnic communities separate geographically and occupationally. Chinese and Indians worked their way into an economically advantaged position while the majority of Malays remained in their traditional occupations of subsistence farming and fishing. At the time of independence, a bargain was struck: In return for granting the "immigrants" the right to become citizens and tacitly accepting their dominance in the economy, the Malays were given control of politics. Their privileged status as the *bumiputra,* or "sons of the soil," is protected in the constitution. Malay is the official language, Islam the state religion, and Malays have preferential treatment in government jobs, business licenses, educational assistance, and landownership.

Dr. Mahathir bin Mohamad, prime minister of Malaysia since 1981.

Source: United Nations photo 178196/E. Debebe.

Ethnic separateness is preserved in communally based political parties and interest groups, and advocacy by non-Malays of a nonracial Malaysian identity is suspect. Malay apprehension in part accounts for the ejection in 1965 of predominantly Chinese Singapore from the Malaysian Federation (which it joined in 1963) after the Singapore majority party campaigned for a "Malaysian Malaysia" policy of multiracialism without special privilege for any group. Even the Communist Party, which from 1948 to 1960 had waged armed struggle against the Malay-privileged federation and continues to exist though fragmented and diminished in support, is predominantly Chinese.

Communal Riots, 1969.   The political alliance among the Malaysian Chinese Association, the Malaysian Indian Congress (MIC), and the senior partner, the United Malays' National Organization, under the leadership of the first Prime Minister Tunku Abdul Rahman managed in the main to keep intercommunal strife under control from independence in 1957 until 1969. Elections that year were preceded by particularly acrimonious campaigning by the Alliance parties and their opponents. The latter were split among five principal parties, like the Alliance organized along ethnic lines. Three of them stressed communal differences in their platforms: the Pan Malaysian Islamic Party, which felt UMNO had sold out Malay interests to its partners, the MCA and MIC; the Democratic Action Party, mainly Chinese who rejected MCA as too closely tied to the Malay elite; and People's Progressive Party, a predominantly Indian party. The other two opposition groups, the radical Malay Partai and the Partai Gerakan Rakyat, nonracial but with a membership mainly of British-educated Chinese and Indian professionals, tried to avoid communal issues and instead focus on corruption in the ruling Alliance.

In the election, the opposition won more than half of the popular vote, but because of electoral districting that favored rural constituencies the Alliance kept nearly two-thirds of the seats in parliament. Rioting broke out in the capital, Kuala Lumpur, between Malays and the other ethnic communities and took a serious toll of lives and property, especially among the Chinese and Indians, before being put down by the army. The government suspended parliament, ruling for nearly two years by decree through a National Operations Council. It reasserted Malay political dominance, arresting many of the non-Malay opposition parties' leaders, and put through a constitutional prohibition on public discussion of racially sensitive issues, such as the special position of the Malays.

The New Economic Policy.   Tun Abdul Razak, who became prime minister in 1970, reconstituted the Alliance as the National Front, by 1973 adding some of the former opposition parties to its ranks. Recognizing that Malay dominance in politics had not resulted in improved economic status, he reneged on the earlier bargain and inaugurated a New Economic Policy (NEP) of active state intervention to reduce Chinese economic power and to increase *bumiputra* ownership of businesses, as well as raise living standards in rural areas where most Malays live.

In the next decades Malaysia's economic progress moved it into the second tier of NICs, with light manufacturing joining commodity production as a leading generator of wealth. The consequent economic changes brought both social and political repercussions in the form of greater diversity in society beyond the stereotype of rich Chinese versus poor Malay and in the form of challenges to the traditional National Front-UMNO dominance. NEP had the effect of differentiating Malay interests, raising some to the status of small businesspeople, incorporating others into the industrial working class, recruiting some as settlers on state-sponsored farms, allocating agricultural development projects to political allies in the countryside, leaving others behind still in the ranks of the rural poor. Principal beneficiaries of NEP were government officials charged with the establishment of state enterprises, often large-scale joint ventures with foreign investors. These enterprises reduced opportunities for small local entrepreneurs while creating opportunities for officials to line their own pockets and gave this new class of state businessmen a strong voice in the UMNO power structure.

Challenges to UMNO.   Criticism of official corruption and mismanagement grew in the 1980s and was joined by other manifestations of discontent with the political status quo. Civil servants were unhappy over the freezing of their salaries, settlers on state farms wanted title to the land, industrial workers chafed under the prohibition of unionization, environmentalists objected to the rapacious exploitation of natural resources, and support grew for the opposition Pan Malaysian Islamic Party (PAS). To these strands of discontent was added the erosion of Malay loyalty to UMNO, caused by the diversification of Malay economic interests.

All these elements converged in 1987 to split the UMNO into two factions, divided over the prime minister's leadership style and allegations of corruption and "money politics." Mahathir barely escaped being ousted as party president and quickly put in place policies to solidify bourgeois support by privatizing some state enterprises and cracking down on reformists and labor strikes and protests. The dissidents in UMNO who lost the intraparty power struggle broke away in 1989 to form an opposition party, Semangat 46.

In the 1990 elections, Semangat 46 allied with two other opposition parties, the multiracial but still predominantly Chinese Democratic Action Party (DAP) and the Islamic PAS. Thus, as one observer put it, "For the first time in Malaysia's electoral history, the ruling Barisan Nasional (national front) was challenged by another Malay-led multiracial opposition that projected itself as a viable alternative to the present government."[11] This contest, which some view as signaling the beginning of a two-party system, resulted in the opposition winning one-third of the seats in the national parliament while the National Front, with about 52 percent of the popular vote, held onto a two-thirds majority. In the states of Kelantan and Sabah the opposition parties won, though the UMNO regained control of the state government in Sabah in 1994. While the myth of Malay unity has been discredited, Malay political dominance remains.

In contrast, the Burman majority in Myanmar has had more difficulty in establishing and keeping control of the state against centrifugal forces at work in that country.

Myanmar/Burma

A British colony from 1885 until 1948, Burma (its official name is now Myanmar) since independence has been bedeviled by ideological differences and also by divisions between the Burman majority and Karen, Shan, Kachin, and other ethnic groups. The Anti-Fascist People's Freedom League (AFPFL), which had organized the resistance to Japanese occupation during World War II and successfully pressured the returning British into granting Burma's independence, became the government party, with U Nu as prime minister.

U Nu's secular civilian government's control of the state was immediately challenged by left factions within AFPFL, by the army, the Communist Party, Buddhist clergy, the Karen National Union, and other groups who wanted local autonomy in a Burma federation. The army, charged with putting down insurrections, became increasingly Burmanized as minority officers and men left its ranks to join the insurgents. The government was unable to maintain law and order or to carry out economic development plans. Conditions deteriorated rapidly until in 1958 the civilian government temporarily turned power over to a caretaker military regime to restore order. In 1960 U Nu returned as prime minister, but renewed internal disorder, expressing peasant and minority dissatisfaction with the government, led in 1962 to a coup under General Ne Win. Burma has had a military-dominated government ever since.

Waving the banner of "The Burmese Way to Socialism," the military's Revolutionary Council moved to gain control of the situation by repressing political opposition and by instituting policies aimed at improving the lot of the peasants. Rejecting the minorities' demand for political autonomy, the government offered instead equality of rights. To replace previous vehicles for political expression, the military sponsored the creation of the Burma Socialist Programme Party (BSPP) and held uncontested elections of BSPP-approved candidates for local, state, and national administrative bodies.

During the past three decades there have been intermittent but unsuccessful attempts by dissident army officers to oust the leadership, as well as antigovernment demonstrations by students and workers. Widespread hostile reaction to the brutal suppression of student protests in 1988 led to Ne Win's retirement from official position (it is assumed that he continues to exercise control from behind the scenes) and to the resumption of overt military rule under the State Law and Order Restoration Council. SLORC instituted martial law (formally lifted in late 1992) and suppressed all dissent. A new National Unity Party was formed to replace the discredited BSPP. SLORC also managed to assure itself of income by asserting its right to a share in the profits of the drug trafficking between Myanmar and its neighbors, China and Thailand.

Elections to the national legislature were held in 1990 under tight restrictions; voting was not permitted in a number of minority areas said to be under heavy security threat. Nevertheless, several hundred parties sponsored candidates and the result was an overwhelming victory for the leading opposition party, the National League for Democracy, over the government-backed National Unity Party. The League won 80 percent of the seats in the People's Assembly, but SLORC has not allowed it to meet and many members of the opposition have been arrested or fled into exile. The

General Ne Win, who led the 1962 coup against U Nu's government, marking the beginning of military rule in Burma.
Source: United Nations photo 95021 TC/jr.

League's General-Secretary Aung San Suu Kyi, daughter of the leader of the Burmese independence movement, has been under house arrest since 1989 and was prevented from going abroad to accept the Nobel Peace Prize awarded her in 1991.

Faced with challenges from pro-democracy forces, from the fragmented communist guerrilla movement, from Karen and other minority separatist forces, and pressure from its neighbor to the west, Bangladesh, to protect the rights of the Moslem minority, the military government has moved since 1992 to strike some form of bargain with its opponents and critics. SLORC refuses to talk with the Democratic Alliance of Burma, the front organization of ethnic and other political groups, preferring instead to negotiate with each of them separately. International efforts to end the Burmese civil war have come from the governments of Thailand and China and former U.S. President Jimmy Carter. Cease-fires have been reached with the Shan, Wa, Pa-O, and Palaung rebel armies, with the four communist insurgent forces, and in late 1993 with the Kachin Independence Army. Peace talks began early in 1994 between SLORC and the Karens, Karenni, and Mons leaders, against the opposition of Burma pro-democracy activists whose bases of operations up to now have been in minority-controlled areas of the country. The government's strategy of offering separate deals to each of the various ethnic groups seems to be succeeding in preventing coordinated actions by all of those who have been opponents of the military regime. Finally, having refused to allow the National Assembly elected in 1990 to meet, the junta convened a national convention of carefully selected delegates to draw up a new constitution; the convention met briefly in 1993, with no outcome, and is scheduled to reconvene in September 1994.

Laos

Laotian politics since independence in 1953 has been significantly affected by three factors: First, lowland Lao constitute only one-half of the country's small and diverse population, which includes more than forty other ethnic groups living in the uplands and mountainous areas; second, the development of Lao nationalism has been retarded partially as a consequence of this ethnic mixture, brought together within borders arbitrarily drawn by the French during the colonial period; and finally, foreign influence in Laotian affairs has been marked, especially Communist Vietnamese influence, through ties to Laotian Communists and U.S. political intervention and extensive bombing during the Vietnam War.

From independence until the peaceful takeover by the Communists in 1975, the government (ostensibly a monarchy) was in fact the prize in a continuing contest for power among Lao princes and their supporters representing rightist, centrist, and leftist positions. For stretches of time in that period, all three factions participated in a coalition government under centrist Prime Minister Souvanna Phouma, following a neutralist foreign policy. But the coalition periodically fell apart, the United States-supported rightist faction taking over while the leftist Pathet Lao, supported by China and North Vietnam, turned to guerrilla warfare against the rightist government.

As the war in Indochina wound down, Pathet Lao and North Vietnamese military victories mounted, and in 1974 a new coalition, the Provisional Government of National Union, was formed with the Pathet Lao in the dominant position. The provisional government lasted until the end of 1975, when the monarchy was abolished and the People's Democratic Republic was inaugurated in a peaceful transition. In 1988 elections to the National Assembly were held for the first time since the Communists came to power and a new constitution was adopted in 1991, recognizing the leading role of the Communist Lao People's Revolutionary Party. Kaysone Phomvihane, chosen president by the National Assembly after the 1988 elections, died in 1992 and was succeeded by Finance Minister Nouhak Phoumsavan; the prime minister is Khamtay Siphandone.

Laos's geographic location between Vietnam, Thailand, and China makes it vulnerable to outside influences. Vietnamese troops have withdrawn, and progress is being made in cooperation with Thailand on curbing insurgents and drug smugglers along the Lao-Thai border and with the United States on investigating the fate of American service people missing in action in the Indochina war. Economic development remains slow due to a shortage of trained personnel, internal communications, and capital. Laos, of little interest to France in colonial days, remains a poor, traditional backwater, just now attracting the attention of foreign aid donors and investors. Economic reforms, stimulated by the loss of financial support from the Soviet Union and Vietnam, are opening the way to increased trade and investment, mainly involving Thailand. That trend is likely to be accelerated with the 1994 opening of the first bridge across the Mekong River, the border between the two countries. Foreign aid comes from the World Bank, the International Monetary Fund (IMF), the Asian Development Bank, and from the Australian, Japanese, French, and Swedish governments.

Next, in recognition that authoritarian regimes differ in the degree and nature of control they exercise, we look at cases of "soft," "hard," and "softening" systems.

"SOFT," "HARD," AND "SOFTENING" AUTHORITARIANISM

The distinction between *soft authoritarianism* and *hard authoritarianism* is not precise, the two being ideal types at the opposite ends of a continuum along which real-world political systems can be ranked as more or less authoritarian. Most observers would agree, for example, that Myanmar and North Korea are toward the hard end of the continuum and Japan far over toward the soft end, Malaysia somewhat less soft than Japan, and Singapore even less so, while South Korea and Taiwan seem to have been moving since the late 1980s from their prior position on the hard side toward a "softening" form of authoritarianism.

In neither hard nor soft authoritarianism is politics truly participatory and competitive. Elections may be held, but who runs the government and sets policy is predetermined by the reality that one group has an effective monopoly on political power. Opposition candidates and parties, where they exist, lack the strength to pose a real challenge to those in power. The "ins" use the "stick" of repressive measures or the "carrot" of positive inducements to keep themselves in power and keep the "outs" out of power.

Soft authoritarianism uses the carrot rather than the stick, although the ultimate power of the state is always there to break up unruly demonstrations, for example, and to set limits on permissible dissent. Opponents are allowed to organize, speak, run for election, and serve in the legislature and as local officials. Citizens may join parties and form pressure groups, civil and political rights are protected, the press is reasonably free, the judiciary reasonably independent. Co-optation rather than confrontation is the preferred style. But the paramount position of the dominant party is effectively unchallenged. Japan is an example of soft authoritarianism, at least until 1993, when the Liberal Democratic Party was driven from office for the first time in thirty-eight years.

In *hard authoritarianism* the stick is more often the weapon of choice, or necessity, though the carrot may be held out to favored individuals or groups. The officials may be in civilian clothes or in uniform and they may rule with or without elections, but if elections are held, they are in effect *plebiscites,* carefully controlled to demonstrate how well-loved the in-group is. Organized political groups may be allowed, but the government "front" organization has the advantage of being able to use the state apparatus—the police, the army, the intelligence agencies—as well as access to the treasury and "protection" money from the private sector to keep itself in power. Opposition parties and interest groups (if they are not just puppets for the appearance of democratic competition) are cowed, harassed, denied access to the media, infiltrated, jailed, tortured, driven into exile, or denied office if they manage somehow to be elected. No holds are barred in the ruling group's determination to hang on to power. Burma/Myanmar since 1962 is a case where opposition parties are allowed to exist at various periods, while North Korea is an example where (as in China) noncommunist but nonopposition organizations are represented in the national legislature.

Soft Authoritarianism in Japan

The rise of Japan, like the legendary phoenix from the ashes of its own destruction, to become the world's second economic power is well known, and the government's role in that "miracle" will be analyzed in Chapter 5. What is striking about Japanese politics in the decades from the end of the American occupation in 1952 until mid-1993 is the *continuity* in leadership provided by the durable coalition of party, government, and business. The Liberal Democratic Party (LDP) and its predecessors, the Liberal and Democratic Parties, controlled all postwar governments except for a brief stretch of Socialist Party government in 1947, until it lost a vote of confidence in June 1993 and failed to win in the elections that followed in July 1993. A new coalition of parties then took over the government with the LDP in opposition. That coalition disintegrated in June 1994 and the LDP, in an unprecedented alliance with the Social Democratic Party of Japan, returned to power in a new government headed by a socialist prime minister. Such an improbable partnership between long-term opponents seems unlikely to last, but it is difficult to predict whether the chaotic political maneuvering that began in 1993 will lead to a restoration of LDP dominance or to a permanent reshaping of Japanese party politics. We will look first at the period of LDP dominance and at the circumstances that led to its loss of control in 1993, then at the performance of the reform coalition that replaced it until it was succeeded by the LDP-Socialist government in June 1994, and conclude with an analysis of the complex forces in contention at this juncture in Japan's postwar history.

Party-Bureaucracy-Business Collaboration in the Period of LDP Dominance.
United in a shared devotion to maximizing their own interests by promoting economic growth, the LDP, bureaucracy, and big business produced the stability and predictability needed for postwar economic recovery and expansion. It did so under a political system labeled "soft authoritarian" to distinguish it from competitive pluralist systems on the one hand and "hard authoritarianism" on the other. The party's dominance was achieved without formal legal restrictions on or covert interference with the opposition parties' right to organize and compete for voter approval. The opposition parties included the Social Democratic Party of Japan (SDPJ), the United Social Democratic Party (USDP), the Democratic Socialist Party (DSP), the Komei ("Clean Government") Party, loosely affiliated with a Buddhist sect, Soka Gakkai, and the Japan Communist Party (JCP). The two centrist parties, Komei and DSP, cooperated with the LDP to give it control in the upper House of Councillors when the LDP lost its majority there in 1989.

LDP's share of the popular vote fluctuated and its cohesiveness at times seemed on the verge of being blown away in the heat of ferocious fights between organized factions in the party, loyal to leading members of parliament. But LDP kept voters' support by using pork barrel enticements, by an electoral districting system that over-represented rural constituents who are staunchly pro-LDP, and by co-opting issues raised by critics (such as environmental deterioration) and adopting programs to correct the problems. But above all, its appeal has come from the country's phenomenal economic success, which has brought benefits to almost everyone. Also contributing to LDP dominance was the inability of the other parties to form a united opposition and to project to the voters the image of people capable of actually running the government. In the Kabuki drama of politics, they seemed destined to be cast as minor players, never as principal actors.

The LDP's role was to elect members of parliament and to name the prime minister but to leave the initiation of public policy, especially in matters of trade, finance, business, and other economic affairs, in the hands of the highly professional and prestigious bureaucracy, particularly the Ministry of International Trade and Industry (MITI) and the Ministry of Finance. License to formulate policies without legislative and partisan "meddling" allowed the ministries to do long-term planning and to involve big business, especially Keidanren, the Federation of Economic Organizations, in the process of policymaking and implementation. Since government relies more on persuasion than on compulsion to get private sector compliance with its plans, much depended on the maintenance of a working relationship between the bureaucrats and the businesspeople. As its part of the bargain, business provided campaign funds to LDP candidates and positions as corporate managers and members of the board to officials when they decided to retire from public service. The LDP gave legislative approval to the ministry-initiated policies and opened up seats in the Diet for bureaucrats ready for a career change.

For decades LDP dominance and the three-way collaboration with big business and the bureaucracy survived the tremendous changes that affluence has wrought in Japanese society. But the sense of national crisis that had brought them together in the early postwar period had faded, social and economic interests had become more diverse, factional and generational differences within the LDP had begun to weaken it, and campaign financing scandals eroded the party's appeal to voters.

The Fall of the LDP Government.   All those factors converged in the summer of 1993 to bring down the government, but it was the defection of leading members of the LDP, more than a sudden rise in popularity of the traditional opposition parties, that dealt the final blow. Revelations about the acceptance of millions in illegal campaign funds by Shin Kanemaru, head of the LDP's largest faction, led to demands by voters and within the party for the government of Prime Minister Kiichi Miyazawa to undertake reforms of election-financing laws and of the election-districting system. When Miyazawa failed to act, a number of LDP legislators led by Ichiro Ozawa and Tsutomu Hata voted against him in a no-confidence vote and formed a new party, Shinseito (Japan Renewal Party), joining two earlier LDP-breakaway groups, the Japan New Party of Morihiro Hosokawa and the Sakigake (New Party Harbinger) of Masayoshi Takemura.

In the elections called by Miyazawa in July 1993, the LDP failed to win the 256 of 511 seats needed for a majority, although it still held the largest number of seats, 223, plus the support of five independents. This opened the way for the three LDP-defector parties and the centrist Komei to join with the Social Democratic Party of Japan (holding the second largest number of seats, 70) and other socialist parties in a diverse multiparty coalition barely large enough to form a new government. Hosokawa became prime minister, Hata foreign minister, and Takako Doi of the SDPJ speaker of the lower house, leaving the LDP and the Communist Party as the opposition.

The Hosokawa Government.   Upon taking office in August 1993, the new prime minister faced a formidable array of domestic and foreign policy problems, the key one being to live up to his promise of electoral reform. The initial proposal was to ban cash donations to individual candidates, to require public disclosure of business and organization contributions, and to switch the majority of parliamentary seats from multimember constituencies to single-member districts, redrawing the districts to reduce the disproportionate weight given to rural areas. LDP members opposed the restrictions on finances. Some of the Socialists were reluctant to support the creation of single-member districts, which tend to favor strong parties, as contrasted with multimember districts where smaller parties have a greater chance of winning seats, according to the formula of representation in proportion to the popular vote each party receives.

The government's proposal passed the lower house, a sufficient number of LDP members voting for it to counter Socialist votes against, but the measure was defeated in the upper house. Forced by lack of unanimous support from his coalition partners, Hosokawa negotiated with the new LDP head, Yohei Kono, to reach a compromise that met LDP objections and allowed passage of the reform legislation in late January

1994. The ban on cash contributions was abandoned, though the amount was limited and the number of single-seat constituencies increased to 300 of 500 seats.

Passage of the electoral reform law exhausted Hosokawa's political capital, and his efforts to adopt a budget and an economic stimulus package to revive the country's sluggish economy and to deal with Japan-United States trade issues were stalemated by policy differences between right and left elements of the governing coalition. Pushed by officials in the Ministry of Finance to advocate a consumption tax increase to offset income tax cuts, Hosokawa was forced to withdraw that proposal in the face of strong objections from the socialists and the New Party Harbinger leader, Masayoshi Takemura. The final blow came with disclosure of questionable campaign and personal financial dealings that led to his resignation in April 1994. Foreign Minister Hata became prime minister after a two-week struggle within the coalition between the more conservative parties led by Renewal Party strategist Ozawa and the more leftist Socialist and Harbinger parties.

The Hata Government.   Hours after his election by a majority in the legislature, the new prime minister moved to consolidate the right and center members of his coalition, including the Democratic Socialist Party, into a single parliamentary group named Kaishin or Reformation, holding more seats than the Social Democratic Party. This maneuver was seen by the SDPJ as part of Ozawa's strategy to split that party and dump its leftist elements from the coalition. But the Social Democrats stuck together and joined the Harbinger Party in refusing to participate in the formation of a new cabinet. Hata remained as prime minister with only minority support in the Parliament until June 25 when he resigned in face of an LDP move to force a vote of no-confidence. Within days, the SDPJ and the LDP joined forces to elect SDPJ chairman Tomiichi Murayama prime minister.

What Now?   The strange marriage of convenience between the two parties that had been ideological opponents for four decades does not resolve the underlying issues that led to the reformist upheaval of 1993. Those issues are dazzlingly complex, involving not only fissures between the old-style parties and the breakaway ex-LDP and other reformist parties and within both sets of parties, but also questions about the relationship between the bureaucracy and business and the international role of Japan in the post–cold war.

Important policies that in the past had been settled by agreement within the LDP-bureaucracy-business triad are now open for contention and are the subject of a new activism among voters, notably consumer and environmental groups. Some business interests and consumers advocate reducing government controls over the economy and politicians would like greater leverage to modify the conservative fiscal and trade policies promoted by the bureaucrats. In the arena of foreign policy Japan's postwar reliance on the security treaty with the United States, long denounced by the Socialists who until recently advocated a neutralist foreign policy and the end of American bases in Japan, is now under fire from nationalists like Ozawa who want the country to take a more active and independent role in global affairs.

How these issues are decided and by whom will depend to a great degree on whether the electoral reforms adopted under the Hosokawa government are put into effect and how candidates and parties adapt to the changed rules of the election game. The redrawing of electoral districts will give greater clout to urban voters; the inauguration of single-member constituencies for 300 of the seats in the lower house will presumably favor the larger parties and encourage consolidation among the smaller ones; changes in campaign financing may affect the influence of special interests in election outcomes, continuing the trend toward reduced business contributions to LDP and its allies since 1993.

Who will gain and who will lose as a result of these changes is unclear, as is the longer-term question of whether Japan will move away from the soft authoritarianism of the LDP-dominated era toward a more competitive two- or multiparty system.

Hard Authoritarianism in North Korea

The Democratic People's Republic of Korea (DPRK) is a socialist state that, since its establishment in 1948, has been ruled by the Communist Korean Workers' Party (KWP). Leadership of government and party was in the hands of President Kim Il Sung until his death in July 1994. Groomed as his political heir is his son, Kim Jong Il, who held the second position in the party and was also supreme military commander. The prime minister is Kang Song San.

Party institutions follow the familiar Leninist pattern: The National Party Congress elected by Provincial Party Assemblies chooses the Central Committee, which elects the Politburo and general-secretary. The KWP's organization parallels and penetrates the governmental institutions. At the national level, the Supreme People's Assembly chooses the president and members of the Central People's Committee, which oversees the National Defense Commission and the Administration Council. Local and provincial governments follow a similar organizational pattern. Party control is exerted over the courts, the media, and mass organizations of youth, women, workers, and farmers, coordinated by the Democratic Front for the Reunification of the Fatherland.

The most salient influences on postindependence North Korean politics have been the domination of party and government by Kim Il Sung and the existence of the "other" Korea, protégé of the United States and perceived threat to the survival of socialism in the North. The torturous, conflict-ridden course of relations between the two Korean governments erupted into a three-year war soon after the establishment of the two states. That war will be discussed in Chapter 7.

Kim's rise to power after returning to Korea in 1945 from exile in Manchuria and Siberia was supported by the Soviets. He first had to establish his primacy not only over the noncommunist Nationalists but also over other Communists who, like him, came home from exile or who came up from the underground in Korea. Working at first through the North Korean Bureau of the Korean Communist Party headquartered in Seoul, the northern Communists created a united front to carry through the "bourgeois revolution." In 1946 they detached themselves from southern authority and launched the Korean Workers' Party. Party membership expanded and subsidiary organizations of labor, young people, and women were created. Governmental institutions were set up and elections held (with underground southern participation), culminating in the end of Soviet occupation and in independence in 1948, following a similar step in the South.

Both governments espoused the goal of Korean unification, and in June 1950 war broke out between them, each side accusing the other of having initiated hostilities. The United States immediately joined on the side of South Korea, and China entered later on the side of the North. Battle raged up and down the peninsula, causing loss of life and widespread devastation on both sides of the thirty-eighth parallel. Military stalemate led finally to an armistice agreement in July 1953 that is still in effect.

Postwar economic reconstruction in the North gave priority to heavy industry and to collectivization of agriculture, accomplished by 1958. Kim announced in 1955 that, having completed the anti-imperialist democratic revolution, North Korea was now making the transition to socialism.

Politically, the period from 1953 to 1958 marked the consolidation of Kim's control over the party and the state, turning back challenges from factions in the party who objected to his monopoly of power and to the continued expansion of heavy industry at the expense of raising living standards. Arguing against uncritical acceptance of the Soviet model of revolutionary change, Kim took the position that the application of Marxist-Leninist principles had to take into account the particular situation in Korea, arrived at through continual contact with the people and through practical struggle. He elaborated as the basis for action his own doctrine of *juche,* self-reliance. This ideological "distancing" from the Soviet pattern signaled also a movement away from Soviet party influence over the Korean party.

From 1958 on, Kim's preeminent position was secure, and he proceeded to strengthen the party by creating a new revolutionary tradition based on a combination of reality and myth about the Korean guerrillas (he had been one) who fought the Japanese in Manchuria in the 1930s. Their example of working among and with the people, he said, should be the role model for the Korean People's Army. Further solidification of Kim's position came with the cultivation of a cult of personality around him as the "Great Leader," extending also to his parents, siblings, and his son, who has moved up over the years in government and party positions.

In recent years the economic accomplishments of the past seem to be unraveling as foreign debt mounts, Soviet aid stops, and responses to efforts to attract foreign capital are slow in coming. Some observers predict economic collapse but, as far as outsiders can judge, the regime is in control and likely to survive the death of the "Great Leader." Dissatisfaction—if there is any—is denied expression.

"Softening" Authoritarianism in South Korea

The Republic of Korea has a presidential form of government that, since 1988, has been moving fitfully away from the authoritarianism that characterized previous governments. The president is Kim Young Sam, elected in December 1992 to succeed Roh Tae Woo, a former general who served from 1988 to early 1993. The president is limited by the constitution to one five-year term. The less important post of prime minister is filled by presidential appointment and its holder frequently changes.

As with North Korea, the division of the country and the goal of reunification have been major concerns for South Korea, but the political history of the two Koreas since 1948 has been strikingly different. In contrast to the apparent stability and continuity of the government in the North, southern politics have been marked by instability and conflict. The founding president, Syngman Rhee (1948-1960), resigned from office under popular pressure, and since then presidential succession on three occasions has been determined extraconstitutionally. Coups brought two military men, Park Chung Hee (1964-1979) and Chun Doo Hwan (1981-1987) to the presidency, and Park was removed from office by assassination.

From the Rhee era on, the power of government was used against domestic opposition. Peasant and army rebellions in the early years and more recent student rebellions were forcibly suppressed. Elections have been punctuated by demonstrations, violence, and charges of fraud. Legislative vote buying, surveillance by internal security police, control of and pressure on the media and labor unions have been employed by the government to tame and undermine opposition. Since the liberal reforms announced by Roh Tae Woo in his 1987 presidential campaign, the government has made efforts to curb the undemocratic features of Korean politics and to move toward a more open and competitive system.

Factionalism based on personalities and on regionalism plagues both government and opposition parties. The government party, the Democratic Liberal Party (DLP), was formed in 1990 by the merger of two opposition parties with the existing government party, the Democratic Justice Party, which lacked a majority in the legislature elected in 1988. The unity of the coalition at first seemed shaky and the DLP failed to win control of the legislature in the March 1992 elections. However, it rallied in the presidential campaign at the end of the year, its candidate, Kim Young Sam, who had run in 1987 against Roh, winning in a three-man race against Kim Dae Jung of the Democratic Party and Hyundai founder Chung Ju Yung of the new United People's Party.

Although there was evidence that intelligence agents and military officers had engaged in clandestine tactics to achieve the DLP electoral victory, since Kim took office he has moved ahead with political reform measures, including legislation to curb the Agency for National Security Planning's notorious penchant for activities aimed at stifling political dissent. The judiciary, long accustomed to being under government control, is being encouraged to assert its independence and to purge itself of corrupt judges. Widespread political corruption among other officials has been a particular target of President Kim's administration; it has brought charges against politicians, ex-military, and businesspeople for tax evasion and bribery and pushed through legislation requiring officials to disclose their financial assets.

Students traditionally play a major role in Korean politics as critics of, and mobilizers of demonstrations against, government policies. They have the assets of numbers, good organization, and popular respect for intellectuals inherited from the Confucian scholarly tradition. In recent years they successfully pressed for investigation of corruption in the Chun government and for more active responses to overtures from the North.

The political liberalization measures undertaken by Roh and expanded by Kim Young Sam seem to have moved South Korea away from the hard authoritarianism of past governments and along the road toward soft authoritarianism. Kim's popularity among the public during his first year in office has enabled him to overcome resistance to reforms from the right wing of the DLP. But the military, discredited in many people's eyes by its past abuses of power, is still a force to be reckoned with, as is big business, feeling the pinch of the world recession. Then too there is the continuing threat of crisis over relations with the North, which might provide an impetus for a return to the garrison state mentality of the past.

The final category of authoritarianism we will use in our comparisons of Asian Pacific governments looks at the *strength* of the state in different countries.

STRONG STATE—WEAK STATE

As with soft and hard authoritarianism, the distinction between *strong* and *weak* states is more impressionistic, even subjective, than precisely measurable. But states *do* differ in their capacity to handle the pressures put on them by the effects of modernization. A strong state has political institutions sufficiently cohesive, flexible, and independent of other forces in society to prevail over challengers to its authority, whether from outside the country (from, for example, multinational corporations and foreign governments) or from inside (for example, from insurgent groups and separatist movements). A weak state lacks that capacity and is therefore liable to manipulation by foreign or domestic forces, or both.[12] Singapore and the Philippines are the examples we have chosen to illustrate this aspect of authoritarianism.

Strong State: Singapore

Although diminutive (only three times larger than Washington, D.C.), this island ministate located at the juncture of peninsular Malaysia and Indonesia survived incorporation into the Malaysian Federation in 1963 and expulsion in 1965 to become a wealthy commercial, financial, and industrial center. Under the leadership of Lee Kuan Yew's People's Action Party (PAP), which has dominated the government since the beginning, Singapore's "administrative state," as a Singaporean political scientist calls it,[13] has managed to invite foreign investment without becoming its captive, to mute Chinese-Malay antagonisms, to keep the rising middle class quiescent, to control labor unions, and to keep political opponents incapable of challenging PAP's dominance.

The government's success in promoting economic development and maintaining stability and order in a previously volatile multiethnic society has been achieved by the benevolent paternalism of Lee's tightly run political party working through a highly competent and uncorrupted bureaucracy, manipulating the institutions of democratic participation by pervasive use of rewards for acquiescence and punishment for opposition.

In the social sphere, government has actively tried through media campaigns, integrated housing, and education to create a "Singaporean" identity above the separate ethnic identities of Chinese, Malay, and Indian. Recognizing that the Malays as a group are at a disadvantage in this society committed to the principle and practice of meritocracy, the government has tried to wean at least some Malays away from traditional habits that impede their adaptation to "modern" society.

In the political sphere, the outward appearance of democracy is preserved. Elections to parliament are held, following brief campaigns in which minor parties run candidates against PAP's. The legislature meets and selects the prime minister according to majority rule. But the reality behind the appearance is different. Electoral districts are drawn to perpetuate PAP's success, and opposition leaders are kept under surveillance by internal security police, frequently harassed, sometimes arrested, and generally neglected by the government-controlled media. Freedom of speech, the press, and assembly is restricted, and unions are either government controlled or kept under close surveillance. Parliament's role is to rubber-stamp policies coming from the executive, and the real locus of power is in the PAP-dominated bureaucracy.

In addition to political controls, the government's paternalistic intrusions into other aspects of people's lives are notorious and to outsiders seem to go beyond the usual requirements for a civil and modern society. Campaigns are waged to curb such undesired behavior as speeding, smoking, gum-chewing, and failure to flush public toilets, and severe fines are imposed on offenders. In an interview in 1992, Lee (now retired from the prime ministership) attributed the need for such regulations of personal behavior to Singapore's rapid transformation from a poor, slum-ridden backwater village to a modern metropolis with cars, high-rise apartments, and other appurtenances of affluence. Asked about the fines for failure to flush public toilets, he said, "Perhaps the reason why they don't flush is because . . . only day before yesterday they were using a hole in the ground, and it really doesn't matter whether you flush it or you don't. It didn't matter."[14]

In recent years, the government has survived without visible difficulty the transition from its larger-than-life founding prime minister to his successor, Goh Chok Tong, who took the top government post in 1990 and the party secretary-generalship in 1992. Lee remains very much involved in politics as senior government minister, and his son Lee Hsien Loong is deputy prime minister and presumably next in line for the top position. PAP's effective monopoly on power seems unshakable.

Weak State: The Philippines

Philippine politics since independence in 1946 has been heavily influenced by American economic and strategic concerns and dominated by Filipino economic elites. For the first two-and-a-half decades the institutions of representative government laid down in the 1935 constitution were maintained, and two major parties, both essentially creations of the wealthy, competed for office. Behind the appearance of Western-style liberal democracy, the political-economic oligarchy controlled not only the political parties but the legislature, the bureaucracy, and elections by the power of money and, where required, by their private armies as well as the military and police. The Filipino state was kept weak and incapable of responding positively to the rising demands of the masses in the cities and the countryside, though not so feeble that it would be unable to serve elite purposes.

While the connection between wealth and political influence is not unique to the Philippines, income and property ownership and consequently political power are highly concentrated in the upper and upper-middle classes, which are estimated to

*Goh Chok Tong, who succeeded Lee Kuan Yew as prime minister
of Singapore in 1990.*

Source: Photo from the Prime Minister's Office, Singapore.

constitute about 10 percent of the population.[15] Elite control of politics was reinforced by the persistence of traditional patron-client relations, which in precolonial
times filled the gap left by the absence of a unified state. The pattern of reciprocal
trust and obligation between patron and client served as the model for political parties and leaders. Votes, jobs in government, favoritism in getting licenses and government contracts were all part of the "currency" exchanged, seen as honorable
fulfillment of one's obligations rather than flagrant corruption.

Family ties are important among the rich, whose wealth often came from
landownership but who after World War II went into industry and commerce. Kinship networks mute the phenomenon found in other developing countries of conflict
between the export agricultural sector tied to and dependent on the world economic
system and the emerging "national bourgeoisie." Although tensions between the two
have surfaced over trade and foreign investment policy issues, they have closed ranks
when mass mobilization under the banner of reform or revolution appeared to
threaten their privileged economic and political position. This was the situation on
the eve of martial law in 1972.

With the support of most of the elite and the military, who had lost confidence in
constitutional government's ability to preserve order against rising demands for social
and political change, President Ferdinand Marcos imposed martial law that year and remained in office beyond the constitutional limit of two four-year terms. He dissolved

congress, suspended elections, intimidated the press, and cowed his opponents, relying increasingly on the military, whom he rewarded with appointments to government posts and expanded scope for the practice of violence against insurgents and dissidents (including the assassination of his leading opponent, Benigno Aquino Jr.).

Domestic and international criticism of Marcos's government gathered momentum in the early 1980s. The mainly middle-class reformist opposition gained mass support after Aquino's death and the Roman Catholic Church under the leadership of Jaime Cardinal Sin lent its influence to the reformist cause. Even worse for Marcos, his base of support in the business community and the armed forces began to erode. Disenchantment among one-time Marcos boosters accelerated as his declining health raised unsettling questions about a potential succession struggle. The destabilizing effects on the economy of such a crisis were feared both by international investors and domestic economic interests, as well as by the technocrats brought into government to promote development. Fissures appeared between the old oligarchy and the newly rich Marcos cronies, between the cronies and the technocrats, between the military and the civilian bureaucracy, and within the military between the Reform the Armed Forces Movement (RAM) group of graduates of the Philippine Military Academy and other officers. Worsening economic conditions adversely affected the business community, farmers, and workers, and contributed to growing support for the radical New People's Army, despite counterinsurgency campaigns against it.

When Marcos ran for reelection in 1986, he was challenged by Aquino's widow, backed by a united opposition. The president's claim to have won was denounced as fraudulent, and the defection of some of the military, combined with mass demonstrations of support for Corazon Aquino on the streets of Manila, brought her into office.

The triumph of Aquino's People Power Revolution over Marcos's authoritarianism did not signal the inauguration of a new, truly democratic order. Instead, the traditional elites (of which she is a member) continued to control the political processes and the use of repression against those who would challenge the status quo, as evidenced by the outcome of land reform efforts and the record on human rights during the Aquino period. Her agrarian reform program was delayed, whittled down in the legislature, and hampered in implementation by opposition from sugar plantation and mill owners. And despite efforts of the Aquino government to curb them, human rights abuses continued because the Philippine state is too weak to prevail over challenges to its authority from the elites who resist efforts to ameliorate the grinding poverty in which most Filipinos live.

Another factor was military resistance to civilian efforts to curb their operational autonomy and put limits on their extraconstitutional techniques for combatting insurgents and other politically suspect individuals and groups. RAM was behind six coup attempts against Aquino's government and sabotaged efforts to negotiate an end to the insurgency of the Communist Party's New People's Army and to accommodate the demands for autonomy of the Mindanao-based Moslem Moro National Liberation Front. Furthermore, the antigovernment insurgents were themselves guilty of abuses and by their very existence created a climate in which violations of rights appear to some to be justified.[16]

The significance of Aquino's years as president is assessed by one observer in these words:

In the end, the transition from authoritarian rule in the Philippines ushered in a political restoration, rather than a revolution. . . . There has been a return to a brand of democratic governance characterized by weak parties, factionalism based primarily on personalities rather than ideology, and the dominance of the traditional, provincial elites. Important elements of the military have resisted a return to a less political role and a nationwide insurgent movement continues to threaten the foundations of the Philippine state.[17]

These problems were inherited by Aquino's successor, retired General Fidel Ramos, who took office in June 1992. A West Point graduate, former head of the constabulary, armed forces chief of staff, and defense secretary, Ramos was elected by less than a quarter of the votes in a contest against candidates of six other parties. HIs own party, Lakas-NUCD, with the help of allies elected by other parties, has a majority in the lower house of the legislature, but the senate is controlled by the LDP, the party of traditional provincial politicians. So Ramos's power base, like the state itself, is weak.

He has undertaken some initiatives toward reconciliation with the rebel military and the Communist and Moslem insurgents. Amnesty for political crimes was offered and talks with the Moro National Liberation Front culminated in an agreement early in 1994 to give more autonomy to Moslem provinces on the islands of Mindanao and Palawan. Counterinsurgency operations against the New People's Army continue and its numbers are declining. A factor contributing to weakening of the Communist insurgency is a split in the Communist Party between its leaders in exile in Holland and groups in the Philippines, the latter favoring negotiation with the government and participation in elections and the former rejecting that course in favor of continued revolutionary activity.

In the economic sphere, Ramos made headlines in mid-1993 by launching an "anti-monopoly" campaign to dislodge certain Marcos cronies from controlling interest in several corporations and replacing them with directors favorable to the government. This move caused some alarm in the business community, elements of which had supported Ramos's presidential bid. A Protestant, he also challenged the Church hierarchy by supporting family planning aimed at curbing the high population growth that adds to the country's deep economic problems, exacerbated by a crushing foreign debt, drastic reduction in U.S. military aid, and the effects of natural disasters. Corruption, a bloated bureaucracy, weak political parties, and an oligarchy unwilling to risk its privileged position by accepting state action to get at the roots of poverty all contribute to the continued weakness of the Philippine state.

THE SPECIAL CASE OF CAMBODIA

The weakest of all Asian Pacific states is Cambodia. It might be argued that it is not a state at all, since whatever "sovereignty" the country possesses is untidily divided between the Khmer Rouge, who control large areas in the countryside, and the new Kingdom of Cambodia government formed in 1993 after UN-sponsored elections. That government resulted from a compromise merger between the Cambodia People's Party's State of Cambodia apparatus and the United Front for an Independent, Neutral and Free Cambodia (FUNCINPEC), the royalist political organization that had waged war against it for years.

Like its neighbors in other parts of what was French Indochina, Cambodia's political history since independence in 1953 has been greatly influenced by external actors, especially communist Vietnam, Thailand, the United States, and China. Like Laos and in contrast to Vietnam, the end of French colonialism came relatively peacefully for Cambodia, but since then its fate has been extremely troubled; in the course of one tumultuous decade its government underwent four abrupt changes.

Sihanouk to Lon Nol

From 1953 to 1970 Cambodia was a constitutional monarchy under Prince Norodom Sihanouk, who in 1955 abdicated the throne to become prime minister. Sihanouk pursued a foreign policy of nonalignment, accepting aid from both East and West, trying to foster national unity and maintain the country's independence by accommodation with China and North Vietnam as counterweights to Cambodia's historical enemies, Thailand and South Vietnam, then allied with and armed by the United States.

The Sihanouk government gradually lost support of the civil service, the middle class, and, most important, the army, which objected to Sihanouk's toleration of the presence of Vietnamese Communist forces on Cambodian territory. In 1970 a rightist military group overthrew him, abolished the monarchy, and put in power the United States-backed anticommunist Marshal Lon Nol. Spillover into Cambodia from both sides in the war in Vietnam brought heavy American bombing and invasion by ground forces to root out the Vietnamese enemy. The consequences were severe economic disruption, corruption stimulated by massive American aid to the Lon Nol government, and an increase in popular support for the antigovernment Communist insurgent Khmer Rouge, backed by China.

Pol Pot to Hun Sen

The Khmer Rouge in turn ousted Lon Nol in 1975 and established Democratic Kampuchea, led by Pol Pot. During the next four years the Khmer Rouge government pushed through radical measures to reorganize society, hunting down foreign-educated people to eradicate foreign influences, abolishing private property and communizing the peasants, forcibly depopulating the cities to which many had fled to escape the bombings and civil war in the countryside, and attempting to eliminate religious institutions through attacks on the Buddhist clergy. More than a million of the country's 5 million people are estimated to have died as a result of these government actions.

Not only did Pol Pot's government turn on its own people, but it turned against its neighbors and historical enemies, the Vietnamese, refusing to negotiate a dispute over territory along their common border. Charging provocation, the Vietnamese, supported by the Soviet Union, invaded in December 1978 to remove Pol Pot and put a more moderate ex-Khmer Rouge group of Communists in his place. The ousted Khmer Rouge, led by Pol Pot and Khieu Samphan and supported by the Chinese, remained an active force, in effective control of areas along the Thai border and carrying on insurgent operations against the Vietnamese-sponsored government in Phnom Penh.

Renamed the People's Republic of Kampuchea and later the State of Cambodia, that government was led by the People's Revolutionary Party (now the Cambodian People's Party) with Hun Sen as prime minister and Heng Samrin as president. Facing almost unanimous international condemnation as a puppet of the Vietnamese, whose troops remained until 1989, the government's legitimacy was challenged internally by the Khmer Rouge and by two Western-supported noncommunist insurgent groups, one headed by Sihanouk and the other by Son Sann, all three of them in 1982 forming a coalition government-in-exile. Finally in 1991, the outside backers of the various Cambodian political groups decided it was in their interest to push for some sort of accommodation. The opposition groups and the government agreed to a cease-fire, to transitional arrangements leading to elections in 1993, and to a new government able to restore peace to this troubled land.

UNTAC

Under that agreement the United Nations Transitional Authority in Cambodia (UNTAC), with some 22,000 military and civilian personnel, monitored the cease-fire

Children play near the memorial at Choeung Ek where bones of Cambodians executed by the Pol Pot government are displayed.

Source: United Nations photo 159733/J. Isaac.

and tried with only limited success to arrange for the partial disarmament of the insurgent forces and the State of Cambodia (SOC) army. Taking over temporary responsibility for running five key government ministries, UNTAC made preparations for the election of a national assembly, registering voters and arranging for repatriation of Cambodians from refugee camps along the Thai border. A Cambodian consultative group, the Supreme National Council, was set up with six representatives from SOC and two from each of the three oppositional groups; Sihanouk, veteran politician and durable symbol of national unity, was chosen president. Contending that SOC's control of the army and the bureaucracy would give it an advantage in the elections, the Khmer Rouge refused to participate. UNTAC decided to go ahead without them.

Election and the New Government

The election was held under close UN supervision in May 1993, the Cambodian People's Party coming in second with 38 percent of the vote behind Prince Norodom Ranariddh's FUNCINPEC, which won 46 percent. The assembly met and drew up a new constitution, restoring a constitutional monarchy with Sihanouk as king. Compromise between Sihanouk's son Ranariddh and Hun Sen led to an unusual power-sharing arrangement, under which the prince became first prime minister and Hun Sen second prime minister, together serving as co-ministers of defense, interior, and public security. The other ministries are divided between the two parties.

Its mission accomplished, UNTAC departed. Staff from UN relief and economic agencies remained to help in rebuilding the economic and social fabric of the country from the ravages of Pol Pot's policies and the years of civil war. The government's capacity to undertake national reconstruction and move ahead with development is severely limited by the division within the government between the two coalition partners, the division of the country between the Phnom Penh government and the Khmer Rouge, and the prolonged absence of King Sihanouk, who spends much of his time undergoing medical treatment in Beijing. The national army, police, provincial heads, and much of the bureaucracy remain under Cambodian People's Party control; although FUNCINPEC people occupy the top positions in ministries allocated to Ranariddh, their influence has yet to penetrate into the lower levels.

Policy differences over how to deal with the Khmer Rouge run deep and hamper the government's ability to pursue a concerted strategy. The alternatives of reconciliation, isolation, and elimination each have their advocates in Phnom Penh. Sihanouk has repeatedly called for efforts at reconciliation between the government and the KR, urging a cease-fire and negotiations on some form of power-sharing. Ranariddh's strategy is to isolate the KR, pressing ahead with economic development as the means of undermining its appeal in the countryside, whittling away at its fighting forces by offering amnesty and resettlement assistance to soldiers who come over to the government's side. Hun Sen's Cambodian People's Party is least sanguine about the possibility of reconciliation, opposes the notion of power-sharing, argues that development efforts will be stymied as long as the KR is capable of sabotaging them, and therefore sees its elimination as the necessary course of action.

In the spring of 1994 the government launched an offensive against KR forces along the Thai border, capturing the city of Pailin and holding it for a month before losing it again. Peace talks then held at Sihanouk's urging failed to produce results, and the KR was reported to have abandoned the goal of power-sharing in favor of a military and political offensive to bring down the Phnom Penh government. In July, after an unsuccessful coup led by one of Sihanouk's sons and another former minister in Hun Sen's government, the parliament passed legislation outlawing the KR, seemingly foreclosing the option of formal talks between the government and the KR, which remains in effective control of large areas of the country.

Hope remains that the way may yet be reopened in the future for gradual national reconciliation and the creation of a single state inspiring the loyalty of all Cambodians. For now, political divisions are tenuously bridged by Sihanouk's personal appeal as the symbol of national unity and by anti-Vietnam feelings of ancient origin, expressed in sporadic outbursts of violence against Vietnamese living in Cambodia and denying them the right to citizenship under the new constitution. Even if the now divided and weak Cambodian state becomes unified and stronger, some form of authoritarianism is likely to continue. If it is able to provide peace and stability, it may be a welcome alternative to its predecessors that Cambodians have endured.

Having looked at manifestations of authoritarianism in each of the countries, now we are ready in the concluding section of this chapter to offer some explanation for its persistence and to speculate on the prospects for democracy in the Asian Pacific.

WHY AUTHORITARIANISM? IS THE TREND TOWARD DEMOCRACY?

To people who expected and hoped that liberal democracy would take root in the Asian Pacific after independence and create the conditions of stability and free choice considered necessary for rapid economic and social development, the record thus far is disappointing. To others who expected that Marxist socialist democracy would be the chosen route to liberation from colonialism and to rapid development under a centrally planned command economy, the record is equally disappointing.

Liberal democracy has been short-lived and where tried did not produce much economic progress. Instead, those countries where economic progress has been most remarkable have had authoritarian political systems, and government has played a much more intrusive role in the economy than expected. In countries where Marxists have come to power, the record in economic development has been considerably less spectacular than hoped for, at least until economic "reforms" began to depart from the orthodoxy of central planning and allow market forces in some sections of the economy to drive growth. There has not yet, however, been a comparable loosening of Communist Party political control.

What accounts for the persistence of authoritarianism in these countries? One explanation is that the attitudes toward authority and patterns of relationships between the ruler and the ruled that existed in the traditional precolonial societies are still powerful influences. In them the norm was a hierarchical social order, presided over by a monarch or a village chief, who was expected to take responsibility for the well-being of his subjects; they in turn owed him obedience and respect for his exalted status. Such norms are clearly not compatible with the modern democratic notions of the accountability of rulers to the ruled and the ruled's right and even responsibility to participate in the selection of rulers and in making policy choices.

Another explanation is that the experience of colonial rule further reinforced the traditions of the precolonial political order. Rather than effectively shouldering the "white man's burden" of preparing the subject peoples for the responsibilities of self-government, colonialism not only encouraged the pattern of "top-down" rule by an alien bureaucracy unaccountable to those governed, but in some colonies propped up local sultans, kings, and emperors as convenient instruments for indirect rule. In some cases, the imperial power made efforts, usually modest and belated, to indigenize the bureaucracy and to involve a select segment of the colonials in appointive or elective positions. But this was far from providing experience in running a modern nation-state. Another legacy of colonial rule that has created a further impediment to democracy was the differential treatment of various national or ethnic groups that created or exacerbated intercommunal hostility and retarded the development of a sense of *national* identity.

Another explanation for authoritarianism is that it is better suited than liberal democracy for handling the difficult transition from a traditional economic and social order to a modern dynamic economy and society. Rather than relying on the invisible hand of the free market to allocate capital and human resources for economic development, it is argued, in the early stages at least government must provide the leadership and coherent view of the course of action the nation needs to take to launch it on the road to a productive modern industrial economy.

In a curious way, both the modernization theorists and the Marxist practitioners in China and the Soviet Union have similarly repudiated the views of their intellectual progenitors. The former, inspired largely by the experience of Japan and the NICs, have departed from Adam Smith, recognizing the necessity of authoritarian governments in the early stages of economic development. The Marxist practitioners in communist states have diverged from Karl Marx, whose position was that capitalism is well suited for making the painful transition from feudalism to industrialism and expanding the society's productive capacity to the point where it can provide the affluence needed for an egalitarian socialist democracy. Rather than wait through the capitalist accumulation process, Lenin, Mao, and other Communist revolutionaries decided not to let pass the opportunity to seize power, and assigned to the Communist Party as trustees for the working class the job of handling the transition from feudalism to industrialism and then to socialism. At that point, according to Lenin, the need for the state as the instrument of the ruling class would vanish and the state itself would wither away.

Of course, as Lenin pointed out and as world system theorists emphasize, the transition to socialism and a stateless society is likely to be delayed, and the need for dictatorial rule continued, by the persistent opposition of international capitalism with its imperialist designs on the rest of the world. Another curious change in communist practice has come in recent years with the introduction of market-oriented policies, reducing the role of government as the sole manager of the economy; this might be interpreted as at least a partial return to the original view of Marx about capitalism's unique capacity for laying the foundation of a modern economy. By whatever route they use to reach it, most observers and practitioners of modernization and development seem to agree that authoritarianism in some degree is either desirable or unavoidable to achieve the conditions of rapid economic growth.

What are the prospects for "democratization" in these authoritarian regimes? One commonly held view is that economic development itself sets in motion social and political changes that lead to demands for more popular control over government. Affluence, diversification of economic interests, education, and the rise of a middle class all are thought to contribute to the trend toward democratization.

But if affluence, or at least progress toward it, is provided by the authoritarian state, why would its beneficiaries want to rock the boat by demanding political change, the initial effect of which is bound to be destabilizing? That runs the risk of killing the goose that lays the golden eggs. And diversification of economic interests from a predominantly agricultural base to a variety of industrial, commercial, and service industries does not necessarily produce political pluralism manifested in parties and pressure groups speaking for those interests. Nor is a growing middle class necessarily an agent of political change.[18] Its potential for challenging the authoritarian status quo is limited in many Asian Pacific countries by its dependence on the state for employment; it is rarely an autonomous class like the property-owning bourgeoisie that pushed through political reforms in Western Europe.

Another view is that, however modest the capacity for and commitment to democratization and however necessary authoritarianism may be to launch economic development, at some point preservation of the status quo becomes an impediment to continued economic advancement; democratic change, however unsettling its initial effects, is a necessity for the long-term stability and legitimacy of the political order.

Others, world system theorists included, are less sanguine about the prospects for democratization, because governments responsive to popular pressure might embark on economic reform programs threatening to powerful domestic and foreign interests, which would by overt or covert means engineer a reversal of the democratic trend, if they allowed it to get underway at all. Even a country that becomes strong enough and determined enough to break out of neocolonial subordination to outside influences is in this view likely to need an authoritarian political system to accomplish this feat and successfully resist pressures to restore the old relationship.

Another perspective on the "democratization" issue raises the question of whether the Western vision of what democracy is might be too ethnocentric, constrained by European political philosophers and institutions and practices that grew out of Graeco-Roman traditions. It is certainly possible to consider that the different cultural grounds of Asia might produce new and different forms of political participation, whether hybrids springing from the contact between indigenous and outside traditions or uniquely Asian varieties.

It is probably too early to hazard a guess whether the trends toward "softening" authoritarianism in Taiwan, South Korea, and Thailand and toward economic liberalization in China, Vietnam, and Laos are harbingers of a democratic "spring" in the Asian Pacific. People outside the region may hope for and support progress toward greater opportunity for political participation and for material well-being, but they should not be demoralized if that progress is fitful, slow, and at times reversed.

SUMMARY

All the Asian Pacific governments are authoritarian. The degree of control varies from country to country, as do the political structures and the techniques by which elites maintain their dominant position in society.

Old-style authoritarianism in the form of colonial rule and unlimited monarchy persists in Hong Kong and Brunei. Communist parties that came to power with the aim of revolutionary transformation still effectively monopolize politics in China, North Korea, Vietnam, and Laos, while in Cambodia one communist regime was ousted by another, which now shares power with noncommunists. In Indonesia, South Korea, and Burma the fragility of postindependence civilian governments led to military takeover. In the first two the armed forces successfully assumed the task of economic development, following in the path of military modernizers in Thailand. Recently civilian governments have succeeded the military in Thailand and South Korea.

Civilian governments under the dominance of a single ethnically based party have ruled multiethnic Malaysia and Singapore since independence. Taiwan's dominant party, transplanted from the mainland, only recently permitted opposition parties to exist. In Japan, the one-party dominant system that lasted until defections from the government party forced it out in 1993 may be restored, or it may be replaced with a new system, the features of which are unclear as of this writing. In the Philippines electoral competition among multiple personalist political parties, a weak state, and politicized armed forces constitute a system suited to the purposes of the economic and local political elites.

The widespread existence of authoritarian rule is variously explained as a continuation of traditional precolonial times, as the reinforcement of those patterns by colonial rule, and as a requirement of nation building and economic development. Whether authoritarianism is a persistent feature of Asian Pacific politics or a temporary phase, to be followed by movement toward more democratic competitive political systems, is not yet certain. In the next chapter, we turn our attention to the connection between politics and economics, in particular to the preeminent role of the state in cases of successful economic development.

QUESTIONS FOR DISCUSSION

1. What are the distinguishing features of *authoritarianism?* Do you think that the label fits the governments of Asian Pacific countries? Why?

2. Do you agree with those who argue that some type of authoritarianism is necessary to guide a country through the processes of modernization and development? Why?

3. Why has the military played such a major role in Indonesia, South Korea, Myanmar, and Thailand? What positive and negative effects do you see in military rule?

4. How durable do you think the trend away from authoritarianism is likely to be in such countries as South Korea, Taiwan, Thailand, and the Philippines? What forces might be working in that direction, or counter to it, in China, Vietnam, North Korea, and Myanmar?

NOTES

1. James C. F. Wang, *Contemporary Chinese Politics: An Introduction,* 4th ed. (Englewood Cliffs: Prentice Hall, 1992), p. 80.
2. Although *Kuomintang,* the earlier romanization, is still used in Taiwan, we use *Guomindang* throughout the book.
3. Cal Clark, *Taiwan's Political Development: Implications for Contending Political Economy Paradigms* (New York: Greenwood Press, 1989), p. 121.
4. Stanley S. Bedlington, *Malaysia and Singapore* (Ithaca: Cornell University Press, 1978), p. 228.
5. R. William Liddle, "Regime in Crisis" (paper presented at the meeting of the Association for Asian Studies, Washington, D.C., 2–5 April 1992).
6. David J. Steinberg, ed., *In Search of Southeast Asia: A Modern History,* rev. ed. (Honolulu: University of Hawaii Press, 1987), p. 426.
7. David Wilson, *Politics in Thailand* (Ithaca: Cornell University Press, 1962), p. 277.
8. Chai-Anan Samudavanija, "Thailand: A Stable Semi-Democracy," in *Democracy in Developing Countries: Asia,* ed. Larry Diamond et al. (Boulder: Lynne Rienner Publishers, 1989), p. 320.
9. Paul Handley, "People's Wrath," *Far Eastern Economic Review,* 28 May 1992, p. 10.
10. The distinction among control, participation, and influence is made in Carolina G. Hernandez, "The Philippines," in *Military-Civilian Relations in South-East Asia,* ed. Z. H. Ahmad and H. Crouch (New York: Oxford University Press, 1985), pp. 157–58.
11. Hari Singh, "Political Change in Malaysia," *Asian Survey* 31, no. 6 (August 1991): p. 712.
12. For a discussion of the distinction between strong and weak states, see Joel S. Migdal, *Strong Societies and Weak States* (Princeton: Princeton University Press, 1988), pp. 4–5.
13. Chan Heng-chee, "Politics in an Administrative State: Where Has the Politics Gone?", cited in Bedlington, *Malaysia and Singapore,* p. 228.
14. Charles P. Wallace, "Making a Case for Kinder, Gentler 'Big Brother,' " *Los Angeles Times,* 19 May 1992, p. H15.
15. David Wurfel, *Filipino Politics* (Ithaca: Cornell University Press, 1988), p. 62.
16. G. Sidney Silliman, "Human Rights Under the Marcos and Aquino Regimes" (paper presented at the meeting of the Association for Asian Studies, Washington, D.C., 2–5 April 1992).
17. Jeffrey Riedinger, "Everyday Resistance to Redistributive Reform: Agrarian Reform in the Philippines" (paper presented at the meeting of the Association for Asian Studies, Washington, D.C., 2–5 April 1992), p. 19.
18. Tun-jen Cheng, "Is the Dog Barking? The Middle Class and Democratic Movements in the East Asian NICs," *International Studies Notes* 15, no. 1 (Winter 1990): pp. 10–17.

FOR FURTHER READING

See the periodicals suggested on page 107 for current information.

Multicountry Studies

Ahmad, Zakaria Haji, and Harold Crouch, eds. *Military-Civilian Relations in South-East Asia*. Oxford: Oxford University Press, 1985.

Diamond, Larry, Juan J. Linz, and Seymour Martin Lipset, eds. *Democracy in Developing Countries*. Vol. 3, *Asia*. Boulder: Lynne Rienner Publishers, 1989, chapters 1, 6-9, 11.

Individual Country Studies

Brown, MacAlister, and Joseph J. Zasloff. *Apprentice Revolutionaries: The Communist Movement in Laos, 1930-1985*. Stanford: Hoover Institution Press, 1986.

Calder, Kent E. *Crisis and Compensation: Public Policy and Political Stability in Japan, 1949-1986*. Princeton: Princeton University Press, 1988.

Clark, Cal. *Taiwan's Political Development: Implications for Contending Political Economy Paradigms*. New York: Greenwood Press, 1989, chapter 5.

Crouch, Harold. *The Army and Politics in Indonesia*. Rev. ed. Ithaca: Cornell University Press, 1988.

Keyes, Charles F. *Thailand: Buddhist Kingdom as a Modern Nation-State*. Boulder: Westview Press, 1987, chapters 4-6.

Lee, Chong-Sik, and Se-Hee Yoo, eds. *North Korea in Transition*. Berkeley: UC Institute of East Asian Studies, 1991.

Ongkili, James P. *Nation-building in Malaysia 1946-1974*. Singapore: Oxford University Press, 1985, chapters 5-7.

Pike, Douglas. *History of Vietnamese Communism, 1925-1976*. Stanford: Hoover Institution Press, 1978.

Rodan, Garry, ed. *Singapore Changes Guard: Social, Political and Economic Directions in the 1990s*. New York: St. Martin's Press, 1993, Part I.

Steinberg, David I. *The Republic of Korea: Economic Transformation and Social Change*. Boulder: Westview Press, 1989, chapters 6, 8, 9.

Taylor, Robert H. *The State in Burma*. Honolulu: University of Hawaii Press, 1987.

Wang, James C. F. *Contemporary Chinese Politics: An Introduction*. 4th ed. Englewood Cliffs, NJ: Prentice-Hall, 1992.

Wurfel, David. *Filipino Politics*. Ithaca: Cornell University Press, 1988.

chapter 5

Political Economy
and Development

A s varied as national states in the Asian Pacific are—the subject of the preceding
chapter—they all share a common objective: to promote the economic growth and
prosperity of the people living within their borders. How well or how poorly states
carry out this task is what confers or revokes legitimacy on them in the eyes of both
their own and the world's population. The fate of the Soviet Union and its Eastern European satellites is a compelling reminder of how a state can fall victim to its own economic failures. This international calamity has drawn attention to the significance of
political economy, of understanding the variety of ways in which state and economy
depend on one another not merely within the boundaries of any single nation-state
but internationally as members of a global community. The relationship between politics and economics at the juncture where national states intersect with the international order is the subject of this chapter.

The astounding economic development of the Asian Pacific since the Second
World War has drawn attention to the role of the state in bringing about economic
progress. From the devastation of defeat in war, the small island nation of Japan has
emerged as the second largest economy in the world, rivaled only by the United States.
Following Japan's example, South Korea, Taiwan, Singapore, and Hong Kong have
successfully transformed themselves into vibrant capitalist economies contributing to
the region's reputation for "economic miracles." Even the economy of the People's
Republic of China—the second largest in the Asian Pacific although it is only one-
eighth the size of Japan's—achieved an impressive 9 percent economic growth rate
in 1991. None of these countries is either a democracy or a "free enterprise" system
as generally understood in the West; authoritarian politics and an interventionist state
are more often the rule either formally or informally. Yet they are at the forefront of
the fastest growing region in the world, challenging a broad range of Western ideas
and practices concerning the role of the state in the economy.

A comparative analysis of political economy in the Asian Pacific raises practical as well as theoretical questions about where global development is headed. Does the state's activist role as manager of the market account for the prodigious productivity and economic success of East Asian national economies? Is their export-oriented strategy a universally applicable model or is it a unique product of its time and place? If it is universally applicable, is there room for all countries to pursue successfully an export-oriented strategy of development or are there inevitably losers in the zero-sum competition of a finite international market? Is there emerging in the Asian Pacific a form of mixed economy distinct from others, possibly a model for global convergence? Through their own developmental achievements, the nations of the Asian Pacific have placed their experiences at the center of the answers to these questions.

We begin with a consideration of the ways in which the political economy of development in the Asian Pacific experience differs from its Western counterpart. Then follows a description of four models of political economy and how they relate to the theoretical perspectives through which development has been viewed in the West. The third section consists of a comparison between the Japanese and the Maoist patterns of political economy, inviting the reader to assess their similarities and differences. The developmental strategy of the "four little tigers"—South Korea, Taiwan, Hong Kong, and Singapore—is examined in the fourth section, followed by a discussion of the market reforms in China, Vietnam, and Laos. Finally, the achievements of the newly exporting countries, the NECs—Malaysia, Thailand, and Indonesia—will be compared and contrasted with the failures of Myanmar and the Philippines to break out of the cycle of Third World underdevelopment.

DISTINCTIVE FEATURES OF DEVELOPMENT IN THE ASIAN PACIFIC

Development is a difficult term to circumscribe. Generally it includes the totality of changes that accompany the process of industrialization: mechanization, urbanization, commercialization, and democratization. In those countries that pioneered industrialization between the sixteenth and nineteenth centuries—the Western European nations and the United States—the process unfolded in a spontaneous manner we call capitalism. Increasingly, however, this process has become more deliberate and planned. Beginning with economic growth in the form of commodity production for an international market, capitalist development was pursued in Western countries by a new class of businesspeople whose activities were supported but not directed by a centralized political order, a national state. As the market expanded in response to the application of new technology, self-generating economies reshaped the social and political institutions of national life. The entirety of these remarkable transformations ushered in the irresistible modern world.

But time warps occur globally as peoples originally left out of this modernizing process are engulfed by its awesome powers. They encounter the modern world as a fait accompli: a delicate filigree of interrelated institutions and beliefs that appear to have neither beginning nor end. Peoples who overnight discover that they are "backward" are compelled to master a bewildering complex of new survival skills or be re-

duced to permanent bondage. This process of large national communities l
act as one in order to reshape their economic, social, and political destiny
in social science circles as *development*. It requires self-consciously unta
complicated strands of a modern way of life that presents itself as a finished product
with few clues as to how or where to begin to duplicate it and which elements to
omit. In the Asian Pacific, this process of development has differed in three major
ways from the experience of the "early developers," and those differences have contributed to the greater role of the state in development.

Late Developers

Historically, all Asian societies are "late developers," a concept widely identified with
Alexander Gerschenkron, who noted the special characteristics of countries, like Germany and the Soviet Union, that joined the global tide of development when it was already in rapid motion. Gerschenkron's hypothesis is that the later a country
industrializes the greater will be the role of the state in compensating for the "missing
prerequisites" that enabled earlier developers to industrialize.[1] Thus when Japan embarked on modernizing its government and economy in the 1880s, the Japanese had
the advantage of learning from a second generation of developers—Germany and
France. This meant starting with a more advanced and foreign machine technology
that required the superior resources of the state to acquire. For countries like China,
South Korea, and Malaysia, which commenced the process even later, the scope and
cost of launching economic development meant an even greater role for the state.
Time, therefore, is one factor in understanding the expanded intervention of the state
in the economic planning of Asian Pacific development.

Imperialism

Another factor is imperialism, the forceful imposition of modernity by foreign rule.
Asian Pacific countries are not merely "late developers" in the manner of Germany or
the Soviet Union but share the experience of colonization (either directly or indirectly) by members of a foreign civilization, an experience unlike any in Europe or the
United States, except that of the Native Americans. Wresting independence from colonial rule requires replacing the colonial government with a state powerful enough not
only to maintain order but to generate massive social and economic change. Among
Asian Pacific peoples, therefore, there is a shared legacy of strong, legitimately interventionist government with sufficient power to secure the economic livelihood of
its people.

Cultural Collectivism

A third factor distinguishing political economies of Asian Pacific countries from those
in the West is cultural: the shared emphasis placed on the collective good, whether
of the family or the state, over and above the individual. The primacy of the common
good requires collective restraints to curb the selfish, narrower pursuit of short-term,
partisan interests. And in the Asian cultural context, this is expressed in the accep-

tance of a state as authoritarian in its preeminence. It is more like an extended family than it is an association of unrelated adults who compete with one another for the acquisition of wealth. The role of the state is not simply to regulate conflicts among individuals but to impose harmony and conformity with proper conduct.

The political ramifications of this preference for harmony have already been evidenced in the pervasiveness of one-party-dominant political systems described in Chapter 4. In this chapter, the widespread acceptance of the state's leadership role in determining the collective economic interest will be discussed as an essential characteristic of successful Asian Pacific political economies. This is as true for the communist command economies of China, North Korea, and Vietnam as it is for the "developmental" states of Japan, Taiwan, South Korea, Malaysia, Singapore, Thailand, and Indonesia.

FOUR MODELS OF POLITICAL ECONOMY

Three models, often with different labels, are used by Western social scientists to describe the broad spectrum of political economies in today's world. At one end is the capitalist *market economy* with its basis in the experiences of Western states since the sixteenth century; at the other end is the communist *planned economy* gleaned from the experiences of the Soviet Union and other communist states since 1917; and in between are all the mixtures or combinations of the two, generally referred to as *mixed economies.* Following descriptions of market, command, and mixed economies and how they are related to the two theoretical approaches we have been using, we will specify a singular conception of the mixed economy as a fourth model, the *developmental state economy* suggested by the common experiences of political economies in the Asian Pacific region.

Capitalist or Market Economy

In the capitalist or market model of development, economics and politics comprise separate spheres of activity in modern society. Adam Smith, as we recall from Chapter 1, prescribed that the economy should be governed by its own rules unfettered by the artificial constraints of the state. Total private control by individuals (usually referring to firms or households) of the factors of production (land, labor, factories, resources) enables the market through principles of competition, supply, and demand to determine what gets produced, at what value goods and resources are exchanged, and how individuals can optimally increase their accumulated value (profit). Thus, the market economy is demand oriented, each actor making decisions on what to produce and/or exchange on the basis of the demand for various goods. The "invisible hand" automatically converts the sum of profit-seeking individuals into the common good of the whole society.

How, then, is government connected with the economy? It creates and preserves the context within which the market operates and provides for the national defense. Examples of legitimate state policies are protecting private ownership of property, guaranteeing the inviolability of contracts, implementing the use of a common currency and uniform weights and measures. Although even Smith recognized a larger role for the state—for example, in providing welfare—to create and maintain the "free" market system than did some of his latter-day acolytes, he nonetheless bequeathed a legacy of reverence for the virtues of an economy completely owned and controlled by private individuals free from state intervention. Is it legitimate for the state to regulate the economy in order to protect competition? to safeguard individuals' rights? Should the state monitor and control consumer goods so individuals are protected from harmful products? Is it also appropriate for the state to correct other flaws of the market as they become apparent? These questions provide great latitude for controversy. It is clear, nonetheless, that the state's role in the market model is both modest and in accordance with the decisions of individuals taking part in the market.

This market model is at the core of modernization theory. Its proponents assume that each developing country will find its interests best served by promoting a free market internally and free trade with the other members of the international community. Whatever assets a state has can thus be transformed into a comparative advantage in trade with others and the earnings used to purchase the advanced technology needed to develop. This is the basis for an *export-led strategy* of development. The exigencies of late development may require a greater role for the state in protecting the market, perhaps even regulating trade to protect infant indigenous industry, but there is never any doubt that the state plays a secondary role, depending upon the market to provide the impetus and mechanics of production and distribution.

Planned Economy

A second, alternative model of modern political economy arises out of the experience of the Soviet Union after 1917. In this model, the state takes over total control of all factors of production, determining what goods will be produced and how they will be distributed to the population. The state draws up a detailed plan specifying what amounts of each good will be produced from what combination of resources and at what prices the goods will be bought and sold. The plan indicates that a dress manufacturing factory, for example, will receive a certain amount of fabric, thread, buttons, and other items to produce a certain number of dresses. From whom the requisite materials will be obtained and to whom the dresses will be distributed are also designated by the plan along with the size, composition, and wages of the labor force. In contrast to the market economy, the planned economy is supply oriented: The state makes production decisions on the basis of supplying citizens with goods and services appropriate to their needs and the state's budget and priorities. All these considerations are guided by a broad social and political vision of the society's destination: a time when all citizens' needs and aspirations can be provided for by a technically sophisticated and prosperous productive system.

The state's role in a planned economy is overwhelming, requiring the central direction of a highly organized and disciplined political party. The Communist Party has performed this function as leader of the state and guardian of its economic goals and socialist aspirations. In their capacity as public officials, high-ranking party members make a staggering number of production decisions that affect the livelihood of the entire population and the fortunes of the country as a whole. The rationale for the party-state's exercise of such extensive economic control is twofold: to catch up rapidly with the already powerful and industrialized nations in the world and to substitute for the weakness of an entrepreneurial class historically charged with carrying out the tasks of capitalist development.

From the world system perspective, the model of a planned economy provides an alternative to the foreign domination brought about by incorporation into the global capitalist economy. Adherents of world system theory argue that underdeveloped peoples are too weak to resist external encroachment by industrialized nations *without* a revolutionary party capable of establishing a strong, highly centralized state. A planned economy, presumably in the context of a socialist revolution, allows a developing country to concentrate its resources, thereby strengthening the autonomy of its state and raising the revenue to pursue an independent economic course of action. With this model of development an *import-substitution strategy* is employed by the state to protect the domestic economy from external competition, enabling it to grow in a self-reliant manner. The state plays the principal role in this approach to economic development by acting as a substitute for the market.

Mixed Economies

The mixed economy is a hybrid model that combines the strengths and avoids the weaknesses of the market model on the one hand and the planned economy on the other. It is a system in which there is a significant sector of state planning to serve the common good while retaining the privately owned market free from state control. The usual examples of this model are Western European states in which a substantial percentage of industries like banking, telecommunications, utilities, and transportation are owned and operated by the state while most other industries remain in the hands of private entrepreneurs and investors. The state engages in economic oversight, making recommendations to private sector industries as well; this is referred to as *indicative planning* in the case of France. Market mechanisms in general determine production decisions in a mixed system because nationalized industries operate within a market context, competing with private industry for resources and markets. But the state can place constraints on the behavior of private enterprises, deciding minimum wages, for example, and in some cases establishing overall guidelines for the economy as a whole.

In the cold war context that followed World War II, it was generally assumed that market and mixed systems fostered democratic political institutions while planned economies invited totalitarian control. In the first two decades after the war, the political map of the Asian Pacific seemed to corroborate this view: China, North Korea, and North Vietnam were planned economies with communist states presumed to exercise totalitarian control while Japan, South Korea, Taiwan, and Singapore were pro-Western and market-oriented states with what appeared to be democratic institutions. By the 1980s, however, the extraordinary economic growth of Japan and the NICs began to appear in a new light. The cold war adversaries, the United States and the So-

viet Union, were entering a period of economic decline and international political retrenchment while the Asian Pacific emerged as a new, vibrant center of economic expansion. This prompted closer scrutiny of how Japan and the NICs had achieved their
dramatic economic ascendance, revealing a pattern of development quite different in
some respects from the one suggested by any of the prevailing models of political
economy.

Developmental State—A Fourth Model

Chalmers Johnson, in his influential book, *MITI and the Japanese Miracle,*[2] introduced the model of a developmental state as a corrective to the misperception that
Japan was following Adam Smith's recipe of the market economy as the way to develop. Johnson demonstrated that Japanese economic development was the consequence not of a democratic state's benign neglect of the market but of an authoritarian
state's active intervention in shaping business decisions. From the beginning of the
Meiji era, according to Johnson, Japan has followed a unique pattern in which a market economy has benefited from self-conscious direction by a bureaucratic authoritarian state. Although the political sphere is formally organized as a representative
democracy, it has actually contained all along two institutionally segregated functions:
ruling, which is the authoritarian decision making of the bureaucracy, and *reigning,*
which is the political give-and-take of competing partisan interests in a parliamentary
forum. Reigning is the domain of democratically elected "politicians," while ruling,
the orchestration and guidance of the national economy, is carried out by technocratic
civil servants in government agencies.

The developmental state that Johnson extrapolates from the Japanese experience
applies equally well to the newly industrializing countries of Singapore, Taiwan, and
South Korea. Economic growth in these countries has followed the same pattern: a
market that is the engine of economic growth and an authoritarian state as the driver
of the engine. For this reason, developmental states have been dubbed BAIRs by Cumings: bureaucratic authoritarian industrializing regimes.[3] However, to distinguish
Japan's postwar democratic system from more blatantly authoritarian regimes (like
South Korea under Park, for example) Chalmers Johnson uses the term *soft authoritarianism* to describe a regime in which persuasion and negotiation rather than command and coercion are used by the governmental bureaucracy to achieve market
compliance. Although it is not clear whether this is a matter of style or substance, the
distinction between *soft* and *hard* authoritarianism is subsidiary in any event to the
category of developmental state.

Four structural elements are identified as characteristic of the developmental
state:

1. bureaucratic autonomy from politics that protects the developmental state
   from bowing to political demands and pressures that might undermine long-
   term national economic growth;
2. close collaboration of public and private sectors directed by a powerful
   planning agency or board;

3. heavy and continuing investment in education for everyone and policies to ensure equitable distribution of the wealth gained through high-speed growth; and

4. the use of incentives and persuasion rather than commands so that the state's economic intervention is based on the price mechanism of the market rather than administratively assigned prices.[4]

There are additional issues surrounding discussion of these and other traits of the developmental state that have attracted considerable attention in recent years: its pragmatic, nonideological character, its suppression of independent labor unions and populist groups, its reliance on paternalistic corporate structures modeled on the family, its role as mediator between the opportunities and dangers of the international market, and the benefit of the domestic national economy. Some of these will be discussed more fully in our comparisons of the political economy of Japan and the NICs.

The significance of this model of a developmental state is its deviation from both the classical laissez-faire Western model of the market economy and the model of economic planning associated with the command economies of socialist states. Though similar in some respects to the mixed economy of Western European countries, which combines substantial sectors of state-owned property with the productive resources and mechanisms of a market economy, the developmental state is more than a mere combination of elements of the command and market systems.

The defining characteristic of the developmental state is not the amount of industry owned and controlled by the state but the degree, scope, and direction of the state's management of the market as a whole. In fact, the state in Japan "is actually smaller in terms of revenues, outlays, and equity ownership than most capitalist countries in the West."[5] Yet the state's role in orchestrating the Japanese, South Korean, and Taiwanese economies is greater than in any of the mixed economies of Western Europe. The developmental state intervenes in the market not only to remove serious obstacles to national economic development and dilute the effects of market failures but to direct the nation's economic growth and ensure its international competitiveness. Primary responsibility for determining national economic priorities is not left to the market but is assumed by a state with sufficient autonomy to pursue developmentally desirable national economic policies. Does this signify that the developmental state is a distinctive type of political economy? If so, is it a unique invention peculiar to the Asian Pacific, a fourth model of political economy?

The practical ramifications attending these as yet unanswered questions are critical: Is it possible for other regimes to duplicate the strategic role of the state in "taming domestic and international market forces and harnessing them to a national economic interest"?[6] Is the developmental state an enduring model, let alone one that other countries can adopt? If it is an enduring model, is it one towards which both command economies and market economies will gravitate? Or with the passage of time will Japan and its acolytes, the NICs and the NECs, begin to behave more like the classical market economies of capitalism? Amidst indications that in Japan, South Korea, and perhaps Taiwan the collaboration between large corporate enterprises and state bureaucracies may be loosening, there is widespread speculation that this "model" may in fact *not* constitute a distinctive model but is merely a detour in the worldwide movement towards a market economy.

These tantalizing questions have theoretical implications as well as practical ones. If, as an increasing number of scholars intimate, Japan, South Korea, Taiwan, Singapore, and the second tier of NECs—Malaysia, Indonesia, and Thailand—do indeed exhibit the characteristics of a hybrid developmental state, they constitute anomalies from both major theoretical perspectives, suggesting a third state-centered theoretical alternative. Both modernization and world system theory underestimate the importance of the state in bringing about modern capitalist development among late developers. The developmental state theory, on the other hand, spotlights the state as indispensable for late developers' entry into and successful industrialization as part of the global economy. This seems to be an additional factor in the flurry of interest in assessments of the Asian Pacific political economies; they constitute important evidence corroborating one or another theoretical and ideological perspective. The reform policies pursued by Communist Parties in China, Vietnam, Laos, and to a lesser extent in North Korea can be interpreted in three distinct ways: as a movement in the direction of convergence with the developmental states in the rest of the Asian Pacific, as an independent mixture of capitalism and socialism captured by the term *market socialism,* or as a step on the road to a full-fledged market economy.

A central issue at the heart of all the questions is the claim that Japan's "developmental state" is actually closer to the experience of the centrally planned economies than it is to the classical market model of the West, which, except perhaps in Hong Kong, is nowhere approximated in the Asian Pacific. The implication of this claim, made by Chalmers Johnson,[7] is that only the planned economy and the developmental state economy are pertinent to the examination of political economies in the Asian Pacific. This is explored in the next section in a comparison of the political economies of Japan from its Meiji roots to the present and Communist China from its inception in 1949 through its Maoist phase, which ended in 1978.

CONTRASTING THE POLITICAL ECONOMY OF JAPAN AND MAOIST CHINA

Among late developers in Asia, Japan and China offer a striking contrast. Japan has a market economy guided by a highly professional government bureaucracy within a parliamentary system; China has a centrally planned economy governed by the Communist Party in a socialist state structure. But neither political economy is quite what it appears to be. Japan's actually has been a collaborative enterprise among government bureaucracy, big business, and (until mid-1993) the Liberal Democratic Party; China's centrally planned economy, in operation from 1949 to 1978, was neither as centralized nor as planned as it claimed. Since adoption of the Reform policy (to be discussed in conjunction with the NICs), China's planned economy seems to be moving more self-consciously in the direction of the Japanese model. The initial conditions under which China and Japan embarked on the road to a modern political economy, however, presented different opportunities.

China's Political Economy: Surviving a Transplant

The kind of development a country follows is never a wide open choice among all rational possibilities but is decisively influenced by which models are available and acceptable to political leaders at any particular point in time. Marxism gained a following in China during the 1920s because it appealed to Chinese nationalism; it offered a successful anti-imperialist alternative to Western models of modernization, a perception the Soviet Union sought to bolster by proposing to return the Chinese Eastern Railway. But the initial allure of Soviet Marxism waned when Soviet advice came into conflict with the needs of the Chinese Communists after 1927. Subsequent events widened the gulf of experience between them and the Stalinist leadership, so that by 1949 their ideas of "revolution" and "communism" were no longer congruent. Nonetheless, faced with an embargo imposed by Western nations, Mao Zedong left China for the first time in his life, traveling to Moscow in 1950 to negotiate a treaty of friendship with Stalin.

The treaty provided China with economic development aid and technical assistance: 156 complete heavy industrial plants accompanied by blueprints, technicians, and a model of the planned economy with which to begin industrialization. With this limited but decisive Soviet assistance, the Chinese began the serious task of large-scale industrial development within a framework of building a new socialist society. The dilemma was how to raise the level of agricultural output high enough to support both an enormous population and the burden of financing a modern industrial sector. Utilizing the Soviet experience as a model, the Chinese adopted a command economy governed by a five-year plan that concentrated on heavy industry directed from the center. Investment in agriculture was kept to a minimum, emphasizing gradual collectivization and projects such as land reclamation that required no financial outlays. It took only two years of applying Soviet practices under the First Five-Year Plan (1953–1957) for the Chinese to show signs of rejecting the transplant.

In the winter of 1957–1958, Mao Zedong introduced the Great Leap Forward, the first of China's attempts to innovate a self-reliant alternative to the highly bureaucratized system of central planning inherited from the Soviet Union. The Great Leap Forward swung the national economy away from sober economic rationality towards experimentation with spontaneous and unconventional means of organizing economic production. Decentralized responsibility for drastically increasing agricultural and industrial production replaced the top-down, orderly management of Soviet-style economic planning. Agriculture took precedence over industry and small- and medium-scale industries were developed *in the countryside* as part of a new form of social organization, the commune, modeled on China's revolutionary base areas. The essential characteristics of the Great Leap Forward were a heady optimism that sought to restore the revolutionary ardor and egalitarian ethic of earlier days, the preference for ideologically minded political activists over technical experts as leaders, and the idea of substituting local initiative and ingenuity for scarce capital and remote planners.

Disastrous harvests, mismanagement, and starvation brought back into power the party advocates of Soviet-style planning, who proceeded to restore an economy in shambles. Mao's solution had turned out to be worse than the problem. A scant six years later the Cultural Revolution, a second, nationwide experimental campaign, was launched in the factories and schools of urban China (discussed further in Chapter 6). From 1953 until Mao's death, Chinese policy oscillated between the two competing conceptions of development: Soviet-style centralized economic planning and Mao's periodic experiments with decentralized antibureaucratic mass politics. The developmental pattern of the Maoist period is thus a zigzag fluctuation that includes both Mao's antibureaucratic and antimarket economics and the return to Soviet-style bureaucratic planning that followed. The common denominator distinguishing both aspects of Maoist development strategy from the Japanese model was the absence of a market economy.

Japan's Political Economy: Transplanting the Past

In contrast to the peripatetic fluctuations of Maoist development, the structure of Japanese development has remained remarkably stable since Meiji times despite catastrophic defeat in war and an American-imposed set of reforms. A market economy has been in place since the nineteenth century, but unlike the Western model it has been governed by close collaboration between state officials and the business elite. This partnership between government and business (described in Chapter 2) began with the modernization of the samurai class, one part of which entered government service while the other became a modern business class. Borrowing heavily from German experience, the Meiji state set up an authoritarian and nationalistic political system based on a powerful bureaucracy and military dedicated to achieving international status. Heavy industrial enterprises thought to be essential for military defense and international competitiveness—steel, shipbuilding, railways, telegraphic communications, and armaments—were initiated by the government and were auctioned off to favored capitalists at a loss when they became a financial burden.[8] Thus like Germany, Japan developed a market economy closely but informally nurtured by its association with government in the form of a strong, bureaucratic authoritarian state.

Government collaboration with industry became even more intense in the late 1920s and 1930s in response to various economic crises: The state assumed powers to forge cartels, approve investments that would expand facilities, or persuade cartel members to curtail production. Thus Japan's postwar governmental authority in the area of licensing and administrative guidance of investments has its origins in policies pursued by the Ministry of Commerce and Industry (predecessor of MITI, the Ministry of International Trade and Industry) in conjunction with the military's expansionist program *before* the Second World War. "Unlike other nations defeated in World War II or torn by revolution in the wake of World War II, Japan did not experience a radical discontinuity in its civilian bureaucratic and economic elites."[9] The same "economic general staff" in charge of industrial planning for purposes of military expansion in the 1930s resumed its position after the war, this time in pursuit of an economic "miracle." The planners' restoration was made possible by a shift in U.S. policy away from its immediate postwar preoccupation with democratizing Japanese institutions.

Shortly after Japan's recovery had commenced under American tutelage, cold war pressures led the U.S. government to reverse its earlier policy of dismantling the prewar bureaucratic-industrial complex, thought to have been responsible for bringing about the war. Instead, faced with union activities, Communist Party activities, and potential instability, the United States sought to restore the strength of prewar institutions as a bulwark against Asian communism. To achieve this aim, the state bureaucracy was given free rein to rebuild the private sector corporate giants, the *zaibatsu*, into new forms of concentrated economic power, the *keiretsu*. These provided the engine of Japan's postwar economic miracle, updating their physical plants, diversifying their holdings, and honing their competitive international edge. The driver of the engine was the state bureaucracy, which had ironically benefited from the one reform that remained intact from the early days of U.S. occupation, the constitutional renunciation of war as an instrument of national policy. Limited to a self-defense role, the military was thus eliminated as the only rival strong enough to check the Ministries of Commerce and Industry and of Finance.

Similarities in the Political Economies of Japan and China

By the late 1950s, when ex-colonies in the rest of the Asian Pacific were prepared to launch their own programs of modernization, the Japanese and the Maoist-Chinese models of political economy offered alternative paths of development. Different from one another in fundamental ways to be contrasted in the following section, they nonetheless share some broad underlying similarities that require mentioning. For both countries, modernization first appeared as an external threat, stimulating an intense nationalism that has accompanied the relentless drive of both governments to seek national economic growth and international recognition. In pursuit of their overriding national purpose of catching up with the highly industrialized nations, both China and Japan prized political stability over individual rights. Japanese "exponents of *national* betterment and [national] rights"[10] have accentuated the obligations of Japanese citizens to their state in the same manner as their Communist counterparts in the People's Republic of China. Both stress national unity at the expense of social and individual diversity, relying on authoritarianism—"soft" in Japan, "hard" in China—to ensure political stability.

Strong government has been the result in both Japan and China. A ruling party's dominant faction has acted as a compression chamber to consolidate the diversity of pluralistic demands into a nationally integrated policy. The outcome is two variants of economic planning. In the case of Japan, incremental industrial planning by the state has relied on a private sector market economy to achieve rapid and sustained economic growth *and* a high per capita income. In the case of Maoist China, a centrally administered plan covering every facet of China's economy has relied on political leadership to obtain high industrial growth rates at the expense of producing ample goods and services for consumption.

Different Forms of Property Ownership

While both China and Japan share strong governments with a self-conscious determination to promote industrialization, they have pursued that end by fundamentally different means. The Japanese state from Meiji times to the present has followed a

Western European model of a market economy, maintaining a separation between privately owned productive property and the public responsibility for national economic growth and prosperity. The Chinese regime under Mao followed the socialist principle of the Soviet Union that productive property belongs to all the people and government is responsible for its management. Stalin's formula for a socialist political economy provided the basis for comprehensive administrative planning in virtually every socialist country. In North Korea and Vietnam as well as in China the proletarian party-state substituted for the capitalist entrepreneurial class to pursue economic development on the basis of self-sufficiency, investment in large-scale heavy industry, the legal elimination of markets (black markets resisted elimination), and collectivized agriculture. These policies were geared toward achieving economies of scale, a sustained high rate of savings, investment, and growth, and the elimination of capitalist inequality and waste.

China. Since 90 percent of the Chinese population lived in the countryside in 1949, the first task of the Communists was to reorganize agricultural production. The initial stage was to provide every Chinese household with title to a piece of land, eliminating the despotic power of the landlords in the process. With land reform completed, the government proceeded to collectivize all the land, integrating the tiny, isolated parcels belonging to individual households into successively larger agricultural cooperatives. During the Great Leap Forward cooperatives were urged to form gigantic communes in the hopes that the economies of scale thereby created would free labor from its household moorings to engage in large-scale irrigation works, construction, and land improvement projects and to begin industrializing the countryside, even building backyard steel furnaces. Despite the rapidity with which these profound social changes were undertaken, they were heralded, much to the chagrin of the Soviet leadership, as "true communism."

In the urban areas, which provided a livelihood for only 20 percent of the population as late as 1980,[11] large, medium, and small industrial enterprises were nationalized in stages, so that by 1958 two forms of property generally prevailed in the cities: the state-owned industrial sector (a significant portion of which—34.7 percent of total industrial output value—had been inherited from foreign owners and bureaucratic capitalists)[12] and the collectively owned light industrial workshops. There were also a small number of privately owned service businesses carried out by tradespeople who repaired pots, sharpened knives, and reconditioned furnishings. The effect of both rural collectivization and urban nationalization was to take investment decisions out of private hands, conferring on government the sole responsibility for centrally administering the country's economy. With total state revenues during the Maoist period constituting about 30 percent of the gross domestic product, the government was able to invest a substantial proportion of national income in the further construction of heavy industry.

Thus property ownership in Maoist China constituted a three-tiered hierarchical system with state-owned urban property at the top, collectively owned rural and urban property beneath it, and private plots and small-scale urban enterprises on the very bottom. Despite official obeisance to the importance of agriculture and peasants,

Chinese workers in a state-owned carpet factory.

Source: Photo by Vera Simone.

the state-owned industrial sector was given top priority and enjoyed higher status over collective, largely agricultural, property. State-owned property obtained the lion's share of investment funds from the government, and workers in state-owned factories enjoyed full-time employment at fixed and generally higher wages *regardless of productivity,* with extensive benefits including housing, health care, food subsidies, pensions, and education for their children. Peasants, on the other hand, received only their share of whatever the collective or commune was able to produce in any one year. If, either as a result of government policy or natural disaster, the harvest was dismal, the peasants' standard of living plunged. They had to build their own homes, fund the commune's clinics, schools, and industries, and pay out of their collective earnings for any goods and services required from the outside. Private enterprise, which in the countryside meant selling produce from one's private plots on the open market, though constitutionally recognized for most of the Maoist period, was ideologically suspect and intermittently vulnerable to curtailment whenever a campaign to put "politics in command" was launched.

Japan. Private property carried no such stigma in Japan, where productive property has been owned by individual families since Meiji times. The Land Tax Revision of 1873–1876 transformed feudal estates into cash-producing commodity enterprises by converting farmers' payments-in-kind to fixed cash sums based on the value of the property. Farmers unable to support themselves on the land under these new conditions were forced into urban factories while successful farmers increased their landholdings. Land eventually became concentrated in the hands of absentee landlords and rich peasants. To rectify this, democratize the country, and neutralize the Communists' demands for a comprehensive rural revolution, the U.S. military government after World War II assisted the Japanese in implementing a land reform program. The policy succeeded in producing an agricultural sector of small-scale family-owned farms that, with the help of the government, revitalized domestic agricultural production.

The government increased its role in agricultural production to furnish rural investment funds formerly provided by the landlords and wealthy farmers. It invested heavily in land improvement (reclamation, irrigation, and drainage), price supports, and subsidies in the form of low interest rates. But the accelerated economic growth in agriculture that resulted from these farm supports did not resolve the problem of income disparities between farmers and their urban counterparts, industrial workers. When farmers organized themselves into powerful associations to pressure the government for a fair return for their labor, the government responded by adopting a formula that tied the price of rice to increases in *non*agricultural wages. Thus the government paid the price of supporting highly capitalized, small, family-owned farms when agriculture, unable to benefit from the economy of scale, lost its developmental role in the economy.

Like land, industrial property in Japan has been privately owned since the Meiji state sold off its industrial holdings to private entrepreneurs in the late nineteenth century. But unlike the agricultural sector, where postwar land reform succeeded in breaking up the large concentrations of land, the attempt to break up the concentrated industrial holdings, the *zaibatsu,* was jettisoned by the U.S. military government in response to the exigencies of the cold war. Instead, the U.S. occupation administration sanctioned the restoration of the two-tiered system of property ownership that had characterized prewar Japan. On the lower level, the small- and medium-sized enterprises, which date back to Admiral Perry's forced opening of Japan to the outside world, are today the labor-intensive suppliers of goods and services to the huge modern, capital-intensive corporate conglomerates. This higher level of extremely large, family-based corporate cartels sprang up out of the successful partnership between early "political merchants" and the Meiji state.

These *zaibatsu,* known since their postwar reorganization as *keiretsu* (Mitsui, Sumitomo, Mitsubishi, and Yasuda are the "Big Four"[13]) are typically diversified holdings under tightly interlocking ownership. Each group is a network of corporate alliances among diverse manufacturers organized around a common bank and trading company and exercising direct control of their subsidiaries through their monopoly of credit. Sumitomo, for example, is not a single manufacturer but a group of distinct companies, each of which owns parts of the others. Constituent members of a *kereitsu* do business with one another rather than with outsiders. And their relations with subcontractors (the suppliers of components) are not strictly contractual, calculated on cost-benefit comparisons among competing suppliers. Instead, the individual enterprises of a *kereitsu* incorporate suppliers into a quasi-permanent network based on personal loyalty and protection. Suppliers are flexible in rendering services to their corporate "patrons" on short notice and providing them with customized components—for example, different grades of plastic for seats and dashboards in the case of an automobile company. In return, the automobile manufacturer guarantees its loyalty as a buyer of its client's suppliers, regardless of competition, the state of the market, or the lure of higher profits with alternative suppliers. A similar pattern of "relational contracting" has evolved between state-owned enterprises in China and their small-scale collective rather than state-owned suppliers.[14]

The reciprocal nature of hierarchical relationships between employers and workers within large corporations and between large corporations and their small family-sized subcontractors is not unlike the situation of large state-owned enterprises in China. In both cases, large enterprises offer workers lifetime employment, retirement and health benefits, and bonuses for high productivity (the latter only adopted in China since the reforms of 1984). Promotion is on the basis of seniority, and one is expected to carry out whatever job the firm may need. In China, for example, teachers of Russian in the Institute of Technology, for which the authors worked in 1984–1985, were required to teach English because of the shift in national language priorities. Both in Japan and China, one's firm is not simply a workplace but an identity. A casual question about what you do, among strangers, is likely to elicit the name of your firm, an indication of the importance of "company culture" as a source of identity. In the United States, by contrast, one's identity is more likely to be expressed in terms of one's individual skill or occupation. The company, in Japan and China, is also the source of one's friends, with social activities revolving around company affairs. But in Japanese companies (and here they differ markedly from Chinese *danwei*) all workers, including managers, are motivated to work long, extra hours without additional pay.

Loyalty to one's company is akin to belonging to a family in Japan; it precludes changing employers on the basis of market opportunities or organizing against employers to obtain higher salaries. In China, until recently, the same result was achieved by the state assigning individuals their jobs. The interests of "company unions" in Japan and trade unions in China, unlike those in the West, are identical with those of management. In Japan, and in China since the reforms, they meet annually with management to fix salaries and bonuses. Since executive salaries are directly tied to the salaries of other workers, with both determined by the profits of the firm as a whole, the company avoids an adversarial zero-sum relationship between labor and capital. Unlike China, however, management in Japan actively seeks to maximize the profits of the enterprise by providing every worker with an opportunity for promotion, even if that means proliferating the hierarchy of job gradations. In China, the tendency is still to reward workers collectively. This was demonstrated in the way the reform policy of bonuses was handled: Instead of rewarding workers individually, bonuses were often used to reward everyone equally for contributing to a factory's increased productivity.

The comparison between businesses and workers at the lower end of the property hierarchy in China and Japan is also instructive. In both Japan and China, workers hired by small-business subcontractors receive lower wages, have less job security, and depend for their livelihood on the vagaries of the market. In recessionary periods, therefore, these family-sized businesses can fire their own workers, though in China these are often collectives that are more likely to absorb the loss collectively. These small-scale enterprises are more dependent on the market for profits, but they are protected from going under by the "relational contracting" mentioned above. As a whole, this two-tiered organization of private property in Japan, though it defies some of the rudimentary "laws" of supply and demand, acts as a flexible and stable system in which predictability is maximized for both business, large and small, and the market as a whole. As we have tried to show in the comparison with China's two-tiered arrangement between state-owned and collective or private businesses, the conception of property ownership implied by this organization of production is quite different from the Anglo-American institutionalization of property ownership.

Planning in China's Socialist and Japan's Developmental State

At the beginning of this chapter, the issue of who *plans* economic growth, second only to who *owns* productive property, was identified as the central distinguishing factor between a planned and a market economy. In a mixed economy, according to that discussion, one would expect state planning to be limited to the productive property owned by the state, which could vary between all and none. Japan, however, does not fit this category of a "mixed economy": The state owns virtually no productive property yet is heavily engaged in quite extensive planning. In China, public ownership of industrial and agricultural property put the state in the business of running the economy. In Japan it was the effect of the boom-and-bust cycles of the capitalist market that brought the government into the business of planning. Rather than to *replace* the market, the function of government planning in Japan has been to *improve upon* the market, compensating for its weaknesses and enhancing its capabilities.

How Are the Plans Carried Out?   The imperfections of the market that require state planning include its narrow short-term pursuit of profit, its concern for individual company interests at the expense of the national interest, its encouragement of opportunistic rather than collectively responsible behavior, its obliviousness to structural changes and social dislocations, and its potential for subordinating national to foreign commercial interests.[15] To counteract these market flaws, the government anticipates the shortcomings of the market and plans a specific course of action to remedy them. Known as an industrial policy, the government's plan determines the parameters within which corporations compete, thereby removing some of the uncertainties and undesirable outcomes of market forces for the best interests of the nation.

The government in Japan alters the expansion, contraction, and direction of corporate investments through a "discriminating use of administrative guidance."[16] This form of "preventive intervention" (as distinct from retrospective or regulatory intercession) requires neither the big government nor the coercive power of a command economy. It achieves maximum economic results with a minimum of public participation, although government intervention in the economy is far greater than in any of the Western capitalist market systems. To some observers it is the source of dynamism and flexibility that has enabled Japan to become an economic superpower.

The key difference between government planning in Japan and Maoist China is that in the latter it was centralized, direct, and comprehensive in scope, covering the entire gamut of human activities from economic production to marriage and population growth, while in Japan state planning has never been either comprehensive or compulsory. In industry as well as agriculture the Japanese government deftly mimics Adam Smith's invisible hand. It seeks indirectly and subtly to orchestrate the actions of private entrepreneurs so as to guide the market in a particular direction. Signals are sent by government bureaucrats to private entrepreneurs, indicating specific industries that need to either increase or decrease production in order to enhance Japan's competitiveness in the international market.

Businesses that follow the advice of the Ministry of International Trade and Industry (the central governmental organ responsible for drawing up industrial policy) are rewarded with easy access to capital, tax breaks, and approval of their plans to establish joint ventures or import foreign technology. With some exceptions, most firms abide by government guidelines because the government's control over credit and licensing can be decisive. Although the extent of the state's power over economic decisions remains controversial, the scope of its planning covers a considerable range, from control of electric power rates and bike racing to how much research and development will take place in different product lines.

By contrast, China's economic planning has been characterized by bureaucratic heavy-handedness. In part this is a function of the sheer magnitude of China's economy, but more essentially it results from the centralized structure of micro- as well as macro-economic planning in such a vast country. By its nature, planning the total economy of China is a multifaceted and complex undertaking in which hundreds of millions of people participate. The comprehensive nature of such planning requires marshaling an extraordinary amount of information from all levels in every sector of economic production. The organization that makes this at all possible, by its thoroughgoing penetration of society down to the lowest level, is the Communist Party of China. Economic policy is decided at the top of both the party and the state pyramids (with their overlapping memberships), followed by a complex process of negotiation and accommodation down the ranks. Even today, when reform policy has structurally decentralized decision making and responsibility, overall planning of the entire economy remains a central function of the state, which retains legal ownership of the productive property.

Who Makes the Plans?   Long-range twenty-year goals of the nation and a strategy for achieving them are formulated by the Politburo, whose Standing Committee represents the prevailing consensus among the top leaders of the Communist Party. Called the General Line of the Party, this overarching program of long-run projections sets the parameters within which medium-term (five-year) and annual plans are drawn up principally by the State Planning Commission (SPC) in conjunction with the State Statistical Bureau and the functional ministries. In addition, the SPC determines the money supply, draws up the budget, and effects the nation's balance of payments, akin in some respects to the U.S. Office of Management and Budget, though on a vaster scale.[17] The State Economic Commission (SEC), immediately below the SPC, assumes responsibility for implementing the shorter-term (one-year) plans by directing the ministries and provinces (and so on down the administrative ladder) to fill in the details relevant for production at each of their levels. All government planning agencies are under the jurisdiction of the State Council, which coordinates all the government's economic work and is formally accountable to the National People's Congress, the highest sovereign body.

In Japan, national economic policy is formulated by the ministerial bureaucracy and centers on industrial policy. Agriculture, by now a small and shrinking sector, is protected by the Ministry of Agriculture, and in the legislative or "political" sphere where until recently it has been overrepresented, agriculture had a disproportionate electoral influence. If agriculture has its special voice in the Diet, big industry has its mainstay in the bureaucracy, most powerfully in the Ministry of International Trade and Industry. Industrial policy is fashioned by MITI and enjoys relative immunity from the pressures of partisan politics. Deriving from wartime planning and continued under postwar conditions of privation and disorganization, MITI's authority to plan for Japan's industrial development was strengthened rather than weakened by American-imposed postwar reforms. In its role as "economic general staff," MITI is assisted by the Ministry of Finance along with other ministries and the Economic Planning Board, and its broad policy mandate for industry requires approval by the legislature.

By contrast, industrial planning in Communist China has from the start been buffeted by tidal waves of political change. The preponderantly peasant composition of the Communist Party that assumed power in 1949 poorly qualified it for the specialized economic task of industrial planning. Compounding the problems of this rural-based leadership in implementing Soviet-style planning were the repeated Maoist campaigns, which disrupted the orderly planning process. They increased the participation of large numbers of peasants and workers in production decisions and injected "mass politics" into the planning process. During the Cultural Revolution, for example, newly founded revolutionary committees at all levels, from provincial government down to the factory floor, were empowered to engage in planning activities: to set quotas and determine the resources needed to meet various targets. Final plans specifying production quotas were then negotiated between the enterprises or communes and the planning officials from the center.

But the Maoist attempts at decentralizing economic decision making, represented by the Great Leap Forward and the Cultural Revolution, were only temporary departures from the Soviet planning model, which, when they failed, delivered the economic system back into the hands of the Soviet-type planners. In this zigzag pattern, the Chinese Communist Party throughout the Maoist era found itself struggling to define a strategy that synthesized its own distinctive revolutionary experience with the professionally rigorous bureaucratic demands made by the Soviet system of central planning. A resolution to this tension was brought about only with the Reform policy, which after 1978 pursued the Maoist goal of decentralization using Western-type market devices in place of the collective or mass politics preferred by the founder of new China.

Comparative Strategies for National Development

The question of which economic strategy a country uses to promote its national economic goals is closely linked to historical contingencies. China's Maoist strategy embracing self-sufficiency evolved in response to a hostile capitalist world economy, while Japan's export-led strategy unfolded in response to international economic opportunities (see box). Beginning with a fortunate coincidence, Japan evolved an outward-looking strategy of manufacturing. By producing for export, private industries acquired both the revenue and the upgraded technology to manufacture successively more sophisticated exports. In this fashion, a virtuous spiral of export-led and import-protected growth was set into motion. The contribution of the Japanese state to this product-cycle sequence of development has been fourfold:

1. It balances the need for exports, which require *low* tariffs or a free trade policy, against the need for imports, which require *high* tariffs to protect new domestic technologies;
2. It acts as a scout for international opportunities, canvasing the world's "technology shelf" for industries "which appear to have future potential for achieving an advantageous position over the next decade, *despite a comparatively disadvantageous position at the time*";[18]
3. It functions as a gatekeeper for the protection of domestic industries against their more advanced foreign competitors; and
4. It administratively sets industrial priorities for curtailing some and expanding other investments.

Maoist strategy moved in the opposite direction, turning its back on a hostile international community to concentrate on the country's internal transformation into a socialist state. In the late 1960s, at the pinnacle of Maoist influence, China was being assailed by both the United States and the Soviet Union. Mao pointed to self-reliance,

---

Development by Accident

Japan was launched on an export-led course by an infection that destroyed all Italian and French silkworm eggs in the 1860s, creating an instant market for its profitable and labor-intensive silk industry. Japan's response to this opportunity resulted in the formation of an internationally oriented entrepreneurial class and the accumulation of valuable export revenue for a government attempting to strengthen its autonomy against the demands of the United States.

By the time the European silk industry had recovered, Japan had a thriving silk-export industry that grew exponentially in subsequent years. Thus began Japan's industrial growth in a sequence of stages that looked to the outside world for clues to its direction. While revenues were raised by exporting resources (silkworm eggs), the Japanese state facilitated the technology transfer and investments necessary to produce labor-intensive light industrial exports (silk and cotton textiles). The state then utilized a system of taxes, subsidies, and direct controls to steer production toward higher-growth industries such as shipbuilding, iron and steel machinery, and chemicals in the second stage, knowledge-based industries in the third stage, and high-tech industries at the cutting edge of world technology in more recent decades.

---

in particular the self-sustained communes, as illustrations of how the country could defend itself from outside attack and build socialism at the same time. But after Mao died, and the damage was surveyed, the cost for China of adopting Maoist strategy was high. By reinforcing the age-old inclination to cut itself off from the rest of the world, China's leadership had lost valuable time in building an infrastructure of roads, transport, and communications to provide the foundation for a modern interdependent economy. The sum of China's immense population, scarcity of arable land, and economic insularity was shared poverty, not socialism.

What is remarkable about the Maoist strategy, however, is its unflinching embrace of experimentation. Its combination of opposites was bold in conception and startling in execution, punctuating the rigidity of a highly centralized planning system with periodic outbursts of mass political participation. The turmoil, uncertainty, and precariousness of life for people faced with an entire society oscillating between two such extremes are almost unfathomable. Two results, however, have been both fortuitous and ironic. Despite all the disruptions, China was able to maintain annual average industrial and agricultural growth rates of 11 and 2.5 percent, respectively, throughout this period; and because of the disastrous economic consequences of these experimental disruptions, the Chinese people were more prepared to embrace economic reforms in 1978 than they might otherwise have been.

Patterns of Securing Compliance

Implementation of government strategies both in China and Japan is a top-down process that involves aggregating information, negotiating differences, making compromises, and persuading opponents to comply with policies deemed by centralized elites to be in the best interests of the nation. In China, the elite Communist Party runs like a spinal cord down the center of the entire body politic, providing coherence and backbone to the task of securing compliance with government policy. In Japan, on the other hand, MITI operates more loosely, exercising its muscle through a complex network of cultural ligaments connecting the corporate economy to the state bureaucracy. Although it may appear in the abstract that the Communist Party, with the full weight of its centralized power reaching directly down through the ranks, would be more effective than MITI in implementing its recommendations, this is not necessarily the case. A great deal depends on the resources of those in command and the willingness of those whose compliance is sought.

Securing Compliance in Japan's Market System.   The Japanese bureaucracy has a combination of resources at its disposal to obtain compliance with its planning priorities. The most widely touted is the high individual and corporate savings rate of the Japanese. Through its postal savings system, the Japanese government has access to extensive financial resources with which to offer subsidies, loans, and credits to industries. Household and firm savings thus accumulated provide 40 to 50 percent of the General Accounting Budget, which together with postal life insurance and pensions constitute a valuable source of capital for the government clearly distinct from tax revenues. MITI also uses its authority to set exchange rates, interest rates, taxes, and the prices of selected factors of production to obtain private sector compliance with its economic policies. Most important, however, is MITI's authority to negotiate, persuade, and arbitrate consensus among private sector enterprises to go along with the government's national economic objectives. "With its self-assertiveness, its strong native nationalism, its loyalist posture, . . . and its terrific 'workism,' MITI reminds us of the General Staff Office of the defunct army."[19]

MITI's clout is evidenced in the weight its stamp of approval carries: a virtual guarantee that a corporation will have access to private loans. The nature of this partnership between government bureaucracy and private enterprise sets the Japanese developmental state apart from the Anglo-American form of capitalism. What is the source of cohesion in this partnership? Two aspects will be briefly reviewed: the institutional interlocking of government, financial, and production organizations; and the cultural interlocking of lifetime employment, the organization of the educational system, and the social conception of "the market" in the Japanese understanding.

Industries in Japan are commonly observed to be in collusion with one another. Research has suggested, however, that rather than being a matter of conspiratorial behavior, this collusion results from the way industrial institutions are organized. The industrial group or *keiretsu,* as discussed above, arranges a diversified group of industries under one roof, so to speak, in an interlocking financial arrangement by which each owns a significant portion of the others' stocks and all are tied closely to a single bank. This manner of financing one another's productive enterprises has three important functions. First, it creates a measure of certainty in supply and demand when members buy and sell among themselves. Second, it counteracts hostile takeovers when substantial blocs of each industry's stock are held by loyal partners in the *keiretsu.* Third, it precludes pressure for short-term high dividends on the part of absentee owners from interfering with management of the long-term interests of the corporation.

Similarly, there is collaboration between private enterprise and the government bureaucracy in the form of an intricate web of personal and informal connections. Personal relationships may be the result of marriage or of having attended the same school or the same class at school. Informal contacts that members of MITI have with businesspeople are extensive and ongoing throughout the lifetime of a civil servant's career. The anticipated outcome of these informal connections is "descent from heaven" (*amakudari*), retirement to a comfortable position in one of the private corporations with which one has worked in the Ministry. From this corporate position one is expected to use one's expertise and connections in the Ministry to help the company secure licenses and approval for projects. The Japanese refer to the relationship between a senior ex-bureaucrat and his or her successor in the bureaucracy as "digging around the roots"—preparing the groundwork for a government-business decision.[20] Altogether these relationships cement the bonds that expedite government's continuous consultations, negotiations, and consensus building with private enterprise.

The same group loyalty that binds companies of a *keiretsu* together also works to forge industrywide cooperation. National trade associations such as the Association of Electric Companies and Keidanren, the Federation of Economic Organizations, which promotes the collective interests of large business enterprises, play an important role in securing industrywide cooperation and sectoral economic management. Though they operate as interest groups, trade associations enjoy quasi-public status among Japanese. They negotiate with MITI to shape official government-approved industrywide policies on the basis of which informal agreements are worked out among individual firms to balance government (cost-based) pricing at the apex of the industry with market pressures that operate at the lower end. MITI's role in the entire process is to settle specific disputes between industries (sometimes sending their representatives on a holiday together to foster trust and cooperation) and provide, in general, the disciplined leadership to spur members of an industry to reach an agreement they fundamentally desire but lack the capacity to bring about.

The extraordinary influence MITI exercises in the economic realm is related to the nature of the educational system and its ties to government. Japan's modern educational system from its origins has been designed to grade abilities for employment, with the effect that it reinforces the "company culture" of corporate employment. Each university (and high school) has a fixed number of entrants solely determined on the basis of performance on nationally standardized exams. Students who rank in the highest percentile of exams upon high school graduation go to the top-ranking Tokyo University, with each next lower percentile going to the next lower-ranking university. Educational background based on a two-track system—university graduate track and high school career track—is therefore the basis for entry level into the corporate world. The top percentage of the most prestigious Tokyo University graduates join MITI, with successively lower ranks of graduates recruited by the other ministries and by corporations. Thus standardized nationwide testing determines who gets to go to college and who, therefore, gets which jobs in the government and corporate hierarchy; it is an open system permitting upward mobility.

Implementing Plans in Communist China.   In Mao's China, compliance with the dictates of central planning is secured by the Communist Party through a combination of ideology and organization. The party, reaching down to the village and enterprise level, uses "mass line" techniques to ensure widespread familiarity with the ideological requirements of government policy. Everyone studies the documents in political study groups, a compulsory activity attached to every work unit (factory, school, mine, retail shop, or residential neighborhood); they are also discussed in mass organizations, like the trade unions or the Women's Federation, and can be the subject of mass campaigns. Thus, to a much larger extent than the Japanese, the Chinese use mobilizational techniques to substitute for market incentives. Production decisions in Japan may be shaped by government planning, but they are implemented by the individual company whose effectiveness is measured by market forces and the monetary rewards of workers. In China, though production decisions are similarly shaped by consultations between party officials and economic managers, during the Maoist period their implementation was effected through involuntary political participation and measured by political rewards.

Unlike Japan, where economic decision makers in administrative positions were shielded from the political conflicts within the ruling party, compliance with the economic policy of the Chinese state inextricably became enmeshed with the political wrangling among factions of the Communist Party. Economic performance in China, therefore, reflected the succession of winners and losers in the political infighting among party factions with contradictory visions of *how* China could best accomplish its economic ends. Party advocates of Soviet-style rapid industrialization favored material incentives to promote workers with greater technical competence. When Maoists came to power, however, political criteria were used to discredit the technically proficient, rewarding those who excelled at political mobilization. Throughout the Maoist period, these contradictory approaches alternated with economic production plagued by unpredictable shifts in economic policy.

Thus economic development in China after 1949 continued to feel the reverberations of the revolution that had ushered in modernization on a nationwide and systematic basis. What in Japan was an orderly administrative process of strengthening the entrepreneurial activities in the private sector was in China a turbulent oscillation between a centrally administered economy and its nemesis, the politics of mass participation. Given this marked contrast between the continuity of Japan's nationalistic political economy and the vicissitudes of China's ideologically driven political economy, it is noteworthy that in both countries it was a strong state that facilitated rapid and impressive economic growth. This question of the relationship of a strong state and economic growth became accentuated when, in the 1970s, the newly industrializing countries (NICs) of the Asian Pacific made their dramatic entry onto the world stage.

THE NICs' DEVELOPMENTAL PATTERN

The unexpected ascendance of the NICs into the world of rapidly industrializing countries led to a reexamination of Japan's development. The NICs, like Japan, employed exports to finance industrialization in a product-cycle sequence of stages (as described earlier). Taiwan and South Korea, as colonies, had been exploited for their comparative advantage as part of Japan's regional development of a coprosperity sphere. Similarly, Manchuria in northeast China had initially been industrialized by the Japanese in this manner. This has led Bruce Cumings to stress the regional nature of industrialization in Northeast Asia: "A country-by-country approach is incapable of accounting for the remarkably similar trajectories of Korea and Taiwan." If, as he suggests, Korean and Taiwanese development occurred within an essentially Japanese context,[21] it may be possible to understand China's reform in 1978 as a similar, if long delayed, resort to the Japanese model of development to rectify its problems with a command system of planning. To pursue this line of discourse, we will juxtapose discussion of the reform program in China with the NICs' pattern of industrialization to explore the possibility that China's opening to the international economy represents a regional convergence of political economies.

With what appeared like startling speed, Taiwan, South Korea, Singapore, and Hong Kong had emerged from Third World poverty and "backwardness" into the front ranks of industrializing countries. In contrast to other developing countries around the world, East Asian NICs exhibited sustained high growth rates (see Table 5.1), a relatively equitable distribution of the product of development, a continuing capability to alter domestic economic structures in alignment with changing international circumstances, and a powerful state capable of mobilizing and deploying domestic economic resources. The question for both scholars and political leaders is how to explain this winning combination of characteristics. Four possibilities have been suggested:[22]

1. It is a result of embracing a market economy with a free trade policy;
2. It is a consequence of "special circumstances" unlikely to be easily duplicated;

TABLE 5.1   GDP Average Annual Growth Rate (in Percent)

Country	1970–1980	1980–1990
China	5.2	9.4
Hong Kong	9.2	6.9
Indonesia	7.2	5.6
Japan	4.3	4.2
Malaysia	7.9	5.7
Philippines	6.0	1.1
Singapore	8.3	6.6
South Korea	9.6	9.6
Taiwan	9.7	7.7
Thailand	7.1	7.9

Source: World Development Report 1993, Oxford University Press, pp. 240–41. *Taiwan Statistical Data Book,* 1993, Council for Economic Planning and Development, Republic of China, pp. 26–27.

3. It is attributable to a shared Confucian heritage emphasizing hard work, frugality, hierarchy, and harmony; and

4. It is the consequence of economic planning by a strong state in close collaboration with a market-driven, export-oriented economy.

After examining the ways in which the political economies of the NICs differ among themselves and from the Chinese or Japanese experience, the reader should be able to determine which of these explanations, in what combination, is most helpful to understand the dynamics of economic development in the Asian Pacific.

Embracing the Market Economy and Free Trade

That Hong Kong, Singapore, South Korea, and Taiwan are all market economies pursuing an open policy of international trade is indisputable. The British colony of Hong Kong is closest among the NICs to the Western market model of a political economy: The government follows a hands-off policy, leaving economic affairs to the international and Chinese business communities. Although highly diversified business groups have existed since the early days of British rule, the preponderance of business enterprises consists of small- and medium-sized manufacturing companies dependent on the flow of refugee labor from the mainland of China. Adhering for the most part to its British colonial role as entrepôt, Hong Kong has industrialized alongside the NICs while remaining atypical by comparison. This means that many of the observations below about the role of the state are not applicable to Hong Kong.

The controversies among observers center on the deviations in the other three NICs from the Western prototypes of a market economy: the substantial state-owned sector in the case of Taiwan, the concentration of economic power in huge conglomerates in the case of South Korea, the heavy reliance on multinational capital in the case of Singapore, and the extensive state intervention in the economies of all three of these NICs. These departures from the Western model raise questions about what a market economy means in the context of Asian Pacific economic development.

Singapore, a city-state like Hong Kong, has a highly internationalized economy, 70 percent of which is owned by multinationals. The shortage of local entrepreneurs, most of whom are in small-scale business, contrasts with the mainly foreign-dominated sector of Singapore's large industrial, export-oriented, high-tech private enterprises, attracted to the island by a highly educated workforce and a modern, sophisticated infrastructure.[23] In both South Korea and Taiwan, on the other hand, state-owned enterprises have played a pivotal role in economic development. The South Korean government, through its state-controlled banks, has exercised a decisive control in shaping the contours of economic growth. In industry as well as external trade, a few very large, privately owned industrial groups, *chaebol,* such as Samsung, Daewoo, and Hyundai, exhibit a remarkable resemblance to the Japanese giants, the *keiretsu* described earlier. At present, the Korean economy is controlled by thirty to fifty of these conglomerate business groups, each owned and managed by a single family. Although the *chaebol* have tended to be more dependent on the Korean state for credit and access to foreign capital than their Japanese counterparts, they have increasingly demonstrated an inclination towards independence from the South Korean state bureaucracy.[24]

In contrast to South Korea, Taiwan has the largest sector of state-owned corporations of all the NICs, and they are disproportionately represented among Taiwan's largest corporations in key industrial sectors. They tend also to be controlled by mainlanders who monopolize government office, while the privately owned sector is composed mostly of small- and medium-sized enterprises predominantly owned by Taiwanese. Based on the criterion of private ownership of property, there is little doubt that the NICs, like Japan, qualify as market economies. Yet there is the separate question: Is it the market forces in these East Asian countries that have driven economic growth, or has the market been propelled, as in Japan, by the state?

Some have argued that trade itself, the adoption of an export-oriented industrialization (EOI) policy, ignited the explosion of industrial activity in the NICs during the 1960s. This line of reasoning suggests it was the early switch of the "little tigers" to an export-led development that triggered their impressive growth rates. With fewer natural resources than Japan, the NICs had no choice but to export manufactured goods if they were to develop at all. They shifted away from the high tariffs of earlier import-substitution policies to lower tariffs that would promote exports of labor-intensive manufactured goods. The sequence was the same as Japan's, except that the NICs followed one step behind in the product cycle: As Japan moved on to high-tech information equipment, the NICs moved into the production of electronic equipment. However, the successful economic ascent of the NICs left them with a far higher trade dependence than Japan, as shown in Table 5.2. The NICs' dependence on Japanese imports (both of technology and capital) has increased as Japan has surpassed the United States as an exporter of intermediate goods and technology. As a result South Korea, Taiwan, Hong Kong, and Singapore are import-dependent on Japan and export-dependent on the United States.

"Special Circumstances"

But the virtuous spiral of economic development created by trade requires an initial outlay of substantial amounts of capital as well as accessible markets capable of absorbing the exports. How did the NICs satisfy these preconditions? One of the explanations for the NICs' unusually rapid development is offered by those who argue that "special circumstances" existed early in their development and gave them a non-replicable advantage.

TABLE 5.2   Ratios of Foreign Trade Turnover to GNP

Country	Percent
Japan	20
South Korea	54
Taiwan	83
Hong Kong	160
Singapore	189

Source: William Nester, *Japan's Growing Power Over East Asia and the World Economy* (New York: St. Martin's Press, 1990), p. 86.

Unlike China or Japan, the NICs are creatures of unusual circumstance. Two are ministates; two are fragments of countries produced by the international rivalry between the United States and the former Soviet Union. As frontline states in the United States' war against communism, South Korea received an annual average of $270 million in economic aid from the United States between 1953 and 1958, and Taiwan received $100 million annually between 1951 and 1965. Military assistance was twice that amount. Singapore and Hong Kong enjoyed advantages from their earlier status as entrepôts: an urbanized population, high literacy rates, a skilled workforce, and long experience in trading internationally. Taiwan and South Korea acquired many of their infrastructural foundations under Japanese colonial rule: a modernized agricultural system, a network of roads and communications, high literacy rates, and linkages with the international economy. American advisers after the Second World War assisted in land reform (as they did in Japan), thus completing the modernization of agriculture begun under the Japanese. As a result of these historical "special circumstances," the NICs were all well located for international trade and ready to "take off" economically at a time of expanding world markets.[25]

Confucian Values

A variation of the "special circumstances" perspective on the economic success of the NICs is rooted in the observation of their common Confucian background. As Chinese-based communities, it is argued, Singapore, Hong Kong, Taiwan, and South Korea share cultural values and traditions that have contributed substantially to their rapid industrialization. Hard work, frugality, the paternalistic family, education, and the ethical responsibilities of political leaders are values that have conditioned Asians growing up in a Chinese cultural setting. It is suggested that "entrepreneurial familism" has provided an economic motor for capitalist development in Confucian-based NICs, particularly in Taiwan and Hong Kong. The paternalistic management of family-owned enterprises fosters the flexibility and inventiveness that enables them to be competitive in a high-risk, rapidly changing international market. And a high level of trust among family members permits cost-cutting financial and labor arrangements, a centralized form of decision making, and informal mechanisms of control and accountability that promote secrecy and preserve entrepreneurial autonomy.[26]

Though it is difficult to measure *the extent* to which these values have contributed to such factors of development as universally high savings rates, the absence of unionization, and compliance with the authority of the state, they undoubtedly have played a role in laying the foundation for a strong authoritarian state that is expected to actively intervene in the economy. Certainly, the belief that a state should be strong and exercise sufficient authority to administer a well-managed economy is widespread in East Asia.

The Role of the State in Economic Planning

The single most compelling factor in the economic development of South Korea, Taiwan, and Singapore is the extensive and intensive ways in which government has pushed economic levers and pulled financial strings to accomplish economic development. The prominence of the state in promoting, financing, shaping, and nudging the economy towards economic growth places the NICs in the same category as Japan and China. All have strong authoritarian regimes aware of the necessity of modern economic growth for their national strength and survival. Among the conditions provided by the governments of the NICs to promote economic growth are land reform, a literate labor force, capital for investments, raw materials, a strong industrialization ideology on the part of the government, a well-trained, efficient, and relatively incorrupt bureaucracy, and institutions for linking the public and private sectors.

Land Reform.   As we have already seen in the case of Japan and China, the initial task of the state in fortifying itself and laying the groundwork for a modern productive system is land reform. For the entrepôts, Hong Kong and Singapore, this was not a problem, but in Taiwan and South Korea, where land was the primary source of wealth, it was essential. Land provides not only food to support a growing nonagricultural sector but raw materials for industry, commodities for export, surplus capital for investment, and labor to fill the nonagricultural jobs.

Though in both Taiwan and South Korea the Japanese had already modernized agricultural production for their home consumption, tenancy rates remained high after the war, with an elite in each case inheriting the greatest proportion of land from the Japanese. The Guomindang leaders who fled to Taiwan in 1949, realizing the significance of land reform as a factor that cost them control of the mainland and in any event not landowners themselves, were eager not to make the same mistake. With the help of American advisers, therefore, they redistributed the land to create a nation of smallholders eager to invest and innovate. This eliminated a powerful internal source of resistance to industrial development and redirected idle capital away from land speculation into manufacturing and commercial enterprises. South Korea, also on the advice of the United States, undertook land reform with similar results. Though land reform did not make the peasantry rich, it did create a more equitable income distribution, which additionally strengthened the centralized authority of the state.[27]

Labor Force.   Another benefit of land reform in South Korea and Taiwan was that it made available a disciplined and low-cost labor force, an advantage that Singapore and Hong Kong had by virtue of being urban centers that attracted a large inflow of refugees. The NICs were in fact unique, as Alice Amsden points out, in garnering world markets "on the *almost* exclusive basis of low wage rates . . . a truly new international division of labor."[28] The Korean government, building on what the Japanese had begun, invested heavily in education, reducing illiteracy, defined as the absence of any schooling whatever, from 40 percent of the work force in 1946 to virtually nil by 1963.[29] It is not only the level but the content of education that has contributed to the NICs' comparative advantage, as Robert Wade points out. In Taiwan and South Korea an increase in the ratios of skilled to unskilled or only basically skilled people in the labor force over the past forty years has enabled their economies to sustain a comparative advantage in progressively more skill-intensive, higher-wage productive enterprises. By ensuring an influx of higher-skilled people into the workforce, government policy in these countries lowers the relative cost of skilled labor, promoting investments in industries that require shifting combinations of skill levels.[30]

Capital.   In the area of capital formation for business investment the government has played an equally activist role in the NICs (with the exception of Hong Kong). The governments of South Korea and Taiwan received massive amounts of foreign aid and military assistance from the United States, providing them with both money and know-how with which to powerfully influence the market. South Korea also received American surplus products under very favorable terms. In addition, the governments of Korea, Taiwan, and Singapore promoted domestic savings and the inflow of foreign capital in a number of important ways. Singapore, for example, introduced a new financial institution to mobilize private sector savings, the Central Provident Fund. The CPF is a means of obtaining forced savings that, while designed to secure economic provisions for old age and health care, is also used by the government to provide housing and other investments for the private sector. Taiwan invested in public sector industries and facilitated the transfer of financial resources from informal (gray) underground networks to legitimate, aboveboard financial institutions. And the government of South Korea owns and controls the banks that, through discriminating lending policies, exercise a considerable influence over investment decisions. Thus, even more than in Japan, government in the NICs has played a dominant role in shaping the nature and direction of economic expansion through its privileged access to domestic savings and foreign investments.

Industrialization Ideology and Efficient Bureaucracy.

Critical to the activist role of government in promoting savings, obtaining resources, and attracting foreign capital are a strong industrialization ideology and a well-trained, efficient, and relatively incorrupt bureaucracy. The core of these officials in the case of South Korea and Taiwan has been American-educated economists, technocrats, aid administrators, and foreign experts working for such organizations as the World Bank, the International Monetary Fund, and the United States Agency for International Development. Singapore, reflecting its origins as a British imperial outpost, along with the British colony of Hong Kong, tend to have British-educated economists and experts both as officials and as advisers. Taiwan is noted for a concentration of engineers among its administrators.

The common denominator of these technocrats, reflective of both their training and the policies of the lending institutions from which they obtain investment funds, is a commitment to investing for economic growth as an end in itself. We call this *industrialization ideology* to differentiate it from liberal, socialist, or communist ideology, according to which there is an end quite distinct from the pragmatic considerations of how best to promote economic growth. Liberal ideology, for example, indicates that free markets and free trade are ends in themselves that ought not to be sacrificed at the altar of growth for growth's sake. Industrialization ideology, however, is a pragmatic adherence to whatever achieves economic growth as measured by the quantities of goods and services produced, labor productivity, and the like.

Public-Private Sector Linkages.   The major way in which governments in South Korea, Taiwan, and Singapore promote economic growth is by linking their public sector policies with those of the private sector. Financially, this is done in a number of different ways. In Singapore the government has established control over savings, which the private sector has responsibility for investing. Thus the government is an intermediary between savers and investors, effectively forging a collaboration with substantial power for the public sector.[31] In South Korea the government achieves this "merging" somewhat more coercively through its state-owned banks, which are the major source of loans for the private sector. But on the positive side, the South Korean government has also monetarily compensated firms for financial losses incurred as a result of exporting commodities at the government's suggestion.[32] In Taiwan private and public sectors are intermeshed through the government's ownership of large corporations in such basic industries as petroleum, steel, and electric power.

Other mechanisms utilized by government in all three NICs include providing an array of incentives for investment in specific areas, control of prices (which in the case of South Korea begins with the price of money), and informal pressures put on manufacturers to procure a larger share of their inputs domestically. The overall principle of public-private relationships is one of cooperation among management, labor, and government in the formulation of plans, much as it is in Japan. In Singapore and Taiwan, the cooperative alliance is among government, foreign enterprises, and local business.

Assessing the NICs' Development

The pattern of economic development in the NICs (with the exception of Hong Kong) is broadly similar to the Japanese model of political economy. The government in each case assumed initiative for creating and has continued to pilot industrial market economies dependent almost entirely upon trade with the outside world, most importantly with Japan and the Western industrialized nations but increasingly with the remaining Southeast Asian nations. By targeting exports that take advantage of a disciplined labor force and by selectively promoting imports that drive the economy up the product-cycle ladder, the government engineers a dynamic market relationship between international demand and domestic supply. A local entrepreneurial class has been strengthened in Taiwan and South Korea, though in Singapore it is the community of international entrepreneurs that has benefited.

"Special circumstances" have played an important role in the NICs' development. In South Korea, for example, a strong military, built up by U.S. aid and training, took over the government in 1961 and systematically engineered economic growth. Under military rule, the windfall profits made by some under the corrupt Rhee regime were used in a new, more growth-oriented direction, giving rise to an entrepreneurial class.[33] In Taiwan the National People's Party, motivated by its defeat on the mainland, embraced land reform, purged its military of corruption, and used martial law to strengthen the state in all areas of life. The role of Confucianism in the development of the NICs has been to preclude any independent opposition on the part of either organized labor or organized interest groups that might fragment the "grand alliance." Thus strong states bolstered by an anticommunist mission, a well-trained military, and Confucian values of hard work, frugality, discipline, and authority undertook planned economic modernization in collaboration with the "free world."

The intriguing aspect of the NICs' political economy is the combination of an authoritarian political regime, economic planning by government, and a market system of exchange. An exchange market, the centerpiece of capitalism, is put into place and directed by the central planning of authoritarian governments. The aspect of this system that sets it apart from the development pattern of the People's Republic of China is that economic planning by the government is market conforming. Indeed, the performance of the market as a stimulant for economic growth in the experience of the NICs was not lost on the socialist countries of East Asia. The recurring inefficiencies and economic stagnation of their planned economies led China and Vietnam in the late 1970s, and North Korea more recently, to take steps in the direction of opening their economies to world trade and the introduction of market mechanisms. This has raised far-reaching questions about the direction of political economy in the Asian Pacific region. Will reforms in the socialist countries lead them to political economies similar to those in Japan and the NICs? Will all the Asian Pacific countries experiencing economic success with some combination of market forces and authoritarian political control then move towards greater democracy? Or will the combination of authoritarian government, whether hard or soft, and a market-based economy become an enduring pattern of development in the twenty-first century?

THE SEARCH FOR A SOCIALIST GUIDED MARKET

Between 1978 and 1985 a series of policies was adopted in China and Vietnam to reform the Soviet-style or Stalinist model of political economy. Although many of these problems had been recognized all along, they assumed critical importance in the changed international circumstances of the late 1970s. The retreat from Vietnam by first the United States and then the Soviet Union drew attention to Japan's position as economic superpower and the impressive strides of the NICs following closely in her footsteps. Though it was not a question of copying either Japan or the NICs, their experiences provided the socialist countries with an Asian alternative to Western-type capitalism and its liberal democratic politics. Looked at from the perspective of this "Japanese model," the socialist or Stalinist pattern of development revealed not merely the full extent of its flaws but a viable direction in which to move to eliminate them. What the Japanese model demonstrated and the NICs confirmed about a successful pattern of development for late industrializers was the efficacy of a market economy guided by authoritarian government planning.

Reform Policy in China

Although the Maoist regime had delivered on some of its promises—an average annual industrial growth rate of 11 percent, full employment, an impressive array of widely distributed social services—the economic system was unable to increase either the standard of living or the labor productivity of its people. The reform policy unveiled at the Third Plenum of the Eleventh Party Congress in 1978 envisioned a revitalization of the economy by opening up to the outside world, emphasizing light and consumer industries, decentralizing production decisions, introducing market mechanisms to determine prices, and separating political power from economic decision making. Over a decade later, these reform policies remain controversial both inside and outside China. Do they portend the gradual shift away from socialism towards a capitalist market economy? Or do they indicate, as the leadership claims, a new intermediate step on the road to communism called "market socialism"?

The Household Contract System.   Economic reform made its debut in the countryside. Referred to as a "household responsibility" system, the policy reversed collectivization by dividing up the land belonging to the production team (the lowest rung of a commune) and leasing it back to individual households. The land was as meticulously parceled out as it had been under land reform: Each household received some of the best-, some of the medium-, and some of the worst-quality land of the team. Leases at first were for fifteen years but later extended to fifty, with the right of children to inherit their parents' land. Each household decided what and how much to produce on the basis of a contract system. The household had a base contract with the state, a tax, to provide a specified quota of a particular crop at a fixed price; anything produced over and beyond that could be sold to the state at a higher (closer to the market) price or to any private party. Each household was thus rewarded on the basis of its work.

Township Industry and Rural Markets.   By the end of 1983 China had reverted to full-scale family farming, with 94 percent of peasant households operating within the system of household responsibility.[34] The range of choices for rural households widened as the government permitted peasants to sublease their land and take up new occupations—providing transport, for example, or starting a new business in the township. As households that excelled at commodity agriculture leased more land from others who gave up farming and moved off into townships, the rural economy diversified and large numbers of people migrated off the land into the townships, the old seats of commune government. *Specialized households* were promoted by the government to concentrate on a narrow range of farm or nonfarm production, raising their level of technical expertise in a single area. In some cases entire rural areas turned into rural commodity markets, specializing in one commodity—all the varieties of buttons, for example, or electrical appliances—and selling wholesale across the nation through the services of peasants-turned-traders.[35]

While some farmers became "10,000-yuan farmers," the equivalent of millionaires, the townships became thriving centers of rural industry. At the core were the industrial collectives that had prospered under the commune system and now operated under contract to the township. Industries like cement and fertilizer, already producing large shares of total national output by the early 1970s, now were joined by a range of industries producing goods and services for rural households. There were small individual entrepreneurs, larger private entrepreneurs who employed eight or more workers, and collectives. Returning to family initiative and incentives produced a lively rural economy, at least in those areas well endowed with factors of production.

Urban Economic Reform.

In 1984, economic reform in the urban areas received the green light in a set of directives described as "socialism with Chinese characteristics." The major problems that inspired reform were the declining efficiency and poor quality of production in state-owned enterprises, the procurement bottlenecks that resulted in underutilization of capacity, the slow pace of innovation, and the lack of separation between governmental functions and enterprise management that stifled worker productivity. Three long-range solutions were envisioned: one was managerial autonomy for enterprises, the second was an industrial contract responsibility system, and the third was price reform. By divesting government of its management role in the economy, making enterprise managers responsible for their profits and losses free from party interference, reducing the scope of mandatory planning, and increasing the role of the market correspondingly, reformers hoped to combine the vigor of the market with the promise of socialism. *Guided Planning* was used to describe the government's function vis-à-vis those goods and services operated in accordance with market forces.

Managerial Autonomy.

To stimulate production in the 400,000 state-owned industrial enterprises employing about 80 million people, the reforms recommended separating ownership from management, that is, the day-to-day control of a plant's operations. The owners, theoretically the state as representative of all the Chinese people but actually the party officials, were to remove themselves from managerial decision making, allowing enterprises to become "independent economic entities," with enterprise managers responsible for the profits and losses of their firms, for determining job descriptions and performance criteria for workers, and for hiring and firing employees. Laws were to be developed to convert individual enterprises into "legal persons with certain rights and duties." Party officials, who for almost thirty years were in the driver's seat of these state-owned enterprises, were now to retreat to the caboose, from where they should "provide active support" without interfering in the enterprise manager's job. Party officials were to confine their activities to carrying out party policy. What this was more precisely was not clear, a loophole that continued to plague party-manager relations during the first decade of reform.

Industrial Contract Responsibility.

As with households in the countryside, workers and their factory director contracted with the state to turn over a specified amount of taxes and profits, keeping for their own use "any or almost any amount above the set quota."[36] Under this contract system, applicable in particular to the larger state-owned enterprises, factory managers would be competitively selected through a system of public bidding. Entire enterprises would also be subject to evaluation: If they could not turn out inexpensively priced commodities of good quality they would be eliminated. By 1986, 75 percent or 9,270 of the 12,380 larger state-owned industrial enterprises had introduced the contract responsibility system, though there were few, if any, reports of enterprises going bankrupt.[37] For those large-scale state-owned enterprises *not* engaged in vital productive activities, it was suggested they voluntarily become joint-stock companies with limited liability. They would thus become shareholding enterprises with stocks purchased by workers as well as individuals outside the enterprise, though the government retained 51 percent of the stock. Management was in the hands of a board of directors. This arrangement would also apply to joint ventures with foreign investors.[38]

Price Reform.   Decontrolling prices is at the heart of economic reform, but politically it is the most nettlesome part of the process to effect. When the prices of products are fixed according to plan they reflect political considerations rather than economic costs. Price reform, therefore, entails reducing the number of products controlled by centralized planning, freeing their prices to rise to a level dictated by the market, while prices of key commodities are kept artificially low by mandatory state controls. In the mid-1980s hundreds of commodity prices were still set by the State Council. Now, according to the World Bank, China conducts "more than half (perhaps two-thirds) of all transactions at market prices."[39] The inevitable corollary of deregulating these prices has been the pressure of demand on available supply. As investment expands and economic growth accelerates in the private sector, consumers with expanded buying power face the lack of available goods and spiraling inflation.

The repercussions of price reform have been politically volatile: Runaway inflation, increased inequality, a frenzy of investment activity, speculative ventures, bad investments, duplication of efforts, and fraudulent deals accompanied the spurt of economic growth in the private sector. The government's response to these problems of an overheated economy and the discontent they aroused among people has been to apply the brakes to economic expansion, attempting to reimpose administrative controls, raise interest rates, and reassert its political clout in the public arena. But it has met with only partial success.

This is because the administrative decentralization brought about by greater enterprise autonomy and managerial control over production decisions has resulted in the central government's loss of control over such critical elements as the growth of the money supply. Now in command of only half of the nation's GNP, the central government finds itself with fewer levers to compel compliance on the part of enterprises at provincial, local, and municipal levels. These enterprises can ignore the government's directives and entreaties to cut back their investments because alternative sources of funds are now available to them. New decentralized financial institutions created by the State Council in its implementation of market-oriented financial reform can extend credit and make loans without approval from the higher-ups, depriving the central government of its control over investment priorities. Thus enterprises at the local and regional levels can collude with private financial sources other than banks to bypass the policies and authority of the central government.

As a result the central bank, the People's Bank of China, has been incapable of controlling the money supply in the manner of the Federal Reserve Bank in the United States. Even its authority over the specialized state banks, like the People's Construction Bank of China or the People's Agricultural Bank of China, is limited. These state banks, like the central bank, are primarily intermediaries, cashiers that allocate funds largely to insolvent state enterprises according to state plan. If the central government were to raise interest rates to reflect the true cost of money the way the informal money market does, it would either have to let firms go bankrupt or increase their subsidies to keep them afloat. Thus the central leadership is caught between a rock and a hard place: inflation on the one hand or mass unemployment on the other.

A Two-Tiered Ownership Structure.   Along with quality control for the larger state-owned enterprises now managed by their factory directors, the reforms encourage experimenting with diverse, flexible forms of cooperative management and economic associations among state-owned, collective, and individual sectors of the economy. Between 1985 and 1987, all small-sized state-owned enterprises with fixed assets of less than U.S. $400,000 were leased out under contract to individuals or cooperatives for a period of five years in the hopes of loosening up the rigidities of production in the state-owned sector. In this category is the vast array of retail services, repair, light industry, catering businesses, transportation, and construction. These private businesses made their own contractual arrangements independently of state supervision, paying only rent and taxes to the state. According to one estimate, this sector of private business accounted for half of the value of total gross industrial output in China in 1985.[40]

These reforms in effect create a two-tiered ownership structure similar to the one existing in Japan. The upper tier consists of large, key enterprises akin to trusts or industrial combines, while the lower tier consists of massive numbers of small enterprises privately run by cooperatives, individual households, or some mixed form of ownership. The private sector does not require state financing yet produces supplies for the large, state-owned enterprises on a more flexible basis than central planning could ever do. It fills the perennial gaps produced by shortages in the planned economy and also absorbs the growing number of workers no longer guaranteed or assigned jobs by the state. Last but not least, it injects innovation and resourcefulness into the top-heavy state-owned enterprise system by creating space for worker initiative. Not only are workers in small private businesses free to manage their affairs through the market, but workers in larger, state-owned enterprises producing *nonessential* commodities can own shares in their enterprises, presumably enhancing their stake and initiative in the enterprise.[41]

Contrasting Purpose and Performance.   Economic reforms represent an attempt to move away from directive planning toward a new form of guided planning. Their purpose is to reproduce within a socialist framework the social, economic, and psychological dynamics of advanced commodity production, which elsewhere in the world were achieved within a capitalist framework. According to Gordon White, three elements are required to find a more productive balance between state control and decentralized initiative and flexibility:

1. the capacity to strengthen technical and institutional information-gathering and communication as well as upgrade new skills;
2. the facility to restructure the overly bureaucratized management system, recruiting and promoting cadres on the basis of technical skills; and

3. the capacity to establish a more rational, less competitive relationship between central and local governments and between different layers of local government.[42]

Though clearly the data is far from being in on the performance of these reforms in practice, there is some preliminary evidence to indicate that it is not merely a question of economic policy but a profoundly political and social process bound to encounter technical problems, institutional resistance, political challenges, and the cultural persistence of older social attitudes and ideological predispositions.[43] In her study of "Urban Reform and Relational Contracting in Post-Mao China," Dorothy Solinger observes that, despite the formal organizational changes brought about by the reforms, the underlying patterns that were built up among bureaucrats and businesspeople under the old party-state system still persist. There is relational contracting between firms based on the loyalty and mutual trust of a long-term commitment that is sheltered from market forces. As in Japan, these relationships, often between large firms and their smaller suppliers, are appropriate to "transactions of a recurring and nonstandardized kind," in which specific readjustments can be made on short notice and short-term losses can be sustained in exchange for certainty and predictability. Thus the "marketizing' of the Chinese economy has resulted in a market system wherein economic exchange paradoxically continues to be structured along lines very similar to those that existed under a more centrally-planned economy."[44]

China's Open Policy and Special Economic Zones (SEZs).   The overall context for China's economic reforms is the opening of the country to the outside world. China's open door policy differs from liberalization in establishing fourteen coastal cities plus the island of Hainan as specialized autonomous zones to attract and absorb foreign technology and capital. These zones are like gigantic industrial parks the government equips with infrastructure and special laws to facilitate international commerce. Their short-term purpose is to exploit their coastal advantages to compete actively in the global marketplace. Foreign direct investment is enticed by the availability of cheap labor and advantageous tax and trade regulations to develop export-oriented industries utilizing imported technology and raw materials. The foreign exchange China earns from its export-led growth can then be used to buy technology for development of capital-intensive heavy industry and mechanized agriculture. The technique is identical to that used by the NICs, though the long-term objective is singularly Chinese: to link the country's vast rural interior with its urban sector in the process of entering into the competition of the global marketplace.

Reform Policy in Vietnam

Establishing a modern political economy in Vietnam has been complicated by both its colonial heritage and the protracted war that further split the country in two until 1975. Vietnam inherited three distinct regional political economies from the French, each separately linked to the international market. The South specialized in rice and rubber production, mostly based on plantation agriculture, while the North was dominated by mining. Trade between North and South was limited under the French, each region oriented toward export commodities, with the railroad, which was to link the two, remaining incomplete until 1936. The only functioning trade link between North and South was coastal shipping.

The Impact of the United States.   This split between North and South was exacerbated by the United States, which supported an economy in the South heavily dependent on military aid and imported goods. The inequities in the land tenure system that led South Vietnamese peasants to support the Communists did finally prompt the United States to undertake land reform in the South, accompanied by a "green revolution" with its application of chemical fertilizers and new seed strains. By 1973 one-third of the cultivated area in the South had been mechanized and modernized. Thus while North Vietnam's development followed a course similar to China's, from land reform to collectivization, which brought with it increased yields, in South Vietnam the beneficiary of land reform (paid for by the United States) was a strong, privately based, highly capitalized agricultural system.

After unification in 1975, therefore, the North faced innumerable problems attempting to extend collectivization and Soviet-style central planning to the South. The withdrawal of American aid to the South and winding down of Chinese aid to the North combined with resistance to collectivization in the South to reduce farm output in both parts of the country. The economic situation deteriorated further under the impact of Vietnam's intervention in Cambodia in 1978 and war with China in 1979. To punish Vietnam for the Cambodian invasion the United States imposed an embargo on all trade and financial relations and opposed any aid from the World Bank, IMF, and other international lending agencies. American allies followed the U.S. move, further limiting Vietnam's access to the world market, foreign aid, and investment. With the economy in crisis, the government responded by making modest moves toward reform that eventually were incorporated into a more comprehensive program of "renovation" known as *doi moi.*

Economic Reforms.   The general direction of reform in Vietnam is the same as in China: to make the transition from a centrally planned economy to a market economy under state direction. In the early phase of piecemeal reform from 1979 to 1981, collectivization was put on hold, and practices that had sprung up at the grass roots as unauthorized ways of coping with the economic crisis were legitimized and extended. After 1981 the contract system was instituted, allowing individual households to lease land from the cooperatives in return for delivering a fixed quota of their crop and selling the rest on the open market. These measures stimulated economic recovery but also contributed to inflation and, especially in Saigon (renamed Ho Chi Minh City), to smuggling and speculation.

Following a brief period of conservative retrenchment in 1982–1985, the party adopted *doi moi* in 1986. A more thorough but flexible approach to devising new forms of ownership and management under the leadership of the Communist Party, *doi moi* involves three related elements: expanding the private sector and the market, decentralizing managerial authority, and cultivating connections to the world economy. Private enterprise was extended to crafts and small industry, and businesses in the South that had been nationalized after unification were returned to their former owners. Lengthened terms for land usage contracts meant de facto family ownership of land. The national currency was allowed to float, and adjustment in interest rates brought inflation under control. Policies were adopted to phase out state subsidies, lift price controls, and require state enterprises to base prices on the cost of production. Privatization of state enterprises was delayed until early 1994, when the first sales of shares in a few companies began.

The enactment of a foreign investment law brought in capital from Europe, other Asian countries, and Vietnamese expatriates. The state monopoly on foreign trade was ended, exporting enterprises were allowed to enter contracts directly with foreign importers, and four cities were authorized to establish their own export-import corporations. Foreign governments gradually ceased to follow the U.S. embargo, and the United States itself relaxed objections to multilateral agencies lending to Vietnam and finally in February 1994 lifted the embargo on American business dealings with Vietnam.

Economic renovation, as in China, has brought costs as well as benefits, among them increased unemployment, greater inequalities in income and regional differences, corruption, and environmental deterioration. But the reformists seem to have successfully fended off objections from the conservatives in the party and to be proceeding on the course they have chosen to raise the living standard of their country.

Laos Embarks on Economic Reform

Somewhat later than Vietnam, and in response to similar problems, the communist government of Laos has also embarked on a course of economic reform. Beginning in 1986, controls on the price of rice and other foods were ended, the currency allowed to float, and trade freed. Some state enterprises have been sold and aid and guidance solicited from the World Bank, IMF, UN Development Program, the Asian Development Bank, and foreign governments.

The results are a 6 to 7 percent GDP growth rate, rising export earnings, currency stability, reduced inflation, and a degree of prosperity in the capital, Vientiane. But Laos's potential for sustained growth is limited by lack of roads and other communications within the country and to neighboring countries and a shortage of educated people with technical and managerial skills. For many of these reasons, business-people in Thailand are better positioned than Laotians to take advantage of trade and investment opportunities, including expansion of hydroelectric power that it already buys and exploitation of coal and other mineral resources. Other areas in Laos marked out for development are raising cattle and pigs for export and upgrading forestry exports from raw timber to processed wood products of greater value. All of this assumes heavy reliance on foreign money and know-how since the internal sources of both are inadequate to the tasks.

Incentives for Reform in North Korea

The Democratic People's Republic of Korea, like China, has adhered to a centrally planned economy supervised by a powerful bureaucracy on the Soviet model. Also like China, it has followed a course of development that stresses heavy industry and self-reliance. More than 30 percent of its budget has been spent on capital construction, with over a third of its import bill going towards the acquisition of capital goods. Despite all the drawbacks and rigidities of this type of development, however, and amassing a substantial foreign debt, "the North Korean economy has performed better than that of any other Asian state outside Eastasia, except possibly Malaysia."[45] In part because of this achievement, which is reason enough to insulate itself from any comparison with South Korea, and in part because of the absence of domestic political turmoil, North Korea has effectively averted stirring up internal pressures to reform. The pressures for change come from without.

The demise of the Soviet Union and disarray in Eastern Europe have disrupted North Korea's major trade network. The reforms undertaken by Russia and China have created additional headaches for North Korea because these countries now insist upon foreign exchange rather than barter as the basis of trade. This highlights the problem with the Stalinist-type political economy: It keeps out not only the undesirable effects of joining the international capitalist economy, but also the foreign exchange required for trade. Thus isolation from the world economy will undoubtedly pressure North Korea into reforms that relink it with the international economy. There are already indications that North Korea has taken some initial steps in the same direction as China and Vietnam, but it looks as if official acknowledgment and full implementation await the completion of the transition occasioned by Kim Il Sung's passing from the political scene.

Thus the decade of the 1980s has witnessed a convergence of sorts between the NICs, who began as weakly dependent appendages of Britain/Japan/United States, and the communist countries who began as fiercely independent revolutionary upstarts opposed to the international capitalist market. The NICs engineered successful industrialization by taking advantage of their political embeddedness in the "free world" to transform their economies into productive links in the global capitalist market. At about the time the NICs were reaping their first rewards, China and Vietnam were acknowledging the limitations of a planned self-reliant development completely cut off from the global economy. Their reforms, decentralizing and "privatizing" agricultural and industrial ownership, have moved them in the direction of the East Asian NICs. As the cold war, which had separated the NICs and the communist countries from each other, dissipated there emerged in its place an expanded international market to which all nations of the Asian Pacific, except perhaps Burma, wanted entry regardless of the ideological underpinnings of their particular form of nationalist government.

SOUTHEAST ASIA: THE NECs AND THE EXCEPTIONS

Among the Southeast Asian countries that were neither NICs nor communist countries, Thailand, Malaysia, and Indonesia not only jumped on the bandwagon of export-led development but managed to hang on, joining the magic circle of states with high economic growth rates. Because they have achieved middle-income status among developing nations by their adoption of export-led growth strategies, these three countries have earned the acronym NECs, for newly exporting countries. Similar to the NICs in combining authoritarian regimes with market economies, the NECs are in three other respects quite different. We will examine the similarities and differences that might account for their status just behind the NICs in the "flying geese" formation.

The two remaining Southeast Asian countries—Myanmar and the Philippines—are exceptions to the Asian Pacific success story on opposing ends of an "openness-to-the-world" continuum. The Philippines' attempt to sustain economic growth rates using an export-led strategy has failed, in part because of a weak state that has made the Philippines too open to international forces and too resistant to the need for fundamental internal changes. Myanmar, on the other hand, is only just pulling up to the starting line in the industrialization process, in part because it has been too closed, until recently shunning interaction with the international community, except for the illicit heroin trade. The Philippines and Myanmar share a handicap that may have contributed to their problem: Neither has achieved the kind of political integration required to pursue truly national economic growth, the Philippines because its economic elite identifies itself too closely with the international community, Myanmar because its military elite has persisted in distancing itself from the international community.

Rapidly modernizing downtown Kuala Lumpur, Malaysia.

Source: Photo by Vera Simone.

Thailand, Malaysia, and Indonesia

Like the NICs, the NECs are privately based market economies with bureaucratic authoritarian states. As in South Korea and Taiwan, the military has played a prominent role in Thailand and Indonesia, related in part to U.S. security interests in the area. And in all three of the NECs, state intervention in the economy has been a noteworthy aspect of their economic development. But three characteristics distinguish the political economies of the NECs from the NICs. The first is that they are well endowed with natural resources of a wide variety; the second is their ethnic pluralism, particularly the presence of Chinese, who have dominated the economic arena in Thailand, Malaysia, and Indonesia. The third is their heavy and enduring dependence on international, increasingly Japanese investment capital, technology, and organizational skills. The governments of Thailand, Malaysia, and Indonesia have accelerated their countries' economic development by luring international capital from production locations where labor costs are rising, in particular the NICs. The opportunity presents itself as a result of the jockeying among the world's leading capitalist states to advance or maintain their relative positions in a rapidly changing international division of labor. For Japan, the region provides a natural location for dispersing its production sites to offset factors like currency appreciation and tariff barriers.

Resource-Intensive Development. Thailand, Malaysia, and Indonesia have large amounts of rubber, rice, palm oil, tin, petroleum, natural gas, and teak and other timber. Since colonization of the region, they have therefore relied on exporting their primary products to generate foreign exchange and investments. In the 1960s, after serious internal conflicts had been settled, the governments of Thailand, Malaysia, and Indonesia, on the advice of international lending institutions, pursued import substitution policies to strengthen domestic production capabilities and the power of the state. By the 1970s, again on the advice of international monetary agencies, the NECs' strategy of development shifted to a policy of export promotion. Following the NICs was a conscious element in the policy of increasing the manufacturing component of their exports. Although the NECs were slower to succeed and their growth rates have not quite reached the level of the NICs, they did dramatically increase the industrial proportion of their exports. Nonetheless, primary products still comprise a significant component of their exports.

Ethnic Pluralism: The Role of the Chinese. A second element the NECs have in common is the vital yet equivocal role the Chinese have played in their economic development. Under colonial rule, the Chinese were merchants, tax collectors, and operators of state trading monopolies. This provided a springboard for Chinese in Thailand, Malaysia, and Indonesia to become the driving force of capitalist development. Because of their position as "outsiders," however, the Chinese were forced to ally themselves with indigenous ruling elites, agreeing to a subordinate political role in return for protection and enhancement of their economic positions. In Malaysia, the wealthy Chinese elite allied itself with the politically powerful, traditional Malay aristocrats who monopolized government positions despite continuous ethnic rivalries. In Thailand it was the upper ranks of the *sakdina* class and in Indonesia the ruling Javanese with whom the economically powerful Chinese cooperated.

As the immigrant communities of ethnic Chinese came to dominate the business world in all three countries, they aroused the resentment of increasingly nationalistic indigenous populations. In Thailand they faced discrimination after 1945 when the state attempted to force Chinese to assimilate;[46] in Indonesia they were massacred after the unsuccessful coup attempt of the PKI in 1965; and in Malaysia they were embroiled in the race riots of 1969. To differing degrees, the singular success of Chinese in the commercial world remains a problem for these three NECs. Thailand has made the most progress toward integrating the Chinese middle class and business community into mainstream Thai society while Indonesia continues policies that fuel hostility, even overt violence, against the Chinese minority. Malaysia occupies a middle ground, promoting the ideal of an ethnic balance among social and ethnic groups; but to achieve that balance, bumiputra are given preferential access to higher education and employment in business and the professions, to the detriment of Chinese.

In Thailand the rapid economic expansion that began (under authoritarian military rule) between 1957 and 1973 was accompanied by a reversal of the anti-Chinese nationalism of the earlier period. By the 1980s economic growth had given rise to a more open political environment in which substantial numbers of Chinese business people had become not only Thai citizens but parliamentarians and cabinet members. The assimilation of ethnic Chinese into Thai society also contributed to a significant number of independently organized business associations with an effective public voice in the economic policymaking process. By contrast the business class in Indonesia remains widely stigmatized as a Chinese enclave, which despite its considerable financial resources is unable to secure a significant share of political power. Generally fearful of publicly asserting their interests in face of government opposition, Chinese business people prefer to work through personal relationships with patrons among senior military and civilian officials. This overshadowing of the Chinese-dominated business sector by the state in Indonesia reflects the relatively small scale of the private sector compared to the state-owned enterprises that dominate key sectors of industry, notably oil and gas. With two-thirds of its revenue coming from these sources, the government has been able to prevent the private business sector from using its economic power as leverage to increase its share of political power.

Foreign Capital and State Intervention.   A third similarity of the political economies of Thailand, Malaysia, and Indonesia is their extensive reliance on direct foreign investments by multi- or transnational corporations to advance their economies. A high percentage of each country's manufacturing and extractive industries is controlled and owned by foreign corporations, which carries with it somewhat higher social costs and political vulnerabilities than is the case in the NICs. Some differences both in the degree of foreign capital and domestic state intervention between Thailand's and Indonesia's political economy will be roughly sketched, as well as the manner in which ethnicity and class intersect in the Malaysian political economy.

The Thai economy, despite sizable U.S. foreign aid and investments, has been most successful in financing important industrial sectors with domestic capital.

Among industries promoted by the Board of Investment, Thai capital accounts for 75 percent of total registered capital. In the textile industry, although the percentage of foreign-owned *registered* capital appears to be higher, it is estimated that the Bangkok Bank alone finances 70 percent of the industry. Thus while foreign companies are a major force in the Thai economy—75 percent of the investment projects approved by the Thai Board of Investments in the late 1980s were from foreign firms[47]—certain key sectors remain dominated by Thai capital. There is, in addition, a wariness of extending the state too far into the business of investing in the economy itself. After 1958, both Thai business and international advisers pushed to confine the government to new investment promotion and infrastructural development and away from state partnerships with business like the National Economic Development Corporation Limited, whose crash had left the government greatly in debt.[48]

Indonesia is at the other end of the spectrum, with international capital extensively involved in its economic development along with a major role of the government as an investor and financier of business enterprises. Under Sukarno, the inability of the state and the national bourgeoisie to generate effective economic development left the generals little choice but to reintegrate Indonesia with the international capitalist economy.[49] Employing American advisers, the Berkeley technocrats, the New Order regime offered funds for projects, loans, and inducements to new foreign investors in the form of tax holidays and guarantees of profit repatriation. The state has also invested directly in production and economic organization through state-owned corporations: banks; state corporations supervising concessions in the resources sector; joint ventures in property, construction, resources, cement, and petrochemicals; and state organizations that organize distribution and pricing of certain procurements, like rice and other basic necessities.[50]

Malaysia began its development with a laissez-faire economic policy that applied equally to domestic and foreign capital. The state provided only infrastructure to facilitate capital accumulation, while foreign and domestic capital was permitted a free hand. On the surface, the alliance between landed, aristocratic Malays who monopolized political bureaucracy and the Chinese who monopolized the urban economy worked smoothly. But beneath the surface Malay resentments against the Chinese mounted: The Malay elites wanted economic control commensurate with their political power, while the Malay peasants were dissatisfied with the class polarization fostered by laissez-faire capitalism in the rural areas. The racial contention came to a head in May 1969. One result was a shift in the role of the state towards greater intervention in economic development and the aggrandizement of the mostly Malay bureaucratic class.

Adoption of the New Economic Policy (NEP) in the early 1970s had a two-pronged purpose: to alleviate the poverty of rural Malay peasants by providing them with access to more land and modern training and to spawn a new Malay capitalist class by supplying urban Malays with a 30 percent share in modern economic enterprises. The objective was to shift 30 percent of the wealth to the Malay community by 1990, decreasing the foreigners' share from 63.3 to 30 percent and increasing the non-Malay share from 34.3 to 40 percent. Redistribution was to come from economic growth rather than existing GNP, making it more palatable for the Chinese, who were understandably worried about losing a share of their wealth. A series of four-year plans detailed the process. The idea was that Malays were not being given but would work for their 30 percent share of corporate capital by expanding the total output through their participation. And in fact, NEP was vigorously pressed by the government, with the major impetus for growth coming from public investment and consumption in areas like transport, manufacturing, utilities, and public administration.

NEP's difficulties, however, stemmed from the underlying economic nature of what the government defined as a racial problem. One difficulty was that the eradication of rural poverty envisioned in NEP failed to address the structural source of rural poverty: landlessness that resulted from a feudal land tenure system. The uneconomic size of most farmholdings and the large numbers of farmers who did not own the land they worked meant that only the already well-to-do rural Malays could avail themselves of the land and infrastructural supports provided by the government. Thus NEP contributed to the rural problem by further increasing income inequality between rich and poor Malays in the rural sector.

A similar difficulty arose from the government's role in expanding the Malay ownership and management of urban corporate wealth. The discretionary power of the government entrusted with the "management shares" allowed it to obtain control of companies, through the use of statutory bodies, with a minimum outlay of cash. The majority of the shares reserved for the Malay community were then purchased by those who could afford them: the small number of richer members of the Malay community who were often politicians, civil servants, and their patrons. Thus by increasing the concentration of economic power under bureaucratic control, NEP further increased the inequality of income and wealth *within* the urban Malay community and in the process adversely affected both private, mainly Chinese, investment and public support for the ruling governmental elite.[51]

The NECs clearly learned some of their lessons in development from the NICs: moving up the product cycle from natural resource exports to manufacturing and higher value-added exports, employing government incentives to encourage domestic capitalist expansion, restricting labor from organizing, and raising the skill level of the labor force. But aspects of the NECs' internal situations as well as the timing of their inclusion into the international economy prompt concerns about the continued viability of an export-driven formula.

The NECs' greater dependency on markets in the developed countries may be more of a short-term problem than that of the more established and technologically advanced NICs, but it is a matter of degree, not of kind. To the extent that the communist countries join the NECs and the NICs in competing for investment capital and markets for their exports, they increase the vulnerabilities of all countries tied into the boom-and-bust cycle of the international economy. The current preoccupation with the threat of a tariff war reflects this recurring worry. Another source of apprehension is how, where, and with what speed new domestic markets can be created to absorb the increased supply of industrial products projected by successful developing countries in the Asian Pacific. A third anxiety concerns the underlying pressures for democratization confronting the authoritarian states that have so successfully piloted their political economies through the treacherous waters of the international econ-

Selling vegetables at an open-air market in Jakarta, Indonesia.
Source: United Nations photo 122601/Wolff.

omy. Will they remain politically in control of their rapidly changing economies? Or will they become subject to the centrifugal democratic pressures that bless and afflict other parts of the world?

Two states chronically subject to centrifugal pressures but lacking in the dynamic qualities of developmental states elsewhere in the Asian Pacific are the Philippines and Myanmar. They are exceptions to the patterns of development that have become so closely identified with the Asian Pacific region.

The Southeast Asian Exceptions

Philippines.   Politics in the Philippines is like a pair of mirrors facing one another in an infinite regression of déjà vu. One mirror is corruption, the other is political violence. As Emmanuel S. de Dios observes, "politics, in an underdeveloped context, is itself a major form of organization of the economy. Political violence may be viewed simply as one form of *investment*, and corruption as a form of *return*."[52] Viewed in this way, the scale of venality that occurs routinely in the Philippine political economy becomes at least more understandable, if not more tolerable. The continuity in policies between Marcos and Aquino, for example, can be understood if one sees the installation of the Aquino regime as a return to the political practices and rules prevailing before martial law was declared by Marcos. The split in the ruling elite at that time gave rise to dictatorship, and the schism continues as an unresolved problem today. But that schism highlighted a deeper problem.

From 1946 until the declaration of martial law in 1972, the dominant elites, divided into two political parties, took turns filling elected offices on the basis of their varying public positions on corruption and political violence. This "elite democracy," a combination of landowning, business, and financial interests, was made up of vertical dyadic relationships between powerful and wealthy patrons and their poor and dependent clients. The political elite was drawn from those who could afford to be patrons: landowners, employers, professionals—people whose occupations permit them to do favors for large numbers of ordinary voters. Once in office, these patrons used their political connections to further their business interests, which also enabled them to contribute to the welfare of their clients. Thus political economy in the Philippines is a vicious circle among elites whose wealth positions them in politics and whose politics in office furthers their accumulation of wealth.

When Marcos illegally extended his political career as president, he adopted populist rhetoric against the "oligarchs"—the older established political clans such as the Lopezes, Osmenas, Aquino-Cojuangcos, and Jacintos—to justify expropriating their holdings and politically persecuting them. But the logic of his regime was an extension of everything that had preceded it. Up until the 1940s the Philippines had a typical colonial pattern of political economy: It exported mineral and agricultural resources in exchange for imported manufactures. In the second phase, beginning in 1948, national policy shifted to an import-substitution strategy to counteract the large balance of payments problem. This gave rise to a manufacturing class that was largely composed of branches of the old landed elite, with the result that no clear line distinguishes the manufacturing interests from the landed aristocracy; both are segments of the same social and economic class with a common interest in preventing any redistribution of the wealth. By the early 1960s, when the Philippine economy had exhausted the benefits from ISS, further industrialization was stymied by the narrow base of incomes constituting the domestic market. Industries were unable to produce on a large enough scale to permit export competitiveness. At the root of this problem of a narrow domestic market was the skewed distribution of land. But to date, land reform has never seriously been implemented because of the identity of interests between manufacturing and landholding factions of the elite who dominate the political arena.

Marcos prevailed under martial law as long as export prices remained high, interest rates low, and international capital continued to flow into the Philippines sufficient to placate the displaced "oligarchs" as well as enrich his "crony capitalists." The expanding role of government under martial law facilitated this process. Government guarantees on foreign loans profited those businesses with ties to the Marcos regime. When, however, these highly leveraged projects failed—because of corruption, incompetence, and/or adverse external circumstances—the government assumed their debts. The government's role in financing these investments and projects, therefore, accounts for the magnitude of the external debt accumulated during the Marcos regime. The bubble broke as a consequence of the international recession of 1980–1981, which threw the Philippines into economic crisis. When in October 1983 a moratorium was declared on debt payments that had skyrocketed as a result of Marcos's attempt to cover bad investments of previous years, international loans evaporated, and the United States withdrew its support of the Marcos regime. With Aquino's reelection, the older elite, the "oligarchs," came back into power, although in order to win the elections, they had initially to enter an uneasy alliance with populist forces making more radical demands.

Structurally the political economy of the Philippines has remained the same under Aquino and now under Ramos. The central problem that underlines the regime's crisis of development is the conflict between growth and debt service. And it is perpetuated by the dynamics of politics as a symbiosis between national and local elites for which Lande's description of premartial law politics remains apt:

> Candidates for national offices need votes, which local leaders with their primary hold upon the loyalty of the rural electorate can deliver. Local leaders in turn need money to do favors for their followers, and this the candidates for high offices can supply. Local leaders also need a constant supply of public works projects and services for their localities. Holders of high elective offices such as senators and congressmen, from whence come most such benefits in the Philippines, can affect the supply of projects and services. The result is a functional interdependence of local, provincial, and national leaders.[53]

The primacy of localism that predates both the Spanish and the American conquest of the Philippines has endured, providing the straitjacket within which the Philippines' development is arrested.

Burma/Myanmar.   The political economy of Myanmar illustrates the complexity and contradictoriness of development. Burma is richly endowed with natural resources—abundant arable land, fertile soil, fish, the best jade in the world, precious gems, water power, timber, gas, coal, and oil—yet it is today the poorest country in the region. At one time the world's largest exporter of rice and considered the "Golden Land" by its Southeast Asian neighbors, Myanmar today has barely enough food to feed its 42 million people. Under a military dictatorship, the country is said to be pursuing the "Burmese Way to Socialism." With two-thirds of its population Buddhist Burmans, the government under a military dictatorship has been at war with its ethnically diverse minority nationalities since independence. And since 1988, when a popular movement for democracy was brutally suppressed, the government has been at war with almost its entire population, leaving a political economy dependent upon selling its natural resources, everything from drugs to timber.

Socialism was adopted in principle as an alternative to both capitalism and communism, each of which was unacceptable. Capitalism was associated with colonial Burma, when Indian moneylenders had dispossessed Burmese cultivators, and under British auspices large-scale rice cultivation for export subjected the entire country to the whims of international commodity prices. Communism, on the other hand, was fundamentally incompatible with Buddhist values. The alternative was some form of democratic socialism adapted to Burmese cultural values. Aung San's commitment to socialism was tempered, as he explained at an AFPFL convention in 1947, by the realization that moving directly to socialism was impossible for precapitalist Burma and that the country would first have to go through a controlled capitalist stage of private enterprise, but without the "old evils of monopoly and exploitation."[54] Landlordism would be ended by giving the land to those who cultivate it, though ultimately it would be nationalized and the central government would own transport, natural resources, communications, and the principal means of production. This stage of economic development was, he said, neither capitalism nor socialism, but something in between.

U Nu was similarly committed to the goal of socialism wedded to the cooperative spirit of Buddhist teachings. During his prime ministership many enterprises formerly in private British hands were nationalized and run as state enterprises and the foreign-owned oil and other industries converted to joint ventures of government and private owners. Logging and export companies were nationalized and the purchase and export of rice were monopolized by a state marketing board. Capital was invested in import-substitution industries and in power generation capacity for industrial growth. Despite these measures, the restructuring of the economy did not proceed very far; "only in the sphere of government expenditure itself was there a significant change in the state's share of the economy from before the war to the end of the 1950s. Even in the state marketing and transportation sectors the independent nationalist state had control over a smaller proportion of all activity than had the colonial *laissez-faire* state."[55]

When the military Revolutionary Council came to power, the founding generation's commitment to socialism was reaffirmed in the "Burmese Way to Socialism," which combined Marxist economic rhetoric, Buddhist ideas about human greed, and the need for strong one-party rule. Initially, the military pursued a radical program of nationalizing banks and all foreign and large local businesses and establishing a government monopoly on both internal commodity and foreign trade. The goal was to liberate the country from dependence on foreign goods, foreign capital, and outside markets. But in the late 1970s economic stagnation led to a change of policy under the Burma Socialist Program Party, which sought limited external aid and allowed the private sector more latitude. Further policy changes in the late 1980s and early 1990s liberalized the grain trade, regularized the lucrative smuggling trade, and increased government revenues by imposing a tax on that trade and creating the Burma Holdings Corporation with capital equal to 20 percent of the country's GNP. State monopoly of banking and natural resources other than agriculture continues. These changes, according to David I. Steinberg, are signs that "Myanmar is moving, hesitatingly, from state socialism to a modified state capitalism, not economic pluralism as understood in the United States."[56]

Recognizing the role that a deteriorating productive sector played in triggering the urban-based mass uprising in 1988, SLORC abandoned the "Burmese Way to Socialism," promoted free enterprise, and courted foreign investments. And despite continued international condemnation of the regime's repression of political opposition, foreign capital responded to the invitation with expanded private investments in Myanmar. By 1992, U.S. companies actually headed the list of foreign investors, with U.S. $163.7 million, mainly in oil, gas, and fisheries; Japan, the Netherlands, South Korea, and France also actively were investing in development of Myanmar's natural resources.

Among ASEAN nations, there is increased interest in drawing Myanmar closer into the orbit of the Southeast Asian organization's regional concerns, because of both the country's lucrative investment opportunities and its strategic significance on China's border. Singapore, now Myanmar's largest trading partner after China and among its top ten foreign investors, is the first noncommunist government to send its top political leader, Prime Minister Goh, on an official visit to Myanmar. This followed Indonesia's invitation to Myanmar's powerful intelligence chief Khin Nyunt to meet with President Suharto, whose principal concern is countering the great weight of China's historical influence over Burma. Khin Nyunt is said to have remarked to Suharto that Myanmar would like to emulate Indonesia's dual military and civilian political framework for development. There is, however, a reluctance among some ASEAN members to move too quickly in embracing Myanmar into their midst without first satisfying their Western partners' objections to Myanmar's human rights violations.

Indications that Myanmar seeks entry into the international economic community have multiplied in 1994. Domestically, the government has come to terms with ethnic insurgents on condition they refuse to provide refuge for prodemocratic activists. In February 1994, one of the largest rebel armies, the Kachin Independence Army, signed a peace treaty with Rangoon (now Yangon). In return for a cease-fire agreement with the central government, insurgents are permitted to turn their attention to commercial opportunities, engaging in business in northern towns. One result of this is Mandalay's growth as an economic center of the country, overtaking the capital city, Yangon.

Militarily and financially the most powerful enemy of the Burmese government is Khun Sa, the warlord of Myanmar's section of the opium-rich Golden Triangle. In a concerted bid to vanquish this remaining center of effective opposition, the Burmese Army in mid-1994 encircled the area and blocked off the cross-border trade into Thailand that has enabled Khun Sa's organization to function. In an attempt to bypass a costly military assault against his highly armed operation, the Burmese government has offered Thailand an incentive to boycott trade with Khun Sa: a dam project on the Salween river, diverting water from Myanmar to Thailand, which badly needs it both for irrigation and hydroelectric power generation. And in July 1994 the government approached the United States with an offer to eradicate Khun Sa's drug empire (the source of most of the heroin entering the United States) in return for military equipment with which to attack his mountain stronghold in eastern Myanmar.

SUMMARY

As latecomers to the process of modernization, Asian Pacific countries share certain cultural and historical experiences that differ from those in the West. Central among these has been the greater dependence on the state as navigator of national economic development. This suggests that a fourth model, the developmental state, be added to the three models traditionally used by Western scholars to understand the variety of political economies in the Asian Pacific. Japan, viewed as a developmental state, demonstrates the advantages of state intervention that is market conforming in contrast to China's Soviet-style state, which attempts to replace the market.

As the analysis of political economy in Japan and China also demonstrates, however, employing one or another type of political economy is not an open-ended choice on the part of political leaders but a complex, historical response to different circumstances and opportunities. The Soviet-style political economies of China, North Korea, Taiwan, Vietnam, and Laos were as determined by the constraints of the cold war and their internal dynamics as were the developmental state patterns of Japan, South Korea, and Singapore. More recently, with dramatic changes occurring in the post–cold war world, China, Vietnam, and Laos have introduced market reforms that move their political economies closer to those pioneered by Japan and then emulated by the NICs and the NECs. Furthermore, they have done so retaining their authoritarian political structures more or less intact. The Philippines and Myanmar are special cases, the former illustrating the drawbacks of being too completely embraced by the international market, the latter illustrating the price of shunning the world economy altogether.

One question to ponder is whether the developmental state that seems to characterize so many Asian Pacific political economies is a distinctive political economy or merely a transitory stage towards a more classically structured market model of political economy. It may be that as these countries develop further, they will converge towards a singular new model of political economy. But whether or not this is the case, the Asian Pacific experience suggests that certain forms of state intervention in the market produce dramatic results in economic growth. When governments in the Asian Pacific underwrite pilot agencies, like MITI in Japan or the Economic Planning Board in South Korea, they insulate them from shareholders or constituents, allowing them to authorize and implement long-term strategies for realizing national economic priorities. Examples might be subsidizing specific industries to make them more internationally competitive, investing in research and development with no immediate prospect of profit, increasing the level of skills of the labor force, or restricting foreign direct investments to serve national economic priorities.

There is another generalization that is warranted by our explorations into the political economy of the Asian Pacific countries. It is that political economy is not something that occurs *within* the territorial boundaries of nations. It is a global phenomenon that often creates these national boundaries to begin with, boundaries that divide real estate and people's allegiances but do not bar capital, labor, or technology. As international capital, which is the currency of development, continues to roam the world in search of the most cost-effective way of combining factors of production, it confronts and interacts with the political dynamics of nation-states. The results, as we are witnessing in today's world, are unsettling and bewildering. This will be the focus of the remaining chapters.

QUESTIONS FOR DISCUSSION

1. What factors distinguish development in the Asian Pacific from development in the West?
2. How do the four models of political economy differ from one another?
3. Why did Soviet-style Marxism appeal to Chinese revolutionaries in search of a development strategy?

4. How was the political economy of Maoist China different from the political economy in modern Japan? How does Reform policy in China compare to development elsewhere in the Asian Pacific?

5. Which factors do you think are persuasive in explaining the NICs' successful economic growth?

NOTES

1. Alexander Gerschenkron, *Economic Backwardness in Historical Perspective* (Cambridge: Harvard University Press, 1962).

2. Chalmers Johnson, *MITI and the Japanese Miracle: The Growth of Industrial Policy, 1925-1975* (Stanford: Stanford University Press, 1982).

3. Bruce Cumings, "The Origins and Development of the Northeast Asian Political Economy: Industrial Sectors, Product Cycles, and Political Consequences," in *The Political Economy of the New Asian Industrialism*, ed. Frederic C. Deyo (Ithaca: Cornell University Press, 1987), pp. 44-83.

4. The characterization of the developmental state used here is based on Chalmers Johnson, "Political Institutions and Economic Performance: The Government-Business Relationship in Japan, South Korea, and Taiwan," in *Asian Economic Development-Present and Future*, ed. Robert A. Scalapino, Seizaburo Sato, and Jusuf Wanandi (Berkeley: University of California, Institute of East Asian Studies, 1985), p. 71.

5. Daniel I. Okimoto, *Between MITI and the Market: Japanese Industrial Policy for High Technology* (Stanford: Stanford University Press, 1989), p. 2.

6. Gordon White and Robert Wade, "Developmental States and Markets in East Asia: An Introduction," in *Developmental States in East Asia*, ed. Gordon White (New York: St. Martin's, 1988), p. 1.

7. Johnson, *MITI and the Japanese Miracle*, p. 31.

8. "By 1912 only 12 per cent of 'factory' operatives were employed in government establishments." W. J. Macpherson, *The Economic Development of Japan c. 1868-1941* (London: Macmillan, 1987), p. 38.

9. Johnson, *MITI and the Japanese Miracle*, pp. 110, 113.

10. From an article by J. W. Hall, "Changing Conceptions of the Modernization of Japan," quoted in H. W. Arndt, *Economic Development: The History of an Idea* (Chicago and London: The University of Chicago Press, 1987), p. 66.

11. Only within the last decade has the state-owned industrial sector reached more than 40 percent of GDP to become the dominant productive sector of the economy.

12. Victor D. Lippit, *The Economic Development of China* (Armonk: M. E. Sharpe, Inc., 1987), p. 135.

13. Two of the "Big Four"—Mitsui and Sumitomo—existed before the Meiji period, in Tokugawa times.

14. Dorothy J. Solinger, "Urban Reform and Relational Contracting in Post-Mao China: An Interpretation of the Transition from Plan to Market" (paper presented at UCLA Center for Chinese Studies and Southern California China Colloquium, 3 June 1989), p. 3.

15. Okimoto, *Between MITI and the Market*, p. 12.

16. Ibid., p. 1.

17. Michel Oksenberg, "China's Economic Bureaucracy," in *The Challenge of China and Japan: Politics and Development in East Asia*, ed. Susan Shirk (New York: Praeger, 1985), pp. 220-21.

18. Miyohei Shinohara, *Industrial Growth, Trade, and Dynamic Patterns in the Japanese Economy* (Tokyo: University of Tokyo Press, 1982), p. 24.

19. Johnson, *MITI and the Japanese Miracle*, p. 154.

20. Chalmers Johnson, "Japan's Economic Bureaucracy," in *The Challenge of China and Japan*, ed. Susan Shirk, p. 229.

21. Bruce Cumings, "The Origins and Development of the Northeast Asian Political Economy: Industrial Sectors, Product Cycles, and Political Consequences," in *The Political Economy of the New Asian Industrialism*, ed. Frederic C. Deyo (Ithaca: Cornell University Press, 1987), pp. 46–47.

22. The following scholars represent each of the four perspectives: (1) free trade: Bela Balassa; (2) "special circumstances": Paul Streeten; (3) Confucian values: Hung-chao Tai; (4) developmental state: Chalmers Johnson.

23. Lawrence B. Krause, Koh Ai Tee, and Lee (Tsao) Yuan, *The Singapore Economy Reconsidered* (Singapore: Institute of Southeast Asian Studies, 1987), pp. 8, 92.

24. An indication of this may be the independent electoral bid launched by the head of the Hyundai group in the 1992 elections.

25. Peter Nolan, "Assessing Economic Growth in the Asian NICs," *Journal of Contemporary Asia* 20, no.1 (1990): pp. 41–85.

26. Siu-Lun Wong, "The Applicability of Asian Family Values to Other Sociocultural Settings," in *In Search of an East Asian Development Model*, ed. Peter L. Berger and Hsin-Huang Michael Hsiao (New Brunswick, NJ: Transaction Books, 1988).

27. Alice H. Amsden, *Asia's Next Giant: South Korea and Late Industrialization* (New York: Oxford University Press, 1989), p. 37.

28. Ibid., pp. 18–19.

29. Ibid., pp. 221–22.

30. Robert Wade, "The Visible Hand: The State and East Asia's Economic Growth," *Current History* 92, no. 578 (December 1993): p. 433.

31. Koh Ai Tee, "Saving Investment and Entrepreneurship," in Krause, *The Singapore Economy Reconsidered*, p. 100.

32. Amsden, *Asia's Next Giant*, p. 70.

33. Ibid., p. 39.

34. Peter Nolan, "Petty Commodity Production in a Socialist Economy: Chinese Rural Development Post-Mao," in *Market Forces in China: Competition and Small Business—the Wenzhou Debate*, ed. Peter Nolan and Dong Fureng (London: Zed Books, Ltd., 1990), p. 8.

35. Zhang Lin, "Developing the Commodity Economy in the Rural Areas," in Nolan, *Market Forces in China*, pp. 97–107.

36. *Beijing Review* 34 (24 August 1987): p. 4, quoted in James C.F. Wang, *Contemporary Chinese Politics* 4th ed. (Englewood Cliffs, NJ: Prentice-Hall, 1992), p. 266.

37. Wang, *Contemporary Chinese Politics*, p. 266.

38. Ibid.

39. Quoted in Lincoln Kaye, "Policies Too Hot to Handle," *Far Eastern Economic Review,* 28 January 1993, p. 37.

40. Wang, *Contemporary Chinese Politics*, p. 266.

41. Ibid., pp. 264–68.

42. Gordon White and Robert Wade, "Developmental States and Markets in East Asia: An Introduction," in *Developmental States in East Asia*, ed. Gordon White (New York: St. Martin's Press, 1988), pp. 13–22.

43. Ibid., p. 22.

44. Solinger, "Urban Reform and Relational Contracting in Post-Mao China," p. 3.

45. Roy Hofheinz Jr. and Kent E. Calder, *The Eastasia Edge* (New York: Basic Books, Inc., 1982), pp. 62–63.

46. Kevin J. Hewison, "The State and Capitalist Development in Thailand," in *Southeast Asia: Essays in the Political Economy of Structural Change,* ed. Richard Higgott and Richard Robison (London: Routledge & Kegan Paul, 1985), pp. 273–75.

47. Wade, "The Visible Hand," p. 439.

48. Hewison, "The State and Capitalist Development in Thailand," p. 277.

49. Richard Robison, "Class, Capital and the State in New Order Indonesia," in *Southeast Asia*, p. 308.

50. Ibid., pp. 310–11.

51. David Lim, "The Political Economy of the New Economic Policy in Malaysia," *Further Readings on Malaysian Economic Development* (Kuala Lumpur: Oxford University Press, 1983), pp. 10, 12.

52. For most of this section on the Philippines we have relied on the article by Emmanuel S. de Dios, "A Political Economy of Philippine Policy-Making," in *Economic Policy-Making in the Asia-Pacific Region*, ed. John W. Langford and K. Lorne Brownsey (Halifax: The Institute for Research on Public Policy, 1990), pp. 109–42.

53. Quoted in de Dios, p. 145.

54. Aung San, *Burma's Challenge 1946*, p. 4, quoted in Josef Silverstein, *Burmese Politics* (New Brunswick, NJ: Rutgers University Press, 1980), p. 143.

55. Robert H. Taylor, *The State in Burma* (Honolulu: University of Hawaii Press, 1987), pp. 259–60.

56. David I. Steinberg, "Democracy, Power and the Economy in Myanmar," *Asian Survey* 31, no. 8 (August 1991): p. 735.

FOR FURTHER READING

Theoretical Perspectives

Berger, Peter L., and Hsin-Huang Michael Hsiao, eds. *In Search of an East Asian Development Model.* New Brunswick: Transaction Books, 1988, pp. 3–23 (Peter L. Berger, "An East Asian Development Model?" and Hsin-Huang Michael Hsiao, "An East Asian Development Model: Empirical Explorations").

Black, Jan Knippers. *Development in Theory and Practice: Bridging the Gap.* Boulder: Westview Press, 1991, pp. 15–44 ("Development in Theory: Meanings and Models").

Gereffi, Gary, and Donald L. Wyman, eds. *Manufacturing Miracles: Paths of Industrialization in Latin America and East Asia.* Princeton: Princeton University Press, 1992, pp. 323–52 and 368–403 (Fernando Fajnzylber, "The United States and Japan as Models of Industrialization" and Christopher Ellison and Gary Gereffi, "Explaining Strategies and Patterns of Industrial Development").

Scalapino, Robert A., Sato Seizaburo, and Jusuf Wanandi, eds. *Asian Economic Development: Present and Future.* Berkeley: University of California Press, 1985, pp. 63–89 (Chalmers Johnson, "Political Institutions and Economic Performance: The Government-Business Relationship in Japan, South Korea, and Taiwan").

Streeten, Paul, ed. *Beyond Adjustment: The Asian Experience.* Washington, D.C.: International Monetary Fund, 1988, pp. 68–105 (Sang-Woo Nam, "Alternative Growth and Adjustment Strategies of Newly Industrializing Countries in Southeast Asia," and Arshad Zaman, "Comments").

Wade, Robert. *Governing the Market: Economic Theory and the Role of Government in East Asian Industrialization.* Princeton, NJ: Princeton University Press, 1990.

Multicountry Studies

Appelbaum, Richard P., and Jeffrey Henderson, eds. *States and Development in the Asian Pacific Rim.* Newbury Park: Sage Publications, 1992.

Brown, Richard Harvey, and William T. Liu, eds. *Modernization in East Asia: Political, Economic, and Social Perspectives.* Westport, CT: Praeger, 1992.

Deyo, Frederic C., ed. *The Political Economy of the New Asian Industrialism.* Ithaca: Cornell University Press, 1987.

Higgott, Richard, and Richard Robison, eds. *Southeast Asia: Essays in the Political Economy of Structural Change.* London: Routledge & Kegan Paul, 1985.

Langford, John W., and K. Lorne Brownsey, eds. *Economic Policy-Making in the Asia-Pacific Region.* Halifax: The Institute for Research on Public Policy, 1990.

Lee, Chung H., and Ippei Yamazawa, eds. *The Economic Development of Japan and Korea: A Parallel with Lessons.* New York: Praeger, 1990.

White, Gordon, ed. *Developmental States in East Asia.* New York: St. Martin's Press, 1988.

Single-Country Studies

Amsden, Alice. *Asia's Next Giant: South Korea and Late Industrialization.* New York: Oxford University Press, 1989, chapters 3–6.

Bowie, Alasdair. *Crossing the Industrial Divide.* New York: Columbia University Press, 1991 (ethnic coalitions and the pattern of industrialization in Malaysia).

Clark, Cal. *Taiwan's Political Development: Implications for Contending Political Economy Paradigms.* New York: Greenwood Press, 1989.

Krause, Lawrence B., Koh Ai Tee, and Lee (Tsao) Yuan, eds. *The Singapore Economy Reconsidered.* Singapore: Institute of Southeast Asian Studies, 1987, chapters 3–6.

Okimoto, Daniel I. *Between MITI and the Market: Japanese Industrial Policy for High Technology.* Stanford: Stanford University Press, 1989.

Riskin, Carl. *China's Political Economy: The Quest for Development Since 1949.* Oxford: Oxford University Press, 1987, chapters 3–5, 7–10, 12–14.

chapter 6

Culture and Ideology

Ideas of who we are as human beings are embedded in two types of *worldview,* one called *culture,* the other *ideology.* Culture is the intricate set of habits (customs), values, beliefs, and attitudes we inherit from those who nurture us in early life. In countless different cultural settings, we learn the elements of behavior, speech, and thought that shape our conduct and govern the way we relate to one another. Like nature, culture is taken for granted and remains unexamined unless we encounter others differently endowed. Yet it is essential to how we find our way around in the world, providing a "pic-tionary" of symbols and images against which we match our perceptions of reality. Thus, culture is more than ideas: It is a symbolic map with which we learn to determine who we are, where we are going, and how to get there. In all its many forms, culture is a constant, a necessary complement to the indefinite and diffuse nature of human genetic inheritance.

Ideologies, by contrast, are ideas that are precipitated by and respond to radical political and social change. When we no longer recognize the social terrain using the habitual language of culture, we find ourselves unable to make appropriate judgments and take effective action. With the advent of modern structures of relations between people, a new set of symbols is required for us to understand how to think, talk, and act in a new environment. Ideologies provide self-conscious patterns of ideas and images that redefine human beings' relationships to one another in terms of the modern state or body politic. Each new ideology describes, explains, and justifies a set of goals and means for social action to either preserve, reform, uproot, or rebuild our social order. As the symbolism of modern ideologies joins that of culture, therefore, it acts as a counterculture, criticizing aspects of political life in need of change and mobilizing people to bring it about.

In individual as well as social life in modern times, there is always tension in the interaction between culture and ideology. The nature of this interaction as it has occurred among the peoples of the Asian Pacific since their encounter with the modern world is the subject of this chapter. What are the similarities and differences among the various cultures in the region, and how have those cultures influenced and been influenced by the ideologies imported from the modern West? The subject is elaborate and imprecise, encompassing not only a large number of distinct cultures in East and Southeast Asia but their interactions with various European ideologies. The complexities are compounded by variations within a single cultural matrix, such as Confucianism, and in various belief systems; there are not only different sects of Buddhism, Islam, and Hinduism and variations within socialist, communist, and liberal doctrines, but there are also mixtures resulting in distinctive blendings of cultural and ideological influences that have traveled throughout the region.

By the mid-nineteenth century, three ideologies destined to have a major impact on the rest of the world—liberalism, conservatism, and socialism—had made their appearance in Western Europe and begun their dispersion abroad. As these ideologies spread throughout the colonial world, they lost their original contexts, changing in curious ways by interacting with cultures and circumstances vastly different from those in the West. When refracted through the prism of Asian nationalism and culture, therefore, they were no longer recognizably Western ideologies; they emerged as distinctively Asian ideologies. All reflected the strong sense of nationalism aroused in Asians by Western imperialism. Thus, although nationalism has already been discussed in Chapter 3, it inevitably permeates much of the analysis in this chapter.

We begin with a summary of how each of our development theories deals with the question of culture and ideology and then consider the argument that culture itself is the decisive factor explaining the extraordinary development among East Asian NICs. A brief description follows of the elements of Western ideologies that appealed to nationalist leaders in their search for a model of modernity. Then comes a discussion of Asian cultural traditions that have endured in the postcolonial era. The remainder of the chapter considers the outcome of the confrontation between Western ideologies and the Asian Pacific cultures they encountered.

CULTURE AND IDEOLOGY IN THE THEORIES OF DEVELOPMENT

Modernization Theory

According to modernization theory, nations that pursue modernization undergo a gradual process of substituting modern scientific ideas for their traditional cultural beliefs, duplicating, with local variations, the original experiences of Western countries. As people learn more advanced ways of cultivating the soil and manufacturing goods, rationality and scientific attitudes are expected to incrementally replace religion and superstition; a progressive linear conception of time and change displaces the relatively static idea of change based on a cyclical conception of time; and individual achievement gradually prevails over the family and socially assigned positions as the determining element of success. This modern substitute for traditional culture is not ideology, however, but a scientific, pragmatic, and presumably universal outlook.

The cultural evolution from "traditional" to "modern" ways of thinking and acting is assumed to follow automatically as a result of the economic and technological changes that spearhead modernization. Yet even in the most advanced modern societies, religion and superstition continue to coexist with science and rationality. And in the most successful examples of late modernization, Japan and the East Asian NICs, the family rather than the individual has remained the prototype for modern industrial organization. This raises two questions left unanswered from the perspective of modernization theory: Why do traditional cultural traits persist alongside modern ideological divisions, and what combination of cultural attributes constitutes a "truly" modern culture?

World System Theory

From the world system/dependency perspective, it is ideology, not culture, that is considered decisive for the capacity of developing countries to industrialize on their own terms, without incurring crippling indebtedness to outside interests. Communism, for example, by which is meant the ideology of Marxist-inspired party regimes, was assumed until recently to be an asset to late-developing nations because it empowered governments to resist the economic and political stranglehold of neo-imperialist forces. But as communism continues to recede from the political agenda of countries seeking the rewards of economic liberalization, like China, Vietnam, Laos, Cambodia, and more tentatively North Korea, the world system/dependency perspective finds itself confronted by new questions. Is it ever possible for peripheral countries to resist incorporation into the world system? Under what conditions can countries embrace modern belief systems without entirely relinquishing their own cultural and ideological distinctiveness?

Indeed, the deficiencies in both world system/dependency and modernization theorists' emphasis on the economic and political aspects of development at the expense of cultural analysis has given rise to a third perspective on development: the cultural approach.

Cultural Theory

The cultural approach views the "habits of the heart," which distinguish one culture from another, as the determining factor in how ably a society adapts to the opportunities of modern capitalist development. Following the lead of Max Weber, the German sociologist who argued that Protestantism was the essential factor in molding Western capitalist thinking, some proponents of the cultural approach suggest that culture shapes attitudes toward time, money, work, saving, and success in ways that either promote or discourage development. It is argued, for example, that Confucian cultural beliefs, which like Protestantism extol the virtues of hard work, frugality, and piety, are uniquely suited to achieving modernization. Some scholars even credit Confucianism with the rise of a singularly effective "oriental model of economic development,"[1] explaining the remarkable economic success of South Korea, Taiwan, Hong Kong, and Singapore. At least one scholar, on the other hand, suggests that the ethical principles of Buddhism may be impediments to industrialization, accounting for Burma's failure to develop.[2]

Other advocates of the cultural approach confine themselves to analyzing the impact of a variety of cultural understandings of power and authority on the style and substance of different cultures' adaptation to modernization. Lucian Pye, for instance, claims that Asian cultural traditions of paternalistic authority not only lead these nations along dissimilar routes toward modernization but will result in modern societies that are distinctively different from those in the West. As Asian cultural traditions adapt to modernization, they necessarily shed some of their traditional differences, developing characteristics common to all modern societies. Yet their distinctive underlying cultural patterns persist, resulting in modern societies unlike those in the West.

Each of the above theories puts a different emphasis on the elements of culture and ideology. Modernization theory emphasizes the universality of modern Western culture. World system theory stresses the role of ideology in enabling newly developing countries to modernize on their own rather than Western terms. Cultural theory asserts the primary importance of indigenous culture as decisive for Asian patterns of development.

THE APPEAL OF WESTERN IDEOLOGIES

Western ideologies have held different and often overlapping appeals to modernizers in the Asian Pacific, depending on the time and circumstances of their nationalist movements for independence, described in Chapter 3.

Liberalism

In general, the appeal of liberalism to nationalists in Asia was its suggestion of liberation, the right to free oneself from the external bullying of foreign powers and from the constraints of antiquated ideas and institutions. Liberalism appeared as a promise of science, progress, power, and prosperity. It signified the choices that exist for individuals, for movements, for countries, to choose an independent path to becoming modern. Often identified with the institution of privately owned property and a free market system of exchange, liberalism was the antithesis of old feudal forms of bondage. In this vague condemnation of all that is old and confining, however, liberalism contained a number of quite different implications.

In early twentieth-century China, liberalism had led intellectuals to embrace the necessity of a revolutionary break with the Confucian past. By contrast, liberalism in Japan and Thailand had resulted in a conception of modernization that emphasized conserving cultural traditions as a veneer for industrialism managed by a state bureaucracy. Among nationalists in British colonies, like Malaya, Burma, and even Singapore, liberalism was understood to mean a bureaucratically organized government capable of providing professional leadership by a political elite based upon merit. In French In-dochina, liberalism was identified with an expanded cultural and intellectual freedom to explore new horizons, a trait that continued to characterize revolutionaries when they adopted socialism. Liberalism for the Filipinos had a distinctively American flavor, stamped by the period of tutelage under the United States. And for all the colonies, lib-eralism meant freedom from foreign rule, the right to self-determination.

Conspicuous by their absence in this list of various appeals that liberalism held out for Asian nationalists are the elements Westerners often assume are its defining features: the human rights of individuals independent of the state and the idea that governments derive their legitimacy from the people. Wherever elements of it were embraced in the Asian Pacific, liberalism seems to have omitted the legalistic, indi-vidualistic, and contractual aspects of the ideology considered so essential by its ad-herents in the West. This raises interesting questions about the nature of Western ideologies commonly identified as liberal, conservative, and socialist. Are they mutu-ally incompatible belief systems based on distinctive premises and principles, or can their component elements be combined in unpredictable ways? Do ideologies con-stitute timeless and universally valid models for social action regardless of cultural con-text? Or are they moving targets that serve the shifting interests of different cultural groups and social classes?

Conservatism

The values associated with conservatism in the West are more consistently appealing to Asian Pacific peoples than are those of liberalism. Its emphasis on authority as com-manding the obedience of individuals is as central to the communist worldview as it is to the official tenets of government in all the noncommunist systems. Throughout the Asian Pacific region, even in Japan, a country generally considered to have a demo-cratic ethos, the state's authority is based on the paternalistic model of family life: Just as the father carries the obligation to provide for the welfare of his family, the gov-ernment has the responsibility to secure the well-being of its citizens. Individuals have determinate duties rather than abstract rights, and power is required by the state to carry out its commitments. All social relations are predicated on the authority of those who are superior over those who are inferior, even when positions are filled on the basis of merit or virtue rather than heredity.

The values identified with conservative ideology in the West, such as loyalty, dis-cipline, and patriotism, are commonplace themes in the culture and rhetoric of poli-tics in all Asian Pacific countries, perhaps with the exception of the Philippines. This is also the case with community, which is so universally considered as taking prece-dence over individuals in Asian Pacific societies that it hardly merits the description of ideology. There is among belief systems in all Asian countries, both traditional and modern, a broad agreement that to live in society requires discipline, obedience to au-thority, and loyalty to the state, without which neither order nor the graces of civi-lization are possible. But in Asia these beliefs are part of an age-old cultural legacy rather than an embattled ideological alternative to mainstream liberal beliefs in indi-vidual rights, as is the case in the West.

Socialism

If the appeal of an ideology were judged by how frequently its label is invoked, socialism in all its varieties (especially Marxist socialism and democratic socialism) might be considered a top contender. Not only China, North Korea, Vietnam, and Laos but also Burma, Singapore, and Indonesia employ socialist rhetoric in justifying public policies. And in Japan, it must be remembered, the Socialists constitute the second largest party. The attraction of socialism for Asian Pacific peoples is its unequivocal commitment to economic and social equality, achieved through the power of collective action rather than by individual effort. In most of these countries, an enormous gulf separates the governing elites from the vast majority of people, who remain very poor. The compelling nature of socialist symbolism for leaders in this situation is its combination of dedication to material prosperity with the promise of social equality in its vision of all citizens sharing in the economic benefits of a modern economy.

An additional element of socialism that has made it appealing to Asian Pacific leaders is its opposition to exploitation and oppression in all forms. It is explicitly anti-imperialist, enabling leaders of ex-colonies to deflect internal discontent over the sluggish pace of progress under postindependence rule. And as a critique of inequality, domestically as well as internationally, socialism addresses continuing imbalances in all Asian Pacific societies between the rich and the poor, urban workers and rural laborers, the politically privileged and the politically underprivileged. Thus for Asian Pacific countries socialism has offered a compelling model of progress, bridging the gap between their tradition-bound way of life and their modern aspirations, with a program for non-Western people to become prosperous and modern without becoming Western and capitalist. In the current transition toward greater liberalization of political discourse in Asia, however, the kind of socialism that is likely to be embraced is more akin to that of Sweden than that of the former communist countries.

DISTINCTIVE FEATURES OF ASIAN CULTURES

"East is East and West is West, and never the twain shall meet" was Kipling's characterization of a supposedly unbridgeable chasm between European and Asian cultures. To many on each side of the divide, the "Other" seemed strange, exotic, inscrutable, even perverse and wrong. But the two sides *did* meet and out of that meeting have come changes in both East and West. Yet even the changes brought by political modernization and economic development in Asia have not eradicated the features of Asian cultures that distinguish them from European and other Western cultures. That distinctiveness persists and strongly influences the political and economic course of contemporary Asian states.

In this section we identify those "Eastern" cultural characteristics that contrast with "Western" views, particularly as they concern attitudes toward political authority; those characteristics have profoundly affected the reception given in Asia to the array of modern secular ideologies of European origin and have shaped the recon-

Buddhism has been a major influence on the cultures of East and Southeast Asia, spreading outward from India and reaching as far as Japan. Shown here is the Great Buddha at Kamakura, Japan.

Source: Photo by Arthur Feraru.

struction of those ideologies in adapting to the Asian context. Certainly there are important differences between the Confucian and Mahayana Buddhist-influenced cultures (China, Japan, Korea, Vietnam, Taiwan, Singapore, Hong Kong), the Theravada Buddhist cultures (Myanmar, Thailand, Cambodia, Laos), the predominantly Moslem Malay cultures (Malaysia, Indonesia, Brunei, and the southern Philippines), and among the countries in each of those groupings.

Still, they have some features in common. These include *collectivism,* a strong identification as members of groups and the expectation that people will subordinate their individual interests to those of the collective; *consensus,* a high value placed on sustaining the harmony of group life by avoiding contentiousness and overt confrontation; *hierarchy,* acceptance of a paternalist pattern of authority and a social order based on superior-inferior rankings in human relationships from husband-wife to emperor-subject; and *power as status,* a traditional reverence toward power as the necessary component for generating order and civilization out of chaos and barbarism.

Collectivism: Loyalty to the Group a Prime Virtue

The solidarity of the stereotypical Asian family is often the object of praise and even envy among non-Asians. It exemplifies the cultural tradition of giving higher priority to the family, the village, the workplace, and the nation, rather than to the individual members of those groups. Responsibility to the "collective" takes precedence over the individual's self- (or selfish) interest, and individual pursuits defer to cooperation with other group members.

Putting a higher value on group solidarity, loyalty, and cooperation than on individual freedom of action is not seen as a starkly simple situation of the group *against* the individual. Rather, it reflects a more "organic" view of the intimate relationship between human beings and the social networks into which they are born. Much like the nested doll of Russian folk art, the individual is the smallest figure encapsulated in successively larger figures—the family, the town, the province, the country—each serving as a protective shell around the smaller figures inside it. Belonging to groups is, in this view, not an option we choose but a necessary condition of being human; our identity is embedded in and defined by the groups to which we belong and our individual well-being depends on the well-being of those groups. The implicit assumption is, "What's good for my family (or my company or my country) is good for me, and in working for its good I am working for my own good."

Indication that group membership is still a higher priority in Asian cultures is found in a study of preschools in China, Japan, and the United States.[3] When teachers, parents, and other adults were asked "What are the most important things for children to learn in preschool?", the Chinese gave first place (37 percent) to "cooperation and how to be a member of a group," with "creativity" (17 percent) and "perseverance" (13 percent) the next most-favored choices. Almost two-thirds of the Japanese selected cooperation and group membership (30 percent) or another group-oriented objective, "sympathy/empathy/concern for others" (31 percent). The top choice for Americans was the individualist virtue of "self-reliance" (34 percent), with (surprisingly?) cooperation and group membership in second place (32 percent).

The expectation that individual interests must be compatible with, and in fact are best served by, loyalty to the group contrasts sharply with the modern Western assumption that the needs of the individual and the group often conflict with each other. The emphasis on individual rights—to "life, liberty and the pursuit of happiness," as Thomas Jefferson put it—derives from an image that is basic to modern Western political and legal thought: that prior to the existence of governments, individuals lived as solitary beings in a "state of nature" and that they set up government by agreement with others for the limited purpose of protecting their individual interests.

The atomistic Western view that humans are naturally unconnected to other humans and the contract theory of the origin of the state are quite alien to Asian cultures. Indeed, their acceptance in the West is neither complete nor without strain. Collectivism still has a hold on Westerners, as witnessed by the willingness of most of them to put their lives on the line for their nation, the ultimate expression of self-abnegation to the "collective." The endemic popularity of "cults" is a similar expression of deep-seated yearning for submerging the individual to a group will to achieve meaning as part of a collective endeavor. Modern society's emphasis on individualism and competition puts strains on people. Substance abuse, violence, suicide, and other forms of antisocial behavior are interpreted as evidence that the stress on individualism overlooks a deep-rooted human need to *belong,* to be part of a community. While individualism frees people to "do their own thing," to be innovative and creative agents of change, it has its dark side too: depriving people of the close bonds of mutual support, leaving them with feelings of detachment, of rootlessness, facing alone the blame for the consequences of failure.

On the face of it, the Asian emphasis on the group seems to be an asset in the process of economic and political modernization. The habit of loyalty to the collective is an advantage to modern enterprises, as demonstrated by the legendary company loyalty of Japanese workers and managers. And, if extended upward to the modern state, it enables government to mobilize its citizens in the task of nation building. But this is true only when a state, as the legitimate power representing all people under its jurisdiction, already exists. Until such a nation-state has established its credibility, loyalty to particularist local, ethnic, religious, and regional groups often produces intergroup conflict and feuds, weakening or impeding attachment to a larger national community. This has certainly been the case in Myanmar and to a significant degree in Indonesia, where ethnic particularism has been detrimental to the formation of a truly integrated, legitimate national power.

The resilience of group loyalties at the local level and (when it exists) the national level in Asian cultures has been promoted by the process of decision making based on consensus building.

Consensus: Harmonious Unity a Desired Goal

The secular Confucian tradition as well as the sacred traditions of Hinduism, Buddhism, and Taoism place a high value on the achievement of harmony. The Confucian ideal of the good society is a pyramid of harmonious interpersonal and intergroup relations from family compounds to palace grounds, while the religions adjure believers to attune themselves to supernatural forces and a cosmic order. With the acknowledgment that it may not always be possible to attain and maintain such a demanding level of correct behavior, it is expected that at least the outward *appearance* of harmony will be preserved. Even though the members of a group may be locked in bitter disputes, good manners require that the disagreement be masked in a formal show of unanimity. Open expression of dissent is considered at minimum in poor taste and at worst high treason. This preoccupation with preserving at least the appearance of unity is attributed by Lucian Pye[4] to a deeply rooted fear of the ever present threat that any significant diminution of civilized authority will open the gates to a takeover by "primitive power," the fang-and-claw rule of the jungle. In short, harmony preserves order and unity keeps anarchy at bay.

The cultural preference for decision making by consensus has its roots in traditional practices at the village level, where the inhabitants gathered to discuss and reach agreement on matters of common importance. Although the village headman may in fact exert the guiding role in determining what is acceptable to all, the appearance of equality in participation to reach agreement is not only preserved but accorded great value. Decisions may benefit some and not others, but the essential objective is the preservation of the group itself. While in Indonesia, consensus has long been a tradition at the village level, in China and Japan the appearance if not the reality of consensus has been a conspicuous aspect of party politics at the highest level. Although to Westerners this may seem an expedient to avoid the onus of individual responsibility, it is in Asia a culturally prescribed way of reaffirming harmony among constituents with diverse views or sharp disagreements over policy. Adherence to consensus as the formal basis for expressing group decisions, even when it is widely speculated that sharp disagreements exist among participants, secures perpetuation of the group by including everyone in the decision and in the responsibility for implementing it.

The priority given in Asian cultures to the value of harmony and consensus is not found in Western liberalism; not that the West courts *dis*harmony and *dis*sensus, but rather that differences of interests and viewpoints are *expected* and can be openly advocated without breaching the etiquette of private or public discourse. Confrontation is neither impolite nor treasonous. Out of the rough-and-tumble conflict of ideas and objectives, conducted within the bounds of accepted "rules of the game," come pragmatic or workable decisions for the group or the government. The decision is what the majority of the participants want, although it is acknowledged that some people carry more weight in the process of decision making than others.

In contrast to the idea that political decisions express group preferences, Asian cultural traditions suggest that group decisions reflect a cosmic order. Truth is not arrived at by contention among rival conceptions but a pattern of righteousness arrived at by everyone through a process of reaching consensus. In this cultural conception, a "loyal opposition" is an oxymoron and majority rule a threat both to continued elite dominance and to the position of ethnic or political or religious minorities. But as Asian societies are transformed into dynamic modern systems with a complex of sometimes dissonant interests, it may no longer be either feasible or desirable simply to declare harmonious assent by fiat from above. Under these circumstances, majority rule as a populist egalitarian form of participation in politics directly challenges another feature of Asian cultures, that is, the assumption that hierarchy is natural in all human relations.

Hierarchy: Reciprocal Obligations of Superior and Inferior

Basic to the traditional Asian concept of authority is the notion of superior-inferior status in all relationships, derived from the model of the father's position in the most basic social unit, the family. This paternalist pattern involves reciprocal obligations between superior and inferior partners in the relationship, the specifics of which may vary as do the roles fathers play in different societies. But the underlying assumption that hierarchy is the natural, legitimate, order of things was and is still quite widely held.

At the top of the pecking order in Confucian China was the emperor and his scholar-officials; ideally, farmers ranked below them but still higher than soldiers and merchants. In two other Confucian societies, Vietnam and Japan, the military were accorded more respect than in China, and the emperor's divine lineage received more credence in Japan than in secularized Confucian China. The Chinese model of a centralized merit-based bureaucracy was more closely followed in Vietnam than in Korea or Japan. In pre-Meiji Japan officialdom was more decentralized, and the Chinese practice of recruitment by examination never really caught on. In Korea, the principle of meritocracy was somewhat diluted when the landed aristocracy laid exclusive claim to eligibility for the examinations to become officials; competition among them for the limited number of available positions and land reached intense levels, contrary to the Confucian ideal of harmonious cooperation. But all the Confucian-influenced countries subscribed to the hierarchical model of a benevolent father-figure monarch, assisted by meritorious officials, ruling over loyal and obedient subjects, setting an example for them of virtue and upholding the moral order so fundamental to a civil society.

In Southeast Asian cultures under the influence of Hinduism and Buddhism, the "god-king" occupied the pinnacle of the hierarchy; his responsibility was to use his divine connection and the power of rituals carefully performed to protect his subjects from the whim of supernatural forces, to keep the society in harmony with the cosmic order. At lower levels of society, superiority-inferiority took the form of more voluntaristic and personalist patron-client relationships, in which the patron provides protection and favors to his clients, who in turn give him loyalty and services. So in all these hierarchical relationships in East and Southeast Asia, the superior and the inferior both had obligations to each other and expected benefits in return; they were linked in a form of mutual dependence, of *inter*dependence presumably satisfying to both partners.

This traditional pattern of hierarchical relationships was reinforced by the experience under colonialism and was continued or revived after independence as a means of attaching legitimacy to the new governments and gathering support for the tasks of modernization. The pattern is only now being challenged by people dissatisfied with their own ranking in the hierarchy or with the hierarchical system in principle. Egalitarianism, for several centuries now in the West a symbolic though incompletely realized goal, is gaining adherents among Asians. Still, hierarchy remains the dominant pattern in political as well as social relations.

Power: The "Antipolitics" of Status and Ritual

The traditional concept of power as responsibility for setting an example of virtue and performing rituals, in return for which the ruler enjoyed the "perks" associated with status, is quite unlike the modern Western notion of power as responsibility for proposing policies and making decisions. To us, the traditional Asian idea of power is profoundly antipolitical, accustomed as we are to expecting that political leaders will use their position to promote change, to carry out programs, to demonstrate their power to *do* things.

But the concept of power as status, rather than as policymaking, seems on reflection to be eminently suited to static societies where change is neither rapid nor a particularly sought-after objective and where the capacity of the state to mobilize resources for major ventures is quite modest. The limited power at the disposal of the rulers and officials fits very nicely with the expectation that the ruler will be free of responsibilities for decision making and that the bureaucracy will handle whatever decisions are required to preserve the status quo. Ritual and administration are the stuff of power, and when used well the outcome is more of the same—that is, the perpetuation of a stable society in which people are given some measure of protection from natural disasters and the wrath of supernatural forces. Pye sums up the historic concepts of power in Asian cultures in these words:

> power had little to do with the concepts of utility, efficiency, and representation which have been central to understanding power in the Western experience. Power as ritual or status was an end value, not to be debased for utilitarian purposes. Since the goals of action were stylized acts performed in support of the collective well-being and not to promote specific policies, there was little sense that more efficient application of power would be desirable or even possible. Those with power tended to conceive of themselves as embodying the collectivity, defending a consensus, rather than representing particular interests. People tried to avoid adopting partisan positions on public "issues," but instead they generally preferred the techniques of intrigue and personalized tactical maneuvering, which were more compatible with conflict in stable hierarchical arrangements.[5]

Such an approach to the uses and management of power would seem to be incompatible with the premises underlying the Western ideologies that were embraced to some degree in all of Asia. In fact, a major dilemma for the postindependence power-holders has been whether to try to plant in Asian soil one or another of the "alien" Western ideologies (much as the "miracle" strains of rice were imported in the "Green Revolution") or to try to graft the "modern" idea of politics as policymaking onto the rootstock of status politics or to cultivate a new variety of politics, grown in Asian soil and well adapted to the new tasks of economic development and social and political modernization. Which choices were made in the various Asian countries, and with what outcomes, are the subject of the next two sections.

EVOLUTION OF IDEOLOGIES IN CONFUCIAN SOCIETIES

East Asian ideologies are indelibly marked by their common Confucian ancestry, some elements of which have been discussed above. Our task now is to describe how Western ideas have been recast to explain and direct the course of modern development in the Confucian-based societies of Japan, China, North and South Korea, Vietnam, Taiwan, Singapore, and Hong Kong. As each of them (excepting Hong Kong, of course) gained its independence, the ideas designed by its nationalist leaders in the course of coming to power became enshrined as the common outlook of the new social order.

There were, of course, a great many contending ideas throughout this period, but we will limit discussion to the dominant worldviews that have prevailed in these countries since independence.

Among the views held in these countries, there are marked differences in attitude toward the function of ideology. In countries adopting the Marxist variety of socialism, ideology is viewed positively, its function being the systematic instruction of people into a modern, revolutionary way of understanding and promoting political change. In China, North Korea, and Vietnam, therefore, the ideas of Soviet Marxism were embraced and energetically incorporated into political life as the emblem of orthodoxy and righteousness. In this sense the ideas Westerners identify as "communism" have served in these countries as a substitute or replacement for Confucian orthodoxy. Marxism-Leninism, like Confucianism, is broad and all-encompassing. It relies heavily upon repetition of standardized formulas to provide the correct guide to thought and behavior. Similarly, the concepts of communist ideology in these countries, although derived from the same Marxist orthodoxy, are subject to divergent interpretations, frequently evoking intense public discussion and private individual scrutiny for signs of the official political disposition.

In Japan, South Korea, and Taiwan, by contrast, ideology has assumed a negative symbolic connotation, one that implies radical change, a sharp break with the past. This has not prevented the actual dissemination of ideas to impart new ways of thinking and acting in these countries. Rather, it has encouraged retention of older cultural ideas, while changing their symbolic significance to adapt to new circumstances. In this manner, progress—the central concept of liberalism—was adopted by making it, in the case of Japan, an essential component of loyalty to the emperor. Leaders in all three of these countries have subliminally if not self-consciously invoked a Confucian heritage to bolster political authoritarianism while selectively appropriating liberal concepts to champion a market economy. But the eclectic combination of Confucian attitudes toward status, hierarchy, and the moral authority of the state with liberal ideas of progress, economic growth, and freedom to defend one's way of life has enabled these countries with an avowedly noncommunist identity and affiliation to evade the "nasty" symbol of ideology.

With this introduction to the political ambiguities of the uses of ideology, we now address the ways in which Western ideas have intermingled with traditional cultural presuppositions in Japan.

Japan: The Meiji Mystique

The dominant belief system in Japan today is still at heart the Meiji amalgam of traditional and modern ideas, minus the militarism and chauvinism that led to defeat in 1945, plus the pacifism and liberal democratic elements introduced by the American occupation.

Meiji Era.   The nineteenth-century samurai-turned-modernizers promoted their program of national renovation by retaining feudal values, expanding on popular attachment to national symbols, and introducing selected elements of conservatism and

Empress Nagako and the late Emperor Hirohito of Japan, whose reign from 1926 to 1989 spanned the rise of the Japanese empire, defeat in World War II, and postwar recovery to become the world's number two economic power.

Source: UN photo 129292/ T. Chen.

liberalism that seemed congruent with traditional values and stimulants to the process of modernization. But they deftly disguised their indebtedness to Western ideas by dressing them in traditional clothes. By explaining their reforms as part of the "restoration of imperial rule," the samurai-statesmen were able, in the name of obedience to the will of the emperor, to promote ideas that would otherwise have been branded unpatriotic, if not treasonous.

Rather than beginning with a systematized ideology, Meiji leaders evolved a national ideology built around the core feudal values of family, social hierarchy, and communal harmony. Novel elements were gradually added, not displacing the older values but fitting themselves into and expanding earlier rules. Loyalty to the emperor and allegiance to the state were among the earliest political precepts to be added to the feudal core in fashioning an ideology for modern Japan. Symbols that glorified the tribal nation were promoted: the emperor as descendant of the sun goddess, the Japanese as the chosen people, and the honor of the nation, which required outperforming the industrial and military might of the Western imperialist powers.

As Carol Gluck points out in her study, *Japan's Modern Myths,*[6] the Meiji oligarchs tailored specific versions of a national ideology to target particular audiences to be transformed from subjects into citizens of a modern monarchy. To farmers being conscripted for military service, the emperor was presented as a majestic object of the spirit of loyalty and Bushido, depending on the virtues of the village as the bedrock of national integrity. Urban folk, on the other hand, were reminded of the obligations of social equality "now that all men are samurai." Whether directed to farmers, artisans, housewives, students, schoolteachers, or local officials these different versions of the nationalistic message were sent in a "dialect" designed for that particular audience.

Nonetheless, the themes of the ideological messages overlapped, reinforcing one another: the emperor as the embodiment of Japan's uniqueness; allegiance to him as the source of national unity and social order; the glory of Japan's empire in the East as proof of Japan's status as a first-class nation; loyalty and patriotism as ideals to which everyone conformed. The result was not only a sense of the nation but a set of ideas delineating the national purposes for which people labored and for which the nation stood. Symbols like loyalty and patriotism, in addition to providing the general civic content of moral education in the schools, were applied to a wide array of worthy causes such as "party loyalty, the entrepreneurial imperative to rise in the world, or the promotion of the sales of domestic—rather than imported—beer."[7]

To these adaptations of feudal and imperial traditions were added Western concepts like progress, liberalism, constitutionalism, and representative government, which at the start of the Meiji period were considered alien in form and meaning, but by the end of that era were accepted as natural elements of the Japanese way of life. Among noted intellectuals exposed to Western ideas, many of whom had close associations with or were themselves members of the Meiji government, liberal ideas were enthusiastically espoused as the means by which Japan would "attain an equal footing with the other powers."[8] In the belief that government had to be broadly representative, Okuma Shigenobu, a senior member of government (later prime minister and founder of Tokyo College), proposed establishing a parliamentary system based on elections contested by political parties. Freedom of speech and the press and the right to hold public meetings were endorsed.[9]

But Japan's traditions favored adopting the "enlightened conservatism" of late-nineteenth-century Germany rather than the individualism of classical liberalism, and it was this ideological route that provided the business class an escape from the inferior rank assigned it by Confucianism to high status in Meiji times, as today. At the beginning of the reform period, Japanese merchants still suffered from a generally contemptuous attitude toward their activities, especially on the part of Meiji officials. They were suspected of the stereotypical sins of merchants: being greedy, corrupt, fraudulent, dishonest, and likely as not unpatriotic. A newspaper editorial in 1895 exhibited Confucian scorn for merchants as a way of mustering patriotic support behind the Meiji oligarchs:

> Examine the speech, appearance, attitudes, character, spirit, and habits of our merchants—all are shameful. They fight over trivial sums and short-range profits, and their only ambition is to feed themselves and their families. They know nothing of sovereign or country, nor are they concerned with the prosperity of the people or the good of society.[10]

The response of businesspeople was to deny that pursuit of profit was their motivation, insisting that national greatness rather than narrow self-interest was what drove business enterprise to succeed. Thus, contrary to the advice of Adam Smith, Japanese business developed an identity of self-sacrifice: to overcome adversity and be successful through dedication to the nation, a sense of duty and patriotism. They became "warriors armed with an abacus,"[11] upholding principles of honor, integrity, and fidelity to one's word.

Thus, starting from a position of inferiority, the business class in Japan evolved an ideology quite distinct from that of its counterpart in the West, fitting itself into rather than rejecting traditions of subservience and loyalty to the state. The Meiji oligarchs, for their part, using a combination of nationalism and Confucian traditionalism to promote industrialization, enhanced the power of government rather than the independent power of the business class. Nationalism served as a rationale both for government aid to private business and for the rejection of the laissez-faire idea of Western liberalism as formulated by Adam Smith. Government accepted private enterprise without reservation and businesspeople for their part accepted the leadership role of the government in the interests of the nation as a whole.

After World War II.   Much of the Meiji ideology of "enlightened conservatism" has survived both defeat in war and economic prosperity in peace. Business resumed its relationship with the state after the war—with United States' blessing—but rather than the military, the Liberal Democratic Party (until 1993) occupied the third side of the triangle. In close collaboration and unchecked by a powerful military, big business and the state bureaucracy once again steer Japan's course in pursuit of international greatness, this time in the direction of conquering foreign markets rather than territory.

Japan's defeat in World War II brought a new ideological direction dictated by the United States. In place of the discredited symbols of Japanese nationalism and militarism, the United States substituted an ideology of peace and freedom for the Japanese people. Peace is symbolized by Article 9 of the new constitution, which renounces the sovereign right to engage in war. Freedom is symbolized by the full range of civil rights found in the U.S. Constitution, to which were added the rights to collective bargaining, full employment, free choice of residence and occupation, and equality, which specified sexual equality and "the right to maintain the minimum standard of wholesome and cultured living."[12] Therefore, Japan today is committed to democracy as the means by which to determine its national purpose and has transferred its former reliance on the military to economic competition as the way to secure Japan's status as a world power.

At the core of Japan's present-day ideology is a self-image of the nation as a corporate entity whose members are involved domestically (as *insiders*) in maintaining economic growth, social harmony, and political stability, while internationally engaging (as *outsiders*) in fierce competition with other businesses and states for increased market shares, global economic penetration, international prestige, and recognition for their nation. This distinction between "insiders" and "outsiders"—an enduring legacy of an earlier cultural pattern—is an important element in understanding what often appears to non-Japanese as a double standard of behavior. In their bid to attain equal status with other powers, Japanese adopt the behavior of outsiders as a means perceived necessary to protect the realm of the "inside." Accompanying this tribal sense of devotion to Japan's self-preservation is the racist aspect—generally unacknowledged—of its nationalism. This aspect of Japanese ideology has implications for Japan's assuming a larger political role as a leader of the world community, a topic to be touched on in Chapter 8.

China: Maoism Eclipsed

Whereas the ideology accompanying modernization in Japan was a reconstructed form of traditionalism, the ideology embraced by Chinese revolutionaries on their ascent to power was decidedly modern and Western. Marxism was adopted by revolutionary intellectuals seeking a new China precisely because it *was* opposed to Confucian culture, a mental straitjacket they viewed as responsible for keeping China weak and backward for over a century. Three questions will be explored in an attempt to understand how and why the Chinese adapted Marxism for their new symbolic framework: Why did Marxism resonate with Confucianism to become the vehicle for transforming China? In what ways did Mao Zedong elaborate and apply communist ideology in the process of fitting it to the framework of Chinese culture? In what ways do the Deng era reforms continue or depart from Maoism?

Affinities between Confucianism and Marxism.   Of all the ideas to engage the minds of Chinese in their long struggle to reunify the country, Marxism succeeded because of its remarkable similarities to traditional Chinese culture. If one tried to construct a modern counterpart to Confucianism one could hardly improve upon Marxism-Leninism-Mao Zedong Thought, as it is officially called. Like Confucianism, Marxism is both empirical and normative, realistic and idealistic. Like Confucianism, Marxism is comprehensive, all-encompassing, secular, and historical. Both have a cosmic vision, but the Marxist vision is of *change,* looking toward the future for its ideal of perfection, not to the idyllic past of Confucianism. Like Confucianism, Marxism assumes the best, not the worst, about human nature; the difference is the promise it holds for all human beings, not merely an educated elite, to fulfill their potential. And like Confucianism, Marxism views the material world as made up of opposite or contradictory forces; the difference is that Marxism looks for the resolution of contradictions rather than accepting them as given elements of the human condition.

Human history, according to Marxist analysis, is a process in which societies pass through successive stages distinguished by how they produce the material things people need to survive and prosper. From low-tech agricultural production dependent on human and animal labor, societies move to vastly more productive industrial technology, using machines of ever increasing sophistication, eventually reaching the stage we now call "postindustrial." At each stage the people who own the means of production—in feudal times the landowning class, in the industrial age the capitalists—dominate political life as well as economic, using the power of the state to protect their privileged position.

For Chinese revolutionaries this analysis fit Chinese reality: Landlords exploited peasants with the connivance of the imperial mandarins; foreign capitalists and their

Chinese collaborators exploited workers and undermined the government's limited capacity and will to resist. But Marxism also held out hope, with the assertion that each stage gives rise by its own inner contradictions to the class struggle that ushers in its successor. Marx predicted that the capitalist stage of production would be succeeded, through the efforts of the more numerous industrial workers, by the communist stage, in which control of the government and of the means of production would pass from the capitalist class to their rightful owners, the working class.

When the transition that Marx had predicted failed to materialize in the most advanced capitalist societies of Western Europe, Lenin modified the theory to fit the opportunity for bringing about revolutionary change in underdeveloped and still largely feudal Russia. Even without a sizable industrial working class or a capital-rich business class, Lenin demonstrated, backward feudal societies could industrialize using the Communist Party as the engine of change. For countries lacking the prerequisites for Western capitalist development, such as China, Lenin's theory, and its successful application in Russia, offered a compelling alternative route to development.

These changes in both theory and historical reality have generated considerable confusion over the term *communism,* which can usefully be clarified here. It is used rather indiscriminately to describe three different things: First, communism is used as the name of the future society that Marxist-Leninists believe will emerge out of the contradictions inherent in the fully developed form of international capitalism. According to Lenin's vision, communism will be a classless society in which, because there is no longer an exploited class to be suppressed, the need for a coercive government disappears and the state will wither away. Nowhere has this stage yet been reached. Instead, countries like China describe themselves as having reached an intermediate stage, "socialism," in which class differences (though no longer exploitation) remain, and government is still needed to complete the process of development and for protection against the outside world.

A second usage of the term *communism,* almost always by noncommunists, is to describe the regimes led by Communist Parties in the former Soviet Union and Eastern Europe and in Asia in China, North Korea, Laos, Cambodia, and Vietnam. Note that these governments do not call themselves "communist"; Vietnam alone uses the term *socialist* in its name and the others variously identify themselves as "people's" and/or "democratic" republics.

A third usage of *communist,* by both Communists and noncommunists, applies to parties and political movements that derive their purpose and their destination from Marxist theory (but curiously, no specifics on how to accomplish that purpose and reach that promised land). Thus in China, the ambiguity of communist ideology stems from its justifying a modern revolution in the name of a mythological future, while in Japan the ambiguity of Meiji ideology resulted from making modern revolutionary changes in the name of a mythological past.

Mao's Contributions to China's Ideology.

The Communists in China embraced the ideology of Marxism as a means for turning around China's humiliating defeat and depredation at the hands of the Western powers. Central to the success of this venture was Mao Zedong's effective conversion of Marxist-Leninist ideology to accommodate China's cultural and historical circumstances. To his credit and discredit, it was Mao's ideology that set the unique course of China's modern destiny. But the enormity of Mao's accomplishments in redefining the way Chinese think and behave, for better and for worse, defies summary. So just four aspects of Mao's contribution to the ideology that guided China's development will be discussed: the rural revolution, the role of the Communist Party, thought reform, and "putting politics in command."

The Rural Revolution.   To throw out the foreigners and set China on an independent course required strength and vision. By 1927 Mao had decided that the peasants alone could provide the strength to bring about revolution in China. The idea of a "rural revolution" was not original with Mao; peasant rebellions were abundant throughout Chinese history and Soviet advisers had counseled their Chinese protégés to take the peasants and their problems seriously. But there was a new element in Mao's formulation, one that was repeatedly to bring the Communist Party into conflict with the traditional elite of China, the intelligentsia, throughout the period of Mao's leadership. His novel suggestion was that China's intellectual elite follow the peasants, joining them, working among them, learning from them in order to become a part of that China from which they had always remained aloof. This belief of Mao's in the revolutionary leadership potential of the peasantry was the foundation of the People's Republic of China.

In 1927 the question Mao posed was whether Chinese intellectuals who had set themselves up as leaders of a Chinese revolution were willing to recognize the masses of illiterate peasants as true revolutionary forces capable of challenging traditional Chinese institutions. In Mao's eyes, this was not only necessary given their numbers and the Communists' base of operations in the countryside but a virtue, enabling them and China to have a "blank page" on which to write China's destiny.[13] It is interesting to note, therefore, that Mao Zedong never actually substituted the peasantry for the working class as "vanguard of the revolution." The party, he carefully reiterated time and again, must be a working-class party. How, then, reconcile a hypothetical working-class party with the fact that its membership is constituted of peasants? One answer is that Mao always exhibited a capacity to play revolution as much by "ear" as by doctrine. Another clue, one that credits Mao with greater theoretical acumen, is his conception of the party as an instrument for the socialization of peasants into revolutionary proletarians.

The Role of the Party.   "Rural revolution" as a means for setting China on a revolutionary course toward communism required redefining the Communist Party's relationship to its followers. Faced with a party that was working class in name only, Mao sought to expand its educational role. Ideology was used to create a curriculum for the mass education of peasant recruits into the party, teaching them everything from literacy and self-discipline to organizational skills and principles of guerrilla warfare. Many of Mao's writings address this task of turning the ideological principles and precepts of Marxist thinking into educational materials to train party recruits from increasingly varied backgrounds. When large numbers of intellectuals climbed aboard during the Yanan period, the "rectification campaign" became the prototype for building "a unified party with common ideals, ideology and goals."[14] Mao's concern was that party cadres understand his ideas about party leadership and how to put them into practice; this was the core of "mass line" politics, a unique result of the party's rural roots.

The idea of the mass line was to ensure that party leaders would serve the interests of the people they led. Among the various techniques of Mao's mass line politics, which included small study groups, criticism/self-criticism sessions, struggle sessions, and mass campaigns covering a range of targets, rectification campaigns were the most unusual. They focused on cadres and how they could improve their work styles. In this process, cadres, or leaders, were expected to criticize their own errors (for example, commanding people with a high-handed attitude). If the criticism was deemed inadequate by other people attending the meeting, additional criticism was invited from the audience. During the Cultural Revolution rectification campaigns turned into direct attacks on party leaders, even the elite of the elite who ran the country, a phenomenon unheard of elsewhere in the world and directly in conflict with the Confucian culture that still influenced people twenty years after the Communists came to power.

Thought Reform.   Much of Chinese communist ideology in the Maoist period, both in word and deed, centered around the question of creating the socialist human being. Thought reform, the core of Mao's strategy for confronting this question, illustrates the singular way in which communist ideology tapped traditional aspects of Chinese culture, creating a novel practice aimed at changing undesirable and misguided behavior among the Chinese citizenry. Regardless of one's feelings about thought reform, its bad connotation in the West is in large part derived from a misunderstanding of what it is and how it works. It is an approach to dealing with behavior that is much like childhood socialization. It addresses the question of how one gets people to "behave in a particular way when either they disagree with you or they have been ignorant of your wishes."[15] Whatever the standards may be for correct socialist behavior (and they change, sometimes radically, over time), they are communicated and implemented by people with whom one works and lives.

When an individual displays antisocial behavior, as defined at a given point in time by prevailing party policy, it is brought up for criticism by one's peers in the small group at work, at school, or, in the case of a youngster stealing a bike, in the residential neighborhood committee. The individual is persuaded to change that behavior because of the "law" (expected norm of behavior), exploring the causes of the behavior, and explaining the consequences. If the behavior recurs, one's immediate peers and/or boss increase the pressure to change in an attempt to raise the discomfort level sufficiently to obtain compliance. Although the method is used systematically in penal institutions, it is more importantly a widespread method for teaching the "law" and ensuring compliance with it. Mass campaigns of thought reform can target a wide assortment of activities to which people must comply, ranging from public sanitation and physical fitness to birth control and increasing outputs of a particular crop.

"Putting Politics in Command" and the Politics of Morality.   Mao's belief in the salutary effects of applying ideology to the task of revolutionizing China extended to all realms. During the Great Leap Forward, when China was short of capital and expertise to increase people's productivity, Mao substituted organizational and ideolog-

School children engaged in manual labor as part of their education during the Cultural Revolution.

Source: Photo taken in February 1976 by Vera Simone.

ical measures to reach the same objective. There were two interrelated aspects to this. First, organizationally, people's lives were radically reoriented as households joined into large communes the size of several villages. Second, ideological resources were applied by exhorting people to put all their hopes for a better future into working harder to increase agricultural output. The belief behind "putting politics in command" appears to be that untapped energies would be unleashed by liberating women from household work, collectivizing the burdens of child rearing, increasing the efficiency of labor management, providing equal pay for equal work, and by community construction of schools, health clinics, and rudimentary backyard steel furnaces.

The Cultural Revolution was, like the Great Leap Forward, presented as "putting politics in command." During this extended campaign, it was the culture rather than the economy that was the target of change. All symbols of either old Chinese or modern Western civilization were defined as "bourgeois" objects, reflecting the decadence and dissipation of a ruling rather than a proletarian class. Young Red Guards were mobilized to raid the homes of those suspected of harboring old paintings, Western books, expensive jewelry, and Ming vases. Proletarian morality was exhibited by austerity in dress, rudeness in manner, the exaltation of manual labor, and confrontational politics between political factions, both on the street and in the government. In schools children did manual labor for half the school day while in factories engineers were required to work on the shop floor. And in the most glaring affront to Confucian values, urban-educated youth were sent to the countryside to labor in the fields along with intellectuals and "capped" party officials who were assigned to do the most menial jobs. The disasters that resulted from this application of Mao's notion of "politics in command" have been amply documented and contributed in no small degree to the ease with which the policy changes known as the Reforms were embraced in China after the Cultural Revolution.

Despite his avowed antitraditionalism, his fervent attempts to undermine Confucian culture in refashioning a modern, proletarian way of thinking, Mao employed ideology in a traditional Confucian manner, as a modeling device for behavior. Ideology, for Mao, was not merely the justification of a preference in policy making, one side's argument winning over another's, but a method or guide for determining the morally correct position. His juxtaposition of politics and expertise, "red vs. expert," insists that expertise does not automatically confer on those who possess it a sense of right and wrong; it may, in fact, obstruct the sense of what is moral. Mao's belief that morality can be embedded in politics is like the Confucian cultural adage that politics consists of setting the proper moral example so that people are inspired to do the right thing for its own sake. It is precisely this moral conception of politics that is rejected in the pragmatism of Reform ideology that has been espoused by Mao's successors.

Reform Ideology after Mao.   Few elements of the Reform policy are entirely new, but the paradigm that has emerged from their combination provides a new ideological perspective, frequently called "market socialism" or more currently "the socialist market." In principle, capitalism and bourgeois pollution are still rejected. The underlying shift has been away from the idea that politics, the will of politically correct leaders, could bring about fundamental economic changes. Reformers substitute the notion that economic progress is governed by its own laws. The activities of political leaders, therefore, have to be limited to ensure that socialist economics operate in accordance with objective economic laws. Economists rather than political pacesetters need to be in charge of making economic policies.

To correct the imbalances that resulted from Maoist strategy requires decentralizing the control of inefficient large-scale collective or state enterprises and diversifying China's ownership system to include private, small-scale cooperative ventures and various forms of hybrid or joint ownership enterprises (described in Chapter 5). This is justified theoretically by separating the juridical concept of ownership from actual control over economic assets. In agriculture, for example, communal lands were subdivided into parcels and leased to individual households, each of which assumes responsibility for making its own production decisions. Although the state retains legal ownership of all the land, control over its disposition is relegated to individual households who can "sell" it or pass it on to their children. Similarly, industries (except large-scale, essential national enterprises such as steel and communications) are granted far-reaching autonomy to make their own production decisions, including the hiring and firing of their labor force.

The central principle and foundation of the Reform outlook is the reintroduction of markets, the operation of the laws of supply and demand to determine which commodities are produced, at what prices they sell, and how profits are reinvested. This amounts to a reversal of the entire edifice of Maoist ideology. In place of state planning, socialist commodity production is to follow market dictates for an indeterminate period, providing the flexibility and dynamism associated with the capitalist state of development. For individual entrepreneurs, directors of factories, households, and co-operatives, this means pursuing profit rather than depending upon state allocations and rewards for fulfilling state targets.

In place of Maoist egalitarianism, getting rich individually is the new first commandment of China's socialist market economy. State planning is reduced to a more selective and restrained intervention in the economic sphere designed to complement market forces. Economic enterprises, though not entirely freed from the pressures of state planning, have greatly expanded operational independence from bureaucratic management. They are responsible for making their own contracts with other enterprises to procure resources and markets for their products. This includes the opening up of China's economy to the capitalist global economy. Special economic zones have been established in an effort to create fast-track market-driven enterprises with foreign capital and Chinese labor. These are governed by special laws exempting joint ventures and foreign-owned enterprises from the constraints of restrictive taxes and regulations that still govern the diverse range of domestic enterprises.

The ideological ramifications of this reform model of "socialism with Chinese characteristics" are momentous and unpredictable. Although the party through the state is clearly in control, economic imperatives will more than likely place constraints on anyone with an ideological agenda. In fact, innumerable questions are raised about the role of the Communist Party, what the separation of ownership and control means in a socialist context, how the relations between managers and workers within enterprises are decided, and how compatible growing income gaps between the rich and the poor are with the socialist egalitarian expectations still fostered by ideological training.

Reformers differ among themselves about how best to achieve an effective interface between state planning and market processes; minor fluctuations occasioned by the relative political influence of different reform groups may continue to occur but within the narrowed range of a fundamental commitment to rapid economic development. Even when they are as economically successful as they have been in China, economic reforms once launched are like a vehicle sent into outer space, subject to unanticipated forces increasingly remote and beyond the ideological control of the political planners.

Taiwan: Familism and Statism

Ideology in Taiwan is composed of two elements that roughly correspond to the age-old split in traditional China between society—life governed by the family—and the state. Among the native Taiwanese, who had emigrated from China centuries earlier, a family-centered commercial orientation flourished under Japanese rule, stimulated by the island's exposure to the international economy. Contained within the social sphere by a repressive Japanese state, this lively market orientation has provided the dynamism and flexibility unique to Taiwanese *guerrilla capitalism.* The term refers to a cultural characteristic of Taiwanese small business strategy: selecting a product the firm is capable of manufacturing, making it quickly, saturating the market with it, and moving on as the price of the product drops in response to increased competition.[16] Familism is the ideology of this small-scale commercial capitalism distinctive of local society in Taiwan.

When the mainlanders arrived in Taiwan after 1945 they brought with them the ideas of Sun Yatsen and enthusiasm for a second chance at implementing them. The ruling party of the mainlanders, the Guomindang (National People's Party), took over from the Japanese both the reins of state power and the large public industrial sector. And by carrying out land reform in the rural areas, the Guomindang laid the groundwork for their own legitimacy and an effective development strategy based on family use of small-scale private property. With islanders pursuing business in the private sphere, mainlanders proceeded on a state-directed or statist course of promoting economic growth, which accorded with both Sun Yatsen's doctrine and the realities of the public ownership of basic industries.[17] Statism is the ideology the mainlanders used to justify an extensive role for the state in redistributing national assets, setting economic objectives, regulating foreign transactions, providing an effective national defense, and directing the national development effort.

Native Taiwanese familism and the statism of the mainlanders have converged to provide the ideological basis for rapid industrialization of the island nation. There is both tension and complementarity in this combination of familism and statism. Familism opposes state regulation, closely guarding traditional family financing from outside scrutiny. It values close competition based upon labor-intensive, low-wage employment, and it is generally sensitive to speculative opportunities for increasing profits. Statism, on the other hand, is an ideology that equates progress with capital accumulation on a scale only government can undertake. Expressing disapproval of the "negative economic effects of private property, particularly speculation in money, commodities, land, and other assets,"[18] mainlanders champion the public enterprises of the state, mismanaged though they may be, as the backbone of state capitalism. It is the form of development prescribed for late-developing countries by Sun Yatsen in the *San Min Chu I* (Three Principles of the People).

Despite Sun's adherence to a form of social democracy, the *San Min Chu I* have provided a perfect ideological instrument for the Guomindang's program in Taiwan. Politically, Sun's first principle, nationalism, acts as a justification for the Republic of China's insistence that Taiwan is an inextricable part of China, an idea that has stirred the opposition of native Taiwanese. Sun's second principle, tutelary democracy, a long period during which people unaccustomed to self-rule learn the culture of democracy, has justified the authoritarian one-party rule exercised by the Guomindang, the mainlanders' party, over Taiwan. But in response to persistent pressure by Taiwanese for a more autonomous state for Taiwan, the ruling party has recently acknowledged that the last stage of constitutional democracy has arrived, when competitive electoral politics previously confined to the local level will be institutionalized at the national level. The third principle is the people's livelihood.

The most intriguing aspect of Sun Yatsen's conception of democratic government is its Confucian paternalism, manifested in the claim that government power and popular sovereignty are always two separate aspects of government. Justification for separating the two is based on his observation that just when modern civilization requires a powerful government to administer the complex affairs of a nation, its people, incapable of understanding the work of government, distrust all government's power because it cannot be held accountable. Sun's solution is to give the operation of government to "the qualified, who must not be hampered by constant interference by the people or representatives of the people."[19] In a democracy, however, since government must be subject to control by the people, sovereign rights must be retained by citizens. Sun "compared government to modern industries, and the president and his staff to experts who know how to manage the company, while the people were like shareholders, retaining control over the president but in general not interfering with the management."[20] Democracy can function in the modern world only in the Confucian spirit of benevolent paternalism on the part of able leaders and deferential consent on the part of subjects who value negotiation and accommodation over confrontation. This Chinese conception of democracy is one with which the founder of the modern city-state of Singapore can heartily agree.

Singapore: Music by a One-Man Band

Some years ago British Foreign Minister George Brown said approvingly to the British-educated prime minister of Singapore (known in his youth as "Harry" Lee), "Harry, you're the best bloody Englishman east of Suez!"[21] No doubt Brown thought he was paying Lee Kuan Yew the highest compliment, and perhaps the prime minister regarded it as such at the time. But in the years since "Harry" returned home from England in 1950 to join the struggle for independence, his ideas may have become less English and more attuned to the cultures of his Asian constituents.

One of the last surviving members of the "first generation" of nationalist leaders, Lee has been a veritable "one-man band" as composer and performer of the sweet music of success during his thirty-year tenure as prime minister and in his current post as senior minister. Although not without critics, he has demonstrated an apparent genius for selecting and adapting Western political values and institutions to harmonize with the multicultural traditions of the people of Singapore and with the twin objectives of political stability and economic development. Having earned the reputation of elder statesman, Lee is now invited to other Asian countries to share his formula for success and offer advice on how to proceed in their own situation.

At the time of independence in 1965 Singapore looked quite unpromising, lacking as it did the conventionally accepted ingredients for survival as a state and for economic viability. The country was small in land and population, ethnically divided, poor, lacking in both natural resources and capital, and the object of suspicion, even hostility, on the part of its neighbors.

Lee's Blend of Confucianism and Western Ideologies.   Out of these inauspicious ingredients and drawing upon ideas from his upbringing in a Chinese family that had been in Singapore for four generations, his education in British schools in the colony and at Cambridge University, living under the Japanese occupation, his train-

Lee Kuan Yew, prime minister of Singapore for
three decades, is still active in government as senior
minister.

Source: Photo from the Prime Minister's Office, Singapore.

ing and practice as a lawyer, his experiences in the united front with Communists in
the anticolonial nationalist movement, and elements of the cultures of his three Asian
constituencies, Lee gradually put together the recipe for success that still seems palatable to most (though not all) Singaporeans. It is a concoction of Confucian principles
of collectivism, consensus, and hierarchy and Western notions of individual freedom
and political participation. It combines democratic socialist attachment to realizing
the goal of equal opportunity and conservative insistence on the need for discipline
and order, free market economics, and state interventionism. Lee's ideas constitute
the reigning ideology of Singapore and have been implemented through government
policies and programs.

To create a Singaporean identity in this multiracial multicultural society, the national ideology promotes the shared values of "Nation before [ethnic] community and society above self; Family as the basic unit of society; Regard and community support for the individual; Consensus instead of contention; Racial and religious harmony."[22] Acceptance of these shared values, it is hoped, will be the glue that holds Singaporeans together while at the same time allowing each group to keep its own cultural heritage.

Government's "4Ms" Policy.   Harmony among the diverse "racial," religious, linguistic, and cultural groups to which Singaporeans belong is the objective of the government's "4Ms" policy of "multiracialism, multilingualism, multiculturalism and multireligiosity."[23] Chinese, Malays, Indians, and the 2 percent of the population who are none of those are to be treated equally and allowed, even encouraged, to keep their identification as members of different groups. The constitution recognizes four official languages—Mandarin Chinese, Malay, Tamil, and English—and bilingualism (English and one of the three Asian languages) is fostered through the education system, although mastery of English confers special advantage. Unlike Malaysia, where Islam has official support as the state religion, Singapore is a secular state, allowing the practice of all religions but favoring none above the others.

The equality of treatment that the 4Ms policy endorses provides justification for insistence on individual merit as the criterion for success. Meritocracy, which was the principle underlying the mandarinate in imperial China, has its modern incarnation in the concept of a civil service recruited on the basis of skills and performance, not on ethnicity or personal connections, and in public sector employment Singapore has recruited the brightest of its technologically qualified university graduates. The combination of equal access to education and employment based on merit is intended to produce a "natural" hierarchy, reflecting differences in individual talent and effort.

Respect for cultural differences, educational opportunity, and nondiscriminatory employment practices have not, however, produced equally successful results for Singapore's Malay minority as for the Chinese majority and the Indian minority. The most cohesive of the ethnic groups, Malays lag behind in education and in business; consequently, since the 1980s the government has encouraged special "affirmative action" programs to raise the school performance of Malay students and self-help projects for Malay entrepreneurs. Still, the government violates its own equal opportunity policy by restricting the numbers of Malays in the Singapore Armed Forces, reflecting doubts about Malay loyalty and evidencing the incompleteness of national integration. The "mixed salad" metaphor for Singaporean society fits the hyphenated identity of Chinese-, Malay-, Indian-Singaporeans better than the "melting pot" of a nonethnic collective Singaporean identity.

Fundamental Concern for Political Order.   The quest for social harmony among Singapore's heterogeneous people has its parallel in the political sphere, where Confucian distaste for overt expression of dissent has combined with a conservative fear of disorder to produce an authoritarian regime where political opposition is suppressed and individual freedoms of expression and organization are curtailed. The People's Action Party's official ideology, proclaimed at its founding, is "democratic socialism." The appearance of Western-style democracy—elections, opposition parties, and so on—exists but, as described in Chapter 4, the reality is otherwise. Some aspects of socialism are retained: the commitment to equality of opportunity, the welfare state programs of social services for its citizens, and government ownership of some enterprises and guidance of the economy, described in Chapter 5.

Lee explains his views on democracy in the Asian context in a way that underlines his overriding concern for order:

> I do not believe that democracy necessarily leads to development. I believe that what a country needs to develop is discipline more than democracy. Democracy leads to undisciplined and disorderly conditions which are inimical to development. The ultimate test of the value of a political system is whether it helps that society to establish conditions which improve the standard of living for the majority of its people, plus enabling the maximum of personal freedoms compatible with the freedom of others in society.[24]

Lee's own political style is notoriously paternalist, even domineering. To behave with the authority and responsibility of a father toward his family is in the Confucian tradition, as is being a model of virtue for others to emulate. But quite *un*Confucian is Lee's approach to power, eschewing the ritual and trappings traditionally associated with power holding; he travels on regularly scheduled Singapore Airline flights for his official trips, and his tastes in personal attire, government office, and residence are simple, even austere. Unlike the Chinese emperors' preoccupation with ceremony and the mandarins' preoccupation with status over policymaking, Lee's idea of power is utilitarian: What use can be made of it to bring about changes in conformity with his vision of what is good for the people of Singapore? Those uses range all the way from government actions to stimulate economic growth and attract foreign capital (described in Chapter 5) to regulating the citizens' personal behavior in the interest of health, safety, and private morality (for example, the ban on spitting and on smoking in public places, the installation of devices on trucks and taxis to warn the driver when the vehicle is exceeding the speed limit, and censorship of "morally offensive"—to officials' tastes—foreign books, periodicals, films).

Some Singaporeans find these and other restrictions intolerable and exercise the option of moving to another country. Others deplore the "cult of materialism"[25] that seems to be the central value driving the citizens of "Singapore, Inc." to conspicuous and competitive consumption, to evaluating themselves and others by their wealth, and to holding a vision of the future as more wealth through high technology and job-related technical education, rather than nonmaterialist "liberal" values in education and in personal and social goals.

Lee Kuan Yew's contribution to the economic development and political stability of Singapore is clear. Whether his particular mix of Asian cultural heritage and imported Western ideologies offers a durable pattern, transferable to other Asian societies, is not so clear. But there is no doubt that Lee has put his personal imprint on the encounter between culture and ideology in the spin-off Confucian society that is modern Singapore.

North Korea: Another Solo Performer

The similarities between Lee Kuan Yew and North Korea's President Kim Il Sung are numerous: Both are "Founding Fathers" and each has been the principal composer and conductor of the ideological themes that have guided and legitimized his particular brand of postindependence politics. Both have ruled through a Leninist-style party, prevailing over opponents by autocratic means; both have groomed a son as successor; and both have given the state a major role in economic development.

But there are differences too. While Lee began with an affinity for democratic socialism as he had observed it in England, Kim's political upbringing was, of course, in Marxism-Leninism. Lee is well educated, and his professional experience as a British-trained lawyer is quite different from Kim's limited education and his experiences as an anti-Japanese guerrilla fighter in Manchuria before returning from exile with the Soviet Army after the Japanese surrender in 1945.

Kim's goal when he came to power was the revolutionary overthrow of the old order, and the political institutions he created followed the Soviet style in both government and party; Lee, with less-than-revolutionary objectives, emulated Western-style governmental institutions. Kim's commitments to command socialism and to a Stalinist emphasis on heavy industry and agricultural collectivization remain unaltered, despite the changes that have occurred in both China and the Soviet Union/Russia; Lee's policies have certainly not displayed any special devotion to socialism. While his road to development led to Singapore's integration into the world capitalist system, Kim's policy was to develop without dependence on foreign capitalists (a policy that has shifted somewhat in the last few years toward efforts to attract foreign capital). Lee has long sought to bring into government and politics the most highly qualified technocrats, a class of people only now beginning to replace the aging guerrilla-fighter generation of political elites in North Korea.

Juche.   Kim Il Sung's contribution to the pantheon of ideologies in the communist world can be pictured as a troika, harnessing a breed of Soviet Marxist-Leninist orthodoxy together with a Stalinist-Maoist-demigod cult of personality behind a lead horse, the doctrine known as *Juche.* Juche, translated roughly as "self-reliance," was explained by Kim in a speech in Jakarta in 1965:

Juche means holding fast to the principle of solving for oneself all the problems of the revolution and construction in conformity with the actual conditions of one's country, mainly by one's own efforts. This is the realistic and creative stand, opposing dogmatism and applying the universal truth of Marxism-Leninism and the experiences of the international revolutionary movement to one's country in conformity with its historical conditions and national peculiarities. This is an independent stand of discarding the spirit of dependence on others, displaying the spirit of self-reliance, and solving one's own affairs on one's own responsibility under all circumstances.[26]

Juche's premise that one must fit Marxism-Leninism to the particular conditions in one's own country serves less as specific guidance for devising policies and programs (what "fits" is largely a matter of subjective choice, in principle testable by trial and error) than as justification for *not* slavishly following other communist countries' revolutionary patterns. As Kim put it in that same 1965 speech:

> It is self-evident that we cannot make a revolution by relying on others, and that others cannot make the Korean revolution in our stead. . . . While resolutely fighting in defense of the purity of Marxism-Leninism against revisionism, our Party has made every effort to establish *Juche* in opposition to dogmatism and flunkyism towards great powers. *Juche* is ideology, independence in politics, self-sustenance in the economy, and self-defense in national defense—this is the stand our Party has consistently adhered to.[27]

Kim's repeated exhortations to avoid the three cardinal sins of "dogmatism," "revisionism," and "flunkyism" have implications for foreign, as well as internal, politics. A simple, even simplistic, formula, "self-reliance" was in a sense forced upon North Korea, located as it is between two rival fraternal communist "protectors" and an array of capitalist "enemies"—South Korea, U.S. forces there, and ex-occupier Japan. Juche put China and the Soviet Union on notice that North Korea was determined not to become a "flunky" of either of them, nor to become too dependent on what North Korea sees as unreliable sources of support. By asserting Korea's right to avoid making a choice between those two contenders for leadership in the world communist camp, Juche left open the possibility of getting help from both of them, as circumstances permitted.

The doctrine's role as a guide to foreign policy is described as "an instrumental principle . . . in coping with the twin alliance security dilemmas of abandonment and entrapment—maximizing allied support in the face of a perceived threat from the South and minimizing the dysfunctional and delegitimizing input of allied control and/or interference."[28] In both foreign and domestic applications, Juche is clearly an expression of nationalism, designed to lend legitimacy to Kim's regime and the primacy of the Workers' Party of Korea as the rightful leaders of their people.

Stalinism and the Cult of Personality.   The two other elements of North Korean ideology are a rigid adherence to the Stalinist model for party-state relations, party organization, centralized planning, and the priority given to heavy industry (even after at least the latter two features have been dropped by the Soviets and the Chinese) and the cult of personality cultivated around the persons of Kim Il Sung and his son, Kim Jong Il. Kim's prescription for the Korean Workers' Party is: "iron discipline should be established in the Party, the unity of its ranks defended, the slightest factionalist tendency not tolerated, and the Party should be firmly protected from infiltration of bourgeois ideas."[29] It seems likely that the fate that befell the Communist

Party in the Soviet Union simply reinforced Kim's conviction about the wisdom of not deviating from Stalinist practices.

The edifice of ideology and institutions built by the elder Kim may survive his passing and enable the younger Kim to succeed in claiming the reins of power in his own right. Kim Il Jong has thus far shown no signs of wishing to reject or depart from his father's political and ideological legacy.

Other Confucian Societies

South Korea. The reigning ideology has been a combination of influences from Korea's political past under the monarchy and then under Japanese colonialism, the contemporary influence of the United States, first as occupier and then as military ally, and the ominous presence of the "Other" Korea, the communist regime in the North. From the monarchical period came the lesson that a strong center is necessary insurance against enemies, both internal and external. From the Japanese came training in "thought police" and other techniques of political repression, and the crippling effect of being denied experience in open political organization and activity. From the West, particularly from the United States, came the idea of constitutionalism, which in South Korea became a ritual exercise intended to legitimize successive authoritarian governments, all operating under the banner of republicanism. Frequent rewriting and amending of constitutions (currently the sixth since 1948) became the tool by which politicians manipulated the structures and powers of government to serve their own purposes. From the looming presence of the North, reinforced by the experience of the Korean War and by the cold war policy of the South's American ally, came an implacable anticommunism that provided justification for repression of dissent, including the use of armed force by the police and the military against civilians.

In recent years, the ruling elite has modified its ideological stance and its practices, allowing space for opposition parties to operate and admitting into its own ranks a leading opponent, Kim Young Sam, who won the presidency in 1992. These changes, described in Chapter 4, have been heralded as evidence that political democracy is being incorporated into the Korean political culture. There is some support for that perception: In a 1991 public opinion survey[30] three of five expressed a preference for democracy over authoritarianism (but two of five did not see democracy as the best system of government); there were important variations by class, age, and region, with greater support for democracy among the better-educated, more affluent younger people and in Cholla Province, long a center of opposition to the military regimes.

Vietnam. Unlike other societies in Southeast Asia, Vietnamese culture became Confucianized during a millennium of intermittent Chinese rule. Although Buddhism remained the dominant religion even after French missionaries enjoyed some success in converting a sizable minority to Catholicism, the prevailing model was the Confucian tradition of a secular state, headed by the emperor and administered by a meritocracy of mandarin scholars. Adoption of Confucianism under the influence of the high culture of China endowed Vietnamese with a sense of superiority over their non-Confucian Southeast Asian neighbors. This is manifest in rivalry with Thailand and competition for influence in Laos and Cambodia, both of which have more cultural affinity with (as well as geographical accessibility to) Thailand than Vietnam.

Like Korea, the division of Vietnam into two states after World War II produced a bifurcation in the ideological development of the country that ended with Vietnam's unification in 1975. In the North Marxist-Leninism, as interpreted and adapted to local conditions by Ho Chi Minh and other leaders, prevailed. In the South no coherent ideology emerged to guide successive governments. Nor did American pressure to create at least the appearance of a liberal democracy in South Vietnam succeed in producing commitment in theory or in practice to such a political vision. With unification under the Communists in 1975, the North's ideology became the orthodoxy for the whole country.

As mentioned in Chapter 4, there has been no modification of the principle of the leading role of the Communist Party in the political life of the state, although there has been some opening up of the political process to popular participation through direct elections to the national legislature and through some relaxation of party screening of candidates for public office. Religion, though not part of official party and government ideology, continues to influence popular attitudes and the clergy.

Government policy toward religion is that religious freedom is to be respected, but relations between the state and religious organizations have not been untroubled. The churches fear government restrictions on their activities and the government fears that foreign and internal opponents will use the Catholic and Buddhist churches as vehicles for antigovernment activities. The arrest and detention of Buddhist monks in Hue is explained by the government as the consequence of their antigovernment political acts, not because of their religious beliefs or observances.

To Buddhists, the distinction between political and religious action is blurred by the long tradition of the "god-king" and of religious involvement in government. The concept of a secular state and the principle of the separation of church and state are unfamiliar, contrary to historical and recent experience.

Hong Kong.   Under British colonial rule, there was no room for direct political participation in the affairs of the territory. This has left a legacy of indifference among a substantial portion of the population. The British government's rather last-minute conversion to the notion that the residents of the colony have some right to participate in their governance is an attempt to change this. Nonetheless, recent opinion surveys[31] show a high degree of distrust of leaders and the many groups now active in local politics. They are seen as excessively concerned with political issues to the neglect of economic and social issues.

Yet at the same time the respondents have high expectations of what political parties could or should do. Public opinion supports the present system of multiple channels of political access: political appointment, patronage, indirect election, as well as direct election. But if direct elections were the only avenue of recruitment to political office, parties could concentrate on competing with each other in mass electoral contests. They might then develop stronger leadership, greater discipline, and a wide popular base. Finally, although there is support in principle for democratization, people still express satisfaction with the colonial system because it has produced stability. One can only speculate whether the high value placed on stability is attributable to a persistent Confucian cultural bias toward order and predictability or to business preference for stable conditions or to a happy conjunction of both factors.

But if public attitudes are a hindrance to the emergence of strong unified Hong Kong Chinese leadership before 1997 it is likely that after 1997, as in colonial Hong Kong, leadership will still be concentrated in the bureaucracy.

Having looked at Confucian societies, we now turn to societies in Southeast Asia where the influences of Buddhism, Islam, and Christianity are strong.

EVOLUTION OF IDEOLOGIES IN OTHER ASIAN SOCIETIES

The predominantly Buddhist countries (Burma,[32] Thailand, Laos, and Cambodia), the predominantly Islamic countries (Malaysia, Indonesia, and Brunei), and the Christianized Philippines each have responded in somewhat different ways to the challenge of incorporating traditional values and practices into postindependence efforts to create or preserve national unity and promote economic development. In this section Burma, Malaysia, Indonesia, and the Philippines have been chosen for examination.

Burma: Socialism, Buddhism, and Nationalism

Burma, like the Philippines, as noted in Chapter 5, is an exception to the economic success story of other Asian Pacific countries. One factor frequently cited to explain Burma's relatively retarded economic growth is its self-isolation from the world economy, a policy at the opposite extreme from that of the Philippines. A second factor often mentioned as responsible for Burma's failure to develop effectively is the government's difficulty in forging national unity out of an ethnically and religiously divided population. Attempts to cobble together an ideology out of elements of nationalism, socialism, and Buddhism have met with little success in achieving national unity and economic growth. A possible explanation for Burma's singularly belated entry into the Asian Pacific developmental dynamic may be found in the way that Buddhist cultural values have combined and clashed with nationalist and socialist ideas in the ideological positions of its three prominent leaders: Aung San, U Nu, and Ne Win.

Socialism was embraced by the first generation of nationalist leaders exposed to Western ideas and has retained its appeal among a broad segment of the population. Even the current rulers of SLORC retain the rhetoric of socialism they inherited from the military junta's official embrace of "The Burmese Way to Socialism." But continuity in the use of "socialism" as an ideological plank in the platform of Burma's various governments obscures significant differences in the mix of traditional Buddhism, nationalism, socialism, and sheer opportunism that has characterized Burmese leadership since independence.

Aung San, U Nu, and Ne Win shared the same purpose: to provide a common moral identity for the new Burmese state, one that would assure popular support for the new government and political unity for both Burmans and the splintered minority populations. Both found capitalism and communism equally objectionable for different reasons: capitalism because it had been discredited as the vehicle used by the British to exploit and subjugate Burma; Marxism because it was materialistic and justified the use of violence; and the Leninist one-party system of the Soviet Union because it contradicted their notion of democracy. Democratic socialism provided the alternative, an ideological formula Ne Win perpetuated even after the military coup of 1962. But the doctrine meant quite different things to each of them.

Aung San's Secular Socialism.   Aung San's understanding of democratic socialism was secular, addressing itself to Burma's economic plight.[33] His vague idea of Burmese socialism as "something in between" capitalism and socialism was never elaborated as a practical ideology but served as an empty receptacle into which the purposes of successive leaders and the underlying patterns of Burmese culture have flowed. For Aung San, because Buddhism was a religion it belonged in the private sphere of civil society; Buddhist faith and the power of the monks needed to be disengaged from politics, not only to promote freedom of religious worship among people with differing faiths but to foster the purity of religious beliefs. "We must draw a clear line between politics and religion, because the two are not one and the same thing. If we mix religion with politics, then we offend the spirit of religion itself."[34] Economic rather than spiritual principles are the underpinning of government in the modern world, which for Aung San meant two things: that the separation of church and state as practiced in the United States was the appropriate model for Burma to follow, and that traditional Buddhist philosophical principles, if they were to become compatible with modern economic institutions and democratic ideas, had to be cleansed of their superstitious beliefs and rituals.

U Nu's Buddhist Socialism.   But this changed under U Nu's political leadership, when the idea of socialism became equated with the traditional Buddhist rejection of Western materialism. U Nu embraced socialism out of a profoundly religious Buddhist conviction that it offered a substitute for the evils of capitalism, which was rooted in human greed and selfishness. This led him to espouse a form of religious revivalism "reminiscent of the Buddhist kings of old."[35] Buddhism, in this tradition, is an integral part of Burmese politics and the backbone of an identifiable Burmese state. Propagating Buddhist faith, therefore, was a way of strengthening Burma's national identity, the power of the state, and the spirituality of its people. To this end, U Nu sponsored ritual efforts to propitiate evil spirits and the construction of 60,000 sand pagodas throughout Burma, further aggravating the economic situation and digressing markedly from Aung San's idea of democratic socialism in Burma. But while U Nu's nationalist-religious resurgence appealed to members of the Burmese urban elite who had been "'culturally disinherited by colonial acculturation' . . . [having] succumbed to western values and ways of life,"[36] it alienated the sizable and varied *minority* of ethnic nationalities for whom Buddhism as a state religion had historically meant a state controlled by and for the Burman majority.

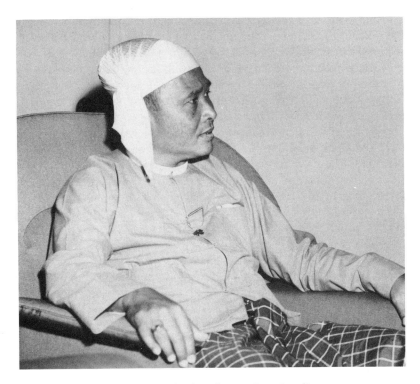

U Nu, devout Buddhist, a leader of Burma's nationalist movement
and first prime minister.
Source: United Nations photo 46405 MB/pcd.

The Military's Socialism.   When the military under General Ne Win came to
power in 1962, "The Burmese Way to Socialism" took another turn. A more secularized rhetoric of socialism stressing the importance of a rational, scientific worldview
replaced the religious denial of the importance of this world and the belief that one's
fate depended on the whim of supernatural forces. Monks were out, technocrats were
in. The Revolutionary Council, through which the military ruled, ended the privileged
position of Buddhism and financial support for it, viewing the clergy as parasitic and
opposed to their socialist program. Though Buddhism was relegated to the private
sphere, the regime nevertheless tried to win popular support by espousing as one of
its goals the spiritual, as well as material, happiness of the people. While *religion*
might be a private matter, the state had responsibility for improving the people's spiritual life, for promoting Buddhist moral values as the ethical foundation of socialism.

Buddhism and National Development.   It is not clear what capacity Buddhism,
the religious anchor of most Burmese, retains to lend or deny political legitimacy, to
promote or retard national integration and economic development. The anthropolo-
gist Edmund Leach suggests "that there is something about the Ethic of Buddhism
which is fundamentally at variance with the Spirit of Capitalism."[37] Wealth that a per-

son accumulates is to be given to support the clergy and build temples, bringing religious "credit" to the donor, but making that capital unavailable for materially productive purposes, such as building factories. As Medford Spiro observes, Burmans are culturally predisposed to use wealth in ways that assure them a more pleasurable rebirth rather than investing in economic enterprises destined to decay in this material world in which one is only a transient.[38] It is not, according to Mya Maung, a question of whether the Burmese want to improve their living conditions but the absence in Buddhist culture of attitudinal incentives to work and its opposition to acquisitiveness.[39]

In the years since independence in 1948, Burma has undergone several metamorphoses. In each of those metamorphoses, leaders claimed to be pursuing socialism, though its form and content have varied over time. But a cynical observer might contend that the present SLORC government is essentially nonideological except in the most primitive form of "conservatism" in the sense of invoking the need for "law and order" to justify continued military control. In a society ethnically fragmented into rival groups, each with its own banner of nationalism, in the absence of an overriding sense of collective identity and minimal consensus to hold the country together as a political community, the military regime can argue that it alone can save Myanmar from a fate like that of the Soviet Union or—worse—Yugoslavia.

So the search continues for an ideological formulation that will succeed in welding a unified nation out of a culturally diverse population and in fostering economic development without subordinating national interests to the world capitalist system. As Steinberg puts it:

> Myanmar needs a cohesive ideological or intellectual underpinning to bind the heterogeneous state together. U Nu's previous attempt to employ Buddhism as such a force and the military's "Burmese Way to Socialism," both failed. Today, the SLORC seems to be employing a *tatmadaw*[military]-led xenophobic nationalism as the ideological cement binding the state together. It may be counterproductive to some of the very goals that the state has set for itself.[40]

Malaysia: Affirmative Action for the Malay Majority

In contrast to China, where Maoist ideology directly challenges both the traditional Confucian hierarchy and Western liberalism, Malaysian ideology encourages both Malay cultural values and elements of British liberalism. Unlike Japan, however, where traditional culture was systematically integrated with German conservatism to form a modern corporate ideology, Malaysia's strategy has been to preserve Malay culture intact while adopting a liberal commitment to representative government and economic progress. This formal endorsement of liberal values makes it possible for non-Malays to acquiesce in the Malay political elite's position as senior partner in the coalition of communal parties that have dominated Malaysian politics since preindependence days and in the special rights accorded to Malays in the constitution.

In the years leading to independence, Malaysian political elites shaped the nationalist ideology to fit certain inescapable realities inherited from precolonial and colonial days: an ethnically and culturally divided population in which Malays had a shaky majority; the influence of Islam, especially among the indigenous rural masses; the territorial division of the country into sultanates; and the acceptance by the Western-educated class of British liberalism as the legitimate model for a modern political system. Ethnic division produced *bumiputerism,* continuing and expanding on the British practice of preferential treatment for Malays; Islam became the state religion; the sultans accepted federalism as the formula for national unification; and liberalism was interpreted as representative government, majority rule, and laissez-faire in economic matters. In the decades since independence, each of those realities has undergone changes, effecting adaptation in the dominant ideology and in government policies.

Bumiputerism.   At the core of national ideology in Malaysia today is the concept of *bumiputerism.* Derived from *bumiputra,* meaning "sons of the soil," it refers to the special rights of Malays (and other non-Malay indigenous people in Sabah and Sarawak) as distinguished from the "immigrant" Chinese and Indians, descendants of laborers the British encouraged to come to extract tin and rubber for the world market. Preferential treatment for Malays in access to higher education and civil service positions had begun as British colonial policy and was incorporated in the constitution drawn up at the time of independence. The tacit agreement then between Malay and Chinese leaders was that politics and economics would be kept separate, with the Malays dominating the former and the Chinese the latter.

But this compact proved less than satisfactory to the Malays, as Chinese wealth brought with it political clout and as the income gap between the Malay masses and the Chinese and Indians widened. The slowness of Malays to move up economically was at least in part the result of British policy encouraging them to preserve their traditional way of life, protected from the inroads of commercialism and urbanization. Tensions between Malays and Chinese increased in the decade after independence, resulting in riots in 1969 and in an expansion of bumiputerism in the New Economic Policy. NEP, a form of "affirmative action" for the benefit of the disadvantaged majority, involved government action to increase the Malay share in business and to improve the lives of rural Malays.

Ethnic separation, which had originated in the alliance between British colonial rulers and the Malay aristocracy, was reinforced during the Japanese occupation, when Malays collaborated with the occupiers while the Chinese waged armed struggle against them. The separatism thus magnified between ethnic Chinese and Malays was further solidified by the postwar "Emergency," pitting mainly Chinese Communist insurgents against the British authorities. Today, it is continued by bumiputerism and inhibits the formation of a national ideology integrating all the citizens of Malaysia.

However, the bonds linking bumiputra may come under pressures generated by economic development, which differentiates interests along occupational, class, and rural-urban lines. And fissures are opening up between Malays and the indigenous people in Sabah who, although they are not Malay and many are Christian, were accorded bumiputra status at the time of joining the union in 1963. Political disagreements between the central government and UMNO on the one hand and the Sabah chief minister and the mainly Christian opposition party in control there have erupted in disputes over logging regulations and in federal prosecution of the chief minister on charges of corruption. These fissures in the bumiputra community further complicate the ethnic impediments to a truly national Malaysian identity.

Federalism.   The British first introduced the concept of federation as a way of bringing the separate sultanates under a common colonial administration without disturbing the traditional relationship between sultans and subjects. However, upon returning to Malaysia at the end of World War II, the British proposed as a step toward independence the creation of a unified state, as well as the abolition of special privileges for Malays and granting citizenship to all long-term residents and all those born in the colony. This proposal aroused vociferous opposition among the Malay community; peasants united behind their aristocratic leaders to fight this threat to their dominant position. They forced the British government to back down on the idea of a Malay Union with equal citizenship for Malays and non-Malays alike. So the constitution was drawn up for an independent Federation of Malaya (renamed the Federation of Malaysia at the time of the addition of Singapore, Sabah, and Sarawak in 1963). Sultans kept their thrones and state governments share power with the central government.

In recent years, Prime Minister Mahathir has come into conflict with the sultans, succeeding in reducing their privilege of immunity from prosecution, publicizing their expenditures for luxuries such as palace renovations and racehorses, and backing a rival claimant to the Kelantan throne. His objective is seen as increasing the power of the central government over the states, a modification of the original federal compact, perhaps signifying a trend toward the unitary state proposed by the British in 1946 and rejected by the Malay majority. Now, in a curious twist, the non-Malay non-Moslem minorities tend to support states' rights against centralization of power because they feel their chances for protecting their rights are greater in a decentralized federal system.

Liberalism.   The alliance between the British colonial authorities and the Malay aristocracy contributed to the latter's embracing British liberalism as the favored ideological orientation. Liberal principles and institutions, including representative government, majority rule, and protection of individual rights, were incorporated in the constitution, and the liberal policy of minimal government intervention in the economy was continued.

With the passage of time, however, adherence to those principles suffered some erosion. The interethnic riots in 1969, in which the police were unable to protect Chinese and Indians from heavy casualties at the hands of Malay mobs, led to a period of suspension of the parliament and rule by decree. Restoration of constitutional government was followed by the adoption of constitutional amendments prohibiting public discussion of sensitive racial issues that might cause social unrest and assigning quotas for bumiputra in universities.

Another sequel to the 1969 riots was the adoption of the New Economic Policy, signaling departure from the principle of laissez-faire in economic affairs. Since "direct government involvement in the economy was associated with socialism, a political ideology that was anathema to the existing leadership,"[41] the shift away from laissez-faire was justified by citing the stellar case of Japan as proof that government intervention in a nonsocialist state could be beneficial in obtaining specific economic results. More recently, Prime Minister Mahathir has denounced the laissez-faire development models promoted by the World Bank and International Monetary Fund.

So the commitment to liberalism made by the early leaders has been modified over time to advance the cause of Malay progress and to defuse the volatile issue of interethnic relations by muzzling public discussion.

Islam.   The final element of Malaysian ideology is Islam. Schooled in British liberalism, the secular-oriented political elite has not only recognized Islam as the state religion but moved in the direction of "Islamization." In order to strengthen its primarily rural political base among conservative Malay Muslims and to counter the appeal of the Islamic opposition party, PAS, UMNO has increasingly incorporated spiritual elements representing the perspective of more orthodox Moslems. This may account for some of the rhetoric of Dr. Mahathir: "Our concept of being developed does not simply focus on per-capita income, but on the quality of life and morality as well. The hedonistic materialism of present [Western] models is not for us. We hope the rest of the world will give us this freedom of choice and not harass us into conformity in the name of freedom."[42]

Still, the prime minister aims at transforming the influence of Islamic beliefs from conservative resistance to the government's goals of economic and social modernization into a moderate progressive force. In 1992 the government created the Malaysian Institute for Islamic Understanding, described by its director as "a policy study body which will offer Islamic interpretations of government policy."[43] Its agenda seems to be to formulate and publicize a Moslem "work ethic," convincing the faithful that hard work and material success are compatible with fidelity to Islamic beliefs and practices. "The idea," according to the head of a nongovernmental youth organization, "is to refocus the ethos of Islam and give progressive principles embodied in the religion more attention."[44] A balance must be struck, in Mahathir's words, "between spiritual attainment and material development."[45]

Vision 2020.   The most current expression of national purpose is the prime minister's projection of what Malaysia will become by the year 2020, called "Vision 2020." Having moved in the years since independence from an economy based almost solely on the export of raw materials to an exporter of light industrial goods as well, Malaysia now aims at reaching the pinnacle of "full development" by 2020. The prime minister's vision is described by Kamal Salih, the executive director of the Malaysian Institute of Economic Research, an influential think tank: "The details are still very sketchy on what it means to become fully developed. But the country closest to what we want to achieve would probably be Sweden. We like their high level of education, their solid industrial base, their advanced technology and their strong social system."[46]

The goal of economic progress may have a broad appeal to all Malaysians sufficiently compelling to diminish the majority-minority differences that have troubled the society and shaped political discourse for more than a century. An expanding "pie" of wealth certainly opens the way to making the bumiputra richer without making the Chinese and Indians poorer. But whether Vision 2020 will hold the center against the challenge of Islamic fundamentalism, the resistance of the sultans to inroads on their prerogatives, the inertia of rural Malay society, the tensions between peninsular and insular states, and the long-standing animosities between the indigenous and "immigrant" communities is impossible to predict.

Indonesia: Industrialization Ideology Holds It Together

In Indonesia as in Malaysia, modern ideology grows out of the nationalist opposition to foreign rule. But unlike Malaysian nationalism, which settled into a moderate blend of Malay culturalism and British liberalism in the context of an amicable transfer of power, Indonesian nationalism has been volatile, shifting from socialist radicalism to military-sponsored industrialization ideology in response to a complicated intermeshing of national and international forces. In the aftermath of a revolutionary struggle for independence against the Dutch, nationalist sentiment was militant. But it was divided both culturally and ideologically.

Cultural Divisions.   Culturally, nationalist sentiment in Indonesia inherited a three-fold division among animist, Hindu-Buddhist, and Islamic "layers," each representing the dominant thinking among people in the archipelago at successive periods in time. Though the majority of Indonesians are Moslem, comprising the largest Muslim population of any nation, this common denominator masks a diversity of religious outlooks deriving from earlier influences that swept across these islands at the crossroads between the Indian and Pacific Oceans. As each "layer" has historically settled on top of the influences of its predecessor, considerable mixing of elements of all three occurred. As Islam slowly spread throughout the archipelago between the thirteenth and sixteenth centuries, it eroded the institutional structures of the earlier religions, animist and Hindu-Buddhist, incorporating some elements and replacing others with Islamic institutions. But for people whose spiritual symbolism had for centuries been shaped by the earlier Hindu-Buddhist and animist beliefs, Islam provided more of a veneer, beneath which the older symbols continued to hold sway, than a substitute for older beliefs.

In Java especially, each of the three "layers" has remained the particular identity of a singular social class that has evolved its own distinct ideological response to the challenge of modernization. Since Javanese are the largest of Indonesia's 300 distinct ethnolinguistic cultures, making up almost half the country's population, and have provided the core of political leadership in modern Indonesia, this tripartite division of Javanese by class and culture has played a significant role in the formation of a dominant ideology for the country. There is an upper class (*prijaji*), with its roots in the court cultures of the great Hindu-Buddhist states; a lower peasant class (*abangan*), with roots in the ancient animist world of spirits, magic, and communal rituals; and a merchant class (*santri*) of coastal traders with a staunch faith in Islam. *Santri* is a term that has come to identify Moslems, both in villages and in towns, whose strict observance of daily prayer and close attachment to the other institutions of Islam are marked off from the rest of Javanese society.[47]

The peasant class was able to adopt Islamic practices without rejecting animist beliefs. The result was the "statistical Moslem," the man who was circumcised, married, and buried by Muslim rites, because there was no institutionalized alternative, but who ate pork, fasted not during Ramadan but on moonless nights, placed trust in magical daggers, took wives and concubines as often as he pleased, and worshipped the spirits of his ancestors and a plurality of gods as much as Allah.[48]

In somewhat different fashion, members of the upper class became secularized Moslems, retaining their Hindu-Buddhist belief in social refinement and self-control as signs of their status as spiritual superiors. But to the more orthodox Moslem religious community of merchants, students, and scholars, the characteristic Javanese pattern of inclusivism, which permitted people to embrace Islam in addition to their other beliefs, was a perversion of the Moslem religion. Thus, accompanying the cultural tolerance of the Javanese tradition for including Islam into the house of Gods, there is the tension between the devout Moslem on the one hand and the "statistical Moslem" on the other.

Ideological Divisions.   The underlying conflicts among these disparate cultural strains found expression in three contending ideological movements. The prijaji had formed the Nationalist Party (PNI), the abangan peasants had found political representation in the Communist Party (PKI), and the santri merchants, the devout Moslems, joined forces with the reformist Moslems in the Masyumi Party. The Nationalists occupied a broadly defined ideological center between the revolutionary social and economic agenda of the Communists on the left and the religious Moslem agenda associated with an Islamic state on the right. Some Nationalists were adherents of Liberalism, advocating science and progress as the foundation of a cosmopolitan Indonesian state; others gravitated more toward either a socialist idea of economic justice or a religious idea of social justice. Sukarno took these traditional cultural strands and modern ideological ideas and wove them into a symbolic design for the new Indonesian state.

Pantja Sila.   First articulated during the latter days of the Japanese occupation, Sukarno's vision of the new republic's symbolic framework was composed of five principles, the Pantja Sila. It was designed as a "sacred" but nonsectarian ideological foundation for rival political forces to live together under the same national roof. As a statement of principles, the Pantja Sila is "short, ambiguous, and impeccably highminded, the five points being 'nationalism,' 'humanitarianism,' 'democracy,' 'social welfare,' and (pluralistic) 'monotheism.'"[49] While in the Javanese tradition of syncretic inclusivism, Pantja Sila provided no clear direction for concrete social and political action and became, in the end, little more than a nationalist slogan for whatever government ruled Indonesia. As such it still constitutes the official ideology of Suharto's New Order military regime.

Sukarno's "Guided Democracy."   During the period of constitutional democracy that followed independence, Indonesia descended toward political chaos under a proliferation of parties and factions within parties. Only the Communists and the religious Moslems formed ideologically driven movements, but neither they nor the military had sufficient power to rule Indonesia. Sukarno, by virtue of his charisma the only person commanding enough to contain all these segments within one regime, imposed authoritarian rule, calling it Guided Democracy.

Like the Pantja Sila, though somewhat more programmatic, Guided Democracy was made up of five elements: the 1945 constitution, Indonesian-style socialism, Guided Democracy, Guided Economy, and Indonesian personality. Couched in an increasingly strident anti-Western and anti-imperialist rhetoric, this program intimated that authoritarianism today would bring about a system of collective production and distribution gradually and without class struggle sometime in the distant future. All groups were to work together as the "people," a concept that became mystically embodied in Sukarno himself. In his words:

> It is because of this that I always urge: unity, unity, and again unity. And we must understand that our revolution can only exert its maximum power when it is truly a national revolution, national and aligned. The revolution of a *people.* And *not* the revolution of one or another class. How often is the word "people" misused. It is used as a mask to camouflage the interests of a particular class. . . . All social and religious sections of our people are without exception revolutionary, because the purpose of the struggle is to annihilate imperialism and the old order, and to accelerate the advent of a new order in the form of national freedom.[50]

While publicly supporting the Communist Party, prohibiting opposition parties, and promoting socialism, Sukarno attempted to retain the loyalty of the military by entrusting it with management of the nationalized Dutch corporate assets in Indonesia. This placed the military in an unusual position. Since 1955 it had received material support and technical training from the United States. Thus military officers were increasingly subject to influence by technocratic ideas of the military-as-modernizers just as they found themselves gaining experience in running the nationalized economic enterprises of Indonesia. In the following years, as the army was called on to suppress the protests, plots, and rebellions (including one instigated by the CIA) precipitated by deteriorating conditions under Sukarno's rule, it strengthened an identity of itself as the only salvation of Indonesian unity with the promise of economic development. Lacking a mass base of his own, Sukarno by 1965 found himself powerless to prevent the squaring off of the two antagonists, the Communists and the military, that he had hoped to balance but who were vying with each other for control of Indonesia's destiny.

Suharto's New Order.

The New Order ushered in by General Suharto was heavily indebted ideologically to the patronage of the United States. It was based on an ethos of staunch anticommunism and modern military professionalism. A thoroughgoing purge of Communists was carried out with the complicity of militant Moslems in the wake of the military "countercoup" of October 1, 1965. One and a half million Indonesians suspected of communist sympathies were massacred and a permanent legal ban was placed on any form of Marxism. Having eliminated the Communists, the military regime used the Pantja Sila as a political weapon against militant Moslems by making it official state doctrine to be adhered to by all organizations. With its stress on a nonsectarian secular state, the Pantja Sila was a convenient device for neutralizing Moslem demands for an Islamic state. In this way, the New Order nullified radical demands from both the left and the right, setting the parameters for a politically stable, secular state that offered appropriate safeguards to acquire loans from international lending institutions and assure foreign capital a safe environment for its investments.

The ideological achievement of the New Order was to substitute pragmatic policymaking on the part of the military for futile ideological conflict among contending parties. What justified the military as the appropriate political actor to carry out this pragmatic policymaking was the doctrine of Dual Function, a constitutional principle that sanctioned the military's carrying out a dual role in both security/political and social/economic affairs. This doctrine was supplemented with the New Order insistence on "monoloyalty," a policy that strictly forbade civil servants (including teachers and faculty members of state universities) from any political affiliation other than absolute loyalty to the government. As the military transformed itself into a civilian party, the general population was forced to abstain from political activity except during elections. This created the political ambiance for the task at hand: "accelerated modernization," a program for rapid industrialization to be carried out with the technical assistance of specialists from the United States and the monetary cooperation of "international lending institutions, friendly foreign governments and private foreign capital."[51]

With the inflow of foreign capital assured by antilabor, anticommunist government policies, military officials of the New Order were able to build a political coalition as a base of internal support. Middle-class beneficiaries of successful development policies were willing to trade their political rights for economic gain. Catholic and Protestant minorities, alarmed by Moslem "extremism," joined civil servants and military officers to suppress Moslem activism. And traditionalist aristocrats, who had fallen from favor in the heyday of the nationalist struggle for independence, made a political comeback, their conservatism bolstering the regime and adding ethnic color for a growing tourist industry. Thus, "industrialization ideology," adopted on the advice of U.S. technocrats in conjunction with the World Bank and other international lending agencies, has been successful at the price of an overall climate of political suppression and loss of human rights. This price is acknowledged by the military regime when it argues that as a developing nation Indonesia cannot afford the luxury of human rights as long as it has to concentrate on the problems of economic development.

The Philippines: Patron-Clientism in American-Style Politics

In the Philippines more than anywhere else in the Asian Pacific, liberalism in its classical sense provided the modern symbolism for the nation-state. Though usually attributed to American influence, popular sentiment for liberal principles of government in the Philippines has its roots in Spanish colonialism. Starting in the 1870s and culminating in the Filipino revolution in 1896, an educated class of Filipinos demanded the same political rights enjoyed by Spaniards under the monarchy. Jose Rizal, the fifth-generation Chinese mestizo novelist, poet, and physician who had studied in Spain and later became a martyr to the cause of Filipino nationalism, advocated elite participation in self-government under Spanish colonial rule. As part of the reform movement of the educated class, the *ilustrados,* Rizal had based his claims for Filipino rights on the Enlightenment principles of natural law.

Thus, in 1899, when the United States annexed the Philippines rather than granting its independence, Americans aborted a revolution committed to liberal principles of the natural rights of individuals. Although the United States suppressed the revolution, it confirmed Rizal's reputation as a national hero in the American-run educational system. This served the purpose of diverting attention from more radical nationalists by assuring the dissemination of a moderate rather than a revolutionary liberal ideology among Filipinos. As a result, by 1935, when the Philippines was preparing for its promised independence from the United States, the economically and politically powerful Filipino elite that was poised to take control of the country identified ideologically with the liberalism of Woodrow Wilson and Franklin Roosevelt.[52]

The Tradition of Patron-Client Relationships. Another element of Rizal's nationalist contribution was the rediscovery of Filipinos' Malay heritage. At the core of this traditional indigenous culture, submerged beneath layers of Spanish and American influence, is the mutual trust that grows out of the debt of gratitude one owes to "someone who has given selfless aid in time of crisis."[53] The prototype for this kind of enduring trust is the relationship between father and son. But in Philippine society it expands beyond the family into "fictive kinship" relationships between individuals occupying unequal positions of wealth and power. The *compadre* system, for example, consists of choosing high-status sponsors for the baptism or wedding of one's children, the choice based on the sponsor's social standing and financial capacity to care for and promote the weaker, more vulnerable "family" charges. In this manner a network of dyadic patron-client relationships is the basis for vertically cementing all social relationships.

The political ramifications of a patron-client system are visible even today in the Philippines. One is the relationship between a politician and the constituents he has assisted in some way (with cash, a job, or a license). They repay their debt by loyally voting for him when he runs for office. Unlike the traditional forms of mutual trust typifying families of old, however, political loyalties are implicit bargains based on expedience and subject to recalculation. Just as ordinary individuals seek the patronage of a politician to solve personal problems, the politician seeks out yet more powerful sponsors, expanding his own fictive kin to assist him with greater resources. In this way limitless patron-client relationships constitute the social and political bonds that tie the weaker to the stronger in vertical networks of dependence. In the Philippines, where neither nationalism nor the state has been strong enough to foster "public trust," this patron-client pattern of personal ties still dominates rural political and, although to a declining degree, urban life.

How does this culturally inherited pattern of face-to-face ties connect with the liberal ideology that emerges from Western rule in the Philippines? First, by defining individuals' "rights" in concrete (rather than abstract) terms as depending on *who* rather than *what* one knows, traditional culture makes the democratic electoral framework a captive of traditional purposes. The demands placed upon democratic political institutions reflect the interests of those with personal connections both in electoral and bureaucratic positions. Such preferential treatment for friends and family on the part of politicians might easily be mistaken for "corrupt" behavior in an American cultural context. Second, the patron-client system in the Philippines promotes political parties that are indistinguishable from one another by ideological principles or programmatic agendas for action. If one's electoral loyalty is governed by calculations of who is wealthy and powerful enough to repay a favor, then switching parties to support an incumbent is a pragmatic, even rational response to political options. If and when bargaining fails to deliver benefits, however, ideologies become important. Discontent with the political system's capacity to function can lead to ideological critique. Ideologies, therefore, are more often invoked by parties in opposition to the government, particularly leftist insurgents.

The Role of Ideology and the Supernatural.   The relative irrelevance of ideologies as a basis for politics is reinforced by the mix of sacred and secular elements in Philippine political culture. A religious conception of politics is, of course, central to Moslem and some Christian communities in the Philippines. But outside the religious communities, a widespread belief among peasants that magic and luck, or *suerte,* determine why people acquire wealth and power discourages more rational explanations of political authority. This sacred element in Filipino attitudes toward political events (for example, the overthrow of Marcos was widely attributed to divine intervention) frequently coexists with attitudes and values of Western origin, like individual rights to freedom of expression and assembly.[54] Filipinos turn out in great numbers for political rallies and express great interest in elections, without necessarily eschewing supernatural ideas about what affects political outcomes.

Thus while Philippine society is observed by many to be both highly democratic and highly politicized as measured by voting turnout and participation in political rallies, its democratic institutions are permeated by older traditional patterns of patron-client relations and sacred (sometimes magical) notions attached to worldly success that impede an identification of politics with public trust and justice for all. In this respect the Philippines is similar to other Asian Pacific nations, which exhibit a unique mixture of Western ideas and Asian cultural precepts carried into the modern age.

SUMMARY

The ways in which Asian nations have borrowed and transformed Western ideologies to express their modern aspirations defy easy generalizations. Countries that were colonized were influenced by the ideology of their rulers: Malaysia absorbed liberalism from the British while the Philippines learned liberalism from the Americans. In practice, then, there were varieties of liberalism as there were of the other Western ideologies introduced to the Asian colonies by imperialist powers. When alternative ideologies were available to modernizers, the particular ideology a country settled on was influenced by such factors as its own cultural heritage, the ethnic homogeneity or diversity of its population, and the "fit" between its own political goals and those favored by the particular ideologies in circulation at the time.

Ideologies were important in shaping the new structures and institutions with which a country began its economic modernization and political development. For Japan, a mixture of conservative ideas from Germany and liberal ideas from England, France, and the United States molded the institutions of government and the economy under Meiji rule, with equal rights and constitutional guarantees of freedom added by the United States-imposed constitution after the Second World War. In China, Vietnam, and North Korea communism meant the institutionalization of economic equality under the dictatorship of the Communist Party. And in the ethnically and religiously pluralist societies of Myanmar, Malaysia, and Indonesia, syncretic ideologies were fashioned to obtain consensus under the leadership of the dominant ethnic group.

But ideologies alone provide only the skeletal outlines of modern political structures; the persistence of inherited cultural ideas flesh out how these structures actually work. Thus, in Asian Pacific countries, cultural values of power-as-status, collectivism, hierarchy, and the harmony produced by consensus continue to define how the new ideas and the structures in which they are embedded actually function. Just as patron-client relationships give substance to the idea of "people power" in the Philippines, the corporate harmony of respected leaders and loyal followers provides the substance of "enlightened conservatism" in Japan and the paternalism of Communist Party functionaries dispenses the justice of "socialism with Chinese characteristics" in China. In Asian Pacific countries generally, therefore, Western ideological influences have been modified in practice by the cultural inheritance of one or more groups of people inhabiting the modern state.

The distinctive blending of Western ideological principles with Asian cultural beliefs and practices has yielded in all these countries a continuing tension between ideology and culture, between the ideals of a modern system of justice and the cultural expectations of equity and fairness. The fulcrum at which these unevenly matched partners balance one another on the scales of justice shifts imperceptibly as states succeed or fail in delivering on their promises.

QUESTIONS FOR DISCUSSION

1. In what significant ways do you see Asian Pacific cultures as similar to and different from your own?

2. How have Asian Pacific leaders adapted Western ideologies to suit the cultural circumstances and practical needs of their people?

3. What similarities and differences do you see between Marxism as a philosophical outlook and Confucianism?

4. What were Mao's contributions to Marxist thought? How do you think they reflected Mao's personal background and/or the cultural fabric of Chinese civilization?

5. What, if any, similarities do you see in the ruling ideas championed in China, Taiwan, Singapore, North Korea, and Vietnam?

6. How do you think religion has influenced the formation of ideologies in Myanmar, Malaysia, Indonesia, and the Philippines?

NOTES

1. Hung-chao Tai, ed., *Confucianism and Economic Development: An Oriental Alternative?* (Washington, D.C.: The Washington Institute Press, 1989), p. 7. A more widely known example of the cultural approach is Lucian Pye, *Asian Power and Politics: The Cultural Dimensions of Authority* (Cambridge, MA: The Belknap Press of Harvard University Press, 1985).

2. David I. Steinberg, *Burma's Road Toward Development: Growth and Ideology Under Military Rule* (Boulder: Westview Press, 1981), p. 176.

3. Joseph J. Tobin, David Y. H. Wu, and Dana H. Davidson, "How Three Key Countries Shape Their Children," *World Monitor,* April 1989, pp. 36–45.

4. Pye, *Asian Power and Politics,* pp. 32–38.

5. Ibid., p. 53.

6. Carol Gluck, *Japan's Modern Myths: Ideology in the Late Meiji Period* (Princeton, NJ: Princeton University Press, 1985), p. 248.

7. The material in this section comes from Gluck, *Japan's Modern Myths,* pp. 248–51. The quotation is found on p. 250.

8. Robert T. Oliver, *Leadership in Asia: Persuasive Communication in the Making of Nations, 1850–1950* (Newark: University of Delaware Press, 1989), p. 30.

9. See Oliver, *Leadership in Asia,* pp. 36–45, for a biographical sketch of Okuma Shigenobu.

10. From an editorial in the *Toyo Keizai Shimpo,* 25 December 1895, quoted in Byron K. Marshall, *Capitalism and Nationalism in Prewar Japan: The Ideology of the Business Elite, 1868–1941* (Stanford: Stanford University Press, 1967), p. 11.

11. Marshall, *Capitalism and Nationalism,* p. 97.

12. Found in Chapter 3 of the Japanese constitution, full English text reproduced in Robert E. Ward, *Japan's Political System* (Englewood Cliffs, NJ: Prentice-Hall, 1978).

13. ". . . we are first 'poor' and second 'blank.' . . . By 'blank' I mean we are like a blank sheet of paper . . . which is good for writing on." "On the Ten Major Relationships," *Selected Works of Mao TseTung,* vol. 5 (Peking: Foreign Languages Press, 1977), p. 306.

14. Mark Selden, "The Yenan Legacy: The Mass Line," in *Chinese Communist Politics in Action,* ed. A. Doak Barnett (Seattle: University of Washington Press, 1970), p. 104.

15. Victor Li, "Law and Penology: Systems of Reform and Correction," in *Deviance and Social Control in Chinese Society,* ed. Amy Auerbacher Wilson et al. (New York: Praeger Publishers, 1977), p. 148. See also Victor Li, *Law Without Lawyers* (Boulder: Westview Press, 1978).

16. Danny Kin-Kong Lam and Ian Lee, "Guerrilla Capitalism and the Limits of Statist Theory: Comparing the Chinese NICs," in *The Evolving Pacific Basin,* ed. Cal Clark and Steve Chan (Boulder: Lynne Rienner, 1992), p. 120.

17. Edwin A. Winckler, "Statism and Familism on Taiwan," in *Ideology and National Competitiveness: An Analysis of Nine Countries,* ed. George C. Lodge and Ezra F. Vogel (Boston: Harvard Business School Press, 1987), p. 180.

18. Ibid., p. 183.

19. Quoted in Chester C. Tan, *Chinese Political Thought in the Twentieth Century* (Garden City, NY: Anchor Books, 1971), p. 129.

20. Ibid.

21. Stan Sesser, "A Nation of Contradictions," *New Yorker,* 13 January 1992, p. 46.

22. John Andrews, *The Asian Challenge* (Hong Kong: Longman Group Far East Limited, 1991), p. 144.

23. Sharon Siddique, "Singaporean Identity," in *Management of Success: The Moulding of Modern Singapore,* ed. Kernial Singh and Paul Wheatley (Boulder: Westview, 1990), p. 563.

24. Lee Kuan Yew, quoted in "Discipline vs. Democracy," *Far Eastern Economic Review,* 10 December 1992, p. 29.

25. Ho Wing Men, "Value Premises Underlying the Transformation of Singapore," in Singh and Wheatley, *Management of Success,* pp. 671–91.

26. Yuk-sa Li, ed., *Juche! The Speeches and Writings of Kim Il Sung* (New York: Grossman Publishers, 1972), p. 45.

27. Ibid., pp. 45–46.

28. Samuel S. Kim, "North Korea and the Non-Communist World: The Quest for National Identity," in *North Korea in Transition,* ed. Chong-Sik Lee and Se-Hee Yoo (Berkeley: University of California Institute of East Asian Studies, 1991), p. 27.

29. Li, *Juche!,* p. 15.

30. Myung Chey, "Democratization in Korea as Perceived by Its Mass Public" (paper delivered at the Association for Asian Studies meeting, Los Angeles, 27 March 1993).

31. Siu-kai Lau, "Hong Kong Chinese Attitude Toward Political Leadership" (paper presented at the Association for Asian Studies meeting, Los Angeles, 27 March 1993).

32. In this chapter "Burma" is used rather than "Myanmar" because that was the country's name during most of the period under discussion.

33. Aung San, *Burma's Challenge 1946,* p. 4, quoted in Josef Silverstein, *Burmese Politics* (New Brunswick, NJ: Rutgers University Press, 1980), p. 143.

34. Donald Eugene Smith, *Religion and Politics in Burma* (Princeton, NJ: Princeton University Press, 1965), p. 118.

35. John F. Cady, "Religion and Politics in Modern Burma," in *Far Eastern Quarterly* 12 (1953): p. 161.

36. Smith, *Religion and Politics in Burma,* p. 124.

37. Quoted in David I. Steinberg, *Burma's Road Toward Development* (Boulder: Westview Press, 1981), p. 176.

38. Quoted in Steinberg, *Burma's Road Toward Development,* p. 178.

39. Quoted in Steinberg, *Burma's Road Toward Development,* p. 177.

40. Steinberg, *Burma's Road Toward Development,* p. 736.

41. Mavis Puthucheary, "The Shaping of Economic Policy in a Multi-Ethnic Environment: The Malaysian Experience," in *Economic Policy-Making in the Asia-Pacific Region,* ed. John W. Langford and K. Lorne Brownsey (Halifax, Nova Scotia: The Institute for Research on Public Policy, 1988), p. 282.

42. Quoted in Karl Schoenberger, "Column One: The Model Here Isn't America," *Los Angeles Times,* 30 January 1991, p. A1.

43. Michael Vatikiotis, "Hearts and Minds," *Far Eastern Economic Review,* 20 May 1993, p. 32.

44. Ibid.

45. Ibid.

46. Quoted in Schoenberger, "Column One," p. A9.

47. Sartono Kartodirdjo, "Agrarian Radicalism in Java: Its Setting and Development," in *Culture and Politics in Indonesia,* ed. Claire Holt (Ithaca: Cornell University Press, 1972), p. 82.

48. Benedict R. O'G. Anderson, "Political Culture in Indonesia," in *Columbia Project on Asia in the Core Curriculum: Case Studies in the Social Sciences,* ed. Myron L. Cohen (Armonk, NY: M. E. Sharpe, 1992), p. 325.

49. Clifford Geertz, "Ideology as a Cultural System," in *Ideology and Its Discontents,* ed. David Apter (London: The Free Press of Glencoe, 1964), p. 67.

50. From a booklet, *Sarinah,* that, though written by Sukarno in 1947, explicitly elaborates on the nature of the Indonesian revolution, quoted in C. L. M. Penders, *The Life and Times of Sukarno* (Teaneck: Fairleigh Dickinson University Press, 1974), p. 110.

51. Benedict R. O'G. Anderson, "Authoritarianism: Indonesia," in Cohen, *Columbia Project on Asia,* pp. 314-15.

52. David Wurfel, *Filipino Politics: Development and Decay* (Ithaca: Cornell University Press, 1988), p. 10.

53. Ibid., p. 34.

54. Ibid., pp. 42, 43.

FOR FURTHER READING

Anderson, Benedict, and Audrey Kahin, eds. *Interpreting Indonesian Politics: Thirteen Contributions to the Debate.* Ithaca: Cornell Modern Indonesia Project, Interim Reports Series, Publication No. 62, 1982, pp. 92-103, 117-130, and 131-148 ("Ideology and Sound Structure in Indonesia," "Indonesia Since 1945—Problems of Interpretation," and "Culture, Politics, and Economy in the Political History of the New Order").

Apter, David, ed. *Ideology and Discontent.* Glencoe: The Free Press, 1964, pp. 47-76 ("Ideology as a Cultural System").

Brainard, Cecilia. *When the Rainbow Goddess Wept.* New York: E. P. Dutton, 1994.

Cohen, Myron L., ed. *Columbia Project on Asia in the Core Curriculum: Case Studies in the Social Sciences.* Armonk, NY: M. E. Sharpe, 1992, pp. 91-104 and 323-35 ("Islam in Indonesia" and "Political Culture in Indonesia").

Dore, Ronald. *Taking Japan Seriously: A Confucian Perspective on Leading Economic Issues.* Stanford: Stanford University Press, 1987, pp. 169-92 ("Goodwill and the Spirit of Market Capitalism").

Gluck, Carol. *Japan's Modern Myths.* Princeton, NJ: Princeton University Press, 1985, chapters 1, 2, 5, 8, 9.

Heywood, Andrew. *Political Ideologies: An Introduction.* New York: St. Martin's Press, 1992.

Kapp, Robert A., ed. *Communicating with China.* Chicago: Intercultural Press, 1983.

Kerkvliet, Benedict J. Tria. *Everyday Politics in the Philippines: Class and Status Relations in a Central Luzon Village.* Berkeley: University of California Press, 1990.

Mackerras, Colin, and Nick Knight. *Marxism in Asia.* New York: St. Martin's Press, 1985.

Milne, R. S., and Diane K. Mauzy. *Malaysia: Tradition, Modernity and Islam.* Boulder: Westview, 1986, chapter 4.

Okimoto, Daniel I., and Thomas P. Rohlen, eds. *Inside the Japanese System: Readings on Contemporary Society and Political Economy.* Stanford: Stanford University Press, 1988, pp. 1-38 ("Culture and Society").

Pye, Lucian W. *Asian Power and Politics.* Cambridge: The Belknap Press of Harvard University Press, 1985, chapters 6-12.

Pye, Lucian W. *The Mandarin and the Cadre: China's Political Cultures*. Ann Arbor: Center for Chinese Studies, Univeristy of Michigan, 1988, pp. 1–108.

Tai, Hung-chao, ed. *Confucianism and Economic Development: An Oriental Alternative?* Washington, D.C.: The Washington Institute Press, 1989, chapters 8 and 9 ("The Impact of Chinese Culture on Korea's Economic Development" and "Modernization and Chinese Cultural Traditions in Hong Kong").

Walder, Andrew. G. *Communist Neo-Traditionalism: Work and Authority in Chinese Industry*. Berkeley: University of California Press, 1986, chapters 4 and 5 ("Principled Particularism: Moral and Political Aspects of Authority" and "Clientelist Bureaucracy: The Factory Social Order").

Wilson, Amy Auerbacher, Sidney Leonard Greenblatt, and Richard Whittingham Wilson, eds. *Deviance and Social Control in Chinese Society*. New York: Praeger, 1977, pp. 14–33 (Donald J. Munro, "Belief Control: The Psychological and Ethical Foundations").

chapter 7

The Global Context of Asian Pacific Development—The Cold War and After

During the second half of the twentieth century the Asian Pacific region has moved from a peripheral to a central place in world politics. The region has ceased to be a minor player overshadowed in the drama of international relations by the "stars" in Europe and America and has become a central actor in the theater of global politics. Taking their place on the international stage in the years after World War II, Asian Pacific countries confronted difficult choices of great significance for their objectives of consolidating national independence and promoting economic growth. The complex course of their involvement in regional and global political, economic, and strategic relationships is the subject of this and the next chapter.

In this chapter, after first surveying the changes in the global political system in the five decades since World War II and suggesting some guidelines for the study of foreign policy, we then move on to the primary focus of the chapter: international politics in the Asian Pacific during the changing phases of the cold war and in the years since it ended. In Chapter 8 the focus is on international political economy, on patterns of trade, aid, and investment, and on regional economic institutions.

THE CHANGING WORLD POLITICAL SYSTEM FROM THE 1940s TO THE 1990s

The process of decolonization that began at the end of World War II brought the former colonies in Asia new status as member states in the international political system. Not only was that system European in origin, but Western countries still dominated it. The modern international system, which emerged in Europe during the seventeenth century, is composed of states, each with a clearly demarcated territory and a population over which its government exercises the sovereign right to rule as it sees fit. International law, rules of behavior voluntarily agreed to by governments as binding on them, regulates relations between states; it rests on the principles of sovereignty, equality, and mutual respect for the territorial integrity and political independence of all states. While these principles are not always adhered to in practice, still a fundamental assumption is that within their own borders governments are supreme, subject to no outside authority without their acquiescence.

The notion of clearly defined territorial boundaries between states that are all legally equal (in principle at least) was alien to precolonial Asia. There, borders between kingdoms were often fluid and permeable, and empires rested on superior-subordinate relations between a central hierarch and less powerful local rulers. The experience of colonialism, when the outside powers imposed borders to define their respective possessions, converted Asian colonials to the European view of the significance of territoriality. Testimony to that significance is apparent in postindependence conflicts between neighbors on jurisdiction over land borders (for example, the Chinese-Soviet border) and over offshore islands (such as the Spratlys) that have strategic, economic, or symbolic significance to the parties.

Bipolarity and the Cold War

In addition to the need to become accustomed to the rules of the game of international relations in this Eurocentric interstate system, leaders of Asian Pacific states also had to make their way through the shoals of a postwar polarization of the world into hostile anticommunist and communist camps in what came to be known as the "cold war." The origin of the cold war is too long a story to go into in detail here. It is sufficient to recall that hostility began as far back as 1917, when the Bolshevik Revolution in Russia and the establishment of a communist Soviet Union met with the antagonism of the capitalist powers. That antagonism was put aside temporarily to form the World War II alliance against Hitler, but it resurfaced after the war as a confrontation over the extent of Soviet influence in Eastern Europe.

What began as an intra-European conflict spread worldwide in the late 1940s as the United States, responding to what it and other Western powers saw as Soviet expansionism aiming at world domination, initiated the policy of "containment" of communism by diplomatic, economic, and military means. The "West," the capitalist anticommunist bloc led by the United States, and the "East," the anti-imperialist communist bloc led by the USSR, each lined up protégés among Asian governments, political parties, and insurgent movements, forming military alliances, providing arms, acquiring bases, and giving various forms of political and economic support and guidance.

The two superpowers took opposing sides in the civil war in China, in the Korean War, in the Vietnam War, and in a number of local insurgencies in Southeast Asian countries before and after independence. Asian states entering this bipolar world were confronted with the need to choose sides in the U.S.-Soviet conflict or to find an alternative to alignment with either side. Burma and Indonesia opted for nonalignment as their official policy, as did Malaysia and Singapore later on, when they became independent. Lined up on the American side in the early phase of the cold war were the governments of Japan, South Korea, the Philippines, Taiwan, Thailand, the French and their supporters in Vietnam, Laos, and Cambodia, and the British in colonial Malaya and Singapore; on the other side were China (after 1949), North Korea, Ho Chi Minh's Democratic Republic of Vietnam, the Pathet Lao in Laos, and various other insurgent groups in Burma, Thailand, Malaya, and the Philippines. Many of the internal political and armed conflicts between Communists and anticommunists within nationalist movements before independence and between governments and political opponents after independence were at least in part an extension of the global contest between the two poles clustered around the superpowers.

Erosion of Bipolarity

The bipolar division that characterized the world political system in the late 1940s to the mid-1950s eroded somewhat in the late 1950s and the 1960s. The superpowers took modest steps toward détente in an effort to reduce tensions that might lead to catastrophic nuclear war between them, and centrifugal tendencies appeared in both East and West camps. In Asia, the alliance between the Soviet Union and China deteriorated into mutual recriminations, and as the split between them came into the open it was mirrored in splits within communist movements in other countries. The Sino-Soviet breakup also confounded American preconceptions about the monolithic nature of the world communist movement and eventually raised questions among U.S. allies about the justification for the pursuit of containment in the war in Vietnam.

Bipolarity was further eroded by the growth of the nonaligned movement in what came to be known as the "Third World," the less-developed, mainly ex-colonial countries, many of which tried to remain outside the orbit of either superpower. Détente did not stop the United States and the USSR from competing for influence in Asia and other parts of the developing world. The Soviets and the Chinese proclaimed their support for wars of national liberation even where the liberation movement was noncommunist and the United States favored nationalists with sufficiently anticommunist credentials. East and West competed with each other in the use of inducements such as economic and military aid to win uncommitted governments to their side, or at least to prevent them from slipping into the other side's orbit. Competition between the superpowers for influence in the Third World provided some leverage for those countries to benefit from both sides.

Evolution toward Polycentrism in the 1970s and 1980s

Although the cold war confrontation between the United States and its allies and the Soviet Union and its allies continued to be a central reality in international politics until the disintegration of Soviet dominance in Eastern Europe in the late 1980s and of the Soviet Union itself in 1991, the world political system in the 1970s and 1980s became in many respects quite polycentric. Groupings of states formed around interests apart from the East-West division; OPEC, the European Community (EC), the League of Arab States, and the Association of Southeast Asian Nations (ASEAN) are some of the organizations that became important centers of attachment for their members and influence in international relations.

Arenas of international cooperation and conflict, such as international trade, aid, investment, the global environment, population growth, and human rights, took their place on the agenda of international relations formerly dominated by military and security issues. And the growing importance of actors other than states, such as multinational corporations, the United Nations, the World Bank, and international nongovernmental organizations, also contributed to the creation of networks of interaction at regional and global levels, which in many respects displaced cold war antagonisms as the central focus of foreign policy and international relations. For Asian Pacific states, these changes created new opportunities and new uncertainties in their relations with each other and with extraregional powers.

Instability in the Global Political System in the 1990s

The decade of the 1990s began with a high degree of instability in the global political system. The end of the cold war and the shrinking of Soviet power have contributed to uncertainty about the U.S. politico-strategic role in the world. Some would label post-cold war global politics a "unipolar" system, since—in their view—only the United States has the economic and military capacity for a truly global reach. Others see American power as waning and already seriously challenged by the economic clout of Japan and the EC, by the proliferation of weapons of mass destruction as well as conventional weapons, and by the upsurge of intergroup violence within states.

None of these challenges is easily met by the application of American military force or economic power. Old political enemies in Asia have become economic partners, and long-time economic partners find themselves at odds over market competition and trade imbalances. The shifting security concerns of the United States and other countries in the post-cold war era require important adjustments for the Asian Pacific region, as for the rest of the world, and the process of adjustment has already begun.

WHAT EXPLAINS FOREIGN POLICY BEHAVIOR?

Three "themes" are implicit in our analysis of international relations in the region and indeed in the whole world. One is that the distinction between "domestic" and "foreign" policies is an artificial abstraction, since in reality the two are inextricably intertwined. A change in Japanese electoral law, for example, that reduces the overrepresentation of rural areas is intimately connected to changes in foreign trade policy on rice imports.

A second theme is that all states in the world are inescapably interdependent, although the intensity and frequency of transactions and interactions among countries does vary considerably. Some states, like Singapore, are heavily enmeshed in global networks of international relationships, while others, like Myanmar, have fewer external ties and mainly with close neighbors. The interdependence may be symmetri-

Chronology of Major Events in Asian Pacific Relations, 1945–1994

1945	Japanese surrender, ending World War II
1948	North and South Korean governments established
1949	People's Republic of China established
	Soviets test A-bomb
	NATO formed
1950	Sino-Soviet Alliance (expired 1980)
	Korean War begins
	Pro-French monarchies in Vietnam, Laos, and Cambodia given limited independence within the French Union
1951	Japan-United States peace treaty signed
	Philippines-United States Mutual Defense Treaty
1952	U.S. occupation of Japan ends
1953	Stalin dies
	Armistice in Korea
1954	First Geneva conference on Indochina; Vietnam divided
	SEATO established (dissolved 1977)
	Republic of Korea-United States alliance
	Republic of China (Taiwan)-United States alliance
1955	Bandung conference of Asian-African states
	Cambodia leaves French Union
1957	Soviets launch *Sputnik* orbiter
	Communist insurgency begins in South Vietnam
1960	Sino-Soviet split
1961	Non-Aligned Movement formed
1962	Sino-Indian border war
1963	Sukarno starts Konfrontasi against Malaysia
	South Vietnamese President Diem assassinated
1964	China detonates nuclear device
	U.S. air strikes against North Vietnam begin
	North Vietnamese army enters South Vietnam
1965	U.S. ground forces sent to Vietnam
	Cultural Revolution begins
	Asian Development Bank established
1967	ASEAN founded
1968	Tet offensive
	Peace talks begin in Paris
1969	Sino-Soviet border clashes
1971	Five-Power Defense Agreement (Australia, New Zealand, Malaysia, Singapore, UK)
1972	China-Japan establish diplomatic relations
	Nixon visits China; Shanghai Communique
	SALT I signed

Chronology of Major Events in Asian Pacific Relations, 1945–1994 (continued)

	PRC takes China's seat in United Nations
	Okinawa returned to Japan
	North and South Korea open talks on normalizing relations
1973	Paris Accords on Indochina
	U.S. troops withdraw from Vietnam
1975	Indonesia annexes East Timor
	South Vietnam falls, Vietnam unified
1976	Mao dies
1978	Soviet-Vietnam Treaty of Friendship
	Vietnam invades Cambodia
	United States-China communique on Taiwan
	Japan-China peace treaty
1979	China invades Vietnam
	Soviets invade Afghanistan
	United States-China establish diplomatic relations
1980	United States-Taiwan treaty ends
1981	China proposes talks with Taiwan on reunification
1983	Soviets shoot down Korean Airlines plane
1984	UK-China agreement on return of Hong Kong
1986	Gorbachev speech in Vladivostok
1987	U.S.-Soviet Intermediate Nuclear Forces agreement
	Portugal-China agreement on return of Macau
	Taiwan lifts ban on travel to mainland
1988	Gorbachev Krasnoyarsk speech
	Seoul hosts Olympics
1989	Gorbachev visits Beijing; Tiananmen Square events
	Vietnamese withdraw from Cambodia
	End of cold war?
1990	China-Indonesia restore diplomatic relations
	USSR-South Korea establish diplomatic relations
1991	Gorbachev visits Japan
	Gulf War
	Paris agreement on Cambodia
	President Bush visits Japan
	Breakup of the Soviet Union
	Philippine Senate ends U.S. bases lease
	North and South Korea admitted to the United Nations
	Taiwan and China establish unofficial bodies to handle contacts between them
1992	UN Transitional Authority in Cambodia (UNTAC) formed
	Non-Aligned Movement summit, Jakarta
	China-South Korea establish diplomatic ties
	Japanese emperor visits China

1993   G-7 summit, Tokyo
President Clinton visits South Korea
UNTAC leaves Cambodia following election of new government
LDP loses election; new Japanese government formed
President Yeltsin visits Japan
APEC summit, Seattle
China issues policy paper on Taiwan
Taiwan seeks membership in UN
1994   United States lifts economic embargo on Vietnam
United States renews China's most favored nation trading status
Japanese Emperor visits the United States
North Korea and the United States hold talks on North Korean
nuclear facilities
North and South Korea agree to hold summit meeting
Kim Il Sung dies

Note: For events since mid-1994, see sources suggested on page 107.

cal, between states more or less mutually dependent, or it may be quite asymmetrical, with one partner dominant and the other subordinate.

The third theme is that the relationships of Asian Pacific states with each other and with non-Asian powers are characterized both by conflict and by cooperation, although the "mix" may vary between partners over time. The United States and Japan, for example, conflict over trade relations and cooperate in military security affairs; China and Taiwan allow person-to-person contacts and are in fundamental agreement that Taiwan is a province of China, while profoundly in conflict over who should govern China.

Explaining Foreign Policies: Three Levels of Analysis

What explains the choice of foreign policy goals and the actions taken by governments? Why, for example, did China respond positively to Nixon administration overtures toward establishing normal diplomatic relations after years of vilifying the United States as an enemy and even while the United States was waging war against communist Vietnam? Was it because Mao had become senile and lost his grip on power to other less doctrinaire leaders? Was it because popular weariness with the disruptions of the Cultural Revolution led to pressure for improving the standard of living, which could be helped by ties to the United States and Japan? Was it because China needed the "America card" to play against a closer enemy, the Soviet Union? Scholars in the field of international relations identify three clusters of factors that are likely to influence the foreign policy choices states make. Those clusters relate to three levels of analysis: the level of the individual decision makers, the level of the nation-state, and the level of the international system in which the state is a participant.

At the individual level are such factors as the personality, the life experiences, the beliefs, the personal political goals, even the health of the decision makers. For example, his age might in part have made it possible for Japanese Prime Minister Hosokawa in 1993 to do what none of his older predecessors had done: to apologize for the terrible deeds done to the people of countries Japan subjugated in World War II.

At the nation-state level are the multiplicity of characteristics relating to the governmental system, the economy, military power, geographic location, topography, natural resources, the society as a whole, its traditions, its history, its people, their religion, their political beliefs. For example, the willingness of the Philippines to align itself with the United States and to have American bases on its soil for more than four decades after independence might be understood in part as a result of the economic benefits derived from U.S. military aid and expenditures in the islands, by the desire of its people to have privileged access to the U.S. market and to emigration to the United States, to the relatively benign historical experience under American colonialism, to goodwill generated by the willing acquiescence to the request for independence, and to the affinity of Filipino political institutions to the American model.

At the system level are such external factors as the configuration of power in the world system, whether it is a multipolar, bipolar, unipolar, or some other type of system; the relative weight of the state in that system, whether it is a small weak state or a major or middle power; the objectives of other states in the system that affect it, the history of relations with neighboring and more distant states; the significance of participation in alliances, in regional or global international organizations. For example, the foreign policy orientation of nonalignment chosen by Burma might be attributed to the fact that it is a small weak state located at the juncture of South, East, and Southeast Asia, bordering on five countries, including a powerful China and Thailand. Or the low-profile political role played by economically powerful Japan might in part have been chosen in recognition that bold initiatives might be resisted by other Asian countries as presaging a revival of Japan's earlier bid for hegemony.

Each level of analysis contributes something to our understanding of foreign policy behavior, although the influence of factors at different levels may vary depending on the characteristics of leaders, of the state, and of the international system. For example, the influence of individual leaders is thought to have greater weight in authoritarian systems than in those where decision making is subject to some degree of oversight by elected officials. In states where the bureaucracy is strong, the idiosyncratic characteristics of top leaders are thought to have less impact than in states where the institutionalization of the foreign policy bureaucracy is incomplete. Economically developed states are presumed to have more latitude in foreign policy choices than less-developed ones. However, it is also recognized that the multiplicity of economic interests in more developed economies may impose constraints on policymakers, as evidenced by the pull and tug of various segments of business and labor organizations over issues of free trade or protectionism in relations among major East Asian trading partners. Influences of actors and conditions outside a state's borders are considered to be greater for small states than for the "movers and shakers" in the international system, but even *they* are subject to pressures from outside as well as within.

Although the relative weight to be assigned to any one factor in explaining a particular foreign policy choice is far from certain, we can state with assurance that *many* influences enter into foreign policy decisions. Looking at causality from the three levels of analysis increases our chances of coming up with plausible explanations for past decisions and possibly some informed predictions about future behavior. Our two theories about development bear some relevance here, although they do not directly set out to explain or predict foreign policies of developing states.

Modernization and World System Theories and Foreign Policy

Modernization theorists assume that newly independent states will take their place in the world political system as sovereign equals, responsible for making choices, as other states do, about what will best serve their national interests in development and security. Their options are to select and use the various instruments of international relations—diplomacy, participation in international organizations, alliances, trade agreements, aid, investments, propaganda, even the threat or use of force—to promote their objectives. Whether they succeed or not depends on individual and societal factors such as the decision makers' skill in choosing appropriate goals and strategies, in mobilizing resources, and in implementing policies. In short, modernization theory implicitly assumes that a developing state has equal opportunity to play the game of international politics to its advantage.

World system theorists, in contrast, warn that formal independence does not mean real independence for former colonies, unless they are able to break out of the invidious connections to the world economic system set up by the imperial powers for their own benefit. But the likelihood is that after formal independence is attained, "neocolonialism" will continue the dependent relationship with the former imperial power or with another advanced industrial patron as the controlling partner. For these "neocolonial" states, control over their own foreign policy is more apparent than real, subject as they are to external influences, whether of other states or nonstate actors such as multinational corporations and international lending agencies. So world system theory would place greater importance on systemic factors than on individual or societal influences on foreign policymaking.

Whichever theory you find more persuasive, the impact of the external reality of the cold war on the foreign relations of the Asian Pacific states cannot be minimized. To that we now turn.

EFFECTS OF THE COLD WAR: WARS AND ALLIANCES

None of the Asian Pacific countries escaped providing the stage and a cast of actors for the dramatic contest being played out between the opposing sides in the cold war. In Burma, Cambodia, Laos, Malaysia, Indonesia, and the Philippines struggles among political parties and between the government and insurgents in each country were battlefields connected to the global struggle between the "East" and the "West." But most profoundly affected by the cold war were Korea, Vietnam, and China. It resulted in the division of each of those nations into two states, one communist and the other anticommunist. Korea and China remain divided and Vietnam, unified after a long and bitter war, still struggles to overcome the effects of partition from 1954 to 1975.

The victory of the Communists in China in 1949 and the signing of the Sino-Soviet treaty of mutual assistance early in 1950 appeared to the United States to signal an alarming extension of the "Red empire." Then came the outbreak of war in Korea in June 1950, seen as validation of the contention that the Soviets were militarily expansionist and as the first major test of the American policy of containment in Asia.

War in Korea: What Led to It and What Resulted from It

There was no reason in 1945 for the Koreans to anticipate that the arrival of Soviet and American troops to accept the surrender of the Japanese forces in Korea would mean the permanent division of their country. True, in Korea's history there had been rival kingdoms centered in the north and in the south, and under the Japanese the north's mineral and power resources had been developed and an industrial base established, while the more populous south remained largely agricultural. But it was also true that Koreans regarded themselves as one people, a sense of identity that had been strengthened and popularized by foreign occupation.

Yet nationalist opposition to Japanese rule, although in principle united behind the Provisional Government in Exile in Shanghai, was deeply divided ideologically and geographically. The movement included right-wing conservatives, propertied elements backed by the Chinese Nationalists, some moderates and noncommunist leftists, and communist elements that looked to the Soviet and Chinese Communists. Many had gone into exile, dispersing to Siberia, Manchuria, Yanan, Shanghai, and the United States, and the ideological divisions among Koreans in exile were paralleled by divisions in the anti-Japanese resistance within Korea. However, as World War II drew to a close, the various factions inside the country agreed to establish a Preparatory Committee for Korean Independence under a leftist, Lyuh Woon Hyung. The committee proclaimed the independence of the People's Republic of Korea, formed local committees to take over government functions from the Japanese, and prepared to welcome the Allied forces.

Two Occupation Zones.   When the Americans arrived in September 1945 to take control of the southern half of the country below the thirty-eighth parallel, they refused to deal with the committees. Instead, the Japanese were put back in their jobs (including the police) until an American military government could begin to function. In the American zone a leading conservative nationalist who had spent years of exile in the United States, Syngman Rhee, succeeded in winning out over rival contenders in the competition leading to the creation of a civilian government in the south. In the north, the Soviets at first worked with local committees under a central committee headed by a noncommunist Christian until the return of anti-Japanese resistance forces from Manchuria, among them Kim Il Sung, who won Soviet support and displaced the early leadership.

The two occupying powers had agreed to work through a joint commission on the formation of a government for all of Korea, but they and various Korean leaders disagreed on which Korean political groups should be consulted on the process. The dividing line between the Soviet and American zones effectively curtailed political connections across the line, and the north and south under foreign occupation grew further apart. In each zone, Korean military forces were formed, land reform programs put through, parties organized, and local elections held. The leader and party favored by each occupying power grew stronger, squeezing out moderate elements that might have prevented polarization between Communists and right-wing anticommunists.

Two States Created.   With negotiations between the United States and the Soviets on reunification of Korea stalled, the United States in 1947 brought the problem to the United Nations General Assembly, in which the American-led bloc then had a controlling majority. The UN Temporary Commission on Korea (UNTCOK) was set up to oversee elections in all of Korea. When the Soviets objected to the conditions UNTCOK laid down for the voting and refused to allow the commission into its zone, the United States went ahead in May 1948 with elections to the National Assembly in the south under UNTCOK observation. In August the Republic of Korea was established with Syngman Rhee as president and the UN General Assembly in December 1948 declared it the legitimate government of South Korea. The United States withdrew its forces except for a small training mission. After the creation of the ROK government, the Soviets withdrew their military from the North and turned over the government to the Democratic People's Republic of Korea with Kim Il Sung as president.

Both North and South expected that the division would be temporary, each anticipating that reunification would soon come about with its side incorporating the other. True believers in the North were convinced that with the tide of history on their side the progressive forces of workers and peasants under communist leadership and with the support of the Soviets would inevitably triumph over reactionary capitalism represented by the United States and its protégé Rhee. In the South Rhee and his supporters were convinced that they could harness the power of the United States, which by then had decided on a course of active resistance to the spread of communism in Europe, to support Rhee's vision of a Korea unified under his regime. So in the months following the separation of Korea into two states, efforts by a new UN Commission on Korea (UNCOK) to bring the two governments into negotiations on unification came to nothing. Verbal volleys were fired from both sides and each built up its military forces with the help of its patron. Cross-border raids occurred frequently, UNCOK duly reporting those incidents back to UN headquarters.

War between North and South.   On June 25, 1950, large-scale hostilities broke out. Each side accused the other of having started the fight. The extent of Soviet and American foreknowledge of or complicity in the launching of the war is still not clear. Some insist that Moscow must have ordered or at least ratified Kim's bid to reunify Korea by force; others suggest that Rhee was the initiator, possibly encouraged by the American diplomat John Foster Dulles to expect U.S. support after the fact for his anticommunist crusade; still others see the war as essentially a civil war, initiated by Koreans, into which the outside powers were drawn by the logic of their mutual suspicions and regional commitments.

Whatever the truth surrounding the initiation of the war, President Truman quickly committed the U.S. military to the South's side, despite the fact that the United States then had no military alliance with South Korea and had publicly announced in January 1950 that the American defense perimeter in East Asia excluded Korea. Truman took the matter to the UN Security Council, which the Soviets were boycotting in protest against the UN's failure to seat representatives of the People's Republic of China in place of the defeated Republic of China government on Taiwan. With the concurrence of all four Asian states then members of the UN (Burma, the Republic of China, the Philippines, and Thailand), the UN approved support for the South and set up a UN command, headed by General Douglas MacArthur, to coordinate military operations. Troops or logistical support were contributed by forty-five countries, including the Philippines, Thailand, Australia, and New Zealand. Still, nine out of ten of the foreign troops fighting on South Korea's side were American.

The battle raged down the peninsula and back up again in early fall 1950 as MacArthur crossed the thirty-eighth parallel with the objective of unifying the country by force. The UN General Assembly reaffirmed its desire for a unified, independent, and democratic Korea and set up the UN Commission for Unification and Rehabilitation of Korea (UNCURK). As UN and ROK forces drew closer to the border between Korea and China, Beijing sent warnings through neutral countries that China would intervene if UN troops continued to move north. MacArthur discounted the warnings, pressed on, and in late November the Chinese counterattacked with nearly a million men. UN forces were driven back deep into the South and then fought back up again to the thirty-eighth parallel, where the military situation stabilized by mid-1951. After two years of diplomatic effort, hampered somewhat by the General Assembly's condemnation of China as an "aggressor" and its refusal to allow the Beijing government to take China's seat in the UN, an armistice agreement was reached in July 1953 and prisoners of war exchanged. The armistice is still in effect and the two sides face each other in periodic meetings at Panmunjom in the demilitarized zone between North and South Korea, which President Clinton visited in the summer of 1993.

Effects of the War.   The Korean War had significant long-term effects on Asian states and on relations between them and the United States. For China, it brought Chinese troops into hand-to-hand combat with Americans, confirming convictions on both sides that the other was implacably hostile and preventing the establishment of normal relations between the two countries for almost thirty years. The war moved China's nemesis, the government on Taiwan, more closely under American protection, which from Beijing's perspective signified continued U.S. interference in the Chinese civil war. Truman's decision to extend the U.S. defense perimeter to include Taiwan and to send the Seventh Fleet to patrol the Formosa Straits thwarted the Chinese Communists from completing their victory over the Guomindang by taking control of the island. Mao's government deeply resented the action but was powerless to prevent the United States from signing a security pact with Taiwan in 1954 and from supplying military and economic aid to Chiang, whose announced aim was to retake the mainland. Aid even included CIA-backing for a remnant Guomindang army that had fled into Burma, from which it launched repeated but unsuccessful invasions into

China. Another affront was U.S. use of the UN to condemn it as the aggressor and to block it from taking China's place in the organization until 1972.

Other Asian countries as well as Taiwan benefited from the intensification of the cold war that the "hot" war in Korea brought. A major beneficiary was Japan. Its economy profited greatly from the stimulus of serving as a crucial staging point and supply source for the war, and its political status was rapidly elevated in 1952 from that of occupied ex-enemy to newly sovereign state and American ally. Over the objections of the Soviet Union, China, Burma, and other countries that had fought the Japanese in World War II, the United States concluded a peace treaty and a security pact that allowed it to continue to occupy bases in Japan in return for the promise of American protection.

The Republic of Korea, like the Republic of China, got a mutual security pact and economic and military aid from the United States, as did the Philippines, where American forces already were stationed. Australia and New Zealand joined the United States in the ANZUS pact, and in 1954 the web of military alliances along the periphery of the Asian mainland was completed with the creation of a regional security pact, the Southeast Asia Treaty Organization. SEATO linked the Philippines, Thailand, and Pakistan with the United States, Britain, France, Australia, and New Zealand, and its protection was extended to the nonsignatory states of Laos, Cambodia, and the Republic of (South) Vietnam.

Another effect of the Korean War was to raise the level of American involvement in the conflict between France and its former possessions in Indochina. Vietnam, Laos, and Cambodia, like Korea, became a local theater for the cold war rivals to carry on their global struggle. What had in 1945 appeared to many Americans as an effort by France to reimpose colonialism now came to be perceived as an integral part of the "Free World" resistance to a worldwide communist conspiracy to seize all of Indochina. Accordingly, the United States began in the early 1950s to provide a generous financial subsidy to France for its military campaign against the Vietnamese independence movement, the Viet Minh. In both Vietnam and Korea, partition into two states was agreed to in recognition of the existence of communist and anticommunist spheres of influence, but each side expected eventual reunification on its terms. Koreans and Vietnamese suffered the agony of internecine war, with American forces heavily involved. War in Korea lasted three years, in Vietnam three decades.

War in Indochina

The Viet Minh, a coalition of various nationalist groups, had been formed on the initiative of the Indochinese Communist Party during World War II to fight against the Japanese occupation and the return of French colonialism. Partisans from the Viet Minh base in the northern part of the country had cooperated during the last months of the war with secret U.S. agents in gathering intelligence and rescuing American flyers who had crashed in Vietnam. In August 1945, in anticipation of the entry of Nationalist Chinese and British forces to accept the surrender of the Japanese, the Viet Minh organized mass demonstrations of popular support and persuaded Emperor Bao Dai to abdicate. On September 2 the Viet Minh leader and long-time Communist Ho

Chi Minh declared the independence of the Democratic Republic of Vietnam. In his speech in Hanoi on that occasion, Ho invoked the words of the American Declaration of Independence to justify Vietnam's claim to self-determination and independence and appealed to President Truman for support of that cause.

When the British landed in southern Vietnam they ousted the Viet Minh committee functioning as the local government in Saigon and used Japanese troops to drive the Viet Minh into the countryside in preparation for the French return to the part of the country they called Cochin China. Meanwhile the DRV government in the north was coping with the presence of almost 200,000 ill-disciplined Nationalist Chinese troops who entered to disarm the Japanese and seized the opportunity to take whatever they could from the local population. Faced with the need for leverage to get the Chinese to withdraw, Ho's government decided to acquiesce in the return of French forces to the north in 1946.

The French Phase (1946–1954).   Once back in, the French rejected the Viet Minh's declaration of independence and for the next eight years the two antagonists were locked in combat on the battlefield and at the negotiating table. To counter the DRV's ambition to liberate all of Vietnam, the French restored Bao Dai to his throne and threw their support in Cambodia and Laos behind monarchs sufficiently tractable to serve French interests. By 1950 France was ready to allow the establishment of three "Associated States" within the French Union, an arrangement giving France continued control of its finances and defense. Western governments accorded diplomatic recognition to those states, as did the communist governments to the Democratic Republic of Vietnam, whose cause had benefited from the Chinese Communist victory in 1949. The DRV backed communist independence movements, the Pathet Lao and the Khmer Issarak, in neighboring Laos and Cambodia.

So the foreign and indigenous players were now in place on the scene and had chosen their parts. To the French, the Americans, and the French puppet monarchs, the contest was a battle against communism, local and international. To China, the Soviets, the DRV government, the communist resistance in Laos and Cambodia, and to many noncommunist nationalists in Indochina, the contest was a struggle of nationalism and self-determination against colonialism. By 1954 the principal international actors were ready to attempt a negotiated settlement and agreed to meet at Geneva to discuss Indochina as well as other issues, including Korea.

The Geneva Conference, 1954.   The conference brought together representatives from the United States, France, the United Kingdom, the USSR, China, the Democratic Republic of Vietnam, and the three Associated States of Vietnam, Laos, and Cambodia. Although the major powers failed to resolve the problem of Korean reunification, the conference did produce agreement on the neutralization and demilitarization of Laos and Cambodia and an armistice between France and the DRV. Viet Minh forces were to withdraw north of the seventeenth parallel and French forces south of it, with all-Vietnam elections to be held within two years to determine the future of the country. An international commission of representatives of Canada, India, and Poland (Western, nonaligned, and Eastern) was created to oversee the armistice and the elections.

The Geneva meeting was significant in other ways. It coincided with the defeat of the French at Dien Bien Phu by Ho's forces. The loss convinced the French that although the enemy might not have the military power to oust them from Vietnam, neither did they themselves have the capacity to defeat the Viet Minh decisively. Facing a colonial struggle closer to home in Algeria, they opted out of Indochina and completed withdrawal of their armed forces in 1956, convinced that the United States could be counted on to continue the struggle against the Communists. President Eisenhower endorsed the "domino theory," according to which the "fall" of Vietnam would topple noncommunist governments in the rest of Southeast Asia and threaten Japan and the West's access to vital raw materials and markets.[1]

Geneva also signaled international acceptance of the PRC as a major participant in world affairs, although the United States still refused to recognize it as the government of China and Secretary of State Dulles declined to shake the hand of Prime Minister Zhou Enlai during the meetings. Neither the United States nor the Bao Dai government in southern Vietnam signed the agreements, objecting to any concession to the Viet Minh, and the United States was already at work on negotiations for SEATO to line up defenses against communist aggression and the alliances with Taiwan and South Korea. Nor was the DRV happy with the concessions it made under pressure from the Soviets and the Chinese in pursuit of their own agenda of "peaceful coexistence." It had agreed to withdraw from areas it controlled south of the seventeenth parallel, to the temporary division of the country at a line further north than seemed fair, and to de facto recognition of the French-created State of Vietnam as a partner in arranging countrywide elections. However, given their assessment of the limited popular appeal of Bao Dai's government even to noncommunists, the Viet Minh had reason to expect they would win those elections.

What was the outcome of the Geneva agreements? As one American journalist put it: "In the end, the Geneva Conference produced no durable solution to the Indochina conflict, only a military truce that awaited a political settlement, which never really happened. So the conference was merely an interlude between two wars—or, rather, a lull in the same war."[2]

The Lull between Wars (1954–1957).   The "lull" after Geneva lasted until the end of the decade. During that time, Vietnamese leaders north and south of the armistice line worked at strengthening their political bases with the help of their chief outside patrons, China and the United States. In the south Ngo Dinh Diem, Bao Dai's prime minister, maneuvered against his political opponents with open and clandestine support from the United States. A Roman Catholic, Diem persuaded influential Americans, including then-Senator John F. Kennedy, that he was the Vietnamese political figure most capable of successful resistance to the Communists. The exodus from the north of nearly a million Catholics, with American encouragement and transport, seemed to demonstrate the magnetism of their coreligionist's government. Again with U.S. support, Diem resisted entering into consultations for the all-Vietnam elec-

Ho Chi Minh

Ho Chi Minh.
Source: Photo AP/Wide World.

The revered founding father whose portrait adorns offices and other public places in Vietnam, "Uncle" Ho was born in central Vietnam in 1890. His birth name was Nguyen Tat Thanh, Ho Chi Minh being one of several pseudonyms he used during his underground political career. His father was an educated man, a minor official until discharged for his anticolonial views. Ho received his secondary education at a *lycée* in Hue and taught in a village school before leaving for Saigon to learn a trade. In 1911 he shipped out as a messboy on a French ship and for the next thirty years did not return to Vietnam.

Ho's travels took him to Africa, Europe, perhaps the United States, in various jobs including restaurant worker in England and photo retoucher in Paris. There during World War I he joined the French Socialist Party and tried to get attention for the cause of Vietnamese independence at the Versailles Peace Conference. When the French socialist movement split, Ho sided with the leftists and became a founding member of the French Communist Party. From then on his time was spent in communist training and organizational activities for the international communist movement (the Comintern) in Paris, Moscow, China, Thailand, Singapore, and Indochina. He met many of the European Communist leaders and gradually fitted his understanding of communist doctrine to the situation in colonial Indochina. One of the founders of the Indochinese Communist Party in Hong Kong in 1930, he was jailed by British authorities in 1931 and deported. He spent most of World War II in China, returning briefly to Vietnam in 1941 with the support of the Chinese Nationalists to form a united front, the Viet Minh, of organizations committed to resisting Japanese and French imperialism. During the Japanese occupation Ho ordered the creation of military units inside Indochina to engage in the dual job of propagandizing among the people and (with less emphasis) in armed struggle against the Japanese, including assistance to downed Allied flyers and to the U.S. Office of Strategic Services' clandestine operations in occupied Indòchina.

Ho finally returned to his native land on the eve of the Japanese defeat and proclaimed the establishment of an independent Vietnam in September 1945. Negotiations with the returning French for some degree of self-rule ended in failure and from 1946 to 1954 Ho, with a cadre of trusted associates, managed the war against the French and other affairs of the Viet Minh, the party, and the government from headquarters in a liberated base area north of Hanoi. When the 1954 Geneva conference brought international recognition of the Democratic Republic of Vietnam, the seat of government moved finally to Hanoi, and from then until Ho's death in 1969, he held various positions as president, prime minister, and party secretary.

The object of vituperation in the United States and among his political opponents in South Vietnam during the American phase of Vietnam's war of independence, Ho is venerated in his homeland as the consummate independence leader and founding father, a person who never married but was like a beloved uncle to many of his people. In life Ho lived simply, even austerely, shunning ostentation; it is ironic that his wish to be cremated and have his ashes scattered in various parts of Vietnam was overridden by his colleagues. Instead his body (like Lenin's and Mao's) was put on display in a huge stone mausoleum in the capital city and is visited by thousands each year.

tions, arguing that fair and free elections would be impossible in areas controlled by the Viet Minh. Instead, he held a referendum in October 1955 to abolish the monarchy and establish the Republic of Vietnam with himself as president, winning more than 98 percent approval, a majority of dubious authenticity. The DRV government protested the South's failure to comply with the Geneva agreement on elections in the whole country, but the protest fell on deaf ears among the great powers, including the Soviet Union.

At that point the Diem government's effective control of the territory south of the seventeenth parallel was mainly limited to Saigon and other cities; much of the Mekong Delta and the rest of the countryside was beyond the reach of his officials and military. So Diem undertook a campaign to win over the peasants with a half-hearted land reform program and to eliminate other resistance by arresting and detaining supporters of the Viet Minh, Buddhists suspected of disloyalty to the regime, the Cao Dai, and other armed sect members. American-trained police and the Army of the Republic of Vietnam (ARVN) used intimidation, torture, and other terror tactics to coerce village chiefs to carry out government orders. One of Diem's projects was the forced creation of *agrovilles*, new rural settlements fortified against Viet Minh infiltration. They did not meet with much success initially, but the concept was revived later by enthusiastic American advisers as the "strategic hamlet" program. Based on the successful use of a similar program by the British in curbing the communist insurgency in Malaya, the lesson turned out not to be transferable to Vietnam. Unlike Malaya, where the insurgents were mainly Chinese and easily distinguished from the Malay population, in Vietnam the insurgents were Vietnamese, indistinguishable from the rest of the population among whom they moved.

NLF Insurgency Begins.   During the early years after Geneva the DRV was concentrating on building up its strength in the North and embarking on socialist economic reconstruction. Its leaders strongly counseled the Viet Minh partisans in the South against initiating full-scale rebellion against Diem, arguing that such action was too risky and doomed to failure. But beginning in 1957 under the impact of Diem's campaign of terror against them, Viet Minh and other targets of RVN who managed to escape arrest reverted to tactics used in the anti-French struggle and went underground, forming guerrilla bases in the countryside and engaging in assassinations of village collaborators, hit-and-run attacks on ARVN and police, and various forms of armed resistance. By 1960 Hanoi conceded legitimacy to insurrection against Diem and authorized the organization of the National Liberation Front (NLF), a coalition of Communists and noncommunists united by their opposition to Diem, with the objective of liberating the South. The NLF (called "Viet Cong" by its opponents) organized its military forces as the People's Liberation Armed Force (PLAF) and in 1969 formed the Provisional Revolutionary Government (PRG), the counterpart of the RVN government in areas in the South under NLF control.

To the United States, the anti-Diem movement in the South was instigated by and directed by North Vietnam as part of the global communist campaign of subversion and aggression, a breach of the cold war line drawn at the seventeenth parallel. The NLF maintained that it was of local southern origin, with little help initially from the North and that it included not just Communists but a broad spectrum of noncommunists opposed to Diem's regime.

In the next few years, Diem's popularity dwindled further despite continuing U.S. aid and advice from American military personnel, whose numbers increased from under 1,000 at the time Kennedy became president in 1961 to 11,000 in 1962 to 16,000 in 1963. The strategic hamlet rural pacification program failed to reduce NLF dominance in the countryside, and Buddhist monks led demonstrations in the cities, using self-immolation as a dramatic form of protest against Diem. Now disenchanted with their protégé, the Americans were willing to see him ousted in a military coup in November 1963, just weeks before President Kennedy's assassination. Unfortunately for the South's government and U.S. purposes, Diem was replaced by a succession of military officers none of whom was able to keep the situation from deteriorating further.

Unites States and North Vietnam at War (1964–1973).   The year 1964 saw an intensification of American involvement, as President Lyndon Johnson authorized support for South Vietnamese commando raids on the North Vietnamese coast. When two U.S. destroyers gathering intelligence in the Gulf of Tonkin reported being fired on by North Vietnamese patrol boats, Johnson asked for a Congressional resolution authorizing him to use force to repel armed attacks on American forces, and he ordered air strikes against North Vietnamese naval bases. Thus the United States moved beyond supplying South Vietnam with weapons, intelligence, and advice to overt military action by American forces, a fateful step further into the quagmire.

A flurry of efforts by third parties at diplomatic settlement met with failure. French President de Gaulle urged an end to foreign intervention and offered to serve as mediator. UN Secretary-General U Thant proposed a meeting in Rangoon, and Soviet Prime Minister Khrushchev pressured North Vietnam to agree to attend. The Soviets and North Vietnamese called for reconvening the Geneva conference. But the Americans, needing time to bolster the disintegrating government in South Vietnam, were not ready to negotiate, and North Vietnam was making preparations to send army units south. In October 1964 the first units of the North's People's Army of Vietnam (PAVN) went into South Vietnam. In December the United States began bombing the network of footpaths and dirt roads leading from the North through parts of eastern Laos and Cambodia that became known as the Ho Chi Minh Trail.

In 1965, faced with further deterioration in the political situation in South Vietnam and convinced that a strategy of mounting military pressure would convince Hanoi to stop its "aggression" against the South, President Johnson rapidly escalated U.S. military participation in the war. Ground combat forces were sent to fight in the South and naval and air forces struck the PLAF and PAVN in the South, the North, Laos, and Cambodia from bases in Thailand, South Vietnam, Guam, and the Philippines. The number of Americans involved rose from 23,000 at the beginning of 1965 to 540,000 in 1968, and they were joined by Thai, Filipino, and South Korean contingents paid for by the United States.

The fighting intensified, with heavy casualties on both sides, reaching an orgy of bloodletting early in 1968 at the time of the Vietnamese new year's holiday, Tet. Departing from their customary small-scale hit-and-run style of warfare, the PLAF and PAVN mounted a countrywide offensive against Saigon and other cities and towns throughout South Vietnam. They did not succeed in holding any of their conquests for long except Hue, which they occupied for nearly a month before American and ARVN troops retook the city in fierce street-by-street fighting. Tet cost both sides dearly. Communist casualties, estimated at 50,000,[3] hit the southerners especially hard, and the vacancies in the NLF organization left by their deaths were filled by northerners. But, while Tet was militarily a defeat for the Communists, it contributed to President Johnson's decision to make a serious offer of negotiation. As evidence of good faith, he stopped air and naval attacks on all except the southern part of the DRV and later in the year ordered a complete halt to bombing of the North.

Talks between the United States and Hanoi began in Paris in May 1968, joined in 1969 by the Provisional Revolutionary Government and a reluctant Saigon government that objected to giving the PRG status as an independent entity. While the war continued, negotiations dragged on for five years, at an impasse over American insistence that PAVN withdraw from the South and the Communists' insistence on PRG inclusion in a coalition government in Saigon. When Richard Nixon became president in 1969 (a year also marked by the death of Ho Chi Minh), he kept up military pressure on the North, bombing their supply lines in Laos and Cambodia and sending ground troops into Cambodia in 1970 to destroy the communist command center for South Vietnam. In 1972, after a new communist offensive, Nixon resumed bombing in the North and ordered the mining of Haiphong Harbor, through which Soviet and Chinese aid came. In the South, Nixon decided, the answer to mounting antiwar pressure at home was to accelerate "Vietnamization." That meant preparing ARVN to take over full responsibility for combat south of the seventeenth parallel, allowing the gradual withdrawal of U.S. ground forces. Nixon announced a new "doctrine" redefining the U.S. security role toward South Vietnam and other Asian countries: America would live up to its obligations to its allies by continuing to provide economic and military aid, but from then on those countries would have to rely on their own troops—not American troops—to defend themselves.

The Paris Accords of 1973 and After.   Finally in 1973 the negotiations reached a conclusion with the signing of the Paris accords. The agreement was for a cease-fire in place (leaving South Vietnam a patchwork of areas under communist and RVN control), for the withdrawal of all "foreign" (that is, U.S.) forces, and for the recognition of the PRG as one of two administrative entities in the South. Negotiations were to follow among representatives of those two and of other South Vietnamese not aligned with either, leading to the creation of a National Council of Concord and Reconciliation and eventually to the peaceful reunification of the whole country at some unspecified future time. A secret commitment was made to North Vietnam for American help in its postwar reconstruction. South Vietnam's President Nguyen Van Thieu had adamantly refused to the terms of the Paris agreement, despite heavy pressure from Washington, until Nixon, in a secret letter, assured Thieu "of continued assistance in the post-settlement period and that we will respond with full force should the settlement be violated by North Vietnam."[4]

American troops withdrew, but the United States continued to be militarily involved, bombing Cambodia until Congress stopped it in August 1973. Although banning use of U.S. funds for military action in Indochina, Congress did approve military aid to Thieu's government for the next two years. Reconciliation talks among the South Vietnamese never began and the cease-fire did not hold. A communist offensive early in 1975 led to the unexpectedly rapid disintegration of the more numerous and better equipped South Vietnamese military. The final collapse of RVN came with the fall of Saigon at the end of April 1975.

Laos fared somewhat better than Vietnam after the Paris accords. A cease-fire and new coalition government were agreed to between the Pathet Lao and the royalists, and the United States ordered an end to the bombing of Laos, begun in 1965 with the consent of the royalist government. When South Vietnam fell in 1975, the Pathet Lao took full control of the Laotian government, and in Cambodia the Khmer Rouge accepted the surrender of the United States-backed Lon Nol government. Three "dominoes" had finally fallen to the Communists.

But the "fall" produced fewer repercussions outside Indochina than had been expected when the contest between the communist and the "imperialist" camps began there thirty years earlier. During the intervening decades, alignments in world politics had shifted (as will be described later in this chapter), blurring the clarity of the sharp dividing lines of the early cold war. In the increasingly complex game of global politics played by the two superpowers and the regional power, China, their protégés in

Indochina were to be protected, but not at all cost, and expended when it served the big powers' interests. For them, the significance of the "fallen dominoes" was less strategic in the long run than hoped for or feared. But to the people of Indochina, the long struggle had incalculable and enduring significance.

Effects of the War.   Deaths and injuries took their highest toll among military and civilians in Vietnam. Bombing by the United States had stalled economic progress in the North, damaged towns, roads, and bridges, and caused evacuation of city-dwellers, but it had not destroyed the will to resist nor the apparatus of government and social order. The South was in much worse shape. Rural areas had suffered from years of American and RVN bombing and spraying forests and fields with 19 million gallons of herbicides[5] to destroy the enemy's cover and food supply, resulting in de-foliated hardwood forests and unusable cropland. To destruction from the air were added the effects of ground combat. The American "search-and-destroy" sweeps through the countryside, the "free-fire zones," and the "pacification" program aimed at taking back the countryside from the NLF left bomb craters, unexploded ordnance, villages destroyed, and local leadership wiped out by one side or the other. Uprooted from their homes and livelihood, many peasants had fled into the towns and cities in search of some measure of safety. The population of Saigon and other urban areas bal-looned; prostitution, black market thievery from the cornucopia of American sup-plies, drug trafficking, and widespread corruption among officials all contributed to demoralization in the South and to the destruction of the fabric of society.

The war accentuated historical differences between the northern and southern regions of the country. Thirty years of socialism in the North contrasted with the fever-ish parody of capitalism in the South, stimulated by the injection of large amounts of American money and matériel into an economy unable to put them to productive uses. Animosity was to be expected between the victors and those who had been of-ficials and supporters of the losing side, but tensions existed too among the victori-ous communist comrades-in-arms. Disagreements had arisen during the war years between the PRG and DRV over military and political decisions. The southerners had of necessity accepted northern leadership in the contest on the battlefield and at the negotiating table. With victory in 1975 they found themselves pushed aside by north-ern "carpetbaggers," insensitive to southerners' expectation of equal partnership in shaping the future of their region.

In Cambodia, Khmer insurgents and NLF-DRV use of territory along the border with South Vietnam called down a torrent of American bombs from 1969 to 1973 (a quarter of a million tons from February to August 1973 alone[6]). As in South Vietnam, country people in the combat areas fled to the capital, Phnom Penh, which like Saigon became bloated beyond its capacity to provide housing, jobs, and services. When the Khmer Rouge took over in 1975, one of their major efforts was to force people back to the countryside. Laos too suffered U.S. bombing from 1965 to 1973, an invasion in 1971 by the South Vietnamese, as well as warfare between the government and Pa-thet Lao-North Vietnamese forces.

All three of the countries needed foreign assistance to rebuild, but the U.S. Con-gress in 1976 forbade government aid to them and in 1977 blocked funding from the

World Bank and other international lending agencies to which the United States belonged. Negotiations in 1977 between Vietnam and the Carter administration on normalization of relations broke down over Hanoi's insistence that Washington honor the secret promise made by Nixon in 1973 to give aid for reconstruction. A U.S. trade embargo imposed on Vietnam in 1979 (and not lifted until 1994) cut off opportunities for private investment and commerce.

Other Asian countries benefited from the Indochina war. The economies of South Korea, Thailand, and the Philippines especially gained from military aid, bases, procurement, expenditures of American servicemen on R and R, and payments for their military's service in Vietnam. However, failure to keep South Vietnam from falling raised doubts about how far other countries could count on the United States to help them in a similar situation. Besides, the world had changed since the bipolarity of the 1950s. The Third World had emerged as a force in world politics, the communist camp was deeply split, and the East-West divide was being crossed in surprising ways, all of which had great significance for the Asian Pacific countries.

EROSION OF BIPOLARITY: NONALIGNMENT AND REALIGNMENTS

Centrifugal forces were at work in both blocs, most dramatically in the East, where the rift between the Soviet Union and China fractured the world communist movement irreparably. But in the West as well, America's dominant position changed with the recovery of Western Europe from the traumas of war and loss of empire and the phoenix-like rise of Japan from the ashes of defeat. The bloc leader's overwhelming preponderance of power diminished and its allies began to assert a degree of independence in foreign policy that was unthinkable in the early years of the cold war. Global politics were also in the process of becoming less Eurocentric, with the rapid increase in the number of newly independent states in Asia, Africa, and the Middle East joining the older ex-colonies of Latin America in a loose affiliation as members of the "Third World." Although some Third World states were formally or informally aligned with the Western or the Eastern camps, they and their nonaligned cohorts shared a sense of themselves as distinct from the "First" and "Second" worlds. In those "worlds" industrialization had already brought the riches and the power to which the Third World aspired and the "developing" countries of the "South" (many of them being in the southern hemisphere) began to see the need for solidarity in dealing with the developed countries of the "North."

The Third World Emerges

In 1955, the year after the Geneva conference, the first meeting of leaders of ex-colonial countries took place in Bandung, Indonesia. Sukarno characterized the gathering as symbolizing "new forces" emerging to challenge the old order in world politics. Sponsored by Indonesia, Burma, and the South Asian countries of India, Pakistan, and Sri Lanka, invitations went to all independent governments in Asia and

Africa except Israel, North and South Korea, Taiwan, South Africa, Australia, and New Zealand. Prime ministers and foreign ministers from twenty-nine governments attended; the East and Southeast Asians represented were Cambodia, the People's Republic of China, Japan, Laos, the Philippines, Thailand, both North and South Vietnam, and the cosponsors, Burma and Indonesia.

Discussions at the conference reflected their common concerns with maintaining their sovereignty and independence and with economic development. The final communique called for a speedy end to colonialism and pledged cooperation in development. Wide support was expressed for Chinese Prime Minister Zhou Enlai's articulation of five principles that should govern relations among countries: mutual respect for sovereignty and territorial integrity, nonaggression, noninterference in others' internal affairs, equality and mutual benefit, and peaceful coexistence. But opinion divided on the issue of alignment with either the Soviet or the American bloc. India's Prime Minister Nehru pushed for the principle of neutrality in the big power conflict. By not taking sides, the newly independent countries would serve their own interests and world peace, acting as a third-party mediator between the two opposing blocs. Some of the countries at Bandung had already chosen sides, so nonalignment failed of endorsement. The issue of alignment or nonalignment continued to divide African and Asian countries and prevented a second conference, planned for 1965, from being held.

However, representatives of twenty-five governments committed to staying out of military alliances with East or West met in Belgrade, Yugoslavia, in 1961, the first in a series of meetings of the Non-Aligned Movement (NAM). NAM membership grew over the years, and it became one of a number of regional and global groupings through which developing countries have exerted pressure on the developed world's governments and the UN and other international organizations. The criteria for qualifying as "nonaligned" are fuzzy. Some NAM members indisputably have had special ties to one side or the other. Singapore and Malaysia, while declaring commitment to nonalignment, have had security links to Britain and other Western countries since independence. Indonesia, which hosted the 1993 NAM summit meeting, also has had military ties to the United States since Suharto came to power, reversing Sukarno's tilt toward the communist side in the early 1960s. And Burma, which had scrupulously avoided foreign attachments, left the NAM at the Havana conference in 1979 on the grounds that the movement was tilting too much toward the Soviet Union.

Incentives for countries to opt for a nonaligned stance in foreign policy were heightened by the superpowers' shift in cold war rivalry from nuclear brinkmanship in central Europe to competition for influence in the uncommitted Third World. Nonalignment made countries eligible for wooing by Moscow and Washington. Governments skillful enough to encourage both suitors and avoid a firm commitment to either might manage to gain benefits from both sides, although détente between the superpowers did not rule out either side's support for antigovernment movements in Third World countries when it served their purposes.

External alignments of governments, Communist Parties, and insurgents in Asian Pacific countries became even more complicated with the fissure that began developing between China and the Soviet Union in the late 1950s and burst into the open in 1960.

The Sino-Soviet Split

From the Chinese perspective, there was ample reason to be wary of the Soviets, despite the shared bond of Marxism-Leninism and China's need for outside help in recovering from years of war and embarking on the task of development. Not only were the Soviets the inheritors of tsarist expansionism into Chinese territory and spheres of influence during the century of China's weakness but, after the 1927 disaster resulting from their advice to the young CPC, Moscow ceased to give aid to the Chinese communist movement. Having come to power in the world's most populous country by their own efforts, the Chinese leaders expected to be treated as equals in relations with their Soviet counterparts. Mao traveled to Moscow in 1950 to negotiate a thirty-year treaty of friendship and Soviet aid in the form of credits and technical assistance. But the seeds of conflict were already in place, finding fertile ground in disputes over their common border, in doctrinal disagreements, in contention over leadership in the communist bloc, and over policy toward the Third World. Abrupt termination of Soviet aid in 1960 signaled the chilling of relations between the two allies.

Border Issues.   After a century of vulnerability to foreign intervention and loss of territory, China's preoccupation with border security was understandable. In the decade following the Korean War, the primary enemy was, of course, America, encircling China through its alliances and bases in Korea, Japan, and Taiwan and its growing involvement in Vietnam. Still, China took issue with its ally over the frontier in the northeast along the Amur and Ussuri Rivers and in Xinjiang in the northwest. Soviet actions increased China's sense of insecurity: Moscow's pursuit of détente and arms control with the United States; Khrushchev's refusal of the Chinese request in 1958 for nuclear protection in the crisis over islands held by Taiwan; Soviet aid to India, with which China also had a border dispute; the buildup of forces along the Sino-Soviet frontier. Clashes between Chinese and Soviet forces erupted in the northeast, reaching a peak in 1969. Later, the 1978 Soviet-Vietnam treaty of friendship and the 1979 Soviet invasion of Afghanistan appeared to China as threats to its southern and western borders.

Doctrinal Disagreement.   Here the issue arose over which country had chosen the correct road to socialism. Mao's departure from the Soviet pattern to launch the Great Leap Forward and the Cultural Revolution was roundly criticized by Moscow. In response, Mao charged Khrushchev with "revisionism," with losing sight of revolutionary goals in pursuit of crass materialism. The exchange of verbal abuse reached amazing depths of vituperation and led to a rupture of party-to-party contacts between the CPC and the Communist Party of the Soviet Union (CPSU). State-to-state relations continued in chilly though correct fashion until Gorbachev's overtures in the 1980s began a slow warming process.

Bloc Leadership and Policy toward the Third World.   Stalin's assumption and Khrushchev's insistence that Mao must acknowledge the leading role of the USSR in the communist camp galled the Chinese. Sensitive to issues of international status after the century of unequal treaties with Western powers, they refused to be treated as subordinate and charged the Soviets with the sin of "hegemonism." From that point on, China successfully challenged the CPSU for dominant influence in Vietnam and Korea and with nonruling Communist Parties in Indonesia, Malaysia, Thailand, and Japan. Policy toward noncommunist Third World governments was also in contention. At issue was whether to support local Communists in pushing for a socialist revolution in those countries (Mao's preference) or to cooperate with noncommunist but anti-imperialist, "bourgeois nationalist" leaders (Khrushchev's choice).

Repercussions of the Sino-Soviet Split.   The immediate effect of the rupture between the leader of the communist bloc and its Asian challenger was to confront ruling and nonruling Communist Parties around the world with a choice of siding with one of them, trying to stay on good terms with both, or splitting into rival Maoist and pro-Soviet parties. In Asia, China had the assets of proximity, of being Asian, and of experience in making a socialist revolution in an overwhelmingly agrarian society. To many Third World Communists, Mao's revision of Marxism-Leninism fit their societies better than the Soviet pattern because they were, as China had been, still preindustrial and lacked an urban working class to be the revolutionary base. But while China might be a more inspiring model than the Soviets to Asian revolutionaries, Moscow was richer and in a better position to give tangible assistance to communist governments and parties.

Longer-term effects on Communist Parties and states of rivalry between China and the Soviet Union were particularly visible in Vietnam and Cambodia after the Indochina War. Though Vietnam received help from both of them throughout the struggle for unification, when the war ended old enmity between China and Vietnam surfaced. It was triggered by Vietnam's refusal to join China in opposition to the Soviet Union, by rival claims to the Spratly and Paracel Islands, by Vietnam's treatment of its Chinese community, and by its assertion of a "special relationship" with Cambodia and Laos. The Khmer Rouge objected to the latter, resenting Vietnam's annexation in the nineteenth century of Cambodian territory in the lower Mekong Delta and the dominant role asserted by Vietnamese in the Indochina communist movement since its beginning in 1930. Pol Pot's Democratic Kampuchea government launched repeated attacks along the border with Vietnam and the Chinese provided him with aid, completing the triangle of tensions. Faced with hostility on two fronts, Vietnam sought assistance from the Soviets, signing a treaty of friendship in November 1978.

The next month Vietnam invaded Cambodia, ousted the Khmer Rouge, and replaced them with a new communist government of former Khmer Rouge more receptive to its interests. Vietnam's intervention and continued occupation of Cambodia met with almost universal condemnation as a violation of that country's territorial integrity and political independence and, despite Pol Pot's record of genocide against his people, Democratic Kampuchea was allowed to keep Cambodia's seat in the United Nations. China and Thailand threw their support behind Khmer Rouge guerrilla warfare against the new government of Heng Samrin, and China launched a brief punitive invasion into Vietnam in February 1979. The United States, by then having restored full diplomatic relations with China, indirectly supported the KR in giving aid to the two other resistance movements led by Prince Sihanouk and Son Sann, which joined with the KR in a coalition government-in-exile. All this produced the curious situation where the leader of the anticommunist bloc, its ally Thailand, and other ASEAN members were lined up on the same side with Communist China and Communist Khmer Rouge against the new communist government in Cambodia, Vietnam, and the Soviet Union. It is hard to imagine any clearer demonstration of the irrelevance of ideological bonds in determining international affiliations.

Finally, the split between China and the Soviet Union made it possible for a new triangular pattern eventually to emerge in Chinese-Soviet-American relations. It gave them room to maneuver in playing the old game of balance-of-power politics, each siding with one against the other to bring about some desired change in the latter's behavior and then switching sides for some other purpose. The guiding principle underlying this intricate improvisation was flexibility, meaning "no permanent allies, no permanent enemies, only permanent interests." Both of the others should be acceptable as a partner when partnership would serve one's national objectives, but no partnership should ever become so firm as to threaten the third power with permanent isolation. Clearly this new game was to be much more complex than the "us versus them" lineup of early cold war bipolarity, and it would require more sophistication and less messianic fervor on the part of foreign policymakers than before. Fortuitously, such men were on the scene in Beijing and Washington as the 1970s began.

Sino-American Accommodation

Recognition of the possibility of radical change in relations came slowly. The rupture between Beijing and Moscow meant that China now had two major enemies, America and the Soviet Union, and the abrupt termination of Soviet aid in 1960 forced it to take the path of self-reliance in foreign relations. Though deprived of help from Soviet weapons experts, Chinese scientists successfully tested a nuclear device in 1964, gaining China entry into the exclusive club of nuclear weapons states. The Cultural Revolution came the next year, turning attention inward and further isolating China from external affairs. America during that period was absorbed in the Vietnam War and in groping toward a redefined relationship with the Soviets that would allow them to compete with each other and at the same time reduce the risks of nuclear war. This trend toward superpower cooperation struck the Chinese as ominous. By the end of the decade, China was emerging from the Cultural Revolution and getting ready to resume contacts with the outside. Nixon and Henry Kissinger were in the White House, and conditions were auspicious for a new era in relations between the two countries. The process culminating in the establishment of formal diplomatic relations in January 1979 took almost eight years from Kissinger's secret visit to Beijing in 1971, the principal roadblock to normalization being each side's position on Taiwan.

Shanghai Communique, 1972.   Americans of the authors' generation, who had followed Richard Nixon's career from his early days as a crusading anticommunist, found it hard to believe the spectacle of the president in Beijing chatting with Chairman Mao and in Shanghai signing the joint communique with Premier Zhou Enlai, the very same person Secretary of State Dulles had snubbed at Geneva two decades earlier. To Chinese who had fought Americans in Korea and who for years had regarded the United States as Enemy #1, the events must have been equally startling. But Nixon's acceptance of Premier Zhou's invitation to visit earned him a secure place in the "friends of China" club, a place that survived Watergate and his resignation in disgrace from the presidency.

The Shanghai Communique[7] expressed the two countries' agreement on principles to govern the conduct of relations between them and named next steps to be taken in developing trade and person-to-person contacts. The basic principles agreed on were the same five principles Zhou had presented at the Bandung conference; added to them were statements that "progress toward normalization of relations between China and the United States is in the interests of all countries," and that "neither should seek hegemony in the Asia-Pacific region" nor "enter into agreements . . . directed at other states" (the latter to allay possible Soviet fears of Sino-American collusion against the USSR).

The communique also contained a statement of each party's views on international affairs and on Taiwan. China expressed support for the "struggle of all the oppressed people and nations for freedom and liberation" and their "right to choose their social systems," while the United States expressed support for "individual freedom and social progress . . . free of outside pressure or intervention." On the subject of Indochina, China favored the PRG's proposal for peace, while the United States supported the Republic of Vietnam's plan. On Korea, China endorsed North Korea's program for peaceful unification, while the United States said it would "maintain its close ties with and support for" South Korea and its efforts "to seek a relaxation of tension and increased communication in the Korean peninsula." China expressed support for "an independent, democratic, peaceful, and neutral Japan" and opposition to "the revival and outward expansion of Japanese militarism." The U.S. statement placed "the highest value on its friendly relations with Japan" and the continued development of "close bonds."

The differences over Taiwan were most marked. China specifically rejected any idea of "two Chinas" or "one China, one Taiwan," which the United States had suggested in 1971 as a compromise on the question of Chinese representation in the United Nations. China's position was clearly stated: that it is the "sole legal government of China, that Taiwan is a province of China," that its "liberation" is "China's internal affair in which no other country has the right to interfere," and that "all U.S. forces and military installations must be withdrawn." The American position moved closer to Beijing's by declaring that the United States "acknowledges that all Chinese on either side of the Taiwan Strait maintain that there is but one China and that Taiwan is a part of China" and that the U.S. government "does not challenge that position." Affirming its interest in "a peaceful settlement of the Taiwan question by the Chinese themselves" and the "ultimate objective" of withdrawing all U.S. forces and installations, the United States stated it would progressively reduce those forces "as the tension in the area diminishes." Domestic matters in both countries stalled further moves until the impasse on United States-Taiwan ties was overcome in 1978.

Joint Communique on Establishing Diplomatic Relations, 1978.   By the agreement on establishing diplomatic relations beginning January 1, 1979, the United States recognized the PRC as the sole legal government of China but specified that cultural, trade, and other unofficial relations with Taiwan would be maintained. This arrangement was modeled on the formula agreed on by China and Japan when they established diplomatic relations in 1972: End official government-to-government ties with Taiwan, but conduct trade and other relations through "private" organizations set up for that purpose.

In statements issued separately from the communique, each government recorded its position on related issues. China reiterated the point that *how* to bring Taiwan "back to the embrace of the motherland . . . is entirely China's internal affair."[8] For its part, the United States announced that with the establishment of diplomatic relations with the PRC, it would end diplomatic relations with Taiwan, start withdrawing its forces, and terminate the 1954 defense treaty a year later. No explicit commitment was made by China to refrain from the use of force to regain Taiwan nor by the United States to stop supplying arms to the island. The arms issue continues to be a bone of contention in Sino-American relations, as is the provision Congress wrote into the 1979 Taiwan Relations Act that the United States has the right to provide Taiwan with defensive armaments. Diplomatic ties between the United States and Taiwan are handled through the technically "private" American Institute in Taiwan and the Coordination Council for North American Affairs in Washington.

After 1979.   The establishment of diplomatic relations was followed by a gradual increase in trade and U.S. private investments and a period of close strategic cooperation in intelligence gathering and military consultations stimulated by the two countries' shared concern over the Soviet invasion of Afghanistan and its support of Vietnam's invasion of Cambodia. The "honeymoon" was marred by China's strong objections to a deal offered in 1981 by President Reagan to sell China high-tech arms it wanted and at the same time sell advanced fighter planes to Taiwan. China maintained that such arms sales were interference in its internal affairs contrary to the U.S. acknowledgment in the Shanghai communique that Taiwan is a part of China.

After long negotiations, another communique was agreed on in 1982 that mitigated, but did not really resolve, the differences on arms to Taiwan or the possibility of forceful unification. The communique referred to the Chinese government's "fundamental policy to strive for a peaceful solution to the Taiwan question" and to American intention to reduce arms sales and not to "exceed, either in qualitative or in quantitative terms, the level of those supplied" since 1979.[9] No date was set for ending arms sales, and controversy flared up again in 1992 when President Bush decided to allow Taiwan to buy American fighter planes.

Sino-Japanese Relations

As a loyal ally, Japan's government had followed American policy by maintaining diplomatic relations with the Chinese Nationalist government to the exclusion of official ties to the communist government. Nevertheless, Japanese companies engaged in trade with the mainland and as that trade grew, so did their pressure on the LDP to distance itself from American policy toward China. When Nixon, without prior notice to the Japanese government, announced that he was going to China, Japan quickly moved ahead of its ally, extending full recognition to the Beijing government in 1972. With China's assent, under the "Japan formula" economic and cultural relations continued between Japan and Taiwan through unofficial associations.

It took six more years of negotiations, complicated by concurrent Japan-Soviet negotiations over fishing rights and over the islands taken from Japan at the end of World War II, for China and Japan to reach agreement on the peace treaty of 1978, which officially ended the state of war between them. At China's insistence, an "anti-hegemony" pledge was written into the treaty, part of China's effort to secure itself against superpower ambitions. Although at times China suggested that Japan should beef up its military defenses against the Soviet threat, the lingering specter of revived Japanese militarism led it to accept continuation of the United States-Japan security relationship as a restraint on that occurring. Increased trade and Japanese loans and investments followed the signing of the peace treaty, all important to China's Four Modernizations program. Strains have appeared over Japan's trade surplus, the treatment in Japanese textbooks of the country's actions in the war in China, and a dispute over possession of Diaoyutai/Senkaku Island in the Yellow Sea.

To China's diplomatic successes in opening relations with the United States and Japan was added the signing in 1984 of the agreement with the United Kingdom for the transfer of Hong Kong to China in 1997 and a similar agreement on Macau with Portugal in 1987.

While bipolarity declined and contacts grew between communist and noncommunist countries, the first steps toward regional cooperation in Southeast Asia were being taken, resulting in the inauguration of ASEAN in 1967.

ASEAN's Role

The founding members of the Association of Southeast Asian Nations were the Philippines, Thailand, Indonesia, Malaysia, and Singapore (Brunei joined in 1985, after it became independent). More seemed to divide them than unite them. Two members were militarily allied with the United States and had American bases on their territory; the others were nonaligned, though Western-leaning, and professed resistance to the presence of foreign bases. Rule by three different colonial powers inhibited the development of ties among them, so that at the time of independence their ties with the United States, Britain, and the Netherlands were much closer than the ties with each other. Furthermore, their economies were competitive, not complementary, and the goal of development set them in competition with each other for external aid, trade, and investment. Finally, there were territorial disputes among them, most over colonial-imposed boundaries, that threatened amicable relations in the region. The most recent flare-up prior to ASEAN's founding had been over the proposal to incorporate the British colonies on the island of Borneo, along with Singapore and Malaya, in a new Federation of Malaysia. Objections were raised by Indonesia and the Philippines, which laid claim to Sabah as having belonged to the Sultan of Sulu. When Britain and Malaya went ahead with the Federation in 1963, Sukarno waged Konfrontasi, a propaganda barrage combined with sporadic raids against Malaysia, which only ended with his ouster in 1965.

The desire to settle future such disputes among themselves, thereby avoiding opportunity for outside powers such as China, the Soviet Union, and Japan to fish in troubled waters, was one motivation behind the establishment of ASEAN. The United States, according to David J. Steinberg,[10] was favorably inclined to closer ties among the anticommunist governments in the neighborhood of Vietnam, where the war was reaching a crescendo. And each of the member states saw that coordinating their foreign policies on specific issues and cooperation in economic, technical, and cultural matters might increase their international clout politically and economically. So they agreed to establish ASEAN, successor to two regional institutions: Maphilindo (Malaya-Philippines-Indonesia), set up in 1963 at Philippine initiative, and the Association of Southeast Asia (Thailand-Philippines-Malaysia), which had held ministerial-level sessions in 1966.

According to ASEAN's founding declaration, its purpose is cooperation to promote economic growth, peace, and stability in the region. The emphasis, in the words of Thanat Khoman, then foreign minister of Thailand and a leading figure in ASEAN's founding, "would be on economic and other nonmilitary activities," purposely excluding military matters "because of the unhappy experience with the Southeast Asia Treaty Organization (SEATO), which failed dismally because of divergent interests between the European and Southeast Asian members."[11] The declaration contained a reference to all foreign bases as "temporary," remaining only with the consent of the host countries, and not "to be used directly or indirectly to subvert" their national independence or the "orderly processes of their national development."[12] Membership was open to all states in the region and a modest institutional framework set up: annual meeting of foreign ministers, and later economic ministers, as needed, with a standing committee to function between those gatherings, and a national secretariat in each member state. A small central secretariat was later formed in Jakarta.

In the first two decades of its existence, ASEAN achieved some success in fostering cooperation on efforts to open markets, stabilize commodity prices, reform the international monetary and trading systems, and deal with extraregional powers on trade, aid, and investment matters. But no progress was made on regional economic integration, either in joint projects or on regional trade liberalization, and intra-ASEAN trade remained quite small. Political cooperation has come more easily since, as Evelyn Colbert[13] points out, the members' foreign policy goals—resist great power interference and get Western help for development—are harmonious and their elites have a similar conservative orientation, seeing political stability as a higher priority than democracy and, as a result of experience with insurgencies, strongly anticommunist and wary of China and the Soviet Union.

One foreign policy initiative taken collectively during this period was the endorsement of the principle of neutrality for the region, the goal being to gain big power acceptance of Southeast Asia as a zone of peace, freedom, and neutrality (ZOPFAN). ZOPFAN and ASEAN's nonalignment as an organization were not regarded as incompatible with existing security ties linking Thailand and the Philippines to the United States and Malaysia and Singapore to the Commonwealth countries. A second issue of more immediate collaborative action concerned Indochina after the end of war there and lessened American presence. At the first ASEAN summit meeting in 1976 in Bali, the leaders agreed that a U.S. "over-the-horizon" military presence was needed for regional stability and that friendly relations with newly unified Vietnam should be sought to wean it away from China and the Soviets and toward closer identification with Southeast Asian countries. Those hopes were dashed by the Vietnamese invasion of Cambodia. From 1979 on ASEAN played a major role in mobilizing international pressure on Hanoi to withdraw and on efforts to negotiate the formation of a representative government in Cambodia, which culminated in the 1991 Paris agreement. The Cambodian issue most directly concerned Thailand, the only "front-line" ASEAN state, while Indonesia, less ready than Bangkok to see Hanoi as China's successor in the role of chief regional threat, countered any anti-Hanoi ASEAN "tilt," keeping channels of communication open and sponsoring informal meetings of interested parties in Jakarta to explore possible ways of settling the Cambodian issue.

ASEAN's stature in international affairs has been enhanced with the waning of the cold war, which opened up new opportunities for creative adaptation to the changing context of global and regional politics. That and other recent developments in international relations are the subject of the next section.

THE END OF THE COLD WAR: NEW AFFINITIES, OLD ENMITIES

Like its beginning, the cold war's ending originated in events in Europe, and Asia felt the repercussions of the momentous changes in Eastern Europe in the late 1980s and the disintegration of the Soviet Union in 1991. As superpower hostility further abated, the international environment provided opportunities for initiatives toward the resolution of long-standing regional conflicts of cold war origin.

The post-cold war international system differs from the cold war era in three major respects: Multipolarity is replacing bipolarity as the dominant pattern in world politics; nuclear deterrence is being replaced by conventional deterrence, likely to be less stable than the "balance of terror"; and national security is coming to depend more on a state's own economic power, as compared to the prior primacy of military power and the protective shield of a superpower ally.[14] In the Asian Pacific region multipolarity also prevails, the major powers being China, Japan, the United States, and Russia, with the NICs and ASEAN constituting two other power groupings. Hsiung foresees that South Korea, Taiwan, and Singapore "will most likely be drawn into the Japanese economic orbit."[15] With the second largest defense budget in the world, Japan has a combined economic and military power that means its influence in the region will increase and U.S. influence decline.[16] In both the Asian Pacific and the world generally, "geoeconomic" concerns will supplant geopolitics as the motivation of foreign policy. The region deviates from the global post-cold war pattern in the continued presence of a group of communist states and the absence, thus far, of a surge of ethnic nationalist conflict on a scale such as that seen in Yugoslavia and several former Soviet republics.

Responses to Moscow's Foreign Policy Initiatives

Initiatives undertaken by Soviet President Gorbachev in the last years before the dissolution of the Soviet Union offered to Asian Pacific countries (as well as to the United States) opportunities to break out of the confrontationist militarized situation that had characterized relations until then. The initiatives were inspired by Gorbachev's "new thinking" about foreign policy, in recognition that success in his program of economic and political reforms required reduction in military expenditures, which in turn required a lessening of international tensions. The development of Siberia and the Far Eastern maritime provinces of the USSR would benefit by more foreign trade and investments, and that required reaching out for new relationships, especially with China, Japan, and South Korea. Accordingly, in speeches at Vladivostok in 1986 and at Krasnoyarsk in 1988, Gorbachev expressed the desire to improve bilateral relations with all countries, to work toward negotiated settlement of regional conflicts such as in Cambodia, and to reverse the military buildup in the region. Asian reaction was generally positive but cautious, awaiting deeds to back up Moscow's words. And the deeds were not long in coming.

Responses from China.   From China's viewpoint, Soviet actions in 1988 went far toward meeting the three conditions Beijing had laid down for normalization of relations: withdrawal of Soviet troops from Afghanistan, withdrawal of Vietnamese troops from Cambodia, and reduction of Soviet troops along the Chinese border. Commitments were made on all three issues, paving the way for President Gorbachev to visit Beijing in May 1989, just as the "prodemocracy" movement took shape in Tiananmen Square. It was hardly an auspicious moment for a summit meeting. The Chinese leaders' reception of Gorbachev was cool, in part because of the distraction and embarrassment of the demonstrators' occupation of the historic center of the capital city, but also because of the Chinese leaders' negative opinion of Gorbachev's glasnost and perestroika policies. Economic restructuring they could accept, even endorse, since their own economic reforms predated and went beyond those of the Soviet Union. But what about the new political ideas of "openness" that were having such a destabilizing effect in Eastern Europe and might infect other communist countries? *That* risk had to be guarded against in China, lest the leadership role of the Communist Party be undermined by such challenges as the misguided, even subversive, students occupying Tiananmen Square. The summit concluded without too much loss of face, and afterward, when the Chinese government forcibly cleared the square, the Soviets refrained from joining international condemnation of the act.

Since then, relations between Beijing and Moscow have continued on a normal basis, even after the breakup of the USSR. Trade has grown and, reflecting its concern with upgrading its armed forces, China took advantage of Russia's sell-off of weapons at bargain prices to buy $1.8 billion's worth in 1992.[17] In November 1993 the two countries signed a five-year military cooperation agreement aimed at further modernization of the Chinese military through technology transfer from the Russians. The removal of intermediary nuclear forces from Soviet Asia, in accordance with a United States-Soviet agreement, as well as withdrawal of Russian military from Mongolia and Vietnam and reduction of troops along the Chinese frontier have done much to mitigate China's apprehensions about the security threat from its northern neighbor. But there is still concern about the possible spillover effects of political instability in Russia and Central Asian states formerly part of the Soviet Union.

Japanese Response.   From Tokyo's viewpoint, Gorbachev's overtures for improved relations were less well received than in Beijing, the sticking point being the "Northern Territories," the four islands in the Kurile chain closest to Japan that the Soviets, in accordance with Allied agreement, occupied at the end of World War II. Although Moscow moved away from its past insistence that ownership of the islands is nonnegotiable and has ceased to condemn the U.S.-Japanese alliance, the Japanese position is that satisfactory settlement of the territorial issue is a requisite for the signing of a peace treaty ending the state of war that has existed since 1945 and for the establishment of normal relations between the two countries. During a state visit to Tokyo in October 1993 Russian President Yeltsin assured his hosts that the peace treaty was his goal and that he would live up to past Soviet commitments (which include a 1956 Soviet promise to give back two of the islands). Yeltsin also apologized for the treatment of Japanese prisoners of war detained in Soviet labor camps after World War II. Prime Minister Hosokawa asserted, "This is a new page in Russo-Japanese relations."[18]

History, economic interests, and domestic politics are underlying impediments to such a qualitative improvement in relations between the two countries. They were rivals for influence in northeast Asia at the turn of the twentieth century, marked by the Russo-Japanese War of 1905, and relations after World War II were chilled by the cold war. Its end, from the Japanese perspective, has not meant the end of the raison d'etre of the security treaty with the United States, and Japanese public opinion still regards Russia as hostile. Nor is potential profit from joint ventures in Siberia sufficiently appealing to lure Japanese capital away from more lucrative investment opportunities in other parts of Asia. The instability of the post-USSR government in Russia also discourages cultivation of more intimate economic relations.

Effects on Korea.   Gorbachev's initiatives got a positive reception in South Korea, fitting nicely with President Roh's "Northern Policy" of seeking full diplomatic relations with communist countries. Discussions about expanding trade between South Korea and the USSR were held in 1989 and diplomatic relations were established in 1990. The Soviets dropped their objection to the admission of the two Koreas to the United Nations and both joined that body in 1991. South Koreans were further reassured by statements from Soviet officials that North Korea had started the war in 1950 and later reports that Stalin had been involved in planning the operation.[19] Trade has grown, but South Korean investment in Russia has been very limited and the government has suspended economic aid because of Moscow's failure to keep up interest payments on earlier loans and to pay compensation for the shooting down of a Korean Air Lines plane that overflew Soviet territory in 1983.[20]

For North Korea the opening of diplomatic relations with Seoul by Moscow and Beijing and the breakup of the Soviet Union brought an increasing sense of isolation, of abandonment by its former protectors. Economic difficulties were exacerbated by Russia's insistence on payment in hard currency for the oil it had previously supplied on generous terms, resulting in shortage of power for industry, transport, and home use. By supporting the admission of both states to the United Nations and opening formal diplomatic relations with Seoul, the Soviets seemed to signal to the North Koreans their virtual abandonment. China's attitude toward Pyongyang remained supportive on the surface, though the Chinese made pointed suggestions about the need for North Korea to undertake economic reforms. This succession of unwelcome events that the ending of the cold war brought contributed to North Korea's sense of being under siege and dampened prospects for progress toward unification of the two Korean states.

The Divided States: Relations across the Thirty-Eighth Parallel and the Taiwan Straits

Although ideological divisions between Communists and noncommunists have become less salient as a consequence of the ousting of ruling Communist Parties in Eastern Europe and the Soviet Union, in Asia that split remains in two cases—Korea and China. Contacts—at first unofficial, now official for Korea and semiofficial for China—have been made between the two sides, but the end of the cold war has not removed the obstacles to reunification of the divided states.

Relations across the Thirty-Eighth Parallel. In the decades since the armistice ending the Korean War in 1953, North and South moved fitfully away from their initial posture of implacable hostility and avowed intention of reunification by force to a grudging acceptance of the other's existence and to the beginning in 1972 of dialogue on peaceful reunification. The talks resulted in a joint communique on principles to guide the discussion but were broken off by the North in 1973. Resumed from 1984 to 1986, and again in 1991, negotiations at the prime ministerial level produced two important agreements signed in December 1991 and ratified by both governments in 1992.

The Agreement on Reconciliation, Nonaggression, Exchanges and Cooperation between the North and the South committed them to respect for each other's government, to refrain from the use of force against each other, to the creation of a joint commission to consider alleged violations of the armistice, to setting up a hotline between Pyongyang and Seoul, and to economic and other contacts across the thirty-eighth parallel. In the second agreement, a joint declaration on nuclear arms, the two sides agreed not to acquire nuclear arms, nuclear fuel reprocessing, or uranium-enrichment capabilities and to establish a joint commission to inspect sites in both countries. (The obstacle to agreement posed by the presence of nuclear weapons in the hands of U.S. armed forces stationed in South Korea had been removed by U.S.

withdrawal of such weapons late in 1991.) North Korea agreed to inspection of its nuclear power and research facilities by the International Atomic Energy Agency (IAEA).

The optimism inspired by the signing and ratification of these two agreements between North and South Korea was not matched by forward movement in relations between them until late June 1994, just on the eve of President Kim Il Sung's death. At that time, a months-long impasse over suspicions that the North was engaged in nuclear weapons development was broken and agreement reached for a July summit meeting between the two Korean presidents. That meeting was foreclosed by Kim's death on July 8 and, as of this writing, it is not known whether it will be rescheduled.

The Nuclear Issue.   Most troubling to North-South relations has been the unwillingness of Pyongyang to allow full international inspection of its nuclear facilities to determine whether it has diverted fuel for weapons purposes. After accepting IAEA monitoring of its nuclear power plants, the North resisted the agency's request for full inspection of research sites at Yongbyon where it was suspected that a plant for reprocessing nuclear fuel was being constructed, a violation of the 1991 North-South agreement and of the North's obligations as a party to the Nuclear Non-Proliferation Treaty. The North Korean government maintained that the plant's purpose is peaceful and denied any intent to develop nuclear weapons. International pressure for inspection continued and in 1993 North Korea announced its intention to withdraw from the nonproliferation treaty, but suspended carrying through on the threat after high-level talks with American officials.

More rounds of talks were held in 1993 and 1994, Pyongyang agreeing in February 1994 to allow resumption of IAEA visits to seven sites, but not to two additional installations suspected of being used for nuclear waste disposal. The IAEA inspectors visited in March, but were denied full access to the Yongbyon laboratory. Tensions mounted in May when the North began replacing fuel rods in a nuclear reactor without international inspectors present to observe the whole process. The IAEA then concluded that it could no longer certify North Korea's compliance with its treaty obligations and the United States, with South Korean and Japanese agreement, declared the intention of seeking UN Security Council sanctions against North Korea, first making a further effort at diplomatic resolution by sending President Jimmy Carter to visit Kim Il Sung. The result was an offer by Kim to resume talks with South Korea and with the United States. Both sets of negotiation began, but were interrupted by Kim's death. The nuclear issue, at this writing, remains unresolved.

North Korea's motive in resisting full international inspection is unclear. It seems contradictory to its overtures toward normalizing relations with Japan, desired because of the economic boost from reparations that Japan is expected to give for damage inflicted during the period of colonial rule. And the nuclear policy certainly supports those in Seoul and Washington who maintain that the North is still a major threat to South Korea's security. Yet the counterargument is that Pyongyang's leaders have no real intention of *using* nuclear weapons, should they develop them, to launch an attack across the thirty-eighth parallel. Instead, the nuclear program might have two other motives. One would be to gain the appearance of having a nuclear deterrent against possible South Korean nuclear capability or the return of U.S. nuclear arms to the South's territory. The second motive might be drawing to itself international attention. Without the nuclear issue, North Korea could be ignored by the rest of the world as a very minor power that has lost its powerful external patrons; with the issue kept alive by uncertainty over its intentions, North Korea is the focus of diplomacy and other forms of attention by the international community. It may hope to use nuclear inspection as a bargaining chip to trade for full diplomatic recognition from the United States and for trade and aid benefits from the outside world.

Plans for Reunification.   Both North and South have offered plans for reunification. The North proposes the creation of a democratic confederal republic under the slogan "one nation, one state, two systems, two regional governments." It would be a unified state with a national council of representatives from South and North in equal numbers (though the South has twice the population of the North). The armed forces of the two sides would be merged, but the two existing governments would remain as "regional" governments, keeping their individual characteristics and conducting relations with other countries while the confederal government would act internationally on behalf of the whole country.[21]

South Korea's proposal, in contrast to the North's idea of unification from the top in one fell swoop, is for a gradual process of step-by-step measures leading eventually to the creation of a unitary democratic state. Articulated by President Roh in 1989, the "Korean National Community Unification Formula" calls for an interim Korean Commonwealth, based on a charter adopted at a summit meeting and approved by the legislatures of the South and North. The commonwealth structures would consist of a joint council of presidents as the supreme decision-making body, a council of ministers of cabinet-level officials from each side to discuss various economic, social, and cultural measures to integrate the two societies, a joint secretariat and liaison offices in each capital, and a council of representatives with equal numbers of legislators from North and South to draw up a constitution for a unified democratic republic. Once the constitution is accepted, general elections would be held to form a single legislature and government for the whole country.[22]

There does not seem to be any strong motivation for or movement toward Korean unification at this juncture, on either side of the thirty-eighth parallel or on the part of interested outsiders. Negotiating from its present position of economic weakness would not be likely to get the North a favorable outcome. With the experience of German unification as an example, South Korea seems reluctant to take on the probable economic burden, especially at a time when its own economy has slowed down. China, with excellent trade relations with South Korea, has no particular reason to encourage an alteration in the status quo, nor do either the United States or Japan. Students and others in South Korea have long espoused the cause of unification, but unless the North collapses in as dramatic and irreversible fashion as did East Germany, leaving no option to the South but to fill the vacuum, unification seems unlikely in the near future.

Relations across the Taiwan Straits.   As with Korea, relations between the People's Republic and the Republic of China have moved from military clashes in the 1950s and 1960s to verbal fusillades from the 1970s on, combining expressions of continued hostility with proposals on unification, to unofficial contacts and a growth in indirect trade beginning in the late 1980s. Those contacts have not reached the official status that relations between the two Koreas have, nor has Beijing reached the point of recognizing the existence of a separate state on Taiwan or acceptance of its presence in the United Nations, as North and South Korea have done. The governments on both sides of the Taiwan Straits do agree that there is only one China and that Taiwan is a province of China; they disagree on the timing and terms of reincorporation of the province in the mainland. This position, however, is disputed by proponents of "independence" in Taiwan, winning international—and China's—recognition of its legal existence as a separate state, which it has been de facto since 1949.

PRC's Efforts to Isolate Taiwan.   In the 1970s, a series of changes in the external environment—the Sino-Soviet split, the opening of Sino-American contacts, the removal of the U.S. Seventh Fleet from the straits, which it had been patrolling since the beginning of the Korean War, and the decision at the UN to allow PRC representatives to take China's seat—combined to reshape relations between Beijing and Taipei. Beijing's strategy was first to isolate Taiwan by insisting that, as a condition of establishing diplomatic relations with PRC, other governments must break official relations with ROC and that Taiwan be denied membership in international intergovernmental organizations before PRC would join. Taipei's response was to counter that isolation and loss of official diplomatic recognition from most of the world's governments by strengthening its economic power and increasing foreign trade. It also set up, with China's tacit consent, "unofficial" trade/diplomatic missions in Japan, the United States, and other countries that had switched from official ties with Taiwan to recognition of the PRC.

PRC Proposal for Unification.   In 1981 Beijing proposed that talks on reunification be held between the ruling parties in the two governments and called for exchanges of mail, trade, and visitors. The terms of reunification, under Beijing's "one country, two systems" formula of 1981 and elaborated in later years, would allow Taiwan considerable autonomy and minimize changes in existing institutions and practices. The proposal was that Taiwan would keep its armed forces and that Beijing would not station PLA troops on the island. Taiwan's local government and socioeconomic system would continue, its officials would participate in national politics, and Beijing promised not to interfere with Taiwan's internal affairs. But it refused international pressure to commit itself unequivocally to using only peaceful means to bring about unification, taking the position that Taiwan's relationship to the mainland is an internal matter to be decided as a sovereign right by the Chinese government.

Taiwan's response to Beijing's proposal on reunification was the "three no's": no official contacts, no compromise, no direct negotiations. Unification would be possible only when Beijing gave up communism and accepted Sun Yatsen's Three Principles and when the Chinese people freely chose reunification. PRC's proposal was regarded as impractical while conditions on the two sides of the straits were so different, and it could have no significance other than an attempt by Beijing to project a favorable image abroad.

Taiwan's Shift on Relations with PRC.   In 1987 Taiwan's policy changed from the negativity of the "three no's" to a more positive mode, signaled by the lifting of the government's prohibition on travel to the mainland. Chang[23] attributes the shift to President Chiang Chingkuo's personal initiative just prior to his death and to the need of Taiwan's small- and medium-sized export-oriented businesses for access to the mainland market. Island entrepreneurs took advantage of the lifting of travel restrictions to increase indirect trade (usually through Hong Kong) with PRC, transferring labor-intensive production to the mainland and entering into joint-venture agreements with mainland enterprises.

In 1990 the government created a cabinet-level council to advise the president on unification policies. It drew up a set of guidelines on principles for unification: recognition that Taiwan and the mainland are parts of one China and that unification must come about by peaceful and democratic means and must serve the interests of the people of Taiwan. In 1991 the Straits Exchange Foundation (SEF), a semiofficial body, was established to handle contacts with mainlanders on cross-straits matters, and Beijing created a counterpart entity, the Association for Relations Across the Taiwan Straits (ARATS). Since then SEF and ARATS have served as the ostensibly nonofficial vehicles for contacts between the two governments, enabling both sides to maintain their mutual nonrecognition as *the* government of China. In August 1993, however, Beijing broke off talks begun earlier that year in Singapore as a demonstration of its displeasure with Taipei's campaign for admission as a UN member.

Taipei's vision of the unification process is similar to that of South Korea, favoring a phased process in three stages. The present stage of increasing unofficial contacts is the preliminary to a second phase of direct links, requiring as a precondition that Beijing renounce the use of force against Taiwan and end its opposition to Taiwan's membership in international organizations. The final stage would be official contacts and negotiations on unification.

The preconditions are unacceptable to PRC, as was made clear in a policy paper, "The Taiwan Question and Reunification of China," issued on August 31, 1993. The paper reiterates the "one country, two systems" position, reviews the basis for Chinese sovereignty over Taiwan, and states Beijing's determination to block efforts to divide that sovereignty by admitting Taiwan to UN membership.[24]

Taiwan's Bid for UN Membership.   Having been evicted from most global international intergovernmental organizations following PRC's seating in the UN in 1972 (though the Asian Development Bank resisted Beijing pressure to oust Taiwan, which is still represented in the ADB and also in APEC, the Asian Pacific Economic Cooperation forum), in recent years Taipei has campaigned for readmission to various international organizations. In 1993 a group of Central American states asked the UN General Assembly to consider membership for ROC. Although the PRC can stop positive action on admission by its veto power in the Security Council, by raising the issue Taiwan gets an international forum to present its viewpoint to the rest of the world.

The case for admission is "based on the principle of universality, and on the precedents of parallel representation for divided nations."[25] Universality of UN membership, it is argued, means that the 21 million inhabitants of Taiwan, who have not been represented in the UN since the seating of the PRC, should be given a voice by the admission of Taiwan as a member. There is the precedent of the representation of the two Koreas and the two Germanies, which did not prevent German unification. To avoid seeming, by seeking separate admission to the UN, to depart from the principle that there is only one China, Taipei points out that ROC has "co-existed with the PRC within China's borders for almost half a century."[26] A further inducement is that Taiwan is able and willing to make substantial financial contributions to the work of the UN. Beijing's 1993 policy paper labels Taiwan's bid for UN membership "an attempt to split state sovereignty" and blames foreign meddling for the continued division of China.[27]

The Movement for Taiwan Independence.   Despite its effort to gain entrance to international organizations, the ruling party on Taiwan shares Beijing's objection to the notion of a declaration of independence by Taiwan. That is, however, a step advocated by the opposition Democratic Progressive Party, most of whose members are native Taiwanese. Beijing has warned that any attempt at independence will be prevented, if necessary by force, so the Taipei government has the task of keeping advocacy of Taiwan independence under control and preserving the status quo in cross-straits relations.

Though progress on political reunification seems at an impasse with irreconcilable demands on both sides—no incentive for Beijing to accept the costs of bringing about unification by force nor economic incentive for Taiwan to seek it voluntarily—the process of economic integration is well underway, notably between Taiwan and the mainland coastal provinces of Fujian and Guangdong. Trade, investment, and travel have boomed in the 1990s and those "nonpolitical" unofficial ties may in the long term overcome or outlive political obstacles to unity. What happens when Hong Kong reverts to PRC control in 1997 will be observed with great interest in Taiwan. Differences between the Hong Kong and Taiwan cases are great; still, the colony's experience with reunification may yield some lessons useful to both Beijing and Taipei in preparations for changing their relationship.

RETHINKING NATIONAL SECURITY IN THE POST–COLD WAR ERA

The perennial search for national "security" takes on different dimensions with the passing of the Soviet Union as a superpower and the end of communist insurgencies everywhere in the Asian Pacific except the Philippines. What are the current and possible future threats that Asian Pacific governments perceive as causes of insecurity? What means are they using to protect their countries and promote their interests? What role in regional security do they see for the United States now that the containment of communist expansionism no longer provides the rationale that it did in the region and globally for almost a half-century? Is Japan's political and military influence in the region likely to expand, commensurate with its preeminent economic position? Is some form of multilateral defense arrangement among the Asian Pacific countries a desirable successor to bilateral alliances with the United States or to the strategy of nonalignment followed by others? Should existing regional bodies, such as ASEAN or APEC, take on new or more responsibilities in conflict resolution and other politico-military matters? These and related issues shaping the post–cold war perspectives and foreign policies of Asian Pacific states are raised in this final section of Chapter 7, starting with a review of actual and potential causes of apprehension.

Threats to Security—Causes of Insecurity

Traditional geopolitical/strategic concerns have not evaporated in the post–cold war age, despite the reality of inescapable economic, environmental, and cultural interdependence. These include calculations of the "balance of power" and the possibility that some action by a major or middle power may upset the balance, thus putting others in jeopardy. Arms races in conventional weapons, as well as the specter of nuclear proliferation, are causes for alarm. Disputes over territory remain unresolved, some over the location of land borders and over rival claims to islands of strategic, economic, or symbolic significance, and are potential causes of armed clashes, particularly the Spratly and Paracels Islands in the South China Sea.

Other matters of concern are the vulnerability of sea lanes to blockage, especially the narrow straits between Malaysia and Indonesia, and the difficulty of preventing spillover along land frontiers from turmoil in neighboring countries, such as antigovernment forces seeking haven in Thailand from Myanmar's SLORC. The dangers that the division of the Chinese and Korean nations will erupt into violence or that a declining U.S. military presence will be met with increased military influence on the part of China or Japan are troubling to some, even most, Asian Pacific governments. Uncertainties about Russia continue to be a source of disquiet. While only the most paranoid would assert that Moscow now has the intent or the political unity needed to threaten its neighbors militarily, it does still have the weapons; the disintegration of the Russian Federation or the rise to power of a xenophobic nationalist movement could have profound effects, especially on Northeast Asia. Finally, mention should be made of competition over spheres of influence and the revival of old hostilities that had been at least partially muted during the cold war. Particularly in Southeast Asia, rivalries between China and Thailand over Myanmar, between Thailand and Vietnam over Cambodia and Laos, and between Indonesia and Malaysia over political leadership are sources of tension and concern among the parties and their neighbors.

To these traditional geopolitico-strategic security issues should be added new-style "geoeconomic" concerns, a reflection of the importance that a healthy economy has for a country's security and of the degree of integration into the world economy of Asian Pacific countries (with the possible exception of Myanmar). Geoeconomics involve such concerns as vulnerability to the loss of foreign markets resulting from competitors' successes or from unilateral or multilateral protectionism; the influx of foreign goods under free (or freer) trade conditions that affect domestic producers adversely; the loss of access to foreign supplies of oil and other vital raw materials; the loss of private foreign investment, perhaps resulting from political instability, environmental regulations, or other conditions in the host country that discourage investors, or from restraints imposed on investors by the home governments for political purposes; and the loss of bilateral or multilateral foreign aid because donors are cutting expenditures or are withholding aid to express displeasure with the recipient government's behavior.

Not all of these concerns apply to every country, of course, but they do show the range of matters that affect foreign policy perceptions in adjusting to changes in the environment of international relations in the post–cold war era. The economic foundation of security may be regarded as more crucial than military capabilities, as Hsiung asserts: "a consequence of the end of the Cold War is the decline of nations' concern for military security in favor of economic security. Under the circumstances, former allies may turn out to be potential adversaries (such as in trade matters). . . . The lines between allies and adversaries are blurring."[28]

Post–Cold War Security: The View from Tokyo

Tokyo's recognition of the importance of economics to national security was expressed in the early 1970s in what came to be known as the policy of "comprehensive security." Having accepted the American-imposed constitutional prohibition on maintaining armed forces and on using war as an instrument of national policy, the Japanese had chosen at the end of the occupation in 1952 to serve as a forward base for the U.S. military and to shelter under the "umbrella" of American nuclear and conventional power for protection against Soviet or Chinese expansionism. Soon, giving in to American pressure to do so, the Japanese government undertook to build a modest army and navy, circumventing the constitutional prohibition by calling them the Self-Defense Forces. Freed of primary responsibility for its own safety by the alliance that committed the United States to Japan's defense (but did not oblige Japan to reciprocate) and assured of access to American markets for the output of its industries being rebuilt with American aid, Japan was able to pursue a pacifist neomercantilist external policy, concentrating on export-oriented growth and protecting its own domestic market from foreign competition.

"Comprehensive Security" Policy.   For the first two decades after regaining its independence, Japan usually followed the U.S. lead on foreign policy issues, notably on the policy of nonrecognition of PRC. But in the early 1970s a series of events (OPEC's quadrupling of oil prices and Nixon's decision to revalue the dollar and to go to China, decisions that directly affected Japan but made without consulting or even notifying the Japanese government) jolted Tokyo into realization of the need for active pursuit of its own interests. The concept of "comprehensive security" was devised, defining security "in a broad sense of economic well-being and invulnerability to disruptions as well as traditional military security, and the active use of diplomatic, economic and cultural initiatives as well as a strong military defence."[29] Still under American protection, Japan could concentrate on strengthening its economic position by diversifying the external sources of oil and other raw materials on which it depends and diversifying its foreign markets so it would not be vulnerable to the loss of any one of them. It also aimed at increasing foreign dependence on Japanese capital through direct foreign investments and official development assistance, and on Japanese technology, goods, and services. Reparations to countries in Southeast Asia for damages suffered during the Japanese occupation have also tied the recipients to Japan's economy. Instrumental in the founding of the Asian Development Bank (ADB) and a major contributor of its capital, Japan actively supports other instruments of multilateral economic cooperation in the Pacific Basin.

With the economic influence it gained in South Korea, China, Taiwan, and the ASEAN countries as an asset, Japan also began to take a more active role in regional political matters. It has undertaken to act as a diplomatic intermediary in regional conflicts. It maintains relations with both PRC and ROC, tries to play a bridging role between South and North Korea and between ASEAN and Vietnam. It worked for a diplomatic resolution of the Cambodian civil war and sent troops abroad for the first time since World War II to serve with the United Nations Transitional Authority in Cambodia, headed by a Japanese UN official. Recognizing the legacy of anti-Japanese sentiment remaining from World War II, government officials have finally in recent years begun to make formal apologies for the treatment of citizens of occupied countries.

Japan's foreign policies now extend beyond the Asian Pacific and are global in scope. It gives bilateral aid to countries in all regions and is now the world's leading provider of foreign aid. The second largest contributor to the UN budget, Japan is an increasingly active participant in the United Nations and affiliated organizations, building a case for a permanent seat on the UN Security Council.

An important element in Japan's security is maintaining good relations with China. Since Japan surged ahead of U.S. leadership and established formal diplomatic ties with Beijing in 1972, relations have been calm, surviving even the Tiananmen affair with only a brief suspension of Japanese aid. The Japanese government has refrained from joining in Western criticisms of Chinese human rights conditions. Prime Minister Kaifu visited China in 1991, and Emperor Akihito made a state visit in 1992.

Military Security.   The military aspect of national security is not neglected by any means, and Japan's military power is formidable, though limited in reach. Even the self-imposed budgetary limit on military expenditure of 1 percent of the GNP is a large amount, given that the GNP is the second largest in the world. It buys technologically advanced equipment for the quarter of a million members of the armed forces. Even so, Japan cannot expect to match either Russia or China in numbers, and so far it has kept to the post-Hiroshima determination not to acquire nuclear weapons, which both of its neighbors do possess, although that option is clearly available. The Japanese government in 1993 indicated reluctance, in light of the threat of North Korea going nuclear, to commit itself indefinitely to the Nuclear Non-Proliferation Treaty. The prospect of an extensive military buildup even in conventional weapons, which might extend Japan's reach beyond the present 1,000 miles from its shores, would clearly be disturbing to other Asian Pacific countries.

A key issue in the post–cold war period is whether the security arrangement with the United States has outlived its usefulness now that communist expansionism is no longer a threat. So far the Japanese government seems reluctant to abandon the special relationship with the United States, despite obvious strains arising from American pressure for Japan to open up its domestic markets to U.S. goods and to share more of the cost of U.S. bases. Not only is there external opposition to such a move, especially among Southeast Asians who see the United States as a restraint against potential revival of a Japanese bid for regional hegemony, but there are also internal constraints on such a departure from traditional security policy. Public opinion in the postwar period has consistently opposed remilitarization and nuclear armaments and supported the alliance with the United States. While the LDP was in power, the opposition Socialist and Communist Parties condemned the presence of American bases and the security treaty, but now that the Socialists are members of the coalition government that replaced the LDP in 1993, their opposition to the security treaty is muted. It seems likely that any major changes in national security policy will be delayed until the new governing coalition's prospects for survival are clearer.

A Bigger Political Role?   There are those inside Japan and outside as well who advocate that Japan accept a political role commensurate with its economic clout. Japanese proponents of the "internationalist" position have in the last decades had some success in overcoming the reluctance of the "neo-mercantilists" to enlarge foreign policy objectives beyond economic matters, but some aspire to a greatly expanded and more visible political and security role for Japan in regional and global relations. The question is, for what purpose? If national security is protected by the present strategies, why take on more? Winning international recognition, perhaps symbolized by a permanent seat on the Security Council, might be appealing to national pride, but would it make Japan any more secure or the lives of the Japanese any more comfortable or meaningful? Taking on more global responsibilities and seeking to be in the global spotlight may be less beneficial than working quietly outside the spotlight to accomplish objectives that serve more modest national goals.

The View from Beijing after the Cold War

The receding of the Soviet threat to China's security has not been an unmitigated blessing, from Beijing's perspective. The breakup of the Soviet Union and the overthrow of the Communist Party in Russia leaves the United States as the sole survivor of the pair of "hegemony-seeking" superpowers and without a world-class rival to counterbalance its ambitions for a "New World Order." The American vision of making the world safe for its version of capitalist democracy conflicts with the worldview of China's leaders, who conclude that self-protection requires convincing other Third World states to join in resisting U.S. ambitions.

Deprived of the prominence it once enjoyed as the pivotal "switch" member of the Moscow-Washington-Beijing triangle, China is now laying the foundation for a new Sino-Japanese-American triangle, with China's influence enhanced by the opportunity to mediate in a growing rift between Washington and Tokyo. Relations with Japan, already good, must be strengthened; the economies of the two countries are complementary and mutual interests in trade and investment powerful enough to weigh against the lingering hostility felt by Chinese as the result of Japanese conquest in the 1930s and 1940s. The chill in relations with the United States since 1989 must be endured, secure in the conviction that Washington will eventually come to realize that it can neither ignore China's key position in Asia, nor cow it into submission to demands for compliance with foreign notions of "human rights" and curbs on China's legitimate arms sales to other countries.

Peaceful Coexistence.   The larger vision of security, of which China's manipulation of the China-Japan-United States triangle is a part, involves elevating the country's status economically, politically, and militarily. Continued economic progress requires internal stability and a benign external environment. To that end, peaceful coexistence with all its neighbors, whatever the past ideological differences, is the theme of Chinese diplomacy. Restoration of normal relations with Indonesia (suspended since 1965) and Vietnam (interrupted in 1979) and the opening of relations with Singapore occurred in the past few years, with the result that PRC now has formal diplomatic relations with all of the Asian Pacific countries. Contacts have been extended beyond the region, with a flurry of visits by top officials to Africa, Latin America, and Europe. The two Koreas and ASEAN are targeted for particular emphasis, not only for economic reasons but also to build up China's political "capital" in dealings with Japan and the United States. Efforts to rebuild ties to Indochina led to PRC's disengagement from the Khmer Rouge and to support for the international peace effort in Cambodia. Even PRC's long-standing antagonism toward India has been mollified by high-level visits between the two countries and by India's recognition of China's possession of Tibet.

Territorial Disputes and Military Modernization.   Territorial issues set China against a number of its neighbors and may at least in part account for efforts to upgrade the technological sophistication of the military. Defense of its claims to the Spratly and Paracels Islands in the South China Sea is thought to be behind the acquisition of airplanes with greater range and for the buildup of "blue seas" naval forces. The dispute over the Paracels pits China against Vietnam, and the Spratlys are claimed by both of them and Taiwan, the Philippines, Malaysia, and Brunei. Offshore oil deposits are a stake in the controversy, and China and Vietnam occupy some of the islands. The PRC National People's Congress in 1992 passed legislation formalizing China's claim and authorizing the use of force to protect areas within the country's territorial waters. The Taiwan government followed suit with similar legislation, though omitting mention of the use of force. (The PRC and ROC positions and the legal arguments on which they base their claims are identical, said to be the outcome of a conference held in 1991 between staff members of government "think-tanks" from Taipei, Shanghai, and Beijing.) When the ASEAN foreign ministers meeting at Manila adopted a declaration calling for a peaceful solution of the territorial disputes, the Chinese foreign minister responded with the suggestion that the claimants consider joint exploitation of the island resources.

In addition to modernizing its conventional forces, China maintains its nuclear weapons and tested nuclear devices in 1992 and 1993. Although PRC's nuclear arsenal is small compared to that of the United States and Soviets (now in the possession of Russia and several other members of the Confederation of Independent States), still it does constitute the key to membership in the exclusive club of nuclear weapons states and a modest deterrent to first use by others. While expressing support for international nuclear arms control measures, the Chinese government has taken the position that the nuclear "giants" must first make substantial reductions in their arsenals.

Regaining Lost Territories and Prestige.   China's perennial goals of regaining territories and prestige lost during its "Century of Humiliation" are still on the agenda and account for Beijing's angry reaction to Hong Kong Governor Chris Patten's proposals for broadening the electorate and the number of elective positions in the colony's government. China charges that the proposed reforms violate the terms of the Sino-British Agreement and warns that it may exercise its right to take over before 1997, should the situation in the colony get out of hand. The return of Macau from Portuguese hands is a done deal, and the efforts to regain Taiwan were discussed earlier in this chapter.

National prestige is at stake in U.S. actions that China regards as meddling in its internal affairs. From the Chinese leaders' perspective, their handling of political dissidents in Tiananmen Square in 1989 and antigovernment Tibetan demonstrations was necessary to protect domestic order and, in any case, not the business of outsiders to criticize. During the Bush administration such criticisms came more often from private organizations and members of Congress than from the Department of State. The Clinton administration, however, took actions in its first year in office that struck China as infringing on its sovereignty. Renewal of China's most favored nation trading status with the United States in 1993 was made conditional on demonstration of progress in human rights, a condition that was effectively dropped in the renewal of most favored nation status in 1994. Also in 1993 the United States charged China with exporting missile components to Pakistan in violation of an international agreement neither country had yet ratified. A few months later it asked for inspection of a Chinese ship bound for Iran carrying, according to U.S. information, substances to be used for manufacturing chemical weapons; inspection turned up no evidence to support that contention. Beijing's sensitivity to actions that seem insulting to its sovereignty and political independence does not, from its viewpoint, constitute an obstacle to the goal of improving relations with the United States; it is, rather, one element in the grand strategy of achieving for China the eminent place in world politics that it feels it deserves.

The Quest for Security by Other Asian Pacific States

The ending of the cold war has affected superpower clients and even nonaligned states to varying degrees. Most adversely affected is *North Korea,* as discussed earlier in this chapter, and *Taiwan*—perhaps paradoxically—the least; its military security has been precarious since the U.S. protective shield was lifted. So, as a deterrent to possible attack from across the straits, Taipei beefs up its air force and surface fleet, spending a third more on defense in 1993 than the PRC, while pursuing the policy of increased unofficial economic, cultural, and family ties with the mainland and with other governments and international organizations.

South Korea and the Philippines.   Both countries continue to be under the protection of security treaties with the United States. Despite student demonstrations calling for the removal of American bases, the South Korean government remains militarily dependent on Washington as the deterrent of last resort to military action by North Korea. Implicit also is the possibility that South Korea might exercise the option of acquiring nuclear weapons to balance such weapons in the North. The success of former President Roh's "Northern policy" in establishing diplomatic and economic relations with China and Russia removes them as serious military threats, and Seoul's "bridge-building" efforts toward Pyongyang, combined with Japanese and American contacts with the DPRK, are aimed at moderating the potential threat from the North. Economic security remains heavily dependent on Japan, on the American market, and on the ability to adjust to competition from the NECs.

Unlike South Korea, the Philippines has taken a step away from its accustomed status as a U.S. client state and toward greater identification with its Asian neighbors. Whether the Philippine Senate's refusal to extend the lease on the U.S. bases at Clark Field and Subic Bay signals the end of neocolonial dependence is not yet clear. Almost a century of the American military presence is over and American aid is drying up, though the security treaty is still alive and the Manila government concurs with other ASEAN members that a precipitous American withdrawal would have a destabilizing effect on the region. Although the Philippines faces no external security threat, economic difficulties have international dimensions. Creating internal conditions that will inspire confidence among private investors and bilateral and multilateral aid donors is imperative; the push is for more investments from overseas Chinese. Diversification of external economic partners may be a way of reducing the Philippines' economic dependence on the United States and Japan.

Other ASEAN States.   Indonesia, Malaysia, Singapore, and Thailand have their own security concerns and ways of managing them. Although none of the countries in Southeast Asia faces imminent external dangers, Indonesia, Malaysia, and Thailand are expanding their navies from "brown-water" coastal protection to "blue-water" capability. Speculation about the motivation behind those moves suggests a number of possibilities: to have the capacity to enforce control over the 200-mile extended economic zones recognized under the Law of the Sea treaty, to back up Malaysia's Spratly claim, to tighten Jakarta's control over its outer islands, and in anticipation of the vacuum resulting from the downsizing of American naval forces in the Western Pacific.

Singapore, nonaligned but pro-United States since independence (like Malaysia and Indonesia since the 1965 coup), took up some of the slack left by the closing of U.S. bases in the Philippines by providing alternative air and naval facilities (scrupulously not called "bases" to comply with ASEAN's declared opposition to foreign bases in the region). The most vulnerable of the ASEAN states, Singapore is also the most ardent advocate for keeping the United States engaged in the region, whether as insurance against the threat of a revived Japanese militarism or outward pressure from the mainland's "awakened giant" China or as an outsider capable of keeping simmering intraregional conflicts from erupting into violent confrontation. The first of those reasons for a continued American presence was expressed obliquely by Senior Minister Lee Kuan Yew, who said in an interview, "We'd all be happier if the American security alliance remains, leaving Japan to concentrate on high-definition television."[30]

Other ASEAN governments also favor a continued American presence, although Malaysia's Mahathir has been an outspoken critic of the U.S. position on human rights and other issues. His proposal for an East Asia Economic Group, without U.S. participation, is a would-be competitor to APEC of which the United States, Australia, New Zealand, and Canada are members. He refused to attend the 1993 APEC summit hosted by the United States. Mahathir's anti-American and (until recently) anti-Chinese attitudes leave Japan as his favored candidate for a greater role in the region. The prime minister's antipathies are not shared by Indonesia's leader, President Suharto; a personal rivalry has developed between the two, reflecting Suharto's irritation with Mahathir's brash bid for leadership of ASEAN, a role Suharto feels should be his as the head of the most powerful member of the group. Indonesia aspires to serve as honest broker among the contestants for the Spratlys and to becoming a more significant naval power with the expected delivery of the former East German navy, bought at bargain prices from the united German government.

Thailand, long a close American ally, has shifted from "client" to a more equal relationship with the United States, playing its "China card" of closer ties to PRC, long regarded as the nemesis to the north. The Thai military purchases Chinese arms at prices so low as to constitute aid, and the two countries were allied in supporting the Khmer Rouge in Cambodia as an antidote to the Vietnam-Soviet alliance. Despite political upheavals in 1992, Bangkok has been busy exerting its influence on matters involving its neighbors. After years of mobilizing the other ASEAN members behind its stubborn opposition to Vietnam and the Vietnam-installed government in Cambodia, Thailand has moderated its stand to the point of promoting Thai trade and investment opportunities in Vietnam and the other Indochinese states and to bringing Vietnam and Laos into ASEAN. In the process of reconciliation between the political factions in Cambodia, the Thai government was officially supportive and tried to convince the Khmer Rouge to participate, but elements of the Thai military who had profited from the transit through Thai territory of Chinese military supplies to the insurgents are now partners in the export of timber and gems from KR-controlled territory through Thailand to the world market. That trade earns the KR money to purchase arms and violates the UN embargo against trade with the KR that Bangkok claims to respect.

Thailand's objective is to become the economic "core" of mainland Southeast Asia and to regain the political influence it once enjoyed in the region before the era of colonialism. Historically, Laos and Cambodia had been the objects of competition between Thailand and Vietnam, and that rivalry persists. At present, Thai influence is in ascendance, having the advantages over Vietnam in the cultural and language affinities with Cambodia and Laos, the magnet of Thai economic assets, and topography favorable to commerce with those neighbors. But an economically revitalized Vietnam will surely become a worthy competitor to Thailand for influence on the other two members of what was once French Indochina. To complete the roster of states toward which Thailand has turned its attention is Myanmar. The two countries share a history of armed conflict as well as a long land frontier permeable to drug traffickers and anti-Yangon insurgents in search of a haven from the Myanmar government's reach. On occasion the Thai government has allowed the Myanmar military to enter Thai territory in pursuit of the insurgents. Bangkok has also taken the initiative in ASEAN to draw the country out of its isolation into "constructive engagement" with the rest of Southeast Asia, resisting U.S. and EC pressures to apply economic sanctions against the SLORC government in protest of its human rights record.

ASEAN.   ASEAN members have gradually expanded the organization's agenda beyond its initial focus on economic cooperation to include regional political and security matters, and this trend has accelerated in the post–cold war period. Consultations occur in the context of the "post-ministerial" conferences held immediately following the annual meetings of ASEAN foreign ministers. Those discussions bring together representatives of the six ASEAN member states with their counterparts from the seven "dialogue partners"—Japan, South Korea, Australia, New Zealand, Canada, the United States, and EC. ASEAN thus serves an ad hoc role as the institutional core around which an informal structure of relationships has formed, linking Southeast Asia, other Asian countries, and outside states with interests in the larger pan-Pacific region. The network was expanded in 1993 at the ASEAN meeting in Singapore, to which China and Russia were invited as guests and Vietnam, Laos, and Papua New Guinea as observers. It was agreed there to set up the ASEAN Regional Forum through which the participating governments are to work on political and security cooperation. The form such cooperation might take is left open, but it seems clear that a NATO-like organization is light-years beyond the desires or capacities of the governments involved. The forum's first meeting took place in 1994 in Bangkok, with a representative of Myanmar present as a guest of Thailand. Of the Asian Pacific States, only Cambodia, Myanmar, North Korea, and Taiwan are not presently in the "loop" for political and security discussions, although Taiwan participates in the APEC gatherings.

Vietnam, Laos, Cambodia, and Myanmar.   The end of the cold war has brought major changes in the external relations of the three former Indochinese states. Deprived of Soviet economic and military support, which it enjoyed from the late 1970s to the 1980s, Vietnam of necessity shelved the ambition to protect its western flank by keeping or putting cooperative communist governments in power in Phnom Penh and Vientiane. Dropping the ideological bent of its previous foreign policy, Hanoi moved to break out of the diplomatic and economic isolation imposed as punishment for the Cambodian intervention by withdrawing its forces and agreeing to the Paris accords on ending the civil war. The thrust is now to reestablish normal relations with China, Japan, and the West as well as ASEAN and to build up its economic strength by inviting foreign investment, trade, and bilateral and multilateral economic aid.

International responses have been positive, particularly from Japan, the ASEAN states (Singapore and Japan are Vietnam's largest trade partners), Australia, and Western Europe. The exception is the United States, which continues to withhold diplomatic recognition, largely because of the influence of a vocal MIA/POW (missing in action/prisoner of war) lobby unconvinced that a satisfactory accounting of the fate of American service personnel has been made. The Vietnamese government maintains that it is cooperating fully with the American mission searching for remains in the countryside and for evidence in Hanoi's military archives; all but a few of the American MIAs have been accounted for, as contrasted with several hundred thousand Vietnamese MIAs from both North and South whose bodies have never been found. Finally, the millennia-old security problem of being one of the frontline states along China's southern border appears at present to be in a "low-threat" phase; normal relations with PRC were reestablished in 1991, but the islands in the South China Sea are objects of dispute between the two governments.

For Laos, a bit player in the unfolding drama of world politics, security is always at risk on a regional stage dominated by China to the north, Thailand to the south, and Vietnam to the east. Laos has little choice but to accommodate to the ebb and flow of external influences. Relations with the PRC have improved since the period when the two countries backed opposing sides in Cambodia, China supporting the Khmer Rouge and Laos siding with the Vietnamese-installed government. China sees Laos as a potential outlet for the transit of goods from interior southern China and itself as a balance to Thai influence, which has increased with the end of the cold war, and to Vietnamese influence, which has declined. Thai investments and trade have grown, and Bangkok dropped its aid to Lao insurgents operating along the Thai border. Granted observer status by ASEAN in 1992, the Vientiane government is moving closer to its noncommunist Southeast Asian neighbors, despite the fact that it, like Vietnam, is one of the few remaining communist governments in the world. Efforts to curb opium production in the "Golden Triangle" in the Lao-Thai-Myanmar border region have resulted in the signing of a treaty of cooperation with those governments.

The specifics of Cambodia's foreign policy under the new coalition government formed in 1993 are yet to be determined, but it seems safe to assume that its position, like Laos's, as a minor power sandwiched between the larger and more dynamic Thailand and Vietnam will continue to be a major influence on policy. Internal security is still precarious both because of Thai tacit collaboration with the Khmer Rouge and the gigantic problem of economic reconstruction. The antipathy toward Vietnam and Vietnamese residents in Cambodia is widespread among Cambodians and is likely to strain relations with Hanoi, as the Khmer Rouge link does to relations with Bangkok. One of the first acts of the new government was to charge both Thailand and Vietnam with illegally occupying Khmer territory. A return to the pre-1970 policy of nonalignment would seem to be the most likely foreign policy orientation, heavily influenced by the eclectic personal connections of the restored monarch Sihanouk and by the providers of external assistance for economic reconstruction.

Finally, we move to Myanmar, the last of the three Southeast Asian "frontline" states on the Chinese border. "When China spits, we swim" is a Burmese saying that expresses graphically, if somewhat inelegantly, the core issue of the country's security: the need to keep on amicable terms with China. That has been accomplished by pursuing a policy of strict nonalignment, combined after 1962 with a degree of self-imposed isolation from which it is now emerging. It rejoined the Non-Aligned Movement in 1992 and has responded to ASEAN overtures toward constructive engagement. China is its main ally and supplier of military equipment. Ties developed during World War II between Japan and the first generation of independence leaders, including Ne Win, are an asset in contemporary relations between Yangon and Tokyo. The Myanmar government ignores or rebuts U.S. and European criticisms of its human rights record and finds support among ASEAN countries in rebuffing Western pressure for an international arms embargo against the SLORC regime. Some small sign of movement in the government's attitude toward dissidents came in July 1994 when the chief of military intelligence announced his willingness to meet with Aung San Suu Kyi, opposition leader who has been under house arrest since 1989. Troubled relations with Bangladesh, its South Asian neighbor to the west, center on members of Myanmar's Moslem minority who have fled across the border to escape mistreatment. In general, however, Myanmar is moving gradually from isolation to closer contacts with other Asian Pacific countries.

With the end of the cold war the international environment seems much more benign for the Asian Pacific states. The diminution of external military threats, even to the still-divided states, holds out possibilities for cooperation in arms control and confidence-building measures aimed at constructing a common security system for the whole region. Relieved of the necessity to devote so much of available human and material resources to protecting national security by military means, countries may now be able to divert some of those resources to improving the quality of their citizens' lives and to reduce the substantial political influence of military officers. The disappearance of ideological correctness as the determinant of friend and foe opens up opportunities for forging relationships with new partners to their mutual gain. The changed context of international relations may stimulate the building of regional institutions, both private and intergovernmental, as stronger and more inclusive networks of economic, cultural, and environmental interdependence overcome the parochialism of national and subnational loyalties. The opportunities for all forms of creative cooperation are legion.

But it is also possible that the post–cold war period will be marked by an upsurge in conflict, both between and within countries, as the restraints imposed by alliance loyalties and fear of being sucked into the maelstrom of superpower battles are lifted and governments have more latitude for risk taking in foreign policy. Old enmities may revive and new ones develop over issues of "turf" in the literal sense of land and territorial waters and extended economic zones, over place in the pecking order, over markets and resources and a whole host of other scarce "goods," material and intangible. Centrifugal forces that had been kept in check by appeals for national unity in the face of external threat may erupt in an orgy of destruction as they have in Eastern Europe. Already we see inauspicious signs in the shape of naval arms races, the threat of nuclear proliferation, antiforeign resentment, vituperative exchanges on human rights, charges of protectionism and unfair trading practices, suspicions of hegemonic designs, foot-dragging on regional institution building. In short, the post–cold war period offers opportunities for more pervasive and more numerous conflicts in a whole range of relationships across and within national boundaries.

SUMMARY

Asian Pacific states' international political relations since the end of World War II have been intimately connected to the global political environment. During the past half-century the world political system has undergone dramatic transformations that have both influenced and been influenced by the states in this region.

The cold war, the global contest between the communist superpower and the anticommunist superpower, impinged on the ex-colonial states' struggle to consolidate their political independence and develop economically. For some, alliance with one or the other superpower brought substantial benefits, helping them to build their economies, although with some loss of autonomy in foreign policy choices. For others, the cold war drew them into disastrous internal or external conflicts, or both, draining the lifeblood of winners and losers alike, dividing three of the Asian nations into two rival states. Even those who tried to remain aloof from the superpower contest were inevitably touched by it.

But the bipolarity that characterized world politics in the early phase of the cold war began to erode, in part as the result of a new assertiveness by some ex-colonial states in Asia and elsewhere. China challenged Soviet leadership of the world communist movement, splitting it irrevocably, and the domination of world politics by the industrialized countries—both East and West—was challenged by a growing solidarity among "developing" states in Asia and other parts of what came to be known as the Third World. The Sino-Soviet rupture opened the way for accommodation across the ideological divide between China and the United States and set the two communist powers in competition for influence over other communist governments and movements. Recognition of common interests among them led to the creation of ASEAN by five noncommunist neighbors in Southeast Asia.

As the cold war hostility between the United States and the Soviets diminished, opportunities opened up for Asian Pacific governments to move toward the resolution of long-standing regional conflicts of cold war origin and to build political and economic bridges across the ideological divide. Koreans and Chinese began to talk about reunification, the American military involvement in Indochina finally ended, and Gorbachev took the initiative in proposing better relations with China, Japan, and other noncommunist states.

The breakup of the Soviet Union dealt the final blow to cold war rationale for Asian Pacific foreign policy alignments and preoccupations and brought new opportunities and problems. The opportunities are for increased international cooperation within the region. The problems include the revival of old enmities temporarily held in check by cold war obligations and the issue of what or who will fill the partial vacuum caused by declining American power in the region. China is a possible candidate, as is Japan, though that country is still committed to sheltering under the U.S. military umbrella, using economic levers as the major instrument of its foreign policy.

Whether the post–cold war period in the Asian Pacific will bring increased cooperation or increased conflict or (more likely) some untidy mix of both, it seems reasonable to anticipate continuation of the trend toward greater importance of economic factors in shaping international relations in the Asian Pacific. Most of the countries are now so embedded in the world economy that issues of trade, aid, and investment are central to their foreign policy behavior. Analysis of regional economic relations is the subject of the next chapter.

QUESTIONS FOR DISCUSSION

1. Why were Asian Pacific countries drawn into the cold war rivalry between the United States and the Soviet Union? Which countries benefited from that involvement? Which were adversely affected?

2. What instances do you see of the influence on the foreign policies of Asian Pacific governments of individual decision makers? of internal factors? of external factors?

3. China's relations with the USSR/Russia and the United States have undergone dramatic changes over the years since 1949. From the Chinese perspective, why did these changes occur? How have they served Chinese national interests?

4. The end of the cold war transformed the global political system. What effects—positive or negative—has that had on international relations in the Asian Pacific?

5. In your view, does the Japan-United States political and security partnership still serve each partner's purposes in the 1990s as it did in the 1950s?

NOTES

1. William A. Williams et al., eds., *America in Vietnam: A Documentary History* (New York: Doubleday, 1985), pp. 156-57, citing *Public Papers of the Presidents of the United States: Dwight D. Eisenhower, 1954* (Washington, D.C.: U.S. Government Printing Office, 1958), pp. 381-90.
2. Stanley Karnow, *Vietnam: A History* (New York: Penguin Books, 1984), p. 199.
3. Ibid., p. 534.
4. Williams, *America in Vietnam*, p. 309, citing *New York Times*, 1 May 1975, p. 16.
5. Marilyn B. Young, *The Vietnam War, 1945-1990* (New York: Harper Collins, 1991), p. 302.
6. Ibid., p. 280.
7. The text is in *Peking Review* 9 (31 March 1972): pp. 4-5.
8. *Peking Review* 51 (22 December 1978): p. 8.
9. "U.S.-China Joint Communique, August 17, 1982," *Current Policy* no. 413 (Washington, D.C.: U.S. Department of State, Bureau of Public Affairs, March 1982).
10. David Joel Steinberg, ed., *In Search of Southeast Asia: A Modern History*, rev. ed. (Honolulu: University of Hawaii, 1987), p. 445.
11. Thanat Khoman, "ASEAN in a Regional and Global Context," in *ASEAN in Regional and Global Context*, ed. Karl D. Jackson et al. (Berkeley: University of California Press, 1986), p. 10.
12. Sudershan Chawla et al., eds., *Southeast Asia Under the New Balance of Power* (New York: Praeger, 1974), p. 119.
13. Evelyn Colbert, "ASEAN as a Regional Organization: Economics, Politics, and Security," in Jackson, *ASEAN in Regional and Global Context*, p. 200.
14. James C. Hsiung, "Asia Pacific in the Post-Cold War Order," in *Asia Pacific in the New World Politics*, ed. J. C. Hsiung (Boulder: Lynne Rienner, 1993), pp. 3-4.

15. Ibid., p. 6.
16. Ibid., p. 9.
17. Tai Ming Cheung, "China's Buying Spree," *Far Eastern Economic Review,* 8 July 1993, p. 24.
18. Laura King, "Moscow-Tokyo Chill's Off," *Sacramento Bee,* 14 October 1993, p. A11.
19. Alex Pravda, ed., *Yearbook of Soviet Foreign Relations, 1991 Edition* (London I. B. Tauris & Co., Ltd., 1991), p. 172, and "Secrets of the Korean War," *U.S. News & World Report,* 9 August 1993, pp. 45-47.
20. Shim Jae Hoon, "Russian Roulette," *Far Eastern Economic Review,* 7 October 1993, p. 30.
21. Rhee Sang-Woo, "From National Unification to State Unification," in *North Korea in Transition,* ed. Chong-Sik Lee and Se-Hee Yoo (Berkeley: UC Institute of East Asian Studies, 1991), p. 136.
22. *To Build a National Community through the Korean Commonwealth: A Blueprint for Korean Unification.* National Unification Board, Republic of Korea, September 1989.
23. Maria Hsia Chang, "Relations Between Taiwan and Mainland China" (paper presented at the Western Political Science Association meeting, 20 March 1992), pp. 18-20.
24. Julian Baum, "Divided Nations," *Far Eastern Economic Review,* 16 September 1993, pp. 10-11.
25. "Divided China in the United Nations: Time for Parallel Representation," paid advertisement in *New York Times,* 20 September 1993, p. A13, National edition.
26. Ibid.
27. *Far Eastern Economic Review,* 16 September 1993, p. 11.
28. Hsiung, *Asia Pacific,* pp. 224-25.
29. William R. Nester, *Japan and the Third World* (New York: St. Martin's Press, 1992), p. 17.
30. Quoted in Charles P. Wallace, "Singapore Proves a Welcome Friend for the U.S. Military," *Los Angeles Times,* 3 January 1992, p. A4.

FOR FURTHER READING

Curtis, Gerald L., ed. *Japan's Foreign Policy After the Cold War.* Armonk, NY: M. E. Sharpe, 1993, parts 1, 3, 4, 5.

Fleming, D. F. *The Cold War and Its Origins.* Garden City: Doubleday and Co., Inc., 1961, vol. 2, part 3, chapters 20-23.

Hsiung, James C., ed. *Asia Pacific in the New World Politics.* Boulder: Lynne Rienner, 1993.

Lee, Chong-Sik, ed. *In Search of a New Order in East Asia.* Berkeley: University of California Institute of East Asian Studies, 1991, parts 1, 3, 4.

Wurfel, David, and Bruce Burton, eds. *The Political Economy of Foreign Policy in Southeast Asia.* London: The Macmillan Press Ltd., 1990.

Young, Marilyn B. *The Vietnam War, 1945-1990.* New York: HarperCollins, 1991.

chapter 8

Political Economy of the Asian Pacific Region

Asian Pacific countries have acquired a regional reputation for vigorous economic growth. Claims of an impending "Pacific Century" in which the Asian Pacific will provide regional dynamism for the entire global economy are buttressed by comparisons with other regions. In the decade between 1980 and 1990, the average annual growth rate of real gross domestic product (GDP) among Asian Pacific countries was 8.4 percent, compared with 3 percent for the industrial countries of North America and Western Europe, 2.9 percent for the Middle East and North African regions, and 1.6 percent for Latin America. It has been suggested that a peculiarly Asian Pacific model of successful development may be responsible for these achievements. Regardless of the validity of this claim, however, regional dynamism in the Asian Pacific has reinforced European regionalism and infused new life into NAFTA, prodding further regionalization of the entire Western Hemisphere. The temptation in the current global atmosphere is to see sustained high growth rates in the Asian Pacific as portending greater institutionalization of the region, both as a defense against potential protectionism on the part of the European Union and NAFTA and to foster a more integrated domestic market for consumption of its own exports.

The conditions for such regional coordination exist in the Asian Pacific. Intraregional trade, aid, and investment are extensive and increasing, the material and human resources to fuel production and furnish markets in the region are abundant, and regionally integrated manufacturing systems are already in operation and rapidly spreading. Furthermore, now that the barriers separating communist from noncommunist nations are receding, new markets are opening for trade and investments in China and Vietnam with Cambodia, Myanmar, and perhaps even North Korea on the horizon. Thus the incentives for Asian Pacific trading partners to increase their economic cooperation are likely to multiply as we move into the twenty-first century.

But it is premature to consider the countries of the Asian Pacific a region in any but the most general sense of geographical proximity. The political and economic obstacles in the way of regional coordination remain overwhelming: the geopolitical disparities among nations in the area, the immense cultural diversity that separates the subregions of East and Southeast Asia as well as the ethnic divisiveness that crosscuts national boundaries in much of Southeast Asia, the historical legacy of mistrust people harbor of their traditional enemies, the economic competition among nations competing for the same markets, and the political fractiousness of new nations maneuvering internal conflicts in an uncertain international order. And these impediments to cooperation pale by contrast to the mistrust all Asian nations share toward the one power that has already contributed substantially toward regionalization in the Asian Pacific, Japan.

In this chapter we focus on the political and economic linkages currently existing among nations of the Asian Pacific. What patterns of economic interpenetration have emerged in relations among countries of the region? How do the economic bonds forged in the process of development intersect with the political interests that define their nations' objectives as sovereign entities? What are the politics of a complex system of economic interdependence that functions both regionally and globally, and how does it impact decision making at the national level? Exploring the answers to these questions involves a shift in our angle of vision: In place of comparing the domestic political economies of Asian Pacific countries from within, as we did in Chapter 5, we now view their political and economic interrelationships from outside and above, evaluating the bilateral and multilateral networks that both connect and divide countries of the region amongst themselves and within the larger global nexus.

We begin by analyzing the relevance of our theoretical models for understanding regionalism as an intermediate layer between the nationalism of the interstate system and the internationalism of the global economy. Then the economic linkages among countries in the Asian Pacific region are traced: the reemergence of regional ties and patterns of trade, investment, and aid both within the region and also between it and extraregional partners in the international market. In the last two sections we discuss the politics of economic interdependence, describing the various multilateral arrangements or regional associations that have been formed to further economic cooperation and speculate on the degree of regionalization likely to occur as a result of the patterns of economic growth in the Asian Pacific.

INTERNATIONAL POLITICS AND THE GLOBAL ECONOMY IN THEORETICAL PERSPECTIVE

International relations are composed of two disparate elements: the configuration of nation-states' interrelationships—the interstate system—and the economic interdependencies of a global production system—the global economy. In their close interaction, which generates both conflict and cooperation, these two components constitute what has come to be known as the international political economy (IPE).

The International Political Economy

The global relationships among a variety of public and private "actors" is the focus of IPE, which addresses the fundamental reality of our times: that the economic and political decisions that affect our livelihoods as producers, consumers, and citizens transcend the boundaries of nation-states. Whether and how one is employed, the nature of our social and educational opportunities, the human "rights" available to us are no longer bounded by the jurisdiction of whatever nation-state defines our citizenship. Human choices and institutional policies are global in their reach, linking all of us economically and politically to one another's destiny.

Not only the scope of international political economy but the large number of diverse actors involved on this global stage are bewildering. National governments (states) are principal actors; in the Asian Pacific setting they include not only the Asian states but the G-7 (the United States, Germany, France, Britain, Italy, Canada, Japan), Russia, and Australia as makers of economic policies and as donors and recipients of aid. Intergovernmental organizations (IGOs) are another important set of actors; these include global financial institutions like the World Bank and the International Monetary Fund and regional organizations such as the Asian Development Bank and ASEAN. Finally there are transnational entities such as multinational corporations (MNCs), international private banks, nongovernmental organizations, overseas Chinese, and a variety of powerful illicit organizations like drug and arms traffickers or immigrant smugglers.

At the global level, the actors that most concern us in understanding the international political economy of the Asian Pacific are multinational corporations and nation-states as they cooperate and contend with each other. Multinational corporations, indifferent to national boundaries, expand operations and shift locations with extraordinary ease, wielding economic power no longer subject to the sovereignty of a single, even the most powerful, state. Using a technology that "renders industrial location and the direction of production less dependent on geographical distance," these multinational corporations become architects of a global economy that inevitably diminishes the capacities of nation-states to function in their traditional role as sovereign bodies. As global entrepreneurs, multinational corporations rely on an organization of labor that decomposes complex production processes into tasks simple enough for an unskilled labor force to learn, giving them access to a worldwide reservoir of labor from which to choose.[1] By contrast, nation-states are deprived of their economic base, left with communities abandoned by industries and citizens powerless to defend their livelihood.

Besieged by a combination of internal and external problems created by the blurring of national boundaries, and the uncertainty of "hegemonic stability" in a world without superpowers, nation-states have sought strength in numbers by increasing interactions with their nearby neighbors. These are the regional associations we know by their acronyms: the European Community (EC), renamed the European Union (EU) in 1994, the Association of Southeast Asian Nations (ASEAN), and the North American Free Trade Association (NAFTA). But regionalization today is an even more pervasive and often less institutionalized phenomenon than these regional organizations suggest. It grows out of the search for some form of mutual security on the part of states that experience increased demands from their citizens for a clean, safe, stable, and prosperous environment in an increasingly chaotic international situation.

The Thai peasant watching his Sony TV after driving home in a Toyota truck and the American suburbanite with a Japanese car, a Taiwanese computer, and a Malaysian-made VCR may be aware of the economic interdependence of prosperity in today's world. What is more obscure to them both is how this international production of prosperity comes into conflict with their national identity and the national community on which they depend for their livelihood. Because material prosperity is increasingly manufactured in component parts produced and assembled in disparate places around the globe, we are all dependent on international trade. But with the lifeline of national economies more than ever dependent on an international economy, there is no clear agreed upon understanding of how transnational economic actors, sovereign nation-states, and competing regional blocs or arrangements fit together as a world political order. Each of our three theories understands this relationship from a different vantage point, though in surveying the following summary remember that our description of each of these approaches necessarily oversimplifies the variety of diverse interpretations that exist within each theoretical perspective.

Modernization Theory

Modernization theory ascribes the success of Asian Pacific economic growth to the adoption of rational market-oriented policies. The state's role is to enact domestic policies encouraging its entrepreneurs to produce for the market. For late-developing countries this means orienting domestic economic production toward the international market. This ensures that each country will specialize in furnishing for export that which it produces best at the lowest possible price, which is called its *comparative advantage*. An international division of labor arises naturally from the principles of the market. When states engage in free trade on the basis of their comparative advantage, each expands its own national wealth through exchange in the international market. The success of newly industrializing economies (NIEs) in the Asian Pacific attests to the validity of these principles: By producing for export commodities of relatively high quality and low price, the NIEs discovered the secret of economic growth in the policy of subjecting their governments to the discipline of the international market, an idea captured in the phrase "getting the prices right."

If the market occupies the central position in an "open trade system," the state nonetheless has a definite if limited international role to play. States must agree to establish the rules and regulations—referred to as *international regimes*—that govern currency exchanges and other economic arrangements between sovereign national entities to ensure that no country or domestic group is hurt by "unfair" international competition. In the real world, of course, nation-states pursue a broad array of political and military as well as economic objectives in the international arena. How, then, are mechanisms of the international market safeguarded from the political interference of powerful states? Modernization theorists assume that each state maximizes its overall utility by calculating the cost-benefit ratios of a wide range of possible options, choosing the course that yields the highest reward or the least objectionable sacrifice. Trade-offs may be necessary and states can and do resort to forms of protectionism to defend or improve their domestic circumstances in certain situations. The essential element from the (neo)classical liberal perspective of modernization theory is that such instances of state intervention in the economic market remain exceptions or temporary departures.

But international trade in the modern age is complicated by the fact that not only goods and services but capital and know-how move freely across national borders. From a modernization perspective the movement of capital and technology—foreign direct investment (FDI)—carries out an essential task: It transmits capital and ideas, spreading economic growth throughout the world. FDI enables economic actors in advanced nations to earn a return on their capital by promoting the economic growth and development of more "backward" areas of the world. Foreign capital brings modern technology, jobs, management skills, and marketing expertise to far corners of the globe, opening developing economies to the opportunities of the world market. As multinational corporations, to whom this missionary task falls, increasingly organize investment, production, and marketing on a global scale irrespective of the needs of isolated national economies, their indifference to national boundaries raises the question of what happens to the sovereignty of states. Because this issue frames the debates among advocates of the contending theories, it will be further discussed below.

World System Theory

To understand the international economy from the world system perspective is to view it as the cause rather than the consequence of nation-states trading with one another on the basis of comparative advantages. From this perspective, modern industrial capitalism, though organized *politically* in the form of sovereign nation-states, is *economically* an international division of labor that is continually expanding and changing its scope and pattern. Thus the world economy is "not . . . a simple addition of its national units, but . . . a powerful independent reality created by the international division of labor and by the world market which dominates all the national markets."[2] The individual nation-states, which are as much the creations as the architects of the international economy, do not interact as equals. Wealthy and powerful states at the core of the international economic system act like magnets, attracting the resources and reaping the profits from incorporating backward areas into the world economy, while peripheral states, instead of benefiting from the diffusion of capital and technology from the core, suffer an increasingly debilitating dependence on their benefactors.

But world system theorists view the international economy as historically evolving. The states comprising the core of the global system after the sixteenth century were Great Britain, joined in the mid-nineteenth century by France, with the United States, Germany, Italy, and Japan moving up from underdeveloped peripheral countries to the middle rank of semi-periphery. By World War II, Germany and Japan were contending with the United States and the Soviet Union for preeminence at the core of a vastly expanded world economy in which the states throughout the rest of Europe and Latin America as well as the colonies of Africa and Asia constituted the semi-periphery and periphery, respectively. This means that at any point in time, although core countries tend to get richer while those on the periphery get poorer, over the long haul major shifts do occur in which core countries descend from their pinnacle of power while countries at the semi-periphery ascend to replace them. In their historical depiction of this drama, world system theorists, though delineating the development of states as a consequence of an expanding international economy, rely on the empirical evolution of history for their analysis.

In general, however, world system theory, in contrast to modernization theory, views the terms of trade as fundamentally unequal, with wealth from the periphery flowing in the direction of the core as the world economic system expands. When capital, technology, and skills in the form of FDI by multinational corporations move from core to periphery, it is in search of cheap labor and easily accessible resources to produce goods for markets in the core. And without the capacity to reproduce or appropriate advanced technology for their own use, national economies in the periphery will generate neither an entrepreneurial class nor a self-sustaining economy to employ all their people. Multinational corporations, on the other hand, benefit from immense and movable assets, rapid changes in technology, worldwide communications and information sources, and ready access to resources, transportation, and competitive labor markets, enabling them to play countries off against one another.

Despite this rather bleak picture that world system theory paints of the marginalization of developing countries in the periphery, it recognizes the historical possibility that some states can move up the international hierarchy. The question this theoretical approach raises, then, is: What are the characteristics that enable some states to effect their own upward mobility in the world system? A similar question might be asked from the more sanguine outlook of modernization theory: Since international cooperation and trade at the international level enable countries to increase their wealth, why are these advantages so vastly underutilized? The developmental state approach, to which we now turn, offers an answer to these questions.

Developmental State Approach

In this view of the industrialization process, it is the systematic leadership of the state that explains how and why developing countries manage the difficult task of sustaining effective economic growth. The premise is deceptively simple: National policies that constructively promote industrialization do not follow automatically from either the international pressures of the advanced industrialized economies or the particular endowments of a particular country. In the absence of a self-confident entrepreneurial class, a state can be instrumental in generating production that is competitive on the international market. It does this by effectively intervening in domestic economic affairs, mobilizing and distributing resources from abroad as well as locally to plan sectoral development in response to evolving international circumstances. To accomplish this end, a state must be capable of directing preferential investments; subsidizing unprofitable industrial ventures; providing infrastructure, technological leadership, tax and production privileges, and marketing assistance; promoting economies of scale in production; and withstanding the domestic political opposition to unpopular policies.[3]

If the developmental state plays the active, critical role in shaping the domestic political economy, it is also a principal player on the international scene. It must protect its national economic interests against the detrimental actions of outsiders while maximizing technological and economic integration into the international system. The underlying logic of this argument is similar to the Realist school of international political economy, which, as Frieden and Lake point out, makes three assumptions:

1. that nation-states are the highest authorities, dominant actors, and the sole judge of their own behavior *in the international economy;*
2. that each nation-state must always be prepared to defend itself by force, if necessary, because no other country or higher authority is obligated to come to its defense; and
3. that nation-states are rational actors in a zero-sum game, each choosing the course that yields the greatest value, in this case, the one that maximizes power.[4]

A developmental state demonstrates its strength in the international arena by controlling and managing foreign capital to enable its domestic economy's technological integration into the international market. Though proponents of the statist perspective share with modernization theorists the view that foreign capital inputs are essential to rapid industrial expansion, they nonetheless display the world system theorists' suspicion that foreign capital is apt to disproportionately benefit investors in the more advanced industrial economies unless the state is capable of breaking down the various components of the production bundle.[5] The "strength" of a developmental state, therefore, consists of having the resources, expertise, and authority to "decouple" foreign capital from its control and management by foreign investors. It must be able to selectively integrate those elements of production–capital and technology, for example—that fit the needs of domestic economic expansion in particular sectors by resisting demands that foreign investment directly control the entire production process from managerial operations and labor through marketing and the repatriation of profits. By restricting foreign direct investment to a particular sector, arranging for technology transfer through licensing or joint ventures, the developmental state protects future market shares and expansion for its domestic industries. But for it to implement such policies that employ foreign direct investment while reserving the domestic market for its own producers, the government must exercise extensive control over market forces within its territory.[6]

"Decoupling" by the developmental state is essential because it facilitates domestic capital accumulation, enabling one's own industries to move up the international product cycle whenever international circumstances present the opportunity. For developing countries to break out of their relative backwardness, according to the developmental state approach, sustained rapid growth is imperative. Only a strong state with centralized access to information, capital, and expertise can direct when and how to expand a nation's comparative advantage, helping to move its industries into new sectors and to acquire the latest technology. The government of a strong state can pursue commercial expansion abroad while providing protectionism at home. It is able to recruit foreign capital/technology with the promise of providing and regulating domestic inputs, a quiescent labor force for example, while protecting and enhancing the competitive advantages of its domestic industries abroad. Thus the officials of a state can lead rather than follow, so long as they can exercise maximum control over both external and internal exigencies.

Applying the Theories to Regional Economic Growth

The actual strategies of Asian Pacific countries fall somewhere between these three theoretical models, mixing and matching on the basis of contingent factors, their own resources, and the degree and type of political integration obtained in each country. Despite their generally authoritarian adaptation to market systems, the differences among them are considerable, as detailed in Chapters 4 and 5. Most countries' policies acknowledge the market as instrumental for rapid economic growth, but none is willing to entrust its economic fortunes entirely to unfettered market forces. Each also empowers the state with significant control over economic affairs to discharge political objectives, albeit in different ways from one another. Yet in none of these countries, including Japan, does the state exercise the kind of independent political force claimed to be essential to the developmental state model.

The world system theory has an equally ambiguous applicability to Asian Pacific experiences. Its profound misgivings that an underdeveloped country can develop within the fold of international capitalism in any but the most crippled form of dependency is unsubstantiated in the outstanding economic performances of the principal players among Asian Pacific countries. Yet might it not be argued that Asian Pacific countries have succeeded precisely to the degree to which they heeded the theory's counsel against the debilitating effects of international capitalism? The impact of the global economy under colonial rule was, after all, the foundation of strong, centralized states throughout the Asian Pacific. Nationalistic sentiment, with the exception of Japan and Thailand, was nurtured on opposition to international capitalism, providing the vocabulary for newly independent nation-states as they pursued modernization in the postwar world. And where it has occurred, their rapid economic growth over the last thirty years is heavily indebted to the political economy of the cold war and Japan's resurrection as a regional core of the expanding global economy. For purposes of exploring the political economy of the Asian Pacific region, therefore, world system theory furnishes the most pertinent perspective for understanding because it underscores the mutual dependence of nations as part of the global economy.

U.S. HEGEMONY AND A REGIONAL
GROWTH ECONOMY

Successful economic growth in the Asian Pacific has been distinguished by an export-oriented strategy pursued by strong nationalistic states and private firms operating in a capitalist market. Even the socialist countries—China and Vietnam, though not yet

North Korea—have opened their economies to international trade and investment, adapting capitalist institutions into a hybrid form of socialist market. How do these countries, all of whom depend heavily on the United States to absorb their exports and on Japan to upgrade their technology and provide capital, relate to one another economically and politically within the larger global context? What underlying patterns have evolved out of their pursuit of prosperity within a postwar global context of expanding opportunities? These questions can only be answered against the backdrop of Japan's ascent to regional power status prior to World War II and the United States' rise to hegemonic status in the postwar world.

Nationalism, regionalism, and the global economy appeared as a triumvirate on the Asian Pacific scene. Nationalism, as described in Chapter 2, was inspired by European political domination and economic exploitation of the region in the nineteenth century. And regionalism was the result of Japan's economic and political participation in the Western-sponsored dismemberment of China. In 1895 Japan acquired access to Korea and Taiwan. Subsequently, as Japan spread its control over northern China, these three territories were integrated into a highly centralized, regional economic empire, the East Asian Co-Prosperity Sphere. As protégé and beneficiary of Western imperialism, Japan enlarged its empire through regional conquest and military occupation so that prior to the end of World War II it encompassed the length and breadth of the Asian Pacific. Thus even before nationalist movements in the rest of the Asian Pacific succeeded in achieving independence from Western political domination, an endeavor in which they were often aided by the Japanese, the peoples of the Asian Pacific had imposed on them a substantial degree of regional integration with Japan at its core.

Japanese-centered regionalism was defeated at the end of World War II by the United States, the new economic center of world power. But with the Asian Pacific and Western Europe in ruins, the wealthy colossus and only creditor nation in the world had first to nurture not only its allies but also its vanquished enemies back to economic health to secure trading partners for itself. Toward this end, the United States organized and funded a new set of global institutions to establish a universal system of liberalized trade throughout the "free world." The International Monetary Fund (IMF), the World Bank (WB), and the General Agreement on Tariffs and Trade (GATT) were designed to promote strong capitalist economies with politically stable pro-American regimes, especially in the frontline states bordering the "communist world."

In conjunction with massive U.S. economic and military assistance, the global economy under the Bretton Woods system of fixed international exchange rates entered a period of robust growth and expansion. The results were immediately visible *in the developed countries* where annual economic growth (real GDP) grew at an average of 5 percent in the period between 1950 and 1970. This was "two and a half times the growth rate in the four preceding decades and twice as rapid as would occur later in the 1970s."[7] Thus, the initial beneficiaries of this new international political regime were the developed countries.

Continuation of the prosperity of the developed world, however, depended upon political stability and the extension of economic development to the rest of the free world. Germany was rehabilitated as the core of an anticommunist Western Europe, and Japan was politically and economically reconstructed as the United States' principal partner in the Asian Pacific. When the Communists came to power in China, the United States dramatically expanded its economic and military assistance to South Korea and Taiwan as well as propping up the interests of the British outposts of Hong Kong and Singapore—together forming the "four tigers."

In Southeast Asia, the United States assumed responsibility for the political stability of countries along the entire perimeter of Communist China, helping to negotiate the independence of colonies from European control, intervening in support of conservative pro-American elites when necessary to "contain communism," and waging war if those elites seemed in danger of collapse. But if the United States shouldered the political leadership and military protection of the noncommunist Asian Pacific, it delegated economic responsibility for its growth and development to Japan. Thus Japan emerged as a strategic economic partner of the United States in Pacific Asia, once again acting as the core of an East Asian regional configuration, this time only economically, with military security provided by the United States.

The U.S.-Japanese Partnership

The irony of postwar reconstruction of a global economy tied to the wealth and productivity of the United States was its ultimate enfeeblement of the giant on which the world depended. To protect its world order ("hegemonic stability") from the perceived threat of communism, the United States engaged in two costly wars in Korea and Vietnam, financed the military security of the entire "free world," and helped rebuild and construct the powerful economies that were to become its competitors.

Even the rules of the United States promoted to facilitate international trade in the postwar world, known as an *open trade regime,* proved to be a mixed blessing for the United States. Although designed to prevent national barriers from raising the costs of selling merchandise throughout the "free world," these rules, if they were to fulfill the multiple objectives of the United States, had to accommodate protectionist policies on the part of its allies while keeping the U.S. market wide open to their exports. Import substitution, after all, was essential for Japan, Taiwan, and South Korea to build the industrial strength necessary to be politically stable partners in the cold war. From the beginning, therefore, American policymakers used a double standard to measure "open trade," a policy referred to as *diffuse reciprocity.*[8] By relying on formal procedures rather than actual outcomes, the United States was able to overlook infractions of free trade rules when it suited the strategic purposes of maintaining "hegemonic stability."[9]

In the Asian Pacific, this meant a convergence of interests between postwar Japan and the United States: reviving the Japanese economy as a regional superpower dependent upon Southeast Asia for its source of raw materials. Toward this end "Washington promoted a triangular economic division of trade between the United States, Japan and Southeast Asia in which America would provide high technology and capital goods, Japan intermediate and consumer goods and Southeast Asia raw materials and energy."[10] This policy was articulated by the Joint Chiefs of Staff in a July 1952 report and implemented in the American practice of linking American aid to the region to the purchase of Japanese goods and services.

The Japanese took advantage of the opportunity provided in the San Francisco Peace Treaty, which required them to pay war reparations to countries devastated in the 1930s and 1940s but left the amount and type to be determined by Tokyo. Between 1955 and 1965, Japan negotiated separate agreements with ten East and Southeast Asian countries, transferring about $1.5 billion in reparations and economic/technical assistance to Burma, Indonesia, the Philippines, South Vietnam, Cambodia, Laos, Malaysia, South Korea, Singapore, and Thailand. "By tying all this aid to purchases of Japanese goods and services, Tokyo opened up vast export markets as each country became dependent on Japanese corporations for spare parts, related products and technical assistance."[11]

From the world system perspective, this partnership between the United States and Japan, which provided the foundation of United States cold war policy in the Asian Pacific, set into motion a subregional division of labor among the countries inhabiting this most recently incorporated part of the global economy. If the United States needed Japan to carry out its postwar mission in the Asian hemisphere, Japan needed Southeast Asia as a source of raw materials to replace its earlier colonial territories in China, Korea, and Taiwan. Accordingly, Japan's reindustrialization acted as a subregional core tied to the availability of raw materials and markets in a subregional periphery, namely the countries of Indonesia, Malaysia, and Brunei. In between these two positions of "flying geese," an intermediate subregional semi-periphery emerged made up of the four tigers, also considered essential to the postwar hegemonic stability of the United States: South Korea, Taiwan, Singapore, and Hong Kong. Thus the regionalization of the Asian Pacific can be viewed, through the lens of world system perspective, as a consequence of the reconstruction of the global economy after World War II.

As long as the United States remained preoccupied with the war in Vietnam, the American economy was assumed to be so far ahead of the rest of the world that Japan's resurgence as an industrial giant attracted little attention. Fundamental cooperation between the victor and the vanquished of World War II was dictated by the defense of the "free world" in the cold war against communism. In the global arena, Japan accepted its junior partnership with the United States while regionally exercising its own hegemonic power as senior partner to the Southeast and East Asian allies of the United States. But the United States found its economy perceptibly weakening under the twin burdens of a costly, not-so-cold war and an insatiable demand by U.S. consumers for goods manufactured in Japan. Alarmed by the relentless expansion of Japan's share of the American market, the United States began reversing its lax policy of tolerating the asymmetry in its trade relationship with Japan. During the 1970s the United States won Japanese agreement to a series of compromises—trigger price mechanisms (TPMs) and voluntary export restraints (VERs)—curtailing the high volume of color televisions, steel, and automobiles it exported to the United States.

In retrospect the major disruptions in the world economy of the 1970s and the political reconfiguration of international relations they triggered set the stage for a new international political economy. Breakdown of the Bretton Woods system of fixed international exchange rates came in the early part of the decade, when the United States went off the gold standard. Two oil crises—in 1973 and 1979—sent shockwaves of recession and inflation rippling through developed and underdeveloped countries alike. And in 1975 and 1979, respectively, the U.S. withdrawal from Vietnam and normalization of relations with the People's Republic of China resulted in similar political aftershocks for governments around the world. After Mao Zedong's death in 1976, China reversed its course, embarking on an economic reform program that by the mid-1980s brought it into the East Asian community of newly industrializing nations, whose primary market for manufactured goods was the United States. Japan by the early 1970s had surpassed the United States as the predominant trade power in East Asia and was accumulating a large trade surplus with the United States. And the U.S. trade deficit was beginning to threaten global financial stability. In this international context, the relationship of Japan and the United States entered a new, more confrontational phase.

By the 1980s, the United States was absorbing an estimated 71 percent of the manufactured exports of the Asian Pacific, with the contribution of the NICs having risen substantially alongside the exports from Japan. The new tensions raised by the Japanese trade surplus with the United States were addressed by the Plaza Agreement reached in February 1985, when the five key-currency countries then known as the Group of Five, made up of the United States, Great Britain, France, West Germany, and Japan, agreed to a policy of bringing the value of the dollar down in relation to the yen. This agreement to manage a depreciation in the American currency that would appreciate the Japanese currency was directed at reversing the enormous growth of Asian Pacific exports that had yielded Japan huge trade surpluses with the United States in the early 1980s. The expectation was that a stronger yen would make Japanese goods in the United States less attractive to consumers while increasing sales of American goods in Japan.

The results were mixed: The U.S. global deficit did decline as the Japanese yen appreciated from 230 to 120 to the dollar, but the Japanese trade surplus with the United States nonetheless remained high ($38 billion) while the NICs benefited by increasing their exports to the United States. Even though the costs of their imports from Japan rose, increasing the NICs' trade deficits with Japan, the NICs accumulated growing surpluses with the United States, edging in on the Japanese market share. Thus, the NICs, as part of a triangular trade relationship, contribute to the increase in both the U.S. deficit and the Japanese surplus, simultaneously strengthening the regional hegemony of Japan and weakening the global hegemony of the United States. In seeking redress for its persistent overall trade deficits with the Asian Pacific, the United States has turned its attention to the value of other Asian currencies and the use of "specific outcomes" to open markets in Asian Pacific countries for American goods.

In the early 1990s, the United States and the European Community still found themselves with recessionary problems of high unemployment and underutilized productive capacity. Japan, with over 40 percent of its investments in the United States, was also in a recession, with substantial losses on its investments, the collapse of real estate and stock markets, and dramatic political turmoil attending the fall from power of Japan's long-standing ruling party. But while the United States grappled with overwhelming trade deficits, Japan contended with enormous trade surpluses. Ambitious public spending programs were launched to counteract the decline in investment spending. If Japan's past performance is any guide, there is a reasonable likelihood that Japan will bounce back from this period of economic retrenchment with a restructured productive capacity geared to exploiting new opportunities and avoiding known hazards in the global economy. Given the persistent deficit problem in the United States and the protectionist sentiments it generates, to what extent can Japan further expand the regional opportunities for economic growth in the Asian Pacific? To address this question, we now turn to a consideration of Japan's trade, aid, and investment patterns as the dominant economic power in the Asian Pacific region.

THE JAPAN-CENTERED STRUCTURE OF REGIONAL TRADE

Japan is fast becoming the major trading partner for all Asian Pacific economies. In 1991, without exception, Japan exported more to each of those economies than did the United States. As recently as 1982 U.S. exports to South Korea and the Philippines were more than Japan's, and to Taiwan they were about the same level. By contrast, in 1991 Japan exported about $5 billion more than the United States to South Korea and $5.6 billion more to Taiwan. Even to the Philippines, which was for so long a traditional U.S. market, the United States now sells less than Japan, $2.27 billion versus $2.66 billion.[12] Although the United States continues to be the largest importer of goods from these countries, with the exception of Indonesia, Japan seems to be closing the gap in the case of Taiwan, South Korea, and Thailand. Only in Singapore has the United States continued to do very well, but even there Japan's 1989–1991 increase was 16 percent, compared to 11 percent for the United States. In the aftermath of Japan's adjustment to the yen appreciation by transferring production to "offshore" locations, the exports of Asian Pacific economies have increased and an increasing share of these exports is going to Japan.

This greater intraregional trade exhibited since 1985 seems to support the Japanese belief in the "flying-geese pattern" of economic growth in the Asian Pacific.[13] The striking aspect of this image applied to Asian Pacific countries is the diversity of "geese" that make up the flock. By their sheer size, capitalist Japan and more recently socialist China—more of a fellow traveler than a member of the flock—cast long shadows over both the more industrialized NICs and the more resource-rich Southeast Asian nations. In everything from size and population to politics and culture, the diversity of countries in the region militates against the kind of economic integration that has occurred in the EC (now the EU). Yet a regional economic pattern has emerged from the flow of merchandise, capital, and aid that links the developmental states of the Asian Pacific with one another and with the global economy. At the center of this regional economic formation is Japan, which acts as model, facilitator, and engine for growth in the region. Though its own growth rate today is lower than all the economies of East and Southeast Asia except Myanmar and the Philippines, Japan dominates the region by the staggering size of its productive output and per capita income. Its position as leader of "the flying geese" suggests two things: It sets the direction in which the flock moves and provides a structure for its economic interrelationships.

In the postwar world, Japan established its regional dominance by a capacity for rapid restructuring of its export-led production to keep one step ahead of technological advances on the global market and of protectionist devices against Japan exports.

While producing toys, electrical appliances, and textiles in the 1950s and 1960s, Japan acquired the technology—through licensing, joint ventures, and "reverse engineering" rather than direct foreign investment—for producing ships, steel, heavy machinery, and automobiles to export in the 1960s and 1970s. When oil crises and protectionist pressures threatened the security of Japan's resources and markets in the 1970s, Japan was quick to alter the structure of its industrial production again, upgrading its technology to produce high-tech electronics like videocassettes and scientific equipment and adopting stringent conservation measures along with diversifying its sourcing for raw materials. Since 1980 Japan has upgraded its technology, shifting its comparative advantage once again, to knowledge-based or information and communication industries.

These shifts in comparative advantage by which Japan propelled itself into the forefront of industrialization are reflected in the composition of Japanese trade. According to data from the Keizai Koho Centre, exports of textiles, ships, and steel products dropped from 29 percent of Japan's total exports in 1977 to 10 percent in 1988, while automobiles increased throughout the 1980s, reaching 20 percent of Japan's total export value in 1986. The leap in Japan's technological sophistication as an industrial producer during this period is evidenced in the declining *share* of total imports, represented by foodstuffs, which remained constant in absolute terms as compared to manufactured goods, whose share of total imports increased from 24 percent in 1983 to 49 percent in 1987.[14]

As Japan restructured its own economy, it exported the capital, machinery, and know-how perfected in the previous phase to its developing neighbors, "the four tigers" or NICs, who could then promote a similar line of exports while avoiding the import restraints targeted at Japan. Most often, this involved Japanese companies moving their investments and production facilities "offshore" to locations in the NICs that offered lower wages and fewer deterrents to exports destined for the United States or the European Community. Offshore production in these so-called "sunset" industries, therefore, continued to profit the Japanese economy as well as boosting regional growth rates by increasing its neighbors' dependence on Japan for spare parts and components. In its move up the industrialization ladder, therefore, Japan not only elevated the economies of its neighbors but tied them more closely to its own. Though Japanese contend that in this way other countries of the Asian Pacific will be able to "catch up" to Japan, the V-shape of the "flying geese" formation suggests no such closing of the ranks, a deduction many of Japan's Asian Pacific neighbors draw from experience. Equally clear, however, is the imprint the Japanese structure of economic growth and trade have had on the phenomenal development of the entire region.

Trade Patterns of the NICs

If domestic adaptation of the Japanese economy had the outcome of regionalizing economic growth during the 1960s and 1970s, the yen appreciation following the Plaza Accord in the mid-1980s had a similar if unintended effect. Designed to lower the Japanese trade surplus with the United States by making Japanese exports to the United States more expensive, its impact in the Asian Pacific was to accelerate the export-led

TABLE 8.1   Japanese Trade with Asian Pacific and Global Partners, 1990 (in U.S. $Millions)

Country/Group of Countries	Japan's Exports to	Japan's Imports from	Japan's Trade Balance
Hong Kong	13,106	2,182	+ 10,924
Singapore	10,739	3,581	+ 7,158
South Korea	17,499	11,743	+ 5,756
Taiwan	15,461	8,506	+ 6,955
NICs: Total	56,805	26,012	+ 30,793
Brunei	86	1,278	− 1,192
Indonesia	5,052	12,744	− 7,692
Malaysia	5,529	5,411	+ 118
Philippines	2,510	2,149	+ 361
Thailand	9,150	4,164	+ 4,986
ASEAN-5: Total	22,327	25,746	− 3,419
China	6,145	12,057	− 5,912
EC	54,046	35,338	+ 18,708
United States	91,121	52,842	+ 38,279

Source: International Monetary Fund, *Direction of Trade Statistics, Yearbook,* 1991.

industrialization of the NICs, linking their trade more closely to Japan. Because their currencies were either pegged to the dollar or appreciated only slightly, the NICs could increase their exports (especially consumer electronics) to the United States after 1985. This enabled them to achieve the highest growth rates in the region during the decade ending in 1990. Their combined exports to the United States almost doubled from 1984 to come within four-fifths of Japan's sizable exports to the United States in 1990.

But if the NICs gained the most from yen appreciation enlarging their trade surplus with the United States, they also increased their dependence on Japanese imports, forming a triangular relationship characteristic of growth in the region. To sustain a high level of exports to the United States, the NICs imported from Japan the intermediate components to produce their consumer and communications products for the American market. As a consequence, the NICs ran a trade deficit with Japan throughout the 1980s, despite an increasing level of exports to Japan.[15] NIC exports to Japan accelerated after the Plaza Accord, mounting from $11 billion in 1985 to $26 billion in 1990. A new element of this trade between the NICs and Japan is the growing proportion of manufactured goods, particularly consumer electronics, that are beginning to make inroads into the Japanese home market. In place of the labor-intensive finished goods, there is a larger component of technology-intensive parts, even capital goods, that make up Japanese imports from the NICs, the proportion increasing from 58 percent in 1980 to 66 percent in 1987.[16]

Between 1984 and 1990 Hong Kong and South Korea substantially reduced their exports to the United States as a proportion of their total, while increasing their exports to Japan, the other NICs, and the European Community. As seen in Table 8.1, all

TABLE 8.2   NICs Trade with Selected Partners, 1984 and 1990 (Percent of Total Exports and Imports)

Two-way Trade		Hong Kong	Singapore	South Korea	Taiwan
To Japan	1984	4.4	9.4	15.8	10.5
	1990	5.6	8.8	20.9	12.4
From Japan	1984	23.6	18.4	24.9	27.2
	1990	16.1	20.1	33.1	28.2
To other NICs	1984	7.9	9.4	7.0	10.6
	1990	9.7	12.3	10.3	17.8
From other NICs	1984	16.5	6.6	3.9	6.7
	1990	17.5	10.2	6.1	12.2
To ASEAN-5	1984	4.9	30.5	3.1	2.5*
	1990	4.0	24.4	4.5	5.2*
From ASEAN-5	1984	3.1	26.0	6.7	4.4
	1990	3.7	20.1	6.7	3.9
To China	1984	17.8	1.0	—	—
	1990	24.8	1.5	0.4	—
From China	1984	25.0	4.7	—	—
	1990	36.8	3.4	0.7	—
To United States	1984	33.2	20.0	36.0	48.8
	1990	24.1	21.2	31.7	32.4
From United States	1984	10.9	14.6	22.5	22.8
	1990	8.1	16.1	27.3	21.1
To EC	1984	14.3	10.1	11.3	5.9†
	1990	17.0	14.4	12.9	9.3†
From EC	1984	11.2	10.4	9.1	10.8
	1990	9.8	12.8	12.8	17.6

*These figures do not include Malaysia and Brunei.
†These figures include only Germany, U.K., and France.
Sources: International Monetary Fund, *Direction of Trade Statistics, Yearbook,* 1991. Republic of China, Council for Economic Planning and Development, *Taiwan Statistical Data Book, 1993.*

four NICs are import-dependent upon Japan, which has consistently enjoyed large trade surpluses with them: in 1990, $5.756 billion with South Korea, $6.955 billion with Taiwan, $10,924 billion with Hong Kong, and $7.156 billion with Singapore. And though all are heavily export-dependent upon the United States, with the exception of Singapore, the huge investments of South Korea and Taiwan in heavy and high-technology industries and of Hong Kong in labor-intensive industries have made them even more dependent on imports of Japanese capital equipment.[17]

All four NICs have expanded their trade with China and the EC as well as with one another. With Taiwan and South Korea relaxing their political opposition to trading with China, Hong Kong became a major conduit for growing trade with China. By 1993, increasing investments from Taiwan and Hong Kong, which take advantage of cheap labor in the growing number of special economic zones set up by the Chinese

TABLE 8.3   Percent of Growth in Gross Domestic Product, NICs and ASEAN-4

NICs	1987–1991	1991	ASEAN-4	1987–1991	1991
Hong Kong	4.6	4.2	Indonesia	n.a.	6.8
Singapore	n.a.	6.7	Malaysia	8.3	8.8
South Korea	9.5	8.4	Philippines	3.8	−.9
Taiwan	7.9	7.3	Thailand	10.4	7.5
NIC average	7.3	6.7	ASEAN-average	7.5	7.7

Source: Far Eastern Economic Review: Asia 1993 Yearbook, pp. 6–7.

government, have turned the major thoroughfares in and out of Hong Kong into parking lots. As increased trade between the NICs and China passed through Hong Kong, ASEAN's share of Hong Kong trade decreased somewhat during the 1980s. But the NICs, especially South Korea, continue to depend on imported raw materials from Indonesia and Malaysia. Altogether, regional trade has become a more significant element in the NIC's overall trade picture, with slightly increased imports from other NICs and significantly expanded exports to China (see Table 8.2).

Just as Hong Kong's trade remains firmly linked to the continent of China, Singapore's retains its special relationship with Malaysia. Though its trade with Thailand and Taiwan grew between 1984 and 1990 from 3.4 percent to 4.5 percent and from 2.5 percent to 3.9 percent of total exports, respectively, Singapore's trade in the Asian Pacific region remains especially high with Malaysia: It was 15.6 percent of the total in 1984, dropping to 13.3 percent of total exports in 1990. But significantly, Singapore's trade with the other NICs *collectively* increased during the period between 1984 and 1990 from 8 percent to 11.2 percent, edging up to its total trade with Malaysia of 13.3 percent in 1990 and with Japan of 14.5 percent. As with Hong Kong, Singapore's trade with the NICs has increased at the expense of the other ASEAN countries, whose trade share has dropped from 28 percent in 1984 to 22 percent in 1990. Compared to its trade with the NICs, however, Singapore's trade with the United States remains at roughly 18 percent while its trade with the EC has increased from 10.3 percent in 1984 to 13.6 percent of its total trade in 1990.[18] Overall, Singapore has moved in the direction of evenly distributing its trade throughout the Asian Pacific region.

Trade Patterns of ASEAN

By the 1980s the ASEAN-4 (ASEAN members except Singapore and Brunei) were also entering the ranks of newly industrializing nations, three of them—Malaysia, Indonesia, and Thailand—overtaking the NICs in their growth performance (see Table 8.3). From their early role as suppliers of raw materials and energy, principally to Japan, the resource-rich ASEAN nations have moved in the direction of diversifying their exports. When Japan and other industrialized countries reduced the proportion of raw mate-

TABLE 8.4   ASEAN-4, NICs, China, Japan, and United States Exports by Sector, 1991 (Percent of Total Exports)

Country	Fuels, Minerals, Metals	Other Primary Commodities	Transport, Machinery	Textiles, Clothing	Other Manufactures
Indonesia	43	16	2	14	25
Malaysia	17	22	38	6	17
Philippines	9	20	14	9	48
Thailand	2	32	22	17	28
Hong Kong	2	3	24	40	32
Singapore	18	8	48	5	21
South Korea	3	4	38	21	34
Taiwan	2	6	38	16	39
China	9	15	19	28	29
Japan	1	1	66	2	29
United States	6	14	48	2	30

Source: World Bank, *Development Report,* 1993, Table 16.

rials and fuel per unit of production after the 1970s, ASEAN nations turned to Japanese and NIC foreign direct investments to upgrade their industrial base. Commodity exports, as a consequence, constitute a smaller share of total ASEAN exports. In 1991 more than half of the exports from Thailand, Malaysia, and the Philippines (as shown in Table 8.4) consisted of manufactures: 67 percent of Thailand's, 61 percent of Malaysia's, and 71 percent of the Philippines'. Even with this shift in composition of trade on the part of the resource-rich ASEAN nations, their relationship with Japan has remained asymmetrical, with ASEAN depending on Japan to buy 35 percent of its commodity exports while Japan's commodity imports from ASEAN constitute only 15 percent of its total.[19]

One solution to the problem of asymmetrical trade relationships is to diversify trading partners. When Malaysia and the Philippines sought to alter their dependence upon their former colonial powers—Great Britain and the United States—however, they found themselves export-dependent on Japan instead. Japan's initial dominance in Southeast Asia—both in the prewar and early postwar periods—as consumer of its natural resources and primary products, has been solidified rather than reduced by its becoming an investor rather than merely a consumer. The trade statistics in Table 8.5 attest to this, and individual country data bear it out. Of Malaysia's exports in 1984, 22.8 percent went to Japan with only 13.5 percent and 13 percent to the United States and Western Europe, respectively. In the same year, 26 percent of Malaysia's total imports were Japanese products, compared to 16.1 percent and 15.5 percent that were U.S. and Western European market shares, respectively.[20] Indonesia, until the late 1960s, was import-dependent on Japan but export-dependent on the United States. But by 1984, 47.3 percent of Indonesia's exports and 23.8 percent of its imports were traded with Japan, while the United States took only 20.6 percent of Indonesian exports and provided 18.4 percent of its imports.[21] In the case of the Philippines, which

TABLE 8.5   Destination of ASEAN-5 Exports, 1984 and 1990 (Percent of Total Exports)

Destination		Indonesia	Malaysia	Philippines	Thailand	Brunei
To Japan	1984	47.31	22.8	19.4	13.0	68.4
	1990	42.54	18.5	19.9	17.4	52.7
To NICs	1984	15.10	29.1	13.9	15.2	12.6
	1990	18.43	39.6	12.4	15.3	14.6
To ASEAN-5	1984	1.65	6.2	3.7	5.8	8.9
	1990	2.38	7.6	4.2	4.2	11.8
To China	1984	.04	1.0	1.1	2.5	*
	1990	3.24	2.5	.8	1.2	.2
To United States	1984	20.58	13.5	38.0	17.2	5.5
	1990	13.10	20.4	38.0	22.7	3.8
To EC	1984	5.02	13.0	13.9	20.7	2.3#
	1990	11.80	18.0	17.8	20.9	12.4#

*amount negligible or nil
#Western Europe
Source: IMF 1991 Yearbook, Direction of Trade Statistics. UN Statistical Yearbook for Asia and Pacific, 1992 for Brunei.

has been export-dependent on the United States since independence, one-third of its trade deficit since the 1970s has been with Japan. Only Thailand, more recently, seems to have avoided being export-dependent on any single trading partner, though its import-dependence on Japan has grown. This "tilting" of ASEAN countries (with the exception of Singapore) in favor of Japan has led William Nester to conclude they are "caught in a classical 'neocolonial' relationship with Japan in which they increase their dependency and Japan increases its surpluses."[22]

However, with the exception of the Philippines and Thailand, export figures for 1990 indicate a shift away from this dependence on Japan. During the 1980s the most significant feature of ASEAN-5 trade was the growth in exports to the NICs compared to the relative decline in importance of exports to Japan. Now Indonesia, Malaysia, and Brunei are exporting proportionately less to Japan and more to the NICs than previously. All of them except for Thailand are trading more with one another. Proportionately, Indonesian exports to China have increased dramatically, with only slight increases by Brunei and Malaysia. Although Japan remains an important trading partner for members of ASEAN, its relative importance for ASEAN exports has remained the same or declined. For Thailand, Japan has increased dramatically as a trading partner, quadrupling its exports and increasing its imports by almost the same amount by 1990.[23] Apart from Japan, Thailand's trade in the Asian Pacific region is primarily with Singapore, though its trade with the NICs has increased, placing it just behind Singapore.[24]

In trade with extraregional partners, Indonesia and Brunei exported a smaller proportion to the United States in 1990 than they did in 1984, while in the same period, all five of the ASEAN countries increased their exports to the EC. Combined exports from ASEAN-5 as a group to the United States and EC increased from 15 percent in 1984 to 18 percent in 1990. If we compare ASEAN-6 exports within the region (that is, with Japan, China, other ASEANs, and NICs) it is clear that only one-third of Philippine and Thai exports are intraregional, while two-thirds or more of the exports of Indonesia, Malaysia, and Brunei are intraregional. Singapore's exports are about evenly divided.

In summary, the pattern of trade that has emerged among Asian Pacific countries is clearly structured around the dominance of Japan's economy in the region but with strong extraregional dependencies on the part of most individual countries (including Japan) on core markets in the larger global economy, in the United States and Western Europe. Japan's economic behavior as regional hegemon has been marked by the inequality world system theory predicts of core countries: It has preserved its own superiority as leading goose in the region, and by intensifying the trade dependency of the flock, has insured that the other geese will continue to fly in formation. The questions we turn to now are what the pattern of investments is in the region and what it might indicate concerning the interrelationship of regionalization and globalization.

INVESTMENT PATTERNS IN THE REGION

Export-led strategy, which has become a trademark of Asian Pacific development, results not only in increased world trade and rapid economic growth for parts of the developing world but vastly expanded opportunities for capital investments from the developed world, the foreign direct investments (FDI) of transnational corporations. FDI in the postwar world has been the late-twentieth-century equivalent of the Portuguese and Spanish explorers of the late fifteenth century. It is capital in search of new economic horizons to chart, conveyed by computer rather than by ship. Among the factors influencing the transformation of today's world economy, FDI has assumed extraordinary importance because it is the medium of technology transfer, a form of DNA for human civilization in the twenty-first century. Not surprisingly, therefore, FDI has grown even faster than world trade and output. As developing countries intensify their efforts to attract FDI and transnational corporations adopt increasingly global strategies to survive and prosper, the gap between the growth rate of exports and that of foreign direct investment continues to widen. It has prompted one writer to observe that "as a means of international economic integration, foreign direct investment is in its take-off phase; perhaps in a position comparable to world trade at the end of the 1940s."[25]

The global pattern of FDI (inward and outward stock and flows) in the early 1980s can be depicted as bipolar, dominated by the United States and the EC, which by 1988 had achieved parity with the United States in terms of stock. In the 1990s the global pattern has become tripolar, with Japan having emerged as an equally important FDI power, at least in terms of *outward* flows. Japan thereby constitutes the third member of a triad. The rapidly declining share of the United States in the triad's total outward stocks and flows has been taken up by the rising share of Japan, which, at least in terms of outward flows, surpassed the United States in 1993 by a substantial margin. In fact, the United States, by becoming a major host (recipient) country for FDI, has promoted the overall rise in world foreign direct investment *located in the triad.* By contrast, Japan, which has so far discouraged the inward flow of FDI, has contributed to the relatively *low share* (about one-half) of worldwide inward stock *located in the triad as a whole.*[26] As a host country for FDI, therefore, Japan is not yet considered an equal triad member.

From a global perspective, then, the triad occupies a dominant position in the marketing strategies of Japanese transnational corporations: Of the total 10.5 trillion yen of manufactured goods sold by Japanese foreign affiliates in 1987, 54 percent were sales *by* affiliates located in the two other triad members (the United States and the EC), and 64 percent were sales *to* a triad country from affiliates in all countries. The second most important market for Japanese affiliates abroad is Asia, where regional core networks are strongly linked not only to Japan but also to the two other legs of the triad: Of the total exports of Asian manufacturing affiliates, 68 percent were to the triad, with 35 percent, 23 percent, and 10 percent exported to Japan, the United States, and the EC, respectively. A large percentage of these exports are semi-finished goods exported from Asia for final manufacture or assembly by another affiliate in the triad or low-cost finished goods to be sold by an affiliated distributor in the triad.[27] This pattern integrates economic markets across regions so that low-cost suppliers based in Asia support the three-legged strategy in the triad. Japan plays an important role in supplying Asian affiliates, which in some cases, like the electrical and electronic equipment industries, create low-cost supply networks to sell manufactured goods back to Japan, while in others, like the automobile industry, supply low-cost components to sell to affiliates in the United States. A major question for the future is what would happen to this interregional economic integration should further regionalization of markets occur in North America and Europe.

The Regional Pattern of FDI

As Table 8.6 clearly indicates, the lion's share of foreign direct investment (FDI) in Asian Pacific countries, with the notable exception of China, comes from the developed countries of North America, Western Europe, and Japan. Shifts occurring between the early and late 1980s continue to distinguish subregional differences between ASEAN and NIC countries. For the NICs, excluding Hong Kong, FDI from developed countries has steadily increased as a share of the total, with a decreasing proportion of FDI coming from developing countries. Unlike the developing countries, for whom higher labor costs have eroded the advantages of the location, developed countries still find production costs lower than at home, with certain advantages like access to a skilled labor force, available infrastructure, and an export orientation. However, they have shifted investments toward more technologically sophisticated industries, manufacturing high value-added products, and increasingly toward services.[28]

For ASEAN countries, with the exception of Malaysia, where the share from developing countries has remained constant, there has been a noticeable growth in FDI from developing countries, especially those within the region, and a corresponding decrease in the share from developed countries. China is the only country where the

TABLE 8.6   Distribution of FDI (Inward Stock) by Home Country, Region, Various Years (Percentage)

Countries	Years	Share of Stock from Developed Area/Developing Area						
		All Developed Countries	North America	Western Europe	Japan	Other Developed Countries	All Developing Countries	Asia and the Pacific
Hong Kong	1989	83.1	38.6	20.0	36.0	5.4	16.9	88.2
	1984	92.0	58.8	16.2	22.9	2.2	8.0	76.5
South Korea	1988	92.8	29.9	13.8	56.1	0.2	5.8	66.5
	1980	89.9	21.9	10.7	67.3	0.1	8.2	26.1
Singapore	1989	94.6	35.1	32.4	32.5	. . .	5.4	. . .
	1980	88.5	33.4	47.7	18.9	. . .	11.5	. . .
Taiwan	1988	72.3	44.4	18.5	37.1	. . .	27.7	61.9
	1980	63.2	55.4	15.3	29.4	. . .	36.8	71.6
Indonesia	1988	72.8	12.2	34.4	38.4	15.0	27.9	82.8
	1980	77.1	6.3	14.0	48.6	31.1	22.9	70.6
Malaysia	1987	59.2	12.4	46.0	33.9	7.6	40.8	93.0
	1981	58.6	11.5	49.4	30.0	9.2	41.4	92.2
Philippines	1987	90.6	65.0	17.2	14.7	3.1	9.4	78.4
	1980	92.0	63.7	13.7	18.3	4.4	8.0	64.6
Thailand	1988	77.3	31.7	19.9	47.5	0.9	22.8	98.4
	1980	80.2	40.5	22.5	36.2	0.8	20.3	99.9
China (PRC)	1987	35.0	48.8	27.2	20.5	3.6	65.0	98.3
	1984	41.8	45.1	34.9	13.9	6.0	58.2	96.6
Vietnam	1989	80.5	0.6	72.7	17.9	8.8	16.1	99.3

Source: United Nations, *World Investment Directory 1992,* vol. 1, *Asia and the Pacific,* Table 8, p. 19.

share of developing countries' FDI exceeds that of developed countries, reflecting the importance of investments coming from Hong Kong, Taiwan, and South Korea into the special economic zones in the coastal areas. The emergence of the NICs as a regionally significant source of FDI, specifically in China, has led some scholars to observe China's potential alongside the NICs to act as an economic counterpoint to Japan's predominance in the region.

Among developed countries, there has been a shift away from North America and Western Europe in favor of Japan as a source of FDI. Since 1989 Japan has become the largest single investor in the region as a whole. Its investments in Taiwan, South Korea, Hong Kong, and ASEAN in 1992 were over $60 million, an amount at least double the United States' investment in the region.[29] More important than the sheer size of Japan's investments in the region's economies has been the dependence fostered by Japan in its relationships with other Asian Pacific countries. Investments flowing from Japan to each of its partners increase each of these countries reliance on Japan as a producer of capital-intensive, high-tech, manufactured goods and as a consumer of their largely labor-intensive intermediate products. The result is a regional network of economic ties comprising de facto economic integration in the region, one in which Japan is the dominant power.

Types of Japanese Investment

Postwar Japanese investments fall into four categories: investment for resource development, investments in import-substitution industries to maintain foreign market share, investment in production for export to third countries, and service sector investments.[30] Japan's earliest postwar foreign direct investment (FDI) was in *resource-extraction development* in Southeast Asia. Its purpose is to assure supplies of minerals, oil, timber, and pulp for home consumption. Indonesia, the recipient of much of this investment, has remained Japan's second largest investment destination after the United States and, along with resource-rich Malaysia and Brunei, is one of the few countries in the region with which Japan consistently runs a trade deficit. A second type of Japanese FDI is in *import-substitution industries.* These are manufacturing firms that set up shop behind another country's import barriers to produce relatively standardized goods for local consumption: textile goods, toys, electrical appliances, consumer electronics, and metal products. Japan relocated much of its labor-intensive industries to South Korea and Taiwan in this way during the 1960s. An important characteristic of this type of Japanese FDI is the large number of small- and medium-sized firms that have invested abroad, often with the capital and technical assistance of Japan's large trading firms. Forty percent of Japan's foreign investments are still made by small- and medium-sized firms that inevitably follow abroad the large corporations with whom they have subcontracting arrangements.[31]

A third type of Japanese FDI is in *production for export to third-country markets.* The purpose of such investments is to take advantage of abundant cheap labor and the investment incentives—income tax exemptions, free plant sites, and duty-free importation of raw materials—provided by countries in export-processing zones. In the 1970s and 1980s, after the Japanese government eased its restrictions on overseas investment, investments of this kind were made in ASEAN countries and in the NICs as well as today in China. With the lifting of restrictions in 1969–1970, Japanese corporations launched large-scale overseas investments in minerals, oil, and raw materials. By 1979, of the Japanese foreign investments in Asia, 39.3 percent were in resources, 44.3 percent in manufacturing, and 16.4 percent in services.[32] And in 1987, according to Nomura Research Institute statistics, 59 percent of the production of Japanese manufacturing subsidiaries in Pacific Asia was for the local market, 17 percent for export back to Japan, and 24 percent for export to the rest of the world.[33]

The fourth type of Japanese FDI is in the *service sector,* which includes investments in finance, real estate, travel, and insurance. "In 1988, 32.4 percent of new Japanese foreign investments were in finance and insurance, followed by 17.9 percent in real estate, 17.1 percent in manufacturing, 8.7 percent in other services, 8.6 percent in natural resources, 8.3 percent in commerce and 7 percent in other categories."[34] Fears that a lingering recession in the United States would preclude further expansion there prompted Japan's "Big Four" securities houses to undertake a major drive into Southeast Asia in the late 1980s, purchasing local securities firms and entering the region's small and volatile but growing stock markets. With Japanese banks, securities, and insurance companies expanding their operations, Singapore and Hong Kong have become major beneficiaries. Seventy-seven percent of Japanese investment into Sin-

gapore in 1988, according to government estimates, was in nonmanufacturing businesses.[35] Japanese department stores have opened branches throughout Southeast
Asia, capturing increasing shares of the retail market as they force local department
stores to sell rather than face bankruptcy. And Japanese tourists flock to these stores
because their prices are lower than comparable items at home.

Three Waves of Japanese Investment.   Japanese investments have swept
across the Asian Pacific in three successive waves. The first, starting in the early
1950s, occurred under restrictions imposed by the occupation authorities to keep capital
from leaving Japan and to preserve Japan's balance of payments. Japanese investments
abroad in this period were approved on a case-by-case basis and only if they promoted
Japanese exports or resulted in overseas development of the natural resources Japan
needed to develop its home industry. Other countries' investments in Japan during
this time were prevented in favor of getting competitive foreign firms to sell their technology to infant Japanese industries. Altogether, however, Japanese FDI in both manufacturing and resource production in this first wave of investment abroad was small,
amounting to $166 million in the ASEAN countries in 1966, which was only one-quar-
ter of the American investment at the time.

A second wave of Japanese overseas investments, spurred by capital liberalization and yen appreciation in 1969–1970, saw Japanese investments throughout the
Asian Pacific reach $4 billion, which was one-third larger than American investments
in the area. By 1976, more than 75 percent of new foreign investment in the Asian Pacific region was Japanese, with eight major recipients—South Korea, Taiwan, Hong
Kong, Singapore, Malaysia, Indonesia, Thailand, and the Philippines—having received
cumulatively 27.2 percent of Japan's total FDI by 1980.[36] Three international events
converged with domestic pressures in Japan in the late 1960s and early 1970s to bring
about this shift in government FDI as part of Japan's comprehensive security policy.
One was Nixon's devaluation of the dollar in 1971 and his subsequent decision to let
the value of the dollar float. A second was the adoption of import-substitution policies
by the NICs and ASEAN countries to foster foreign industrial investments in their
countries. The third international event to push Japan into vastly expanded FDI was
OPEC's temporary oil-export embargo and quadrupling of oil prices in 1973.

Domestic pressures for an easing of government restrictions on FDI in this second "wave" of investments overseas included a shortage of labor within Japan, the
high cost of land, and a nationwide consensus to place restrictions on heavy polluting
petrochemical and metal-refining industries in order to "houseclean Japan."[37] To circumvent Japanese vulnerability and spread around Japan's resource suppliers as
strategically as possible, the government encouraged Japanese corporations to embark on large-scale oil, mineral, and raw material investments. When undertaken in
joint ventures with host countries who depended upon Japan as a market for their
abundant natural resources, the tactic provided leverage for the Japanese. This applied to Malaysia and the Philippines, from whom Japan imported 100 percent and
92.7 percent, respectively, of their bauxite exports. In a classic example of pursuing
"comprehensive security," the Japanese government used a foreign aid program, its
sponsorship of the Asahan industrial complex in Indonesia, to promote overseas in-

vestment in the construction of an immense dam and hydroelectric power station on the Asahan River, which fueled an aluminum refinery and other industries, to obtain low-cost resources.

To put in global perspective the flow of Japanese investment into the Asian Pacific region, however, it must be remembered that it was surpassed by the phenomenal growth of Japanese investments in the United States. Already the largest recipient of Japanese investment, the United States had absorbed $25.290 billion through 1986, a figure three times larger than the second-ranking country, Indonesia, with $8.423 billion.[38] Thus Japanese investment growth within the region, rapid as it has been, has *declined relative to* the extraordinary growth in Japan's extraregional investments. This expansion of intraregional economic ties accompanying an even greater interdependence tends to support Richard H. Solomon's observation of "a unique outward-looking regionalism" characteristic of the Asian Pacific, one that closely links the region to the global economy.[39]

A third "tidal wave" of investments was spearheaded by Japanese banks and securities corporations in the mid-1980s. These new Japanese investments, mostly in service industries, "totaled $1.43 billion, $2.32 billion, and $4.86 billion in 1985, 1986, and 1987, respectively, compared to new American investments in the area of $55 million, $405 million, and $2.2 billion in those same years. In 1988, the Ministry of Finance estimated that Japan's cumulative investments in East Asia were $30 billion or about 21 percent of Japan's total foreign investments."[40]

With the exception of resource-based industries, Japanese investments in the Asian Pacific go down the ranks of the "flying geese" as development among the countries in the region moves up the rungs of the international product cycle. Early waves of Japanese investment in non-resource-based industries were directed to the East Asian NICs, in particular South Korea and Taiwan. With rising wage costs and currency appreciation in the NICs after the mid-1980s, Japanese companies producing key technology-intensive products began moving their operations away from production in the NICs to ASEAN countries. Japanese FDI in South Korea in FY 1988 decreased by about half, increasing more than threefold in Thailand. Mitsubishi Electric, for example, decided to reduce its audio equipment production at its Taiwan affiliate company, increasing its investment in its Thai joint venture, while Asics, the leading Japanese sports equipment manufacturer, shifted all its sports shoe production from South Korea to Indonesia.

As Japanese firms export higher value-added products out of the Asian Pacific region, their investments within the region are increasingly more sophisticated in their use of technology. Sony, for example, has upgraded its investments in Singapore by producing compact disc players that for the first time utilize a large-scale robotized production system for optical pickups, and Fujitsu's plans include building a $25 million semiconductor plant in Malaysia.[41] While the export of higher value-added products improves the trade balances of these host countries, the gain is offset by their increased dependence upon Japan for more, and more expensive, components. As much as Japan's Asian Pacific neighbors seek increased Japanese investments to help them develop, therefore, they are at risk of being compromised by Japan's "economic colonialism." Thus, to the extent that Japan's economic success has been accompanied by an accelerated economic hegemony in the region, it faces continuing political problems that arise from perceptions of its "arrogance and insensitive behaviour."[42]

The NICs' Investments

Until the 1980s, outward investment from the developing countries of the Asian Pacific was small. After the mid-1980s, however, in response to rising costs of labor and currency appreciation, Hong Kong, South Korea, and Taiwan became major foreign investors in the rest of the region, especially among the ASEAN-4 (Indonesia, Malaysia, Philippines, and Thailand) and the coastal provinces in China. Since 1985, Taiwan has invested more than $12 billion in Southeast Asia, becoming by 1991 the largest foreign investor in Indonesia and Malaysia, as well as one of the top investors in other ASEAN countries. Examples of Taiwan's investments include a $220 million petrochemical plant joint venture in the Philippines and a $1 billion "electronics park" in Malaysia. There is also a large capital flow in an ever expanding two-way indirect trade across the Taiwan Strait between Taiwan and the People's Republic of China. With little or no direct official contact, Taiwan's investments in the PRC in 1991 are said to have totaled $5.6 billion, with more than 3,000 Taiwanese firms in operation in China.[43] Hong Kong, reputedly the largest investor in the region, is reported by China as having invested (along with Macao) $15.5 billion in 1979–1987.[44] By the end of 1991, business firms from Hong Kong were employing over 3 million workers in adjacent Guangdong province. South Korea, although it started to invest directly in China later than the other NICs, had already contracted for 141 Korean firms to be established in China, an investment of $1.4 billion.

The NICs in the 1980s, replicating Japan's earlier transfer of its labor-intensive production technologies to the NICs in the 1960s and 1970s, were moving up the high-tech ladder, exporting their own labor-intensive enterprises to ASEAN countries and China as they attracted primarily technologically intensive FDI from Japan. Until the mid-1980s, NIC investments especially in ASEAN countries were primarily in labor-intensive manufacturing; in the case of Taiwan, for example, they were in textiles, chemical products, and electrical equipment. Since then, manufacturing as a proportion of NIC investments in ASEAN has begun to shift somewhat, with increasing diversification in the direction of construction and the service sector. For Taiwan, this has been particularly evident in the Philippines and in Thailand, where the construction industry has grown significantly. For Hong Kong and Singapore, FDI investment has been concentrated in services; for Hong Kong this has been apparent in Indonesia and in Thailand, and for Singapore in Malaysia.[45] In the 1990s, an increasing amount of NICs' FDI in labor-intensive manufacturing has gone to China, whose exports present a challenge to the ASEAN-4, since both China and ASEAN-4 enjoy a comparative advantage in similar product lines. China's exports are predominantly labor-intensive light manufactures combined with resource-based products like crude oil and raw materials, which ASEAN-4 countries rely on for their foreign exchange.

In a study by Chow, applying the "export similarity index" to an evaluation of the overlapping of exports between China and ASEAN-4 in OECD markets, the conclusion was that among Asian Pacific countries Malaysia had the least export similarity with

China, while the Philippines and Thailand displayed the greatest export similarity with China. By 1990 more than 50 percent of China's exports overlapped with those from the Philippines and Thailand in the U.S. and EC markets, and greater than 40 percent with those from Indonesia in the same markets.[46] This might suggest a potential competition between China and the ASEAN-4 countries over similar products sold in the United States and EC. By contrast, many business firms in the NICs—particularly Hong Kong, South Korea, and Taiwan—have instead exported various kinds of domestically produced industrial components to be processed at offshore assembly lines in the neighboring ASEAN-4 or China's coastal provinces for reexport to the world market. The resultant FDI from the NICs has generated an additional momentum in the direction of regional economic integration.

In summary, there has been a rapid growth of FDI in the Asian Pacific, principally as a consequence of the overall economic growth of countries in the region. Japanese TNCs have played the leading role, pursuing a regional core network strategy in their sourcing and supplying activities. Japanese affiliates have thereby contributed to the economic interdependence of Asian Pacific economies, acting as a force for integration in the region. NICs (except for Singapore) have also become major investors abroad, the outward investments of South Korea and Taiwan overtaking those of Hong Kong. The geographical distribution of FDI from the NICs exhibits a pattern similar to Japan's: a larger proportion going to developed countries, with a declining share of total FDI going to developing countries. In 1988, the percentage of total FDI to developed countries was 71.3 percent and 55.5 percent from Taiwan and South Korea, respectively, up from 56.5 percent and 31.8 percent in 1980. And for TNCs home based in South Korea and Taiwan, like those in Japan, the North American market, particularly the United States, is the most important location for outward FDI.[47]

The direction of overseas investments by Japan and the NICs differs according to the strategies and objectives of the home-based TNCs: Investments within the Asian Pacific region seek to maintain the competitiveness of exports while those to developed countries try to overcome existing or future tariff and nontariff barriers. Whether responding to internal and/or external factors, the increase in FDI of countries in the Asian Pacific grows out of the impetus to safeguard export markets, a motive that reflects as much as it affects trade. And if FDI is closely interrelated with trade, so is official development assistance (ODA), considered by some to be another form of investment.

FOREIGN AID

Bilateral foreign aid goes back to colonial rule, when the transfer of funds by governments to their colonial administrations was known as "infant colony subsidies." Once colonial territories became independent nation-states following World War II, the overseas economic aid provided by governments of rich countries to governments of poor countries became known as foreign aid or, more formally, official development assistance (ODA).[48] From a modernization theory perspective, such "foreign aid" is a way of providing new nations with the necessary financial and technical resources to ensure their economic viability and political stability. In the world system view, such financial assistance to new, weak players in the international market is a cost required to sustain and expand a world economy in which rich players, the core countries, are the major beneficiaries. Applying either schematic to the dynamics of foreign aid in the Asian Pacific subregion raises a central question about the purposes and efficacy of Japan's role as principal donor in the region: Does Japanese ODA contribute more to the independence (or dependence) of recipients or to the enrichment (or sacrifice) of Japan?

The Evolution of ODA

Japan views itself as having historical, geopolitical, economic, and strategic interests both in China and in the ASEAN states, each of which receives almost one-half or more of its bilateral ODA from Japan. They are not only an essential source of energy and raw materials but a significant market for both Japanese goods and Japanese capital. Often justified on these grounds, Japan's perception of its own vulnerability was magnified first by its devastating defeat in World War II and thereafter by the humbling experience of reentering the community of nations as a client-state of the United States. Besides its neighbors' fears of recurring militarism, its constituents' insistence on comprehensive security, and poor countries' expectations of financial help, there were continuous demands by the United States for Japan to be economically strong yet suitably accommodating to its patron's interests. This relationship between the United States and Japan has profoundly affected the ways in which Japan has grappled with the issue of foreign aid.

By 1961, when the Development Assistance Committee (DAC) of the OECD (Organization for Economic Cooperation and Development) began coordinating the donations of rich countries to assist developing nations, Japan was already a charter member. A minor aid donor at first, Japan rose rapidly to become, in absolute volume, the fourth largest donor in the DAC by the end of the 1970s and the first by 1989, with an annual ODA expenditure of $9 billion between 1988 and 1990.[49] In Asia, which Japan considers as vital to its own security as Latin America is to the United States', Japan surpassed the United States as principal aid donor by 1977. The heaviest concentration of Japanese ODA all along has been in the ASEAN states (and more recently, China) where Japan began outspending all other DAC donors by 1987 (see Table 8.7).

Compared to the 1960s and early 1970s, when as much as 90 to 100 percent of Japan's aid was concentrated in the Asian Pacific, Japanese aid to the ASEAN states as a proportion of its total aid has actually been reduced, reflecting Japan's increasing acknowledgment of its global responsibilities. After the international crises of the 1970s, Japanese ODA began to move out into the larger global arena, with larger donations going to the Middle East, Africa, and Latin America. As a result, its Asian share of ODA dropped to about 63 percent, with half of this, approximately 30 percent, going to ASEAN countries. This led to the 7:1:1:1 regional distribution formula widely believed to be employed by the Foreign Ministry, according to which roughly 70 percent of Japan's aid is set aside for Asia, with 10 percent each assigned to Latin America, the Middle East, and Africa.[50] Table 8.8 shows the actual figures for 1988.

TABLE 8.7   Percent of Total Foreign Aid Received by ASEAN-5 (1987) and China (1979–1984) from Major Donors

	Donors		
Philippines	53.7 Japan	32.6 United States	13.7 others
Thailand	69.4 Japan	8.0 United States	6.9 West Germany
Malaysia	78.5 Japan	11.0 Australia	10.5 others
Indonesia	63.1 Japan	12.5 Netherlands	24.4 others
Singapore	50.6 Japan	20.2 West Germany	16.1 Australia
China	45.0 Japan	14.0 IMF	12.0 UN

Sources: Compiled from Japan's Ministry of Foreign Affairs, cited in Robert M. Orr, Jr., *The Emergence of Japan's Foreign Aid Power* (New York: Columbia University Press, 1990), Table 4.3, p. 76. Information for China is from Zhao Quansheng, "Japan's Aid Diplomacy with China," in Bruce M. Koppel and Robert M. Orr Jr., eds., *Japan's Foreign Aid: Power and Policy in a New Era* (Boulder: Westview Press, 1993), p. 165.

The second major turning point for ODA policy, initiated by the United States, was the Plaza Accord, which decreased the value of the dollar by appreciating the yen. The net result was to precipitate an outflow of private sector FDI from Japan (and the NICs) as well as to change the focus of ODA in the ASEAN states from securing natural resources to assisting the development of export industries. Japan extended concessional loans for government projects to improve economic and social infrastructures in Indonesia, Malaysia, the Philippines, and Thailand. This raised the concerns of the United States because Japan, with its protected domestic markets, was unable to absorb additional manufactured goods, raising the likelihood that increased exports from ASEAN would end up in the United States with its already huge trade deficit. Among ASEAN members, complaints addressed both the indebtedness that high interest payments resulting from the rising value of the yen would exact on ASEAN nations and the "growing feeling that Japan has not adequately met ASEAN's request to

TABLE 8.8   Japan's Bilateral ODA by Region (1988)

Region	**U.S. $ Millions**	**Percent of total Japanese ODA**
Asia (total)	4034.35	62.8
Northeast Asia	724.64	11.3
ASEAN	1930.21	29.9
Other Southeast Asia	266.38	4.3
Southwest Asia	1109.21	17.3
Unspecified	3.64	0.3
Middle East	582.52	9.1
Africa	883.93	13.8
Latin America	399.29	6.2
Other	521.78	8.1

Source: Robert M. Orr Jr., *The Emergence of Japan's Foreign Aid Power* (New York: Columbia University Press, 1990), Table 4.1, p. 70.

dismantle its remaining trade barriers."[51] Clearly, the long-term pressure would be in the direction of Japan's replacing the United States as an import market for manufactured goods produced in Southeast Asia.

Another shift in direction of Japanese aid within the Asian Pacific occurred in the 1980s when the NICs, who had been early recipients of significant amounts of aid themselves, became donors. South Korea and Singapore, for example, were among the top ten recipients of Japanese aid in 1970 but no longer appear among the top ten recipients in 1986. By contrast, aid to the Philippines and China has steadily, in some years even dramatically, increased. In fact, China became Japan's largest recipient of ODA from 1982 until 1987, when Indonesia resumed its number-one spot. In 1987 and 1988, the Philippines and China joined Indonesia as the top three recipients of bilateral Japanese ODA, receiving $534.72 million, $673.70 million, and $984.91 million, respectively, in 1988.[52]

Japan has grown into China's largest aid donor since 1979, when both countries set a precedent, Japan in providing and China in accepting for the first time a (yen) loan package from a DAC member. Having severed diplomatic ties with Taiwan, Japan was encouraged in this role by the United States, which had a strategic interest in promoting an open and moderate China but was prohibited from extending aid because the Foreign Assistance Act regarded China as a "member of the international communist movement."[53] Typical of Japan's overall ODA, only a very small proportion of Japanese ODA to China is in grants; the overwhelming proportion is in the form of concessional yen loans, which, to allay U.S. fears of Japanese domination of the fabled lucrative China market, is atypically untied to procurements.[54]

NICs' aid to the region, beginning in 1987, has exhibited the same clear-cut links with investments as Japan's. South Korea started an economic cooperation fund in 1987 to distribute 55 billion won of currency loans as part of a five-year 300 billion won foreign aid loan plan to developing countries, while Taiwan in 1988 established a soft-loan fund of $1.2 billion for disbursement over a five-year period to "friendly" developing countries in Southeast Asia and Africa. In Taiwan, it was hoped that foreign aid, including such projects as funding technical cooperation, would be beneficial in a number of overlapping ways: to offset the huge foreign-exchange reserves Taiwan had accumulated, to finance infrastructural projects that could assist Taiwanese investments abroad, to enhance trade, and to further diplomatic relations vis-à-vis China. Foreign assistance by the South Koreans was given to development projects and financing the purchase of capital goods from South Korea.

ODA: Attributes and Accusations

More important and controversial than the sheer size of Japanese aid have been the national objectives ODA serves as part of Japan's overall foreign policy. From the outset, Japan has openly acknowledged the close link between foreign assistance and its need to promote the Japanese economy. Japan's preoccupation with its vulnerabilities as a national entity has made its underlying objectives in providing ODA quite different from those of the United States. For Japan, trade, aid, and investment are essential for survival, a condition that by extension can be said to be true of its protégés, the NICs. This is expressed in the five policy objectives of Japanese foreign assistance programs:

1. to further Japanese economic interests by promoting exports, securing raw materials, and creating a favorable climate for commercial business activities in the recipient country;
2. to establish and strengthen diplomatic ties in order to counteract the lingering negative image of Japan that was the legacy of World War II;
3. to bolster the political stability of neighboring Asian countries;
4. to become a good partner of the other aid-giving, industrialized nations of the world; and
5. to establish Japan's status and influence in both regional and global international affairs.[55]

In its postwar reindustrialization, Japan once again confronted the necessity of cultivating markets both for resources and manufactured goods. Official foreign assistance was the form in which this was achieved. But an additional vulnerability had to be compensated for by ODA: winning friends and acceptability among the nations of both the region and the world. This objective, embedded in Japan's postwar foreign policy, has coincided with the interests and needs of its principal partner. The United States, finding itself in retreat from the Asian Pacific theater after virtual defeat in Vietnam, needed a friendly and reliable power to fill the vacuum of its own diminished role. And if Japan's constitution (written and imposed by the United States) precluded military rearmament of the sort sought by the United States in the heyday of the cold war, then Japan's presence as a source of foreign assistance in the region would have to suffice.

But winning friends with ODA has not been easy for Japan. Major criticisms have been voiced from all quarters on every aspect of Japanese foreign aid. First and foremost, Japan has been faulted for primarily considering her own national economic interests rather than the needs of recipient countries. At first criticism was directed at Japan's preference for commercially tied loans rather than concessional aid. Japan is notorious for offering the smallest number of grants as a proportion of total ODA. There is widespread suspicion that Japan uses foreign assistance simply to create markets for Japanese goods and services, and a number of attributes of the administration of Japanese ODA lend credence to this perception. Foreign aid is administered largely by bureaucrats in a bewildering number of competing ministries, each having its own agenda for evaluating the worth of foreign assistance projects. Those agencies with the greatest clout often have the least interest in overseas aid expenditures.

The party with the most interest in Japan's aid policy is business, and Japan's preference for infrastructural aid projects reflects the considerable influence of construction companies and engineering consulting firms in the determination of which projects to fund. Japan administers sizable amounts of aid money in recipient countries with extremely small staff contingents. The lack of trained development specialists means there are no field missions abroad. This results in the private sector's moving in to fill the void. "In 1986 engineering consulting firms alone did 43.7 billion yen worth of ODA-related business."[56] They often do the feasibility studies used to make project selections and then provide the contractors to do the work once they are approved.

The request basis of the aid process, which mandates that proposals for all aid projects come from the recipient government, enables Japan to justify maintaining such a small bureaucracy professionally trained to administer development assistance. In theory, the recipient governments are responsible for implementation of the projects. But since they too lack the requisite expertise, assistance on the part of the Japanese private sector fills a need. Thus the trading companies with their amply staffed overseas offices have played an active role in implementing Japan's aid program. It is hardly surprising, therefore, that this familiar cooperation between the public and private sectors in the determination and implementation of Japanese foreign aid has led some observers to view ODA as "a thinly disguised export promotion program."[57]

TRADE, AID, AND INVESTMENT AMONG THE "RENEGADES": MYANMAR, VIETNAM, LAOS, CAMBODIA, AND NORTH KOREA

The pattern of postwar trade, aid, and investment in the Asian Pacific was shaped, as we have seen, in the context of the cold war. With Japan as Asian buffer between the United States and the communist world, the political lines were drawn to isolate China, along with North Korea, North Vietnam, and Laos, from the rest of the Asian Pacific, which was to be a model of "free world" development. Cambodia remained in contention and wracked by war and political dissension as it was drawn into the strife between its neighbors—Thailand and Vietnam—and their powerful patrons, the United States and the USSR. Burma, like Cambodia, was not only wedged between even more gigantic powers—India and China—but had similarly been the scene of massive destruction by both sides—Japan and the Allied forces—during World War II. But in contrast to Cambodia, which did not have the opportunity to remain above the fray, Burma chose self-isolation and neutrality. These five countries, then, for different reasons, had in common an antipathy toward the Western world. This placed them outside or with only tenuous ties to the flourishing international economy.

For all these countries the end of the cold war and the disintegration of the Soviet Union have meant fundamental changes in their international relations. The future of countries within the socialist orbit, whose trade, aid, and investment had been linked with the command economy of the Soviet Union, depended upon how determinedly they pursued a program of economic reform. China, having faced the most serious difficulties both domestically and in its relationship with the Soviet Union, was the first to implement economic reform, pursue an export-led strategy with an infusion of private investment capital, and receive large amounts of Japanese ODA. By the late 1980s, with a short hiatus in the aftermath of the Tiananmen affair, China was successfully incorporated in the Japanese regional orbit of trade, aid, and investment. Japan had assumed the role of mentor with the blessing of a more distanced United States. Vietnam and Laos also embarked on the path of economic reform in the 1980s, almost immediately inviting the economic attention of Japan and Thailand. In 1994 North Korea alone remained outside the fold of the international market economy, though there were indications this would change once succession to Kim Il Jung was resolved.

North Korea and Myanmar

At either end of the east-west arc of the Asian Pacific, North Korea and Myanmar are at the very periphery of postwar regional economic development. North Korea receives no ODA from Japan, though from a perspective of Japan's policy of comprehensive security it could well be argued that this is unwarranted. But it is likely to remain the case as long as three purely political conditions continue to exist: North Korea's militaristic rather than economic approach to international relationships, South Korea's opposition to Japan's establishing a diplomatic relationship with North Korea, and Japan's alignment with the United States' Korean policy.

In light of the recent fragmentation of Japan's once-dominant Liberal Democratic Party, it may be significant that proponents of a closer relationship with North Korea have existed within Japan for some time. Not only the Japan Socialist Party and the Japan Communist Party but also the liberal faction in the Liberal Democratic Party, led by Masayoshi Ohira and Zenko Suzuki, have maintained for the last twenty years that the entire Korean peninsula was important to the security of Japan. This has occasioned diplomatic strain between South Korea and Japan, as when the then-minister of foreign affairs (a member of Ohira's faction) went so far as to state in 1974 that he believed North Korea had no aggressive intentions toward South Korea.[58] In late 1993, however, such expressions of optimism were overshadowed by concerns that North Korea may be arming herself with nuclear weapons.

Burma/Myanmar presents an equally paradoxical case study of Japanese foreign assistance because, despite its spurning of international assistance, it has been a recipient of large amounts of Japanese ODA since the November 5, 1954, signing of a peace treaty between Japan and the Union of Burma. Heedless of Aung San's written legacy warning against Burma's dependence upon foreign assistance, Burma received assistance from a number of different quarters: Initially there was minimal aid from the Colombo Plan nations, the United States, and even the Soviet Union, with quite substantial aid from Japan after 1954. Japan provided products and technicians for a total value of $200 million over a ten-year period, with $2 million of this amount for Japanese-Burmese joint ventures and an additional $5 million annual grant for technical assistance. In 1963 (after the military coup) Burma requested a renegotiation of the reparations agreement and received an additional $200 million over twelve years beginning in 1965; $140 million of the amount was in grant reparations and $60 million in concessional loans.[59] Since then, except for a brief hiatus during 1990, Japanese ODA has come to about $2.2 billion, one of the largest in the world measured on a per capita basis.

This Japanese aid was extended despite indications that, far from contributing to Burma's development, the aid was being siphoned into support of an increasingly militarized administration of a corrupt regime. Japan even admonished Burmese officials in "a dialogue" in 1988 on the need to engage in economic reform. After the Burmese military disallowed the 1990 elections, Japan did suspend its aid. But irrespective of SLORC, the inadequacies of economic reform, the failures of four major Japanese industrial projects, and the enormous debt burden that has led the Burmese government into destructive sales of forest resources and the drug trade, Japan has been Myanmar's sole source of assistance since independence in the full knowledge, apparently, of its inefficacy as a tool for that country's development. A new joint venture between the Burmese and Japanese was announced on April 11, 1990, a month before Myanmar's democratic elections were held and dismissed. According to the Myanmar-Japan Concord, the construction of seven major projects will be undertaken, including new international airports in Rangoon and Mandalay, at a cost expected to be about $14 billion over a ten- to fifteen-year period and involving the participation of 240 Japanese firms.[60]

A number of reasons are used to explain this state of affairs, some that are singular to Myanmar, some that speak to the characteristics of Japanese ODA in general. There is first and foremost the intrinsic wealth of Myanmar, both as a source of rice and of energy. Second are the close personal ties of the Burmese nationalist leadership to Japan—General Ne Win was trained and supported by the Japanese prior to 1945—and the physical destruction at the hands of the Japanese that marred this relationship toward the end of the war. Third is the absence of any Japanese oversight for its aid or any third-party evaluation of its effectiveness, an intrinsic aspect of the recipient-request nature of the process as described earlier. But most importantly, it can be suggested, is that the Japanese have through their ODA made themselves indispensable to Myanmar. "Their relations are critical to Burma, their support vital to the Burmese economy, and their access exceptional. Should Burma prosper, both Burma and Japan will benefit."[61] And there are indications that other countries, South Korea prominent among them, are lining up to invest in Myanmar as soon as the political climate permits.

Vietnam, Cambodia, and Laos

Embroiled in war with the United States until 1975, these three countries have come within view of normalizing their international relations and being incorporated into the global economy. Principally this is due to the dramatic changes in the international circumstances surrounding the end of the cold war. Even before U.S. troops were withdrawn from Vietnam, Japan was prepared to normalize diplomatic relations with North Vietnam and provide economic aid to both North and South Vietnam as soon as the Paris Peace Accord was signed in January 1973. When laying out the nonideological principles on which economic aid to Vietnam would be based at the conclusion of the Paris Peace Accord between the United States and Vietnam in 1973, Foreign Minister Ohira disclosed that 500 million yen had already been given to Vietnam, as a whole, through the International Red Cross. Its first official aid package to North Vietnam was 8.5 billion yen in grants in 1975, with another 5 billion in 1976. When Vietnam invaded Cambodia in December 1978, however, Japan suspended its aid commitments, and the Cambodian imbroglio became the major stumbling block to Japan's resumption of aid to Vietnam.

Behind the conflicts raging in Cambodia and among the great powers over its destiny as a state was the economic and military presence of the Soviet Union as an ally of Vietnam. The Vietnamese economy was propped up by Soviet and East European aid and preferential trading arrangements after 1975. When these arrangements were terminated, therefore, Vietnam's difficulties provided the opportunities for resolving the Cambodia stalemate and bringing about an enduring stability in that troubled area of the Asian Pacific. Japan has contributed substantially to bringing this about by playing a more political role than ever before and using the prospect of economic aid to Vietnam as a lever to obtain Vietnam's cooperation. In turn, the ASEAN nations have reduced their mistrust of Vietnam in favor of changing Indochina "from a battlefield to a marketplace."[62] Thailand has become increasingly active in Indochina, former Prime Minister Chatichai Choonhavan personally requesting Japan in 1990 to resume aid to Vietnam. President Suharto of Indonesia visited Hanoi in the same year to sign an economic and scientific technology agreement and express interest in Vietnam's joining ASEAN. The following year, Singapore, France, and Italy all announced resumption of economic aid to Vietnam.

In 1993, as reported by the Vietnamese government, there was a total of 390 projects worth close to $3 billion invested in Vietnam by companies from Taiwan, Hong Kong, the Netherlands, Britain, Australia, Singapore, France, Japan, South Korea, Canada, Malaysia, Sweden, Thailand, and the Philippines. Of special interest is the development of Vietnam's offshore oil fields, an area in which joint enterprises have made their largest investments. Japan's private investments have been eighth among the largest investors, with only twenty-four projects valued at $160 million. This may be related to the fact that the United States until 1994 imposed an embargo on doing business with Vietnam. But American companies have signed business contracts and hope to have some advantages in construction, machinery, hotel development, and, given the large numbers of Vietnamese Americans, air travel. The United States has also removed its objections to the IMF's granting loans to Vietnam, which is likely to lead to hundreds of millions of dollars in loans from the World Bank, the Asian Development Bank, and other lending institutions. With two of its major conditions for resuming economic aid to Vietnam having been met—a new coalition government in Cambodia and improved relations between the United States and Vietnam—Japan has promised $500 million a year in ODA through 1995, and Brunei is said to be negotiating a multibillion-dollar aid package.[63]

As in the case of Vietnam, which liberalized its foreign investment policy in 1988, Laos has moved in a more market-oriented direction. It has been on the receiving end of trade agreements, substantial investment, and charitable aid projects from bilateral and multilateral aid-giving agencies. The Thais have extensive contracts to log Laotian tropical hardwood forests. Australia is helping to build a bridge across the Mekong, which widens the trade link with Thailand. American companies, until recently blocked from even making commitments to invest in Vietnam, have become the second largest foreign investors in Laos, concentrating on two oil-exploration contracts in southern and central parts of the country.

The Japanese government has provided Laos with economic aid in the form of grants and technical cooperation (economic consultants) amounting to a total of 2.6 billion yen since 1989. To address the Laotian need for educational opportunities

Japan accepts foreign students from Laos. In August 1990, Foreign Minister Nakayama, in the first visit of a Japanese foreign minister to Laos in thirty-one years, announced a policy of wholehearted cooperation in helping Laos to develop a market economy.[64] The marked interest by Laotians in the benefits of a market economy has elicited a lively response on the part of some of its neighbors. While Vietnam's influence has waned, Thai and Chinese (PRC) influence has increased.

The political economy of Cambodia remains a glint in the eyes of its neighbors as a new constitutional regime takes shape. The new coalition government faces an economy in shambles, an empty government treasury, and the Khmer Rouge still in control of large areas of the country, profiting from the lucrative trade in timber and gemstones. Years of civil war destroyed much of the village-based economy, which the Draconian measures taken by the Pol Pot government failed to restore. The arrival of UNTAC has brought a massive infusion of dollars into the Cambodian economy in the form of salaries and local purchases, overwhelming the Hun Sen government's precarious hold on the economy. In Phnom Penh this has stimulated feverish private business activity in construction, hotels, and restaurants, partially financed by overseas Cambodian money. Runaway inflation has prompted underpaid civil servants to take on sideline businesses in order to survive.

Many Cambodians remain in refugee camps along the Thai border; still to be paid for somehow are the costs of resettling those still resident now that UNTAC has departed. The new government faces great dependence on outside economic aid to create the conditions that will make direct foreign investment attractive. Like Laos, however, Cambodia suffers from the absence of a skilled labor force, and the virulent anti-Vietnamese sentiment among *all* political groups may deprive Cambodia of the skilled labor available from her more populous neighbor. These problems notwithstanding, with a political economy yet to be shaped in Cambodia, there is undoubtedly interest in expanding trade and investments among the French, who still have a presence in Cambodia, the Thais, the Japanese, and, unwelcome as they may be in Cambodia, the Vietnamese.

REGIONAL ASSOCIATIONS FOR ECONOMIC COOPERATION

Public Goods and the Leadership Role

Dictated by the sheer size of Japan's economy, there is no doubt it will continue to play the core leadership role in promoting economic growth of the Asian Pacific region. But exports, imports, and capital exports are the result of free trade in the private market that, in order to function smoothly, requires that certain international conditions, "international public goods," be provided. Among these are security, maintenance of a free trade system, and some mechanism for international redistribution of income. Overall security in the postwar world, as we have seen in Chapter 7, was largely provided in the context of the cold war. Similarly, maintenance of the free trade system and an international redistribution of income was furnished by the international organizations set up under the aegis of the United States: GATT, the UN and its numerous agencies, the international financial organizations—the World Bank, the International Monetary Fund—and a variety of nongovernmental organizations.

With the United States in decline, Japan has taken over some of the financial burden of providing these public goods. We have seen this principally in the growth of bilateral official direct assistance for countries in the Asian Pacific. It is also argued that Japan's regional economic strategy of deepening asymmetrical trade and investment relationships is part and parcel of its policy of comprehensive security. In that case, Japan is providing quasi-hegemonic security not only for itself but for the region as a whole within the larger global hegemony of the United States. This is, of course, the central dilemma of the region: whether and in what manner Japan will be able to assume the political leadership role for the region while simultaneously accommodating its global political responsibilities as a major player on the international stage.

The demand for Japan to shoulder political responsibilities commensurate with its global role as an economic superpower is most vocal in the developed world, though there are undoubtedly domestic pressures in the same direction. On the other hand, whether it is desirable or not for Japan to act as political leader for the region, and there is widespread ambivalence throughout the Asian Pacific over this question, Japan is likely to dominate the region with the sheer magnitude of its economic presence. Only China, when it catches up to Japan, will be in a position to counter or join Japan as a core economy in the Asian Pacific region.

Japan has, in fact, played an active role in furthering regional economic integration by initiating and encouraging the formation of regional organizations like the Asian Development Bank. But in promoting Asian Pacific cooperation, the Japanese have been keenly aware of the profound mistrust their weaker neighbors retain toward Japan's leadership in the region. This is apparent in both the rhetoric and caution with which all countries in the Asian Pacific have moved toward greater regional economic and political association. Japan's predilection to separate economics from politics in the "parallel development" of economic and political foreign relations is reflected in the process by which movement toward regional association has occurred in the postwar world.

The Stimulus toward Cooperation

Economic growth in the Asian Pacific region has been both contagious and contingent on an expanding global economy. Though Japan, the NICs, and China all export the largest proportion of their products to North America and the EC, they have in the process of pursuing an export-led dynamic crisscrossed one another's territories with an increasingly integrated network of economic and political interaction. The rapidly multiplying private contacts, mostly economic and bilateral, among people of different nationality across the entire Asian Pacific have been accompanied almost from the start by a spirited awareness of the advantages of regional cooperation on a wide range of issues. This identification among academics, professionals, government officials, and business groups has resulted in the formation of a number of all-regional organizations to collect, assess, and disseminate information of mutual interest. These have been at the heart of a movement considered by some scholars as a potential foundation of Asian Pacific regionalization.

Despite its geographical location and obvious Asian identity, however, Japan's preeminent status as a highly developed state within the region sets its interests apart from, perhaps even in conflict with, its developing neighbors. As a global economic power Japan plays a dual role, as a "Western" extraregional partner of the United States and as a core of the dynamically growing Asian Pacific region, the leader in the "flying geese formation." It is necessarily Janus-headed, with one face in the direction of the global world economy, the other facing its home base, the Asian Pacific region. There is some tension, therefore, among those regional associations that were created at the initiative of one of the global powers, including Japan, and/or that include powerful extraregional partners and those in which the Asian Pacific states, including Japan, as principal members have taken both the initiative for their formation and the command of their membership and internal organization.

Regional organizations in our usage are intergovernmental and nongovernmental organizations that are both geographically and substantively centered on the Asian Pacific. Both can be considered *international;* in some cases the term refers to the relations among states within the region, in other cases the term more broadly refers to all relations (official and unofficial) across national boundaries. The largest number of regional associations surveyed below fall into the category of nongovernmental organizations (NGOs); only ASEAN, APEC (Asian Pacific Economic Conference), and ADB (Asian Development Bank) are intergovernmental organizations (IGOs).

All-Regional Organizations

The forerunner of Asian Pacific nongovernmental organizations (NGOs) in the postwar period, the Institute of Pacific Relations was a private regional forum in existence from 1925 until it fell victim to McCarthyism in 1961. IPR brought academics, journalists, and business and labor leaders together with politicians, bureaucrats, and state officials. Within a short period after the demise of IPR two new NGOs appeared, one principally an academic forum, the other a business association.

PAFTAD.   The Pacific Free Trade and Development Conference, originally convened in 1968 at the initiative of the Japanese to consider a proposal for a Pacific free trade area, invites academics to participate in research on economic policy issues of common interest to countries in the region. By bringing concrete research results to the attention of practitioners in government and the business world, PAFTAD hopes to be able to promote regional economic cooperation. Although dominated by liberal, market-oriented economists from the developed countries of Japan, Australia, New Zealand, Canada, and the United States, PAFTAD included academics with diverse views from countries in Southeast Asia, the Soviet Union, China, and Pacific Latin America. Early research focused on alternative trading arrangements; more recent research explores industrial policy, technology, and trade in services.

PAFTAD has played the role of trailblazer in the early stages of institutionalizing economic cooperation in the region. Given the age-old, colonial, and cold war legacies of divisiveness and mutual antagonisms, PAFTAD as a nongovernmental structure bypasses the participation of states in any official capacity while still incorporating the policy viewpoints of political practitioners. The policy orientation of PAFTAD research has been strengthened by the government background of many of the delegates. They have brought to the organization an accumulation of expertise from a wide range of economies, an extensive network of societal and political contacts, and a commitment to regional cooperation. In the informal setting provided for by PAFTAD, these scholars were able to highlight significant areas of potential economic cooperation.[65]

PBEC.   A second commercially oriented NGO launched by business leaders from the same countries and at about the same time as PAFTAD is the Pacific Basin Economic Council (PBEC). Joined by firms and individuals from South Korea, Taiwan, Mexico, Chile, Hong Kong, Peru, Indonesia, Malaysia, the Philippines, Singapore, and Thailand, PBEC is nonetheless narrowly based among the business community. It also is torn by dissension among those members who see the organization as the voice of business in regional politics and those members who see it as a "rich man's club" for renewing contacts and professing their faith in free enterprise.

PECC.   PBEC and PAFTAD are full members of the third regional NGO that plays a role in influencing regional economic cooperation, the Pacific Economic Cooperation Conference (PECC). Growing out of a conference of scholars, business leaders, and state officials meeting in Australia in 1980, PECC is a logical next step in the institutionalization of regional cooperation. It is based on a principle of nonexclusiveness that promotes reaching out to representatives of any country or organization as long as it is dedicated to the cooperation theme. Currently it includes members from ASEAN (Brunei, Indonesia, Malaysia, Philippines, Thailand, Singapore), the OECD (Japan, the United States, Canada, Australia, and New Zealand), South Korea, and the South Pacific islands as well as PAFTAD and PBEC. Its conferences and research programs are supervised by an international steering committee that includes many longtime leaders of PAFTAD and PBEC.

The tripartite membership structure of PECC brings together state officials acting as individuals in a nonofficial capacity (a polite fiction to circumvent protocol requirements) with scholars and business leaders. This ensures that state interests are expressed and defended alongside those of the private sector. The decision to form PECC as a new and more comprehensive type of cooperative forum was accompanied by a decision to make PECC an unofficial rather than an official organization. Based on a consensus that direct governmental interaction in the Asian Pacific area is premature, PECC solicits no formal consent by governments but uses task forces to "develop trusting relationships with government officials and researchers on an informal basis."[66] This unofficial mode of operating has enabled PECC to include both China and Taiwan as regular members, the Soviet Union with observer status, and the ASEAN states, a major step toward a more inclusive Asian Pacific forum for economic cooperation. Its informal nature promotes flexibility and depth of discussion, and a consensual style of decision making forces state participants to negotiate and compromise with their societal counterparts for the organization to move forward on any particular issue. PECC has begun the process of formal institutionalization with the formation of a Singapore-based permanent secretariat in 1990.

APEC.   Both the PECC and ASEAN are informally interlocked with two broader diplomatic fora that include the United States, Australia, Canada, and New Zealand along with the Asian Pacific nations. The fifteen-member Asia-Pacific Economic Co-operation forum (APEC), first convened in 1989, is composed of the six ASEAN nations along with South Korea, Taiwan, Hong Kong, China (PRC), and Japan and the United States, Canada, Australia, and New Zealand. Its principal focus on preserving an open trading system among its members was a response to a drift toward protectionism and the formation of regional trading blocs. Prime Minister Nakasone first floated the idea for a trans-Pacific alliance to protect the multilateral trading system, but it was Australian Prime Minister Bob Hawke who provided the impetus for the first ministerial-level conference in 1989. Despite the diversity of the group, agreement was reached on the following guiding principles, which were subsequently endorsed by ASEAN:

1. APEC was to be outward looking and not oriented toward the formation of a regional bloc;
2. the process of consultations was to be nonformal, based on building consensus on a gradually broader range of economic issues;
3. APEC would not develop into a formal intergovernmental negotiating process in which some sought to force their views on others;
4. APEC would complement existing regional organizations such as ASEAN and PECC; and
5. participation was to be open-ended, assessed on the basis of the strength of economic linkages with current participants rather than on ideological grounds.

A specific agenda of tasks was undertaken by APEC members in 1990. These included monitoring the regional and global economic outlook and improving data on regional trade in goods and services and on investment flows; technology transfer and trade promotion; and sectoral cooperation in energy, telecommunications, transport, fisheries, and marine resources conservation. The United States announced an initiative for regional human resource development, and Singapore was to set up a regionwide data base on trading opportunities. An agreed-upon definition of trade liberalization was to be consistent with GATT principles and not to the detriment of other economies inside or outside the region. The agreement to avoid actions that would damage market access of those outside the region meant that APEC could not move in the direction of a trading bloc. At a special meeting of APEC trade ministers in 1990, agreement was reached on phasing out the trade-distorting multifiber arrangements and phasing in a comprehensive framework for subjecting trade in services to normal GATT disciplines.[67]

The APEC meeting in Seattle in November 1993, on the heels of successful passage of NAFTA in the United States, received much publicity. But despite the fanfare,

Leaders of APEC at November 1993 meeting in the United States. From the left are: Prime Minister Paul Keating, Australia; Prime Minister Goh Chok Tong, Singapore; President Suharto, Indonesia; President Fidel Ramos, Philippines; President Bill Clinton, United States; Chairman Vincent Siew, Chinese Taipei; Prime Minister Morihiro Hosokawa, Japan; Hong Kong Financial Secretary Hamish MacLeod; President Jiang Zemin, China; Prime Minister Chuan Leekpai, Thailand; President Kim Young Sam, South Korea; Prime Minister Jean Chretien, Canada; and Sultan Hassanal Bolkiah, Brunei.

Source: Photo from AP by Doug Mills.

the meeting did more to illuminate fundamental differences between the Asian and the Anglo-American contingents of the Pacific Rim than to move the organization toward agreement on trade procedures. Mexico, Papua New Guinea, and Chile gained entry, but Australia and Southeast Asian members raised objections to admitting other Latin American countries. A decision was reached to bar entry of new members for three years while the group better defined its mission. The most tangible outcome of this APEC meeting was to prod resolution of the subsequent Uruguay round of the GATT. The trepidation with which Asian Pacific "member economies" welcomed joint participation with the United States was captured by Pyong Hwoi Koo, chairman of the South Korean conglomerate, Lucky Star International, when he compared Asia's smaller nations to "shrimps" in danger of being devoured by the U.S. "whale."[68]

EAEG.   If APEC represents the powerful link that ties Asian Pacific countries to the United States, EAEG represents a sentiment, if not quite a movement, in the opposite direction. Malaysian Prime Minister Mahathir (who refused to attend the 1993 APEC meetings) in December 1990 proposed the formation of an East Asia Economic Group that would look to Japan for leadership rather than including extraregional powers whose interests were not necessarily those of the culturally Asian Pacific nations. By excluding not only the United States and Canada but Australia and New Zealand as well, the implication of EAEG as an organizational forum was that "Asian" aspirations were fundamentally different from those of Western nations. As an expression of an underlying tension between Asian Pacific nations and those identified with the West as a culturally distinct grouping, EAEG elicited only a cautious, nervous response among other Asian Pacific countries. Indonesia insisted it be redefined as a caucus (EAEC) before ASEAN considered approving it. The cold reception of Mahathir's exclusively Asian Pacific economic group is understandable since it flies in the face of the region's fundamental reliance upon the West as a market for its exports. But Malaysia's refusal to attend the 1993 APEC meetings in Seattle indicates an enduring alternative posture to that of the majority, expressing a diffuse concern that the immense disparity between the developing nations of the Asian Pacific and their powerful Pacific neighbors can result in an association like APEC becoming a vehicle for great power dominance.

ASEAN's "Dialogue Partners."   It is notable, in light of the underlying paradox that Asian Pacific countries face in their relationship with the West, that ASEAN remains the most widely respected regional organization. Organizationally, ASEAN, which represents Southeast Asian countries with the exclusion of the Indochinese nations of Cambodia, Laos, and Vietnam, has informally broadened its scope by encompassing the foreign ministers of the United States, Japan, Canada, Australia, and New Zealand and a representative from the EC as informal "dialogue partners." Thus an informal, unofficial organization not unlike APEC has emerged out of the "postministerial" meetings that have become the standard practice following the annual meetings of ASEAN. At these informal meetings between the foreign ministers of the English-speaking nations of the Pacific Rim and a representative of the EC and their ASEAN counterparts, the emphasis is on maintaining communication and exchanging ideas on regional affairs of mutual interest. Most important among them are economic problems and international tensions in the area: the problem of the "boat people" and developments in Cambodia and Vietnam. Out of these annual meetings with "dialogue partners" has emerged a broad network of linkages, tying ASEAN to *all* the major market-oriented economies in the world. An example of expanded cooperation that has resulted from these regular contacts between ASEAN and their "dialogue partners" is the joint business clubs and councils that each "dialogue" country has established with business representatives of ASEAN states.[69] Thus, ASEAN has grown as an Asian Pacific regional organization by maintaining its identity as a distinctively Asian grouping while simultaneously expanding to include, at least informally, other countries within the wider Pacific Rim market economy.

ADB.   The most comprehensive of the all-regional associations is the Asian Development Bank, established at the initiative of Japan in 1966. Headquartered in Manila with a membership of thirty-two countries inside the region and fifteen outside, the ADB is a major source of concessional loans to poorer countries for economic development projects in the region. Both Taiwan (Taipei, China) and China (PRC) are members, North Korea is not, and the Soviet Union has observer status. Japan and the

United States are the two major financial contributors, together controlling 30 percent of the votes on its board of governors, which selects the president and determines overall policy. Every president so far has been a Japanese financier.

The twenty-second annual meeting held in Beijing in 1989 established a number of "firsts" against the dramatic backdrop of Chinese pro-democracy students occupying Tiananmen Square. It was the first meeting to be held in a communist country, the first visit of any Taiwan delegation to the PRC, with the position of finance minister of this delegation occupied by a woman for the first time, and the first time South Korea attended the meetings as a donor rather than a recipient. It was decided at this meeting to pursue new directions, in principle, in the forthcoming decade, despite serious disagreements on how these agreed-upon changes should be implemented. The membership called for an ADB-led multilateral dialogue to boost economic policies in developing member countries, encouragement for stepped-up environmental protection, and the creation of an Asian Finance and Investment Corporation (AFIC) to act as a bridge between ADB and commercial banks to expand participation in private enterprise.[70]

Retarded Regional Institutionalization.   What is apparent from the overview of regional associations is that formal institutionalization of regional economic cooperation in the Asian Pacific lags far behind de facto economic integration as measured by trade, aid, and investment patterns. As one might expect from the extreme diversity in size, population, resource endowments, cultural-historical circumstances, ideological bent, and stages of economic development of Asian Pacific countries, all-regional associations tend to be sprawling, amorphous bodies that are open-ended, outward looking, and largely consultative in nature. Regional organizations are for the most part NGOs that offer opportunities for academics with expertise, government officials, and businesspeople from throughout the Asian Pacific to interact, pool their resources, set up data banks, and seriously explore the issues, strategies, and obstacles involved in promoting greater regional economic cooperation.

Three factors perpetuate the reluctance on the part of Asian Pacific countries to move toward more formalized governmental institutions of a regional nature. One is the heavy economic dependence of these countries on markets outside the region, particularly in the United States and the EC, to buy their exports. A second is Japan's overwhelming economic dominance and its dual identity as a developed "Western" and an Asian regional power. The third factor is the difficulty of defining membership to accommodate one colony, two Chinas, and three or more subregional and multinational entities in the process of formation.

Members of ASEAN, one of the region's most successful multinational organizations, are concerned that their newly found identity not be diluted by incorporation into a larger international organization. At the opposite end from this well-established regional organization are a number of new subregional *growth triangles*. The term, originally used to describe Singapore's plans to develop a subregional industrial park with Indonesia and Malaysia, has also been applied to the multinational development zone in northeastern Asia. The Tumen River Delta Project, where North Korea, China, and Russia converge, is a $20 billion development project initiated by China and sponsored by the United Nations Development Program. This multinational development zone has its roots in the same concept as the special economic zones (SEZs) established in the southeastern region of China. The prospect of Hong Kong returning to China has occasioned speculation that the commercially developed southeastern region of China might join Hainan and Taiwan to force the regime in Beijing to acknowledge its special characteristics. The prospect of such subregional growth areas raises the novel question of how their participation in regional associations might be handled.

Given the enormous challenges to greater regional institutionalization in the Asian Pacific, what is remarkable is the widely expressed intuitive perception that regionalism is definitely on the Asian Pacific agenda. What are the origins of this perception, and does it have any validity? In the final section of this chapter we address these questions.

TO BE OR NOT TO BE: THE QUESTION OF ASIAN PACIFIC REGIONALISM

The core and cause célèbre of regionalization in the Asian Pacific is, of course, Japan. The dynamic postwar economy of Japan, which provided both the impetus and a model for development in the region, has made Japan the principal champion of greater regional association. Until the demise of the Soviet Union, the mere suggestion that Japan favored a particular regional formation was sufficient to heighten the suspicions of her neighbors. Since then, however, it is no longer commonplace to assume that Japanese domination of the region would always be opposed by the ever watchful victims of earlier Japanese aggression. Japanese economic dominance of the region has appeared more benign, even advantageous, to other Asian Pacific countries than before, altering considerably their perceptions of a mutual common interest in regional development. By 1990 Japan's bilateral aid and foreign investments had stimulated a level of intraregional trade that surpassed that of any other region, creating a formidable economic network of regional interdependence.

But regionalization in the Asian Pacific must be understood as distinct from that in Western Europe since the 1960s. It does not occur as a result of attempting to coordinate fully developed national economies into a regionally more effective competitor in the global economy. Rather, regionalization in the Asian Pacific is itself the process by which national economies are enabled to grow and develop. As countries become incorporated into the dynamics of aid, trade, and investment not only in the region but via the region into the global economy, they generate a virtuous circle of exports-capital goods imports-capital formation-productivity improvements-exports. The outcome of this export-led strategy has been the singular development of effectively organized national economies within the NICs, ASEAN states, and China.

However, it is not exports or trade alone that accounts for this development. A second aspect of this regionally based strategy of capital formation involves the dynamic process of an evolving international product cycle. Based on the ever expanding technological capacity of Japan to produce increasingly more sophisticated goods and services that lend themselves to production in different stages and in different places, adjacent national economies are able to import not only finished products but intermediate capital goods with which to embark on a vertical ascent from less capitalized, labor-intensive production to higher value-added, more capital-intensive production. The outcome of this international product cycle is an increasing horizontal trade within the region and between countries of the region and the global economy. Instead of operating on the basis of fixed comparative advantage(s) that countries use as a basis of exchange, this development of the capitalist market elevates mass production and assembly principles to a new international division of labor. As a result, the trade relationship between Japan and its regional neighbors has gradually been transformed from an interindustry vertical type, in which primary commodities, for example, are exported and manufactured products are imported, to an intra-industry horizontal type of division of labor, in which the intermediate goods to produce sophisticated products like automobiles are imported and finished automobiles are exported. Japan serves as the source of intermediate goods and the United States as the destination of exports.

With an increasing horizontal division of labor, the development of industrialization in one country induces the upturn of industrial production in another country. Horizontal trade in the Asian Pacific through this accelerating reciprocal interrelationship has benefited the development of national economies. The sizable trade in intermediate goods, for which the developing nations of the Asian Pacific depend on Japan, plays a pivotal role not only for reciprocally inducing increased production and high growth rates but also for ensuring a closer integration among trading countries throughout the region.

Thus, the Asian Pacific may not have the conditions the European community had in its formative years—two nations of similar size and economic capacity, West Germany and France—but it does offer an alternative model of regional formations that is closely tied to its innovative, state-centered, developmental strategy. With strong states capable of seizing the regional and global opportunities for development of their national economies, the countries of the Asian Pacific are presently contributing to a momentous global transformation. Frequently referred to as a new international division of labor, this unfolding transformation constitutes a new stage in the evolution of the world economic system.

Two general but necessarily speculative conclusions may be drawn with respect to the future of regionalization in the Asian Pacific and its challenge for the world system. One is that Asian Pacific regionalism may force us to think about regionalism in a different way. What may be emerging in the Asian Pacific is a new, dynamic regional economic structure encompassing a sizable number of nation-states, cutting across the territorial boundaries equated with national sovereignty throughout the nineteenth and twentieth centuries. It would be a mistake, however, to conceive of these regional formations as made up of equal members or as closed regional blocs. They are more likely to have the internal unevenness of present-day nation-states. With a highly integrated horizontal division of labor, these regional economies will have a capacity for autonomously generating continued sources of economic growth and technological innovation far greater than the nation-state.

Regions in this sense are not mere aggregations of nation-states for defensive purposes. Gilpin suggests they be called "trading regions" rather than "economic blocs."[71] But while they are "open," even interlocked with the global economy, in contrast to the colloquial connotation of "economic blocs," these regional centers can nonetheless be in competition with one another. This is the second conclusion to be drawn about the embryonic regionalism emerging in the Asian Pacific. If it develops along lines similar to the patterns described in this chapter, it is likely to engage with other regional centers of economic power in a struggle for control of the "world product." Such an economic struggle for control of the world product among regional centers may then be presented as a competition between various forms of capitalism organized on both a regional and global scale. As a replacement of the cold war clash of ideologies, therefore, this type of economic competition among regional centers of power, far from eliminating the existing power of military forces throughout the world, may be likely to use them in support of one or another system of political economy.

These speculative suggestions have avoided discussion of the fate of nation-states and the thorny question of their sovereignty. But they attempt to account for the widespread preoccupation with regionalization in the context of existing evidence. This includes the various ways in which protectionism is set into motion by what seems to be an inexorable process of globalization and transnational integration. Industrial planning, managed markets, and colossal mergers are the order of the day. As rapidly as tariff barriers come down, nontariff barriers are erected to take their place. What the United States calls "specific targets" in its demands for parity in trade with Japan are quantitative restrictions that are the functional equivalents of tariffs and operate on a regional as well as a national basis. Important sectors of the economy of Japan, the United States, and the EC are protected in this way. Gilpin estimates that "as much as 40 percent of world trade is 'managed trade' of some kind, rather than simply subject to market forces."[72]

SUMMARY

In this chapter, we have traced the patterns of trade, investment, and aid that have increasingly tied the countries of the Asian Pacific into a subregion of the world economy. With China and Vietnam embracing market reforms and participation in the global economy, the degree of de facto economic cooperation among businesses throughout the Asian Pacific has increased dramatically. By the early 1990s Japan's bilateral aid and foreign investments had stimulated a level of intraregional trade that surpassed that of any other region, creating a formidable economic network of regional interdependence.

Among ASEAN states, those with a history of colonial subjugation to European powers—Malaysia, Singapore, and Indonesia—have diversified their trading partners *within the region,* hoping thereby to loosen the strings that bound them so implacably to a single Western power. By contrast, Thailand and the Philippines have two-thirds of their trade with extraregional powers. Yet all the countries in the region have found themselves increasingly dependent upon Japan as the regional economic superpower. Japan's economy along with the others' is dependent upon the United

States, whose hold on its hegemonic reins has weakened. The inevitable result has been a complex network of interdependence in which regional economic growth is contingent upon extraregional trade and investment. This interdependence of countries in the region upon one another and the developed countries is reflected in the growing significance of regional associations.

The question of whether or not the Asian Pacific moves in the direction of what is popularly referred to as a "yen bloc" is part of the larger question of regionalization throughout the global economic system. Though the manner in which globalization will proceed is a matter of pure conjecture, the process continues unabated, knocking the ground out from under many of our most comfortable suppositions. The challenge is to provide at least some heuristic ways of thinking about the implications of different paths that global events might take in the twenty-first century. These will be addressed in the final chapter.

QUESTIONS FOR DISCUSSION

1. How has the growth of trade, aid, and investment in the Asian Pacific promoted and/or impeded the institutionalization of regional associations?
2. What, in your view, are the opportunities and pitfalls of greater regionalization not only in the Asian Pacific but throughout the world?

NOTES

1. Michael Stohl and Harry R. Targ, *Global Political Economy in the 1980s* (Cambridge, MA: Schenkman Publishing Co., 1982), p. 15.
2. James Caporaso, "European Industrial Policy and the Evolving Global Division of Labor," in *Global Political Economy in the 1980s,* ed. Michael Stohl and Harry R. Targ (Cambridge, MA: Schenkman Publishing Co., 1982), p. 81.
3. Russell Mardon and Won K. Paik, "The State, Foreign Investment, and Sustaining Industrial Growth in South Korea and Thailand," in *The Evolving Pacific Basin in the Global Political Economy: Domestic and International Linkages,* ed. Cal Clark and Steve Chan (Boulder: Lynne Rienner, 1992), p. 150.
4. Jeffry A. Frieden and David A. Lake, *International Political Economy: Perspectives on Global Power and Wealth,* 2d ed. (New York: St. Martin's Press, 1991), p. 10; emphasis added.
5. The term *production bundle* is used by Steve Chan to refer to the variety of inputs required for industrial production, in "Catching Up and Keeping Up: Explaining Capitalist East Asia's Industrial Competitiveness," *The Journal of East Asian Affairs,* no. 5 (1991): p. 80.
6. Russell Mardon and Won K. Paik in Clark and Chan, *The Evolving Pacific Basin in the Global Political Economy,* p. 151.
7. Mark Borthwick, *Pacific Century: The Emergence of Modern Pacific Asia* (Boulder: Westview Press, 1992), p. 508.
8. Stephen D. Krasner, "Trade Conflicts and the Common Defense: The United States and Japan," in *Pacific Dynamics: The International Politics of Industrial Change,* ed. Stephan Haggard and Chung-in Moon (Boulder: CIS Inha University-Westview Press, 1989), p. 252.

9. Robert Keohane discusses the distinction between diffuse and specific reciprocity, indicating the implications of each approach, in his article "Reciprocity in International Relations," *International Organization* 40 (Winter 1986): pp. 1–27.

10. William Nester, *Japan and the Third World: Patterns, Power and Prospects* (New York: St. Martin's Press, 1992), p. 121.

11. Ibid., p. 122.

12. Bernard K. Gordon, "Japan: Searching Once Again," in *Asia Pacific in the New World Politics,* ed. James C. Hsiung (Boulder: Lynne Rienner Publishers, 1993), p. 62.

13. K. Akamatsu is credited with having applied the term to the characteristic growth pattern of the region, in "A Historical Pattern of Economic Growth in Developing Countries," *The Developing Economies,* no. 1 (March-April 1962): pp. 3–25.

14. Masahide Shibusawa, Zakaria Haji Ahmad, and Brian Bridges, *Pacific Asia in the 1990s* (London and New York for the Royal Institute of International Affairs: Routledge, 1992), p. 11.

15. Ibid., p. 12.

16. Ibid., p. 13.

17. Nester, *Japan and the Third World,* p. 103.

18. Data is from the International Monetary Fund's *Direction of Trade Statistics, Yearbook,* 1991.

19. Nester, *Japan and the Third World,* p. 134.

20. Ibid., p. 135.

21. Ibid.

22. Ibid., p. 134.

23. See IMF, *Direction of Trade Statistics, Yearbook,* 1991, p. 378.

24. Shibusawa, *Pacific Asia in the 1990s,* p. 16.

25. The quote, attributed to DeAnne Julius, *Global Companies and Public Policy: The Growing Challenge of Foreign Direct Investment* (London: Royal Institute of International Affairs/Pinter Publishers, 1990), is found in United Nations Centre on Transnational Corporations, *World Investment Report 1991: The Triad in Foreign Direct Investment,* p. 3.

26. United Nations, *World Investment Report 1991: The Triad in Foreign Direct Investment,* p. 33.

27. Ibid., pp. 46–47.

28. United Nations, *World Investment Directory 1992, vol. 1, Asia and the Pacific,* p. 18.

29. Gordon, "Japan," p. 62.

30. Shibusawa, *Pacific Asia in the 1990s,* p. 20.

31. Nester, *Japan and the Third World,* pp. 54–57.

32. Ibid., p. 65.

33. Quoted in Shibusawa, *Pacific Asia in the 1990s,* p. 20.

34. Nester, *Japan and the Third World,* pp. 65–66.

35. Quoted in Shibusawa, *Pacific Asia in the 1990s,* p. 20.

36. Nester, *Japan and the Third World,* p. 103, and Shibusawa, *Pacific Asia in the 1990s,* p. 20.

37. Nester, *Japan and the Third World,* pp. 60, 103.

38. Ibid., p. 65.

39. Richard H. Solomon, Director of the Policy Planning Staff, U.S. Department of State, "Pacific Development and the New Internationalism" (address before the Pacific Future Conference, Los Angeles, CA, March 1988), *Current Policy* No. 1060, Bureau of Public Affairs, U.S. Department of State.

40. Nester, *Japan and the Third World*, p. 103.

41. Shibusawa, *Pacific Asia in the 1990s*, p. 22.

42. The terms were used by Malaysian Prime Minister Mahathir, as quoted in Nester, *Japan and the Third World*, p. 116.

43. Gordon, "Japan: Searching Once Again," p. 199.

44. Shibusawa, *Pacific Asia in the 1990s*, p. 23.

45. Ibid., p. 24.

46. Gordon, "Japan," p. 200.

47. United Nations, *World Investment Directory 1992: Asia and the Pacific*, pp. 28-31.

48. Robert M. Orr Jr., *The Emergence of Japan's Foreign Aid Power* (New York: Columbia University Press, 1990), p. 2.

49. Orr, *The Emergence of Japan's Foreign Aid Power*, p. 3, and Yoshio Okawara, "Japan's Global Responsibilities," in *Japan's Emerging Global Role*, ed. Danny Unger and Paul Blackburn (Boulder: Lynne Rienner, 1993), p. 61.

50. Orr, *The Emergence of Japan's Foreign Aid Power*, p. 55.

51. Quoted in Orr, *The Emergence of Japan's Foreign Aid Power*, p. 78.

52. The table listing the top ten recipients of largest amounts of Japanese bilateral ODA from 1970 to 1988 is found in Orr, *The Emergence of Japan's Foreign Aid Power*, pp. 70-71.

53. Ibid., p. 73.

54. Ibid., p. 74.

55. Koppel, *Japan's Foreign Aid*, p. 136.

56. Orr, *The Emergence of Japan's Foreign Aid Power*, p. 28.

57. This section has relied on Orr's analysis of the evolution of aid policy, pp. 52-68. The quote is on p. 59.

58. Hosup Kim, "Japanese ODA Policy to the Republic of Korea," in Koppel, *Japan's Foreign Aid*, p. 226n. 38.

59. David I. Steinberg, "Japanese Economic Assistance to Burma," in Koppel, *Japan's Foreign Aid*, pp. 138, 142.

60. Ibid., p. 162n. 44.

61. Ibid., p. 156.

62. Juichi Inada, "Stick or Carrot? Japanese Aid Policy and Vietnam," in Koppel, *Japan's Foreign Aid*, p. 124.

63. Associated Press, "U.S. Firms Prepare for Vietnam," *The Sacramento Bee*, 30 August 1993, D1.

64. Inada, "Stick or Carrot?" p. 129.

65. Lawrence T. Woods, "Non-Governmental Organizations and Pacific Cooperation: Back to the Future?" *The Pacific Review* 4, no. 4 (1991): pp. 313-14.

66. Norman D. Palmer, *The New Regionalism in Asia and the Pacific* (Lexington, MA: Lexington Books, 1991), p. 142.

67. Andrew Elek, "The Challenge of Asian-Pacific Economic Cooperation," *The Pacific Review* 4, no. 4 (1991): pp. 324-27.

68. Quoted in "Clinton Targets Pacific Rim for Trade Crusade," by Karl Schoenberger and Leslie Helm, *Los Angeles Times*, 19 November 1993, A13.

69. Palmer, *The New Regionalism*, p. 72.

70. Ibid., pp. 148-51.

71. Robert Gilpin, "The Debate About the New World Economic Order," in *Japan's Emerging Global Role*, ed. Danny Unger and Paul Blackburn (Boulder: Lynne Rienner, 1993), p. 26.

72. Ibid., p. 26.

FOR FURTHER READING

Brown, Richard Harvey, and William T. Liu, eds. *Modernization in East Asia: Political, Economic, and Social Perspectives.* Westport, CT: Praeger, 1992, chapter 2.

Dixon, Chris. *South East Asia in the World-Economy.* Cambridge: Cambridge University Press, 1991, chapters 5 and 6.

Frieden, Jeffry A., and David A. Lake, eds. *International Political Economy: Perspectives on Global Power and Wealth.* 2d ed. New York: St. Martin's Press, 1991.

Haggard, Stephan, and Chung-in Moon, eds. *Pacific Dynamics: The International Politics of Industrial Change.* Inchon & Boulder: CIS-Inha University and Westview Press, 1989.

Higgott, Richard, Richard Leaver, and John Ravenhill, eds. *Pacific Economic Relations in the 1990s: Cooperation or Conflict?* Boulder: Lynne Rienner Publishers, 1993.

Hsiung, James, ed. *Asia Pacific in the New World Politics.* Boulder: Lynne Rienner Publishers, 1993.

Lee, Chong-Sik, ed. *In Search of a New Order in East Asia.* Berkeley: Institute of East Asian Studies, University of California, 1991, part 2.

Martin, Linda G., ed. *The ASEAN Success Story: Social, Economic, and Political Dimensions.* Honolulu: East-West Center, 1987.

Palmer, Norman D. *The New Regionalism in Asia and the Pacific.* Lexington, MA: Lexington Books, 1991.

Shibusawa, Masahide, Zakaria Haji Ahmad, and Brian Bridges. *Pacific Asia in the 1990s.* London and New York for the Royal Institute of International Affairs: Routledge, 1992.

Unger, Danny, and Paul Blackburn, eds. *Japan's Emerging Global Role.* Boulder: Lynne Rienner Publishers, 1993.

chapter 9

Summing Up and Looking Ahead

To appreciate the development of Asian Pacific nations, assess the "miracle" of their economic growth, and to speculate on their increasingly interdependent destiny as a regional center of global economic activity, we have attempted in this book to weave the strands of our explorations into a single piece of fabric. Cut originally from the whole cloth of human history, this fabric is necessarily reconstituted out of the odds and ends, traces and fragments of human communities sometimes stitched together, sometimes torn asunder by events far beyond their control. With varied beginnings in precolonial villages, small kingdoms, and majestic empires, Asian Pacific people have passed from local and imperial traditions, through colonial rites of passage, into their place as modern actors on the global stage of history.

Comparing the politics of the Asian Pacific has been a vast and complex endeavor. The diversity of the fifteen countries included in our delineation of the region is extraordinary. In size, resource endowment, ethnic and religious configuration, and economic and political organization their differences defy categorization and resist attempts at generalization. Geographically, these countries range from the size of a city-state (Singapore) to the size of a continent (China), from one or more islands to a vast stretch of interior landmass. The cultural variation is equally daunting, from the intricate ethnic mosaic of Southeast Asia to the dense homogeneity of civilizations in China, Japan, and Korea. Yet despite the diversity, there are common threads that bind these disparate peoples together, distinguishing their development from that of the West. How those threads have interwoven with the patterns and designs coming from the West has fashioned the material of this book.

In Chapters 2 through 8, we followed the Asian Pacific peoples' experiences with colonialism, their nationalist struggles, their efforts to survive as modern states in a capitalist-dominated world economy, their adaptation to a global political system rent by cold war conflict, and then their adjustments to the fluidity and uncertainties of the post–cold war era. This final chapter is devoted to summing up and looking ahead at the course of modernization and development in the Asian Pacific. How far have the people of these countries come since their encounter with the dynamic expansionism of a more technologically advanced West? How has their development been similar to and different from the Westerners from whom they learned the importance of becoming modern? How far do the theories of development explain what has happened in Asian Pacific countries? What problems will they confront in the twilight years of this century and the first decades of the next one? What is the future likely to hold in the evolving power relations between states in the region and between the region and the rest of the world?

In this chapter we offer partial and tentative answers to those questions for you to evaluate in the light of your own knowledge and insights. We hope that your reward for reading this far will be to discover that you have your own answers, drawing on your interpretation of what you now know about that fascinatingly complex and rapidly changing region of the world, the Asian Pacific.

THE RECORD OF POLITICAL AND ECONOMIC ACHIEVEMENTS

Survival as States

We begin with the obvious: All of the states that gained their independence still exist, with the sole exception of South Vietnam, now rejoined to the rest of Vietnam. None has reverted to colonial rule, and the two remaining colonial possessions are soon to be returned to Chinese sovereignty. None of them, despite deep cleavages among their people, has disintegrated into a number of quarreling successor states, as have Yugoslavia and the Soviet Union. Even in the case of Malaysia, its brief marriage with Singapore was annulled with a degree of civility that made subsequent cooperation between the two states possible. So the record of survival for Asian Pacific states is impressive.

Survival, like the process of liberation from colonialism, has not been without costs, many imposed by the international struggle between the superpowers and internal struggles between Communists and non- or anticommunists. The two Koreas fought a war with each other in which China joined, responding to what Beijing perceived as the beginning of an American campaign to "liberate" the mainland from the "Reds." The government on Taiwan has since 1949 felt its survival threatened by the possibility of attack from the mainland and so has built up its military strength, at first with generous American aid, now self-financed. The struggle for survival was particularly costly for the Indochinese states. All were embroiled politically and militarily in the contest between North Vietnam and Communist insurgents in South Vietnam, Cambodia, and Laos on one side and the United States and South Vietnam on the other, and all suffered heavy damage from ground and air warfare. Cambodia's independence was subsequently jeopardized by Vietnamese intervention and again by civil war, from which it began to emerge in 1993. In Malaysia and Indonesia, communist movements once posed challenges before being forcibly suppressed. Communist and ethnic rebels have waged guerrilla war against the governments in Myanmar and the Philippines for decades, but negotiations seem to be bringing about an end to their armed opposition.

Sovereignty and Independence

But survival means more than just the *appearance* of independent statehood. A major objective of Asian Pacific governments in throwing off colonialism was to assert their national sovereignty in the international arena, to control their destiny through foreign policy decisions of their own making. Of the countries allied with the United States, the Philippines was least successful in escaping from the bonds of "neocolonialism," remaining under the American shadow at least until recently, when the country's strategic significance diminished and Japan's economic stake surpassed America's. Japan, while asserting its independence in economic matters, has chosen to follow U.S. leadership in most external political affairs. Its unprecedented self-abnegation on the use of military power as an instrument of foreign policy may be interpreted as evidence either that Japan is dependent on the United States for its security or that it is better able to achieve its foreign policy goals by purely economic means. The Japanese economic stake in many countries in the region carries with it the possibility of Japanese influence over their economic policymaking, but Japan's low profile in international politics seems thus far to have kept to a minimum any effort to extract obedience in foreign policy as the price for economic support.

South Korea's military dependence on the United States circumscribes its latitude for independence in external political affairs. American leverage over Taiwan since the termination of the alliance is difficult to judge; Taiwan's ability to *buy* expensive American military hardware and the American need to *sell* the excess output of the weapons industry may tip the balance of influence more to the island's favor. Although deprived of legal recognition as a sovereign state by the international community and thus of formal membership in most international intergovernmental organizations, the Republic of China government's de facto control of Taiwan is indisputable, however vulnerable it may be to takeover by the PRC. Thailand, another ally of the United States once quite dependent on American military aid and a staunch supporter of American policy in Indochina, has distanced itself from Washington. It has diversified its weapons suppliers, moved toward accommodation with China and Myanmar, and reasserted its traditional influence in Laos and Cambodia.

The sovereignty and independence of those two states appear quite precarious. Laos's vulnerability stems from Vientiane's loose grip over the hinterland and the government's eager receptivity to almost any form of external help, whatever the source or terms, for the country's stagnant and backward economy. Cambodia's future depends on the ability of the two-headed coalition government formed in 1993 to wean itself from financial dependence on international aid, to gain control of areas still under the Khmer Rouge, and to put an end to Thai collaboration with the KR in the timber and gem trade. Both states' prospects gain at least in the short run from Vietnam's abandonment of its aspirations to reassert the dominant role Vietnamese played in the rest of Indochina under French colonialism. Hanoi's effort to establish its credentials as "good neighbor" to China and ASEAN, its military power, large population, and attractiveness to foreign investors all seem favorable to protecting Vietnam's sovereignty and independence.

Nonalignment and isolation bought Myanmar independence from outside control of its foreign policy, but limited the range of actions it could take. Brunei, Malaysia, and Singapore have managed to remain officially nonaligned while retaining a degree of security dependence on their former colonial overlord, Great Britain, supported by the United States, Australia, and New Zealand. In contrast, Indonesia's rupture with the Netherlands was quite abrupt, and its political, economic, and military ties to other Western powers, particularly the United States since Sukarno's departure, have been on more equal terms of reciprocal influence.

Of all the countries, China—particularly after the break with the Soviet Union—seems to have most effectively pursued an independent course in its foreign relations. Even the opening to foreign business interests does not seem to have impaired significantly its determination to defy other governments' actions that appear to the Chinese as insults to their national sovereignty and prestige. North Korea, having kept a substantial margin of freedom from domination by either of its neighboring communist patrons by maneuvering between them, as of this writing has resisted external pressures to change its course on nuclear site inspection. However intransigent and even irrational Pyongyang's behavior may appear to outsiders, the North's policies do seem to demonstrate its independence of foreign domination.

National Unity

The degree of success attained by Asian Pacific states in "nation building," in creating or tightening the bonds of national unity, depends in large part on the extent of ethnic, regional, religious, and political diversity in each country when it achieved independence. Colonialism brought the gospel of nationalism everywhere in the region, catching on faster and winning more converts in some places than others. Sometimes the spread of modern nationalism reinforced bonds of solidarity already felt by the people, as in the case of countries with long histories of separate political identity (such as Japan, China, and Korea), national unity being equally fervently espoused by both Communists and anticommunists in China and Korea. In Indonesia and the Philippines, the potential for nation building was enhanced by colonial rule, which gave the people of those islands their first experience of union. However, the emergence of some form of pan-Malay nationalism uniting the people of Malay stock inhabiting what are now Malaysia, Indonesia, and the Philippines was foreclosed by their separate administration as colonies of three different Western powers.

Borders drawn around Laos and Burma by the colonial powers and the migration of foreign laborers into British Malaya meant that at independence the governments of Malaysia, Singapore, Burma, and Laos inherited ethnically diverse populations lacking a sense of common identity. In Malaysia, the Chinese and Indian minorities have accepted the government's policy of discrimination in favor of the Malay majority as the price they must pay for being left in relative peace to pursue economic activities. Singapore seems to have worked out an accommodation between the Chinese majority and the minority Malay and Indian citizens and claims to be aiming at greater psychological unity in the form of a Singaporean identity. Thus far, however, in both

Singapore and Malaysia successful *state* building has not yet been matched by successful *nation* building. In Burma, divisions between the Burman majority and a daunting array of non-Burman groups, some in almost continuous rebellion against the central government, have made state building difficult and nation building impossible. By 1993 SLORC seemed to have negotiated an ad hoc form of shared sovereignty with all of the insurgents except the Karens, a compromise that falls far short of the goal of national unity. Similarly fractionated between Lao-speakers and non-Lao mountain people, Laos's identity as a nation after independence was further stalled by ideological divisions, and the abolition of the monarchy after the Communists consolidated power removed it as a possible symbol around which some semblance of national unity might be forged.

The monarchies in Thailand and Cambodia, on the other hand, have retained their potency as symbols of national unity and even preserved some of the political influence they once enjoyed in the era of unlimited royal power. The Thai king's contribution to national unity and stability was demonstrated in 1992, when he intervened after a bloody confrontation between rival political groups and insisted that peace be restored. Norodom Sihanouk, having survived four decades of assaults on the integrity and independence of Cambodia, returned to the throne in 1993, still the (perhaps the *only*) symbol of national unity for the Khmer people. Ahead are the problems of overcoming political divisions within the Khmer majority and incorporating (or evicting) the Vietnamese minority.

Some governments still face challenges from minority groups demanding autonomy or independence, such as China's Tibetan population, the Karens in Myanmar, Moslems in the Philippines and Thailand, and Acehnese, Timorese, and Irianese in Indonesia. Brunei's sultanate has thus far escaped serious challenge from the large non-Malay minority, although it would be difficult to claim that all the residents of that ministate share a sense of Bruneian national identity or that the sultan's government wants them to.

Although the Chinese and Korean nations are still divided, the general picture of Asian Pacific states is that they are reasonably in control of centrifugal forces and unlikely to disintegrate. Varying degrees of coercion underlie the extent of stability and cohesiveness their leaders have achieved since independence.

Political Leadership

Some form of authoritarianism has typically been chosen by postcolonial leaders as the means either to bring about political, social, and economic revolution or to make more modest economic and social progress or to defend the status quo against internal or external threat. In a few countries, such as South Korea, Taiwan, Thailand, and the Philippines, authoritarian rule seems to be in the process of self-transformation toward a more consensual, less coercive system. In others, such as China and Myanmar, the leadership has responded to challenges from critics and opponents by tightening, rather than loosening, political controls.

There has been a surprising continuity in leadership in the period since independence for most of the Asian Pacific governments. Communist Parties have held the reins of power in China since 1949, in North Korea since 1948, in North Vietnam since

1945, and in all of Vietnam since 1975. Noncommunist one-party rule has prevailed in Singapore and Malaysia since independence, in Taiwan since 1945, in Japan until 1993, while in Brunei the sultan has reigned supreme since the end of the British protectorate. The military has been in power in Myanmar since 1962, in Indonesia since 1965, and in Thailand from 1932 to 1992. The four remaining states—Laos, the Philippines, South Korea, and Cambodia—have experienced more discontinuity in leadership than the others. Laos, after years of shifting coalitions among a trio of princes, has been led since 1975 by the Communist Party. The Philippines have gone from a competitive two-party civilian system to Marcos's dictatorship with major military participation to the post-Marcos multiparty civilian government with the military still politically significant. South Korea's political history since 1948 has seen civilian rule overthrown by the military, who dominated the government until the end of 1992. Cambodia has had the most checkered history of all, going from limited monarchy to military dictatorship to Khmer Rouge Communists under Pol Pot to more moderate Communists to limited monarchy again under a coalition government of Communists and noncommunists.

Whether the continuity in leadership that characterizes most of the Asian Pacific countries will survive the passing of aging leaders, and whether the power holders will deal successfully with pressures for political change are problems that will be discussed below. But the continuity experienced thus far has brought the benefit of political stability (with some exceptions, like the upheavals of the Great Leap Forward and the Cultural Revolution and the periodic outbursts against military rule in Thailand and Myanmar). In the case of Japan, the NICs, the NECs, and now China, continuity of leadership and stability are thought to have contributed to their progress in economic development. Burma's economic stagnation, and North Korea's of late, suggest that the connection among continuity in leadership, political stability, and economic development is not a simple one.

Economic Progress

It is in economic development that Asian Pacific countries have excelled, redirecting world attention to the idea that manufacturing exports for a global economy provides an effective means for accomplishing sustained and rapid economic growth, even for countries with few natural resources starting out in a world dominated by rich and powerful developed nations. Although the region as a whole has astounded the world with its economic growth rates, the record of accomplishment is—as we have seen—mixed. Some countries have been gloriously successful, most have made considerable progress, substantially raising the standard of living of many (though not all) of their people, while a few are still no better off than they were at the time of independence.

While the market appears to have triumphed, even in the self-styled socialist countries, as the most effective mechanism for generating and distributing wealth, the process of development in the Asian Pacific region, as in other parts of the world, has costs as well as benefits. The physical quality of life, improved in some respects, has also been adversely affected by runaway urbanization, unsafe working conditions, profligate consumption of forests and other natural resources, and environmental degradation on a scale equaling or surpassing that in the West. A 1993 report by the UN Economic and Social Commission for Asia and the Pacific pointed out that rapid economic growth has caused air and water pollution of crisis proportions and contributed to the large, ever increasing numbers of urban poor living in slums, even in high-income countries such as South Korea. In many countries the income gap between the newly affluent and the rest of the population has widened, and the focus on industrial development leaves the rural population behind. In recent years the economies in Japan and South Korea in particular have demonstrated that even those cases of "miracle" growth are subject to the boom-and-bust cycle well known in Western economic history.

A Distinctive Pattern of Development

The costs notwithstanding, an impressive record of achievements followed the adoption of an export-led strategy lending support to the idea that a distinctive national-regional pattern of development has taken shape in the Asian Pacific. The roots of this strategy go back to Western colonial incorporation of the entire region into the imperialist world system. Under the impact of Western and Japanese imperialism, people in the Asian Pacific were introduced to the idea of the modern nation-state, to the global economy, and to the regional implications of economic integration as mutually compatible, perhaps even complementary, developments. When Asian nationalists pursued independence, therefore, they were keenly aware that the objective of national development facing them after liberation had to be undertaken within the larger context of the global economy.

In the aftermath of Japan's defeat, the United States became the economic center of power in a world ideologically divided into two armed camps. Although nationalism had not abated and strong states in the Asian Pacific retained their decisive role in guiding domestic economic development (with notable exceptions), they now pursued development on one or the other side of the political and military fence. Exempt from playing an independent political and military role in the world, Japan rapidly reemerged as a powerful engine of regional economic growth within an expanding global network of markets. While China, North Korea, and Vietnam, along with Laos and Cambodia, became embroiled in war against the United States, domestic political turmoil, and socialist economic planning (described in Chapters 4 through 7), the economies of Japan, South Korea, Taiwan, Hong Kong, and the ASEAN nations were beneficiaries of the boom in the capitalist world economy.

The political and economic relationships built up in the Asian Pacific during this era laid the foundation for the distinctive national-regional pattern of economic growth and expansion, described in Chapter 8 and variously alluded to as "the flying geese formation," the East Asian developmental model, or Confucian capitalist model of development. But the international context providing the incubator for this developmental pattern (described in Chapter 7) has now ceased to exist. Viewed against the backdrop of this shifting international context, how well do the four theoretical approaches covered throughout the book explain the nature of development in the Asian Pacific?

HOW WELL DO THE THEORIES EXPLAIN DEVELOPMENT?

One conclusion about the theories of development seems inescapable: The road to economic progress mapped out by the modernization theorists was not the one taken by Japan and the newly industrializing nations of the Asian Pacific, nor has incorporation in the global capitalist economy been the roadblock to development that dependency theorists predicted it would be. Contrary to modernization theory's assumption, Asian Pacific countries did not follow the incremental course presumed to have characterized Western nations. Rather then emulating the self-reliant, market-driven Western way of modernizing, Asian Pacific countries relied heavily on the world economy, their own interventionist states, and important elements of their traditional cultures to promote rapid sustained economic growth. On the other hand, despite dependency theorists' grim expectations that less developed nations would be prevented from improving their prospects, some developing countries, by adopting export-led strategies, have in fact been able to propel themselves into the middle rank of newly industrializing countries. What, then, of the other theories?

World System Theory

Existing evidence on the whole seems to corroborate the three-tiered hierarchy of core, semi-periphery, and periphery that world system theorists use to understand nation-states' development as parts of a single expanding world capitalist system. [1] Two additional elements of world system theory appear substantiated by the evidence. One is that countries do in fact move up and down the ladder of successful development, not as a simple consequence of their own domestic efforts, but as a complex response to a dynamically changing set of global opportunities. The second is that this upward and downward mobility is confined to a relatively small number of countries; worldwide, the larger number of peripheral countries remain at the bottom and the smaller number of core countries retain their advantageous positions at the top of the wealth and development hierarchy.

The central question, not only for theory but for the policymaking of state officials, therefore, is: What explains the successful upward mobility of Asian Pacific countries? The developmental state approach contributes significantly to answering this question.

The Developmental State Approach

This approach draws attention to the ways in which an effective, developmentally oriented state can facilitate a virtuous circle between the market decisions of domestic entrepreneurs and the global opportunities for economic expansion and upgrading. When a state has sufficient autonomy from partisan domestic interests to exercise national leadership closely attuned to the growth of a global economy, it can promote the country's rapid and sustained development and upward mobility in the international status hierarchy. The developmental state approach thus turns out to be a strategy for successful industrialization that places a premium on the political autonomy and economic leadership of the state. As a theoretical explanation of development, the statist approach rests on the opposite assumption from both modernization and world system theories: that economic power cannot exist outside the framework of politics provided by a state. What the theory proposes (and the Asian Pacific experience seems to support) is that the power of politics is autonomous and preeminent, the necessary precondition for harnessing and managing economic power organized on the basis of the market.

Critics of the developmental state theory, especially those who have studied Latin America, argue that *which* pattern of development a weak developing state chooses when it embarks on modernization may depend on the particular model provided by a neighboring core country. Fernando Fajnzylber[2] suggests that a reason for the success of East Asian NICs may be that they took Japan as their model and followed its emphasis on strategic, long-term industrialization, high savings rates, international competitiveness, education as a national priority to compensate for the dearth of natural resources, the "conquest" of external markets, and social integration as a legitimating device for ruling elites. Latin American countries, by contrast, followed the U.S. pattern of development based on a tactical, short-term orientation toward industrialization geared primarily toward the domestic rather than the international market, high levels of consumption rather than savings, reliance on natural resources in international trade, and a social order structured and legitimized largely by market forces, with the state playing a far less innovative and critical role in planning and financing development than in the Japanese model. "These models represent not only the ideological hegemony of the U.S. and Japan in propagating developmental paradigms but also the concrete historical impact of their colonial and neocolonial legacies in shaping the production, consumption. and distribution patterns in their respective follower nations."[3]

Cultural Theory

Criticism of the developmental state theory also comes from adherents of the cultural theory of development. From the vantage point of cultural theorists, alternative types or models of development are shaped by the varying cultural environments of people. People's cultural beliefs and values set limits on and shape both their pattern of development and the kind of state that carries it out. Thus whether a strong or a weak state is employed as a framework for development is itself an outcome of a people's culture; different cultures produce different styles of modernization. Cultural theorists argue that cultural attributes like the relatively high social prestige of bureaucrats, the importance of education, frugality, deferred gratification, reciprocal social obligations, and an appreciation of the authority of the state promote development while others, like conspicuous consumption and unrestrained competition among self-interested individuals, do more to obstruct development. It is the Confucian-based culture of East Asian states that, for cultural theorists, accounts for their success in moving up the international ladder of economic achievement.

Although no one disputes the significance of culture as one of many variables explaining the success or failure of particular developmental states, advancing the nebulous concept of culture as the sole causal factor to explain differences in developmental patterns invariably results in contradictory arguments. Thus Confucianism has been used to explain both why China did not industrialize and why Taiwan and Hong Kong did. There is, in addition, the fact that a significant number of non-Confucian countries, Southeast Asian nations among them, have been able to adopt the pattern of development first exhibited by East Asian countries, which argues that culture may not be as essential a component for successful development as emulation of a regional patron-state and integration into the regional and global division of labor.

The cultural theory may nonetheless have explanatory value for the transnational economic role Chinese have played in fueling growth not only in Taiwan, Hong Kong, and Singapore but in the other countries of the Asian Pacific to which they have migrated for centuries. The contribution of "overseas Chinese" as a transnational economic force in the development of the region cannot be overestimated. They have energetically promoted business and trade in the development of nation-states throughout Southeast Asia and they continue to form an "invisible" regional network of economic activity linking development cross-nationally.

Having celebrated the impressive political and economic accomplishments of Asian Pacific countries and assessed the different theories' power to explain their development, we are ready finally to turn our attention to the future, to the hazards and opportunities facing them in the last years of the twentieth century and the early years of the twenty-first. In the next section, the focus is on prospects for political change and in the concluding section on the region's place in the global economic and political system.

PROSPECTS FOR POLITICAL CHANGE: SUCCESSION AND HUMAN RIGHTS

Change is inevitable in human institutions as it is in the lives of individuals. Sometimes change occurs almost imperceptibly, at a glacial pace; at other times, like our own, the speed of change is dizzying. This is especially true for the people of the Asian Pacific, many of whom, in the span of a generation or two, have been swept from the familiar moorings of traditional society to the excitement, uncertainty, and opportunities generated by rapid modernization. The political figures who have provided the leadership for development face the reality of their own mortality, and the political organizations through which they have exercised control over the masses face growing pressures generated by the very economic and social transformations they themselves have brought about.

The Problems of Succession

What will happen in China when Deng "goes to meet Marx," in Indonesia when Suharto dies or retires, in Cambodia when Sihanouk succumbs, in North Korea now that Kim Il Sing has departed? Are the military back in the barracks for good in South Korea, Thailand, Indonesia, and the Philippines, and will SLORC follow them in accepting civilian supremacy? Will UMNO in Malaysia, PAP in Singapore, the DLP in

South Korea, the Guomindang in Taiwan continue to win out in elections over opposition parties, or will they be ousted as was the LDP in Japan in 1993? In China, Vietnam, Laos, and North Korea, will the Communist Parties hold on to their monopoly of power, or will they be so divided by internal conflict or undermined by the effects of economic liberalization that they suffer the fate of Communist Parties in the Soviet Union and Eastern Europe? Is the Sultan's throne secure in Brunei? What will 1997 mean for the fledgling political parties in Hong Kong?

Questions of succession in political leadership are the subject of lively interest and speculation everywhere, but especially in countries where procedures for orderly and peaceful transfer of power from one set of leaders to another are not well established or widely accepted as legitimate. Political succession is often difficult in cases of highly personalized rule by a "supreme leader" or where one group has monopolized power for a long time. Attempting to anticipate the outcome is admittedly risky and the predictions even of so-called "experts" are frequently wrong. Mindful of the limitations of forecasting, we nevertheless offer our analysis of what the future is likely to hold.

First, those countries with aged leaders—China, Indonesia, Cambodia—and North Korea, where one has recently died. In both of the communist countries, political heirs have been designated. Deng Xiaoping's is Jiang Zemin, who already holds top government and party positions, as well as Deng's former post as chair of the military commission, and Kim Jong Il has succeeded his father. Members of each party's Politburo make the decision, probably choosing the expected successor quickly to assure the appearance of a smooth transition. That will be followed by a period of behind-the-scenes struggles as the new leader seeks to consolidate his control over the party, government, and military. Both policy and personality will enter in.

China.   Deng's legacy of economic reform is presumed to be irreversible, but serious differences exist within the party over the speed of growth. On one side are the Dengist "the-faster-the-better" proponents and on the other the "slower growth" advocates associated with Premier Li Peng and Vice Premier Zhu, whose concern is to keep or restore central regulation of growth through control of banking, credit, and currency. At heart is disagreement over how much central control is essential to meet the two objectives of raising the standard of living and keeping social order under the leadership of the Communist Party.

Out in the country, fast-growth policies have their enthusiastic supporters among provincial and local officials, banks, and enterprises, especially in the coastal areas, which have benefited most from the relaxation of central control to launch land-development projects, expand industrial production, and make money. The military also have a stake in economic growth, both as recipients of a share of the government budget and as managers of profit-making enterprises from which they earn additional income. But the risk that fast-growth policies may lead to loss of control and a descent into anarchy is also of concern to the military, having been called on in the past to restore order when party-government authority broke down as it did during the Cultural Revolution.

If external conditions in the world market and relations with principal trading partners are favorable to sustained growth, the "fast track" group coalesced around Jiang Zemin is likely to consolidate power simply on the principle that "nothing succeeds like success." If the economy falters, if inflation and corruption get out of control and work widespread hardship, then to Li (if his health holds out), Zhu, and the more "conservative" elements in the party will fall the difficult job of pushing austerity measures on the country.

North Korea.   The younger Kim's chances of consolidating his own power over the Korean Workers' Party, the state apparatus, and the military are quite difficult to assess, in part because little is known about whatever factional disagreements exist between conservatives and reformists in the KWP and in part because of the precarious domestic economic and international situation. As the old anti-Japanese partisan cronies of the elder Kim are replaced in the top party posts by younger people, that presumed base of support for Kim Jong Il erodes. Prior to his father's death, the son occupied key positions related to the military and is likely to have their support initially, though if he fails to revive the economy and maintain political stability, the military may turn elsewhere. Some form of "collective leadership" by Kim with either conservatives or reformists is possible, but whether he as the son of the old-style leader would survive for long in a reformist collectivity is doubtful.

Indonesia.   Elderly, but apparently in good health, Indonesia's President Suharto may decide to serve another term when his present one ends. Even so, who will—sooner or later—succeed him is already under discussion. The military, key political players since before independence, will have to approve of the candidate, whether he is one of them or not; their uneasiness over the selection in 1993 of a civilian as chairman of the ruling political organization, Golkar, suggests that a nonmilitary person might have difficulty overcoming their opposition. Particularly suspect in their eyes is Suharto's close adviser, Minister of Research and Technology B. J. Habibie, an enthusiastic advocate of high-tech projects and head of an association of Islamic intellectuals. A civilian president might be more appealing internationally because the army is associated with repression of human rights, especially in East Timor. However, lacking a tradition for choosing a successor and making a peaceful transition in leadership, the process in Indonesia is likely to be prolonged and difficult.

Cambodia.   What happens in Cambodia when Sihanouk dies depends on whether the hybrid government created in 1993 survives and establishes its legitimacy and effective control over the whole country. The chances of that happening are not brilliant. If it does not, then Prince (now Prime Minister) Ranariddh's succession to the throne as Sihanouk's eldest son would alone not be enough to hold the country together. If the government should succeed in solidifying its control before Sihanouk dies, then who becomes king will be less important; there might even be no need to continue the monarchy at all, especially since none of his children seems to have inherited Sihanouk's charismatic appeal to the Cambodian people.

Though with less dramatic attraction than cases where a well-known leader's departure is anticipated, the future of the ruling parties in states where one group has monopolized political leadership for decades is also a subject of interest. In noncommunist one-party dominant systems, such as Malaysia, Singapore, Taiwan, and South

Norodom Sihanouk returned to the throne of Cambodia in 1993. It will be difficult to find a successor to the king who, for half a century, has been the symbol of national unity for his people.

Source: United Nations photo 178131/J. Su Doc. 0059p.

Korea, the ruling party might be deposed, as was Japan's LDP in 1993. Each case has its own particular features, but all share the risk that complacency, corruption, internal squabbling, loss of vision, and loss of touch with their constituents may undermine their capacity to rule effectively. Further, economic progress has had the effect of strengthening, diversifying, and multiplying a variety of interest groups that make demands on government to respond to their particular aims. Success in accommodating those interests within the ruling party is crucial to its continuing in power, for which the political assets of incumbency give it an advantage.

Malaysia and Singapore.   The dominant parties in both countries seem to be in solid positions. The minority populations lack the sheer numbers to oust them at the polls and opposition parties so far have not succeeded in breaking out of their separate ethnic bases and forming broad cross-ethnic coalitions to challenge either the

National Front in Malaysia or PAP in Singapore. There are generational, regional, secular-Islamic fissures within UMNO, but there is nowhere else for disaffected partisans to go if they hope to have a share in exercising political power. UMNO can always raise the specter that turning it out of office risks a return to intercommunal violence. A similar situation prevails in Singapore, where people who object to the government's paternalism and curbs on freedom can emigrate. In both countries, government controls on the media and restrictions on political organizations inhibit the growth of opposition movements capable of mounting a serious challenge to the dominant party. Unless the economic situation deteriorates and the expanding pie of wealth that now keeps most people content stops growing, UMNO and PAP should be able to adapt to social and economic changes without losing their political grip. But if the goose that lays the golden eggs stops producing, it may find itself stewing in the pot of class or communal conflict.

Taiwan.   The Guomindang has survived the passing of the Chiang dynasty, the transition from mainlander domination to power sharing with the islanders, and the legalization of opposition parties. In the 1993 local government elections, its majority fell below 50 percent for the first time, but it kept control of a majority of the positions against the challengers, the Democratic Progressive Party and the Guomindang-breakaway Chinese New Party. The DPP's chances of ousting the Guomindang are curbed by voter uncertainty about the possible consequences of its avowed objective of declaring Taiwanese independence. As long as the Guomindang can keep enough of the voters convinced that its policy of caution in dealings with the mainland is better than a precipitous declaration of independence, it should be able to stay in power.

South Korea.   The Democratic Liberal Party is, of course, a recent creation resulting from the merger of the ruling Democratic Justice Party and the former opposition party headed by Kim Young Sam. Since he became president in 1993, Kim has launched efforts to strengthen civilian control over the military, to fight campaign finance corruption, to spur economic recovery, and to deal with the uncertainties of North-South relations. It is too early to judge either his presidency or the durability of the DLP merger, but with the opposition in eclipse at present, unless the DLP splits apart, its dominance in the near future seems reasonably secure.

Japan.   Here the questions are whether the latest LDP-SDPJ coalition will last, or the eight-party coalition that displaced the LDP in 1993 will regroup and return to power, or whether the LDP will regain its earlier position as the dominant political force. Additional questions are whether the powerful financial bureaucracy will acquiesce in the new government's stated policy of reducing government supervision of the economy, and where the Keidanren will put its money, now that it has said it will stop bankrolling LDP candidates. Like Mark Twain's death, reports of the LDP's demise have proven premature. It is entirely possible that a renovated, more unified party, less corrupted by the scramble for individual campaign chests will emerge, attract back some of its former members whose defection brought about its fall in 1993, enabling it to drop the 1994 alliance with the socialists and return to power on its own.

The One-Party Communist States.   While there is evidence of discontent and opposition from religious, ethnic, and political interests, the dominant position of the ruling parties in these countries seems unchallengeable for the present. (The sudden collapse of Communist Parties in Eastern Europe, however, counsels caution on such an assertion.) Despite social changes occurring as a result of economic reforms in China, Vietnam, and Laos, and differences of opinion within the parties in China and Vietnam about the pace of economic liberalization and even hints of contention over the need for political reforms in the future, none of those parties seems headed for a breakup into contending parties. As long as they resist centrifugal forces, there is little or no chance for noncommunist opposition parties to organize in the face of government surveillance through police and military and control of the media. In the absence of any alternative to it, the Communist Party, particularly in China, can play on the fear of descent into chaos and anarchy in appealing for public support for its continued leadership.

Finally, the Military.   Even in governments now headed by civilians, such as Thailand and the Philippines, the military are not going to drop out of politics or let themselves be pushed aside in the drive for economic development. Post-cold war uncertainties have heightened interest in national security issues and increased military expenditures in a number of countries, and these developments enhance rather than diminish the political influence of the military. In Myanmar, the junta's latest effort to create a civilian front organization along the lines of Indonesia's Golkar may be no more successful in attracting public support than was the National Unity Party in 1990. But the opposition party, the League for Democracy, seems to have been crushed as an organization inside the country by the generals who continue to evoke preservation of national unity as their ultimate justification for staying in power.

In all of these countries the forces of change brought about by economic development are at work and are certain to have political effects. Tensions are inevitable between technocrats and ideologues, between bureaucrats and politicians, between central and local governments, between regions, between city and countryside, between industry and farmers, between business and environmentalists. Old leadership is being challenged to change from inside and outside, and human rights is one of the most controversial of those challenges.

Prospects for Expanding Human Rights

In approaching this subject, we need to acknowledge the human propensity to assume that *our* way of doing things is the right, the *only,* way to do things and that others' persistence in doing things *their* way is perverse error from which they should be rescued by persuasion or even coercion. This propensity is particularly manifest where such emotionally charged issues as individual rights and democracy are concerned. Americans more than other Westerners seem to exhibit a special zeal for the mission of converting the rest of the world to their vision of those ideals.

Although governments everywhere endorse the principles of democracy and human rights, they do not agree on precisely what are the essential features of democracy, on which are the rights that ought to be protected, and even on whether any universally applicable standards are possible. Some argue that the Western emphasis on individual civil and political rights (such as freedom of expression, the right to vote, to equal protection of the laws) neglects economic and social rights (such as the right to a decent living standard, to a job, education, health care) and the rights of *groups* of people to keep their cultural identity, language, autonomy. Even when it is agreed that all of those rights are important, disagreement arises over which ones should be given priority, if they all cannot be promoted simultaneously.

In the Asian Pacific as elsewhere, that lack of consensus is a cause of controversy in both international and domestic politics, pitting governments, political parties, non-governmental organizations, and individual citizens against each other in a struggle to have their own versions of democracy and rights prevail. Asian Pacific governments rarely criticize each others' practices, but that restraint is exercised selectively by Western governments. Their criticisms are most often directed against China, Indonesia, North Korea, Vietnam, and Myanmar, and the U.S. administration wants to link continuation of trade advantages for the first two countries to improvements in their human rights record. The most outspoken responses to Western critics have come from China, Singapore, Malaysia, Indonesia, and Myanmar. The differences center on three issues: cultural distinctiveness versus universality; economic development first versus full rights to political participation along with development; and respect for national sovereignty over internal affairs versus the right of governments to set conditions for amicable relations.

Universality versus Cultural Distinctiveness.   To the Western argument in favor of the principle of universality, that human rights standards are or should be the same everywhere, Asians counter with the cultural distinctiveness argument, that Asian cultures and political traditions are different from the West's, so Asian concepts of rights and democracy are necessarily different too. As Kishore Mahbubani, deputy secretary in the Singapore Foreign Ministry, says:

> There is no unified Asian view on human rights and freedom of the press. These are Western concepts. Asians are obliged to react to them. Predictably, there is a whole range of reactions from total acceptance to total rejection. The truth is that in most Asian societies there is little awareness, let alone understanding, of these concepts. The vast and populous continent of Asia, preoccupied with more immediate challenges, has not had the time or energy to address these issues squarely.[4]

Even so, he continues:

> both Asians and Westerners . . . can agree on minimal standards of civilised behavior that both would like to live under. For example, there should be no torture, no slavery, no arbitrary killings, no disappearances in the middle of the night, no shooting down of innocent demonstrators, no imprisonment without careful review. These rights should be upheld not only for moral reasons; there are sound functional reasons. Any society which is at odds with

its people and shoots them down when they demonstrate peacefully, as Burmese did, is headed for trouble. [5]

Development before Rights. Some Asians reject the argument that the exercise of democratic rights to political participation and expression is a prerequisite for economic development, saying instead that development must take place first because exercise of individual rights is meaningless until people enjoy basic material well-being. Rapid economic progress requires stability and allowing dissenters to sabotage that effort is impermissible. For example, President Jiang Zemin, when asked about China since Tiananmen, responded:

> China has enjoyed political stability, and economic development and living standards of the people have greatly improved. . . . China is constantly strengthening its democracy and legal system. It is not an easy job. Managing a country . . . to ensure food and clothing to China's 1.2 billion people is a contribution in itself [to world peace and stability].[6]

Implicit here is that when there is a choice between political freedom and material progress, most people will choose the latter; further, by meeting their expectations for improvement in their lives, government is in fact being responsive to the people it governs. An American journalist with years of experience in China comments:

> From afar, it sometimes seems as if the fundamental dynamic in China is brutal repression of dissent. In reality, political dissent plays an inconsequential role in most people's lives, particularly in the countryside [where three-quarters of China's people live]. . . . Most Chinese say that if the Communist Party were suddenly to announce free elections, it could count on the votes of the peasants to win overwhelmingly.[7]

Criticism Infringes Sovereignty. Finally, the principle of sovereignty is used against Western governments' criticisms of Asian governments' human rights records and in particular against efforts to make trade and aid conditional on changes laid down by the trade partner or aid donor. At the 1993 APEC meeting in Seattle, President Jiang reminded President Clinton that governments should show respect for each other and not meddle in each other's internal affairs. Prime Minister Mahathir of Malaysia has charged that the West uses human rights to reimpose dominance over other countries; "This is what the West wants—not democracy, not free trade and not human rights."[8] The writer of a letter to the editor of the *Far Eastern Economic Review* concurs in that assessment of Western motives: "it seems that free trade and human rights have replaced colonisation and Christianity as the new banners under which Western nations can continue to dominate the world."[9]

A parting shot from Singapore against Western hypocrisy in criticizing others while ignoring conditions in their own countries:

> In the face of growing evidence of social, economic and occasionally moral deterioration of the fabric of many Western societies, it would be increas-

ingly difficult for a Westerner to convince Asians that the West has found universally valid prescriptions for social order and justice . . . the West should stop lecturing Asians.[10]

Conventional wisdom has it that greater affluence brings more widespread expectation of and pressure for participation in politics. In the cases of South Korea, Taiwan, and Thailand, this seems to have occurred and, if generalized to other countries, augurs well for the advancement of political and civil rights. But prosperity does not always follow an upward curve, and unless protection of rights becomes firmly entrenched in the political culture and effectively defended in political and legal institutions, their durability in times of economic adversity is uncertain. In a fundamental sense, citizenship requires constant vigilance to keep the governors responsive to the needs and wishes of the governed. In actuality, in the West as well as Asia, this responsibility falls most of the time on a few, those who are politically active in parties and other organizations. In some Asian Pacific countries, national NGOs have formed to monitor and advocate for human rights. If they can escape being seen as tools of foreigners trying to embarrass or subvert their governments, those NGOs have potential for promoting and protecting rights.

Outside pressures, on the other hand, particularly public government-to-government "shaming" exercises, are likely to be counterproductive. No government wants to appear to be caving in to foreign demands, and "face-saving" is important, in the West as well as in Asia. In our view, the prospects for improvements in economic and social rights for most of the people are good and for some, more opportunity to exercise political and civil rights is opening up, fitful and painful though progress may be.

THE NEW GLOBAL ORDER AND PROSPECTS FOR THE REGION

The convergence of an economically vibrant Asian Pacific, the end of the cold war, the political dissolution of the Soviet Union and states in Eastern Europe, and a diminution in the economic base of U.S. power have set into motion a new international configuration of wealth and power. Although the United States remains the solitary hegemon of world order, it is principally on the basis of its political influence and military might. The dynamism for global economic growth no longer emanates from any one country or region, a situation that has led scholars to use "multipolarity" as a descriptive label for the emerging world order. Chapter 8 analyzed the distinctive regional growth pattern that evolved by using export earnings to import capital, intermediate goods, and technologies. The resulting intra-industry horizontal trade within the region has strengthened the international competitiveness of manufactured exports among an expanding number of countries in the region. By providing the capital goods and capital-intensive intermediate goods to its neighbors, Japan has induced industrialization among its trading partners and in the process has stimulated a transformation of trade relationships from the interindustry vertical type to an intra-industry horizontal type of division of labor.

The success of this regional development pattern has had a dramatic effect on international relations, changing not only the priorities from military to economic competition but potentially also the numbers and kinds of international actors as well as the nature of their interaction in pursuing cooperation and competition in the global economic arena. First we focus on some problems and dilemmas posed for international political economy by this global transformation from a cold war international regime to one that will eventually reflect the emergent new international division of labor. Three interrelated problems will be addressed. One is the "Japanese problem," stemming from the perception that the Japanese have unfair trade advantages; the second is the dilemma of resorting to a strategy of aggressive unilateralism; and the third is the dilemma posed by globalization. In the final section, we discuss the impact of the new global landscape on the prospects for the Asian Pacific. Here we will concentrate on the political possibilities of alliances among Asian Pacific countries as they attempt to pursue two contradictory objectives: increasing market shares to sustain the international competitiveness of their national economies, and economic cooperation through regionalization to counter the potential effects of the already institutionalized regions in Europe and the Western Hemisphere.

The Dilemmas of a New Global Configuration

The cold war international regime established after World War II served as an incubator for the formation of an economically powerful Asian Pacific region with Japan at its core and a frontier for expansion in Myanmar, Vietnam, the newly constituted Cambodia, North Korea, and the northeastern region where China, Korea, and Russia converge. As the architect of this international regime, the United States used its special relationship as victor over a defeated Japan to construct a regional bulwark against communism in the Asian Pacific. In exchange for relinquishing autonomy over its own national security (Article 9 of the Japanese constitution), Japan would reap favorable conditions for economic growth along with military security from the United States. This "implicit bargain," built into the foundation of the postwar international system, set the parameters for what "free trade" was to mean in the postwar world.[11] The United States would tolerate Japan's restrictive and aggressive trade and investment policies while opening wide its own market to Japanese (and other Asian Pacific countries') exports because it served the best interests of both the United States and the "free world" to strengthen the economies of allies in the Asian Pacific region.

"The Japanese Problem."   From the start, therefore, what was heralded as a system of "free trade" was actually a complex historical compromise including a large number of "safeguards, exemptions, exceptions and restrictions—all designed to protect the balance of payments [of nation-states] and a variety of domestic social policies."[12] Though the objective of GATT was to lower tariff barriers and promote nondiscrimination in trade between nations, the right of national governments to protect their own domestic markets remained sacrosanct. The United States obtained a GATT waiver to exempt its own agricultural price supports from international negotiation; it also recognized Japan's protection of its postwar industries as national prerogatives implicitly protected by the framework of liberalization. But this system of "embedded liberalism" became problematic once Japan rather than the United States was the paramount exporter of industrial goods. At this point, the perception that imports were permitted by Japan only in areas where they did not compete with domestic production became "the Japanese problem."

Ironically, it was the very success of the international regime represented by GATT that brought "the Japanese problem" into the limelight. As the vast majority of nations in the world, including Japan, successfully reduced and eliminated tariff barriers, the flood of exports into the United States, which it must be recalled was the biggest buyers' market in the world, submerged domestic industries' capabilities to compete. The result was a series of attempts on the part of the U.S. government to redress its own vulnerabilities in a world market with cost-effective competitors. Nontariff barriers (NTBs) were erected to slow down or limit the rate of increased in (Japanese) imports, Japanese currency was appreciated to increase American capital and goods exports to Japan, and the Japanese government's acquiescence to a series of quid pro quos within the framework of the Structural Impediments Initiative (SII) was obtained. When the United States still found itself stymied from lowering its deficits with Japan and significantly increasing its share of the Japanese domestic market, policymakers concluded that Japan's "unfair trade practices" stemmed from the unique nature of Japan's internal industrial structure.

Thus, "the Japanese problem" refers to the fact that Japan's developmental political economy differs qualitatively from the political economy prevailing in other advanced capitalist countries. This difference between Japan's capitalist system and that of Western countries is perceived as a problem for the continued growth of both the U.S. and the world economy.[13] As we have seen throughout this book, there is no agreement on what explains the singular nature of the Japanese model of development. Some scholars argue that it is a distinctive cultural matrix, others argue that it is the industrial structure of a corporate economy informally wedded to the state bureaucracy. There is also no agreement on whether or not these structural differences are likely to diminish over time or remain as a more permanent feature of Japanese and some of the other Asian Pacific political economies. These uncertainties surrounding the intractability of U.S. deficits and Japanese current account surpluses have resulted in an endemic strain in the partnership between the two countries. Considered a "Japanese problem" in the United States and a weakness of the American economy in Japan, this mutual discontent underlies "Japan bashing" in the United States and the variety of racial and other slurs directed by Japanese officials at U.S. society.

But as John Ruggie surmises, a problem would exist with the GATT framework of international order regardless of Japan's situation. It was inevitable, once formal trade barriers were reduced to insignificant levels as intended by GATT, that the domestic policies and practices that shape the structure of foreign trade of different countries would assume center stage in international trade. At that point, whatever differences emerged in the domestic policies and practices among countries would be cause for an international problem. It is the consequence of an inherent conflict between the limited nature of the GATT mission "to maintain a balance of [external] concessions and obligations, not to restructure nations," and the increasingly interventionist objective of an international trade game in which powerful players in the global economy seek to harmonize the international effects of divergent domestic economic structures.[14] Because GATT relies upon multilateral agreements for reaching symmetrical quid pro quos, there is no way to use GATT to transform a fundamental asymmetry between Japan's domestic economic structure and that of the United States.

The Strategy of Aggressive Unilateralism.   This conflict between the asymmetry of Japan's domestic economy and that of the other capitalist countries led the United States unilaterally to undertake an aggressive form of "managed trade" by passing into law Section 301 of the Omnibus Trade and Competitiveness Act of 1988. In Super 301, as it is called, Congress mandates the executive branch of the United States to assess and take unilateral action against any policy it deems to be an "unfair trading practice." Thus, Super 301 targets Japanese (and others') trade policies unilaterally rather than through GATT-sponsored negotiations. And it targets Japan not because Japan is "cheating" on formal GATT rules but because "The structure of Japan's trade is simply, and importantly, different from the established norm around which the international trade regime revolves."[15] Japan's low level of manufactured imports, intra-industry trade, and preference for unprocessed or the least refined raw materials are used as evidence of a closed market. Super 301 is a form of retaliation for Japan's pursuing a policy to prevent U.S. corporations from establishing majority-owned subsidiaries within Japan.

The objective of such unilateral action on the part of the United States is to pry open the Japanese market, bringing Japan's trade structure into greater harmony with those of its trading partners. Though it may not in and of itself constitute protectionism, the policy evokes charges and countercharges of protectionism, portending increasing problems between Japan and the United States because it is clearly GATT-illegal and tends to erode the efficacy of the multilateral arrangements that are at the foundation of the existing international regime represented by GATT. Although the danger is mitigated by Japan's continued acquiescence to U.S. demands in a manner that sidesteps Japanese refusal to formally negotiate under terms of Super 301, the underlying problem remains irresolvable within the confines of an international regime created to serve the cold war configuration. International trade disputes that stem from fundamental differences in the way industries and trade are domestically organized and managed in different countries and regions are inherently beyond the scope of the GATT framework as it has functioned in the cold war era. And forecasts that the end of the cold war would usher in universal victory for liberal economics and democratic politics have been premature. It is far from clear what these terms mean in the global economy that has emerged while the world's attention was fixed on the possibility of nuclear annihilation.

Globalization.   Regional economic development in the Asian Pacific has coincided with an extraordinary period of technological innovation and foreign direct investments to fundamentally alter the structure of global relationships. Computer technology, the science and application of which have come to be known as cybernetics and cybernation, respectively, has generated new products and services, produced old ones with new processes, and brought about a new way of linking production systems internationally.[16] There are various terms to capture the newness of this global process we are witnessing: a new international division of labor, complex interdependency, a borderless economy. It is a transformation that breaks down production processes and fragments them so they are spread across a vast and shifting array of countries covering the entire surface of the globe. Production components are designed, manufactured, assembled, and marketed in different locations. As a result, intra-industry trade grows more rapidly than interindustry trade. And like traded services that have also expanded dramatically, intra-industry trade is not amenable to collecting uniform and universal statistics because it "does not exist in conventional economic theory."[17]

The effects of globalization on world markets have been drastic because it changes what, how, when, and where things are produced and distributed. Products have shortened lives, and choosing among a number of competing technologies and production locales can have a rapid and profound effect on profits, losses, and the prospects that a firm will be taken over or disappear. The survival of firms increasingly dictates entering into cross-national alliances with competitors, which brings with it new problems and new demands on the abilities of executives. Diplomacy is no longer the specialized preserve of state officials but an attribute required of corporate managers when multinational corporations enter into negotiations with states to avail themselves of the best locations for different aspects of their production processes.

The global economy would not be possible if not for the changes in how firms organize their financial affairs. These have occurred with great rapidity in recent decades as nationally centered financial markets that engaged in some buying and selling of credit across the exchanges have grown into a closely integrated "global system, in which national markets, physically separate, function as if they were all in the same place."[18] New credit instruments have been devised by banks, transnational corporations, and states, all of which issue tradable commercial paper that acts as the equivalent of money to sustain investments and lubricate trade. The extraordinary mobility of capital and the creation of new forms of credit have been facilitated by the revolution in communications and information. This technology is capable of generating international financial flows in any week or month that are fifty times greater in value than the flow of goods.[19]

These structural changes in financial and production markets have only begun to have a noticeable impact on the policies of the United States. In contrast to the Asian Pacific, where inward foreign direct investment has been an integral part of postwar development, extensive foreign direct investment going into the United States has been of only small consequence until recently. The result has been dramatic, though not necessarily widely understood among people. Generally described in the United States as a shift away from foreign to domestic policy, it is actually a shift in priorities away from a foreign policy defined in military terms to a domestic policy defined in global economic terms. The melting of the cold war has exposed a new international rivalry among states that the Asian Pacific has helped to define: It is the development game.[20]

The development game is one in which states enhance their prestige by pursuing greater market shares of global economic development; economic rather than military weapons are critical to win in this game. Expressed somewhat differently, nation-states in the postwar world pursue higher standards of living for their populations by actively involving themselves with multinational firms pursuing global strategies. In place of seeking control over more territory, the first priority of states now is to compete for the means to create wealth within their own territory. This leads states to interact with each other as well as with multinational corporations in pursuit of economic rather than military security. As they seek to arm themselves economically, they no longer employ the "blunt, unsophisticated and easily targetable weapon"—the tariff—substituting in its place the newer "stealth" weapons consisting of "that panoply of administrative arrangements and 'voluntary' agreements that exist under the collective title of the Non-Tariff Barriers (NTBs)."[21]

Since Japan has developed the equivalent of a "Star Wars" system to detect other countries' threats to its economic security, the new global configuration of political economy raises important questions of how Japan and the other countries of the Asian Pacific are likely to respond to the United States' having joined the development game. Which national populations will have the greatest advantages in attracting market shares of the global economy in the new "triangular diplomacy"—among states, among firms, and between states and firms? What alliances will be made or unmade in pursuit of winning? Will the EU and NAFTA develop as open trading regions or as protectionist regional blocs? Will the Asian Pacific move toward greater institutionalized economic and political cooperation? Or will the combination of old conflicts and new rivalries leave the Asian Pacific politically fragmented and economically contentious? These questions are, of course, unanswerable but tantalizing and we will in the final section indulge ourselves in that time-honored human need to gaze into the crystal ball or throw the I Ching.

Which Way the Asian Pacific?

How will the newly industrializing countries fare in the new global economy? With a regional pattern so dependent upon exports to the United States, what strategies can be developed to adjust to the increasing regionalization of the world's countries? Will the Japanese continue to have the advantages that have been attributed to their distinctive developmental system, or will they, as developed countries ahead of them, begin to suffer from the problems of old age and decay while the United States engages in its own restructuring to face the new tasks of the twenty-first century?

These questions draw attention to the possibility that what has passed for a superior model of economic growth and development among Asian Pacific countries may yet turn into the familiar capitalist system with all the flaws already afflicting developed capitalist countries. Japan's declining growth rates, increasing unemployment, and other dislocations of its current recessionary downturn are used as evidence for the argument. On the other hand, it is at least plausible that Asian Pacific development will continue to evolve in its own distinctive fashion while industrial restructuring in the United States will exhibit its own particular imprint. The purpose of this book has been to provide an understanding of the singular pattern of Asian Pacific development so readers can make their own comparisons. As all countries readjust to the new global economy, contrasts among different organizational models of production will become the basis for how countries attempt to restructure their advantages. Perhaps no single paradigm of perfection or universal agreement will emerge, but countries with sophisticated and well-maintained infrastructure, a highly skilled and well-disciplined labor force, a resilient educational system, and an effective and internationally savvy political leadership are likely to have a competitive edge in the contest for global market shares.

The Japan-United States Relationship.   At the heart of the question of the Asian Pacific future is the U.S-Japanese partnership that has provided the foundation for the region's development in the postwar period. Trade tensions between the two countries, as amply demonstrated, are bound to increase, especially if the gap between Japan's surpluses and the United States' deficits continues to widen. Internal divisions among Japanese over the issue of opening Japan's domestic market to outsiders are already complicated by the necessity of political reform. The dramatic ousting of the LDP from its political position of stable authority in the postwar world has had controversial consequences: The symbolically significant Japanese rice market has been opened for the first time, and electoral changes to undermine the dominance of the LDP have been introduced. But the internal structure of the Japanese political economy remains intact. It continues to enable Japan, as it has throughout the postwar period, to publicly acquiesce to pressures from the United States without actually implementing agreements so they achieve the desired outcomes. But it seems clear that if the openness of the Japanese market is measured by the United States in terms of outcomes rather than the formalities of bilateral agreements, the United States-Japan partnership will be in for some rocky times. Ironically, this result is equally likely should political reform in Japan succeed.

On the U.S. side, resistance to industrial restructuring to increase the country's international competitiveness is just as contentious. Judging from the divisiveness over NAFTA, advocates of protectionism are capable of mustering considerable national political support. It is far easier, given historical prejudices and the transparency of the political system in the United States, to impose a "fairness" doctrine on Japan holding the Japanese responsible for U.S. deficits than it is to undergo fundamental domestic restructuring. But, as in Japan, though there is movement in the direction of industrial restructuring and some form of industrial planning as an instrument of national policy could shore up the partnership between Japan and the United States, the nationalistic sentiments that favor protectionism as a solution to trade problems with Japan are as powerful in the United States as they are in Japan. Thus the future of the United States-Japan partnership will depend ultimately on the capacities of both Japan and the United States to reform the historical and cultural biases underlying their relationship since the Second World War.

Regionalism Led by Japan and China?   The relationship between the United States and Japan is closely intertwined with the question of regionalism. Heightened tensions between Japan and the United States lead in the direction of more protectionist-oriented regional development on both sides of the Pacific Ocean. As we have seen, Japan has followed a course of trade, aid, and investment that has fostered economic regional integration. For Chalmers Johnson, "There is no doubt that Japan has the capacity to create a yen-based regional economic grouping in the Asian Pacific region."[22] How rapidly this occurs, what institutionalized shape such a regional grouping might assume, and what direction it moves in are contingent on all the interrelated domestic and international factors. If both the EU and NAFTA develop as open regions committed to multilateralism rather than as protectionist blocs seeking to exclude the exports of Asian newcomers, then more leeway will be available for Asian Pacific countries to develop a rather closely integrated economic cooperation while maintaining close dependent ties with the United States both militarily and economically. The successful conclusion of GATT negotiations in 1993 coming on the heels of the high-profile APEC meetings offers some promise for the openness of the regions being formed in Europe and the North American continent. But Asian Pacific countries will cautiously await the impact of these regional formations on their own export markets.

China will play a principal role in affecting the outcome of both United States-Japan relations and the Asian Pacific's prospects for greater regionalization. By its size, resource endowments, historical importance in the region, global stature, and success at achieving economic reforms within a framework of political stability, China stands apart from and somewhat above the rest of the Asian Pacific, sharing this position with its former archenemy, Japan. Alone among all the Asian Pacific countries, China has successfully pursued an independent foreign policy, first distancing itself from both the United States and the Soviet Union at the height of the cold war and then enlisting as a third party in disputes between the superpowers. The People's Republic is well qualified, therefore, to complement Japan's diffidence in its role as global leader while at the same time acting as a countervailing force to Japan's economic power in the region. As a third party in a triangular relationship with the United States and Japan, China's position on international issues can be pivotal in either increasing or decreasing tensions between the Asian Pacific and North American regions. By asserting its independence or throwing its weight behind one or the other economic superpower, China is likely for the foreseeable future to act in a stabilizing manner to further its ambitious economic development plans. Essential to these plans are the successful integration of Hong Kong and the de facto merging of Taiwan with the economy of the mainland.

Pressures toward increased regionalization seem certain to continue in the coming years. Of major importance in deciding the pace of change toward greater institutionalization of regional cooperation will be the degree of openness or protectionism of the U.S. market. Rising protectionism on the part of the United States can act as a unifying force among the disparate Asian Pacific countries. There is already some overt sentiment, as indicated earlier in this chapter, for excluding the United States from any Asian Pacific organization. This could be strengthened by heightened tensions between the United States and Japan. A possibility that their exports would no longer find an outlet in the United States might prompt the governments of Asian Pacific countries to open their domestic markets to one another. Increased formal agreements regarding the creation of such a "common market" may be only a glimmer on the horizon, along with Korean unification and Vietnam joining ASEAN, but they are surely already in the minds of the leadership.

Clearly, the obstacles to an Asian Pacific region taking shape in the manner of the EU are formidable. How Japan carries out its leadership role in the region will be critical. But judging the effectiveness of Japanese leadership can be culturally biased. It may be, as Alan Rix points out, that Japan's style of "leadership from behind"[23] will make Japanese economic and political power in the region more acceptable than any overt dominant behavior would allow. A style of leadership that stresses negotiation and skill in brokering the interests of many actors may be more appropriate to the task of forming the equivalent of an "international regime" at the regional level.

Conjecture about the short-term outlook of the Japan-United States partnership runs the gamut: Some argue it will result in bigemony or "Amerippon," others suggest either a Pax America II or a Pax Nipponica. In the long run, regionalism as a way of increasing the market size of nation-states will mean a great many more regions in the world. Multipolarity might take the form of a sizable number of regional nodes of power, not in isolation from each other but in competition and collusion over the resources of the global economy.

But getting from here to there is a daunting enterprise, the possibilities or impossibilities of which are beyond the scope of this book. Trying to understand development in and among Asian Pacific countries will be a continuing quest. What we have attempted in this book is to provide a historical and cultural context for understanding the issues and problems that face each of these countries. We have not shied from covering the breadth of the terrain, an endeavor we hope has not prevented our doing justice to our neighbors across the Pacific.

QUESTIONS FOR DISCUSSION

1. Looking back over their record of political and economic achievements during the last four decades, what grade would you assign to each of the fifteen Asian Pacific countries and Hong Kong? Why?

2. Imagine that you, an expert on theories and models about development, have been hired by the government of one of the less affluent Asian Pacific countries (such as Vietnam or Myanmar) to brief top officials on what lessons are to be learned from other countries' experience in development and modernization. What important points about each of the various theories or models of development would you point out to them as relevant guidelines to consider in policy making?

3. What (if anything) should the U.S. government, private organizations, and individuals do about human rights in Asian Pacific countries?

4. Do you agree with some who forecast that the twenty-first century will be the "Pacific Century"? What role will the United States have in the region? Japan? China?

NOTES

1. Steve Chan and Cal Clark, "The Rise of the East Asian NICs: Confucian Capitalism, Status Mobility, and Developmental Legacy," in *The Evolving Pacific Basin in the Global Political Economy: Domestic and International Linkages,* ed. Cal Clark and Steve Chan (Boulder: Lynne Rienner Publishers, 1992), p. 39.

2. Fernando Fajnzylber, "The United States and Japan as Models of Industrialization" in *Manufacturing Miracles: Paths of Industrialization in Latin America and East Asia*, ed. Gary Gereffi and Donald Wyman (Princeton: Princeton University Press, 1992), pp. 323–352.

3. Chan and Clark, p. 43.

4. Kishore Mahbubani, "Live and Let Live," *Far Eastern Economic Review*, 17 June 1993, p. 26.

5. Ibid.

6. Stephen Magagnini, "Chinese Leader Scores PR Coup at Conference," *The Sacramento Bee*, 21 November 1993, p. A32.

7. Nicholas D. Kristof, "Riddle of China: Repressions As Standard of Living Soars," *New York Times*, 7 September 1993, p. A6, National Edition.

8. Michael Vatikiotis and Robert Delfs, "Cultural Divide," *Far Eastern Economic Review*, 17 June 1993, p. 20.

9. T. P. Huang, Letter to the Editor, *Far Eastern Economic Review*, 26 August 1993, p. 4.

10. Mahbubani, "Live and Let Live," p. 26.

11. A point made with respect to Europe by B. J. Cohen in 1974, quoted in *Pacific Economic Relations in the 1990s: Cooperation or Conflict?* ed. R. Higgott, R. Leaver, and J. Ravenhill (Boulder: Lynne Rienner Publishers, 1993), p. 3.

12. John Gerard Ruggie, "Unravelling Trade: Global Institutional Change and the Pacific Economy," in Higgott, *Pacific Economic Relations*, p. 16.

13. An article that details evidence for the existence of the "Japan problem" is "The 'Japan Problem' in Pacific Trade" by John Ravenhill in Higgott, *Pacific Economic Relations*, pp. 106–32.

14. Ruggie, "Unravelling Trade," p. 29.

15. Ibid., pp. 25–26.

16. The best work on the subject to which this entire section is heavily indebted is *Rival States, Rival Firms: Competition for World Market Shares*, by John M. Stopford, Susan Strange, with John S. Henley (Cambridge: Cambridge University Press, 1991).

17. Ruggie, "Unravelling Trade," p. 33.

18. Stopford, *Rival States, Rival Firms*, p. 41.

19. Ibid., p. 44.

20. Shumpei Kumon and Akihiko Tanaka use the concept of "the development game" in their alternative framework to the hegemonic power explanation of changes in the current world system. See "From Prestige to Wealth to Knowledge," in *The Political Economy of Japan*, vol. 2, *The Changing International Context*, ed. Takashi Inoguchi and Daniel I. Okimoto (Stanford: Stanford University Press, 1988), pp. 66–82.

21. Richard A. Higgott, *Some Alternative Security Questions for Australia*, Canberra Papers on Strategy and Defence, No. 51 (Canberra: Australian National University, 1989), p. 21.

22. Chalmers Johnson, "History Restarted: Japanese-American Relations at the End of the Century," in Higgott, *Pacific Economic Relations*, p. 53.

23. Alan Rix, "Japan and the Region: Leading from Behind," in Higgott, *Pacific Economic Relations*, pp. 62–82.

FOR FURTHER READING

Akaha, Tsuneo, and Frank Langdon, eds. *Japan in the Posthegemonic World*. Boulder: Lynne Rienner Publishers, 1993.

Caporaso, James A., ed. *A Changing International Division of Labor*. Boulder: Lynne Rienner Publishers, 1987.

Hersh, Jacques. *The USA and the Rise of East Asia Since 1945: Dilemmas of the Postwar International Political Economy*. New York: St. Martin's Press, 1993, chapters 3 and 4.

Morley, James W., ed. *Driven by Growth: Political Change in the Asian-Pacific Region*. Armonk, NY: M.E. Sharpe, 1993.

Nanda, Ved P., et al. *Global Human Rights: Public Policies, Comparative Measures, and NGO Strategies* (Boulder: Westview Press, 1981).

Stopford, John M., Susan Strange, with John S. Henley. *Rival States, Rival Firms: Competition for World Market Shares*. Cambridge: Cambridge University Press, 1991.

Acronyms

ADB	Asian Development Bank
AFIC	Asian Finance and Investment Corporation
AFPFL	Anti-Fascist People's Freedom League, Burma
ANZUS	Australia-New Zealand-United States security treaty
APEC	Asian Pacific Economic Cooperation forum
ARATS	Association for Relations Across the Taiwan Straits, China
ARVN	Army of the Republic of (South) Vietnam
ASEAN	Association of Southeast Asian Nations
BIA	Burma Independence Army
BSPP	Burma Socialist Programme Party
CPC	Communist Party of China
CPF	Central Provident Fund, Singapore
CPPCC	Chinese People's Political Consultative Conference
CPSU	Communist Party of the Soviet Union
DAC	Development Assistance Committee, OECD
DAP	Democratic Action Party, Malaysia
DLP	Democratic Liberal Party, South Korea
DPP	Democratic Progressive Party, Taiwan
DPR	People's Representative Council, Indonesia
DPRK	Democratic People's Republic of Korea
DRV	Democratic Republic of (North) Vietnam
DSP	Democratic Socialist Party, Japan
EAEG	East Asia Economic Group
EC	European Community, now European Union (EU)
EOI	export-oriented industrialization policy
FDI	foreign direct investment
FUNCINPEC	United Front for an Independent, Neutral, and Free Cambodia

GATT	General Agreement on Trade and Tariffs
G-7	Group of seven major industrialized countries
GCBA	General Council of Buddhist (Burmese) Associations
GDP	gross domestic product
GNP	gross national product
IAEA	International Atomic Energy Agency
ICP	Indochinese Communist Party
IGO	intergovernmental organization
IMF	International Monetary Fund
IPE	international political economy
ISDA	Indies Social Democratic Association
FY	fiscal year
JCP	Japan Communist Party
KPRP	Khmer People's Revolutionary Party
KR	Khmer Rouge
KWP	Korean Workers' Party
LDP	Liberal Democratic Party, Japan and Philippines
MCA	Malay Chinese Association
MCP	Malayan Communist Party
MIA/POW	missing in action/prisoners of war
MIC	Malaysian Indian Congress
MITI	Ministry of International Trade and Industry, Japan
MNC	multinational corporation
MPAJA	Malayan People's Anti-Japanese Army
MPR	People's Consultative Assembly, Indonesia
MRLA	Malayan Races Liberation Army
NAFTA	North American Free Trade Association
NAM	Non-Aligned Movement
NATO	North Atlantic Treaty Organization
NEC	newly-exporting country, referring to Indonesia, Malaysia, and Thailand
NEP	New Economic Policy, Malaysia
NIC	newly industrializing country, referring to Hong Kong, Singapore, South Korea, and Taiwan
NIE	newly industrializing economies, both NIC and NEC
NGO	nongovernmental organization
NLF	National Liberation Front, South Vietnam
NPC	National People's Congress, China
NTB	nontariff barrier
ODA	official development assistance
OECD	Organization for Economic Cooperation and Development
OPEC	Organization of Petroleum Exporting Countries
PAFTAD	Pacific Free Trade and Development Conference
PAP	People's Action Party, Singapore
PAS	Pan Malaysian Islamic Party

PAVN	People's Army of Vietnam
PBEC	Pacific Basin Economic Council
PCI	per capita income
PDI	Indonesian Democratic Party
PECC	Pacific Economic Cooperation Conference
PKI	Indies (later Indonesian) Communist Party
PLA	People's Liberation Army, China
PLAF	People's Liberation Army Force, Vietnam
PNI	Indonesian Nationalist Party
PPP	Islamic United Development Party, Indonesia
PRC	People's Republic of China
PRG	Provisional Revolutionary Government, South Vietnam
RAM	Reform the Armed Forces Movement, Philippines
ROC	Republic of China
ROK	Republic of Korea
SALT	Strategic Arms Limitation Talks
SEATO	Southeast Asia Treaty Organization
SDPJ	Social Democratic Party of Japan
SEC	State Economic Commission, China
SEF	Straits Exchange Foundation, Taiwan
SEZ	special economic zone
SI	Sarekat Islam, Indonesia
SII	Structural Impediments Initiative
SLORC	State Law and Order Restoration Council, Myanmar
SOC	State of Cambodia
SPC	State Planning Commission, China
TNC	transnational corporation
TPM	trigger price mechanism
UMNO	United Malays' National Organization
UNCOK	UN Commission on Korea
UNCURK	UN Commission for Unification and Rehabilitation of Korea
UNTAC	United Nations Transitional Authority in Cambodia
UNTCOK	UN Temporary Commission on Korea
USDP	United Social Democratic Party, Japan
VER	voluntary export restraint
WB	World Bank
YMBA	Young Men's Buddhist Association, Burma
ZOPFAN	zone of peace, freedom, and neutrality

Index

399